The Rise of Mormonism: 1816-1844

H. Michael Marquardt

Longwood, Florida
2005

Copyright © 2005 by H. Michael Marquardt

The Rise of Mormonism: 1816-1844
by H. Michael Marquardt

Printed in the United States of America
Includes bibliographical references and index

ISBN 1-59781-470-9

All rights reserved solely by the author. No part of this book, or
parts thereof, may be translated or reproduced in any form or by
any media without the permission of the author. The views
expressed in this book are not necessarily those of the publisher.

1. Mormonism. 2. Mormon Church-History-19th Century. 3. Comparative Religions. 4. The Church of Jesus Christ of Latter-day Saints. 5. Joseph Smith, 1805-1844, revelations. 6. Book of Mormon. 7. Doctrine and Covenants. 8. Joseph Smith Translation of the Bible. 9. Book of Abraham.

www.xulonpress.com

CONTENTS

PREFACE

When I first conceived the idea of presenting my insights into the development of the genesis of Mormonism it was with the thought that the various aspects of the founding prophet of Mormonism—Joseph Smith—would have to be examined in the context of his times. What were some of the things he did, what were his claims, and what relationship did he have with his converts? As a religious prophet Smith had a following from the time he first told of his experiences with the supernatural.

With this in mind it became evident that this book would need to be intertwined with the theology of Joseph Smith from his simple teachings through to its more complex development. What we find is that in the process of time Smith's story became text, with believers believing, and spiritual experiences becoming physical realities. In presenting this research I bring into this picture the underlining beginnings not only of the largest church organization, The Church of Jesus Christ of Latter-day Saints (headquartered in Salt Lake City, Utah), but also the Community of Christ, formerly and still officially the Reorganized Church of Jesus Christ of Latter Day Saints (headquartered in Independence, Missouri). The smaller churches, groups, and individuals are also considered as they also rely in part on the story of Joseph Smith.

In this study it appears to me that Joseph Smith was motivated by a desire to present his experiences as a basis for others to obtain faith. Story telling became a way of life for him as he was able to explain to family and friends what was most dear to his heart. Consequently this book covers Mormonism's foundational years, its scripture and theological development.

My interest in Mormonism began in the 1961. It was in this year that I was introduced to the story of Joseph Smith's visionary experiences. I was baptized into the LDS church in March of that year and commenced my study. Fifteen years later I resigned my membership. One of my research principles has been to assist other students and writers of Mormonism. This has been very rewarding as indicated in my papers housed in the Manuscripts Division, J. Willard Marriott Library, University of Utah, in Salt Lake City.

Whenever possible I have used primary sources. These include court records, letters, journals, and contemporary newspapers. This has given me a better understanding of the social, economic, and political happenings at the time discussed in this book. It has also been valuable in evaluating the various conflicts that involved the Mormons and those who were critical of their activities and beliefs.

I have followed original spelling as far as possible when quoting various documents. In presenting quotations from manuscripts some punctuation and capital letters have been supplied to facilitate readability. Words in manuscripts that appear above the line are indicated by angled brackets <>. Crossed-out and repeated words are usually deleted. Source notations and comments are presented in footnotes.

Special appreciation is given to the late Wesley P. Walters for his research which appeared in our co-authored book *Inventing Mormonism: Tradition and the Historical Record.*[1] The chapters in the above work have been revised for the current book with new documentation where appropriate. Chapter 9 also received his input.

—H. MICHAEL MARQUARDT

SANDY, UTAH, JULY 2005

---

[1] San Francisco: Smith Research Associates, 1994; paperbound 1998, distributed by Signature Books, Salt Lake City.

Common Abbreviations

1830 BOM = Joseph Smith, *The Book of Mormon: An Account Written by the hand of Mormon, Upon Plates Taken from the Plates of Nephi.* By Joseph Smith, Junior, author and proprietor (Palmyra, New York: Printed by E. B. Grandin for the author, 1830), cited with page number and followed by LDS and RLDS chapter and and verse

Abraham = Book of Abraham in *The Pearl of Great Price* (Salt Lake City: Church of Jesus Christ of Latter-day Saints, 1981)

BC = A Book of Commandments, for the Government of the Church of Christ (Zion [Independence, Missouri]: Published by W. W. Phelps & Co., 1833)

D&C = *Doctrine and Covenants*

JST = *The Holy Scriptures* (Independence, Missouri: Herald Publishing House, Reorganized Church of Jesus Christ of Latter Day Saints, 1991); also known as Joseph Smith Translation of the Bible [revision of King James Bible]

KJV = King James Version of the Bible

LDS = The Church of Jesus Christ of Latter-day Saints (Mormon), headquartered in Salt Lake City, Utah

LDS archives = Archives, Church of Jesus Christ of Latter-day Saints, Salt Lake City, Utah

LDS D&C = *The Doctrine and Covenants of The Church of Jesus Christ of Latter-day Saints* (Salt Lake City: Church of Jesus Christ of Latter-day Saints, 1981)

Moses = Selections from the Book of Moses in *The Pearl of Great Price* (Salt Lake City: Church of Jesus Christ of Latter-day Saints, 1981)

NT = New Testament

OT = Old Testament

RLDS = Reorganized Church of Jesus Christ of Latter Day Saints (official name but now known as the Community of Christ), headquartered in Independence, Missouri

RLDS archives = Community of Christ Library-Archives, Independence, Missouri

RLDS D&C = *Book of Doctrine and Covenants* (Independence, Missouri: Herald Publishing House, Reorganized Church of Jesus Christ of Latter Day Saints, 1990)

Libraries

I would like to give special thanks to the following repositories where research was conducted. I express my appreciation to these institutions and their staffs.

Illinois:
Hancock County Historical Society, Carthage
Illinois State Historical Society, Springfield
Land Records Center, Nauvoo
Leslie F. Malpass Library, Western Illinois University, Macomb
Lovejoy Library, University of Southern Illinois at Edwardsville

Missouri:
Genealogy and Local History Branch, Mid-Continent Public Library, Independence
Jackson County Historical Society, Independence
Library-Archives of the Community of Christ (RLDS archives), Independence
Mercantile Library Association, St. Louis
Missouri Historical Society, St. Louis
St. Louis Central Library, St. Louis
State Historical Society of Missouri-Columbia, Columbia
Thomas Jefferson Library, University of Missouri, St. Louis
Western Historical Manuscripts Collection, Ellis Library, University of Missouri, Columbia

New York:
Baker Library, Fredonia
Board of Supervisors, Chenango County Office Building, Norwich
Broome County Public Library, Binghamton
Buffalo & Erie County Historical Society Research Library, Buffalo
Buffalo and Erie County Public Library, Buffalo
Chenango County Clerk's Office, Norwich
Division of Rare and Manuscript Collections, Carl A. Kroch Library and Olin Library, Cornell University, Ithaca
Green Library/Moore Memorial Library, Green

Guernsey Memorial Library, Norwich
Office of History, Chenango County Historical Society, Norwich
Ontario County Clerk's Office, Canandaigua
Ontario County Historical Society, Canandaigua
Ontario County Records Center and Archives, Canandaigua
Oxford Memorial Library, Oxford
Palmyra King's Daughters Free Library, Palmyra
Palmyra Village Offices, Palmyra
Richmond Memorial Library, Batavia
Rochester Public Library, Rochester
Seneca County Clerk's Office, Waterloo
Seneca Falls Historical Society, Seneca Falls
State University of New York (SUNY) Fredonia
State University of New York (SUNY) Geneseo
Town Clerk's Office, Bainbridge
Town Clerk's Office, Manchester
Town Clerk's Office, Palmyra
Warren Hunting Smith Library, Hobart and William Smith
Colleges, Geneva
Waterloo Library and Historical Society, Waterloo
Wayne County Clerk's Office, Lyons
Wayne County Historical Society, Lyons

Ohio:
Chardon Public Library, Chardon
Geauga County Archives and Records Center, Chardon
Geauga County Clerk's Office, Chardon
Kirtland Stake Family History Library, Kirtland
Kirtland Temple Historic Center, Kirtland
Ohio Historical Society, Columbus
P. K. Smith Research Library, Lake County History Center, Lake
County Historical Society, Mentor
Western Reserve Historical Society, Cleveland

Pennsylvania:
Erie County Public Library, Erie
Historical Society of Pennsylvania, Philadelphia
Latter Day Saint Research Center, Jenkintown

Presbyterian Historical Society, Philadelphia

Utah:
Family and Church History Department of the Church of Jesus
Christ of Latter-day Saints (LDS archives), Salt Lake City
International Daughters of Utah Pioneers Library, Salt Lake City
LDS Family History Library, Salt Lake City
L. Tom Perry Special Collections, Harold B. Lee Library, Brigham
Young University, Provo
Manuscripts Division, J. Willard Marriott Library, University of
Utah, Salt Lake City
Merrill Library, Utah State University, Logan
Salt Lake Public Library, Salt Lake City
Utah State Historical Society, Salt Lake City

Other repositories include:

American Antiquarian Society, Worcester, Massachusetts
Amistad Research Center, New Orleans, Louisiana
Bancroft Library, University of California, Berkeley, California
Beinecke Rare Book and Manuscript Library, Yale Collection of
Western Americana, Yale University, New Haven, Connecticut
Bodleian Library, Oxford University, Oxford, England
Boston Public Library, Boston
Daughters of American Revolution Library, Washington, D.C.
Kansas State Historical Society, Topeka
Library of Congress, Washington, D.C.
State Historical Society of Wisconsin, Madison

1

Relocation to Palmyra and Manchester, New York

In 1816 forty-five year old Joseph Smith Sr. left his wife
Lucy and eight children in Norwich, Vermont and traveled to the
village of Palmyra in western New York state. A history of the
Smith family was written twenty-eight years later by Lucy Mack
Smith, Joseph's wife.[1] Her history of the Smith family in New
York covers about ninety pages in her rough manuscript.
Undoubtedly Lucy Smith's narrative contains some errors, but it
remains a valuable record of her family's life.

From contemporary records and accounts we learn many
interesting details of the family's move to Palmyra and later to
Manchester, the next township south of Palmyra. It can be
established, with reasonable certainty, the chronology of the move
of the Smith family. The records described in this chapter help
determine when the family was living in the village of Palmyra,
their move to the log cabin on Stafford Road, and finally their
residence on the farm in Manchester.

Lucy describes her husband departing for Palmyra, New
York. Leaving Vermont Joseph Sr. was followed for a short
distance by his eldest sons Alvin and Hyrum who watched as their
father left alone for Palmyra. He would send for his family when
he was ready for them.

Lucy was joyful at the reunion with her husband early in
1817. Lucy was forty-one years old though she considered herself
one year younger, being born in 1775 rather than 1776. She

---

[1] Notes were taken from the dictation of Lucy Mack Smith and made into a
manuscript draft in 1844-45 by Martha Jane Coray and her husband Howard.
The original manuscript draft is in the archives of The Church of Jesus Christ of
Latter-day Saints, Salt Lake City, Utah (hereafter LDS archives). The history
was revised in 1845 and first published as *Biographical Sketches of Joseph
Smith the Prophet and His Progenitors for Many Generations* (Liverpool:
Published for Orson Pratt by S. W. Richards, 1853). See Lavina Fielding
Anderson, ed., *Lucy's Book: A Critical Edition of Lucy Mack Smith's Family
Memoir* (Salt Lake City: Signature Books, 2001), cited hereafter as *Lucy's Book*.
This work includes a textual history, a parallel comparison of the rough draft,
the 1853 printing, and notations of important manuscript and printed variants.

1

described the family's long-range plans after locating in the village of Palmyra:

> We <all> now Sat down and maturely councilled [counseled] together as to what course i was best to take how we sho[u]ld proceed to buisness [business] in our then destitute circumstances It was agreed by each one of us that it was <most> advisable to ap[p]ly all our energies together and endeavor to obtain a Piece of land as this was then a new country and land was bow [low] being in its rude state but it was almost a time of famine wheat was $2.50 per bushel and other things in proportion. how shall we, said My Husband, be able to sustain ourselves and have anything left to buy land[?] As I had done considerable at painting oil cloth coverings for tables stands &c. I concluded to set up the buisness [business] and if prospered I would try to supply the wants of the family. In this I succeeded so well that it was not long till we not only had an abundance of good and wholesome provision but I soon began to replenish my household furniture a fine stock of which I had sacraficed [sacrificed] entirely in moving[2]

This recollection compresses a number of years prior to 1820. Lucy represents her important role as wife and helpful caretaker in reestablishing the family in Palmyra. Lucy's craft enterprise prospered, and later the family contracted for one hundred acres in the township of Farmington (the area that became Manchester in 1822), immediately south of Palmyra Township.

Joseph Sr. is first mentioned in Palmyra on the road tax list for April 1817 as a resident on Main Street.[3] At this time their family consisted of six sons and two daughters: Alvin (nineteen),

---

[2] Lucy Mack Smith, Manuscript Draft. See Anderson, *Lucy's Book*, 318.

[3] Palmyra Highway Tax Record, Palmyra, New York, Copies of Old Village Records, 1793-1867, LDS Family History Library, Salt Lake City, Utah, microfilm #812869. A copy is also in the King's Daughters Library, Palmyra, New York. The record is labeled at the beginning, "A Copy of the Several Lists of the Mens Names Liable to Work on the Highways in the Town of Palmyra in the Year 1804." The original record itself cannot be located at the present time, but a typescript made by Doris Nesbitt, is presently the only copy available.

Hyrum (seventeen), Sophronia (thirteen), Joseph Jr. (eleven), Samuel Harrison (nine), William (six), Catherine (four), and Don Carlos (one).

New York law established a system for maintaining roads which required that each township be divided into road districts and that all men in each district were required to work on the roads. Each district was under the supervision of a path master or overseer elected at an annual town meeting held on the first Tuesday of April. At the same meeting three commissioners of highways were elected. The overseer had sixteen days from the date of his election to list every male living in his district who was twenty-one years or older (a free man) or property owner (a freeholder). Each man devoted at least one day a year to keeping the roads in repair in the district in which he lived. This included clearing brush, stones, and fallen trees; repairing bridges; filling holes; and in the winter clearing paths through the snow. One could hire someone to serve in his place, but failure to fulfill the obligation in person or by proxy resulted in a fine enforceable by law.[4] The office of Overseer of Highways was not to be taken lightly. The overseer was liable to a fine of ten dollars for each failure to notify those who were required to work on the roads and for each delinquency in performing any other task assigned him. Two weeks prior to the town meeting the following year he was required to certify what work had been done, by whom, and to report anyone who had not fulfilled his obligation.

The name of Joseph Sr. first appears in Road District 26 for April 1817, consistent with his having arrived in the latter part of 1816. The town's "Record of Roads" shows that District 26 began on Main Street in the center of the village of Palmyra (the so-called "Four Corners" where four churches now stand) near where the road from Canandaigua intersected and ran west until it crossed into what is now Macedon Township. The district included a small portion of the present Walworth road on the north side of Mud Creek and also a road running south toward the adjoining township of Farmington (now Manchester).[5]

---

[4] New York Legislature, *Laws of the State of New York*, 2 vols. (Albany: H.C. Southwick, 1813), 2:125, 128-29, 271-75, 309.

[5] Palmyra, New York, "Record of Roads of the Town of Palmyra, 1793-1901," 94-95, 104; microfilm copy in the State Library, Albany, New York.

This 1817 list basically follows the order in which individual properties were situated as one moves west on Main Street, with Joseph Smith Sr., listed as living at the west end of Main Street. Joseph Sr.'s name occurs again at the same location in District 26 in 1818 and 1819. Horace Eaton wrote concerning the residence of the Smith family on Main Street:

> Where Asa Chase now resides there once stood a house built by Saml. Jennings. This house was occupied by the father of Joseph Smith, the founder of Mormonism, who cam[e] from Sharon [sic] Vt. 1817. Afterwards Levi Daggett resided there & here occurred the wedding of Henry Wells & Sarah Daggett.[6]

As explained by the Woman's Society of the Western Presbyterian Church, "Henry Wells married his first wife—Sally Daggett—in the little weather beaten house that stands opposite Stafford street on the north side of Main street."[7]

In April 1820, the name of Alvin Smith appears for the first time on the road tax list among the merchants on Main Street. Alvin turned twenty-one in February 1819 and his absence from the 1819 road list may indicate he had been hired out or was not considered twenty-one years old that year. Residing on Main Street may represent the cake and beer shop the Smiths reportedly operated in town.[8] However, Joseph Sr.'s name appears at the end of the list, showing he is now living outside the business district and near the Palmyra-Farmington town line, where the road district ended.

The Smith family now lived in a cabin on property south of the village owned by Samuel Jennings, who had built the house

---

[6] H[orace]. Eaton, "Continuation of the History of Palmyra, A Sermon preached on the Annual day of Thanksgiving, Nov. 26, 1863," Palmyra King's Daughters Library, Palmyra. Eaton was pastor of the Western Presbyterian Church from 1849 to 1879.

[7] The Woman's Society of the Western Presbyterian Church, comp., *Palmyra, Wayne County, New York* (Rochester, New York: The Herald Press, 1907), 27. The marriage between Henry Wells and Sarah Daggett (daughter of Levi Daggett Sr.) took place on September 5, 1827.

[8] Pomeroy Tucker, *Origin, Rise, and Progress of Mormonism* (New York: D. Appleton & Co., 1867), 12.

which they occupied on Main Street. It appears that in early 1820 Alvin Smith was still using the house in Palmyra while his father and family members had removed to the new location near the southern border of Palmyra Township. This residence would be mentioned two months later in the "Palmyra Town Book" as "Joseph Smiths dwelling house," located about fifty feet north of the line dividing Palmyra from Farmington. It stood about two miles south of Main Street on property owned by Jennings, a merchant with whom the Smiths did business and extended him credit.[9] When the road survey crew on June 13, 1820 laid out the extension of Stafford Road to join Main Street to the north, they used the cabin as a reference point. The survey read: "Minutes of the survey of a public Highway beginning on the south line . . . in the town of Palmyra three rods fourteen links southeas[t] of Joseph Smiths dwelling house.[10]

The Smith cabin location is further supported by Orsamus Turner, who in 1818 began as a young apprentice printer at the office of the *Palmyra Register*. He recalled that he first saw the Smith family in the winter of 1819-20 living "in a rude log house, with but a small spot underbrushed around it" near the town line.[11] This cabin on the outskirts of the village of Palmyra should not be confused with a cabin the family eventually built on land in nearby Manchester and mentioned by Lucy Mack Smith.

Lucy subsequently reported that the family contracted for 100 acres of "Everson" (Evertson) land held by the estate of Nicholas Evertson, an attorney in New York City, who had

---

[9] Samuel Jennings, Estate Papers, June 5, 1822, Ontario County Records Center and Archives, Canandaigua, New York, 10, line 23, and 12, line 10, for Joseph Smith Sr.'s debts of $11.50 and $1.00 respectively at the time of Jennings's death on September 1, 1821.

[10] "Palmyra Town Book," (Old Town Record [1793-1870]), 221. Also in "Record of Roads," (1793-1901), 120, Town Clerk's Office, Palmyra, New York. The "Record of Roads" book reads "dwelling home," while the "Town Book" reads "dwelling house." Both are recopied from a now missing original road record book, but the latter reading was transcribed earlier. A 1982 excavation confirmed a dwelling site at this location.

[11] O[rsamus]. Turner, *History of the Pioneer Settlement of Phelps and Gorham's Purchase* (Rochester, NY: William Alling, 1851), 212-13, 400. A full analysis is contained in Dan Vogel, ed., *Early Mormon Documents*, 5 vols. (Salt Lake City: Signature Books, 1996-2003), 3:415-21.

acquired considerable land holdings in western New York before his death in 1807. It was June 1820 before his executors conveyed to Caspar W. Eddy, a New York City physician, power of attorney to sell his holdings. Eddy traveled to Canandaigua, New York, the seat of Ontario County, and on July 14, 1820 transferred his power of attorney to his friend Zachariah Seymour.[12] Seymour had long been a land agent in the area and was a close associate of Oliver Phelps, who with his partner Nathaniel Gorham had opened a land office in Canandaigua and had instituted the practice of "articling" for real estate.

Articling was a way for hard working but cash-poor pioneers to obtain possession of land by buying on the installment plan. Under this arrangement a schedule of payments was outlined in an "Articles of Agreement" which stipulated the following conditions: the deed was held by the seller until the final payment was made and if the buyer defaulted he lost all right to the land as well as to any improvements, and the seller could then resell it.[13]

It was by this method that the Smiths worked to become property owners. The land deed of Squire Stoddard, who in November 1825 acquired the lot adjoining the Smith Manchester farm, noted that the north line of his property was "the south line of lands heretofore articled to Joseph and Alvin Smith."[14]

The usual pattern of payment involved breaking the price down into three or more installments, each due a year apart on the original date of the contract. Often the first payment was further broken into easily met segments, such as $10 down, $18 within 90 days, and the balance within the year. When the anniversary date of the contract arrived, the entire second payment was then due. Although title was retained by the seller, the property tax was

---

[12] For the probate of Nicholas Evertson's estate, see County of New York, Manhattan Borough, Surrogate's Court, Wills, 47:7-11. On the power of attorney, see Miscellaneous Records, C:342-44, 347-48, Ontario County Records Center and Archives, Canandaigua.

[13] On Oliver Phelps's "articling" innovation, see John W. Barber and Henry Howe, *Historical Collections of the State of New York* (New York: S. Tuttle, 1842), 406-407, reprinting an extract from the *Rochester Directory* of 1827. A number of Seymour's papers are in the Phelps's papers both at the State Library in Albany and the Ontario County Historical Society in Canandaigua.

[14] Deed recorded in Deed Liber 44:220, Ontario County Records Center and Archives, Canandaigua.

ordinarily paid by the buyer and is expressly stipulated in some contracts. Sometimes specific requirements were added, such as building a cabin at least eighteen feet by eighteen feet within a year or clearing a specified acreage of land within that period. Often the record of payments was kept on the back of these Articles of Agreement.[15]

Joseph Sr., and Alvin would have had to "article" for their land shortly after July 1820. Joseph Smith Sr. is listed in the Farmington (Manchester) 1820 census (which was enrolled between August 7, 1820 and February 5, 1821), suggesting that the articling was completed no later than February 1821. The ages of the male family members were: under 10, 2 (William and Don Carlos); 16-26, 2 (Alvin and Hyrum); over 45, 1 (Joseph Sr.). Female members were: under 10, 1 (Catherine); 16-26, 1 (Sophronia) and 26-45, 1 (Lucy Mack Smith). Both Joseph Jr. (age fourteen) and his younger brother Samuel Harrison (age twelve) are missing from the census.[16]

The new Smith farm encompassed approximately one hundred acres, one third of the original Lot No. 1 in Farmington Township. According to the assessment roll for June 22, 1820, the entire three hundred acres of Lot 1 were taxed to the heirs of Nicholas Evertson at that time. In the following year's assessment (July 7, 1821) only two hundred acres were taxed to the Evertson heirs, while the balance was assessed to Joseph Smith.[17]

After contracting for the farm, Lucy reports, "In one year's time we made nearly all of the first payment. The Agent adivised [advised] us to build a log house on the land and commence clearing it, we did so. It was not long till we had 30 acers [acres] ready for cultivation. But the second payment was now coming

---

[15] Examples of printed forms requiring the payment of the assessment tax, building a cabin, clearing acreage and the reversion clause can be found in the State Library, Albany, New York, among the Phelps papers.

[16] See *Ontario Repository*, Aug. 8, 1820, 3; "Census of 1820," *History and Growth of the United States Census* (Washington, D.C., 1900), 134, 137); U.S. 1820 Census Records, Farmington, Ontario County, New York, LDS Family History Library, microfilm #193717, p. 318, Family #524, Salt Lake City. The *Palmyra Register* of August 16, 1820, asked residents to help prepare the census information themselves.

[17] Farmington, New York, Assessment Roll, July 7, 1821, 25, 32, Ontario County Records Center and Archives, Canandaigua.

due and no means as yet of meeting it."[18] In the draft memoir Lucy stated, "So that in 2 years from the time we entered Palmyra, strangers destitute of friends, home or employment, We were able to settle ourselves upon our own land [in] a snug comfortable though humble habitation built and neatly furnished by our industry."[19] The two-year time period after arriving in Palmyra mentioned by Lucy appears to be an inaccuracy on her part.

As a result Alvin left Palmyra in an effort to raise "the second payment and the remmainder [remainder] of the first," and he returned with "the necessary amount of money for all except the last payment." If they contracted for the land soon after Seymour received his power of attorney to sell it, around August 1, 1820, then the rest of the first payment and all of the second payment would have been paid to Seymour by August 1, 1821. Mother Smith adds that they were unable to make the third and last payment (which would have been August 1, 1822) because the land agent died. Seymour did indeed die on July 2, 1822, corroborating this part of her story and establishing the fact that the Smiths contracted for the land sometime after mid-July 1820.[20]

Lucy mentioned that "in one year's time" after they contracted for the property, the land agent told them they should build a cabin on their land, which "we did." However, it cannot be precisely determine from her account when this log structure was built. That this refers to their Farmington farm and not the Palmyra property is clear from several key facts. First, the Smiths were living in the Palmyra cabin when the road supervisors mentioned it in June 1820 before the Smiths could have contracted for the Farmington land. In addition, William Smith wrote concerning the Farmington-Manchester property, "The improvements made on this farm was first commenced by building a log house at no small expense, and at a later date a frame house at a cost of several hundred dollars."[21] William would hardly call a cabin built on

---

[18] Anderson, *Lucy's Book*, 319-20.

[19] Ibid., 321.

[20] Ibid., 321-23. On Zachariah Seymour's death, see the Walter Hubbell Papers, Princeton Library, Princeton University, Princeton, New Jersey: letter from Henry Panquis to James Kent, August 8, 1826, 1; and his eulogy in the *Ontario Repository*, July 16, 1822, a reprint of the previous week's *Ontario Messenger*.

[21] "Notes Written on 'Chamber's Life of Joseph Smith.' by William Smith,"

Samuel Jennings's land in Palmyra an improvement on their farm across the line in Manchester.

From the Palmyra road tax list it is clear that at least Joseph Sr. and Alvin were still living in Palmyra as late as April 1822. It is probable that the Smiths did not move to the Manchester farm until after the summer of 1822. It could not be earlier than July 1821 because the Smith family genealogy mentions the birth of Lucy, the youngest child of the family. The genealogy specifically states that Lucy was "born in Palmyra."[22]

That some members of the Smith family did not move until after April 1822 is witnessed by the Palmyra road tax list. In 1821, the name of Hyrum Smith, who had become twenty-one in February, appeared with Alvin and Joseph Sr. on the Palmyra road tax list. In the April 1822 road tax list, the elder Smith and Alvin again appear, so that as of April the father and oldest son had not yet moved to their Manchester farm, since they were taxed as Palmyra residents. Hyrum's name is missing from the 1822 list. This could indicate that other members of the family had been working on their one hundred acres and had built a cabin sometime in 1821. It is also possible that Hyrum and perhaps some other Smith children had moved there to relieve the crowded conditions in their Palmyra cabin. But it could also indicate that Hyrum had hired out to work.

When the one hundred acres first went on the assessment roll in July 1821, taxed to Joseph Sr., the parcel was valued at $700, $7 an acre. This was approximately what uncleared land in the area was selling for at that time. The remaining two hundred acres of Lot No. 1 were taxed to the Evertson heirs at a value of $1,400.[23] The same value appeared in the June 29, 1822 assessment.[24] However, by July 24, 1823 the value of the Smith

---

about 1875, typescript, 17, LDS archives.

[22] "Genealogy," Manuscript History, A-1:10 [separate section], LDS archives, reads, "Lucy Smith, born in Palmyra, Ontario Co. N.Y. July 18, 1821." See Dean C. Jessee, ed., *The Papers of Joseph Smith: Autobiographical and Historical Writings* (Salt Lake City: Deseret Book, 1989), 1:19. *William Smith on Mormonism* (Lamoni, IA: Herald Steam Book & Job Office, 1883), 5, gives 1821 as the date for the move to Manchester.

[23] For examples of land prices, ranging from $3 to $10 an acre, see the Phelps papers in Albany, New York.

[24] Manchester, New York, Assessment Roll, June 29, 1822, 16, Ontario County

property had jumped to $1,000. This is an increase of over 40 percent, yet the average property value for the whole township rose only 4 percent that year. This indicates that for the first time a cabin had been built and sufficient land had been cleared so that under New York law the assessed value had to be raised.[25]

Lucy's narrative corroborates the assessment roll evidence for an 1822 move to the Manchester property. She introduces events leading up to her son Alvin's death by saying: "In the spring after we moved onto the farm we commenced making Mapel [Maple] sugar of which we averaged 1000 lbs per year. We then began to make preparations for building a house, as the Land Agent of whom we purchased our farm was dead and we could not make the last payment."[26] William Smith wrote that the family moved into the township of Manchester and "Here my father purchased one hundred acres of new land heavely [heavily] timber[e]d and in the clearing up of this land which was mostly done in the form of fire."[27]

Next Lucy remarks that the third harvest had "arrived since we opened our new farm and all our sons were actively employed in assisting their Father to cut down the grain and storing it away." Wheat harvest in New York State fell during the latter part of July. By contracting for the property sometime after mid-July 1820, the harvest for that year was over. The first harvest for the Smiths would have fallen in the summer of 1821. Accordingly the third harvest would bring us to the summer of 1823. At this point she relates the story of an angel's visit informing her son of gold plates. She reported that he attempted in September to obtain the plates but was denied permission. Finally she says that in November they succeeded in raising their frame house and had the necessary materials on hand for its completion. However, Alvin's sudden sickness on November 15 and his death four days later on November 19, 1823 left the house incomplete. Lucy remembered

---

Records Center and Archives, Canandaigua.

[25] Manchester, New York, Assessment Roll, July 24, 1823, 17. The four percent increase was arrived at by comparing the dollar value per acre of property from 1820 to 1823 and averaging the increase shown in 1823. On increase in evaluation, see *Laws of the State of New York* 2:510.

[26] Anderson, *Lucy's Book*, 322-23.

[27] "Notes Written on 'Chamber's Life of Joseph Smith.'" 20.

that on his death-bed Alvin told Hyrum, "I now want you to go on and finish the House."[28]

To summarize, the first location where the Joseph Smith Sr. family lived outside of the village of Palmyra was a log house on Samuel Jennings property. That they resided there is mentioned in a June 1820 survey. There is no indication that they built this log house. While living there they were told by the land agent to build a log house on their newly acquire hundred acre farm. This is according to Lucy Mack Smith. Improvements such as a log structure and clearing of land are reflected in the July 1823 assessment of the property.

Lucy mentioned that Alvin commenced building a frame house just before his death which occurred in November 1823. The home may not have been actually finished but the Smiths moved into it. There was only one frame house in Manchester. As will be explained in chapter four Lemuel Durfee purchased the farm and its improvements in December 1825. The Smith family then became renters and lived in the home until about April 1829 when they moved in with Hyrum's family in the log home built on the hundred acres. There is no contemporary record showing the family living in Palmyra Township after their move to what became Manchester.

Once it is clear that the frame house was not raised until November 1823 then the increase of $300 in the assessed valuation, four months earlier in July 1823, must refer to some other improvements, including the completion of the log cabin on their farm. This conclusion receives further confirmation when Lucy introduces the events of 1823 with the words, "In the spring after we moved onto the farm." This clearly fixes the date of their move to the farm as occurring in 1822.

---

[28] Anderson, *Lucy's Book*, 335-36, 349-52. Lucy says that the frame house was still being built when Alvin died but has the year as 1822, which is incorrect. She gives Alvin's death variously as 1822 and 1824. Early sources for the year of Alvin's death include the gravestone in the General John Swift Memorial Cemetery, Palmyra, inscribed: "In memory of/ Alvin. Son of Joseph/ & Lucy Smith. who/ died Nov. 19. 1823./ in the 25. year of/ his age." (See photograph in Alma P. Burton, *Mormon Trail from Vermont to Utah* [Salt Lake City: Deseret Book, 1966], 35.) and *Wayne Sentinel* 2 (Sept. 29, 1824):3, Palmyra, contains an ad put in the newspaper by Joseph Sr., dated "Sept. 25th, 1824," stating he had exhumed Alvin's body to refute rumors that it had been removed for dissection.

Some indirect evidence supporting an 1822 date for the Smiths' move onto their Manchester property comes from the dating of the Palmyra revival. The account that young Joseph Jr. gave in 1838-39 places the excitement on the subject of religion as occurring in the second year after they moved to the farm, although mistakenly dating it to 1820.[29] Lucy's account specifically places the revival as occurring after Alvin's death. Contemporary evidence shows that the revival occurred during the last months of 1824 and early months of 1825. Thus if the revival, which broke out in 1824, occurred two years after the Smiths moved to their Manchester farm then their move to the farm would have indeed occurred in 1822.

---

[29] Manuscript History, Book A-1:1, LDS archives; Jessee, *Papers of Joseph Smith* 1:269.

2

Palmyra Revival of 1824-1825

When Joseph Smith Jr., described his first vision in his 1838-39 account, he dated it to the spring of 1820 and affirmed that this vision was the result of a religious revival, "an unusual excitement on the subject of religion." Smith stated that the excitement that stirred him also led his mother, brothers (Hyrum and Samuel Harrison), and sister Sophronia to join the Presbyterian Church, while he was drawn to the Methodists.[1] An examination of newspaper accounts, religious periodicals, church records, and personal narratives shows that there were no significant gains in church memberships or any other signs of excitement or revival in Palmyra in 1820. There was a stirring and momentous revival there with all the features that Joseph Smith's history mentions during the fall and winter of 1824-25.

In the draft of his mother's history, Lucy adds details which suggest an 1824 date for the revival as well. She begins by linking the revival to the death of her son Alvin, who died in November 1823. After relating the family's sorrow after his death, when "we could not be comforted because he was not," she adds a short statement, subsequently crossed out: "About this time their [there] was a great revival in religion and the whole neighborhood was very much aroused to the subject, and we among the rest flocked to the meeting house to see if their [there] was a word of comfort for us that might relcive [relieve] our over charged feelings."[2]

Her "over-charged feelings" were the result of her oldest

---

[1] See Manuscript History, Book A-1:1-2, LDS archives; Jessee, *Papers of Joseph Smith* 1:269-70. The fact that the names of Smith's mother and brothers appear later as members of the Palmyra Presbyterian Church who were dropped for nonattendance is further evidence that the revival Joseph Smith had in view affected the local Presbyterian Church. See "Records of the Session of the Presbyterian Church in Palmyra," 2:11-12, microfilm, film #900, reel 59, Harold B. Lee Library, Brigham Young University, Provo, Utah. Volume 1, which may have listed the Smiths as members, has been missing since at least 1932.

[2] Anderson, *Lucy's Book*, 356-57. Another portion crossed out included: "The circumstance of this Death aroused the neighborhood to the subject of religion" (355).

son Alvin dying suddenly the previous year. A year later Lucy was still seeking consolation for her wounded soul and hoped to find it at the town meeting house where the revival was in full progress and frequent meetings held. Her manuscript continues:

There was <at this time> a man then laboring in that place to effect a union of all the churches, that all denominations might be agreed to worship God with one mind, and one heart. This I thought looked right, and tried to persuade my Husband to join with them as I wished to do so myself and it was the inclination of them all [her children] except Joseph. He refused from the first to attend the meeting with us. He would say, Mother, I do not wish to prevent you from going to meeting or joining any church you like or any of the Family who desire the like, only do not ask me to <do so> for I do not wish to go. But I will take my Bible and go out into the woods and learn more in two hours than you could if you were to go to meeting two years. My husband also declined attending the meetings after the first but did not object to myself and such of the children as chose <going or becoming> church members.

Lucy notes that her son Joseph warned her about those involved, and her description of his warning suggests that the church she was intending to join was indeed the Presbyterian Church:

Now you look at deacon <Jessup>. . . . suppose that (one of his poor neighbors) owed him the value of one cow. This man has eight small children; suppose the poor man should be taken sick & die leaving his wife with one cow but destitute of every means of support for herself and family. Now I tell you that deacon Jess<u>p, <religious> as he is, would not hesitate to take the last cow from the widow and orphans rather than loose the debt.[3]

---

[3] Ibid., 357-58. In the Coray revised manuscript Joseph Smith's 1838-39 account, as published in the *Times and Seasons* (Nauvoo, Illinois) in 1842, was inserted into Lucy's history, making it contain two accounts of the same revival but with different dates. See Anderson, *Lucy's Book*, 331.

Henry Jessup was a long-time Presbyterian, one of the original trustees of the Western Presbyterian Church of Palmyra at its incorporation on March 18, 1817.[4]

According to Joseph, his older brother Hyrum joined the Presbyterian Church along with his mother as a result of the religious excitement. Willard Chase, a neighbor, mentioned that in 1825 Hyrum asked to borrow a stone (called a seer stone) found earlier while digging a well. Though reluctant to let the stone go, Chase said he honored Hyrum's request because Hyrum "had made a profession of religion" and Chase felt he could now be trusted to return it.[5]

In his 1838-39 account Joseph Jr. remembered that great multitudes joined the Baptist, Methodist, and Presbyterian churches during the revival. Church membership rolls are carefully kept, and in most cases can still be traced.

Membership rolls of "the first Baptized Church in Palmyra," which had a frame meetinghouse west of the village of Palmyra in Macedon Township, reveals that during the entire year of 1820 only eight people were received on profession of faith and baptized. However during the period between October 1824 and April 1825, even though the church was without a pastor at the time, ninety-four individuals were baptized and added to membership rolls.

For Baptists the awakening began on October 20, 1824, when church minutes show that "Michael Egleston, Erastus Spear, Lorenzo Spear, Abagail Spear, Belena Byxbe, Minerva Titus, Sophia Rogers, and Harriot Rogers told their Christian experience to the Church and were fellowshipped by the Church and on Thursday following were Baptized by Elder Bradley and Received into the Church." The minutes of November 20 mentioned eight more individuals baptized; the November 24 minutes name an

---

[4] Incorporation papers of the Western Presbyterian Church of Palmyra, March 18, 1817, in Miscellaneous Records, Book C:209, Ontario County Clerk's Office, Canandaigua. Henry Jessup was referred to as Deacon Jessup; see *Western Farmer* 1 (Dec. 12, 1821):4.

[5] Affidavit of Willard Chase, Manchester, Ontario County, New York, Dec. 11, 1833, in E.D. Howe, *Mormonism Unvailed* (Painesville [Ohio]: Printed and Published by the Author, 1834), 241. See also Vogel, *Early Mormon Documents* 2:66.

additional twelve. In December nineteen more were added by conversion. In the first four months of 1825 there were forty-five additional baptisms. For the one year period from October 1824 to the end of September 1825 there were a total of ninety-four persons baptized, an increase of eighty-seven members. Membership increased from one hundred thirty-two to two hundred and nineteen (sixty-five percent).[6]

The same pattern characterizes Methodist membership records, which give the total membership of the dozen or so preaching points serviced by a circuit-riding preacher. The increase of two hundred and eight reported in the summer of 1825 for the previous year demonstrates that this had proved to be a banner year for the Ontario circuit on which Palmyra was located. In contrast, the circuit had constantly lost members during the period between 1819 and 1821 — twenty-six in 1819, six in 1820, and forty-nine in 1821.[7]

Presbyterian membership rolls paint an identical picture. Although the first volume of the local church's minutes is missing, records of the Geneva Presbytery to which the church belonged and reported are still extant, and these clearly reflect the revival in the congregation at Palmyra. The minutes show that by September 21, 1825 when figures were in for a revival over the winter of 1824-25 "99 have been admitted on examination." As early as February 1825 the Presbytery was called on, in glowing terms, to

bless the Lord for the displays of sovereign grace which

---

[6] For 1820, see Minutes of the Palmyra Baptist Church under the dates of March 18; June 17; and Aug. 19, 1820. For 1824-25, see the Minutes of the Palmyra Baptist Church, Oct. 16; Nov. 20, 24; Dec. 4, 5, 18, 1824; Jan. 1, 15, 29; Feb.19; March 5, 19; and April 3, 1825. See *Minutes of the Ontario Baptist Association* (Rochester: Printed by Everard Peck, 1825), 5, for published membership figures for the conference year 1824-25. The records of "The First Baptized [sic] Church in Palmyra" are now in the American Baptist Historical Society in Rochester, New York. In 1835, when part of the congregation organized the Baptist Church within the village of Palmyra itself, the original records remained with the part of the church that would eventually become the Macedon Baptist Church in the next township to the west.

[7] *Minutes of the Annual Conferences of the Methodist Episcopal Church* (1773-1828), published in 1840, report: 446 (1824), 471 (1825), 330 (1819), 345 (1820), and 366 (1821). The records of the Palmyra Methodist Church were burned in a fire at Rochester in 1933.

have been made <within our boundaries> during the past year. In the congregation of Palmyra, the Lord has appeared in his glory to build up Zion. More than a hundred have been hopefully brought into the kingdom of the Redeemer. The distinguishing doctrines of grace have proved eminently the sword of the Spirit, by which the rebellion of man's heart has been slain. The fruits of holiness in this revival even now are conspicuous. The exertions for the promotion of divine knowledge are greater than formerly. Sabbath Schools, Bible classes, Missionary & Tract Societies are receiving unusual attention, & their salutary influence is apparent.[8]

Evidence of the increase of "Sabbath Schools, Bible Classes, Missionary & Tract Societies" also can be seen in the following excerpts printed in the local newspaper the *Wayne Sentinel*:

Messrs. Editors -- Please to allow the subscriber . . . the privilege of expressing his gratitude to God, for what He is doing for the people of Palmyra, and likewise his thanks to a number of friends in that village, for assisting him in printing Tracts, and in setting up Sabbath Schools.

The collection taken up on the Sabbath evening, amounting to $7[.]72, by the recommendation of the Rev. Mr. STOCKTON, will afford the subscriber some assistance, and it being divided and partly appropriated to a Juvenile Library, for a Sunday School in Palmyra, it will probably be the means of commencing a Library there for the benefit of the rising generation. . . .

By a Sabbath School Society is meant an institution for

---

[8] Geneva Presbytery "Records," Sept. 21, 1825, Book D:40; Geneva Synod "Records," Oct. 6, 1825, 431, both in the Presbyterian Historical Society, Philadelphia, Pennsylvania. In the Presbytery's Report to Synod, the Palmyra church reported for the year between September 10, 1824 and September 23, 1825 additions of 103 members and a membership jump from seventy-nine to one hundred seventy-eight members (one hundred thirty percent) with forty adult baptisms. See "Presbyterial Reports to the Synod of Geneva," Presbyterian Historical Society. For the quote, see Geneva Presbytery "Records," Feb. 2, 1825, Book D:27-28.

collecting the children and youth, of all denominations, whenever most convenient, for the purpose of giving them instructions from the word of God without any attempt to build up any peculiar sect or party. Such parts of the Holy Scriptures ought to be committed to memory as are of the most practical nature, and such as may be considered most useful in pointing out the duty of man to his Maker, and to his fellow creatures; such, for instance, as the Lord's Prayer, the Ten Commandments, Christ's Sermon on the Mount, the xii. of Romans, iii. of Colossians, and iv. of Ephesians. ...

A MEETING will be held in the Presbyterian house of worship, in this village, on *Thursday evening, the 16th inst.* at half-past 6 o'clock, for the purpose of organizing a RELIGIOUS TRACT SOCIETY. All who feel disposed to encourage the circulation of Scripture truth in the form of small and familiar publications, are invited to attend.[9]

A look at the Presbytery records for 1820 suggest some anticipation of a revival in the church of Phelps (located at Oaks Corners some fourteen miles from Palmyra) and at Canandaigua (some thirteen miles away), but nothing for the Palmyra church. The "Presbyterial Reports to the Synod of Geneva" confirms the scarcity of converts in the conference year of 1820. The presbytery reported to synod only fourteen additions to the Western Presbyterian Church of Palmyra for the period between February 1820 and March 1821. The additions include eight infant baptisms. If four Smiths joined that year, this would have left only two others to join all year.[10] But if the four members of the Smith family united with the Western Presbyterian Church of Palmyra by April 1825 there ages would be: Lucy (49), Hyrum (25), Samuel

[9] *Wayne Sentinel* 2 (Dec. 15, 1824).
[10] Geneva Presbytery "Records," Feb. 2, 1820, Book C:37 and "Presbyterial Reports to the Synod of Geneva." The membership for Palmyra shows an increase over the previous year's report from sixty-one to seventy-one members. This figure includes those who transferred in by letter of recommendation from another congregation as well as those joining upon profession of faith, off-set by those transferring out and those who either died or were dropped from membership.

Harrison (17), and Sophronia (22).

This pattern of growth is confirmed by Reverend James Hotchkin, who in 1845 began writing the official history of the rise of the Presbyterian denomination in western New York. The Synod of New York backed this effort and requested all the churches to open their records to him. Hotchkin was especially interested in revivals. His account for the Palmyra church shows revivals in 1817 and in 1824 but nothing in the intervening years.[11]

The revival over the winter of 1816-17, which affected mainly the Presbyterian Church of Palmyra, received coverage in at least a dozen periodicals, including among others the *Christian Herald and Seaman's Magazine*, the *Religious Remembrancer*, the *American Baptist Magazine*, and the *Boston Recorder*.[12]

The 1824-25 revival likewise received enthusiastic write-ups in an equal number of publications.[13] But there is total silence in these same periodicals about any revival in Palmyra between 1819 and 1821.[14]

---

[11] James H. Hotchkin, *A History of the Purchase and Settlement of Western New York, and the Rise, Progress, and Present State of the Presbyterian Church in that Section* (New York: Published by M. W. Dodd, 1848), 378.

[12] See accounts in *The Christian Herald and Seaman's Magazine* (Sept. 28, 1816; May 10; June 7, 1817): 2:16; 3:103f, 164; *Religious Remembrancer* (Oct. 5; Nov. 2, 1816; May 17, 1817), 4th Series, 24, 39, 151f; *American Baptist Magazine* (July 1817) 1:153; and *Boston Recorder* (Sept. 17, 1816; May 13; Oct. 21, 1817): 1:151; 2:88, 180. See also Joshua Bradley, *Accounts of the Religious Revivals . . . from 1815 to 1818* (1819), 223.

[13] Accounts of the revival in Palmyra during 1824-25 are reported in *New-York Religious Chronicle* 2 (Nov. 20, 1824): 154; 3 (April 9, 1825): 58; *Western New York Baptist Magazine* 4 (Feb. 1825): 284; *Western Recorder* 1 (Nov. 9, 1824): 90; 2 (March 29, 1825): 50; *Boston Recorder* 10 (April 29, 1825), 70; 10 (May 20, 1825): 82; *Baptist Register* (Utica), Dec. 3, 1824; March 11, 1825, 7; *American Baptist*, Feb. 1825; *Zion's Herald* 3 (Feb. 9; May 11, 1825), a Methodist weekly in Boston; *American Baptist Magazine* 5 (April 1825):124-25; and the *New York Observer*, May 7, 1825.

[14] The following periodicals were examined without finding a single reference to a Palmyra revival: Baptist: *American Baptist Magazine* (Jan. 1819-Nov. 1821); *Latter-day Luminary* (Feb. 1818-Nov. 1821); *Western New York Baptist Magazine* (Feb. 1819-Nov. 1821). Presbyterian: *Religious Remembrancer* (Jan. 1818-18 Aug. 1821); *The Christian Herald and Seaman's Magazine* (Jan. 2, 1819-Jan. 6, 1821); *Evangelical Recorder* (June 5, 1819-Sept. 8, 1821). Methodist: *The Methodist Magazine* (Jan. 1818-Dec. 1821). Other: *Boston Recorder* (Jan. 1818-Dec. 1821); *Palmyra Register* (Jan. 13, 1819-Dec. 27,

The 1824-25 dates can also be confirmed by checking the names of reported participants. William Smith, Joseph's brother, was interviewed in June 1841 by James Murdock, who read back his notes for correction. William recalled that "About the year 1823, there was a revival of religion in that region, and Joseph was one of several hopeful converts."[15] In his own book, *William Smith on Mormonism*, published in 1883, William wrote, "In 1822 and 1823 [sic], the people in our neighborhood were very much stirred up with regard to religious matters by the preaching of a Mr. Lane, an Elder of the Methodist Church, and celebrated throughout the country as a 'great revival preacher.'"[16] In addition to Lane, William, who was thirteen years old at the time, recalled the involvement of Benjamin Stockton:

> Rev. Stockton was the president of the meeting and suggested that it was their meeting and under their care and they had a church there and they [the Smiths] ought to join the Presbyterians, but as father did not like Rev. Stockton very well, our folks hesitated and the next evening a Rev. Mr. Lane of the Methodists preached a sermon on "what church shall I join?" And the burden of his discourse was to ask God, using as a text, "If any man lack wisdom let him ask of God who giveth to all men liberally."[17]

1820). The *Palmyra Register* has revivals reported in the state of New York but not in Palmyra (June 7; Aug. 16; Sept. 13; Oct. 4, 1820). Even when it describes a Methodist camp meeting in the vicinity of the village, it reports only that a man got drunk at the grog shops on the edge of the campground and died the next morning (3 [June 28; July 5, 1820]:2).

[15] Letter of Rev. James Murdock, dated New Haven, June 19, 1841, to the *Congregational Observer* 2 (July 3, 1841):1, Hartford and New-Haven, Connecticut. Interview of William Smith aboard an Ohio River boat on April 18, 1841. Original of *The Congregational Observer* is located in the Connecticut State Historical Society, Hartford. This interview was republished in the *Peoria Register and North-Western Gazette* 5 (Sept. 3, 1841).

[16] William Smith, *William Smith on Mormonism*, 6.

[17] Interview of William Smith by E. C. Briggs as reported by J. W. Petersen to *Zion's Ensign* 5 (Jan. 13, 1894):6, Independence, Missouri; see also, with minor inaccuracies, *Deseret Evening News* 27 (Jan. 20, 1894):11; *Latter-day Saints' Millennial Star* 56 (Feb. 26, 1894):133-34. William stated that "My mother, Lucy Smith, and my brothers Hyrum and Samuel and my sister Sophronia were members of the Presbyterian church situated in the town of Palmyra" (*Zion's*

William's description of the revival fits the pattern of the period. Once a revival had broken out, regular and frequent meetings would be scheduled at the town meetinghouse to advance the enthusiasm. Since Presbyterians were dominant in Palmyra, one could well expect Reverend Benjamin Stockton, their pastor, to preside and to expect the converts to join the church located in the village itself. The Baptist building was about a mile west of the center of the village, and Methodists were a mile east on Vienna Road, so Joseph Smith's expression of an unusual excitement in that "region of country" was a good way to describe the situation.

It is important to note that any extended series of revival meetings at which Stockton presided must fall in 1824 or later because he did not become pastor of the Palmyra Presbyterian Church until February 18, 1824.[18] Reverend James Hotchkin in cataloging the revivals in the churches of Geneva Presbytery wrote of the Palmyra church that a "copious shower of grace passed over this region in 1824 under the labors of Mr. Stockton, and a large number were gathered into the church, some of whom are now pillars in Christ's house."[19]

Stockton was pastor of the Skaneateles church in central New York from March 4, 1818 until June 30, 1822.[20] He visited Palmyra for a speech to the Youth Missionary Society in October 1822, and the newspaper described him then as "Rev. Stockton of Skaneateles."[21] He appeared again in the Palmyra paper when he

---

Ensign 3 [Aug. 27, 1892]:2), which he described as the "Church, of whome the Rev. Mr. Stoc[k]ton was the Presiding Paster" (William Smith, "Notes Written on 'Chamber's Life of Joseph Smith' by William Smith," typescript, 18, LDS archives).

[18] For his installation, see *Wayne Sentinel* 1 (Feb. 18, 1824):3; (Feb. 25, 1824):2. Also Geneva Presbytery "Records" C:252-54, 274; and Hotchkin *History*, 377. Stockton asked for permission to resign on September 5, 1827 (Geneva Presbytery "Records" D:83) which was agreed to by the local congregation on September 18 (D:85).

[19] Hotchkin, *History*, 378.

[20] For his installation date, see *Evangelical Recorder* 1 (March 7, 1819):111; or *Religious Intelligencer* 2 (May 2, 1818):800. On the terminal date, see Hotchkin, *History*, 341. Stockton remained a member of Cayuga Presbytery, which included Skaneateles, through 1823 (see Geneva Synod "Records," 1:211, 238, 258, 374) until he transferred to Geneva Presbytery on February 3, 1824 (see Geneva Presbytery "Records" C:252).

[21] *Palmyra Herald* 2 (Nov. 6, 1822):3.

performed a wedding on November 26, 1823, just a week after Alvin's death.[22] According to William Smith, Stockton was present the previous week and preached Alvin's funeral sermon. In this sermon Stockton implied that Alvin "had gone to hell, for Alvin was not a church member, but he was a good boy and my father did not like it."[23] William noted that when the revival meetings closed and Stockton insisted that the converts join the Presbyterian Church, "our folks hesitated" because of his insinuation about Alvin.

The "Rev. Mr. Lane," the other person mentioned by William Smith as participating in the revival, is George Lane, a talented Methodist preacher.[24] Lane is also mentioned by Oliver Cowdery, who worked with Joseph Smith beginning in 1829. In the Mormon periodical, *Latter Day Saints' Messenger and Advocate*, Cowdery commenced a "full history of the rise of the church of Latter Day Saints," published during 1834-35. For details of this account he said he relied on information furnished by Joseph Smith. Cowdery wrote:

> That our narrative may be correct, and particularly the introduction, it is proper to inform our patrons, that our brother J. SMITH jr. has offered to assist us. Indeed, there are many items connected with the fore part of this subject that render his labor indispensible [indispensable]. With his labor and with authentic documents now in our possession,

---

[22] *Wayne Sentinel* 1 (Dec. 31, 1823; Jan. 7, 14, 21, 28, 1824).

[23] *Zion's Ensign* 5 (Jan. 13, 1894):6; *Deseret Evening News* 27 (Jan. 20, 1894):11 and *Latter-day Saints' Millennial Star* 56 (Feb. 26, 1894):133. See also *Zion's Ensign* 3 (Aug. 27, 1892):2.

[24] For sketches of Lane's life, see *Minutes of the Annual Conference of the Methodist Episcopal Church* 8 (1860):40-41; William Sprague, *Annals of the American Methodist Pulpit* 7 (1861):810-11; Hendrick B. Wright, *Historical Sketches of Plymouth, Luzerne Co., Penna.* (Philadelphia: T.B. Peterson & Brothers, 1873), 309, 346ff; Oscar Jewell Harvey, *The Harvey Book* (1899), 128-34; George Peck, *The Life and Times of Rev. George Peck, D.D.* (New York: Nelson & Phillips, 1874), 96-97, 104, 108-9; George Peck, *Early Methodism Within the Bounds of the Old Genesee Conference from 1788 to 1828* (New York: Carlton & Porter, 1860), 492-95, and scattered references 166-67, 235-38, 309, 346, 428, 431, 441-42, 447-49, 509. Lane's portrait appears in *The Methodist Magazine* 9 (April 1826), and later in H. Wright, *Historical Sketches*, facing 346.

we hope to render this a pleasing and agreeable narrative, well worth the examination and perusal of the Saints.[25]

Then Cowdery begins with Smith as a young man of seventeen who is stirred by a revival in 1823 through the preaching of Lane:

One Mr. Lane, a presiding Elder of the Methodist church, visited Palmyra, and vicinity. Elder Lane was a tallented man possessing a good share of literary endowments, and apparent humility. There was a great awakening, or excitement raised on the subject of religion, and much enquiry for the word of life. Large additions were made to the Methodist, Presbyterian, and Baptist churches.—Mr. Lane's manner of communication was peculiarly calculated to awaken the intellect of the hearer, and arouse the sinner to look about him for safety—much good instruction was always drawn from his discourses on the scriptures, and in common with others, our brother's mind became awakened. For a length of time the reformation seemed to move in a harmonious manner, but, as the *excitement* ceased . . . a general struggle was made by the leading characters of the different sects, for proselytes.

Oliver Cowdery then mentioned members of the Smith family joining one of the churches:

In this general strife for followers, his mother, one sister, and two of his natural brothers, were persuaded to unite with the Presbyterians. . . . After strong solicitations to unite with one of those different societies, and seeing the apparent proselyting disposition manifested with equal warmth for each, his mind was led to more seriously contemplate the importance of a move of this kind.[26]

---

[25] *Latter Day Saints' Messenger and Advocate* 1 (Oct. 1834):13, Kirtland, Ohio. Cowdery's eight installments were copied in the fall of 1835 and are located in Manuscript History, Book A-1:46-103 [a separate section], LDS archives. See Jessee, *Papers of Joseph Smith*, 1:26-96.

[26] *Messenger and Advocate* 1 (Dec. 1834): 42-43, emphasis in original.

When Oliver Cowdery first published this account, he gave Smith's age as the "15th year of his life." He corrected this in his next letter, and said that in his previous letter the time of the religious excitement should have been in Smith's seventeenth year: "You will recollect that I mentioned the time of a religious excitement, in Palmyra and vicinity to have been in the 15th year of our brother J. Smith Jr.'s, age—that was an error in the type—it should have been in the 17th.—You will please remember this correction, as it will be necessary for the full understanding of what will follow in time. This would bring the date down to the year 1823."[27]

The 1823 Palmyra excitement, as Cowdery printed it, was placed prior to the reported first appearance (September 1823) of the angel who guarded the golden plates of the Book of Mormon. Oliver Cowdery's correction of the date to the year 1823 has the incorrect year since Lane was not the presiding elder of the local Methodist circuit until he was appointed a year later in 1824. That Cowdery has not overdrawn the effectiveness of Lane's preaching is evident from the comments of a fellow minister in the Methodist Genesee Conference, George Peck:

As a preacher he [Rev. George Lane] was thoroughly orthodox, systematic, and earnest. His sermons exhibited a thorough acquaintance with the Scriptures and with the human heart. In the palmy days of his itinerancy he was often overwhelmingly eloquent. Sometimes under his powerful appeals vast congregations were moved like the trees of the forest before a mighty wind. Many a stout-hearted sinner was broken down, and cried aloud for mercy under his all but irresistible appeals. His language was unstudied, but chaste, correct, simple, and forcible.[28]

In 1823 Lane was living in the area of Wilkes-Barre, Pennsylvania, and was not appointed presiding elder of the Ontario District in which Palmyra was located until July 1824.[29] He

---

[27] Ibid., 1 (Feb. 1835): 78.

[28] George Peck, *Early Methodism*, 494. George Lane was born on April 13, 1784 and died on May 6, 1859.

[29] For official confirmation of Lane's assigned field of labor, see *Minutes of the*

presided only until January 1825 when illness in his family forced him temporarily to leave the ministry.[30]

As presiding elder Lane was responsible to ride from circuit to circuit in the Ontario District and hold the quarterly business meetings for each circuit. Each preaching point or congregation on the circuit sent delegates to the quarterly meeting, and at its conclusion the presiding elder would travel on to the next circuit of the district to preside at its quarterly meeting.

According to Lane's report, published in the *Methodist Magazine* (April 1825), the Lord's work in Palmyra and vicinity "commenced in the spring, and progressed moderately until the time of the quarterly meeting, which was held on the 25th and 26th of September" 1824.[31] A note in the local Palmyra newspaper of September 15 showed the progress of the work over the spring and summer, shortly before Lane came on the scene at the September conference:

> A reformation is going on in this town to a great extent. The love of God has been shed abroad in the hearts of many, and the outpouring of the Spirit seems to have taken a strong hold. About twenty-five have recently obtained a hope in the Lord, and joined the Methodist Church, and many more are desirous of becoming members.[32]

This supports Joseph Smith's description of the religious excitement or revival as having "commenced with the Methodists." By September the revival had not yet touched the Baptist church, for at the annual meeting of the Ontario Baptist Association held on September 22, the church reported only two baptisms for the

---

Annual Conferences (1773-1828), 1:337, 352, 373, 392, 418, and 446. In 1823 Lane was serving in the Susquehanna District in central Pennsylvania. In July 1819 Lane went with Reverend George Peck to the annual eight-day business meeting of the Genesee Annual Conference. This was held at Vienna (now Phelps), a village some fifteen miles from the Smith home. The "Journal" of the conference does not indicate that any preaching services were held, and there is no indication of any revival touched off at Vienna or Palmyra.

[30] *Minutes of the Annual Conferences* (1825), 470.

[31] "Revival of Religion on Ontario District," letter of George Lane, Jan. 25, 1825, in *Methodist Magazine* 8 (April 1825):158-59.

[32] *Wayne Sentinel* 1 (Sept. 15, 1824):3.

entire previous year.[33] Similarly the local Presbyterian Church remained untouched, for the report of the Presbytery for September 8 stated, "there has been no remarkable revival of religion within our bounds."[34]

George Lane's personal report dated January 25, 1825 presents a detailed account of the revival's progress. He describes events occurring in the vicinity of Palmyra, focusing on how youth were especially affected:

> From Catharine [circuit] I went to Ontario circuit, where the Lord had already begun a gracious work in Palmyra. . . . About this time [September 25 and 26, 1824] it appeared to break out afresh. Monday evening, after the quarterly meeting, there were four converted, and on the following evening, at a prayer meeting at Dr. Chase's, there were seven. Among these was a young woman by the name of Lucy Stoddard.

Nineteen-year-old Lucy Stoddard was a cousin of Calvin Stoddard, who would later marry Smith's sister Sophronia and who would a few months after this also be touched by the revival.[35]

From this point Lane's account is largely taken up with Lucy Stoddard's conversion experience. Her calm and joyful acceptance of illness and death, just a few weeks after her conversion the last week of September 1824, helped fan the flames of revival among the young people of the village:

> The great deep of her heart was broken up; she saw clearly that she was a child of wrath, and in danger of hell. With this view of her sad condition, she fell prostrate at the feet of her offended sovereign, and in the bitterest anguish cried

---

[33] *Minutes of the Ontario Baptist Association* (Convened at Gorham, Sept. 22-23, 1824), 4.

[34] Geneva Presbytery "Records," Sept. 8, 1824, D:16.

[35] Calvin W. Stoddard, twenty-three years old at the time, was baptized by Elder Malby of the Palmyra Baptist Church on Sunday, April 3, 1825, along with his sister Bathsheba. His parents (Silas and Bathsheba), who were in their sixties, had been baptized the month before (Minutes of the Palmyra Baptist Church, March 5 and April 3, 1825). Stoddard married Sophronia Smith, who was then a member of the Palmyra Presbyterian Church, on December 30, 1827.

for mercy. In this situation, however, she was not suffered long to continue before she obtained a most satisfactory evidence of her acceptance with God through the merits of Jesus Christ. Her soul was unspeakably happy, and with great emphasis she exhorted others to come and share with her the inestimable blessing.

A week after her conversion she married Hiram Wilcox. Lane continued his report:

The same week she was married she was attacked by a bilious remittent fever, which terminated in a typhus fever. . . . at length, her disorder took such a turn as to convince her and others, that her stay in this world would be but short. The patience with which she endured her afflictions, which were sometimes very severe, was remarkable; not a murmur was heard to escape her lips. . . . From Saturday night to the time of her dissolution, which took place on Monday following, she seemed wholly swallowed up in God.

Lane then described her dying moments and the dramatic impression left on her friends. He reported that

when life appeared almost extinct, she raised her trembling hands, and clapped them three times, crying, "Hallelujah! hallelujah! hallelujah! glory to God in the highest!" From this time she lay in perfect composure until twelve o'clock on Monday, November 1st, when she breathed her last without a struggle or a groan, after an illness of three weeks and two days, and just five weeks from the time of her conversion. The effect produced by this death was the happiest. While it confounded the infidel, it greatly strengthened believers, especially young converts.[36]

Stoddard was not the only one whose death challenged

---

[36] *Methodist Magazine* 8 (April 1825):159-60. Lucy Stoddard Wilcox died on November 1, 1824.

friends to prepare for heaven. In Manchester Township, which joined Palmyra on the south, a deadly epidemic broke out and spread through Phelps Township to the east. This "sweeping mortality," as it was called by Benjamin Farley, a Christian-Connection preacher, was regarded by him as an act of God to prepare people's hearts to seek salvation. Writing from Phelps, he reported in a letter to the *Gospel Luminary* dated January 28, 1825:

> It has been a great time of lament[a]tion and mourning; children removed from parents, and parents from children. The scene has been truly alarming. . . . I was called upon almost every day to attend on funeral solemnities, and often two in a day; until I was attacked myself with the same fatal disorder, which brought me near to the grave.

Such widespread deaths inevitably made people think of the need to prepare for eternity. Farley continued:

> Since those d[a]ys of death and mourning, the Lord has graciously visited this place in mercy. Many have been brought to sing the new song, while scores are enquiring what they must do to be saved. The work is not confined to one neighborhood, but is becoming general. In Palmyra it is judged that more than one hundred have recently experienced salvation; and in the vicinity of Sulphur Springs [now Clifton Springs, Manchester Township] about the same number. The work in the above mentioned places is among the methodists and presbyterians. Congregations are uncommonly large and attentive. . . . the harvest truly is great.[37]

The actual numbers of converts in Palmyra may have been larger than Farley's January 1825 letter estimated, for two months previously the *Western Recorder* had already reported "one hundred or more" converts for Palmyra:

A revival of religion has lately commenced in the town of

---

[37] *Gospel Luminary* 1 (March 1825):65-66, West Bloomfield, New York.

Palmyra, N.Y. It is stated by one of the subjects of this glorious work, that one hundred or more persons, it is thought, have lately been brought out of darkness into marvelous light.—Persons of all ages and classes are the subjects of this work of grace.[38]

By mid-December the number was said to have swelled to near two hundred. Reverend Reuben Winchell in a letter dated "Dec 20th, 1824" written from Avon, New York, reported that while he was recently preaching at West Bloomfield he heard that the number of converts was about two hundred. He wrote: "In Palmyra, a town about 30 miles North East of this, God has triumphed gloriously. About 200, as I am informed, are sharers in this great and precious work."[39]

Even these figures may be too conservative; for Lane placed the number of Methodist converts alone at "upward of one hundred and fifty" by mid-December:

December 11th and 12th our quarterly meeting for Ontario circuit was held in Ontario. . . . Here I found that the work which had for some time been going on in Palmyra, had broken out from the village like a mighty flame, and was spreading in every direction. When I left the place, December 22[n]d, there had, in the village and its vicinity, upward of one hundred and fifty joined the [Methodist] society, besides a number that had joined other churches, and many that had joined no church.[40]

By the time Lane left the area the third week in December, many people needed only an invitation in order to be baptized. On Christmas day a Baptist preacher wrote to a friend: "As I came on my journey this way, I tarried a few days, and baptized eight."[41]

Meanwhile revivals were spreading as well in the neighboring towns. By February revivals were reported in Williamson and Ontario to the north, in Manchester, Sulphur

---

[38] *Western Recorder* 1 (Nov. 9, 1824):90.

[39] *American Baptist Magazine* 5 (Feb. 1825):61-62.

[40] *Methodist Magazine* 8 (April 1825):160.

[41] *The Latter Day Luminary* 6 (Feb. 1825):61.

Springs, and Vienna to the southeast, in Lyons to the east, and in Macedon to the west. Even towns at a greater distance from Palmyra began to experience revival fires, with Mendon to the west and Geneva to the southeast sharing in the divine outpouring.

A steady stream of reports of the spreading revival continued to flow from the papers and periodicals in early 1825. On January 13 Methodist preacher J. B. Alverson wrote from Canandaigua about Methodist gains:

> In Geneva the work has increased considerably. . . . On Ontario circuit . . . the prospects are very promising. Two hundred have been added since conference [i.e. July 1824]. On Lyons [circuit] the Lord continues to visit the people in great mercy. At Clyde the prospect is great . . . Sixty-one have experienced religion since this revival commenced, and forty-one have joined the society.[42]

By February townships bordering on Lake Ontario were described as touched by revival fires. According to West Bloomfield's *Gospel Luminary* for February 1825, "We learn that a powerful reformation has been spreading for several months past, in the towns of *Palmyra, Williamson* and *Ontario*. The work we are informed still continues in those places."[43]

West Bloomfield itself tasted the reformation blessing. "It has been a gr[ad]ual scene of reform[a]tion with us ever since April last" (1824), wrote David Millard in a communication dated February 25, 1825. Though not as powerful as the revival had been, still he found that "Our meetings are yet crowded and solemn, and some appear to be seeking the one thing nee[d]ful. On the 11th, inst. I baptized *twenty* happy converts. . . . On the 19th I baptized *five* more. Several others are expected to go forward in this ordinance soon." Millard, who had been preaching at West Bloomfield since 1817, closed his report by noting: "Such a season of extensive and powerful revivals, was probably never known in this western country, since its first settlement."[44]

By March the work was subsiding in the village of

---

[42] *Methodist Magazine* 8 (April 1825):161.
[43] *Gospel Luminary* 1 (Feb. 1825):42, emphasis in original.
[44] Ibid., 1 (March 1825):65, emphasis in original.

Palmyra, but it continued to spread in adjacent towns. Gorham, considerably south of Vienna, was followed by the area of Clyde, farther east beyond Lyons, where during the first part of May about one hundred and fifty were reported, converted. By this time "no recent cases of conviction" were reported from Palmyra itself, but the work was advancing in the Sulphur Springs area and still continuing at Geneva, twenty-five miles distant.[45] This generalized 1824-25 revival activity fits completely Joseph Smith's statement that the excitement occurred not only in the place where he lived but "became general among all the sects in that region of country, indeed the whole district of Country seemed affected by it."[46]

As converts began filling churches, leaders took stock of their numbers. By January Methodists estimated that on their Ontario circuit two hundred had joined their society. A Baptist pastor in Bristol, New York, reported to a friend under the date of March 9, 1825 that in the immediate area of Palmyra, "Multitudes have abandoned their false hopes and false schemes. . . . About three hundred have united with the Baptist, Presbyterian, and Methodist churches; and to each in about equal numbers."[47]

The Palmyra newspaper for March 2, 1825 reprinted a report from the *Religious Advocate* of Rochester:

> More than two hundred souls have become the hopeful subjects of divine grace in Palmyra, Macedon, Manchester, Phelps, Lyons, and Ontario, since the late revival commenced.—This is a powerful work; it is among old and young, but mostly among young people. Many are ready to exclaim, "what hath God wrought!" "It is the Lord's doing, and it is marvellous in our eyes." The cry is yet from various parts, "come over and help us." There are large and attentive congregations in every part, who hear as for their lives. Such intelligence must be pleasing to every child of God, who rightly estimate the value of immortal souls, and wishes well to the cause of Zion.

---

[45] *Western Recorder* 2 (May 10, 1825):74.

[46] Manuscript History, Book A-1:1, LDS archives; Jessee, *Papers of Joseph Smith* 1:270.

[47] *American Baptist Magazine* 5 (April 1825):125, Solomon Goodale writing from Bristol, New York, March 9, 1825.

Since the *Religious Advocate* was a Presbyterian-related periodical, the figures undoubtedly reflect Presbyterian gains. A note in the same issue of the Palmyra paper adds this balancing information: "It may be added, that in Palmyra and Macedon, including Methodist, Presbyterian and Baptist Churches, more than 400 have already testified that the Lord is good. The work is still progressing. In the neighboring towns, the number is great and fast increasing."[48]

By September 1825 the results of the revival for Palmyra had become a matter of record. The Presbyterian Church reported ninety-nine admitted on examination; Baptists had received ninety-four by profession of faith and baptism; the Methodist circuit showed an increase of two hundred and eight. Oliver Cowdery's mention of "large additions" and Joseph Smith's statement that "great multitudes united themselves to the different religious parties" were scarcely overstatements. Thus the revival matching the detailed descriptions of both Cowdery and Smith took place in 1824-25 both "in Palmyra" (Cowdery) and "the neighborhood" (Smith), as well as in the surrounding "vicinity," "region," and "whole district of Country."[49]

Contemporary evidence requires an 1824-25 date for the religious revival or excitement in the area of Palmyra which Joseph Smith and Oliver Cowdery described in their respective histories. Certainly memory at times conflates events, and perhaps Smith in retrospect blended in his mind events from 1820 with a revival occurring four years later.

---

[48] *Wayne Sentinel* 2 (March 2, 1825):3, 4. Unfortunately these reports have been mistakenly misdated to 1820 and used in several Mormon publications to establish an 1820 revival. However, the *Religious Advocate* did not begin publication at Rochester until about 1825, and its account quoted above refers to the 1824-25 revival. For an example of this account being used to support an 1820 revival date, see Gordon B. Hinckley, *Truth Restored: A Short History of the Church of Jesus Christ of Latter-day Saints* (Salt Lake City: Deseret Book, 1979), 1-2.

[49] For a response for an 1820 revival date, see H. Michael Marquardt and Wesley P. Walters, *Inventing Mormonism: Tradition and the Historical Record* (San Francisco: Smith Research Associates, 1994), 28-31.

3

Secular and Religious Background

Joseph Smith Jr.'s formal education was limited and sporadic. He received some of his earliest instruction from his parents. His mother, Lucy, explained that her children had been "deprived of school," but that after her family moved from the hills of Vermont to Lebanon, New Hampshire, in 1811, those children "who were old enough attended a school near by."[1]

After the family moved to western New York, Joseph Jr. apparently attended school in the Palmyra area. According to his own account, schooling was irregular because of economic pressures on the family: "as it required the exertions of all that were able to render any assistance for the support of the Family therefore we were deprived of the bennifit [benefit] of an education. Suffice it to say I was mearly [merely] instructid [instructed] in reading, writing and the ground <rules> of Arithmatic [Arithmetic] which const[it]uted my whole literary acquirements."[2]

Young Joseph owned a book on arithmetic titled *First Lines in Arithmetic, For the Use of Young Scholars* published in Hartford, Connecticut in 1818. His name appears in the book: "Joseph Smiths Book[,] January 31st, 1818" also the name of his sister Catherine.[3] At a later date Joseph Smith owned *Sacred Geography or a Description of the Places Mentioned in the Old and New Testament* by Thomas T. Smiley. This twelve page booklet intended to promote knowledge of the Holy Scriptures and

---

[1] Anderson, *Lucy's Book*, 300. Joseph Jr. would have been about six years old at the time.

[2] Joseph Smith, "A History of the life of Joseph Smith Jr.," (1832) MS, 1, LDS archives; Dean C. Jessee, ed., *The Papers of Joseph Smith: Autobiographical and Historical Writings* (Salt Lake City: Deseret Book, 1989), 1:5. Orson Pratt wrote in 1840: "He could read without much difficulty, and write with a very imperfect hand; and had a very limited understanding of the ground rules of arithmetic" (*Interesting Account of Several Remarkable Visions* [Edinburgh: Printed by Ballantyne and Hughes, 1840], 3).

[3] Photocopy in the Wilford C. Wood Collection, Wilford C. Wood Museum, Bountiful, Utah.

contained three maps of the Holy Land.[4]

Isaac Butts attended school with Smith in the Palmyra area,[5] as did Christopher M. Stafford, who remembered Joseph as "a dull scholar."[6] William Stafford's son, John Stafford, recalled, "Joe was quite illiterate. After they began to have school at their house, he improved greatly. . . . they had school in their house, and studied the Bible."[7] Young Joseph most likely received some training from his father who at one time had been a school teacher.[8]

Another young boy who attending school with Joseph Jr. was Peter S. Morrison. Morrison lived a short time in the Joseph Sr. family home and recalled, "I went to school in school session with Joseph and Hyrum Smith. I well remember that Joseph was considered somewhat of a dull pupil—that is, whenever he took up a book to study he would soon forget all about it and go off into absent-mindedness."[9]

Joseph Jr.'s lack of formal schooling sometimes yielded the erroneous impression that he was illiterate. In the latter part of 1825 while Smith was working in northern Pennsylvania, Isaac Hale, his future father-in-law, remarked that he was "not very well educated."[10] Perhaps in response to such impressions, Smith,

---

[4] Published in Philadelphia and printed for the author by W. P. Bason, Charleston, South Carolina, 1824, in RLDS archives. The names "Joseph Smith Jr" and "M J Whitehead" are written in the booklet.

[5] Statement of Isaac Butt, in *Naked Truths About Mormonism* 1 (Jan. 1888):2, original publication in the Yale University Library.

[6] Statement of C. M. Stafford, ibid., 1 (April 1888):1. For a listing of books in the Manchester Rental Library, see Robert Paul, "Joseph Smith and the Manchester (New York) Library," *Brigham Young University Studies* 22 (Summer 1982):333-56.

[7] *Saints' Herald* 28 (June 1, 1881):167. This material comes from the notes of the interviewer, William Kelley. His notes about John Stafford are "Joe was quite illit- [illiterate] until after they began to have school at their house - they had school at their house. and studied their Bible" (William H. Kelley Papers, Library-Archives, Community of Christ, formerly the Reorganized Church of Jesus Christ of Latter Day Saints, Independence, Missouri, cited hereafter RLDS archives).

[8] Anderson, *Lucy's Book*, 294, 299.

[9] "Founder of Church Known by Visitor," *Salt Lake City Herald*, Dec. 31, 1912.

[10] *The Susquehanna Register, and Northern Pennsylvanian* 9 (May 1, 1834):1; also E. D. Howe, *Mormonism Unvailed* (Painesville [Ohio]: Author, 1834), 263.

though almost twenty years old, enrolled in school in the Bainbridge, New York area while he was working for Josiah Stowell during the winter of 1825-26. While being examined before Justice Albert Neely on March 20, 1826, Smith testified that he had been "going to school."[11]

Other accounts confirm this. Stowell's son Josiah remembered Joseph as "about 20 years old or there about. I also went to Schoal [School] with him one winter."[12] Asa B. Searles reported that he was a fellow student with Joseph in Bainbridge when his brother, Lemuel Searles, was a teacher there.[13] Local tradition holds that "Smith, while here, attended school in District No. 9."[14]

With opportunities for formal education limited, the Smith family, like others on the frontier, relied on other avenues of instruction and information. One source of wide ranging information was the newspaper, which the Smiths received weekly in Palmyra. Orsamus Turner, who served a five-year printer's apprenticeship in Palmyra between 1818 and 1822, recalled that young Joseph came to the village to pick up his father's newspaper:

> He used to come into the village of Palmyra with little jags of wood, from his backwoods home; sometimes patronizing a village grocery too freely; sometimes find an odd job to do about the store of Seymour Scovell; and once a week he would stroll into the office of the old Palmyra *Register*, for his father's paper.[15]

---

[11] Charles Marshall, "The Original Prophet. By a Visitor to Salt Lake City," *Fraser's Magazine* 7 (Feb. 1873):229.

[12] Josiah Stowell, Jr., to John S. Fullmer, Feb. 17, 1843, LDS archives. See Mark Ashurst-McGee, "The Josiah Stowell Jr.—John S. Fullmer Correspondence," *Brigham Young University Studies* 38, no. 3 (1999):108, 113; and Vogel, *Early Mormon Documents* 4:80.

[13] *History of Lee County* [Illinois] (Chicago: H. H. Hill and Company, Publishers, 1881), 397. Searles "had many a wrestle [with Joseph]; but young Smith was a large, strong fellow and could handle any of the boys."

[14] James H. Smith, *History of Chenango and Madison Counties, New York* (Syracuse, NY: D. Mason & Co., 1880), 154.

[15] O[rsamus]. Turner, *History of the Pioneer Settlement of Phelps and Gorham's Purchase*, 213-14.

After they moved to their Manchester farm, the Smith family received the *Wayne Sentinel*, a successor to the *Register* and the *Herald*. A notice giving the subscription cost and the published amount of Joseph Sr.'s delinquent bill suggest that the Smiths received the paper for more than two years. The *Sentinel* cost $2.00 per year if picked up at the office. The August 11, 1826 issue listed "Joseph Smith" among the delinquent subscribers with the amount due $5.60.[16]

Certainly the Smith family made use of this newspaper. In September 1824 Joseph Sr. placed an advertisement in the *Sentinel* which ran for six weeks. The advertisement concerned a rumor that his oldest son Alvin's buried remains had been disturbed:

> To the Public. Whereas reports have been industriously put in circulation, that my son *Alvin* had been removed from the place of his interment and dissected, which reports, every person possessed of human sensibility must know, are peculiarly calculated to harrow up the mind of a parent and deeply wound the feelings of relations— therefore, for the purpose of ascertaining the truth of such reports, I, with some of my neighbors, this morning repaired to the grave, and removing the earth, found the body which had not been disturbed.
>
> This method is taken for the purpose of satisfying the minds of those who may have heard the report, and of informing those who have put it in circulation, that it is earnestly requested they would desist therefrom; and that it is believed by some, that they have been stimulated more by a desire to injure the reputation of certain persons than a philanthropy for the peace and welfare of myself and friends. JOSEPH SMITH.[17]

The newspaper ran stories on the Hebrew origin of American Indians, a topic subsequently discussed by Joseph Jr. Mordecai M. Noah had embraced this popular theory, and on

---

[16] *Wayne Sentinel* 1 (Oct. 1823):1, and 3 (Aug. 11, 1826):3.

[17] Ibid., 2 (Sept. 29, 1824):3, emphasis in original. The ad is dated Sept. 25, 1824. This notice also appeared in the issues of Oct. 6, 13, 20, 27 and Nov. 3, 1824.

October 11, 1825 the *Sentinel* reprinted an address detailing his opinion: "Those who are conversant with the public and private economy of the Indians, are strongly of [the] opinion that they are the lineal descendants of the Israelites, and my own researches go far to confirm me in the same belief." He then lists a number of reasons for his belief:

> The Indians worship one Supreme Being as the fountain of life, and the author of all creation. Like the Israelites of old, they are divided into tribes. . . . their language and dialect are evidently of Hebrew origin. They compute time after the manner of the Israelites. . . . They have their prophets, High Priests, and their sanctum sanctorum. . . . They have their towns and cities of refuge

After concluding his list of evidences, he reflected:

> If the tribes could be brought together, could be made sensible of their origin, could be civilized, and restored to their long lost brethren, what joy to our people, what glory to our God, how clearly have the prophecies been fulfilled, how certain our dispersion, how miraculous our preservation, how providential our deliverance.[18]

The newspaper also followed contemporary religious events, which clearly affected young Joseph and his family. The Smiths could have read of the visions and revelations of Asa Wild, a religious seeker like Joseph's uncle Jason Mack.[19] The paper published in 1823 Asa's claim that God told him that in seven years "there would scarce a sinner be found on earth" and "that every denomination of professing christians had become extremely corrupt; many of which never had any true faith at all."[20]

Wild's claim that existing churches were in error would have found sympathetic ears in the Smith family. Even by the time

---

[18] Ibid., 3 (Oct. 11, 1825):1.

[19] Anderson, *Lucy's Book*, 230.

[20] *Wayne Sentinel* 1 (Oct. 22, 1823):4. See Elden J. Watson, "The 'Prognostication' of Asa Wild," *Brigham Young University Studies* 37, no. 3 (1997-98):223-30.

of young Joseph's birth in 1805, both of his parents had come to rely on personal interpretation of the Bible as the primary guides to religious life. A crucial context for the background and education of young Joseph thus becomes the broader religious questing and experiences of his extended family.

The family of Joseph Sr. originally had ties to the Congregational Church. According to records of the Topsfield, Massachusetts church, his father, Asael, had been baptized as an infant on March 11, 1744. Nearly twenty-eight years later on March 8, 1772, Asael had three of his children baptized: Jesse (about four years old), Priscilla (about two years old), and Joseph (infant).[21] After Asael's family moved to Tunbridge, Vermont, his son Joseph, at the age of twenty-four, was married to Lucy Mack on January 24, 1796 by Seth Austin, a justice of the peace in Tunbridge.[22]

A year later Joseph, along with his father and his brother Jesse, professed belief in the doctrine that all people will be saved. They were among the dozen men who on December 6, 1797 stated that they had "formed our Selves into a Society and wish to be known by the Name or forme of universalists." As a result they also informed the town clerk that they did not want "to be Charged with any Tax towards the Support of any teacher of any Diferant [Different] Denomination."[23]

Years later Joseph Sr.'s son William remembered that his father's "faith in the universal restoration doctrin[e], however, often brought him in contact with the advocates of the doctrin[e] of

---

[21] George Francis Dow, in section titled: "Baptismal Records of the Church in Topsfield," *The Historical Collections of the Topsfield Historical Society* 1 (Topsfield, MA: Published by the Society, 1895, 2d ed.):15, 37-38. See also Richard L. Anderson, *Joseph Smith's New England Heritage: Influences of Grandfathers Solomon Mack and Asael Smith* (Salt Lake City: Deseret Book and Provo, Utah: BYU Press, 2003), 246n118, 249n127.

[22] Tunbridge Town Records, Book A:129, located in the Tunbridge Town Clerk's Office, Tunbridge, Vermont. Lucy mentions that Austin married them, but this was not included in the 1853 printing of her book (Anderson, *Lucy's Book*, 258).

[23] Tunbridge Town Records, Book A:188. See also Vogel, *Early Mormon Documents* 1:633-34 and Larry C. Porter, *A Study of the Origins of The Church of Jesus Christ of Latter-day Saints in the States of New York and Pennsylvania* (Provo, Utah: Joseph Fielding Smith Institute for Latter-day Saint History and BYU Studies, 2000), 5.

endless misrey [misery]." Because of his "belief in the ultimate and final redem[p]tion of all mankind," William claimed it "brought down upon my father the aprobiem [opprobrium] or slur of Old Jo Smith."[24]

Although following a different path, Lucy Mack Smith also came to be of independent religious leanings, emphasizing the Bible and personal experience rather than organized religion. While in Tunbridge she attended Methodist meetings. She wrote that she persuaded her husband to attend with her a few times: "But as soon as his Father and brother Jesse heard that we were attending Methodist meeting they were much displeased and his father came to the door one day and throw Tom Pain[e]'s age of reason into the house and angrily bade him read that untill he believed it."[25] Thomas Paine's *Age of Reason*, which expounded deism, was widely regarded as an atheistic tract. It taught that true religious knowledge is not revealed or taught by any church but attained by reason and that God, after creating the world according to rational laws, withdrew and no longer interacts with nature or humankind.

Lucy was concerned about her husband's spiritual condition and prayed about him. That night she had a dream in which she saw two trees. She understood that one of the trees was her husband's brother Jesse and the other tree was her husband, who would hear and receive the gospel with his whole heart.[26] This belief in visions and dreams formed a significant part of the Smith family's religious life.

In 1802 the Smith family, by then Joseph, Lucy, and their two young sons, Alvin and Hyrum, moved from Tunbridge to Randolph, Vermont. At Randolph Lucy became seriously ill. She promised God that she would serve him if she recovered from her illness. "<I> covenanted with God if he would let me live I would endeavor to get that religion that would enable me to serve him right whether it was in the Bible or where ever it might be found

---

[24] William Smith, "Notes Written on 'Chambers Life of Joseph Smith.' by William Smith," typescript, 18, LDS archives.

[25] Anderson, *Lucy's Book*, 291. The *Age of Reason* incident is not in the Coray finished manuscript.

[26] Anderson, *Lucy's Book*, 292-94.

even if it was to be obtained from heaven by prayer and Faith."[27] She prayed to God and heard a voice then say, "Seek and ye shall find, knock and it shall be opened unto you. Let your heart be comforted, ye believe in God, beleive [believe] also in me."[28]

Lucy later remembered hearing a Presbyterian give a discourse and afterward she "returned saying in my heart there is not on Earth the religion which I seek, I must again turn to my bible. Taking Jesus and his deciples [disciples] for an ensample I will try to obtain from God that which man cannot give nor take away."[29] She followed this course for a number of years, later recovered her health, and "found a minister who was willing to baptize me and leave me free from membership in any church."[30]

Thus by the time of young Joseph's birth his father had embraced the doctrine that all people will be saved, while his mother avoided joining any church, regarding all churches as devoid of "the religion which I seek." Eventually the Smith family moved from Randolph to Sharon, Vermont, where they rented land from Solomon Mack, Lucy's father, and farmed, and "in the winter he [Joseph Sr.] taught school."[31] Here their son Joseph was born two days before Christmas on December 23, 1805.

Religion remained an important focus of the Smith family during young Joseph's childhood. In 1811, when he was five years old, his grandfather, Solomon Mack, published *A Narraitve of the Life of Solomon Mack*, an account of his life's experiences and religious conversion.[32] After its publication Mack rode on

---

[27] Ibid., 277-78. For additional information on the religious background of Joseph and Lucy Smith, see Dan Vogel, *Religious Seekers and the Advent of Mormonism* (Salt Lake City: Signature Books, 1988), 25-28.

[28] Anderson, *Lucy's Book*, 278. See Matt. 7:7, Luke 11:9, and John 14:1.

[29] Ibid., 280.

[30] Ibid., 281.

[31] Ibid., 299, 294. William Smith wrote about his father, "his occupation in early life was that of a school teacher he was a man well letter[e]d in the common branches of our english studies" ("Notes Written on `Chambers Life of Joseph Smith,'" 20).

[32] Solomon Mack, *A Narraitve of the Life of Solomon Mack, Containing An Account of the Many Severe Accidents he met with during a long series of years, together with the Extraordinary Manner in which he was converted to the Christian Faith* (Windsor [Vermont]: Printed at the Expense of the Author [1811]). For the text and dating of this work, see Richard L. Anderson, *Joseph Smith's New England Heritage*, 43-73, 201-202n1.

horseback through the surrounding countryside, selling copies of his self-published book. In his narrative, Mack informs readers that until the winter of 1810-11 he gave very little thought to God. In spite of crippling illnesses, he wrote, "I never once thought on the God of my salvation or looked up to him for blessing or protection." He had never read the Bible and "could only recollect some taught parts such as I had heard and laid up for the purpose of ridiculing religious institutions and characters."

But at the age of seventy-six, while incapacitated because of illness, he came under conviction of his sins when he "saw a light about a foot from my face as bright as fire. . . . I thought by this that I had but a few moments to live. . . . I prayed that the Lord would have mercy on my soul and deliver me from this horrible pit of sin." The same appearance of light occurred some nights later, and on another occasion he thought he heard the Lord call him by name. Each time he thought he had but a moment to live.

Finally seeking a sign of his acceptance and pardon by God, he asked to have one night entirely free from pain. He wrote, "And blessed be the Lord, I was entirely free from pain that night." He continued: "And the Lord so shined light into my soul that everything appeared new and beautiful. Oh how I loved my neighbors. How I loved my enemies—I could pray for them. Everything appeared delightful." He found this especially so with regard to the Lord: "The love of Christ is beautiful. There is more satisfaction to be taken in the enjoyment of Christ one day, than in half a century serving our master, the devil."[33]

Young Joseph's grandfather was not the only one to tell of seeing lights and encountering God in dreams. At about the same time, his father, according to his mother's later recollections, was having similar experiences: "my husband's mind became much excited upon the subject of religion; yet he would not subscribe to any particular system of faith, but contended for the ancient order, as established by our Lord and Saviour Jesus Christ, and his Apostles."[34]

In April 1811, a month after William was born, Joseph Sr. had what Lucy termed his first vision. In this vision he saw a field

---

[33] Solomon Mack, *A Narraitve of the Life of Solomon Mack*, 11, 20, 22-24.
[34] Anderson, *Lucy's Book*, 294.

and the attendant spirit said, "this field is the world which lies ina[n]imate & dumb as to the things pertaining to the true religion or the order of Heavenly things; all is darkness."[35] As the result of this vision, he, like his wife Lucy, came to the opinion that all churches were in darkness. Lucy wrote that her husband "seemed more confirmed than ever, in the opinion that there was no order or class of religionists that knew any more concerning the Kingdom of God, than those of the world, or such as made no profession of religion whatever."[36]

Joseph Sr. had other visions intermittently during young Joseph's childhood. In May 1818 his father had his sixth vision. In this vision he saw himself on judgment day traveling toward "the meeting house" upon which crowds of people were converging. He was told he had arrived too late and the door was shut. "I soon felt that I was perishing and began to pray but my flesh continued to wither on my bones." An angel appeared and asked him if he had done everything necessary to be admitted. The messenger reminded him, "Justice must have its demands and then mercy <has its> claims." Upon hearing this, it entered his mind "to ask God in the name of Jesus and I cried out in the agony of my soul, Oh, Lord, I beseech Thee in the name of Jesus Christ to forgive my sins. I then felt strengthened and My flesh began to be restored. The angel then said, you must plead the merits of Jesus for he is an advocate with [the] Father and a mediator between God and man. I now was made quite whole, and the door was opened and upon entering I awoke."[37]

Perhaps as the result of such visions Joseph Sr. seems to have consistently avoided organized religion. After he attended one meeting during the 1824-25 revival, Lucy remembered her husband refused to attend further meetings.[38]

William recalled that his father had morning and evening prayers: "I well remember father used to carry his spectacles in his vest pocked [pocket] . . . and when us boys saw him feel for his

---

[35] Lucy Mack Smith, manuscript draft. Variant reading in Anderson, *Lucy's Book*, 295.
[36] Ibid., 296.
[37] Ibid., 324-25.
[38] Ibid., 358.

specks, we knew that was a signal to get ready for prayer."[39]
William told about his father's instructions to the family:

> My father's religious customs often become earksome
> [irksome] or tiresome to me, while in my younger days as I
> made no profession of Christ[i]anity. Still I was called upon
> to listen to pray[e]rs boath [both] night and morning. My
> father's favourit [favorite] evening humn [hymn] runs thus:

> > The day is past and gone
> > The evening shades appear
> > O may we all remember well
> > The night of death draws near.

> Again and again this was hymn sung while upon the
> bending knees. My parents, father and mother, pour[e]d out
> their souls to God the doner [donor] of all blessings, to
> keep and g[u]ard their children and keep them from sin and
> from all evil works.[40]

In 1834 Joseph Sr. told of his efforts to provide a religious
education for his children, emphasizing the comfort he found in his
visionary experiences:

> I have not always set that example before my family that I
> ought: I have not been diligent in teaching them the
> commandments of the Lord, but have rather manifested a
> light and trifling mind: But in all this I have never denied
> the Lord. Notwithstanding all this my folly, which has been
> a cause of grief to my family, the Lord has often visited me
> in visions and in dreams, and has brought me, with my
> family, through many afflictions, and I this day thank his

---

[39] *Zion's Ensign* 5 (Jan. 13, 1894):6; *Deseret Evening News* 27 (Jan. 20, 1894);
and *Latter-day Saints' Millennial Star* 56 (Feb. 26, 1894):133.
[40] William Smith, "Notes Written on 'Chambers Life of Joseph Smith,'" 18. The
hymn, written by John Leland, a Baptist minister, was published in the first LDS
hymnal. See *A Collection of Sacred Hymns* (Kirtland, Ohio: F.G. Williams &
Co., 1835 [1836]), 62-63.

holy name.[41]

The Smith family was not unique in this emphasis on visionary experience as the basis of enlightenment.[42] This was evidence of the working of the Holy Spirit of God in the life of the individual and a prominent part of the revivalistic religious experience. The assurance of forgiveness often came in the form of a vision.

This visionary forgiveness came to youthful seekers as well as more mature ones. In 1816 Elias Smith (no relation) published his account of a very similar experience. For some time as a youth in his early teens he felt a deep sense of being lost:

> My mind was greatly distressed by considering myself a sinner, justly condemned to die. . . . Every wrong ever committed, whether in thought, word, or deed, appeared before me, and things which before appeared small, now rose like mountains between me and my Creator. It appeared to me that I was a criminal brought to the bar, and proved guilty, and deserving death, without one plea in his own behalf.

With such thoughts pressing on his mind, this youth slipped while carrying a piece of timber. He was pinned on the ground next to a log:

> While in this situation, a light appeared to shine from heaven, not only into my head, but into my heart. This was something very strange to me, and what I had never experienced before. My mind seemed to rise in that light to the throne of God and the Lamb. . . . The Lamb once slain appeared to my understanding, and while viewing him, I felt such love to him as I never felt to any thing earthly. My

---

[41] Remarks made by Joseph Smith Sr., on December 9, 1834 and recorded in Patriarchal Blessing Book, 1:1 (LDS archives). See Mark L. McConkie, *The Father of the Prophet: Stories and Insights from the Life of Joseph Smith, Sr.* (Salt Lake City: Bookcraft, 1993), 75-76.

[42] See for example, Richard L. Bushman, "The Visionary World of Joseph Smith," *Brigham Young University Studies* 37, no. 1 (1997-98):183-204.

mind was calm and at peace with God through the Lamb of God, that taketh away the sin of the world. The view of the Lamb on mount Sion gave me joy unspeakable and full of glory.[43]

A few years later, Billy Hibbard published his spiritual vision. Writing about it in 1825, he described an event that took place about 1782 when he was nearly twelve years old. He saw himself as a helpless, hopeless sinner:

I found to my unspeakable grief and dismay, that I was altogether unholy in my nature; my sins had corrupted every part, so that there was nothing in me that was good; I was a complete sink of sin and iniquity; I looked to see if there was no way to escape, if God could not be just and have mercy on me: but no . . . all my hopes of obtaining mercy and getting to Heaven at last, are gone, and gone forever!

Hibbard continued in this depressing state of guilt for some days, hoping to find pardon for his sins. Then on a Sunday while reading about the sufferings of Christ, he "had an impression to go in secret and pray":

when I came to the place of prayer, had kneeled down, and closed my eyes, with my hands uplifted toward the heavens, I saw Jesus Christ at the right hand of God looking down upon me, and God the Father looking upon him. The look of Jesus on me removed the burden of my sins, while he spoke these words, "Be faithful until death and this shall be thy place of rest."

After thus seeing both the Father and the Son in vision the burden of his guilt suddenly was lifted:

I never had seen Jesus Christ before, nor heard his voice,

---

[43] Elias Smith, *The Life, Conversion, Preaching, Travels, and Sufferings of Elias Smith* (Portsmouth, New Hampshire: Printed by Beck & Foster, 1816), 1:56, 59.

nor ever had a sense of his intercession at the right hand of God for me till now; and now I could see the justice of God in shewing mercy to me for the sake of his Son Jesus Christ; and not only to me, but to all that would come to him forsaking their sins, and believing that his death and suffering were the only satisfactory sacrifice for sin.

Finally he described the ecstasy of the visionary experience:

the love of God in Christ and of Christ in God, so completely overcame me, that I was all in tears, crying, Glory! Glory! Glory! Beholding the glory of God by faith, was a rapturous sight. . . . I opened my eyes therefore, while still on my knees; and behold all nature was praising God. The sun and firmament, the trees, birds, and beasts, all appeared stamped with the glory of God. I leaped from my kneeling posture, clapped my hands, and cried, Glory! Glory! Glory! Heaven and earth is full of thy glory.[44]

Another youth, Eleazer Sherman, described a similar deliverance from the guilt of sin. On January 10, 1815 at the age of nineteen, he concluded that "misery and despair must be my lot forever":

I sunk down in tears, and sorrow overwhelmed my sinking soul. While in this distress, I heard as it were a soft and pleasant voice saying to me, Behold the Lamb of God, that taketh away the sin of the world: And then was presented to my mental view the dear Saviour, from his birth to his death. He seemed one of the most innocent looking persons ever beheld by mortal eyes.

After appearing on his throne of mercy, the Savior seemed to ask the young man to surrender his life to him. "As soon as I had given up all," he wrote, "I found peace, and the glory of God filled my soul."[45]

---

[44] B. Hibbard, *Memoirs of the Life and Travels of B. Hibbard* (New York: Printed for and Published by the Author, 1825), 22-24.
[45] Eleazer Sherman, *The Narrative of Eleazer Sherman* (Providence: H. H.

The seventh and last vision of Joseph Sr. occurred, according to his wife, while he was living in Palmyra in 1819 or 1820.[46] It was about this time that young Joseph would say that he experienced his first vision. The earliest account of that vision survives from 1832 in Joseph Jr.'s own hand. He begins his narration by pointing out that his parents "spared no pains to instructing me in <the> christian religion." He then described his youthful religious questing:

> At about the age of twelve years my mind become seriously imprest [impressed] with regard to the all importent [important] concerns for the wellfare of my immortal Soul, which led me to searching the scriptures, believeing [believing] as I was taught, that they contained the word of God. Thus applying myself to them and my intimate acquaintance with those of differant [different] denominations led me to marvel exce[e]dingly, for I discovered that <they did not> adorn their profession by a holy walk and Godly conversation agreeable to what I found contained in that sacred depository, this was a grief to my Soul. Thus from the age of twelve years to fifteen I pondered many things in my heart . . . my mind become exce[e]dingly distressed for I become convicted of my sins and by searching the scriptures I found that <mankind> did not come unto the Lord but that they had apostatised from the true and liveing faith and there was no society or denomination that built upon the gospel of Jesus Christ as recorded in the new testament.

However, he continued, "I learned in the scriptures that God was the same yesterday, to day and forever." By observing the wonders of nature, Joseph confirmed for himself "well hath the wise man said <it is a> fool <that> saith in his heart there is no God." Thus by considering both the Bible and creation he concluded: "All, all these bear testimony and bespeak an omnipotant [omnipotent] and omnipreasant [omnipresent] power, a

---

Brown, 1830), 1:20-21.
[46] Anderson, *Lucy's Book*, 330.

being who makith Laws and decreeeth and bindeth all things in their bounds, who filleth Eternity, who was and is and will be from all Eternity to Eternity." Thus convinced that the God of the Bible existed, but no denomination any longer taught the New Testament gospel, he continued praying:

> I cried unto the Lord for mercy for there was none else to whom I could go and obtain mercy and the Lord heard my cry in the wilderness and while in <the> attitude of calling upon the Lord <in the 16th year of my age> a piller [pillar] of light above the brightness of the sun at noon day come down from above and rested upon me and I was filled with the spirit of god and the <Lord> opened the heavens upon me and I saw the Lord and he spake unto me saying, Joseph <my son> thy sins are forgiven thee. . . . behold I am the Lord of glory, I was crucifyed for the world.[47]

Several observations can be drawn from this earliest written narration of Smith's teenage religious experience. First, like his mother, he found the Bible a reliable guide and his interpretation of it the only correct one. Second, like his parents before him, he realized that no church any longer had the truth; everyone else had apostatized. Finally, like his parents and many others of that period, he felt a conviction of his sins and found forgiveness through a direct vision of the Savior granting him pardon.

Orsamus Turner, the young apprentice working at the Palmyra *Register* newspaper office, noted young Joseph's presence at a Methodist camp meeting. He recalled that "after catching a spark of Methodism in the camp meeting, away down in the woods, on the Vienna road, he [Smith] was a very passable exhorter in evening meetings."[48] The reference to "camp meeting"

---

[47] "A History of the life of Joseph Smith Jr.," 1-2, LDS archives, and Jessee, *Papers of Joseph Smith*, 1:5-6. In June 1830 there was a brief reference to Joseph's experience of forgiveness recorded in the Book of Commandments: "For, after that it truly was manifested unto this first elder [Joseph Smith], that he had received a remission of his sins, he was entangled again in the vanities of the world" (BC 24:6). Joseph saw this experience in 1832 as his call to start into the ministry. In this 1832 recollection he wrote that he was in his sixteenth year of age (1821) when he received forgiveness.

[48] O[rsamus]. Turner, *History of the Pioneer Settlement of Phelps and Gorham's*

alludes to a camp grounds site used by Methodists at that time. This camp was about a mile outside the village of Palmyra, "away down in the woods" on the road running southeast to Vienna. At this site in 1822, Methodists built their first house of worship.

The Methodist work in Palmyra was still only a "class meeting" on the circuit at this time. It was not until July 3, 1821 that the Methodist Society of Palmyra was incorporated as a church "by the name of the first Methodist Episcopal Church of Palmyra."[49] Four days later, on July 7, 1821, Durfee Chase deeded to the Methodist Church his property on Vienna Road.[50] It was not until 1822 that they were able to begin construction of a meeting house.[51]

In the Methodist style of worship, a sermon was preached in which points were drawn from a given text or passage from the Bible. After the message, an exhortation was usually given by another speaker who would reemphasize the points made in the preacher's exposition and plead with the people to take seriously the message they had just heard. The Methodist structure provided for the licensing of official exhorters by the District Conference.[52] However, in more informal situations, such as camp meetings and evening services (where the liturgical format used at the morning worship was dispensed with), even those as young as twelve or thirteen could rise and give exhortations.[53] Since Turner completed his apprenticeship and left Palmyra in the summer of 1822, his words provide a valuable insight into Joseph's religious activities before his seventeenth birthday.

Purchase, 214, 400. See also Calvin N. Smith, "Joseph Smith as a Public Speaker," *Improvement Era* 69 (April 1966):277.

[49] See Miscellaneous Records, Book C:385-86, in the County Clerk's Office, Ontario County, Canandaigua.

[50] See Deeds of Ontario County, Book G:345, Ontario County Records Center and Archives, Canandaigua.

[51] See Palmyra *Herald* 2 (June 19, 1822):2.

[52] *The Doctrines and Discipline of the Methodist Episcopal Church* (New York: J. Emory and B. Waugh, 1828), 28, 43, 45, 64, 74, 80. For background on the Methodist Class, see David Lowes Watson, *The Early Methodist Class Meeting: Its Origins and Significance* (Nashville, TN: Discipleship Resources, 1987). Members of the class were to "bear one another's burdens" (94) and "there was no prerequisite for Methodist membership other than a desire for salvation, the societies were open to all, regardless of their spiritual state" (108).

[53] *Doctrine and Discipline of the Methodist Episcopal Church*, 71.

Joseph did not become a licensed exhorter because such persons had to be members in full standing with the denomination. However, Pomeroy Tucker, another early resident of Palmyra, remarked concerning Joseph, "at one time he joined the probationary class of the Methodist church in Palmyra, and made some active demonstrations of engagedness . . . [but] he soon withdrew from the class."[54] Formal church membership would have required Joseph's meeting with the class leader "at least six months on trial."[55]

Joseph attended a debating club in Palmyra Village and Turner recalled the following:

> Joseph had a little ambition; and some very laudable aspirations; the mother's intellect occasionally shone out in him feebly, especially when he used to help us solve some portentous questions of moral or political ethics, in our juvenile debating club, which we moved down to the old red school house on Durfee street, to get rid of the annoyance of critics that used to drop in upon us in the village[56]

Joseph Jr. was involved with the local Methodist class and wrote about his "intimate acquaintance" with persons in different denominations during his youth. By the time he was approaching nineteen, during the 1824-25 revival meetings, he was somewhat partial toward the Methodists but felt little need for organized religion. He later wrote in his 1838-39 account:

> During this time of great excitement my mind was called up to serious reflection and great uneasiness; but though

---

[54] Pomeroy Tucker, *Origin, Rise and Progress of Mormonism*, 18.

[55] *Doctrines and Discipline of the Methodist Episcopal Church*, 80.

[56] Turner, *History of Phelps and Gorham's Purchase*, 214. This statement by Turner is cited in John Henry Evans, *Joseph Smith, An American Prophet* (New York: Macmillan, 1933), 32. The *Western Farmer* 1 (Jan. 23, 1822):3, Palmyra, contained the following: "NOTICE. The young people of the village of Palmyra and its vicinity are requested to attend a Debating school at the school house near Mr. Billings' on Friday next." Notice dated January 19, 1822.

my feelings were deep and often poignant, still I kept myself aloof from all these parties, though I attended their several meetings as occasion would permit."[57]

His mother recalled, "Joseph never said many words upon any subject but always seemed to reflect more deeply than common persons of his age upon everything of a religious nature."[58]

According to his later colleague Oliver Cowdery, Joseph was impressed by the revival preaching of Reverend George Lane. As mentioned in chapter two, Lane was the Methodist presiding elder of the Ontario District from July 1824 until January 1825. Cowdery wrote, "much good instruction was always drawn from his [Lane's] discourses on the scriptures, and in common with others, our brother's [Joseph Smith's] mind became awakened."[59] Joseph would have been eighteen years old when he heard Lane preaching.

After the family discussed "the subject of the diversity of churches," Lucy Smith recalled that Joseph saw an angel who revealed to him the gold plates:

After we ceased conversation, he went to bed <and was pondering in his mind which of the churches were the true one> but he had not laid there long till <he saw> a bright <light> enter the room where he lay. He looked up and saw an angel of the Lord <standing> by him. The angel spoke, I perceive that you are enquiring in your mind which is the true church. There is not a true church on Earth. No, not one, <and> has not been since Peter took the Keys <of the Melchesidec priesthood after the order of God> into the Kingdom of Heaven. The churches that are now upon the Earth are all man made churches.[60]

Lucy Smith later remembered "listening in breathless

---

[57] Manuscript History, Book A-1:2; Jessee, *Papers of Joseph Smith* 1:270.

[58] Anderson, *Lucy's Book*, 335, not in Coray revised manuscript.

[59] *Messenger and Advocate* 1 (Dec. 1834):42.

[60] Anderson, *Lucy's Book*, 335, not in Coray revised manuscript.

anxiety to the <religious> teachings" of her son Joseph, "for Joseph was less inclined to the study of books than any child we had but much more given to reflection and deep study."[61] These teachings would have been the theological expositions resulting from Joseph's deep study expressed within the Smith family.

Joseph Smith's childhood vision, as his 1832 narrative describes, of Christ's appearing and granting him forgiveness for his sins was similar to those of other young people of his day. The later 1838-39 version of his first vision introduces a revival before his vision and creates a chronologically implausible picture.

From what we can learn about the religious background of the Smith family, Joseph Jr.'s parents taught religious values to their children. Though his father did not regularly attend church, he did sing and pray with his family. Joseph's religious instruction included hearing minister's sermons, revival homilies, private family worship, and personal Bible study. Joseph was not uninformed, ignorant, or illiterate.

While the Smith family held Christian beliefs, they also believed in treasures supernaturally buried in the earth which could be obtained only through magical rituals. It is to the well-documented period of what Joseph Jr. called glass looking that we turn our attention in the next chapter.

---

[61] Ibid., 344.

4

Manchester Scryer

The possibility of finding buried treasure fascinated many in late eighteenth and early nineteenth century America. Reports of searching for such riches were widespread in the Palmyra area,[1] and extant accounts show that treasure was generally sought through supernatural means. Locations for buried wealth and lost Spanish mines were sometimes located through dreams. Treasures could also be located by using divining rods, often made from "witch hazel," or by looking in special stones or crystals. Sometimes when a stone was used, a person would place the stone in a hat and then conjure the guardian treasure spirit. After finding a spot where the cache was supposedly hidden, the seekers would draw a magic circle on the ground around the hidden treasure. Sometimes they would maintain absolute silence, but other times they would recite magical charms or religious verses used as charms. Whatever the means, money-diggers needed to overcome the guardian spirit who had enchanted the treasure, otherwise the treasure would slip back into the earth.

In his official history, Joseph Smith downplayed his experience as a money-digger and sought to cast this activity in the context of manual labor. However, Smith was involved in such endeavors for years in two widely separated areas and enjoyed an established reputation as a gifted seer. He was thought to be able to located lost goods with a special seer stone and magical religious ceremonies.[2] Rodger I. Anderson explained some background to

---

[1] Newspaper articles mention unnamed individuals who claimed to have found vast treasures. The *Orleans Advocate* published in Albion, New York, contains the following: "A few days since was discovered in this town, by the help of a mineral stone, (which becomes transparent when placed in a hat and the light excluded by the face of him who looks into it, provided he is fortune's favorite,) a monstrous potash kettle in the bowels of old mother Earth, filled with the purest bullion" (reprinted in *Wayne Sentinel* 3 [Dec. 27, 1825]:2). Republished in the *Livingston Register*, December 28, 1825, Geneseo, New York.

[2] Wayland D. Hand, "The Quest for Buried Treasure: A Chapter in American Folk Legend[a]ry," in *Folklore on Two Continents: Essays in Honor of Linda*

53

this practice and belief:

> the practice of money digging by no means originated with Smith. Long before Smith's neighbors accused him of hunting for buried money by occult means, the art of magical treasure hunting was already widespread in America. Accounts of men pursuing enchanted treasures with divining rods appear throughout the eighteenth century, and in combination suggest that the practice had very early become ritualized. The treasure was located by a divining rod, immobilized by charms, magic circles, or special steel rods driven into the ground for that purpose, and incantations recited to protect the diggers from "certain malicious Demons who are said to h[a]unt and guard such Places." Any deviation from these prescribed rituals on the part of the treasure hunters, any "Mistake in the Procedure, some rash Word spoken, or some Rule of Art neglected, the Guardian Spirit had Power to sink it deeper into the Earth and convey it out of their reach."[3]

Young Joseph was assisted by his father and his older brothers Alvin and Hyrum.[4] In addition neighbors of the Smith family were money diggers, including Willard Chase, Samuel

---

Degh (Bloomington, Indiana: Trickster Press, 1980), 112-19; D. Michael Quinn, *Early Mormonism and the Magic World View* (Salt Lake City: Signature Books, rev. ed., 1998).

[3] "Joseph Smith's Early Reputation Revisited," *Journal of Pastoral Practice* 4 (1980):77-78; see also Rodger I. Anderson, *Joseph Smith's New York Reputation Reexamined* (Salt Lake City: Signature Books, 1990), 12-13.

[4] In January 1859 Martin Harris, an early Mormon convert then residing at Kirtland, Ohio, was interviewed by Joel Tiffany. This account was subsequently published in *Tiffany's Monthly* 5 (Aug. 1859):163-70, a spiritualist publication at New York City. See also the affidavit of Peter Ingersoll, Palmyra, Wayne County, New York, Dec. 2, 1833, in Howe, *Mormonism Unvailed*, 233. Philastus Hurlbut (a former member of the Mormon church) visited Palmyra and Manchester townships during November and December 1833 and obtained, besides two general statements, a number of statements from some Joseph Smith family acquaintances. These were subsequently printed in Howe's compilation *Mormonism Unvailed* in 1834. For a convenient compilation of the statements collected by Hurlbut, see Vogel, *Early Mormon Documents* 2:13-77.

Lawrence, as well as John, Joshua, and William Stafford.[5] Others in the area also claimed to have special stones, including Sarah or Sally Chase; also Joshua and William Stafford.[6] Donna Hill wrote, "there is testimony from early Mormons that Joseph had searched for treasure, that to some extent he had accepted the myths which often accompanied belief in buried treasure at that time and that a number of his close friends in the church were 'money-diggers' and rodsmen."[7]

In southern New York and northern Pennsylvania, William Hale, Oliver Harper, and Josiah Stowell also searched for treasures.[8] Financial support was supplied, among others, by Abraham Fish in Manchester and by Asa and Josiah Stowell in Bainbridge.[9]

When Joseph Smith recalled his money-digging activities, he wrote only about searching for a lost mine in 1825 for Josiah Stowell. But contemporary records suggest that this had been one of the Smith family occupations in the Palmyra/Manchester area since the early 1820s. For example, Joshua Stafford of Manchester recalled that he "became acquainted with the family of Joseph Smith, Sen. about the year 1819 or 20. They then were laboring

---

[5] *Tiffany's Monthly* 5 (Aug. 1859):164; John Stafford in *Saints' Herald* 28 (June 1, 1881):167; and C. R. Stafford, statement of March 1885, in *Naked Truths About Mormonism* 1 (Jan. 1888):3.

[6] Statement of C. R. Smith, March 1885, in *Naked Truths About Mormonism* 1 (April 1888):1; interview of John Stafford in William H. Kelley papers, Library-Archives, Community of Christ, Independence, Missouri (hereafter RLDS archives); see *Saints' Herald* 28 (June 1, 1881):167.

[7] Donna Hill, *Joseph Smith: The First Mormon* (Garden City, New York: Doubleday, 1977), 66. See Dan Vogel, "The Locations of Joseph Smith's Early Treasure Quests," *Dialogue: A Journal of Mormon Thought* 27 (Fall 1994):198-231.

[8] Joseph and Hiel Lewis, "Mormon History", *The Amboy Journal* 24 (April 30, 1879):1; Frederic G. Mather, "The Early Mormons," *Binghamton Daily Republican,* July 29, 1880, see also *Lippincott's Magazine of Popular Literature and Science* (Philadelphia: J.B. Lippincott and Co., 1880), 26:200, 202; *Tiffany's Monthly* 5 (Aug. 1859):164.

[9] Copy of a letter from six leading citizens of Canandaigua, New York, dated Jan. 1832, in answer to a query about Mormons from Rev. Ancil Beach, in the Walter Hubbel papers, Princeton University, Princeton, New Jersey; Statement of W. R. Hine, in *Naked Truths About Mormonism* 1 (Jan. 1888):2; and A. W. Benton, "Mormonites," *Evangelical Magazine and Gospel Advocate* 2 (April 9, 1831):120.

people, in low circumstances. A short time after this, they commenced digging for hidden treasures . . . and told marvellous stories about ghosts, hob-goblins, caverns, and various other mysterious matters."[10] Willard Chase, another friend of the family, similarly recalled, "I became acquainted with the Smith family . . . in the year 1820. At that time, they were engaged in the money digging business."[11]

One of the most detailed accounts of this early period was given by William Stafford, a neighbor who lived in Manchester and whose family gave the name to Stafford Road where the Smiths' house still stands.

> I first became acquainted with Joseph, Sen., and his family in the year 1820. They lived, at that time, in Palmyra, about one mile and a half from my residence. A great part of their time was devoted to digging for money . . . I have heard them tell marvellous tales, respecting the discoveries they had made in their peculiar occupation of money digging. They would say, for instance, that in such a place, in such a hill, on a certain man's farm, there were deposited kegs, barrels and hogheads of coined silver and gold--bars of gold, golden images, brass kettles filled with gold and silver—gold candlesticks, swords, &c, &c.[12]

Joseph Sr. believed he could locate objects that were lost or hidden from sight under the ground. A neighbor, Peter Ingersoll, recalled that "he requested me to walk with him a short distance from his house, for the purpose of seeing whether a mineral rod would work in my hand, saying at the same time he was confident it would. . . . he cut a small witch hazel bush and gave me direction how to hold it."[13] In a letter of Jesse Smith to "Hiram" Smith written on June 17, 1829, Jesse wrote concerning a person who

---

[10] Statement of Joshua Stafford, Manchester, Ontario County, New York, Nov. 15, 1833, in *Mormonism Unvailed*, 258.

[11] Affidavit of Willard Chase, before Justice of the Peace, Frederick Smith, Dec. 11, 1833, in *Mormonism Unvailed*, 240.

[12] Affidavit of William Stafford, Manchester, New York, Dec. 8, 1833, in *Mormonism Unvailed*, 237.

[13] Affidavit of Peter Ingersoll, Dec. 2, 1833, in *Mormonism Unvailed*, 232.

discussed the Smith family, "he says your father has a wand or rod like Jannes & Jambres who withstood Moses in Egypt—that he can tell the distance from India to Ethiopia."[14] Fayette Lapham, who interviewed Joseph Sr., said that Smith "believed that there was a vast amount of money buried somewhere in the country; that it would some day be found; that he himself had spent both time and money searching for it, with divining rods, but had not succeeded in finding any, though sure that he eventually would."[15]

The younger Joseph learned to work the witch hazel rod from his father. Mrs. S. F. Anderick recalled that Joseph Jr. claimed "he could tell where lost or hidden things and treasures were buried or located with a forked witch hazel." She continued:

Willard Chase, a Methodist who lived about two miles from uncle's, while digging a well, found a grey smooth stone about the size and shape of an egg. Sallie, Willard's sister, also a Methodist, told me several times that young Jo Smith, who became the Mormon prophet, often came to inquire of her where to dig for treasures. She told me she would place the stone in a hat and hold it to her face, and claimed things would be brought to her view. Sallie let me have it several times, but I never could see anything in or through it. I heard that Jo obtained it and called it a peep-stone, which he used in the place of the witch hazel. Uncle [Earl Wilcox] refused to let Jo dig on his farm. I have seen many holes where he dug on other farms.[16]

---

[14] Copy of letter in Joseph Smith Letterbook 2:60, LDS archives.

[15] "The Mormons," *Historical Magazine* 7 (May 1870):306.

[16] Statement of Mrs. S. F. Anderick, June 24, 1887, in *Naked Truths About Mormonism* 1 (Jan. 1888):2. See William W. Phelps to E. D. Howe, Jan.15, 1831, in *Mormonism Unvailed*, 273. Benjamin Saunders said, "I have seen Sally (Sarah) Chase peep or look in her seer stone a many a time. She would look for any thing. I have had it in my hand" (W. H. Kelley Collection, "Miscellany 1795-1948," RLDS archives). Sallie (named Sarah) was born on October 20, 1800 to Clark and Phebe Chase. Her father died in 1821. The records of the Clark Chase family are found in William E. Reed, *The Descendants of Thomas Durfee of Portsmouth, R.I.* (Washington, D.C.: Gibson Bros., 1902), 213-14, and George Grant Brownell, comp., *Genealogical Record of the Descendants of Thomas Brownell 1619 to 1910* (Jamestown, New York, 1910), 200.

Willard Chase employed Joseph Smith Jr. to help him dig a well on the Chase property where the seer stone was discovered. Willard was twenty-four years old and Joseph was sixteen. Chase gives details of the discovery from his perspective:

> In the year 1822, I was engaged in digging a well. I employed Alvin and Joseph Smith to assist me; the latter of whom is now known as the Mormon prophet. After digging about twenty feet below the surface of the earth, we discovered a singularly appearing stone, which excited my curiosity. I brought it to the top of the well, and as we were examining it, Joseph put it into his hat, and then his face into the top of his hat. It has been said by Smith, that he brought the stone from the well; but this is false. There was no one in the well but myself. The next morning he came to me, and wished to obtain the stone, alledging [alleging] that he could see in it; but I told him I did not wish to part with it on account of its being a curiosity, but would lend it. . . . He had it in his possession about two years.[17]

The magical stone is now in the possession of the Church of Jesus Christ of Latter-day Saints in Salt Lake City.[18]

William Stafford, who helped Joseph Smith Sr. and team with their digging, later recalled how young Joseph used the stone to search for treasure:

---

[17] Affidavit of Willard Chase, Dec. 11, 1833, in *Mormonism Unvailed*, 240-41. Smith later borrowed the stone and returned it at Chase's insistence. The stone was subsequently borrowed by Hyrum Smith and never returned. Joseph in his examination before Justice Albert Neely on March 20, 1826 said that he "had occasionally been in the habit of looking through the stone to find lost property for 3 years" or since about 1823. Fayette Lapham learned from Joseph Sr. that after the stone was found when working on a well "Joseph spent about two years looking into this stone, telling fortunes, where to find lost things, and where to dig for money and other hidden treasure" (*Historical Magazine* 7 [May 1870]:306). On Joseph Smith's use of seer stones, see Richard Van Wagoner and Steven Walker, "Joseph Smith: 'The Gift of Seeing,'" *Dialogue: A Journal of Mormon Thought* 15 (Summer 1982): 49-68. For additional information on seer stones, see Quinn, *Early Mormonism and the Magic World View*, 32-64, 145-46, 158-77, 242-46.

[18] Ibid., 243.

They would say, also, that nearly all the hills in this part of New York, were thrown up by human hands, and in them were large caves, which Joseph, Jr., could see, by placing a stone of singular appearance in his hat, in such a manner as to exclude all light; at which time they pretended he could see all things within and under the earth, —that he could see within the above mentioned caves, large gold bars and silver plates—that he could also discover the spirits in whose charge these treasures were, clothed in ancient dress.

Stafford also recalled that young Joseph "had been looking in his glass" and saw some kegs of gold and silver underneath the earth. He went with both Smiths and the elder Joseph made a circle and said that the treasure was within the circle. Hazel sticks were then put in the ground "around the said circle, for the purpose of keeping off the evil spirits." After putting a steel rod in the center of the circles and digging a trench, the older Smith consulted his son who had been "looking in his stone and watching the motions of the evil spirit." It was determined that they "had made a mistake in the commencem[e]nt of the operation; if it had not been for that, said he, we should have got the money."[19]

The Smiths obtained no gold or silver, but witnesses claimed young Joseph helped find other objects. Martin Harris, who became a close friend of the Smith family, was impressed when Joseph used his stone to find his lost toothpick. He recalls:

I was at the house of his [Joseph's] father in Manchester, two miles south of Palmyra village, and was picking my teeth with a pin while sitting on the bars. The pin caught in my teeth, and dropped from my fingers into shavings and straw. I jumped from the bars and looked for it. . . . I then took Joseph on surprise, and said to him—I said, "Take your stone." I had never seen it, and did not know that he had it with him. He had it in his pocket. He took it [out] and placed it in his hat—the old white hat—and placed his face in his hat. I watched him closely to see that he did not look [to] one side; he reached out his hand beyond me on the

---

[19] Affidavit of William Stafford, Dec. 8, 1833, in *Mormonism Unvailed*, 237-39.

right, and moved a little stick, and there I saw the pin, which he picked up and gave to me. I know he did not look out of the hat until after he had picked up the pin.[20]

An early 1832 letter written at Canandaigua, New York, south of Manchester, reported that Joseph "had been engaged for some time in company with several others of the same character in digging for money . . . and for a time were supported by a Mr. Fish an illiterate man of some property."[21] Mr. Fish is Abraham Fish of Manchester, New York, a neighbor of the Smith family. Abraham Fish was acquainted with Joseph and his father.[22] Fish lived south of the Smith/Durfee farm. That Fish was illiterate is evidenced in the Nathan Pierce Docket Book when he signed his name with an "X" identified as "his mark." A receipt dated March 10, 1827 received by the younger Joseph from the Thayer store in Palmyra reads: "Palmyra, 10th March 1827, Recd of Joseph Smith Jr Four dollars which is credited to the account of A. Fish" and signed J & L Thayer. Joel and Levi Thayer were the owners of the store.[23]

Josiah Stowell was a farmer with substantial holdings in the town of Bainbridge, Chenango County, in southern New York[24]

---

[20] *Tiffany's Monthly* 5 (Aug. 1859):164. Lucy Harris, Martin's wife, stated, "About a year previous to the report being raised that Smith had found gold plates, he became very intimate with the Smith family, and said he believed Joseph could see in his stone any thing he wished" (*Mormonism Unvailed*, 255).

[21] Copy of a letter from six leading citizens of Canandaigua, New York, dated Jan. 1832, in answer to a query about Mormons from Rev. Ancil Beach, in the Hubbel papers, Princeton University Libraries, Princeton. See Vogel, *Early Mormon Documents* 3:15.

[22] Abraham Fish was born about 1773 and died on July 17, 1845 at the age of seventy-two (*Wayne Sentinel* [July 23, 1845], 2). The probate of the will of Lemuel Durfee, Sr., lists "One note signed by Joseph Smith [Sr.] and Abraham Fish, thirty-seven dollars and fifty cents" with interest of $1.42 (Probate Papers, Surrogate's Court, Wayne County Courthouse, Lyons, New York). After Durfee's death on August 8, 1829 (*Wayne Sentinel* 6 [Aug. 14, 1829]:3), Durfee's son, also named Lemuel, brought suit against Joseph Smith, Sr. and Abraham Fish on January 19, 1830 for $39.92, which was eventually paid (Docket Book of Nathan Pierce, Town Hall of Manchester, Manchester, New York). Pierce was a justice of the peace in Manchester where Joseph Sr. was residing and Durfee was a resident of Palmyra.

[23] Joseph Smith Collection, under Receipts, in LDS archives.

[24] Josiah Stowell was married to Miriam Bridgman. They had eight children, four sons and four daughters: Simpson (or Simson; also listed as Simeon), b.

and a deacon in the First Presbyterian Church. In the mid-1820s Stowell organized a money digging company to search for a mine he believed had been hidden by Spaniards in northern Pennsylvania near the home of Isaac Hale.[25] Stowell hired Joseph Smith and his father to help. It was while digging and boarding at the home of Isaac Hale that Smith met his future wife Emma Hale. She was born in July 1804 and was a year and a half older than Smith.

Two of Emma's cousins, Joseph and Hiel Lewis, later recalled how the possibility of a treasure came to light:

> We are unable at this time to give precise dates, but some time previous to 1825, a man by the name of Wm. Hale, a distant relative of our uncle Isaac Hale, came to Isaac Hale, and said that he had been informed by a woman named Odle, who claimed to possess the power of seeing under ground, (such persons were then commonly called peepers) that there was great treasures concealed in the hill northeast from his, (Isaac Hale's) house. By her directions, Wm. Hale commenced digging, but being too lazy to work, and too poor to hire, he obtained a partner by the name of Oliver Harper, of [New] York state, who had the means to hire help. But after a short time, operations were suspended for a time.[26]

Josiah Stowell eventually took up the search. In the fall of 1825 he went north to the Manchester area to visit his son Simpson Stowell. While there he heard about the Smiths' ability to locate

---

July 29, 1791; Martha b. Sept. 10, 1793; Horace b. March 10, 1796; Miranda b. Sept. 6, 1798; Thomas b. Sept. 28, 1800; Rhoda b. March 11, 1805; Miriam (Mary) b. May 22, 1807; and Josiah b. April 16, 1809. See William Henry Harrison Stowell, *Stowell Genealogy* (Rutland, Vermont: Tuttle Co., 1922), 229-30.

[25] Stowell "became infatuated with the idea that he must go in search of hidden treasures, which he believed were buried in the earth" (James H. Smith, *History of Chenango and Madison Counties, New York*, 153). This was based on the 1877 recollection of William D. Purple. The name "Isaiah Stowel" in the recollection should be Josiah Stowell.

[26] *The Amboy Journal* 24 (April 30, 1879):1, Amboy, Illinois. See Vogel, *Early Mormon Documents* 4:301-302.

buried treasure. Reportedly Joseph Jr. told Stowell that he could see the treasure Stowell had been looking for in Harmony through his peep stone even while still in Manchester. He also, according to Stowell's account, "described Josiah Stowel[l]'s house and outhouses" accurately.[27] Stowell was impressed and hired Smith and his father to help locate the treasure.

Oliver Cowdery, who became a friend of the Smith family in 1829, wrote of Stowell's project and of his hiring Joseph Smith:

This gentleman, whose name is Stowel[l], resided in the town of Bainbridge, on or near the head waters of the Susquehannah river. Some forty miles south, or down the river, in the town of Harmony, Susquehannah county, Pa. is said to be a cave or subterraneous recess. . . . where a company of Spaniards, a long time since, when the country was uninhabited by white settlers, excavated from the bowels of the earth ore, and coined a large quantity of money. . . . Enough, however, was credited of the Spaniard's story, to excite the belief of many that there was a fine sum of the precious metal lying coined in this subterraneous vault, among whom was our employer [Stowell]; and accordingly our brother [Joseph Smith] was required to spend a few months with some others in excavating the earth, in pursuit of this treasure.[28]

In his own history Joseph Jr. also mentioned this work with Stowell:

In the month of October Eighteen hundred and twenty five I hired with an old Gentleman, by name of Josiah Stoal [Stowell] who lived in Chenango County, State of New York. He had heard something of a silver mine having been

---

[27] See Stowell's 1826 testimony in Charles Marshall, "The Original Prophet. By a Visitor to Salt Lake City," *Fraser's Magazine* 7 (Feb. 1873):229.

[28] *Messenger and Advocate* 2 (Oct. 1835):201. This account may have been written in response to Isaac Hale's 1834 affidavit, which is mentioned in the article. Although Cowdery's letter claims Smith worked for Stowell as "a common laborer" (200), Smith's mother indicated he was hired because Stowell had heard Joseph saw things which the natural eye could not (see note 31).

opened by the Spaniards in Harmony, Susquahana [Susquehanna] County, State of Pen[n]sylvania, and had previous to my hiring with him been digging in order if possible to discover the mine. After I went to live with <him> he took me among the rest of his hands to dig for the silver mine, at which I continued to work for nearly a month without success in our undertaking, and finally I prevailed with the old gentleman to cease digging after it. Hence arose the very prevalent story of my having been a money digger.[29]

Smith's father and mother indicated that he was more than a hired hand for Stowell. Joseph Sr. reportedly told Fayette Lapham that his son went to Harmony, Pennsylvania, "at the request of some one who wanted the assistance of his divining rod and stone in finding hidden treasure, supposed to have been deposited there by the Indians or others."[30] Similarly Lucy recalled that Stowell had sought her son's help because he heard Joseph "possessed certain keys, by which he could discern things invisible to the natural eye."[31]

In other words it was because of Smith's reputation that father and son made the trip of over one hundred miles to Harmony, Pennsylvania, where Stowell employed them to help locate the mine. Smith was now nineteen and his father fifty-four.

On November 1, 1825, soon after their arrival in Harmony and in anticipation of their discoveries, Stowell's treasure digging company drew up "Articles of Agreement." This agreement

---

[29] Manuscript History, Book A-1:7-8, LDS archives; Jessee, *Papers of Joseph Smith* 1:282. Joseph's account records that he worked "for nearly a month," Lucy's book has "by the month," and Oliver Cowdery's account "a few months." Much of Lucy's printed history is similar in wording to the Joseph Smith account published in the *Times and Seasons* 3 (May 2, 1842):772. In the *Elder's Journal* Joseph responded to a question of whether he had been a money digger with this answer: "Yes, but it was never a very profitable job for him, as he only got fourteen dollars a month for it" (1 [July 1838]:43, Far West, Missouri; see B. H. Roberts, ed., *History of the Church of Jesus Christ of Latter-day Saints* [Salt Lake City: Deseret Book, 1959], 3:29). It is not known whether the fourteen dollars was in addition to his room and board.

[30] "The Mormons," *Historical Magazine* 7 (May 1870):307.

[31] Anderson, *Lucy's Book*, 360.

stipulated, "if anything of value should be obtained at a certain place in Pennsylvania near a Wm. Hale's, supposed to be a valuable mine of either Gold or Silver and also to contain coined money and bars or ingots of Gold or Silver," each member would receive a share, including a share to the Oliver Harper's widow. According to this agreement, Joseph Sr. and his son Joseph (who both signed the agreement) would receive "two elevenths of all the property that may be obtained."[32]

It was while they were away in southern New York that the new land agent in Canandaigua agreed to sell the Smith's delinquent Manchester farm to Russell Stoddard who wanted to add it to his holdings. Only panic-stricken appeals by Lucy and Hyrum Smith to sympathetic neighbors and the return of Joseph Sr. prevented eviction. A kindly Quaker, Lemuel Durfee, bought the land and allowed the Smiths to remain as tenants.[33]

In 1834 Isaac Hale recalled the treasure-seeking venture:

[Joseph] Smith, and his father, with several other "money-diggers" boarded at my house while they were employed in digging for a mine that they supposed had been opened and worked by the Spaniards, many years since. Young Smith gave the "money-diggers" great encouragement, at first, but when they had arrived in digging, to near the place where he had stated an immense treasure would be found—he said the enchantment was so powerful that he could not see. They then became discouraged, and soon after dispersed. This took place about the 17th of November, 1825; and one of the company gave me his note for $12[.]68 for his board, which is still unpaid.[34]

---

[32] *Daily Tribune*, April 23, 1880, 4, Salt Lake City, from the *Susquehanna Journal,* March 20, 1880. See Vogel, *Early Mormon Documents* 4:407-13.

[33] Lemuel Durfee purchased it on December 20, 1825 (Deed Liber 44:232-34, Ontario County Records Center and Archives, Canandaigua). The Smith family eventually lost the farm.

[34] Affidavit of Isaac Hale, March 20, 1834, in *Susquehanna Register, and Northern Pennsylvanian* 9 (May 1, 1834):1, original newspaper in the Susquehanna County Historical Society, Montrose, Pennsylvania. The testimonies from the *Register* were reprinted in *The New York Baptist Register* 11 (June 13, 1834):68, original in Colgate University Archives. Also published in Howe, *Mormonism Unvailed*, 263.

Others in the area also recalled Smith's activities and placed them within the context of religious and supernatural practice. Michael Morse described the treasure forays around Harmony to an interviewer in 1879:

> Joseph came into Harmony with a Mr. Stowell, to dig for treasure - silver in oars [ores] - which was said to have be[e]n mined & hid by Spaniards a long time before. He thinks three different companies had been digging for it in all and that Mr. Stowell with his company were one of the three Says Joseph at that time (about 1825) was a green, awkward, and ignorant boy of about 19 yrs of age Says he <then> made no profession of religion. Said Mr. Stowell was a religious man, as was also Mr. Isaac Hale at whose house Mr. Stowell, Joseph and the other hired men boarded, and that prayers were had of mornings before the company set off to work.[35]

In 1842 Joel K. Noble of Colesville, New York, placed the money digging within the context of occult ritual. He recalled that young Joseph "came here when about 17-18 Y[ears]. of age in the capacity of Glass Looker or fortune tel[l]er."[36] Noble summarized the story of the company's alleged sprinkling the ground with a dog's blood while offering prayers.[37]

---

[35] William W. Blair Journal, May 8, 1879, RLDS archives. Blair interviewed Michael Morse in Amboy, Illinois. In his journal Blair wrote Morse's first name as "Gabriel" rather than Michael. Blair also wrote to the editor of the *Saints Herald* about what he learned from Michael Morse. See *Saints Herald* 26 (June 15, 1879):190, letter dated May 22, 1879.

[36] Joel King Noble to Jonathan B. Turner, March 8, 1842, in answer to an inquiry from Professor Turner of Illinois College, Jacksonville, Illinois. Located in the Turner Collection of the Illinois State Historical Library, Springfield, Illinois. See Vogel, *Early Mormon Documents* 4:107.

[37] Ibid. 4:109. William R. Hine, who lived in Colesville at the time, stated that Joseph "claimed to receive revelations from the Lord through prayer, and would pray with his men, mornings and at other times." *Naked Truths About Mormonism* 1 (Jan. 1888):2. Compare similar statements by Henry A. Sayer (ibid., 1:3) and Joseph Rogers (ibid., 1 [April 1888]:1). Joseph's use of sacrifice in his Palmyra diggings is referred to in William Stafford's testimony (*Mormonism Unvailed*, 239); Pomeroy Tucker, *Origin, Rise and Progress of Mormonism*, 24-25; Stephen S. Harding's letter in Thomas Gregg, *The Prophet*

While Joseph Smith was working for Josiah Stowell, he was brought before a court on charges sworn against him by a nephew of Josiah Stowell, Peter G. Bridgman (or Bridgeman). Apparently Bridgman became concerned that his uncle's money was being spent in the pursuit of elusive treasure.[38] Accounts of these charges corroborate Smith's treasure hunting in southern New York and Pennsylvania.

In 1831 Abram W. Benton, a young man about the same age as Joseph Jr., recalled the arrest for disorderly conduct and the judgment of guilt, adding, "considering his youth, (he then being a minor,) and thinking he might reform his conduct, he was designedly allowed to escape. This was four or five years ago."[39] In Noble's 1842 recollection, Smith was charged with vagrancy, condemned, and "whisper came to Jo. off off—took Leg Bail (or Gave [Leg Bail])."[40]

For over a hundred years three different published versions of the actual 1826 court record taken from Albert Neely's docket book have been available as well as an account told by William D.

---

of Palmyra (New York: John B. Alden, 1890), 56; C. R. Stafford's statement in *Naked Truths About Mormonism* 1 (Jan. 1888):3. The same ritual in the Pennsylvania diggings is recorded in Emily C. Blackman, *History of Susquehanna County, Pennsylvania* (Philadelphia: Claxton, Remsen & Haffelfinger, 1873), 580; and in Frederick Mather's interviews in *Lippincott's Magazine* 26 (Aug. 1880):200. See also *Binghamton Daily Republican*, July 29, 1880.

[38] Within a month after swearing out the warrant, this crusading twenty-two-year-old was licensed as an exhorter by the Methodists and within three years helped establish the West Bainbridge Methodist Church.

[39] Letter written by A. W. Benton of South Bainbridge, New York, dated March 1831, in *Evangelical Magazine and Gospel Advocate* 2 (April 9, 1831):120, Utica, New York. Dr. Abram Benton, according to the family Bible record, was born on July 16, 1805. He was later received into the Medical Society in October 1830 (see James H. Smith, *History of Chenango and Madison Counties, New York*, 100, 144). For a while he lived on the east bank in South Bainbridge just north of the bridge (Chenango County Deeds RR:587). About 1838 he moved to Sterling, Illinois, and then to Fulton, where he died on March 9, 1867.

[40] Noble to Turner, March 8, 1842. The letter arrived too late to be included in Turner's book, *Mormonism in All Ages*, (see correspondence from Absalom Peters, Jan. 1 and July 6, 1842, regarding the printing, in another Turner Collection in the Illinois State Historical Survey Library, Urbana). Noble after 1850 moved to Hartland Township, Huron County, Ohio, where he died on February 19, 1874.

Purple. But because the pages from the original docket book had been lost, the authenticity of these published accounts was questioned. However, in 1971 two itemized bills were discovered which had been submitted by Justice Neely and Constable Philip De Zeng to cover costs incurred in the arrest and examination of Joseph Smith, and they confirm many of the details of both the Purple account and the published versions of the record.[41]

Because of the multiplicity of documents concerning the March 20, 1826 examination of Joseph Smith, it is possible to reasonably reconstruct the order of events as the young glass-looker would have experienced them. When Smith was arrested, he would have been brought before Justice Neely for a preliminary examination, often referred to loosely as a "trial" but specified by Neely on his bill as an "examination." The examination was to determine whether Smith should be released as innocent of the charges or, if the evidence seemed sufficient, actually brought to trial. During the examination Smith's statement was taken (not under oath), and witnesses for and against the accused were sworn in and examined and their statements taken down.[42] Both before and during the examination Joseph remained under guard by Constable De Zeng, who charged the county for "attendance with Prisoner two days & 1 nigh[t]"—the day of the examination and the day and night preceding.[43]

As indicated, Bridgman had sworn out the warrant. Neely's court record begins with the complaint: "State of New York v. Joseph Smith. Warrant issued upon written complaint upon oath of Peter G. Bridgeman, who informed that one Joseph Smith of Bainbridge was a disorderly person and an impostor."[44] New York

---

[41] For a detailed description of each of these documents, see H. Michael Marquardt and Wesley P. Walters, *Inventing Mormonism: Tradition and the Historical Record*, 222-30 and Vogel, *Early Mormon Documents* 4:239-66.

[42] "The examination of the prisoner should not be upon oath" (*A New Conductor Generalis: Being a Summary of the Law Relative to the Duty and Office of Justices of the Peace, Sheriffs, Coroners, Constables, Jurymen, Overseers of the Poor* [Albany: Published by E. F. Backus, 1819]), 142.

[43] Compare Constable Redfield's 1829 bill, May 19 re: Jacob Lee, for "keeping him part of two days & one night and attending the Examination."

[44] *Fraser's Magazine* 7 (Feb. 1873):229. Peter Bridgman was a nephew of Josiah and Miriam Bridgman Stowell (Burt Nichols and Joseph Clark Bridgman, *Genealogy of the Bridgman Family* [n.p., Hyde Park, Massachusetts, 1894], 129,

law collected various types of vagrancy under the broad heading of "Disorderly Persons" and included, along with beggars, prostitutes, and those who neglect their wives and children, "all persons pretending to have skill in physiognomy, palmistry, or like crafty science, or pretending to tell fortunes, or to discover where lost goods may be found."[45] Since Smith had never actually led the diggers to anything of value, Bridgman considered that Joseph was indeed pretending to discover lost items.

According to Neely's court record, as published in *Fraser's Magazine*, Smith first made a statement in his own defense:

Prisoner examined: says that he came from the town of Palmyra, and had been at the house of Josiah Stowel[l] in Bainbridge most of time since; had small part of time been employed in looking for mines, but the major part had been employed by said Stowel[l] on his farm, and going to school. That he had a certain stone which he had occasionally looked at to determine where hidden treasures in the bowels of the earth were; that he professed to tell in this manner where gold mines were a distance under ground, and had looked for Mr. Stowel[l] several times, and had informed him where he could find these treasures, and Mr. Stowel[l] had been engaged in digging for them. That at Palmyra he pretended to tell by looking at this stone where coined money was buried in Pennsylvania, and while at Palmyra had frequently ascertained in that way where lost property was of various kinds; that he had occasionally been in the habit of looking through this stone to find lost property for three years, but of late had pretty much given it up on account of its injuring his health, especially his eyes, made them sore; that he did not solicit business of this kind, and had always rather declined having anything to do with this business.[46]

116, 118-19).

[45] *Laws of the State of New York, Revised and Passed . . .*, 2 vols. (Albany: H.C. Southwick & Co., 1813), revisers William P. Van Ness and John Woodworth, 1:114, 410, usually cited as Revised Laws, or R.L. See *Conductor Generalis* (1819), 108; also *Revised Statutes* (1829), 1:638.

[46] *Fraser's Magazine* 7 (Feb. 1873):229.

Joseph Smith made a passing remark about attending school and Josiah Stowell Jr., who was almost seventeen years old at the time remembered, "I also went to Schoal [School] with him one winter. He was a fine likely young man & at that time did not Profess religion."[47] The next witness called was Josiah Stowell Sr.:

[Stowell] says that prisoner [Joseph Smith] had been at his house something like five months; had been employed by him to work on farm part of time . . . that prisoner had looked [in his stone] for him sometimes; once to tell him about money buried in Bend Mountain in Pennsylvania, once for gold on Monument Hill, and once for a salt spring; and that he positively knew that the prisoner could tell, and did possess the art of seeing those valuable treasures through the medium of said stone; that he found the [1883 printing: "digging part"] at Bend and Monument Hill as prisoner represented it; that prisoner had looked through said stone for Deacon Attleton for a mine, did not exactly find it, but got a [1883: "piece"] of ore which resembled gold, he thinks; that prisoner had told by means of this stone where a Mr. Bacon had buried money; that he and prisoner had been in search of it; that prisoner had said it was in a certain root of a stump five feet from surface of the earth, and with it would be found a tail feather; that said Stowel[l] and prisoner thereupon commenced digging, found a tail feather, but the money was gone; that he supposed the money moved down. That prisoner did offer his services; that he [Joseph Smith] never deceived him; that prisoner looked through stone and described Josiah Stowel[l]'s house and outhouses, while at Palmyra at Simpson Stowel[l]'s, correctly; that he had told about a painted tree, with a man's head painted upon it, by means of said stone. That he had been in company with prisoner digging for gold, and had the most implicit faith in

---

[47] Josiah Stowell Jr., to John S. Fullmer, Feb. 17, 1843, LDS archives. See Mark Ashurst-McGee, "The Josiah Stowell Jr.—John S. Fullmer Correspondence," *Brigham Young University Studies* 38, no. 3 (1999): 108, 113; and Vogel, *Early Mormon Documents* 4:80.

prisoner's skill.[48]

Stowell's comment about Smith searching for ore at
Monument Hill and looking for salt is confirmed by William R.
Hine's recollection that "Asa Stowel[l] furnished the means for Jo
to dig for silver ore, on Monument Hill." He also mentions that
Smith "and his workmen lived in a shanty while digging for salt.
When it rained hard, my wife has often made beds for them on the
floor in our house."[49]

Another witness, Jonathan Thompson, also testified in
support of Smith's skills in locating treasure:

> that prisoner [Joseph Smith] was requested to look for chest
> of money; did look, . . . that prisoner, Thompson, and
> Yeomans went in search of it; that Smith arrived at spot
> first; was at night; that Smith looked in hat while there, and
> when very dark, and told how the chest was situated. After
> digging several feet, struck upon something sounding like a
> board or plank. Prisoner would not look again, pretending
> that he was alarmed on account of the circumstances
> relating to the trunk being buried, [which] came all fresh to
> his mind. That the last time he [Joseph Smith] looked he
> discovered distinctly the two Indians who buried the trunk,
> that a quarrel ensued between them, and that one of said
> Indians was killed by the other, and thrown into the hole
> beside the trunk, to guard it, as he supposed. Thompson
> says that he believes in the prisoner's professed skill; that
> the board which he struck his spade upon was probably the
> chest, but on account of an enchantment the trunk kept
> settling away from under them when digging; that
> notwithstanding they continued constantly removing the
> dirt, yet the trunk kept about the same distance from them.
> Says prisoner said that it appeared to him that salt might be
> found in Bainbridge, and that he is certain that prisoner can
> divine things by means of said stone. That as evidence of
> the fact prisoner looked into his hat to tell him about some

---

[48] *Fraser's Magazine* 7 (Feb. 1873):229; Daniel S. Tuttle, "Mormons," *New
Schaff-Herzog Encyclopedia* (New York: Funk and Wagnalls, 1883), 2:1,576.
[49] W. R. Hine, in *Naked Truths About Mormonism* 1 (Jan. 1888):2.

money witness [Thompson] lost sixteen years ago, and that he described the man that witness supposed had taken it, and the disposition of the money.[50]

William Purple was impressed by Thompson's detailed description of their search:

many years before a band of robbers had buried on his [Thompson's] flat a box of treasure, and as it was very valuable they had by a sacrifice placed a charm over it to protect it, so that it could not be obtained except by faith, accompanied by certain talismanic influences. So, after arming themselves with fasting and prayer, they sallied forth to the spot designated by Smith. . . . Mr. Stowell went to his flock and selected a fine vigorous lamb, and resolved to sacrifice it to the demon spirit who guarded the coveted treasure. Shortly after the venerable Deacon [Josiah Stowell] might be seen on his knees at prayer near the pit, while Smith, with a lantern in one hand to dispel the midnight darkness might be seen making a circuit around the pit, sprinkling the flowing blood from the lamb upon the ground, as a propitiation to the spirit that thwarted them. They then descended the excavation, but the treasure still receded from their grasp, and it was never obtained.[51]

Dr. Purple reported that he heard the testimony of Joseph's father, though this testimony is not mentioned in the official record, which only had to "put in writing" as much of the testimony "as shall be material to prove the offence."[52] Purple stated that "Joseph Smith, Sr., was present, and sworn as a witness" and that "He swore that both he and his son were mortified that this wonderful power which God had so miraculously given him should be used only in search of filthy lucre, or its equivalent in earthly treasures." According to Purple, Joseph Sr. "trusted that the Son of Righteousness would some day

---

[50] *Fraser's Magazine* 7 (Feb. 1873):229-30.
[51] W. D. Purple, "Joseph Smith, the Originator of Mormonism," *Chenango Union* 30 (May 3, 1877):3. See Vogel *Early Mormon Documents* 4:136.
[52] *Laws of New York* (1813) 2:507.

illumine the heart of the boy, and enable him to see His will concerning him."[53]

After hearing the testimony, Justice Neely concluded that there was enough evidence to indicate that the prisoner, Joseph Smith the Glass Looker, had claimed to have the skill to discover lost goods, a misdemeanor under the Vagrant Act, and had not actually found anything. Neely wrote in his court record, "And therefore the Court find the Defendant [Joseph Smith Jr.] guilty."[54] He ordered the constable, Philip De Zeng, to notify two other justices and prepare for trial. The material witnesses, three in this instance, were put under recognizance to appear at the forthcoming Court of Special Sessions.[55]

At this point the course of events becomes somewhat difficult to trace. Certainly many people found guilty in a pre-trial hearing do not go to trial. The bills of the four justices have been found, and they show that no Court of Special Sessions was held. Justice Noble writes that Joseph took "Leg Bail" an early slang expression meaning "to escape from custody."[56] What may have happened is that the three justices discussed the case, and considered that since this was Joseph Smith's first offence, privately made a deal with him. Dr. Purple who was present at the examination recalled that Smith was discharged. Years later Smith's co-worker Oliver Cowdery, probably getting his information from Smith, recalled that "some very officious person complained of him as a disorderly person, and brought him before the authorities of the county; but there being no cause of action he

---

[53] Purple, "Joseph Smith, the Originator of Mormonism," *Chenango Union* 30 (May 3, 1877):3.

[54] *Fraser's Magazine* 7 (Feb. 1873):230.

[55] "A bond or recognizance, 25," *Conductor Generalis* (1819), 482. "The fees of a Justice for his services in apprehending, binding, committing, &c for crimes and misdemeanors, are—for every oath, 12 1/2 cents; warrant, 19; recognizance, 25; mittimus, 19; which are audited and allowed by the board of supervisors as county charges" (Thomas G. Waterman, *The Justice's Manual: or, A Summary of the Power and Duties of Justices of the Peace in the State of New-York* [Binghamton, New York: Printed by Morgan & Canoll, 1825], 199). On defendant and witness recognizance see *Revised Statutes* (1829), 2:707, Sec. 8; 709 Sec. 21.

[56] Eric Partridge, *A Dictionary of Slang and Unconventional English* (New York: Macmillan Co., 1967 ed.), 476.

was honorably acquitted."[57] It is true that no penalty was administered. Edwin Brown Firmage and Richard Collin Mangrum have written:

> Dr. Purple's account suggests that Smith was discharged. The trial [examination] record indicates Smith was found guilty but mentions no sentence. Noble's letter and Benton's article agree that Smith was condemned, but Noble suggests Smith jumped bail and left. Benton, however, suggests that the court took into account Smith's age and hoped his conduct might be reformed, and therefore "he was designedly allowed to escape." In any case, it seems no sanction was imposed, and the court did not pursue the matter any further.[58]

Dale L. Morgan concluded: "From the point of view of Mormon history, it is immaterial what the finding of the court was on the technical charge of being 'a disorderly person and an impostor;' what is important is the evidence adduced, and its bearing on the life of Joseph Smith before he announced his claim to be a prophet of God."[59]

Whatever the outcome may have been, it is clear from the testimonies recorded at the examination and also from other statements by neighbors and witnesses, both from the Bainbridge-Harmony area and also from Manchester-Palmyra area nearly one hundred miles away, that young Smith had for several years earned part of his livelihood by hiring out as a glass looker to locate hidden treasures by gazing into his seer stone. It is also evident that Joseph surrounded his activities with a religious atmosphere flavored with the supernatural, although he himself at this time made no profession of religion. He looked into his peep stone to see: hidden mines and treasures under ground; Stowell's house and

---

[57] *Messenger and Advocate* 2 (Oct. 1835):201. See Jessee, *Papers of Joseph Smith* 1:95.

[58] *Zion in the Courts: A Legal History of the Church of Jesus Christ of Latter-day Saints, 1830-1900* (Urbana: University of Illinois Press, 1988), 382n1.

[59] John Phillip Walker, ed., *Dale Morgan on Early Mormonism: Correspondence and a New History* (Salt Lake City: Signature Books, 1986), 373n44.

farm a hundred miles away; a miscreant who stole Thompson's money ten years earlier; the murder of a Native American whose spirit was guarding a treasure; and the location of treasures and ghosts or spirits of dead guardians who moved them around under the ground.

These activities led the two widely separated communities to associate him with divination and necromancy. In fact early adherents of the Mormon faith claim that Joseph located the gold plates from which he dictated the Book of Mormon by gazing into his seer stone. He also used this stone to obtain the text of the book as well as to receive instructions from God for his early followers.

One valuable discovery which Joseph Smith did make during this period was Emma Hale. Smith told her that as soon as he saw her, he recognized that she was the one who had to be with him to enable him to find the treasure which he had been promised.[60] She was won over, but her father was not. Isaac Hale later stated that "young Smith made several visits at my house, and at length asked my consent to his marrying my daughter Emma. This I refused, and gave him my reasons for so doing; some of which were, that he was a stranger, and followed a business that I could not approve."[61]

Without her father's permission, Emma and Joseph eloped and were married on January 18, 1827 by Zachariah Tarble, a justice of the peace in Bainbridge. As she later told the story to her son:

I was visiting at Mr. Stowell's, who lived in Bainbridge, and saw your father there. I had no intention of marrying when I left home; but, during my visit at Mr. Stowell's, your father visited me there. My folks were bitterly opposed to him; and, being importuned by your father, aided by Mr. Stowell, who urged me to marry him, and preferring to marry him to any other man I knew, I consented.[62]

---

[60] *Historical Magazine* 7 (May 1870):307.
[61] Isaac Hale, *Susquehanna Register* 9 (May 1, 1834):1; Howe, *Mormonism Unvailed*, 263.
[62] *Saints Herald* 26 (Oct. 1, 1879):289. This interview was conducted by her son Joseph Smith III in February 1879.

Joseph had turned twenty-one years old; Emma was twenty-two. Since Isaac Hale did not approve of the marriage, the couple lived with Joseph's parents in Manchester. Emma's parents were Methodists and she was probably also a Methodist.[63]

Sometime after their marriage, they hired Peter Ingersoll to help pick up Emma's personal possessions and furniture. Isaac Hale related that "Smith stated to me, that he had given up what he called 'glass-looking,' and that he expected to work for a living, and was willing to do so."

Emma's brother Alva reported that "Joseph Smith Jr. told him that [']his (Smith's) gift in seeing with a stone and hat, was a gift from God,' but also states 'that Smith told him at another time that this *'peeping'* was all d—d nonsense. He (Smith) was deceived himself but did not intend to deceive others; — that he intended to quit the business, (of peeping) and labor for his livelihood.'"[64] Ingersoll described his trip with Smith to Harmony:

I was hired by Joseph Smith, Jr. to go to Pennsylvania, to move his wife's household furniture up to Manchester, where his wife then was. When we arrived at Mr. Hale's, in Harmony, Pa., from which place he had taken his wife, a scene presented itself, truly affecting.

His father-in-law (Mr. Hale) addressed Joseph, in a flood of tears: "You have stolen my daughter and married her. I had much rather have followed her to her grave. You spend your time in digging for money —pretend to see in a stone, and thus try to deceive people." Joseph wept, and acknowledged he could not see in a stone now, nor ever could; and that his former pretensions in that respect, were all false. He then promised to give up his old habits of digging for money and looking into stones.

Mr. Hale told Joseph, if he would move to Pennsylvania and work for a living, he would assist him in getting into business. Joseph acceded to this proposition.

---

[63] Mary Audentia [Smith] Anderson, *Ancestry and Posterity of Joseph Smith and Emma Hale* (Independence, Missouri: Herald House, 1929), 302.
[64] Alva Hale, *Susquehanna Register* 9 (May 1, 1834):1, emphasis in original; Howe, *Mormonism Unvailed*, 268.

Peter Ingersol then returned with Joseph Smith to Manchester and related the following:

> Joseph told me on his return, that he intended to keep the promise which he had made to his father-in-law; but, said he, it will be hard for me, for they will all oppose, as they want me to look in the stone for them to dig money: and in fact it was as he predicted.[65]

Joseph now had a wife to support. He promised his father-in-law he would stop crystal-gazing and work hard for a living. About June 1827 Smith's father told his friend Willard Chase that his son had discovered a hidden record written on plates of gold.

---

[65] Affidavit of Peter Ingersoll, Palmyra, Wayne County, New York, Dec. 2, 1833, Howe, *Mormonism Unvailed*, 234-35.

5

The Treasure

By the summer of 1827, when newlyweds Joseph and Emma Smith[1] were living with Joseph's family in Manchester, New York, people began to hear from the Smith family about a treasure Joseph had found. They told the story of a book written on plates of gold which had been buried in the ground in a Manchester hill (later called the Hill Cumorah) about two miles southeast from their home. This glacial drumlin had been, according to one scholar, "the site of treasure digging both before and after Joseph Smith's receiving the golden plates."[2]

This chapter attempts to recover from available sources the earliest versions of this saga. Certainly no single account gives a complete picture of events pieced together years later. But important patterns and similarities recur among the various early accounts. In contrast to the account which was later told, the earliest versions linked the finding of the plates with the practice of searching for buried treasure. They also linked obtaining the plates with magical rituals traditionally associated with winning treasure from its guardian spirits.

Willard Chase was a neighbor and friend of the Smith family. He had known them since 1820 and later recalled that the family followed the money-digging business "until the latter part of the season of 1827." That June, Joseph Smith Sr. told Chase a remarkable story, whose beginnings went back more than three years to September 1823:

---

[1] Joseph Knight Sr. wrote that Joseph Smith "looked in his glass and found it was Emma Hale" who was the right person to bring with him to the hill to obtain the book (Joseph Knight Reminiscences, LDS archives). See Dean C. Jessee, ed., "Joseph Knight's Recollection of Early Mormon History," *Brigham Young University Studies* 17 (Autumn 1976):31; see also Vogel, *Early Mormon Documents* 4:13.

[2] Ronald W. Walker, "The Persisting Idea of American Treasure Hunting," *Brigham Young University Studies* 24 (Fall 1984):435.

That some years ago, a spirit[3] had appeared to Joseph his son, in a vision, and informed him that in a certain place there was a record on plates of gold, and that he was the person that must obtain them, and this he must do in the following manner: On the 22d of September, he must repair to the place where was deposited this manuscript, dressed in black clothes, and riding a black horse with a switch tail, and demand the book in a certain name, and after obtaining it, he must go directly away, and neither lay it down nor look behind him.[4] They accordingly fitted out Joseph with a suit of black clothes and borrowed a black horse.

Chase reportedly was told that Smith in fact went to the stone box in which the gold record was deposited and removed the book:

but fearing some one might discover where he got it, he laid it down to place back the top stone, as he found it; and turning round, to his surprise there was no book in sight. He again opened the box, and in it saw the book, and attempted to take it out, but was hindered. He saw in the box something like a toad, which soon assumed the appearance of a man, and struck him on the side of his head.

---

[3] Joseph Smith Jr. evidently did not give the messenger a name while he was in New York. In his 1838-39 history he mentioned that the personage who appeared to him stated "his name was Nephi" (Manuscript History, Book A-1:5; also in duplicate Book A-2:6, both in LDS archives). In other sources the person who buried the gold plates and appeared to Smith is named "Moroni," son of Mormon. In the manuscript history above the name "Nephi" has been added the name "Moroni" with a footnote added after Smith's death giving three references where the name was published as "Moroni" (*Messenger and Advocate* 1 [April 1835]:112; 1835 D&C 50:2 [p. 180], name added to the 1830 text in 1835 [see LDS D&C 27:5 and RLDS D&C 26:2]; and *Elders' Journal* 1 [July 1838]:42-43, Far West, Missouri).

[4] It is noteworthy that no scriptural passages were cited in Joseph Smith's 1832 account of the messenger's visit, unlike his later account. In Oliver Cowdery's description published in the 1835 *Messenger and Advocate*, the angel quoted many biblical verses. In Smith's 1838-39 narrative history, passages of scripture appear but are revised with new emphasis.

Smith tried to take the book again but was struck by the spirit. On asking "why he could not obtain the plates," he was told that he had not obeyed the orders of the spirit. He was then instructed to bring his oldest brother Alvin:

> come one year from this day, and bring with you your oldest brother, and you shall have them. This spirit, he said, was the spirit of the prophet who wrote this book, and who was sent to Joseph Smith, to make known these things to him. Before the expiration of the year, his oldest brother died; which the old man said was an accidental providence!

When Smith returned a year later, the spirit asked about his brother. Learning he was dead, the spirit "commanded him to come again, in just one year, and bring a man with him. On asking who might be the man, he was answered that he would know him when he saw him."

According to Chase's account, filtered through his and Joseph Sr.'s perspectives, Joseph Jr. first decided that the next year he should bring Samuel Lawrence, another treasurer seeker and seer in the Manchester area:

> Joseph believed that one Samuel T. Lawrence was the man alluded to by the spirit, and went with him to a singular looking hill, in Manchester, and shewed him where the treasure was. Lawrence asked him if he had ever discovered any thing with the plates of gold; he said no: he then asked him to look in his stone to see if there was any thing with them. He looked, and said there was nothing; he told him to look again, and see if there was not a large pair of specks with the plates; he looked and soon saw a pair of spectacles, the same with which Joseph says he translated the Book of Mormon.
>
> Lawrence told him it would not be prudent to let these plates be seen for about two years . . . Not long after this, Joseph altered his mind, and said L[awrence]. was not the right man, nor had he told him the right place.[5]

---

[5] Affidavit of Willard Chase, Manchester, Ontario County, New York, Dec. 11,

One hundred miles to the south, a resident of Colesville for whom Smith worked briefly, recounted a very similar story. Joseph Knight Sr., whose recollections were written sometime between 1835 and 1847, when Knight died, also told of the spirit requesting that Joseph bring Alvin to the hill. Knight does not mention Lawrence, but his account adds the identity of a third person Smith felt compelled by the spirit personage to take to the hill in order to obtain the treasure—his future wife Emma Hale:

> From thence he [Joseph Smith] went to the hill where he was informed the Record was and found no trouble for it appeared plain as tho[ugh] he was acquainted with the place it was so plain in the vision that he had of the place he went and found the place and opened it and found a plane [plain] Box he oncovered [uncovered] it and found the Book and took it out and laid [it] Down By his side and thot [thought] he would Cover the <place> over again thinkinking [thinking] there might be Something else here But he was told to take the Book and go right away and after he had Covered the place he turned round to take <the> Book and it was not there and he was astonished that the Book was gone he thot he would look in the place again and see if it had not got Back again
>
> he had heard People tell of such things and he opened the Box and Behold the Book was there he took hold of it to take it out again and Behold he Could not Stur the Book any more then he Could the mount[a]in he exclaimed why Cant I stur this Book[?] and he was answer[e]d you have not Done rite [right] you Should have took the Book and a gone right away you cant have it now Joseph Says when Can I have it[?] the answer was the 22nt Day of September next if you Bring the right person with you Joseph Says who is the right person[?] the answer was your oldest Brother
>
> But before September Came his oldest Brother Died then he was Disap[po]inted and did not [k]now what to do

---

1833, in Howe, *Mormonism Unvailed*, 240, 242-43, emphasis omitted. See Vogel, *Early Mormon Documents* 2:66-68.

But when the 22nt Day of September Came he went to the
place and the personage appeared and told him he Could
not have it now But the 22nt Day of September nex[t] he
mite [might] have the Book if he Brot with him the right
person Joseph Says who is the right Person[?] the answer
was you will know then he looked in his glass and found it
was Emma Hale Daughter of old Mr Hail [Hale] of
Pensylvany a girl that he had Seen Before for he had Bin
Down there Before with me[6]

Catherine Smith, younger sister of Joseph Jr. and a teenager
in September 1827, told about her brother receiving instructions to
bring Alvin to the hill:

He raised the lid again, and there was the record, just as it
laid before. He reached forth his hands to take it and he felt
a pressure pushing him away. He tried the second time, and
the third time he fell to the earth with the pressure, and he
cried in the bitterness of his soul: Lord, what have I done,
that I can not get these records? Moroni said: You have not
obeyed the commandments as you were commanded to;
you must obey His commandments in every particular. You
were not to lay them out of your hands until you had them
in safe keeping. Joseph said: What shall I do? He said:
Come here again next year at this time and bring your
oldest brother with you, and you can receive the records.[7]

---

[6] Joseph Knight Reminiscences, LDS archives. See Jessee, "Joseph Knight's
Recollection," 30-31 and Vogel, *Early Mormon Documents* 4:12-14. Joseph
Knight Jr., recalled the following: "I think it was in November [1826] that he
[Joseph Smith Jr.] made known to my Father and I that he had seen a vision, that
a personage had appeared to him and told him where there was a gold book of
ancient date buried, and that if he would follow the direction of the angel, he
could get it. We were told it in secret" ("Joseph Knight's incidents of History
from 1827 to 1844," comp. Thomas Bullock, from loose sheets in Joseph Knight
Jr.'s possession, Aug. 16, 1862, LDS archives, as cited in William G. Hartley,
*Stand by My Servant Joseph: The Story of the Joseph Knight Family and the
Restoration* [Provo, Utah: Joseph Fielding Smith Institute for LDS History and
Salt Lake City: Deseret Book, 2003], 11).
[7] Reported in "An Angel Told Him. Joseph Smith's Aged Sister Tells About
Moroni's Talk," *Kansas City Times*, April 11, 1895, 1, Kansas City, Missouri,
quotation marks omitted. Catherine's name is also spelled Katharine.

About 1830 Fayette Lapham visited the Smith family with a friend, Jacob Ramsdell, and talked with Joseph Sr. about finding the buried record. Lapham's narrative, which was published in 1870, is very similar to the versions related by Chase and Knight—including the details about bringing Alvin and then Emma to the hill in order to placate the guardian spirit:

He [Joseph] then told his father that, in his dream, a very large and tall man appeared to him, dressed in an ancient suit of clothes, and the clothes were bloody. And the man said to him that there was a valuable treasure, buried many years since, and not far from that place; and that he had now arrived for it to be brought to light, for the benefit of the world at large; and, if he would strictly follow his directions, he would direct him to the place where it was deposited, in such a manner that he could obtain it. He then said to him, that he would have to get a certain coverlid, which he described, and an old-fashioned suit of clothes, of the same color, and a napkin to put the treasure in. . . . when he had obtained it, he must not lay it down until he placed it in the napkin. . . . Joseph mounted his horse. . . . Taking up the first article, he saw the others below: laying down the first, he endeavored to secure the others; but before he could get hold of them, the one he had taken up slid back to the place he had taken it from.

Smith was struck down and fell on his back. The personage then told him that

when the treasure was deposited there, he was sworn to take charge of and protect that property, until the time should arrive for it to be exhibited to the world of mankind; and, in order to prevent his making an improper disclosure, he was murdered or slain on the spot, and the treasure had been under his charge ever since. He said to him [Joseph] that he had not followed his directions; and, in consequence of laying the article down before putting it in the napkin, he could not have the article now; but that if he would come again one year from that time, he could have them.

The year passed over before Joseph was aware of it, so the time passed by; but he went to the place of deposit, where the same man appeared again, and said he had not been punctual in following his directions, and, in consequence, he could not have the article yet. Joseph asked when he could have them; and the answer was, "Come in one year from this time, and bring your oldest brother with you; then you may have them." During that year, it so happened that his oldest brother died; but, at the end of the year, Joseph repaired to the place again, and was told by the man who still guarded the treasure, that, inasmuch as he could not bring his oldest brother, he could not have the treasure yet; but there would be another person appointed to come with him in one year from that time, when he could have it.

Smith was told about an important person he soon would meet:

Joseph asked, "How shall I know the person?" and was told that the person would be known to him at sight. During that year, Joseph went to the town of Harmony, in the State of Pennsylvania, at the request of some one who wanted the assistance of his divining rod and stone in finding hidden treasure, supposed to have been deposited there by the Indians or others. While there, he fell in company with a young woman; and, when he first saw her, he was satisfied that she was the person appointed to go with him to get the treasure he had so often failed to secure.[8]

In 1879 Hiel and Joseph Lewis, cousins of Emma Hale Smith, wrote a joint account on how Joseph Smith discovered the plates. Their account is likely based upon Joseph Lewis' recollections as he was twenty years old in early 1828. The account

[8] Fayette Lapham, "Interview with the Father of Joseph Smith, the Mormon Prophet, Forty Years Ago. His Account of the Finding of the Sacred Plates," *Historical Magazine* 7 (May 1870):306-307. See Vogel, *Early Mormon Documents* 1:458-61. William R. Hine said, "Jo told Emma he had a revelation about the plates, but that he could not obtain them until he had married her" (*Naked Truths About Mormonism* 1 [Jan. 1888]:2).

recalled the importance of their cousin Emma to Smith's narrative:

> He [Joseph] said that by a dream he was informed that at such a place in a certain hill, in an iron box, were some gold plates with curious engravings, which he must get and translate, and write a book; that the plates were to be kept concealed from every human being for a certain time, some two or three years; that he went to the place and dug till he came to the stone that covered the box, when he was knocked down; that he again attempted to remove the stone, and was again knocked down; this attempt was made the third time, and the third time he was knocked down.
>
> Then he exclaimed, "Why can't I get it?" or words to that effect; and then he saw a man standing over the spot, which to him appeared like a Spaniard, having a long beard coming down over his breast to about here, (Smith putting his hand to the pit of his stomach) with his (the ghost's) throat cut from ear to ear, and the blood streaming down, who told him that he could not get it alone; that another person whom he, Smith, would know at first sight, must come with him, and then he could get it. And when Smith saw Miss Emma Hale, he knew that she was the person, and that after they were married, she went with him to near the place, and stood with her back toward him, while he dug up the box, which he rolled up in his frock.[9]

Smith's mother, Lucy, added her own recollections about the gold record to her memoir. She dates Joseph's first trip to the nearby hill just before Alvin's death in November 1823 and emphasizes Alvin's place in these events. She thus indirectly suggests why Joseph may have felt the guardian spirit required Alvin's presence at the hill:

> <He vis[i]ted the place where the plates were laid and thinking> he could keep every commandment given him

---

[9] Joseph and Hiel Lewis, "Mormon History. A New Chapter, About to Be Published," *The Amboy Journal* 24 (April 30, 1879):1, Amboy, Illinois. See Vogel, *Early Mormon Documents* 4:303-304. Rather than an iron box it should be a stone box.

<supposed> that it would be possible for him to take them from their place and carry them home. But said the divine messenger you must take them into your hands and go straight to the house without delay <and put them in immediately and lock them up>.

Accordingly when the time arrived he went to the place appointed and removed the moss and grass from the surface of the rock and then pryed [pried] up the flat stone according to the directions which he had received. He then discovered the plates laying on 4 pillars in the inside of the box. After some further conversation Joseph he put forth his hand <and> took them up <but> when he lifted them from their place the thought flashed across his mind that there might be something more in the box that would be a benefit to him in a pecuniary point of view. In the excitement of the moment he laid the record down in order to cover up the box least some one should come along and take away whatever else might be deposited there.

When he turned again to take up the record it was gone but where he knew not nor did he know by what means it was taken away. He was much alarmed at this. <He> kneeled down <&> asked the Lord why it was that the record was taken from him. The angel appeared to him and told him that he had not done as he was commanded in that he laid down the record in order to secure some imaginary treasure that remained.

Joseph was then permit[t]ed to raise the stone again and there he beheld the plates the same as before. He reached forth his hand to take them but was <thrown> to the ground. When he recovered the angel was gone and he arose and went to the house.[10]

William Smith remembered that Joseph had told the family concerning his first attempt to receive the plates:

When he went to get the plates he found them as he was told he should. He took them from the stone box in which

---

[10] Lucy Mack Smith, draft manuscript. See Anderson, *Lucy's Book*, 345-47.

they were found, and placed them on the ground behind him, when the thought came into his mind that there might be a treasure hidden with them. While stooping forward to see, he was overpowered, so that he could not look farther. Turning to get the plates, he found they had gone; and on looking around found that they were in the box again; but he could not get them.[11]

According to Mother Smith, Joseph was instructed that "when you get the record take it immediately into the house and lock it up as soon as possible."[12] She adds that Alvin told Joseph that they would "have a fine long evening <and> all set down and hear you talk." Joseph told the family about the plates and asked them not to discuss what he said outside their family. She then describes how in the evenings the Smith family would meet and listen to Joseph's religious teachings. They also heard Joseph tell stories of the continent's former civilizations.[13]

Alvin, his mother remembers, was especially interested in the record. On his death bed he told Joseph, "I want you to be a good boy & do everything that lays in your power to obtain the records be faithful in receiving instruction and keeping every commandment that is given you."[14] According to Lucy:

Alvin had ever manifested a greater zeal and anxiety if it were possible than any of the rest with regard to the record which had been shown to Joseph and he always showed the most intense interest concerning the matter. With this before our minds we could not endure to hear or say one word upon that subject, for the moment that Joseph spoke of the record it would immediately bring Alvin to <our> minds.[15]

---

[11] "The Old Soldier's Testimony. Sermon preached by Bro. William B. Smith, in the Saints' Chapel, Detroit, Iowa, June 8th, 1884. Reported by C. E. Butterworth," *Saints Herald* 31 (Oct. 4, 1884):643.

[12] Anderson, *Lucy's Book*, 340, see also 346. Not in Coray final manuscript.

[13] Ibid., 342-45.

[14] Ibid., 352.

[15] Ibid., 356.

Lucy continues her narrative, "but none were more engaged than the one whom we were doomed [to] part with, for Alvin was never so happy as when he was contemplating the final suc[c]ess of his brother in obtaining the record. And now I fancied I could hear him with his parting breath conjureing his brother to continue faithful that he might obtain the prize which the Lord had promised him."[16]

Clearly the gold plates story had been repeated outside the Smith family before September 1827, and no doubt seemed familiar to those who heard it and were acquainted with stories about the treasure-digging activities of the Smith family. A number of accounts have survived describing how Smith claimed he finally obtained possession of the gold plates.

According to his mother's detailed account, on September 20, 1827 Joseph Knight Sr. and his friend Josiah Stowell arrived at the Smith family frame house.[17] Knight heard that Joseph was to get the record on September 22. This was why he was at the Smith home before Joseph went to get the plates,[18] and "they remained with us untill the 22."[19]

On the morning of the twenty-second, Joseph and Emma left the Smith home "taking Mr. Knight's horse and wagon" without his knowledge to travel to the hill about two miles away.[20] When they arrived at the hill, Joseph left Emma with the wagon

---

[16] Ibid., 465.

[17] Ibid. 376. See Jessee, "Joseph Knight's Recollection," 32. Martin Harris said that Josiah Stowell "was at this time at old Mr. Smith's digging for money" (*Tiffany's Monthly* 5 [Aug. 1859]:165). According to Knight, it was Stowell who took Joseph and his new wife to Manchester after their marriage.

[18] Joseph Knight Sr. wrote that Joseph "had talked with me and told me the Conversation he had with the personage which told him if he would Do right according to the will of God he mite [might] obtain [the plates] the 22nt Day of Septem[b]er Next and if not he never would have them" (Joseph Knight Reminiscences; see Jessee, "Joseph Knight's Recollection," 32).

[19] Anderson, *Lucy's Book*, 376. Lucy's narration has Joseph Knight Sr. and Josiah Stowell still at their home after Joseph locked up the plates in a chest. Knight wrote, "I went to Rochester on Buisness [Business] and return[e]d By Palmyra to be there about the 22nt of September. I was there Several Days" (Joseph Knight Reminiscences; see Jessee, "Joseph Knight's Recollection," 32). Stowell and Knight appear to have visited with the Smith family for more than a week after they arrived on the twentieth.

[20] Anderson, *Lucy's Book*, 376.

while he went to the side of the hill. Joseph said he then took the plates out of a box in the ground and hid them in a fallen treetop, concealing them with the bark of the tree.[21] He returned to Knight's wagon, where Emma was waiting, and they started back to the house.

Meanwhile at the Smith home, according to Lucy, "When the male part of the family sat down to breakfast Mr. Smith enquired for Joseph, <for no one but myself knew where he was> (as no one knew where he had gone but myself). I told him that I thought I would not call Joseph, that I would have him set down with his wife." That "no one knew" where Joseph had gone that morning is questionable. Joseph Knight Sr. knew Joseph Jr. was expected to retrieve the plates. One of the reasons why Knight and Josiah Stowell were at the Smith home was because of the importance of the September twenty-second date. Lucy asked her husband to cover her son's absence—"do let him eat with his wife this morni<n>g."[22]

Joseph Knight soon discovered his "Horse and Carriage was gone."[23] Lucy remembered that "Mr. Knight came in quite disturbed. Why, Mr. Smith, said he, my horse is gone. I can't find him on the premises and I want to start home in half an hour. Never mind the horse, said I, Mr. Knight does not know all the nooks and corners in the pasture. I will call William (this <was> my 5th son), he will soon bring him. This satisfied him for a little while but he soon made another discovery, his waggon was gone, & now he concluded that the Horse and waggon had gone together and some rogue had gone with them both." Knight evidently went out to look for them, and "while he was absent Joseph returned."[24] Knight recalled, "after a while he [Joseph] Came home and he

---

[21] Here we follow Martin Harris (*Tiffany's Monthly* 5 [Aug. 1859]:165) and Willard Chase (*Mormonism Unvailed*, 216) that the hiding place was in a fallen tree top. As to the type of tree, Lucy Smith said that Joseph hid the plates "in a cavity in a birch log" (*Lucy's Book*, 385), and Martin Harris mentioned that they were hidden "in an old black oak tree top" (*Tiffany's Monthly* 5 [Aug. 1859]:165, see also 166).

[22] Anderson, *Lucy's Book*, 377.

[23] Joseph Knight Reminiscences; see Jessee, "Joseph Knight's Recollection," 33.

[24] Anderson, *Lucy's Book*, 377-78. Whether Joseph Knight was really planning on returning home "in half an hour" or waiting until Joseph told him about recovering the gold plates is not known.

turned out the Horse all Come into the house to Brackfirst [Breakfast]. But no thing said about where they had Bin [Been]."[25]

The plates were now, according to Joseph, hidden in a fallen treetop,[26] but a better place to deposit them was needed. According to Lucy, Joseph "asked my advice what it was best to do about getting a chest made." They decided to have one made but lacked the money to pay for it until

> The next day <Mr. Warner> came to him and requested <Joseph> to go with him to a widow's house <in Macedon by the name of Wells>, that she wanted <a wall and as she wanted some labor done in a well>, would pay him the money for it. He <he accompanied> Mr. Warner to Macedon <according to> Mrs. Wells <request. This> woman [no] one of the family had ever seen or heard of before although she sent purposely for Joseph. We considered it a provision of Providence to enable us to pay the money we were owing the cabinet maker.[27]

The story now went abroad from the Smith family that Joseph Jr. had obtained some gold plates which had been buried in the ground. Since Joseph and his father had been involved with a treasure-seeking group, his former partners wanted their share of the find. As Martin Harris explained, "The money-diggers claimed that they had as much right to the plates as Joseph had, as they were in company together. They claimed that Joseph had been [a] traitor, and had appropriated to himself that which belonged to them. For this reason Joseph was afraid of them."[28]

---

[25] Joseph Knight Reminiscences, see Jessee, "Joseph Knight's Recollection," 33.

[26] Affidavit of Willard Chase, Dec. 11, 1833, in Howe, *Mormonism Unvailed*, 246. Joseph Sr. asked Emma "if she knew aught of the record, whether Joseph had taken them out or where they were. She said She did not know" (*Lucy's Book*, 382).

[27] Lucy Mack Smith, draft manuscript. Variant reading in *Lucy's Book*, 379-80. Lucy stated, "there was not a shilling in the house."

[28] *Tiffany's Monthly* 5 (Aug. 1859):167. David Whitmer in a newspaper interview said: "I had conversations with several young men who said that Joseph Smith had certainly golden plates, and that before he attained them he had promised to share with them, but had not done so, and they were very much incensed with him" (*Kansas City Daily Journal*, June 5, 1881; reprinted in the

According to Lucy, Joseph Sr. was informed that a group of "10 or 12 men were club[b]ed together with one Willard Chase a Methodist class leader at their head," and they had sent for an unnamed conjuror "to divine the place where the record was deposited by magic art." "Accordingly," she continued, "the morning after we heard of their plans Mr. Smith went over a hill that <lay> east of <us> to see what he could discover among the neighbors there. At the first house he came to he found the conjurer, Willard Chase and the company all together. This was the house of one Mr. Laurence."[29] Joseph Knight later wrote: "I will Say there w[as] a man near By By the name Samuel Lawrance [Lawrence] He was a Seear [Seer] and he had Bin [Been] to the hill and knew about the things in the hill and he was trying to obtain them."[30]

While Joseph Jr. was working in Macedon, helping Mrs. Wells with her well, Emma took a stray horse that had been on the Smiths' premises two days (according to Lucy) and rode to Macedon. Joseph came up out of the well because he had perceived that Emma was coming to see him. She informed him that the money-diggers claimed to have located where he had hidden his golden book. Joseph looked in his peep stone and said to Emma that the plates were safe. Joseph promised Mrs. Wells that he would come back when he could, then mounted a horse "in his linen frock" (smock or work apron), and rode back home with Emma.[31]

Joseph then walked by himself to where he hid the gold plates on or near the hill. Several people remember the story they heard of how he brought the plates back to the Smith house. According to Lucy's version Joseph:

took the plates from their [hiding] place and wrapping them

Deseret Evening News, June 11, 1881; *Saints Herald*, 28 [July 1, 1881]:197; and *Latter-day Saints' Millennial Star* 43 [July 4, 1881]:422).

[29] Anderson, *Lucy's Book*, 381.

[30] Joseph Knight Reminiscences; see Jessee, "Joseph Knight's Recollection," 32. Exactly when Joseph Sr. went to the Lawrence home is not known. Lucy has the visit after Joseph recovered the plates and this is the account followed in our reconstruction. Knight has the visit to the Lawrence home occurring the night of September 21.

[31] Anderson, *Lucy's Book*, 383-84.

in his linen frock put them under his arm and started for the house. After walking a short distance in the road, he concluded it would be safer to go across through the woods. In a moment he struck through the timber where there was a large windfall to cross. He had not proceeded far in this direction till, as he was jumping over a log, a man spran[g] up and gave him a heavy blow with a gun. Joseph <leveled> him to the ground.[32]

Smith claimed he knocked down several men as he ran home, arriving out of breath. When all the commotion settled, Joseph showed those present his dislocated thumb, which his father put back in place.[33] Joseph Jr. then "related to our guests [Joseph Knight and Josiah Stowell] the whole history of the record."

Josiah Stowell was still at the Smith home at the end of September. Martha L. Campbell wrote, referring to Stowell, "if I understood him wright [right] he was the first person that took the Plates out of your hands the morni<n>g you brought them in."[34] After this Joseph went to Willard Chase's house and talked with him. Chase recalled the story that Smith told him, which is similar to the accounts of Smith's mother and Joseph Knight:

> That on the 22d of September, he arose early in the morning, and took a one horse wagon, of some one that had stayed over night at their house, without leave or license; and, together with his wife, repaired to the hill which contained the book. He left his wife in the wagon, by the road, and went alone to the hill, a distance of thirty or forty rods from the road; he said he then took the book out of the

---

[32] Ibid., 385-86. This is the only account that mentions a gun. Martin Harris understood that he was struck by a club (*Tiffany's Monthly* 5 [Aug. 1859]:166).

[33] Anderson, *Lucy's Book*, 386-88. The story at this point is taken from Lucy Smith's account. Benjamin Saunders said, "I saw his hand all swel[l]ed up" (Benjamin Saunders interview, 1884, in the W. H. Kelley Collection, "Miscellany 1795-1948," 23, RLDS archives. During the scuffles Smith was struck on his side (*Tiffany's Monthly* 5 [Aug. 1859]:166; *The Reflector* 2 [Feb. 14, 1831]:101, Palmyra, New York; *Historical Magazine* 7 [May 1870]:307).

[34] Martha L. Campbell (by the request of Josiah Stowell) to Joseph Smith, Dec. 19, 1843, Joseph Smith Collection, LDS archives. See Vogel, *Early Mormon Documents* 4:83.

ground and hid it in a tree top, and returned home.

He then went to the town of Macedon to work. After about ten days, it having been suggested that some one got his book, his wife went after him; he hired a horse, and went home in the afternoon, staid long enough to drink one cup of tea, and then went for his book, found it safe, took off his frock, wrapt it round it, put it under his arm and run all the way home, a distance of about two miles. He said he should think it would weigh sixty pounds, and was sure it would weigh forty.

On his return home, he said he was attacked by two men in the woods, and knocked them both down and made his escape, arrived safe and secured his treasure.—He then observed that if it had not been for that stone, (which he acknowledged belonged to me,) he would not have obtained the book.[35]

Martin Harris, a wealthy farmer of Palmyra who knew the Smiths as treasure seekers, heard about the find. Harris indicated that he "had a revelation the summer before, that God had a work for me to do."[36] Lucy Smith mentioned that Harris was aware of the existence of the gold plates for sometime: "here let me mention that no one knew anything of this buisness [business] <from us> except one confidential friend of My Husband's to whom he named it some 2 or 3 years before."[37] Martin said he heard about the gold plates "about the first of October, 1827." Harris said:

The first time I heard of the matter, my brother Presarved [Preserved] Harris, who had been in the village of Palmyra, asked me if [I] had heard about Joseph Smith, jr., having a golden bible. My thoughts were that the money-diggers had probably dug up an old brass kettle, or something of the

---

[35] Affidavit of Willard Chase, Dec. 11, 1833, in Howe, *Mormonism Unvailed*, 245-46.

[36] *Tiffany's Monthly* 5 (Aug. 1859):163.

[37] Anderson, *Lucy's Book*, 380. Lucy further stated, "The reader will notice, that on a preceeding [preceding] page I spoke of a confidential friend to whom Mr. Smith [Joseph Sr.] mentioned the existence of the record 2 or 3 years before it came forth. This was no other than Martin Harris" (394).

kind. I thought no more of it. This was about the first of October, 1827.

Martin also recalled being told by the Smith family how Joseph obtained the gold plates. (The horse and wagon which Harris remembered belonging to Stowell was owned Joseph Knight):

After this, on the 22nd of September, 1827, before day, Joseph took the horse and wagon of old Mr. Stowel[l], and taking his wife, he went to the place where the plates were concealed, and while he was obtaining them, she kneeled down and prayed. He then took the plates and hid them in an old black tree top which was hollow. Mr. Stowel[l] was at this time at old Mr. Smith's, digging for money. . . .

When Joseph had obtained the plates he communicated the fact to his father and mother. The plates remained concealed in the tree top until he got the chest made. He then went after them and brought them home. While on his way home with the plates, he was met by what appeared to be a man, who demanded the plates, and struck him with a club on his side, which was all black and blue. Joseph knocked the man down, and then ran for home, and was much out of breath. When he arrived home, he handed the plates in at the window, and they were received from him by his mother. They were then hidden under the hearth in his father's house. But the wall being partly down, it was feared that certain ones, who were trying to get possession of the plates, would get under the house and dig them out.

Harris said that the above events occurred before he talked with Joseph:

A day or so before I was ready to visit Joseph, his mother came over to our house and wished to talk with me. I told her I had no time to spare, she might talk with my wife, and, in the evening when I had finished my work I would talk with her. When she commenced talking with me, she told me respecting his bringing home the plates, and many other things, and said that Joseph had sent her over and wished me to come and see him.

Harris "waited a day or two," had breakfast, and then "told my folks I was going to the village, but went directly to old Mr. Smith's." While there Harris requested Smith "to tell me the story, which he did as follows. He said: 'An angel had appeared to him, and told him [Joseph] it was God's work.'" According to Harris, the angel "told him he must quit the company of the money-diggers."[38]

Harris discussed Smith's story with the Reverend John A. Clark. Clark later recalled, "According to Martin Harris, it was after one of these night excursions, that Jo, while he lay upon his bed, had a remarkable dream. An angel of God seemed to approach him, clad in celestial splendor."[39]

Almost all who heard versions of the story remembered in particular Smith's interaction with this messenger or spirit associated with the gold record. Abigail Harris remembered a visit by Smith's parents: "They told me that the report that Joseph, jun. had found golden plates, was true, and that he was in Harmony, Pa. translating them—that such plates were in existence, and that Joseph, jun. was to obtain them, was revealed to him by the spirit of one of the Saints that was on this continent, previous to its being discovered by Columbus."[40]

Henry Harris heard about the gold plates from Joseph Jr. and remembered Smith's interaction with an angel and his use of a stone known as a seer stone:

> After he pretended to have found the gold plates, I had a conversation with him, and asked him where he found them and how he come [sic] to know where they were. He said he had a revelation from God that told him they were hid in

---

[38] *Tiffany's Monthly* 5 (Aug. 1859):164-69.

[39] *The Episcopal Recorder* 18 (Sept. 5, 1840), Philadelphia, Pennsylvania, letter dated Aug. 24, 1840; Clark, *Gleanings by the Way* (Philadelphia: W. J. & J. K. Simon; New York: Robert Carter, 1842), 225. Oliver Cowdery wrote to William W. Phelps that Joseph had previously been acquainted with the place where the record was deposited (*Messenger and Advocate* 1 [Feb. 1835]:80, Kirtland, Ohio).

[40] Statement of Abigail Harris, Nov. 29, 1833, in Howe, *Mormonism Unvailed*, 253.

a certain hill and he looked in his stone and saw them in the place of deposit; that an angel appeared, and told him he could not get the plates until he was married, and that when he saw the woman that was to be his wife, he should know her, and she would know him.[41]

Benjamin Saunders, who was thirteen years old at the time, remembered hearing the story at his home:

I heard <Joe> tell my Mother and Sister how he procured the plates. He said he was directed by an angel where it was. He went in the night to get the plates. When he took the plates there was something down near the box that looked some like a toad that rose up into a man which forbid him to take the plates. He found a big pair of spectacles <also with the plates>. As he went home some one tried to get the plates away from him. He said he knock[ed] the man down and got away. Had two or three skirmishes on the way. I saw his hand all swel[l]ed up and he said it was done in hitting the enemy.[42]

During the time Smith reportedly had the gold plates in Manchester, they were said to have been hidden in various places. Several accounts have survived which detail the help of Alvah Beeman. Lucy Smith remembered that Beeman "came from the village <of Livonia>, a man in whom we reposed much confidence. . . . it was resolved that a portion of the hearth should be taken up and the plates buried under the same." This was just before a "large company of men came rushing up to the house armed with guns" looking for the gold plates.[43]

Martin Harris mentioned "old Mr. Beman" as one of the treasure seekers who had been "digging for money supposed to have been hidden by the ancients."[44] The gold plates were

---

[41] Statement of Henry Harris, Ibid., 252.

[42] Benjamin Saunders interview (1884), 22-24, RLDS archives. See Vogel, *Early Mormon Documents* 2:137-38.

[43] Anderson, *Lucy's Book*, 391.

[44] *Tiffany's Monthly* 5 (Aug. 1859):164. Alvah (or Alva) Beeman (also spelled Beman and Beaman) was born on May 22, 1775. Joseph Knight wrote, "Beeman

eventually "put into an old Ontario glass-box." Harris said, "Old Mr. Beman sawed off the ends, making the box the right length to put them in, and when they went in he said he heard them jink [clink], but he was not permitted to see them. He told me so."[45]

Beeman's daughter Mary related what she heard about her father and the gold plates:

> Father [Alvah Beeman] became acquainted with Father Joseph Smith, the Father of the Prophet, he frequently would go to Palmira to see Father Smiths and his family, during this time Brother Joseph Smith came in possession of the plates which contained the Book of Mormon.
>
> As soon as it was noised around that there was a golden Bible found (for that was what it was called at that time) the minds of the people became so excited and it arose at such a pitch that a mob collected together to search the house of Father Smith to find the records. My Father was there at the time and assisted in concealing the plates in a box in a secluded place where no one could find them.[46]

After being hidden under the hearth, they reportedly were placed in the Smith's cooper's shop.[47] Finally the plates were "nailed up in a box and the box put into a strong cask made for the purpose, the cask was then filled with beans and headed up."[48].

Fearing the hostile money-diggers around Manchester, Emma's family allowed her and her husband to move back home to

---

took out his [divining] Rods and hild [held] them up and they pointed Dow[n] to the h[e]arth whare [where] they ware [were] hid. there Says Beeman it is under that h[e]arth" (Joseph Knight Reminiscences; Jessee, "Joseph Knight's Recollection," 34). Since Lucy Smith and Mary A. Noble said that Alvah Beeman helped hide the plates in the hearth, perhaps he was just demonstrating the power of his rods.

[45] *Tiffany's Monthly* 5 (Aug. 1859):167. Joseph B. Noble (son-in-law of Alvah Beeman) wrote that Beeman "was permit[t]ed to handle the plates with a thin cloth covering over them" (Joseph B. Noble Journal, LDS archives).

[46] Mary Adeline Beeman Noble Journal, written after Sept. 1834, LDS archives. See Vogel, *Early Mormon Documents* 3:308.

[47] Anderson, *Lucy's Book*, 392.

[48] Ibid., 401. Also Martin Harris in *Tiffany's Monthly* 5 (Aug. 1859):170. Orson Pratt wrote in 1840 that the plates were put "into a barrel of beans" (Jessee, *Papers of Joseph Smith*, 1:401).

Harmony, Pennsylvania. Her brother Alva helped transport the couple and their barrel of beans to the Hale property where Joseph would start dictating the text of his book. In 1829, after the dictation was completed and the type was being set, Smith wrote a letter from Harmony to Oliver Cowdery about their stay in southern New York and Pennsylvania: "the people are all friendly to <us> except a few who are in opposition to ev[e]ry thing unless it is some thing that is exactly like themselves and two of our most formadable [formidable] persacutors [persecutors] are now under censure and are cited to a tryal [trial] in the church for crimes which if true are worse than all the Gold Book business."[49]

Emma's father Isaac later remembered his daughter's and son-in-law's stay at his home:

> I was informed they had brought a wonderful book of Plates down with them. I was shown a box in which it is said they were contained, which had, to all appearances, been used as a glass box of the common sized window-glass. I was allowed to feel the weight of the box, and they gave me to understand, that the book of plates was then in the box—into which, however, I was not allowed to look.[50]

In the spring of 1828 Martin Harris arrived at Harmony to assist Smith as a scribe during the process of translating. Surviving accounts of the translation process suggest that Smith worked without directly using the plates—this despite all of the difficulty in obtaining, hiding, and bringing the plates along. When it came to translating the crucial plates, they were no more present in the room than was John the Beloved's ancient parchment, the words of which Joseph also dictated the next year.[51] Richard Van Wagoner

---

[49] Copy of letter of Joseph Smith to Oliver Cowdery, Oct. 22, 1829, transcribed in 1832 into Joseph Smith's Letterbook 1:9, LDS archives; Dean C. Jessee, comp. and ed., *Personal Writings of Joseph Smith*, rev. ed., (Salt Lake City: Deseret Book and Provo, Utah: Brigham Young University Press, 2002), 251-52.

[50] Affidavit of Isaac Hale, March 20, 1834, in *The Susquehanna Register, and Northern Pennsylvanian* 9 (May 1, 1834):1; reprinted in Howe, *Mormonism Unvailed*, 264.

[51] H. Michael Marquardt, *The Joseph Smith Revelations: Text and Commentary* (Salt Lake City: Signature Books, 1999), 33; BC 6; LDS and RLDS D&C 7

and Steven Walker in their study observe:

> The plates could not have been used directly in the translation process. The Prophet, his face in a hat to exclude exterior light, would have been unable to view the plates directly even if they had been present during transcription. A mental picture of the young Joseph, face buried in a hat, gazing into a seer stone, plates out of sight, has not been a generally held view since the early days of the Church. The view raises some difficult questions. Why, for example, was such great care taken to preserve the plates for thousands of years if they were not to be used directly in the translation process?[52]

Isaac Hale's summary of the process suggests his incredulity: "The manner in which he [Joseph] pretended to read and interpret, was the same as when he looked for the money-diggers, with the stone in his hat, and his hat over his face, while the Book of Plates were at the same time hid in the woods!"[53]

David Whitmer of Fayette, New York, an early disciple of Joseph Smith who became acquainted with him in 1829 while the book was still being dictated, recalled in 1881: "He [Joseph] did not use the plates in the translation, but would hold the interpreters to his eyes and cover his face with a hat, excluding all light, and before his eyes would appear what seemed to be parchment" on which he would see the characters on the plates and the translation. Joseph would then read the words that he saw to his scribe.[54] In an 1885 interview, Whitmer said that Joseph used a seer stone "placed in a hat into which he buried his face, stating to me and others that the original Character[s] appeared upon parchment and under it the

---

(April 1829).

[52] "Joseph Smith: 'The Gift of Seeing,'" *Dialogue: A Journal of Mormon Thought* 15 (Summer 1982):53.

[53] *Susquehanna Register* 9 (May 1, 1834):1; reprinted in Howe, *Mormonism Unvailed*, 265.

[54] *Kansas City Daily Journal*, June 5, 1881, 1; reprinted in the *Deseret Evening News*, June 11, 1881; *Saints Herald* 28 (July 1, 1881):198; *Latter-day Saints' Millennial Star* 43 (July 4, 1881):423; and Vogel, *Early Mormon Documents* 5:76.

translation in english which [enabled him] to read it readily."[55]

It is not clear from the early accounts whether Smith used a single seer stone or, in another tradition, two seer stones as a pair of spectacles to read the meaning of the text. Either way the various accounts emphasize Smith's continued use of a seer stone.[56] In Joseph Smith's 1832 account he mentions there were spectacles "to read the Book."[57] Joseph Knight, who visited Smith in Harmony, wrote:

Now the way he translated was he put the urim and thummim into his hat and Dark[e]ned his Eyes then he would take a Sentance [Sentence] and it would appe[a]r in Brite [Bright] Roman Letters then he would tell the writer and he would write it then <that would go away> [and] the next Sentance [Sentence] would Come and so on. But if it was not Spelt rite [right] it would not go away till it was rite [right]. So we See it was marvelous thus was the hol [whole] translated.[58]

---

[55] Interview of David Whitmer by Zenas H. Gurley, Jr., Jan. 14, 1885, typescript, LDS archives. The bracketed words "enabled him" came from *Autumn Leaves* 5 (1892):453, Lamoni, Iowa. See Lyndon W. Cook, ed., *David Whitmer Interviews: A Restoration Witness* (Orem, Utah: Grandin Book Company, 1991), 157-58.

[56] On the method that the Book of Mormon was said to have been translated, see, under various titles, James E. Lancaster in *Saints Herald* 109 (Nov. 15, 1962):798-802, 806, 817; reprinted in *John Whitmer Historical Association Journal* 3 (1983):51-61; *Restoration Studies III* (Independence, Missouri: Herald Publishing House, 1986), 220-31; and Dan Vogel, ed., *The Word of God: Essays on Mormon Scripture* (Salt Lake City: Signature Books, 1990), 97-112. James Lancaster wrote, "An examination of the eyewitness testimony produces the following consensus on the method of translation of the Book of Mormon: . . . the plates were not used in the translating process and often were not even in sight during the translation" (*Restoration Studies III*, 226).

[57] Jessee, *Papers of Joseph Smith* 1:9.

[58] Joseph Knight Reminiscences; see Jessee, "Joseph Knight's Recollection," 35. Regarding the Urim and Thummim, see Kenneth Sowers, Jr., "The Mystery and History of the Urim and Thummim," *Restoration Studies II* (Independence, MO: Herald Publishing House, 1983), 75-79. Concerning the seer stone in a hat, see J. L. Traughber, Jr., "Testimony of David Whitmer," *Saints Herald* 26 (Nov. 15, 1879):341; and David Whitmer, *An Address to All Believers in Christ* (Richmond, Missouri: author, 1887), 12, 30, 37.

The biblical term "Urim and Thummim" in Knight's account seems to be a later term used to apply to the seer stone and sometimes to two magical stones in frames like spectacles. Lucy Smith remarked, "Joseph kept the urim and thum[m]im constantly about his person," even having it with him while he was working down in a well.[59] It was by the "Urim and Thummim," according to Lucy, that Joseph received a commandment that he should baptize Oliver Cowdery and that Cowdery should baptize him.[60] At one time an intimation "was given through the urim and thum[m]im" as Joseph "one morning applied the latter to his eyes to look upon the record, instead of the words of the book [of Mormon] being given him, he was commanded to write a letter to one David Whitmore [Whitmer]."[61]

Accounts also differ about what supposedly happened to the gold plates.[62] David Whitmer told an interviewer in 1884 that the plates "were taken away by the angel to a cave, which we saw by the power of God while we were yet in the Spirit."[63] William Smith said in 1841 that Joseph "was directed by a vision to bury the plates again in the same manner; which he accordingly did."[64]

Brigham Young, who joined the church in 1832, spoke of Joseph Smith and Oliver Cowdery going to the Hill Cumorah and "the hill opened, and they walked into a cave." Orson Pratt referred to "numerous records of the ancient nations of the western continent," in another area of the hill."[65]

---

[59] Anderson, *Lucy's Book*, 384.

[60] Ibid., 439. See Marquardt, *Joseph Smith Revelations*, 46; BC 15:6-7; LDS D&C 18:7; RLDS D&C 16:2.

[61] Anderson, *Lucy's Book*, 446.

[62] Folklore has it that Joseph returned the gold plates into a cave in the Hill Cumorah in Manchester, New York. For a collection of these stories, see Paul Thomas Smith, "A Preliminary Draft of the Hill Cumorah Cave Story Utilizing Seven Secondary Accounts and Other Historical Witnesses," March 1980, privately circulated.

[63] Interview of David Whitmer by Edmund C. Briggs, in *Saints Herald* 31 (June 21, 1884):396; and Cook, *David Whitmer Interviews*, 127.

[64] William Smith interview, *The Congregational Observer* 2 (July 3, 1841):1.

[65] Brigham Young in *Journal of Discourses* 19:38, June 17, 1877; quoted in *The Contributor* 3 (Feb. 1882):137; *The Juvenile Instructor* 31 (Sept. 1, 1896):514; and Daniel H. Ludlow, ed., *Encyclopedia of Mormonism: The History, Scripture, Doctrine, and Procedure of the Church of Jesus Christ of Latter-day Saints* (New York: Macmillan Publishing Co., 1992), 3:1,427-28. Young

Taken together, these earliest accounts about the gold plates place the event within the larger context of treasure hunting. Smith reported that he obtained the gold plates from the ground where they had been hidden for 1,400 years. Like his earlier attempts to locate lost objects and valuable treasures in the earth, he located the plates by means of the stone.[66] He removed his find from its depository and laid it down. After laying it down, however, it suddenly disappeared and went back into the box. This is similar to another treasure dig he participated in, with the guardian standing by and protecting the item.

The guardian spirit is a consistent focus of these early stories. Whether the guardian of the plates was a spirit or angel, its purpose was to watch over the buried box and its contents. Smith went to great lengths to obey the spirit's commands. He wore special clothes. He was given a simple command not to lay the plates down. When he did, the spirit struck him and kept him from obtaining the treasure. Because he did not do as he was instructed, Joseph was told to come in another year and bring Alvin with him.

Many aspects of the story told in New York and Pennsylvania were later revised. This included Joseph Smith having looked into the stone and instructed to bring Emma Hale to the hill, and especially details which linked the gold plates and treasure hunting. Rodger I. Anderson commented on why such details were omitted from Smith's historical accounts:

> His earlier story of the mobile plates which vanished and reappeared so mysteriously was not mentioned because of its similarity to the elusive treasures he was accused of hunting; the spirit's command to bring Alvin to the hill and after Alvin's death, Emma, was deleted because it smacked more of ritualistic magic than religion "pure and undefiled"; and Joseph Knight's recollection that Smith had "looked in his glass" to find the right person was discarded

---

remembered that "Joseph Smith said that Cave Contained tons of Choice Treasures & records" (Scott G. Kenney, ed., *Wilford Woodruff's Journal*, typescript, 1833-1898, 9 vols., 1983-85 [Midvale, Utah: Signature Books], 6:509, entry for Dec. 11, 1869, original in LDS archives). Orson Pratt's comments are in the *Latter-day Saints' Millennial Star* 28 (July 7, 1866):417.

[66] Interview of Martin Harris, *Tiffany's Monthly* 5 (Aug. 1859):163, 169.

because of its resemblance to the glass looking charge he had been convicted of in 1826. Smith had learned from bitter experience that not all regarded such activities as divine.[67]

In the 1832 retelling of the gold plates story, Smith was not given elaborate tasks to break the spell but was simply informed by the angel that in "due time thou shalt obtain them."[68] By the time of Smith's 1838-39 account, he was instructed from the very start that there would be a four-year waiting period: "I made an attempt to take them out but was forbidden by the messenger and was again informed that the time <for> bringing them forth had not yet arrived, neither would untill four years from that time."[69]

The early story as Joseph Smith related it was important since it was to establish the belief that he had a record. His immediate family was also essential to him as they were among the first to believe him. Chapter six will summarize the activities of the Joseph Smith Sr. family after they arrived in Palmyra.

---

[67] "Joseph Smith's Early Reputation Revisited," *Journal of Pastoral Practice* 4 (1980):98; see also Rodger I. Anderson, *Joseph Smith's New York Reputation Reexamined* (Salt Lake City: Signature Books, 1990), 47.

[68] Jessee, *Papers of Joseph Smith* 1:8.

[69] Manuscript History, Book A-1:7, LDS archives; Jessee, *Papers of Joseph Smith* 1:281; Joseph Smith-History 1:53, Pearl of Great Price.

6

Smith Family Activities

After the Smith family joined Joseph Sr. in Palmyra, New York, they first lived on Main Street in the village of Palmyra. Pomeroy Tucker, who was personally acquainted with the Smith family at this period, recalled:

At Palmyra, Mr. Smith, Sr., opened a "cake and beer shop," as described by his signboard, doing business on a small scale, by the profits of which, added to the earnings of an occasional day's work on hire by himself and his elder sons, for the village and farming people, he was understood to secure a scanty but honest living for himself and family. . . . Mr. Smith's shop merchandise consist[ed] of gingerbread, pies, boiled eggs, root-beer.[1]

While residing in Palmyra village Joseph Smith Sr. worked on Jeremiah Hurlbut's land. The elder Smith is listed in the 1817-1819 road records as living close to Hurlbut.[2] Jeremiah was a son of John Hurlbut an early settler of Palmyra. His mother Hannah and her family owned property in Palmyra. The assessment rolls has Jeremiah being taxed for thirty acres with eight acres on the north side and twenty-two acres on the south side of Main Street.[3] There appears to have been an arrangement for Joseph Sr. to pay one half of the taxes on the land to Hurlbut. The elder Smith and his sons worked on the Hurlbut land for a few months.

---

[1] Pomeroy Tucker, *Origin, Rise, and Progress of Mormonism*, 12. James Gordon Bennett in his diary, entry for Aug. 7, 1831, recorded: "Old Smith [Joseph Sr.] . . . made gingerbread and buttermints &c&c" (in Leonard J. Arrington, "James Gordon Bennett's 1831 Report on 'The Mormonites,'" *Brigham Young University Studies* 10 [Spring 1970]:355). This was published as "the manufacture of gingerbread" in *The Morning Courier & Enquirer* (New York), Aug. 31, 1831.
[2] Palmyra Highway Tax Record, Palmyra, New York, Copies of Old Village Records, 1793-1867, LDS Family History Library, microfilm #812869.
[3] Palmyra, New York, Assessment Roll, 1816-18, Ontario County Records Center and Archives, Canandaigua.

On March 27, 1818 Joseph Sr. and Alvin Smith gave a promissory note to Jeremiah Hurlbut for the sum of sixty-five dollars:

Forvallue Received i Promise to Pay to
Pay to Jeremiah Hurlbut Or Barer the sum
Of Sixty five Dollars to be Paid in good
Merchant Grain at the market Price by
the first January next with use forva
lue Receivd March the 27<th> 1818 Jos. Smith
$65.00   Alvin Smith[4]

There appears to have been a falling out between both men. Forty-seven year old Joseph Sr. brought suit against twenty-seven years old Jeremiah Hurlbut.[5] Most of the note (fifty-three dollars) was considered paid by Smith on August 10, 1818 with "Crops on the ground." Joseph Sr. saw the necessity of taking Jeremiah Hurlbut to court because he felt cheated on the purchase of a span of horses and also Hurlbut owed for work already performed worth about forty dollars. Smith also considered that Hurlbut had not worked the land according to their agreement.

At the office of Justice of the Peace Abraham Spear the parties appeared on January 22, 1819. Spear's summary on the case states:

Plaintiffs Declaration was for several articles of account and one Item was for Damages which Plaintiff sustained in the purpose of a span of horses of Defendant which horses was said to be unsound. Defendant Denies the Charge and pleads a set off of a balance Due on a note and several articles of account

The court was finally held on February 6, 1819 with a jury at the request of Joseph Sr. The twelve man jury consisted of some of the prominent citizens of Palmyra. Five witnesses for the

---

[4] Court of Common Pleas, 1818 January–May, Affidavits, Box Location AM01-187, Box No. 11211, Ontario County Record Center and Archives.
[5] "Court Common Pleas 1819, Narratio," AM01-185, Box No. 11203, Ontario County Records Center and Archives.

plaintiff included Smith's sons Hyrum and Joseph Jr., also George Proper. There appeared on behalf of Hurlbut seven witnesses. After hearing the evidence of both parties the jury "found for the plaintiff $40.78."

The evidence presented by plaintiff Smith and defendant Hurlbut consisted of, besides the original 1818 note, their individual listing of work or expenses performed for each other. Joseph Smith Sr.'s listing of costs started in May 1818 and included such items as:

To hyrum half Day fenceing	0.50
To my self & Hyrum & teem one Day	3.00
To making fence one Day	1.00
To Hyrum & horses <half Day> Drawing Rales	1.50
up to the 22nd may	
July the 10th Dr. to half Day mowing	0.50
To one Day mowing & c.	$1.00
To part of two Days myself & Boys <haying>	0.75
To Joseph half Day Drawing hay	0.25
To Hyrum & teem part of a Day Drawing hay	1.00

Additional work occurred in the south and north fields at seventy-five cents a day. The list included entries that show that Hurlbut took Smith's horses without asking and used the horses and wagon for drawing wood, corn, and wheat. But the horses used by Hurlbut could account for why Smith left the crops on the ground on August 10. The last two items added by Smith were for "Damages Sustained by means of warranty & fraud or ducet [deceit] in the Sale of Horses &c" asking for $80.00 and "To Not performing contrat [contract]" $25.00.

Hurlbut's list included such items as "To ho[e]ing corn 2 days on the west lot," amount: $1.50; "To 3d days works ho[e]ing corn on the east lot & Mowing myself," amount: $3.00; and "To paid Smith half of Tax on Land," amount: $1.62½. The total amount of taxes to be paid on real estate by Jeremiah Hurlbut for 1818 was $3.26.[6] This indicates that Joseph Smith Sr. was working

---

[6] Palmyra, New York, Assessment Roll, 1818, Ontario County Records Center and Archives.

on the 30 acres owned by the heirs of John Hurlbut with taxes to be paid this year by Jeremiah. Added at the end of the list is: "To damage for not working land according To agreement" $25.00 and "To 28 dollars damage sustained in the wrong apprisal [appraisal] of crops." Hurlbut's list appears to have been adjusted twice (evidently by the justice of the peace) for items that Joseph Sr. had previously paid him, probably in labor.

Not including the damage claim in the sale of horses ($80.00), Joseph Smith Sr.'s list was adjusted for two items. The amount of $64.75 (out of $65.00) included the $25.00 for not performing according to contract and was the amount Hurlbut owed Smith. This amount was reduced because Joseph Sr. owed Hurlbut $10.08 for services rendered and the $13.89 (including interest) remaining on the note of March 27, 1818. This brings the amount of the judgment to $40.78 that Hurlbut owes Joseph Smith Sr. plus the cost of suit $4.76 for a total cost to Hurlbut of $45.54. Justice Abraham Spear wrote, "the summons Issued in the above sent was for trespass on the Case for fifty Dollars or under."

Hurlbut, through his attorney Frederick Smith (no relation to Joseph Smith), appealed the judgment against him with Justice Spear forwarding the documents relating to the case to the Ontario County Court of Common Pleas. Hurlbut's complaint was against Joseph and Alvin Smith because they signed the note promising to pay Hurlbut or bearer $65.00 in good merchantable grain. The two Smiths "ought to have paid and delivered" to Hurlbut the money by January 1, 1819. Evidently the crops on the ground reportedly worth $53.00 was not considered fulfilled and Hurlbut appealed the case claiming that Joseph and Alvin "have not paid said note or any part thereof" and that they "wholly refused, and still do refuse" to the damage of $140.00.

A bond was made to the court for $81.56 (twice the amount of judgment) and was signed by Jeremiah Hurlbut, William Jackways, and Solomon Tice who was married to Jeremiah's sister Anna. A transcript of the proceedings was forwarded to the Court of Common Pleas in Canandaigua.

The Common Pleas Court Minutes book recorded on cases heard on appeal listed: "The like as the 2^d above" under default with the wording for the second entry: "The defendants default in not pleading having been duly entered On motion of [named]

Attorney for the Plaintiff Ordered Interlocutory Judgement and that the Clerk assess the damages."[7] No record has been located indicating the amount assessed to Joseph and Alvin Smith. So it is not clear at this point the total outcome of the appeal. This case shows that Joseph Sr., Hyrum, and Joseph Jr., who was twelve years old, worked for Jeremiah Hurlbut during a brief period in 1818.

The record of Road District 26 for April 1819 list Joseph Smith Sr. and Jeremiah Hurlbut next to each other. By the next year Joseph Sr. is listed at the end of the list indicating he was living on Samuel Jennings's property where the Smith family lived until they moved onto the 100 acres in Manchester after April 1822.

Pomeroy Tucker described the family's Manchester cabin as "a small, one-story, smoky log-house, which they had built prior to removing there. This house was divided into two rooms, on the ground-floor, and had a low garret, in two apartments. A bedroom wing, built of sawed slabs, was afterwards added."[8] Tucker also recalled the family's economic activities during this period:

> The chief application of the useful industry of the Smiths during their residence upon this farm-lot, was in the chopping and retailing of cord-wood, the raising and bartering of small crops of agricultural products and garden vegetables, the manufacture and sale of black-ash baskets and birch brooms, the making of maple sugar and molasses in the season for that work, and in the continued business of peddling cake and beer in the village on days of public doings.[9]

The male members of the Smith family hired out to others

---

[7] "Common Pleas Minutes August Term 1819 by the Bar," AM01-188, Box No. 5022, County Records Center and Archives.

[8] Tucker, *Origins, Rise, and Progress of Mormonism*, 13. Pomeroy Tucker continued, "Subsequently this property was purchased by Mr. Smith on contract." Tucker wrote that the land the Smith family lived on was included in the farm of Seth T. Chapman who owned the Manchester property at the time Tucker wrote his book.

[9] Ibid., 14.

in the community. John H. Gilbert, a resident of Palmyra since 1824, recalled "Hyrum Smith was a common laborer, and worked for any one as he was called on."[10] Orsamus Turner remembered young Joseph bringing "little jags of wood" to the village and obtained an odd job at Seymour Scovell's store.[11]

Coopering or making barrels, the essential containers for all sorts of goods and commodities at the time, was a Smith family trade. Asael Smith, Joseph Sr.'s father, was a cooper.[12] Mrs. Anderick recalled that Joseph Sr. and his son Hyrum "worked some at coopering."[13] Besides making barrels, they also made related items such as slipwood chairs, baskets, and birch brooms.

Christopher M. Stafford remembered, "Old Jo claimed to be a Cooper but worked very little at anything. He was intemperate. Hyrum worked at cooperage. . . . I exchanged work with Jo but more with his brother Harrison, who was a good, industrious boy."[14] Other neighbors agreed that Samuel Harrison was an asset to the family. "Harrison was a good worker for one day or a month," said Hyram Jackaway.[15]

Benjamin Saunders, another neighbor living near the Smiths, remembered them as "good workers by days work. They were coopers by trade. Did not like to make steady business of it. <They were> Big hearty fellows. Their morals were good. The old man sometimes would drink until he felt quite happy at our log rollings and raisings: but he was not quarrelsome. He was not a bad man."[16] Isaac Butts mentioned that old Joseph "taught me to

---

[10] Memorandum dated Sept. 8, 1892, Palmyra, New York, in Wilford C. Wood, *Joseph Smith Begins His Work*, 2 vols. (Salt Lake City: Deseret News Press, 1958), Vol. 1, introductory pages. "Hyrum, another son, helped his father at the trade of a cooper" (Frederic G. Mather, *Lippincott's Magazine of Popular Literature and Science* 26 [1880]:198).

[11] O[rsamus]. Turner, *History of the Pioneer Settlement of Phelps and Gorham's Purchase, and Morris' Reserve*, 213-14.

[12] Richard L. Anderson, *Joseph Smith's New England Heritage: Influences of Grandfathers Solomon Mack and Asael Smith*, revised ed., (Salt Lake City: Deseret Book and Provo, Utah: BYU Press, 2003), 120, 251n134-35.

[13] Statement of Mrs. S. F, Anderick, 1887, in *Naked Truths About Mormonism* 1 (Jan. 1888):2.

[14] Statement of C[hristopher]. M. Stafford, 1885, in Ibid. 1 (April 1888):1.

[15] William H. Kelley Notebook, March 1881 [p. 12], RLDS archives.

[16] Interview of Benjamin Saunders, William H. Kelley Collection "Miscellany 1795-1948" (1883-85), [19-20], RLDS archives.

mow. I worked with old and young Jo at farming."[17]

According to his mother, Alvin Smith was the one who took charge of acquiring materials and beginning construction of a frame house for the family. However, after the house was raised, Alvin became sick. Because their own doctor was away, they called a doctor from the next town who over Alvin's objection gave him a large dose of calomel (mercurous chloride), a toxic compound used as a digestive remedy. The calomel had to be followed by a powerful purgative for removing it promptly from the body. When this did not work, Alvin realized he was dying. On his death bed he called Hyrum to his side and told him, as Lucy later recalled, "I must die and now I want to say a few things to you that you must remember. I have done all that I could do to make our dear Parents comfortable. I now want you to go on and finish the House, take care <of> them in their old age, and do not ever let them work hard any more."[18] Joseph Sr. was fifty-two and Lucy was forty-eight years old when their son died.

At the autopsy performed by Dr. Robinson and the Smiths' own doctor, Dr. McIntire, the calomel was found untouched in the upper bowel, surrounded by gangrene. Thereafter, according to Lucy, Robinson "spoke long and earnestly to the younger physicians upon the danger of administering powerful medicines without a thorough knowledge of <the practice of> physick." He expressed regret that as fine a youth as "ever trod the streets of Palmyra" was "murdered, as it were, by him at whose hand relief was expected." Apparently another person grieved at Alvin's death--"a lovel[y] young woman who was engaged to be married to my son."[19] Alvin's death was a shock and heartbreak to the whole family.

Work on the house continued until it was habitable, and the family moved in. This frame house was an improvement over the log cabin, which later became Hyrum's home. The Smith family would reside on the Manchester portion of the Stafford Road for eight years.

Work during this period included treasure seeking for the

---

[17] Statement of Isaac Butts in *Naked Truths About Mormonism* 1 (Jan. 1888):2.

[18] Anderson, *Lucy's Book*, 352.

[19] Ibid., 355. This portion of the 1844-45 manuscript was crossed out with an X, evidently to alert the compiler not to include it in the final version.

older male members. "There was a company there in that neighborhood," Martin Harris later recalled, "who were digging for money . . . Of this company were old Mr. Stowel[l] – I think his name was Josiah – also old Mr. Beman, also Samuel Lawrence, George Proper, Joseph Smith, jr., and his father, and his brother Hiram Smith."[20] Alvin helped young Joseph dig a well on the Chase farm in 1822 when they discovered a seer stone.[21] Lucy Smith described treasure-seeking activities as balancing other family occupations such as farming:

I shall change my theme for the present, but let not my reader suppose that because I pursue another topic for a season that we stopt our labor and went <at> trying to win the faculty of Abrac, drawing Magic circles or sooth saying to the neglect of all kinds of bus<i>ness. We never during our lives suffered one important interest to swallow up every other obligation but whilst we worked with our hands we endeavored to remmember [remember] the service of & the welfare of our souls.[22]

About two years after the Smith family settled on their hundred-acre farm, Lucy, Hyrum, Samuel, and Sophronia joined the local Western Presbyterian Church of Palmyra. As a result,

---

[20] *Tiffany's Monthly* 5 (Aug. 1859):164. Pomeroy Tucker wrote, "Smith's father and elder brothers generally participated in the manual labors of these diggings" (*Origin, Rise, and Progress of Mormonism*, 23).

[21] Affidavit of Willard Chase, Dec. 11, 1833, in Howe, *Mormonism Unvailed*, 240-41. Willard, a son of Clark Chase (1770-1821), was on born February 1, 1798. His brother Mason was born on November 19, 1795 (Wm. E. Reed, *The Descendants of Thomas Durfee of Portsmouth, R.I.* [Washington, D.C.: Gibson Bros., 1902], 213-14, and George Grant Brownel, comp., *Genealogical Record of the Descendants of Thomas Brownell 1619 to 1910* [Jamestown, New York: 1910], 200). Martin Harris stated, "Joseph had a stone which was dug from the well of Mason Chase, twenty-four feet from the surface" (*Tiffany's Monthly* 5 [Aug. 1859]:163).

[22] Anderson, *Lucy's Book*, 323. This comment by Lucy in the draft manuscript was not included in the Coray final manuscript. Abrac derives from Abracadabra and Abraxas, both of which were used on magic amulets. Members of the Masonic Lodge of the eighteenth century claimed they knew "the way of obtaining the faculty of <u>Abrac</u>" (James Hardie, *The New Free-Mason's Monitor* [New York: n.p., 1818], 203).

family activities during the mid-1820s included some church going. As William Smith recalled in 1883:

> My mother, who was a very pious woman and much interested in the welfare of her children, both here and hereafter, made use of every means which her parental love could suggest, to get us engaged in seeking for our souls' salvation, or (as the term then was) "in getting religion." She prevailed on us to attend the meetings, and almost the whole family became interested in the matter, and seekers after truth.[23]

Participating family members would have taken part in the instruction, confession of faith, membership vows, baptism, and welcome by the elders and congregation which constituted active membership in the church.

The family was given a reprieve of sorts during this period after Zechariah Seymour, the land agent who collected their mortgage payments, died in July 1822. But the Evertson heirs in New York City hired John Greenwood, a lawyer, to replace Seymour and conferred to him power of attorney on May 17, 1824.[24]

Work on the family's frame house continued after Alvin's death. Lucy Smith mentioned that a Mr. Stoddard was "the principle workman on the house."[25] One event not mentioned by Lucy was that her husband was not able at the time to pay Russell Stoddard, who was about 35 years old. The money owed was for work on the frame home and some lumber used in the project. Stoddard went before Peter Mitchell, who was a Justice of the Peace in Manchester, with his complaint of non payment of $66.59. Justice Mitchell heard the case on February 18, 1825. Joseph Sr. confessed owing Russell the money but he did not intend to defraud any creditor. The transcript of the judgment against Joseph Smith Sr. was sent to the Common Pleas in Canandaigua the county seat. Part of the document reads:

---

[23] *William Smith on Mormonism*, 6.

[24] Miscellaneous Records, Book C:458, Ontario County Records Center and Archives.

[25] Anderson, *Lucy's Book*, 359.

Joseph Smith the said defendant in this Cause being duly
sworn saith that he is honestly & justly indebted to the
plaintiff in the above suit in the sum of sixty six dollars &
fifty nine cents money of account of the United States it
being for work & labour & lumber Which the said plaintiff
did for me in building a dwelling house which said sum is
over & above all just demands which he the said defendant
had against Russell Stoddard the said plaintiff & that the
confession of judgment about to be made by him the said
defendant for the sum of sixty six dollars & fifty nine cents
is not to be made for the purpose of defrauding any
creditor[26]

This sworn testimony was signed by Joseph Smith Sr.
Included in the transcript is a copy of another document which
indicated like the above that the elder Smith did owe Stoddard for
services rendered the Smith family:

I Joseph Smith the defendant in the above Cause do hereby
confess that I am honestly & justly indebted to Russell
Stoddard the above named plaintiff in the sum of sixty six
dollars & fifty nine cents money of account of the United
States & do hereby authorize you the said Justice to enter
judgment against me the said defendant in favour of
Russell Stoddard the said plaintiff for the same Given
under my hand this 18h day of Feb 1825   Joseph Smith

What financial arrangement was made by Joseph Sr. to pay
Russell Stoddard is not known. This does show that Joseph Sr.
acknowledge his debt and was willing to pay it.

Lucy remembered a time after the appointment in May
1824 of John Greenwood, the new land agent, when the family
"received intelligence of the arrival of a new land agent for the
Ever[t]son Land, of which our farm was a portion. This caused us
to bethink ourselves of the remmaining [remaining] payment
which was still due and which we would be under the necessity of

---

[26] "1825 Common Pleas Transcripts," AM21-101, Box No. 19302, Ontario
County Records Center and Archives.

112

making <prior> to obtaining the deed <which> our bonds called for." The death of Zachariah Seymour in July 1822 prevented their final payment on the land. According to Lucy, her husband "sent Hyrum to the new Agent at Canandaguia [Canandaigua] to inform him that the money should be forthcoming as soon as the 25th of <Dec>[em]ber [1825] which the Agent said would answer every purpose and agreed to retain the land untill that time."[27]

About this time Joseph Jr. sent his brother Hyrum to again borrow the seer stone from Willard Chase. As Chase recalled it:

I believe, some time in 1825, Hiram Smith (brother of Joseph Smith) came to me, and wished to borrow the same stone, alledging [alleging] that they wanted to accomplish some business of importance, which could not very well be done without the aid of the stone. I told him it was of no particular worth to me, but merely wished to keep it as a curiously, and if he would pledge me his word and honor, that I should have it when called for, he might take it; which he did and took the stone. I thought I could rely on his word at this time, as he had made a profession of religion.[28]

Soon thereafter Joseph Sr. and his namesake were hired by Josiah Stowell to come south and help him dig for treasure near Harmony, Pennsylvania.[29] They were there until about November 17, 1825, when they returned to Bainbridge.

Lucy said that Mr. Stoddard ("the principle workman on the house") offered to purchase their home but was flatly refused by the Smiths.[30] As indicated previously this was Russell Stoddard.[31] It is of interest that another Stoddard, Squire Stoddard,

---

[27] *Lucy's Book*, 361-62.

[28] Affidavit of Willard Chase, Dec. 11, 1833, in Howe, *Mormonism Unvailed*, 241.

[29] A November 1, 1825 agreement was signed by Stowell, Joseph Smith Sr., Joseph Smith Jr., and others. It was published in the Salt Lake *Daily Tribune*, April 23, 1880, 4; Vogel, *Early Mormon Documents* 4:407-13. See statement of Isaac Hale in *Susquehanna Register, and Northern Pennsylvanian* 9 (May 1, 1834):1; Howe, *Mormonism Unvailed*, 263.

[30] Anderson, *Lucy's Book*, 359.

[31] In June 1907 George Albert Smith talked to Russell Stoddard, son of Russell,

bought the Evertson land south of the Smith farm on November 2, 1825.[32] His land was south of the land "articled to Joseph and Alvin Smith" and north of land deeded to Russell Stoddard.

Lucy said Stoddard told the land agent that the elder Smith and young Joseph had both left town and that Hyrum was cutting the sugar maple trees for fire wood and doing damage to the farm. He offered to buy the farm for cash, and since the Smiths were in default, John Greenwood agreed and gave Stoddard the deed. Afterward Stoddard and two friends went to the Smiths and asked them to leave the property. Panic ensued. The family sent to Harmony for Joseph Sr., and he hurried north to Manchester. As Lucy told the story:

> Hyrum went straightway to Dr. Robinson, (an old Friend <of ours who lived in Palmira)>. . . . [he] sat down and wrote [about] the charecter [character] of <my> family our industry and faithful exertion's to obtain a home in <the> forest, where we had set[t]led ourselves, with many commendations ca[l]culated to beget confidence in us as to buisness [business] transactions. This he took in his own hands and went through the village and in an hour there was attached to the paper the names of 60 subscribers. He then sent the same by the hand of Hyrum to the land Agent in Canandaguia [Canandaigua].[33]

Mr. Greenwood was enraged that he had been misled by Stoddard and sent a messenger to obtain the deed. The Smiths then turned to a friend who directed them to Lemuel Durfee. Durfee, his son Lemuel, and Joseph Sr. went to Canandaigua, where Durfee paid $1,135 on December 20, 1825 for the farm.[34] Stoddard "gave up the deed to Mr. Durfy [Durfee] . . . who now came into

---

who said "he heard his Father say he built the Smith house for Jos[eph] Smith Senior assisted by others" (George Albert Smith Journal, entry for June 7, 1907, LDS archives).

[32] Deed Liber 44:219-21, Ontario County Records Center and Archives.

[33] Anderson, *Lucy's Book*, 367.

[34] Deed Liber 44:232-34, Ontario County Records Center and Archives. Lucy stated in her manuscript they were told that "if Hyrum could raise $1000 by Saturday at 10 o'clock in the evening they would give up the deed" (*Lucy's Book*, 369).

posses[s]ion of the Farm. With this Gentleman," said Lucy, "we were now to s[t]ipulate as renters." Durfee allowed the Smiths to remain in the frame house and on the farm. According to Lucy, Durfee "gave us the priviledge [privilege] of the place one year with this provision that Samuel our 4th son was to labor for him 6 months."[35]

Almost one year after the family became renters, the *Wayne Sentinel* announced, "MARRIED - In Manchester . . . Mr. Hiram Smith, to Miss Jerusha Barden." They were married on November 2, 1826.[36] Jerusha was twenty-one years old, and Hyrum was twenty-six. Lucy heartily approved, noting in her history, "My oldest son [Hyrum] . . . Married him a wife that was one of the most excellent of Women."[37] Two months later Joseph Jr. married Emma Hale in Bainbridge on January 18, 1827, bringing her back to live in the family home in Manchester.[38] That same year, Sophronia married Calvin Stoddard on December 30.

Young Joseph was often hired by Martin Harris to work "on his farm, and that they had hoed corn together many a day, Brother Harris paying him fifty cents per day. Joseph, he [Harris] said, was good to work and jovial and they often wrestled together in sport, but the Prophet was devoted and attentive to his prayers."[39]

Samuel Harrison Smith worked for the elder Durfee in 1827, according to one of Durfee's account books: "April the 16 day the year 1827 S. Harrison Smith Son of Joseph Smith began to

---

[35] Anderson, *Lucy's Book*, 372.

[36] *Wayne Sentinel* 4 (Nov. 24, 1826):3. See photo of Hyrum Smith's Bible in *Ensign* 14 (Jan. 1984):33, "November the 2d 1826."

[37] Anderson, *Lucy's Book*, 364.

[38] Bible of Joseph and Emma Smith; see photo in *Ensign* 11 (March 1981):62 and 14 (Jan. 1984):33; "Genealogy of President Joseph Smith Junior," in Manuscript History A-1:9 [separate section] (see Jessee, *Papers of Joseph Smith* 1:18). The Smith-Cowdery Bible purchased in 1829, and used for Joseph Smith's revision of the Bible, contained the following under "Marriages," "Joseph Smith Junr Emma Hale was married Jan 18 1827 Bainbridge, Chenango County State of New York" (RLDS archives). See Anderson, *Lucy's Book*, 265. In Lucy Smith's manuscript draft, Joseph's and Hyrum's marriages are placed previous to the Smiths becoming renters on the farm.

[39] Edward Stevenson in *Latter-Day Saints' Millennial Star* 48 (June 21, 1886):389. Stevenson heard this from Martin Harris on their journey from Ohio to Utah Territory in 1870.

Work for me by the month. [He] is to Work 7 Months for the use of the place Where Said Joseph Smith Lives."[40]

Hyrum continued working as a cooper and with his father and brothers for local farmers including Lemuel Durfee. They apparently took their wages in credits toward their purchases. In Durfee's account book for 1827 he noted:

> Joseph [Sr.] and Hiram Smith Dr [debit] to three barrels of Cider at 9/ per barrel May the Last 1827 [9 shillings per barrel]
>
> June the 26 day Joseph Smith Dr. to Veal hind Quarter 23 pound $0.69 also one fore Quarter Wt. 22 pounds $=55 55
>
> august Credit by Joseph Smith by mo[w]ing three days & Joseph Smith Ju Jnr. two days mowing & Hiram Smith one day mowing even
>
> Sept. first to two barrels of Cider racked of[f] to Joseph & Hiram Smiths at 9/ per barrel $2=25[41]

Hyrum Smith was now living in the log house with his wife Jerusha, who was expecting their first child. Hyrum had previously joined the Masonic Lodge in Palmyra and was listed as a member of the Mount Moriah Masonic Lodge No. 112 for the period June 1827 to June 1828. Levi Daggett, Pomeroy Tucker, and other respected citizens were also members of the lodge.[42] Hyrum was

---

[40] Lemuel Durfee Account Book (1813-29), 15, Ontario County Historical Society, Canandaigua.

[41] Lemuel Durfee Account Book, 41-42, location of original in the King's Daughters Library, Palmyra, New York, in 1973. The present location of the account book is unknown. This is a separate account book and should not be confused with a similar ledger cited in note 40.

[42] "Return of Mount Moriah Lodge No. 112 held in the town of Palmyra in the County of Wayne and State of New York from June 4th AL 5827 [1827] to June 4th AL 5828 [1828]," Grand Lodge Free and Accepted Masons of the State of New York, Library and Museum, New York City. Also the Nauvoo, Illinois, Lodge listed Hyrum as having previously been a Mason in New York, entry for Dec. 30, 1841: "Hyrum Smith, Mount Moriah, No. 112, N.Y." (Mervin B. Hogan, ed., *Founding Minutes of Nauvoo Lodge, U.D.* [Des Moines, Iowa: Research Lodge No. 2, 1971]), 8. See Richard L. Anderson, *Investigating the Book of Mormon Witnesses* (Salt Lake City: Deseret Book, 1981), 149nn28-29.

still attending the Palmyra Presbyterian Church.[43] Hyrum and Jerusha's first child, a girl named Lovina, was born on September 16, 1827.[44]

Joseph Jr.'s interest in prehistoric America affected family life during these years. Lucy recalled the recitals about the land's ancient inhabitants which Joseph recounted during his teenage years:

In the course of our evening conversations Joseph would give us some of the most ammusing [amusing] recitals which could be immagined [imagined]. He would de[s]cribe the ancient inhabitants of this continent, their dress, thier [their] man[n]er of traveling, the animals [upon] which they rode, The cities that were built by them, the structure of their buildings, with every particular, of their mode of warfare [and] their religious worship - as particularly as though he had spent his life with them.[45]

The family became directly involved in Joseph's passion after the gold plates were said to have been retrieved from the fallen treetop where he reportedly left them. According to Lucy, her son Don Carlos was sent to Hyrum's home to let him know that Joseph needed a chest:

Carlos went into Hyrum's house he found him at tea with 2 of his wife's sisters, Carlos touched his brother's shoulder just as he was raising his cup to his mouth. Without waiting to hear a word of the child's errand Hyrum dropped his cup & sprang from the table and ketched [caught] up the chest,

---

[43] "Records of the Session of the Presbyterian Church in Palmyra," 2:11, minutes of March 10, 1830, microfilm, film #900, reel 59, Harold B. Lee Library, Brigham Young University, Provo, Utah.

[44] Anderson, *Lucy's Book*, 268. See photo of the "Family Record" in Hyrum Smith's family Bible in *The Friend* 18 (Jan. 1988):35, entry: "Lovina Smith the Daughter of Hyrum & Jerusha Smith was Born September 16th 1827." This Bible is dated to the Kirtland, Ohio period. Lovina was born in Manchester. See Vogel, *Early Mormon Documents* 1:584-85 and George Albert Smith Family Papers, Manuscripts Division, Marriott Library, University of Utah, Salt Lake City.

[45] Anderson, *Lucy's Book*, 345.

turnend [turned] it upside down and leaving the contents on the [floor] left the House in an instant with the chest on his shoulder. The young ladies were much surprized at his singular behaviour and protested to his wife (who was bedfast her oldest daughter Lovina being but 4 days) that her husband was positively crazy. She laughed heartily, O! not in the least said she. [Hyrum] has just thought of something that he has neglected and it's just like him to fly off in a tangent when he thinks of anything that way.[46]

Joseph permitted the family to feel and handle what he said were the plates before depositing them in the chest. William Smith remembered that he "did not see them [the plates] uncovered but I handled them and hefted them while [they were] wrapped in a tow frock." He mentioned that his "Father and my brother Samuel saw them as I did while in the frock. So did Hyrum and others of the family."[47]

Joseph then locked the record in the box and with the family's help hid it under the brick hearth in the west room of the house.[48] This hearth surrounded the fireplace where the Smith family discussed the events of the day and where Joseph talked to his family about his adventures. It was probably in this room that he related to Josiah Stowell and Joseph Knight "the whole history of the record, which interested them very much." They listened and believed "all that was told them" by Joseph.[49]

Still concerned about the safety of the plates, Joseph took the box from the hearth and carried it out to the "cooper shop across the road." He put the box under the floor of the shop. The money-diggers located it there and smashed the box to pieces but

---

[46] Ibid., 387. Lucy has Lovina being four days old. She should have been eleven days old (or more), as Joseph did not immediately return home with the record.

[47] "Wm. B. Smith's last Statement," *Zion's Ensign* 5 (Jan. 13, 1894):6; reprinted in the *Deseret Evening News* 27 (Jan. 20, 1894):11; *Latter-day Saints' Millennial Star* 56 (Feb. 26, 1894):132. Ten years earlier William Smith wrote, "I was permitted to lift them [the plates] as they laid in a pillow-case; but not to see them" (*William Smith on Mormonism*, 12).

[48] Joseph Knight Reminiscences, LDS archives; Dean C. Jessee, ed., "Joseph Knight's Recollection of Early Mormon History," *Brigham Young University Studies* 17 (Autumn 1976):33.

[49] Anderson, *Lucy's Book*, 388.

did not find the plates.[50] According to Martin Harris, Joseph had taken the plates out of the box and hidden them in the loft under some flax.[51] Alvah Beeman, a friend of the family, helped make a new container from a wooden box made to hold window glass, and Joseph worked "with his Father on the farm in order to be near the treasure that was commit[t]ed to his care."[52]

Lucy Smith went to the Harris home just north of the village of Palmyra and invited Harris' wife and daughter to come and see the container. Harris recalled, "My daughter said, they were about as much as she could lift. They were now in the glass-box, and my wife said they were very heavy. They both lifted them."

Martin arrived later but found that Joseph had gone to Peter Ingersoll's farm to get some flour. Harris talked with Emma and the Smith family and they said that Joseph "found them [the plates] by looking in the stone found in the well of Mason Chase [older brother of Willard]. The family had likewise told me the same thing."

While at the Smith home, Harris hefted the plates and thought that they weighed about forty or fifty pounds. Harris told Joseph that if this was the Lord's work, "you can have all the money necessary to bring it before the world." He then went home, prayed, and was "satisfied that it was the Lord's work" and that he "was under a covenant to bring it forth."[53]

Although several people felt the plates under a cloth before

---

[50] Ibid., 392.

[51] Martin Harris who was interviewed in 1859 reported, "After they had been concealed under the floor of the cooper's shop for a short time, Joseph was warned to remove them. He said he was warned by an angel. He took them out and hid them up in the chamber of the cooper's shop among the flags [flax]. That night some one came, took up the floor, and dug up the earth, and would have found the plates had they not been removed" (*Tiffany's Monthly* 5 [Aug. 1859]:167).

[52] Anderson, *Lucy's Book*, 389.

[53] *Tiffany's Monthly* 5 (Aug. 1859):168-70. Edward Stevenson wrote, "Martin's Wife had hefted them & felt them under cover as had Martin" (Interview of Martin Harris by Edward Stevenson, Sept. 4, 1870, LDS archives). Willard Chase talked with Joseph about the same time that Harris asked the family how the plates were found. Chase recalled, "He then observed that if it had not been for that stone, (which he acknowledged belonged to me,) he would not have obtained the book" (*Mormonism Unvailed*, 246).

they were put in a box or held the box while it was in a pillow case, others were dissatisfied and determined to see the actual plates. As a result Joseph and Emma went to her parents' home in Harmony to work on the translation of the plates away from the curious. Harris paid off Joseph's debts and gave him $50 for the journey.

Alva Hale, Emma's brother, came north to Manchester to move their belongings. The box containing the plates was said to have been put into a barrel of beans for the trip. Before leaving, Joseph arranged with Martin Harris to come south to Harmony and pick up an alphabet transcribed from the Egyptian characters said to be on the gold plates. Harris wanted copies of the writing on the plates verified by experts. According to Lucy, when Harris went to Harmony a few months later to get the copy, "Hyrum went with him."[54]

Meanwhile the life and work of the Smiths in Manchester went on as before. Lemuel Durfee noted in his account book for 1828:

> May the 13th Joseph [Sr.] & [Samuel] Harrison Smith Dr. [debit] to three barrels of Cider the Liqure at $3=38
>
> June the 18 day the year 1828 Credit By Hiram & Har[r]ison Smiths a hoeing one Day a piece
>
> June the 20 day Joseph & Harrison Smiths Dr. to the Liqure of three barrels of Cider at 9/0 per barrel $3=38
>
> July 7 day Credit by J. Smith & Rockwell by hoeing three days
>
> July 20 Jos. Smith & Harrison Cr. by Work binding Wheat one day of william and three days of Harrison Work
>
> august 7 Credit <by> Rockwell to two days Mowing for me by Harrison Smith by three days a Mowing for me [55]

On September 11 Joseph Sr. went to Gain C. Robinson, the family physician in Palmyra, and obtained medicine for "Boy Harrison" who was twenty years old at the time.[56]

---

[54] Anderson, *Lucy's Book*, 402.
[55] Lemuel Durfee Account Book, 43-44; see footnote 41.
[56] Gain C. Robinson Day Book, Sept. 1, 1827-Feb. 12, 1830, Palmyra's King's Daughters Free Library, Palmyra New York, entry for Sept. 11, 1828, as cited in

Lucy Smith mentions a trip she took with her husband to Harmony to visit Joseph and Emma. They met for the first time Emma's parents, Isaac and Elizabeth Hale, and family members. This apparently occurred about October 1828. When they returned home they found Sophronia and Samuel very sick.[57] In early 1829 Joseph Sr. and Samuel went south to visit Joseph and Emma.

Because Hyrum Smith was one of the trustees of the local school, he was responsible for hiring teachers. Lyman Cowdery applied but soon encountered a scheduling conflict and recommended his brother Oliver, who was hired.[58] Oliver boarded with the Smith family where he heard the story of Joseph and the record. Cowdery decided that as soon as the school term was ended, he would like "the priviledge [privilege] of writing for Joseph."[59] In early April Oliver Cowdery and Samuel Harrison left for Harmony, Pennsylvania. Lucy remembered, "The time was now drawing to a close. We now began to make preparations to remove our family and effects to the log house <which> was now occupied by Hyrum" and his family.[60]

The Smith family's place of residency after their move to the log house of Hyrum and his family is referred to in every case as Manchester. All of the Smiths' legal and personal documents dating from 1829-30 are dated at Manchester. This includes Joseph Smith's revelations; letters written by Oliver Cowdery while living with the Smith family; law suits against Joseph Sr. and Hyrum; the 1830 census; and the 1830 Manchester assessment roll where Hyrum Smith is taxed for fifteen acres on Lot 1.

Vogel, *Early Mormon Documents* 3:439.

[57] Anderson, *Lucy's Book*, 423-31.

[58] Ibid., 431. William and Oliver Cowdery were evidently living in the township of Arcadia, Wayne County. See list of letters unclaimed at the Newark Post Office, Oct. 1, 1827, in the *Lyons Advertiser* 6 (Oct. 17, 1827). For Lyman Cowdery, see list of unclaimed letters at the Palmyra Post Office, *Wayne Sentinel* 5 (July 11, 1828):3.

[59] Anderson, *Lucy's Book*, 432.

[60] Ibid., 434. The earlier reading "we had formerly lived in" is crossed out in the manuscript. There were two log homes that the Smiths lived in prior to residing in the frame house. The first one was in Palmyra Township, to which they did not return, and the other one was built by the Smiths in Manchester Township. Lucy Mack Smith, William Smith, and Pomeroy Tucker each mention a cabin being built on land in Manchester.

There is no evidence of Hyrum Smith residing in Palmyra after his marriage since the highway road tax lists do not include his name on any road district for 1827 or 1828. The road leading from the south boundary of the Corporation of the Village of Palmyra to the town line in 1828 was in Road District 1 and was Stafford Road. There were only six men over twenty-one years of age in this road district.[61]

At Manchester Hyrum's wife Jerusha, who was expecting the couple's second child, was sick. He went to Dr. Gain C. Robinson and obtained medicine on March 25, 1829 for Jerusha.[62] A daughter was born to them on June 27, 1829 who they named Mary.[63] This added another person to live in the log home.

Chapter seven returns us to the end of 1827 when Alva Hale, his sister Emma, and Joseph Jr. arrive at the Isaac Hale home in Harmony, Pennsylvania.

---

[61] Palmyra Highway Tax Record, Palmyra, New York, Copies of Old Village Records, 1793-1867, LDS Family History Library, microfilm #812869.

[62] Gain C. Robinson Day Book, Sept. 1, 1827-Feb. 12, 1830, Palmyra's King's Daughters Free Library, Palmyra New York, entry for March 25, 1829, as cited in Vogel, *Early Mormon Documents* 3:439.

[63] Anderson, *Lucy's Book*, 268; see Pearson H. Corbett, *Hyrum Smith: Patriarch*, 57, 103. See photo of the "Family Record" recorded in Hyrum Smith's family Bible in *The Friend* 18 (Jan. 1988):35, entry: "Mary Smith was Born June 27th 1829."

Life in Harmony, Pennsylvania

In December 1827 Emma and Joseph left Manchester for the 150 mile trip to the township of Harmony, Susquehanna County, Pennsylvania.[1] Emma's brother Alva helped move them. There Joseph became more acquainted with the Emma's family and relatives. Smith discussed with the close knit Hale family about finding the plates. The book was said to contain the word of the Lord that had been delivered to the ancient inhabitants of the American continent.

Isaac Hale, known as a great hunter in Susquehanna County, was born in 1763 and was 64 years old when Joseph Smith returned with his daughter Emma. Isaac's wife was 60 year old Elizabeth. They were members of the Methodist Episcopal Church. The family included five sons (Jesse, David, Alva, Isaac Ward, and Reuben) and four daughters (Phebe, Elizabeth, Emma, and Trial).

The elder Isaac indicated that Joseph and Emma lived in his house and brought a box with them that was said to contain the gold plates. Hale informed Joseph if there was anything in his house like that and he was not allowed to see it "he must take it away; if he did not, I was determined to see it. After that, the Plates were said to be hid in the woods."[2] The couple moved to a nearby house that Jesse Hale had lived in not far from Emma's father Isaac.

Prior to Joseph and Emma leaving Manchester in December, "it was agreed that Martin Har[r]is should follow him as soon as Joseph should have sufficient time to transcribe the Egyptian alphabet which Mr. Harris was to take to the east and through the country in every direction to all who were professed linguists to give them an opertunity [opportunity] of showing their

---

[1] Anderson, *Lucy's Book*, 402.
[2] "Mormonism," *Susquehanna Register, and Northern Pennsylvanian* 9 (May 1, 1834):1, Montrose, Pennsylvania. See Vogel, *Early Mormon Documents* 4:286.

talents."[3]

It was not until about February 1828 that Martin Harris came to take a sample of the reported ancient characters to find out if any learned person could confirm their authenticity or translate them. Of those languages the Egyptian language was considered mysterious and untranslatable.

For all practical purposes if you do not know a foreign language you would start with learning the alphabet and rules of grammar. It appears that Joseph Smith copied and worked on writing an Egyptian alphabet. The alphabet was said to have come from the gold plates. The work probably included Smith's understanding of the characters. When Martin Harris arrived at Harmony the copied page or pages of characters were given to him. This was an alphabet to the Book of Mormon as described by Lucy Smith.

Joseph Smith's father understood that the last plate of the Book of Mormon contained characters of the alphabet. He explained this to Fayette Lapham, a visitor at his home: "The remaining pages [of the gold plates] were closely written over in characters of some unknown tongue, the last containing the alphabet of this unknown language."[4]

Martin Harris visited men in Utica and Albany before he arrived in New York City.[5] He first visited Dr. Samuel L. Mitchill (also spelled Mitchell), the fifty-one year old was the vice president of Rutgers Medical College that was located in lower Manhattan and who resided in New York City. Mitchill was a well known scholar. His name is often found in newspaper articles of the period. Mitchill referred Harris to Professor Charles Anthon of the same city.

Anthon was known for his scholarship as he published in 1825 a revision of John Lempriere's *A Classical Dictionary*.[6] In

---

[3] Anderson, *Lucy's Book*, 402.

[4] "The Mormons," *Historical Magazine* 7 (May 1870):307; Vogel, *Early Mormon Documents* 1:462-63.

[5] William W. Phelps to E. D. Howe, Jan. 15, 1831 in Howe, *Mormonism Unvailed*, 273.

[6] J[ohn]. Lempriere, D.D., *A Classical Dictionary; Containing a Copious Account of all the Proper Names mentioned in Ancient Authors*, Fifth American Edition, Corrected and Improved by Charles Anthon, Adjunct Professor of Languages and Ancient Geography in Columbia College (New York: E.

1828 Charles Anthon was a classical scholar at Columbia College (now Columbia University) who knew French, German, Greek, and Latin. Harris was forty-four years old while Professor Anthon was near the age of forty.

Martin Harris told a wide variety of persons about his trip to New York City and his visit to Charles Anthon in his office-residence at Columbia College. In the history of Joseph Smith Professor Anthon's name was spelled "Anthony" rather than "Anthon" the correct spelling of his name. The history includes what is reported to be a statement made upon the return of Martin Harris to Joseph Smith. It is not clear whether Harris made a written statement or if this was Joseph Smith's recollection of Harris' oral report. The history reads:

I went to the City of New York and presented the Characters which had been translated, with the translation thereof, to Professor <Charles> Anthony [Anthon] a gentleman celebrated for his literary attainments. Professor Anthony [Anthon] stated that the translation was correct, more so than any he had before seen translated from the Egyptian.

I then shewed him those which were not yet translated, and he said that they were Egyptian, Chaldeak, Assyriac, and Arabac, and he said that they were true characters. He gave me a certificate certifying to the people of Palmyra that they were true characters and that the translation of such of them as had been translated was also correct.

I took the Certificate and put it into my pocket, and was just leaving the house, when Mr Anthony called me back and asked me how the young man found out that there were gold plates where he found them. I answered that an Angel of God had revealed it unto him. He then said to me, let me see that certificate, I accordingly took it out of my pocket and gave it [to] him when he took it and tore it to pieces, saying that there was no such thing now as ministering of angels, and that if I would bring the plates to him, he would

---

Duychinck, G. Long [etc.], 1825). The book by Lempriere was originally published in 1788.

translate them.[7]

According to this account Anthon told Harris to bring the plates to him and when Harris replied that he could not Anthon said "I cannot read a sealed book." There is a question of whether the word "translation" is the proper word to use or if "transcription" would more accurately described the handwritten characters shown by Harris to Anthon. Either way the above account is a religious statement of support for Joseph Smith. The purpose of showing the learned what was copied was to produce evidence that the characters on the gold plates were authentic ancient characters from gold plates in the possession of Smith.

There is no indication that Charles Anthon tried to work on making a translation. Certain questions linger, did or did not Anthon decipher some characters? If he did not decipher anything why did he write out a statement? Why tear up a useless statement? And finally did Anthon say "I cannot read a sealed book"? Anthon would most likely not have destroyed a statement if, as he said, his statement was that there was no meaning to the characters. There was probably something more to it. Anthon owned a copy of Jean Francois Champollion's *Précis du Systéme Hiéroglyphique des Anciens Égyptiens* (Paris, 1824) in his library.[8]

It is possible that Harris may have returned to see Samuel Mitchill after visiting Anthon but we do not know this for sure. Mitchill died in 1831 and did not record his encounter with Harris. Charles Anthon is known to have responded to three inquiries about the visit. The first letter was written to Eber D. Howe, publisher of the Painesville, Ohio *Telegraph* in 1834, the second letter to Rev. Thomas W. Coit, Rector of Trinity Church in New Rochelle, New York in 1841, and the third letter to another minister in 1844.

Anthon's letters appear to answer the particular inquiry of each individual. For example, in his 1834 letter he wrote that no letter or note was made for Harris while in the 1841 letter he said

---

[7] Manuscript History A-1:9, LDS archives, written 1838 and recopied in 1839. See Jessee, *Papers of Joseph Smith* 1:285; Joseph Smith-History 1:64-65, Pearl of Great Price.

[8] Division of Rare and Manuscript Collections, Carl A. Kroch Library and Olin Library, Cornell University, Ithaca, New York.

he did write one. His letters described from memory what he saw years earlier when Martin Harris brought to him a sheet of paper not knowing the name of the man who visited him.

Harris had the impression that Professor Anthon thought some of the writing may have the appearance or resemblance of Arabic, Assyrian, Chaldean, Egyptian, Greek, Hebrew, or Syriac characters. Whether he said this is not known. But from what Anthon wrote there were not enough characters in any one language to interpret them. He concluded that none were Egyptian hieroglyphics.

Charles Anthon gave a description of the sheet of paper shown to him by Martin Harris. It confirms that the placement of the various characters appeared to be from a variety of different ancient languages, in vertical columns, and drawn on the paper like some type of alphabet. Anthon described in 1834 the writing:

> It consisted of all kinds of crooked characters disposed in columns, and had evidently been prepared by some person who had before him at the time a book containing various alphabets. Greek and Hebrew letters, crosses and flourishes, Roman letters inverted or placed sideways, were arranged in perpendicular columns, and the whole ended in a rude delineation of a circle divided into various compartments, decked with various marks, and evidently copied after the Mexican Calender [Calendar] given by Humboldt, but copied in such a way as not to betray the source whence it was derived.[9]

Seven years later Professor Anthon still maintained the basic way the paper appeared to him:

> A very brief examination of the paper convinced me that it was a mere *hoax*, and a very clumsy one too. The characters were arranged in columns, like the [C]hinese mode of writing, and presented the most singular medley that I had ever beheld. Greek, Hebrew, and all sorts of letters, more or less distorted, either through unskilfulness

---

[9] Anthon to Eber D. Howe, Feb. 17, 1834, in Howe, *Mormonism Unvailed*, 271-72; Vogel, *Early Mormon Documents* 4:380.

or from actual design, were intermingled with sundry delineations of half moons, stars, and other natural objects, and the whole ended in a rude representation of the Mexican zodiac.[10]

Martin Harris told Joel Tiffany in 1859 that Joseph Smith found the plates of gold upon which was "recorded in Arabic, Chaldaic, Syriac, and Egyptian, the Book of Life, or the Book of Mormon."[11] The transcript in the possession of the Community of Christ Library-Archives (from David Whitmer heirs) with seven horizontal lines is apparently not the same sheet of paper that Anthon saw in vertical columns. It may represent the type of characters presented by Harris to Anthon.[12] To have Arabic, Assyrian, Chaldaic, and Egyptian together on a sheet of paper as described by Martin Harris indicates that the characters may have been copied as mentioned by Professor Anthon. The sample of the characters was reported to include Egyptian.[13]

Mitchill, Anthon, nor any other American scholar could work with Egyptian writing much less translate Egyptian with confidence. Why the trip to New York City? To convince Harris that Joseph Smith had in his possession ancient writing. Thus insure that the characters that Joseph Smith interpreted were real. To Harris only Smith had the divine gift to render the copied characters with the message of the gold plates into English. That Anthon would say the "translation was correct" is probably something he did not say. This appears to be a misunderstanding by Harris.

Professor Anthon wrote about six years later in February

---

[10] Anthon to Rev. Thomas W. Colt, April 3, 1841, in *Church Record* 1 (April 17, 1841):231, Flushing, New York, emphasis retained; Vogel, *Early Mormon Documents* 4:383.

[11] "Mormonism-No. II," *Tiffany Monthly* 5 (Aug. 1859):163; Vogel, *Early Mormon Documents* 2:302.

[12] Paul M. Hanson, "The Transcript from the Plates of The Book of Mormon," *Saints Herald* 103 (12 Nov. 1956):5-7.

[13] The text of the Book of Mormon mentioned the Egyptian language: "And now behold, we have written this record according to our knowledge in the characters, which are called among us the reformed Egyptian, being handed down and altered by us, according to our manner of speech" (1830 BOM, 538; LDS Mormon 9:32; RLDS 4:98). See also LDS 1 Nephi 1:2; RLDS 1:1.

1834 that a farmer called on him "with a note from Dr. [Samuel L.] Mitchell, of our city, now dead, requesting me to decipher, if possible, the paper which the farmer would hand me. Upon examining the paper in question, I soon came to the conclusion that it was all a trick – perhaps a *hoax*." Then he explained, "He requested an opinion from me in writing, which of course I declined giving."[14]

When writing another letter in 1841 concerning this visit Anthon wrote: "he requested me to give him my opinion in writing about the paper which he had shown to me. I did so without any hesitation . . . The import of what I wrote was, as far as I can now recollect, simply this, that the marks in the paper appeared to be merely an imitation of various alphabetic characters, and had in my opinion no meaning at all connected with them. The countryman [Harris] then took his leave, with many thanks, and with the express declaration that he would in no shape part with his farm or embark in the speculation of printing the golden book"[15]

It may be that Anthon declined giving an opinion relating to one aspect of the paper while making another statement without hesitation. According to the foregoing account Martin Harris said that Anthon destroyed a certificate after he was told that the plates were found by the assistance of an angel.

Harris confirmed that he was warned by Anthon. According to Martin "Professor Anthon then gave me a certificate certifying that the characters were Arabic, Chaldaic, and Egyptian. I then left Dr. Anthon, and was near the door, when he said, 'How did the young man know the plates were there?' I said an angel had shown them to him. Professor Anthon then said, 'Let me see the certificate!' – upon which, I took it from my waistcoat pocket and unsuspectingly gave it to him. He then tore it up in anger, saying there was no such thing as angels now – it was all a hoax."[16]

---

[14] Anthon to Eber D. Howe, Feb. 17, 1834, in Howe, *Mormonism Unvailed*, 270-71, emphasis retained; Vogel, *Early Mormon Documents* 4:378-79.

[15] Anthon to Rev. Thomas W. Coit, April 3, 1841, in *Church Record* 1 (April 17, 1841):231; Vogel, *Early Mormon Documents* 4:384-85.

[16] David B. Dille, "Additional Testimony of Martin Harris (One of the Three Witnesses) to the Coming Forth of the Book of Mormon," *Millennial Star* 21 (Aug. 20, 1859):545), statement of September 15, 1853 shortly after Dille talked to Harris. See Vogel, *Early Mormon Documents* 2:298-99.

In a third letter written by Professor Charles Anthon he again repeated what he told Harris:

I told him very frankly that the whole matter was a hoax and cautioned him against being cheated out of his property. You will perceive from this what a monstrous lie, the Mormons are uttering when they say that I promised to decipher the piece of writing in question—if the original records were brought to me. I told the man at once that he was imposed upon and that the writing was mere trash. What Dr. Mitchell may have said I know not.[17]

The trip of Martin Harris appeared in newspapers the next year. It was also used by early church missionaries telling the story about the Book of Mormon to prospective converts. The following is a sample of what newspapers reported:

So blindly enthusiastic was Harris, that he took some of the characters interpreted by Smith, and went in search of some one, besides the interpreter, who was learned enough to *English* them; but all to whom he applied (among the number was Professor Mitchell, of New York,) happened not to be possessed of sufficient knowledge to give satisfaction! Harris returned, and set Smith to work at interpreting the Bible.[18]

Newspaperman William W. Phelps, editor of the *Ontario Phoenix*, published in Canandaigua, New York, wrote in January 1831 that he understood that some characters "were shown to Dr. Mitchell, and he referred to professor Anthon who translated and declared them to be the ancient shorthand Egyptian."[19] Whether

---

[17] Anthon to "Rev. and Dear Sir," August 12, 1844, in *New-York Observer* 23 (May 3, 1845):69, New York. Brought to my attention by Erin Jennings.

[18] *Niagara Courier* 2 (Aug. 27, 1829), Lockport, New York, emphasis retained. Also published in the *Rochester Daily Advertiser and Telegraph* 3 (Aug. 31, 1829). This was a reprint from an article in the *Palmyra Freeman*, Aug. 11, 1829, no known copy extant.

[19] Phelps to Howe, January 15, 1831 in Howe, *Mormonism Unvailed*, 273; Vogel, *Early Mormon Documents* 3:6-7.

Phelps obtained this information from Harris is not known but it is possible. As stated above it is doubtful if Anthon could have translated ancient Egyptian. Repeating such claim was common. If there were Egyptian characters (hieroglyphic, hieratic, or demotic) on the paper, Anthon told Harris that it "contained any thing else but *'Egyptian Hieroglyphics.'"*[20]

William E. McLellin, an early church missionary, was reported to have preached the following about the gold plates:

> At the place appointed he [Joseph Smith] found in the earth a box which contained a set of thin plates resembling gold, with Arabic characters inscribed on them. The plates were minutely described as being connected with rings in the shape of the letter D, which facilitated the opening and shutting of the book. The preacher [McLellin] said he [Smith] found in the same place two stones with which he was enabled by placing them over his eyes and putting his head in a dark corner to decypher the hieroglyphics on the plates![21]

Again if Anthon made the statement, as reported by Harris, that the characters were true characters this does not mean that they had any coherent meaning. Who destroyed the statement? In Anthon's letters he wrote nothing about the destruction of a statement. Harris said it was the professor who did it after hearing the plates were revealed by an angel. But the main conclusion in this case is that no translation or reading was made.

An important aspect of the visit is the account of what Harris told Anthon on how the Book of Mormon was being produced. Martin described this as happening before he became a scribe to Joseph Smith. This explains the way the work was being done when Reuben Hale and his sister Emma worked as Smith's scribes. Smith already had his alphabet and Martin wanted to see learned men to ascertain if the characters were genuine.

Anthon wrote in 1834 what he remembered from Harris

---

[20] Ibid. 4:380, emphasis retained.

[21] *New-Hampshire Gazette* 76 (Oct. 25, 1831), Portsmouth, New Hampshire. The article was a reprint from the *Illinois Patriot* of Jacksonville, Illinois, no copy extant. McLellin preached in Jacksonville on September 10, 1831.

about a gold book. The book consisted "of a number of plates of gold," dug up in New York state and with the book a pair of spectacles:

These spectacles were so large, that, if a person attempted to look through them, his two eyes would have to be turned towards *one* of the glasses merely, the spectacles in question being altogether too large for the breadth of the human face. Whoever examined the plates through the spectacles, was enabled not only to *read* them, but fully *understand* their meaning. All this knowledge, however, was confined at that time to a young man, who had the trunk containing the book and spectacles in his sole possession. This young man was placed behind a curtain, in the garret of a farm house, and, being thus concealed from view, put on the spectacles occasionally, or rather, looked through one of the glasses, decyphered the characters in the book, and, having committed some of them to paper, handed copies from behind the curtain, to those who stood outside.[22]

Martin Harris traveled to Harmony and reported to Joseph Smith his experience with Mitchill and Anthon. Smith and Harris now understood the trip to New York City as being predicted in the book of Isaiah 29:11-12, it being a fulfillment of prophecy:

And the vision of all is become unto you as the words of a book that is sealed, which men deliver to one that is learned, saying, Read this, I pray thee: and he saith, I cannot; for it is sealed: And the book is delivered to him

---

[22] Anthon to Eber D. Howe, Feb. 17, 1834, in Howe, *Mormonism Unvailed*, 270, emphasis retained; Vogel, *Early Mormon Documents* 4:378-79. Others who heard about the finding of the spectacles include: Fayette Lapham (Ibid., 1:462), Willard Chase (2:68), Benjamin Saunders (2:137), John H. Gilbert (2:546), and Lucy Mack Smith (*Lucy's Book*, 379, 389). The spectacles are described in the Book of Mormon as "two stones which was fastened into the two rims of a bow" (1830 BOM, 216; LDS Mosiah 28:13; RLDS 12:18). See also Joseph Smith's mention of "spectacles for to read the Book" (Jessee, *Papers of Joseph Smith* 1:9). Both the spectacles and seer stone were later known as the Urim and Thummim. See also *Niagara Courier* 2 (Aug. 27, 1829), Lockport, New York.

that is not learned, saying, Read this, I pray thee: and he saith, I am not learned.[23]

Harris then returned to his home in Palmyra. Shortly afterwards Martin took a trip to Harmony with Lucy his wife. After they arrived Lucy Harris searched for the plates in and around the Smith home but found nothing. Harris then took Lucy back to Palmyra.

Joseph Smith dictated the text while a scribe wrote the words on manuscript pages. Emma and her brother Reuben acted as scribes for Joseph. Elizabeth Lewis McKune remembered that "Reuben Hale, younger son of Isaac Hale, acted as scribe, writing down the words from Joseph Smith's mouth, but after a short time Martin Harris did the writing."[24] Others such as Emma Smith, Joseph Knight Sr., Joseph Fowler McKune, and Samuel Brush mentioned that seventeen year old Reuben was a scribe.[25]

Michael Morse when interviewed by William Blair in 1879 "says Joseph told him he found the plates in a *stone* box. Says he many times called in at Jos[e]phs on business, when J[oseph]. would be engaged [in] translating the plates. J[oseph]. put the seer stone in a hat and leaning forward would place his face in the hat, and then Dictate to his scribe, Sentence by Sentence."[26] Smith would dictate the contents of the gold plates without the plates being in his presence.

The claim of having plates with ancient writing on them was to increase faith. It was not necessary for Joseph Smith to use plates to produce the story that was represented to be contained on

---

[23] This text with a little variation was incorporated into the Book of Mormon, though some of its features are different, with the understanding of Martin's 1828 trip to New York City. See 1830 BOM, 111; LDS 2 Nephi 27:15-20; RLDS 11:136-142 for a commentary on the passage.

[24] Comments of Elizabeth McKune quoted in a letter of Hiel Lewis, Sept. 29, 1879 published in *Daily Tribune* 18 (Oct. 17, 1879):2, Salt Lake City. See Vogel, *Early Mormon Documents* 4:320.

[25] Ibid., 1:537, 541 (Emma Smith); 4:18 (Joseph Knight); 4:402 (Joseph McKune); 4:359 (Samuel Brush). See also Rhamanthus M. Stocker, *Centennial History of Susquehanna County, Pennsylvania* (Philadelphia: R. T. Peck and Co., 1887), 556.

[26] William W. Blair Journal, May 8, 1879, emphasis in original, RLDS archives. See Vogel, *Early Mormon Documents* 4:340-44.

them. To assist others in having religious faith in Jesus Christ was the overriding purpose in telling about plates. Some would believe by having a vision of the plates while others did not need to have such experience. For Smith the struggles and experiences he told necessitated maintaining that the writings of native peoples were from an ancient record whether or not he physically had them in his possession. The story on the record was presented to Joseph Smith in the form of revelation. It is claimed by Alva Hale, Nathaniel Lewis, Levi Lewis, and Joshua McKune that Joseph Smith promised them that they would be able to see the plates but they never saw them.[27]

In April Martin Harris returned to Harmony to be Joseph's scribe. The writing would have been in the book of Lehi. The dictation occupied, according to Smith's history, from April 12 to June 14 just before the expected birth of Emma and Joseph's first child.[28] These fifty days were spent mainly with Smith continuing his dictation from when Reuben Hale and Emma were scribes. Martin Harris asked and obtained permission to take home a large portion of the manuscript to show to family members.

On June 15 a son was born who was deformed. Sophia Lewis said that she "was present at the birth of this child, and that it was still-born and very much deformed."[29] Joseph attended Emma for about two weeks. The grave stone reads:[30]

In Memory of An
Infant Son of
Joseph And Emma
Smith June 15th 1828

Martin Harris made a covenant to show the handwritten manuscript only to five individuals who were family members. The

---

[27] Mormonism," *Susquehanna Register* 9 (May 1, 1834):1, Montrose, Pennsylvania. See Vogel, *Early Mormon Documents* 4:291, 294, 297, and 325.

[28] Manuscript History, A-1:9, LDS archives; Jessee, *Papers of Joseph Smith* 1:286.

[29] "Mormonism," *Susquehanna Register* 9 (May 1, 1834):1. See Vogel, *Early Mormon Documents* 4:298; also 4:320.

[30] McKune Cemetery, Oakland (formerly Harmony), Susquehanna County, Pennsylvania. The infant was not named at the time.

persons who were to be shown the writings were his wife Lucy, her sister Polly Harris Cobb, his father and mother Nathan and Rhoda, and his brother Preserved. He was to keep the manuscript safe and not show it to anyone else.[31] William W. Blair reported an interview with Martin Harris in 1860:

> he in reply to direct inquiries, told me that he obtained the one hundred and sixteen pages manuscript of the Book of Mormon from Joseph [Smith], and took them to his home, where he read them in the evenings to his family and some friends, and that he put them in his bureau in the parlor, locking both the bureau and parlor, putting the keys of each in his pocket, and so retired for the night, after which he never saw them. He seemed to be still conscience-smitten for permitting them to be stolen.[32]

Martin kept his promise until friends, other than his family, asked to see the manuscript. At the Smith home Emma was recovering from the effects of child birth and sadness of the loss of their first born son. About July first Joseph departed for his parents' home in Manchester.

Shortly after his arrival Smith requested Martin to come to the Smith home. Harris went to his drawer where he last kept the manuscript and it was gone, where he knew not. It is suspected that Lucy Harris removed it or had someone take it so the one hundred plus handwritten manuscript was indeed not to be found. It is not clear if Lucy destroyed the manuscript or gave it to others.

According to Lucy Smith when called for Martin usually came in haste to the Smith home.[33] The family waited about four hours before he arrived. When he finally came into the house and sat at the table he did not eat, but cried out "Oh! I have lost my

---

[31] Jessee, *Papers of Joseph Smith* 1:286. In Smith's 1832 account he says that Harris was to show it to only four persons (Ibid. 1:10).

[32] Lucy [Mack] Smith, *Biographical Sketches of Joseph Smith the Prophet, and His Progenitors for Many Generations* [Plano, Illinois: Reorganized Church of Jesus Christ of Latter Day Saints, 1880], 131, footnote by W. W. Blair, interview about August 9, 1860 at Kirtland, Ohio. Reprinted in *Saints Herald* 35 (May 12, 1888):297). See Anderson, *Lucy's Book*, 422n179.

[33] Anderson, *Lucy's Book*, 417.

soul I have lost my soul." Joseph asked Martin if he had lost the manuscript. When Harris replied in the affirmative Joseph in anguish walked the floor and said according to his mother:

Oh! My God My God, said Joseph, clenching his hands together, all is lost [all] is lost what shall I do[?] I have sinned, it is me that tempted the wrath [of] God by asking him to that which I had no right to ask as I was differently instructed by the angel.[34]

Soon Joseph left for Harmony knowing that he would tell Emma that the manuscript pages were lost. It would not be possible to produce the same words that were on the lost pages.

A class of the Methodist Episcopal Church was formed in Harmony by 1812. "All of the names of the first class cannot be given with certainly, but it is well known that John Comfort and his wife, Nathaniel Lewis and his wife, Isaac Hale and his wife, Marmaduke Salisbury and his wife, and James Newman and his wife were members of this class."[35] Michael Morse, husband of Emma's sister Trial Hale, was the leader of the class in Harmony. In 1879 Joseph and Hiel Lewis, cousins to Emma Hale, stated that Joseph briefly joined the Methodist Episcopal Church or class in Harmony, Pennsylvania, in the summer of 1828. There was disagreement about how long Joseph's name remained on the class rolls, three days or six months.

The Lewis brothers said that Joseph Smith presented himself before the class and asked that his name be put on the class book. This was done and a few days later a member of the class, Joseph Lewis, objected and asked Smith to have his name taken off the class record. Smith went before the class and withdrew his name from probation.[36]

It is possible that Joseph attended class with his wife Emma because of the death of their first son. Emma had been a Methodist since she was a young girl. That Joseph was a member of the class

---

[34] Ibid., 418.

[35] Stocker, *Centennial History of Susquehanna County*, 587.

[36] For the series of articles see *Amboy Journal* 24 (April 23, 30; May 21; June 4, 11; July 2, 9, 30; Aug. 6, 1879), Amboy, Illinois; Vogel, *Early Mormon Documents* 4:299-321.

was not questioned; only the length of time his name remained on the class record. Smith did not want to become a full member after his encounter with Joseph Lewis. The date Joseph Smith had his name put on the class book was probably in early July shortly after he returned from Manchester. Like so many of the early Methodist records, the early class books of the Harmony (now Lanesboro) church are lost, so it will never be known for certain the length of time remained on the rolls for only three days or for about six months. It would not have been out of the ordinary for Joseph to attend the Methodist class at this time.[37]

Soon after Smith said he asked God how it could be that the manuscript was lost. The response was Joseph Smith's first recorded revelation believed to have been given to the young prophet through his seer stone:

> The works, and the designs, and the purposes of God, can not be frustrated, neither can they come to nought, for God doth not walk in crooked paths; neither doth he turn to the right hand nor to the left; neither doth he vary from that which he hath said: Therefore his paths are strait and his course is one eternal round.[38]

Then Smith was given a serious rebuke, "behold, how oft you have transgressed the commandments and the laws of God, and have gone on in the persuasions of men: for behold you should not have feared man more than God, although men set at nought the counsels of God, and despise his words, yet you should have been faithful and he would have extended his arm, and supported you against all the fiery darts of the adversary; and he would have been with you in every time of trouble." If Joseph would repent he would be afflicted for a season and still be chosen and not lose his gift. The gift was the "sight and power to translate" that God had given to him. As to the contents of the lost writings the revelation explained:

for as the knowledge of a Savior has come into the world,

---

[37] "Was Joseph Smith a Methodist?" *Saints Herald* 26 (Dec. 15, 1879):376.
[38] Marquardt, *Joseph Smith Revelations*, 24; BC 2:1; LDS D&C 3:1-2; RLDS D&C 2:1 (July 1828).

even so shall the knowledge of my people, the Nephites, and the Jacobites, and the Josephites, and the Zoramites, come to the knowledge of the Lamanites, and the Lemuelites and the Ishmaelites,[39] which dwindled in unbelief, because of the iniquity of their fathers, who have been suffered to destroy their brethren, because of their iniquities, and their abominations: and for this very purpose are these plates preserved which contain these records.[40]

As mentioned it was about October 1828 when Lucy and Joseph Sr. visited their son and daughter-in-law. According to Lucy this occurred after September 22. They became acquainted with Emma's parents, sisters, and brothers. In January 1829 Samuel, after recovering from his sickness, went with his father to the Knight's home. Joseph Knight wrote:

in January his father [Joseph Sr.] and Samuel Came from Manchester to my house when I was Buisey [Busy] a Drawing Lumber. I told him they had traviled [traveled] far enough I would go with my Sley [Sleigh] and take them Down [to Harmony] to morrow. I went Down and found them [Joseph Jr. and Emma] well and the[y] were glad to See us we conversed about many things. in the morning I gave the old man ahalf [a half] a Dollar and Joseph a little money to Buoy [Buy] paper to translate I having But little with me.[41]

Joseph received a revelatory message for his fifty-seven year old father. The revelation like the religious text he was dictating incorporated phrases from the King James Version (KJV) of the Bible (references in brackets):

---

[39] The names Nephites, Jacobites, Josephites, Zoramites, Lamanites, Lemuelites, and Ishmaelites are found in three places in the Book of Mormon. See 1830 BOM, 124, 517, 519; LDS and RLDS Jacob 1:13; LDS 4 Nephi 1:36-38; RLDS 1:40-42; and LDS and RLDS Mormon 1:8-9.

[40] Marquardt, *Joseph Smith Revelations*, 24; BC 2:3, 6; LDS D&C 3:6-8, 16-19; RLDS D&C 2:3, 6.

[41] Joseph Knight Reminiscences, LDS archives.

Now, behold, a marvelous work [Isaiah 29:14] is about to come forth among the children of men [Psalm 12:1], therefore, O ye that embark in the service of God [Ezra 6:18], see that ye serve him with all your heart [Deuteronomy 11:13], might, mind and strength [Luke 10:27], that ye may stand blameless before God at the last day: Therefore, if ye have desires to serve God, ye are called to the work, for behold, the field is white already to harvest [John 4:35], and lo, he that thrusteth in his sickle [Revelation 14:16] with his might, the same layeth up in store [1 Timothy 6:19] that he perish not [Jonah 1:6], but bringeth salvation to his soul, and faith, hope, charity [1 Corinthians 13:13], and love, with an eye single to the glory of God, qualifies him for the work.[42]

Isaac Hale remembered a time when Martin Harris wanted to see the plates of gold. Hale recounted the following:

I went to the house where Joseph Smith Jr., lived, and where he and Harris were engaged in their translation of the Book. Each of them had a written piece of paper which they were comparing, and some of the words were "*my servant seeketh a greater witness, but no greater witness can be given him.*" There was also something said about "*three that were to see the thing*"—meaning I supposed, the Book of Plates, and that "*if the three did not go exactly according to orders, the thing would be taken from them.*"[43]

Harris made this trip to Harmony in March because he still needed confirmation that Joseph "had in his possession the record of the Nephites" and wanted a witness that it was so. The revelation gave Harris a second chance and that he would need to enter again into covenant. Martin was told he would be a witness

---

[42] Marquardt, *Joseph Smith Revelations*, 25; LDS and RLDS D&C 4 (Feb. 1829). See Grant H. Palmer, *An Insider's View of Mormon Origins* (Salt Lake City: Signature Books, 2002), 46-47.

[43] "Mormonism," *Susquehanna Register* 9 (May 1, 1834):1, emphasis retained. It is possible that the Hale remembered the wording of the original text which predated other copies.

to the plates if he humbled himself in prayer and faith. The revelation continued:

> & if this be the case Behold I say unto you Joseph when thou hast translated a few more pages & then shalt thou stop for a season even untill I command thee again then thou mayest translate . . . for this Cause have I said stop & stand still untill I Command thee & I will provide means whereby thou mayest accomplish the thing I have commanded thee[44]

Isaac Hale asked Joseph or Emma whose were the words he read. He was answered "they were the words of Jesus Christ." Hale said he considered it a delusion and asked them to abandon it. Hale continued: "The manner in which he [Joseph] pretended to read and interpret, was the same as when he looked for the money-diggers, with the stone in his hat, and his over his face, while the Book of Plates were at the same time hid in the woods!"[45]

On April 5, 1829, Samuel Harrison Smith and Oliver Cowdery arrived at Harmony from Manchester. Joseph Smith made arrangements for the purchase from Isaac Hale of some property and house the couple was living in.[46] Cowdery became a new scribe for Joseph's religious history. Thereafter the writing of the manuscript of the Book of Mormon progressed more rapidly. Cowdery was reportedly shown the plates in a vision before he left Manchester. Joseph wrote concerning Cowdery's vision that the "Lord appeared unto a young man by the name of Oliver Cowd[e]ry and shewed unto him the plates in a vision and also the truth of the work . . . now my wife had writ[t]en some for me to translate and also my Brother Samuel H. Smith."[47]

---

[44] Marquardt, *Joseph Smith Revelations*, 28; BC 4:10-11; LDS D&C 5:30, 34; RLDS D&C 5:6 (March 1829).

[45] "Mormonism," *Susquehanna Register* 9 (May 1, 1834):1.

[46] See agreement dated April 6, 1829 signed by Smith and Hale in the presence of Oliver H. Cowdery and Samuel H. Smith, LDS archives. On September 7, 1834 Oliver Cowdery wrote, "On Monday the 6th, I assisted him [Joseph] in arranging some business of a temporal nature" (*Messenger and Advocate* 1 [Oct. 1834]:14, Kirtland, Ohio).

[47] Joseph Smith's 1832 account, 6, LDS archives; Jessee, *Papers of Joseph Smith* 1:10.

Joseph Smith had a keen interest in religious teachings for the last ten years. He was a married man twenty-two years old. He had been talking to his family about obtaining a special record for the last four years. Smith could dictate about three pages a day and produce a lengthy manuscript. For the period from October 1828 to March 1829, before Cowdery became a scribe, it would be possible to have written on many pages. With three scribes helping the only drawback would be if there was not enough paper to write on (which did occur according to Joseph Knight Sr.) or not having a scribe available and if this was the case Smith could do his own writing.

Joseph Smith continued to dictate the text of the Book of Mormon with Oliver Cowdery as scribe. Smith, for example, worked on what is known as the Sermon on the Mount preached by Jesus and printed in the King James Bible. A comparison with the text in the Book of Mormon shows that Joseph documented the visit of Jesus to a New World people using the New Testament Gospel of Matthew.

In May 1829 Oliver Cowdery and Joseph Smith felt called to enter the waters of baptism. The early story is that they received a commandment to baptize each other.[48] On May 15 Oliver was baptized by Joseph and then the ordinance was performed wherein Oliver baptized Joseph for the remission of sins in the nearby Susquehanna River. They may have received this commandment from an angel.[49] They ordained each other with authority to administer baptism and waited until further instructions. This was mentioned in a June revelation that confirmed that Cowdery had been "baptized by the hand of my servant [Joseph], according to that which I have commanded him: Wherefore he hath fulfilled the thing which I commanded him."[50]

During the same month Hyrum visited Joseph at Harmony

---

[48] Anderson, *Lucy's Book*, 439.

[49] The date of May 15, 1829 was recorded by Oliver Cowdery September 15-28, 1835 in Patriarchal Blessing Book 1:8, LDS archives. The name of the angel was identified as John. Additional wording was added in 1835 to a commandment given in 1830 indicating that John was the son of Zacharias, also known as John the Baptist, who was sent to Smith and Cowdery. See Marquardt, *Joseph Smith Revelations*, 72-76.

[50] Ibid., 46; BC 15:6-7; LDS D&C 18:7; RLDS D&C 16:2 (June 1829).

to see how the translation was coming. While there Joseph received revelation directed to Hyrum personally:

> Keep my commandments, and assist to bring forth my work according to my commandments, and you shall be blessed. Behold thou has a gift, or thou shalt have a gift, if thou wilt desire of me in faith, with an honest heart, believing in the power of Jesus Christ, or in my power which speaketh unto thee: for behold it is I that speaketh: behold I am the light which shinneth in darkness, and by my power I give these words unto thee. . . . cleave unto me with all your heart, that you may assist in bringing to light those things of which have been spoken: Yea, the translation of my work: be patient until you shall accomplish it.[51]

About the beginning of June David Whitmer came to Harmony and took Joseph and Oliver in his wagon to the Peter Whitmer Sr. home in Fayette Township, Seneca County, New York to complete writing the Book of Mormon. Smith later returned to Harmony arriving on October 4 while the type was being set for the forthcoming book.[52] Oliver Cowdery stayed in Manchester at the home of Hyrum Smith and worked on making a copy of the original Book of Mormon manuscript for the printer.

---

[51] Marquardt, *Joseph Smith Revelations*, 42-43; BC 10:4-5, 9; LDS D&C 11:9-11, 19; RLDS D&C 10:4-5, 9 (May 1829).

[52] Smith to Cowdery, Oct. 22, 1829, Joseph Smith Letterbook 1:9, LDS archives. This is a copy of the original letter.

8

Publication of the Book of Mormon

After returning from Fayette to Manchester in June 1829, Hyrum Smith received a letter from Oliver Cowdery to strengthen Hyrum's resolve since his baptism. Cowdery wrote about "feeling anxious for your steadfastness in the great cause of which you have been called to advocate."[1] A few days later Hyrum received correspondence with a very different thrust from his Uncle Jesse Smith, who resided in Stockholm, New York:

Again you say, if you are decieved [deceived] God is your deciever [deceiver], Blasphemous wretch - how dare you utter such a sentence, how dare you harbor such a thot - aye, you never did think so, but being hardened in iniquity, you make use of the holy name of Jehovah! for what, why to cover your neferious [nefarious] designs & impose on the credulity of your Grandfather, one of the oldest men on the earth, Blackness of darkness! . . . You state your father cannot write by reason of a nervous affection this is a poor excuse, worse than none, he can dictate to others and they can write, If he knows not what to write, he can get your Brother's spectacles he would then be as able to dictate a letter, as Joe is to decipher hieroglyphics, if more should be wanting he can employ the same scoundrel of a scribe, and then not only the matter but manner and style would be correct.[2]

In the same month Joseph Smith had some of his gentlemen believers testify as witnesses to the Book of Mormon gold plates.

[1] Cowdery to Hyrum Smith, June 14, 1829, transcribed in 1832 into Joseph Smith Letterbook 1:5, LDS archives.

[2] Jesse Smith to Hyrum Smith, June 17, 1829, Joseph Smith Letterbook, 2:59-61, LDS archives. The letter was copied into the letterbook in 1839. See Vogel, *Early Mormon Documents* 1:552-53.

This took place at the end of June when he finished writing the Book of Mormon. The first set of three witnesses included two known scribes, Martin Harris and Oliver Cowdery, and their Fayette friend David Whitmer. Within a few days the second group of witnesses met at Manchester. They included Joseph Smith's father, his brothers Hyrum and Samuel, and members of the Whitmer family who traveled from Fayette. The four Whitmer brothers were Christian, Jacob, Peter Jr., and John. A friend by marriage, Hiram Page, also became a witness. The spiritual experiences they had and their testimony represent a religious statement about the reality of the Book of Mormon plates.

All eleven witnesses said they saw the engravings that were on the plates. The three men represented their experience as seeing an angel and the plates. For the additional eight men they indicated that they also saw engravings on the plates and with their hands felt the plates that Joseph Smith showed them.

Both the three and eight witnesses believed that Joseph Smith had what appeared to be gold plates. Smith was present at the time with the men at the Fayette and Manchester locations when they made their statements. Because the testimony is not dated nor notarized many persons wondered how serious their testimony should be taken. Also whether the gold plates were objective or subjected has been a question for many inquirers. Whatever one may think about these statements no physical plates were put on display for the general public to look at.

The Palmyra newspaper, *The Wayne Sentinel*, started noticing the claims of Joseph Smith Jr. in its pages. The June 26, 1829 issue included the following background:

> Just about in this particular region, for some time past, much speculation has existed, concerning a pretended discovery, through superhuman means, of an ancient record, of a religious and divine nature and origin, written in ancient characters, impossible to be interpreted by any to whom the special gift has not been imparted by inspiration. It is generally known and spoken of as the *"Golden Bible."* Most people entertain an idea that the whole matter is the

result of a gross imposition, and a grosser superstition.[3]

The article stated, "It is pretended that it will be published as soon as the translation is completed." Shortly afterwards, Egbert B. Grandin the editor of the *Wayne Sentinel*, entered into an agreement to publish the Book of Mormon. For $3,000 Grandin would print and have bound 5,000 copies of the book. As a man of some wealth Book of Mormon witness Martin Harris was looked upon as supplying the financial backing to have the book printed. Harris together with Joseph Smith traveled to Rochester, New York to find a good printer. *The Gem*, a newspaper in Rochester, published the following account of Harris and the story that he told:

A man by the name of Martin Harris, was in this village a few days since endeavouring to make a contract for printing a large quantity of a work called the Golden Bible. He gave something like the following account of it. "In the autumn of 1827 a man named Joseph Smith of Manchester, in Ontario County, said that he had been visited by the spirit of the Almighty in a dream, and informed that in a certain hill in that town, was deposited a Golden Bible, containing an ancient record of divine origin. He states that after a third visit from the same spirit in a dream, he proceeded to the spot, removed earth, and there found the Bible, together with a large pair of spectacles. He had also been directed to let no mortal see them under the penalty of immediate death, which injunction he steadfastly adheres to. The treasure consisted of a number of gold plates, about 8 inches long, 6 wide, and one eighth of an inch thick, on which were engraved hieroglyphics. By placing the spectacles in a hat and looking into it, Smith interprets the characters into the English language.[4]

---

[3] *The Wayne Sentinel* 6 (June 26, 1829):3, emphasis retained. The *Sentinel* included the first known publication of the title page of the Book of Mormon. See Vogel, *Early Mormon Documents* 2:218-19.

[4] *The Gem, of Literature and Science* 1 (Sept. 5, 1829):70. For a similar account see the *Niagara Courier* 2 (Aug. 27, 1829), Lockport, New York or the *Rochester Daily Advertiser and Telegraph* 3 (Aug. 31, 1829), which reprinted

Smith and Harris decided that it was best to have the work done locally in Palmyra and Harris worked out an agreement with Egbert Grandin for printing the book. On August 23 Martin Harris made an indenture between himself and Grandin "in consideration of the sum of three thousand dollars" for typesetting, printing, and binding the Book of Mormon. This was secured by a mortgage for "the same tract of land or farm upon which the said Martin Harris now resides" and was to be paid in eighteen months.[5]

Oliver Cowdery squeezed into the log home, where the entire Smith family was living, and began making a copy of the manuscript of the Book of Mormon for the printer to use in typesetting. According to Lucy, "Peter Whitmer was commanded to remain at our house to assist in guarding the writings."[6] The manuscript Oliver prepared is known as the printer's manuscript of Book of Mormon. Enough of the text from the original manuscript was copied to supply the typesetter twenty-seven year old John H. Gilbert.

The printing was explained by Gilbert, "one sheet of [printed] paper made two copies of 16 pages each, requiring 2500 sheets of paper for each form of 16 pages. There were 37 forms of 16 pages each,—570 [sic; 592] in all. The work was commenced in August 1829, and finished in March 1830—seven months."[7] The majority of the typesetting was done by John Gilbert, who recalled years later:

When the printer was ready to commence work, [Martin] Harris was notified, and Hyrum Smith brought the first installment of manuscript, of 24 pages, closely written on common foolscap paper,;—he had it under his vest, and [his] vest and coat closely buttoned over it. At night Smith came and got the manuscript, and with the same precaution

---

the article from the *Palmyra Freeman*. The *Niagara Courier* included in its article the title page to the book.

[5] Mortgages, Liber 3:325, Wayne County Courthouse, Lyons, New York.

[6] Anderson, *Lucy's Book*, 459. Both the printer's and the original manuscripts were used for the typesetting the Book of Mormon.

[7] Memorandum, Sept. 8, 1892, Palmyra, New York, in Wilford C. Wood, *Joseph Smith Begins His Work*, 2 vols. (Salt Lake City: Deseret News Press, 1958), Vol. 1, introductory pages. See Vogel, *Early Mormon Documents* 2:545.

carried it away. The next morning with the same watchfulness, he brought it again, and at night took it away. This was kept up for several days. . . . After working a few days, I said to [Hyrum] Smith on his handing me the manuscript in the morning; "Mr. Smith, if you would leave this manuscript with me, I would take it home with me at night and read and punctuate it." His reply was, "We are commanded not to leave it." A few mornings after this, when Smith handed me the manuscript, he said to me:—"If you will give your word that this manuscript shall be returned to us when you get through with it, I will leave it with you." I assured Smith that it should be returned all right when I got through with it. For two or three nights I took it home with me and read it, and punctuated it with a lead pencil. . . . Martin Harris, Hyrum Smith and Oliver Cowdery were very frequent visitors to the office during the printing of the Mormon Bible.[8]

After each stick of type was set it was put in a galley until everything was ready to print. Each sheet was printed with thirty-two pages on each side. After drying the paper was then turned over and printed on the reverse. The sheet was then cut in the center to make two half-sheets. Then a half-sheet was folded to make a signature of sixteen pages. When the printing was completed the thirty-seven signatures were bound. When the books were ready for sale not all of the copies had yet been bound.

Typographical errors were corrected while the sheets were being printed. Some word variations occur in the signatures so that many copies of the first edition actually have a few differences.[9] Nearly one-sixth of the Book of Mormon text was typeset from the original manuscript and not from the printer's copy because the copying fell behind. Part of Heleman through Mormon of the original manuscript was used by the composer to set type for the book.[10] In the 1830 edition this would cover pages 443-538. When

---

[8] Ibid. 2:543-44. Gilbert also wrote: "Hyrum Smith was the only one of the family I had any acquaintance with, and that very slight" (2:526).

[9] Later in 1837 the text was modernized and some corrections made.

[10] From about LDS Heleman 13:18 through Mormon 9:37 and RLDS Heleman 5:23 through Mormon 4:103.

the "printer's manuscript" was produced for this section (but not used by the typesetter) it contained some words that were different than the printed text and the original manuscript. The copying was not done word by word. In fact there are mistakes by the scribes in both manuscripts.

Many persons were involved as the wording of the 1830 Book of Mormon text was produced. It appears from the manuscripts extant that Joseph Smith dictated most of the text to his scribe. Each scribe would take down the dictation differently as far as their particular spelling and make minor mistakes. When the printer's manuscript was made even there copying errors occurred but also some corrections were made. When it got to the typesetter he had the responsibility to produce the book as he thought the author intended it to be. Mistakes were made in reading the handwriting of whatever manuscript was used.

Of interest is what John H. Gilbert said in relation to the text used in the Book of Mormon that has corresponding wording from the King James Version of the Bible. In an interview a reporter wrote, "Gilbert, perceiving that large portions were stolen verbatim from the Bible, used to have a copy of that book on his [type] case to aid him in deciphering the manuscript and putting in the proper punctuation marks."[11]

Thomas B. Marsh arrived in Palmyra from Massachusetts after hearing from a lady about a golden book found by Joseph Smith. Marsh described visiting the Grandin printing office:

> I returned back westward and found Martin Harris at the printing office, in Palmyra, where the first sixteen pages of the Book of Mormon had just been struck off, the proof sheet of which I obtained from the printer and took with me. As soon as Martin Harris found out my intentions he took me to the house of Joseph Smith, sen. . . . Here I found Oliver Cowdery, who gave me all the information concerning the book I desired. After staying there two days I started for Charleston, Mass., highly pleased with the

---

[11] "Joe Smith. Something About the Early Life of the Mormon Prophet. Story of the Mormon Bible From the Man Who First Printed it. The Men Who Figured in Its Production and Publication," *The Post and Tribune*, Dec 3, 1877, Detroit, Michigan, as cited in Vogel, *Early Mormon Documents* 2:519.

information I had obtained concerning the new found book.[12]

Later Thomas Marsh corresponded with Cowdery. It was in November when Cowdery wrote to Joseph Smith: "My dear Brother I cannot hardly feel to close this letter as yet without informing you that we received one [letter] from Mr. Marsh from Boston, Masacuchusetts [Massachusetts] dated the 25th Oct. he informs us that he wishes to hear from us and know of our wellfare he says he has talked conside[r]able to some respecting ou[r] work with freedom but others could not because they had no ears."[13]

Stephen S. Harding, another visitor, remembered that during the summer of 1829 he went to the *Wayne Sentinel* office and to the Smiths' residence in Manchester, which he described as "a log house, not exactly a cabin. Upon our arrival, I was ushered into the best room in company with the others." Oliver Cowdery read from the Book of Mormon manuscript. When Harding returned to the printing office a few weeks later, he was given a copy of a proof sheet that included the title page.[14] Another interested individual was Solomon Chamberlain who also stopped in Palmyra and visited the Smith family:

I soon arrived at the house, and found Hyrum walking the floor; as I entered the room, I said peace be to this house; he looked at me and said "I hope it will be peace." I then said is there any one here that believes in visions and revelations. He [Hyrum] said yes, we are a visionary house. I then said I will give you one of my pamphlets, (which

---

[12] "History of Thos. Baldwin Marsh," *Deseret News* 8 (March 24, 1858):18, Fillmore City, Utah Territory.

[13] Cowdery to Smith, Nov. 6, 1829, Manchester, New York, transcribed in 1832 into Joseph Smith Letterbook 1:8, LDS archives.

[14] Letter of Stephen S. Harding, dated Feb. 1882, in Thomas Gregg, *The Prophet of Palmyra* (New York: John B. Alden, 1890), 41, 48, 52. Harding mentioned that after the candle had burned "Mother Smith loaded a clay pipe with tobacco, which she ground up in her hands" (43). Compare Pomeroy Tucker, *Origin, Rise, and Progress of Mormonism*, 284. For a photograph of the title page Harding received and on which Joseph Smith was identified as "author and proprietor," see *Church History in the Fulness of Times* (Salt Lake City: Church of Jesus Christ of Latter-day Saints, 1989), 64.

was visionary and of my own composition)[15]

From another account of his experiences Solomon wrote:

They then called the people together, which consisted of five or six men who were out at the door. Father Smith was one and some of the Whitmer's. They then sat down and read my pamphlet. Hyrum read first, but was so affected he could not read it, He then gave it to a man, which I learned was Christian Whitmer, he finished reading it. I then opened my mouth and began to preach to them, in the words that the angel had made known to me in the vision, that all Churches and Denominations on the earth had become corrupt, and [that] no Church of God [was] on earth but that he would shortly raise up a Church, that would never be confounded nor brought down and be like unto the Apostolic Church. They wondered greatly who had been telling me these things, for said they we have the same things wrote down in our house, taken from the Gold record, that you are preaching to us.[16]

Chamberlain then asked the Smiths whether they were a visionary household:

if you are a visionary house, I wish you would make known some of your discoveries, I think I can bear them. Then they began to make known to me, that they had obtained a

---

[15] Account of Solomon Chamberlain, published in Dean C. Jessee, ed., "The John Taylor Nauvoo Journal," *Brigham Young University Studies* 23 (Summer 1983):45, copied into Taylor's diary in the spring of 1845. One pamphlet which contained some background material on Chamberlain was titled *A Sketch of the Experience of Solomon Chamberlin, to Which Is Added a Remarkable Revelation, or Trance, of His Father-in-Law Philip Haskins: How His Soul Actually Left His Body and Was Guided by a Holy Angel to Eternal Day* (Lyons, New York, 1829), copy at the Harold B. Lee Library, Brigham Young University. See Larry C. Porter, "Solomon Chamberlain's Missing Pamphlet: Dreams, Visions, and Angelic Ministrants," *Brigham Young University Studies* 37, no. 2 (1997-98):113-29.
[16] Larry C. Porter, "Solomon Chamberlain—Early Missionary," *Brigham Young University Studies* 12 (Spring 1972):316-17, dated July 11, 1858.

gold record, and had just finished translating it. Here I staid [stayed], and they instructed me in the manuscripts of the Book of Mormon; after I had been there two days, I went with Hyrum and some others to [the] Palmyra printing office, where they began to print the Book of Mormon; and as soon as they had printed sixty-four pages I took them and started for Canada.[17]

During the last week of October, Martin Harris and Hyrum Smith went to Fayette to visit the Whitmers. Oliver Cowdery wrote to Joseph, "Hyram and Martin went out to Fayette last week they had a joyful time and found all in as good health as could be expected."[18]

Abner Cole, a free-thinking Palmyra lawyer, had his office located in the center of town on Main Street as early as 1812. Coe began in September 1829 a satirical paper called *The Reflector*. He presented his commentary on village life under the pen name of Obadiah Dogberry. Cole arranged to use the press of the *Wayne Sentinel* on evenings and Sundays to print his paper. A "New Series" continued with the issue of December 22, 1829. At a later date Cole moved to Rochester and started another newspaper, the *Liberal Advocate*, using the same pen name, Obadiah Dogberry. The masthead, like that of the Palmyra *Reflector*, included the quote from Alexander Pope: "Know then thyself, presume not God to scan! The proper study of mankind is man."[19] Abner Cole probably heard much talk around town about Joseph Smith's new Bible and was intrigued by the sheets of the Book of Mormon that

---

[17] "John Taylor Nauvoo Journal," 45-46. Chamberlain would have picked up four signatures of sixteen pages each for the total of sixty-four pages.

[18] Cowdery to Joseph Smith, Nov. 6, 1829, Joseph Smith Letterbook 1:8, LDS archives.

[19] Cole died on July 13, 1835, and the local newspaper reported his death: "In this city, on the 13th inst Abner Cole, Esq. Editor of the 'Liberal Advocate'" (*Rochester Daily Democrat*, July 15, 1835). For additional material on "Obadiah Dogberry" (Abner Cole), see M. Hamlin Cannon, "Contemporary Views of Mormon Origins (1830)," *The Mississippi Valley Historical Review* 31 (June 1944):261-66; Russell R. Rich, "The Dogberry Papers and the Book of Mormon", *Brigham Young University Studies* 10 (Spring 1970):315-20; and Joseph W. Barnes, "Obediah Dogberry Rochester Freethinker," *Rochester History* 36 (July 1974):1-24.

he found around the printing office.

Lucy Smith remembered that in January 1830 on "One Su[n]day <afternoon> Hyrum became very uneasy, he told Oliver that his peculiar feellings [feelings] led him to believe that something <going> was [sic; was going] wrong at [the] printing Office." Oliver and Hyrum went to Grandin's printing establishment and found Abner Cole "at work printing a paper which seemed to be a <weekly> periodi<cal>." Hyrum discovered that Cole was printing portions of the Book of Mormon in his paper. Thus *The Reflector* became the first publication to print extracts from the text of the Book of Mormon even before its issuance in March 1830.[20]

"Mr. Cole, said he [Hyrum], what right have <you> to print the book of Mormon in this way, do you not know that we have secured a copy right." Lucy continued:

> Hyrum <&> Oliver returned immediately home and after counciling with Mr. Smith it was considered neces[s]ary that Joseph should be sent for. Accordingly My husband set out as soon as possible for Penn.[21]

Joseph made a trip north from Harmony to talk to Cole and told him to desist from publishing any more from his book. The last issue of *The Reflector* that printed any text from the forthcoming Book of Mormon was an "Extra," dated January 22, 1830. The Smiths maintained control over the printing and sale of the book. Joseph Sr. signed the following agreement with Martin Harris:

> I hereby agree that Martin Harris shall have an equal privilege with me & my friends of selling the Book of Mormon of the Edition now printing by Egbert B. Grandin until enough of them shall be sold to pay for the printing of the same or until such times as the said Grandin shall be

---

[20] Lucy Mack Smith, manuscript draft; see *Lucy's Book*, 470-71. Lucy recalled the newspaper as "Dogberry paper [on] Winter Hill." In fact, *The Reflector* was issued from "his `Bower' on Winter Green Hill" (*The Reflector* 1 [Sept. 2, 1829]:1).

[21] Anderson, *Lucy's Book*, 472-73.

paid for the printing the aforesaid Books or copies.
Manchester January the 16th 1830   Joseph Smith Sr.
Witness Oliver H P Cowdery[22]

The cost of printing each book, including binding, was sixty cents. As mentioned with a total of 5,000 copies printed, the total cost was $3,000. Martin Harris was assured of having enough books to sell to recover his investment in the printing. One incident which occurred about January 1830 while the Book of Mormon was at the printer throws light on the importance Joseph Smith placed on his copyright to the book.

Hiram Page told about Joseph Smith Jr. wanting to sell the copyright to the Book of Mormon in Canada. Page, one of the eight witnesses to the book, related his experience to William E. McLellin in 1848, eighteen years later. In his letter Hiram Page criticized Joseph Smith because the expected outcome of their trip was unfulfilled (corrected spelling in brackets):

Joseph herd [heard] that there was a chance to sell a copyright in canada for any useful book that was used in the states. Joseph thought this would be a good opertunity [opportunity] to get a handsom[e] sum of money which was to be (after the expencis [expenses] were taken out) for th[e] exclusive benafit [benefit] of the Smith famaly [family] and was to be at the disposal of Joseph accordingly oliver Cowdery. Joseph Knights. Hiram Page and Joseah Stoel [Josiah Stowell] were chosen ([as I understoo]d by revilation [revelation]) to do the buisaness [business]; we were [living from] some 30 to 100 miles apart the necesary [necessary] preperation [preparation] was [made] (by them) in a sly manor [manner] So as to keep martin Haris [Harris] from dra[w]ing a s[hare] of the money, it was told me we were to go by revilation [revelation] but when we assembled at father Smiths; the[re was] no revilation

---

[22] In Simon Gratz Autograph Collection, Case 8, Box 17 (American Miscellaneous), under Smith, Joseph, Sr., Historical Society of Pennsylvania, Philadelphia. Used by permission. Photographs have been published in *Ensign* 13 (Dec. 1983):44; *Church History in the Fulness of Times*, 65; and Marquardt and Walters, *Inventing Mormonism*, after the conclusion.

[revelation] for us to go but we were all anctious [anxious] to get a r[evila]tion [revelation] to go; and when it came we were to go to kingston where we were to sell if they would not harden their harts [hearts]; but when [we] got their [there]; there was n[o] purcheser [purchaser] neither were they authorised [authorized] at kingston to buy rights for the provence [province]; but little york was the place where such buisaness [business] had to be done; we were to get 8000 dollars [we] were treatid [treated] with the best of respects by all we met with in kingston — by the above we may ~~see~~ learn how a revilation [revelation] may be receved [received] and the ~~one~~ person receving [receiving] it not be benafitid [benefited][23]

As indicated the travelers returned empty-handed. The text of this revelation though written at the time is not known to be extant. Eight thousand dollars was a great deal of money in Smith's time. It is unlikely that anyone would have invested such a large amount of money for a copyright. Page said they went to Kingston, Ontario, Canada, and "were treated with the best of respects." He indicated, however, that Smith was "not benefited."

Hiram Page did not see anything wrong with Joseph Smith wanting to sell the copyright. David Whitmer, who recounted the event many years later, did not seem concerned either, but was disturbed because Smith received a revelation through the seer stone that did not come to pass.[24] The revelation to sell the copyright in Canada was written down and recorded but never published. William McLellin, who joined the church in August 1831, wrote in 1872 the following:

But again, Joseph [Smith] had a revelation for Oliver [Cowdery] and friends to go to Canada to get a copy-right secured in that Dominion to the Book of Mormon. It proved so false that he never would have it recorded,

---

[23] Page to McLellin, Feb. 2, 1848, Fishing River, Missouri, photocopy, RLDS archives.
[24] David Whitmer in an interview published in the *Des Moines Daily News*, Oct. 16, 1886, and David Whitmer, *An Address to All Believers in Christ* (Richmond, Missouri: author, 1887), 30-31.

printed or published, I have seen and read a copy of it, so that I know it existed.[25]

William McLellin's comment that the revelation was not recorded evidently refers to its not being included in the Book of Commandments manuscript produced in 1831. There was no plan to have it published in that compilation. McLellin also wrote in 1877, "J[oseph] Smith's revelation for Cowdery to go to Canada was never printed. M[artin]. Harris had the copy that I read in Manuscript."[26]

David Whitmer wrote about the return of the men from Canada. Whitmer said that he was present with Joseph Smith in Fayette:

> Joseph was at my father's house when they returned. I was there also, and am an eye witness to these facts. Jacob Whitmer and John Whitmer were also present when Hiram Page and Oliver Cowdery returned from Canada. Well, we were all in great trouble; and we asked Joseph how it was that he had received a revelation from the Lord for some brethren to go to Toronto [sic] and sell the copy-right, and the brethren had utterly failed in their understanding. Joseph did not know how it was, so he enquired of the Lord about it, and behold the following revelation came through the stone: "*Some revelations are of God: some revelations are of man: and some revelations are of the devil.*"[27] So we

---

[25] McLellin to Joseph Smith III, commenced July 1872, RLDS archives. McLellin also related that the revelation was received in 1829. See Joseph Fielding Smith, comp., *Life of Joseph F. Smith, Sixth President of The Church of Jesus Christ of Latter-day Saints* (Salt Lake City: Deseret News Press, 1938), 240, and in a Notebook (21), J. L. Traughber Collection, Manuscript 666, Manuscripts Division, J. Willard Marriott Library, University of Utah, Salt Lake City.

[26] McLellin to John L. Traughber, May 7, 1877, copied by Traughber, Traughber Collection, Accession 1446, Box 2, Manuscripts Division, J. Willard Marriott Library, University of Utah.

[27] A March 1831 revelation says, "that ye may not be seduced by evil spirits, or doctrines of devils, or the commandments of men, for some are of men, and others of devils" (Book of Commandments 49:9; LDS D&C 46:7; RLDS D&C 46:3).

see that the revelation to go to Toronto [sic] and sell the copy-right was not of God, but was of the devil or of the heart of man.[28]

In another area of concern was an old debt incurred by Joseph Sr. which resulted in legal action against him. When Lemuel Durfee Sr.'s estate was inventoried, it included a note signed by Joseph Sr. and by Abraham Fish with his "x" for the amount of $36.50 plus interest. On January 19 Durfee's son entered a plea before Justice Nathan Pierce against Smith and Fish, and the two signed consent for judgment. It was turned over to Constable S. Southworth for collection and it was resolved in September.[29]

Since about September 1828, Lucy as well as Hyrum and Samuel Harrison stopped attending the Palmyra Presbyterian Church and partaking of the sacrament of the Lord's Supper.[30] By the spring of 1830 the pastor and elders of the church had become concerned:

March 3d 1830 Session met pursuant to notice - opened with prayer Present Revd Alfred E. Campbell Moderr [Moderator]
    Henry Jessup
    Geo Beckwith
    David White   Elders
    Pelatiah West
    Newton Foster
   . . . Resolved that the Revd A. E. Campbell and H

---

[28] Whitmer, *An Address to All Believers in Christ*, 31, emphasis in original. See also interview with Whitmer in the *Omaha Herald*, Oct. 17, 1886; reprinted in Lyndon W. Cook, ed., *David Whitmer Interviews: A Restoration Witness* (Orem, UT: Grandin Book, 1991), 203.

[29] Probate Papers, Box 053, filed by executors Oliver Durfee and Lemuel Durfee Jr., filed on Jan. 22, 1830, Surrogate's Court, Wayne County Courthouse, Lyons, New York. For collection process, see Nathan Pierce Docket Book, 1827-30, Manchester Town Office, 25. The signature of Joseph Smith Sr., appears to be different from the one in the Simon Gratz Autograph Collection. This could be accounted for by the "nervous affection" Jesse Smith mentions, by the quill he used to sign his name, or by his using a different angle when signing.

[30] "Records of the Session of the Presbyterian Church in Palmyra," 2 (March 10, 1830):11.

Jessup be a committee to visit Hiram Smith Lucy Smith
and Samuel Harrison Smith and report at the next meeting
of session
> Closed with prayer -
> Recorded from the Moderators minutes
> [Signed] Geo. N. Williams Clk [Clerk]

A week later the session met again and received the report
of their committee's visit: "The committee appointed to visit Hiram
Smith Lucy Smith and Samuel Harrison Smith reported that they
had visited them and received no satisfaction. They acknowledged
that they had entirely neglected the ordinances of the church for
the last eighteen months and that they did not wish to unite with us
anymore." The session accordingly cited them to appear before it
in two weeks to answer the charge of "Neglect of public worship
and the sacrament of the Lord's Supper for the last eighteen
months."[31]

Lucy Smith remembered the visit from three men, one of
whom she called "Deacon Beckwith." George Beckwith had been
appointed to be the advocate to manage their defense and either
went with the committee or on his own to do what he could to
bring them back to the church. Lucy reported her firm resistance to
Deacon Beckwith's pleas:

> No sir, said I, it is <of> no use; you cannot effect any thing
> by all that you can say - he then bid me farewell and went
> out to see Hyrum. They asked him if he really did believe
> that his brother had got the record which he pretended to
> have. Hyrum <testified boldly to the truth and>, told him
> that if he would take the book of Mormon when it was
> finished [being printed and bound] and read it asking God
> for a witness to the truth of [it] he would receive what he
> desire<d> and now, sa<i>d he [Hyrum], Deacon Beckwith
> just try it and see if I do not tell you [the] truth.[32]

---

[31] Ibid., 11-12.

[32] Lucy Mack Smith, manuscript draft; see *Lucy's Book*, 469. The 1853 edition
reads: "Hyrum. 'I will tell you what I will do, Mr. Beckwith, if you do get a
testimony from God, that the book is not true, I will confess to you that it is not
true.'" Lucy stated in her manuscript that one of the men said that they had

Beckwith remained unconvinced.

When the Smiths did not appear before the session on the appointed day, they were cited to appear five days later. Pelatiah West was appointed to serve the citation and be sure they received it. The Palmyra session records for the trial read:

March 29th 1830 Session met pursuant to adjournment
Opened with prayer
Present Revd Alfred E. Campbell Modr
    Geo Beckwith
    Newton Foster
    Pelatiah West   Elders
    Henry Jessup

The persons before cited to wit. Hiram Smith Lucy Smith and Samuel Harrison Smith not appearing and the Session having satisfactory evidence that the citations were duly served Resolved that they be censored for their contumacy Resolved that George Beckwith manage their defense. The charge in the above case being fully sustained by the testimony of Henry Jessup, Harvey Shel, Robert W. Smith and Frederick U. Sheffield (see minutes of testimony, on file with the clerk) the Session after duly considering the matter were unanimously of opinion that Hiram Smith, Lucy Smith and Samuel Harrison Smith ought to be Suspended. Resolved that Hiram Smith, Lucy Smith and Samuel Harrison Smith be and they hereby are suspended from the Sacrament of the Lord's Supper.

Closed with prayer - Adjourned
Recorded from the minutes of the Moderator.
[Signed] Geo. N. Williams Clk[33]

As this was occurring, the Book of Mormon was being offered for sale.[34] The book was first sold for fourteen shillings

---

"belonged to our church a whole year." This is clearly an error on her part as they were active for three years.

[33] "Records of the Session of the Presbyterian Church in Palmyra" 2:13.

[34] Copies of the Book of Mormon were ready for sale by March 26, 1830. See *Wayne Sentinel* 7 (March 26, 1830):3. Compare Tucker, *Origin, Rise, and Progress of Mormonism*, 55.

($1.75), and later the cost was reduced to ten shillings ($1.25). Henry Harris recalled talking with Martin Harris: "After the Book was published, I frequently bantered him for a copy. He asked fourteen shillings a piece for them; I told him I would not give so much; he told me [they] had had a revelation that they must be sold at that price. Sometime afterwards I talked with Martin Harris about buying one of the Books and he told me they had had a new revelation, that they might be sold at ten shillings a piece."[35]

A week later the Church of Christ was organized at the Manchester log house on April 6, 1830. Joseph Jr. returned to his home in Harmony and Hyrum became the central figure in the new church in the Palmyra area. For example, in August 1830 Hyrum was visited by Parley P. Pratt, who later recalled:

I accordingly visited the village of Palmyra, and inquired for the residence of Mr. Joseph Smith. I found it some two or three miles from the village. As I approached the house at the close of the day I overtook a man who was driving some cows, and inquired of him for Mr. Joseph Smith, the translator of the "Book of Mormon." He informed me that he now resided in Pennsylvania; some one hundred miles distant. I inquired for his father, or for any of the family. He told me that his father had gone [on] a journey; but that his residence was a small house just before me; and, said he, I am his brother. It was Mr. Hyrum Smith. . . . He welcomed me to his house.[36]

Pratt left for a few days but soon returned to Hyrum's house:

---

[35] Howe, *Mormonism Unvailed*, 252. Sylvia Walker remembered that the price of the Book of Mormon was lowered: "The Mormons said the price of the 'Book of Mormon' was established at $1.75 by revelation. It did not sell well and they claimed to receive another to sell it at $1.25" (*Naked Truths About Mormonism* 1 [April 1888]:1).

[36] Parley P. Pratt [Jr.], ed., *The Autobiography of Parley Parker Pratt* (New York: Published for the Editor and Proprietor by Russell Brothers, 1874), 38-39; (1994 ed.), 20. Pratt recalled, "He [Hyrum] invited me to his home, where I saw mother Smith and Hyrum Smith's wife, and sister Rockwell, the mother of Orin Porter Rockwell" (*Journal of Discourses* 5:194, discourse delivered on Sept. 7, 1856).

I now returned immediately to Hyrum Smith's residence, and demanded baptism at his hands. I tarried with him one night, and the next day we walked some twenty-five miles to the residence of Mr. Whitmer, in Seneca County. Here we arrived in the evening, and found a most welcome reception. . . . I found the little branch of the church in this place [Fayette] full of joy, faith, humility and charity. We rested that night, and on the next day, being about the 1st of September, 1830, I was baptized by the hand of an Apostle of the Church of Jesus Christ, by the name of Oliver Cowdery. This took place in Seneca Lake, a beautiful and transparent sheet of water in Western New York. A meeting was held the same evening, and after singing a hymn and prayer, Elder Cowdery and others proceeded to lay their hands upon my head in the name of Jesus, for the gift of the Holy Ghost. After which I was ordained to the office of an Elder in the Church.[37]

Parley P. Pratt returned to Manchester in October 1830 after baptizing his brother Orson. Parley wrote the following:

I now took leave, and repaired again to the western part of New York, and to the body of the Church. On our arrival, we found that brother Joseph Smith, the translator of the Book of Mormon, had returned from Pennsylvania to his father's residence in Manchester, near Palmyra, and here I had the pleasure of seeing him for the first time. . . . On Sunday we held meeting at his house; the two large rooms were filled with attentive listeners, and he invited me to preach. . . . We repaired from the meeting to the water's edge, and, at his request, I baptized several persons.[38]

---

[37] *Autobiography of Parley Parker Pratt* (1874), 42-43; (1994 ed.), 24, 27. That Joseph Smith was in Harmony, Pennsylvania see Book of Commandments 28, "given in Harmony, Pennsylvania, September 4, 1830" (Marquardt, *Joseph Smith Revelations*, 72) and the reverse side of the deed of land from Isaac Hale to his son-in-law, dated April 6, 1829, noting that payment was received in full "Harmony August 26th 1830" (Joseph Smith Collection, LDS archives). The Indenture was made on August 25, 1830 and witnessed by John Whitmer. See Vogel, *Early Mormon Documents* 4:428-30.

[38] *Autobiography of Parley P. Pratt* (1874), 46-47; (1994 ed.), 31. Pratt's

One of those baptized at this time was Ezra Thayer. He recalled that his half brother and a nephew also heard Hyrum preach before Joseph returned. What follows are excerpts from his account:

I had a half brother living with me and a nephew, and they took my horses and went to meeting, to hear Hyrum preach while I was gone. . . . My half brother said that Hyrum said that Joseph had seen an angel. My nephew said that there was something in it, and that I had better go and hear him. . . . The next Sunday I went and there was a large concourse of people around his father's house, so that they extended to the road, filling up the large lot. . . . Hyrum began to speak. . . . Joseph was then in Harmony, Pa., and the next Sunday he came to his father's house, and we assembled to see him. . . . He then asked me what hindered me from going into the water, as Oliver Cowdery's mother was going to be baptized. . . . Then we started to the water. . . . We were baptized just below the mill. . . . Parley P. Pratt baptized us.[39]

In August 1830, about the time Parley Pratt visited Hyrum,

---

description of the log home agrees with that of Pomeroy Tucker who stated, "This house was divided into two rooms," adding that a bedroom wing was added later (*Origin, Rise, and Progress of Mormonism,* 13). Pratt wrote elsewhere: "Then, after finishing my visit to Columbia Co., I returned to the brethren in Ontario Co., where for the first time, I saw Mr. Joseph Smith, Jr., who had just returned from Pennsylvania, to his father's house, in Manchester" (Pratt, *Mormonism Unveiled* [New-York: Published by O. Pratt & E. Fordham, Third Edition, 1838], 41). The "History of Parley P. Pratt" also mentions "I saw for the first time Joseph Smith, the Prophet, at his father's house, in Manchester" (*Deseret News* 8 [May 19, 1858]:53).

[39] *True Latter Day Saints' Herald* 3 (Oct. 1862):79-83. When Thayer asked what was the price of the Book of Mormon, "Fourteen shillings" [$1.75] was the reply. He bought a copy (80). See Book of Commandments 35:14; LDS D&C 33:15; RLDS D&C 32:3, where it is clear that Thayer and Northrop Sweet had already been ordained elders in the church because they could lay hands on individuals for the gift of the Holy Ghost. The "History of Parley P. Pratt" states that Pratt preached and at the close of the meeting there were "baptized seven persons" (*Deseret News* 8 [May 19, 1858]:53). Those baptized included Ezra Thayer, Northrop Sweet and Oliver Cowdery's step mother Keziah Cowdery.

the census was taken of those living in the Smith family house in Manchester. It had been a decade since the previous census and the families of both Joseph Sr. and Hyrum were listed as one household.[40] The ages of the male family members were: 10-15, 1 (Don Carlos); 15-20, 1 (William); 20-30, 2 (Hyrum and Samuel Harrison), and 50-60, 1 (Joseph Sr.). Females members were: under 5, 2 (Lovina and Mary, daughters of Jerusha and Hyrum); 5-10, 1 (Lucy); 20-30, 1 (Jerusha); 30-40, 1 (not identified), and 50-60, 1 (Lucy Mack Smith). Catherine (age seventeen) was not listed.

By August growing financial complications would shortly result in the family quitting the area entirely. On the day after the founding of the Church of Christ, April 7, 1830, Hyrum Smith signed a note for shoeing horses with Levi Daggett of Palmyra. When this was not repaid, Daggett brought suit before Nathan Pierce, a justice of the peace in Manchester.[41]

The fact that this summons was brought before Justice Nathan Pierce of Manchester, Ontario County, is further evidence that in June 1830 Hyrum Smith resided in Manchester rather than in Palmyra, Wayne County.[42] A summons was served by Constable Southworth on June 8, the day before the first church conference in Fayette. Ten days later another summons was issued. On the 28th Joseph Sr. appeared on his son's behalf. The Docket Book reads:

> 28th June 1830 Joseph <Smith> father of the Defendant appeared and the Case was called and the plaintif[f] declared for a note and account Note dated 7th April 1830 for $20.07 on Interest and on account for Shoeing horses of ballance due on account $0.69 Joseph Smith sworn and saith that his Son the Defendant engaged him to Come

---

[40] 1830 U.S. Census, Manchester, Ontario County, New York, 170, Family #124, microfilm #017161, LDS Family History Library.

[41] Nathan Pierce Docket Book, Manchester Town Office; microfilm of docket book, film 900, reel #62, Harold B. Lee Library, Brigham Young University.

[42] See *Laws of the State of New York* (Albany: Printed by Leake & Croswell, 1824), 280. In the 1830 assessment records Hyrum Smith is taxed for fifteen acres on Lot 1. See 1830 Assessment Records of Manchester, New York, July 5, 1830, 23, Ontario County Historical Society, Canandaigua. Don Enders brought this document to our attention.

down at the return of the summons and direct the Justice to enter Judgment against the defendant for the amount of the note & account Judgment for the plaintif for twenty one dollars seven cents $21.07

August came and Daggett still had not been paid. Thus on August 14 Pierce issued an execution:

THESE are therefore to command you to levy on the goods and chattels of the said defendant (except such as are by law exempted from execution) the amount of the said judgment, and bring the money before me, on the *13th-* day of *September* 1830 at my office in the town of *Manchester.* . . . And if no goods or chattels can be found, or not sufficient to satisfy this execution, then you are hereby commanded to take the bod<u>y</u> of the said defendant and convey *him* to the common Jail of the county aforesaid.[43]

Constable Nathan Harrington collected $12.81 from Hyrum and after court costs paid Daggett $9.94 of the amount owed him on September 13. This was not quite half of the debt. On September 27, the execution was renewed by Justice Pierce with additional fees and again the threat of jail. After nearly a month Harrington came with the execution to collect the remainder and found neither Hyrum nor anything of value. He wrote on the execution: "No property to be found Nor Boddy [Body] and I return this Execution October the 26 1830."[44] Hyrum had left for Colesville, New York.

In these hard times, when people heard that their neighbors

---

[43] Printed Execution found unbound in Nathan Pierce Docket Book, Manchester Town Office. The use of italics indicates where handwriting was filled in on the printed form. The reverse side of the Execution records that $9.94 was received for "Levi Daggett by A K Daggett." This is probably Augustus K. Daggett, son of Levi Daggett, Sr. (see microfilm #017177, LDS Family History Library). See also Samuel Bradlee Daggett, *A History of the Doggett-Daggett Family* (Baltimore: Gateway Press, Inc., 1973), 149-50, 199.

[44] The final item written in the docket book for this case was "Paid by Justice 4th April 1831," and the amount of $21.07 plus $1.60 for a total of $22.67. The reverse side of the execution contains the amount of $24.75, probably including the $12.81 already paid.

were going to move they wanted hard cash.[45] Lucy commented concerning Hyrum's leaving the house about October 1830: "Hyrum had settled up his business, for the purpose of being at liberty to do whatever the Lord required of him." Thus Hyrum, his wife, and their two daughters were to "go immediately to Colesville."[46]

About the same time Hyrum left for Colesville an elderly Quaker came to the house with a note owed by Joseph Sr. and demanded payment. According to Lucy, the man offered to forfeit the note if Smith would burn the copies of the Book of Mormon, but he received neither payment nor satisfaction. A constable was ordered to arrest Smith and take him to the Canandaigua Jail, where he became "an imprisoned debtor."

Samuel Harrison visited his father in jail. Lucy reported that her "husband [was] confined in the same dungeon with a man committed for murder." The elder Smith remained at the jail yard "until he was released, which was thirty days."[47] The man mentioned by Lucy was Eli Bruce. Bruce had been convicted on charges dealing with the abduction and murder of William Morgan, reportedly by Masons. In his diary Bruce recorded:

November 5th – Not so much pain in my head as yesterday. Had a long talk with the father of *the Smith*, (Joseph Smith,) who, according to the old man's account, is the particular favorite of Heaven! To him Heaven has vouchsafed to reveal its mysteries; he is the herald of the latter-day glory. The old man avers that he is commissioned by God to baptize and preach this new doctrine. He says that our Bible is much abridged and deficient; that soon the Divine will is to be known to all, as written in the *new Bible*, or *Book of Mormon*.[48]

---

[45] Richard L. Bushman, *Joseph Smith and the Beginnings of Mormonism* (Urbana: University of Illinois Press, 1984), 172.

[46] Anderson, *Lucy's Book*, 487.

[47] Ibid., 493, 495-97.

[48] Diary of Eli Bruce, Nov. 5, 1830, as cited in Rob Morris, *The Masonic Martyr: The Biography of Eli Bruce, Sheriff of Niagara County, New York* (Louisville, KY: Morris & Monsarrat, 1861), 266-67, emphasis retained.

Samuel helped move the family to Waterloo, near the Peter Whitmer farm in Fayette. There were still threats from creditors. Joseph Jr., who had since moved to Kirtland, Ohio, warned Hyrum in March 1831 that David Jackaway was planning to arrest his father. "I <have> had much Concirn [Concern] about you but I always remember you in <my> prayers Calling upon God to keep <you> Safe in spite <of> men or devils. I think <you> had better Come into this Country immediately for the Lord has Commanded us that we should Call the Elders of this Chursh [Church] to gether unto this plase [place] as soon as possable [possible]." In a postscript he wrote:

Harrison [Smith] and O[r]son Prat[t] arrived here on Feb. 27th. They left our folks well. David Jackways has threatened to take father with a supreme writ in the spring. You had <bet[t]er> Come to Fayette and take father along with you. Come in a one horse wagon if you Can. Do not Come threw [through] Buf[f]alo for th[e]y will lie in wait for you. God protect you. I am Joseph.[49]

That December Orson Pratt arrived from Fayette with a letter from Joseph Smith and John Whitmer. Pratt and Hyrum traveled from Colesville to Fayette to attend the third church conference on January 2, 1831.[50] Previous to the conference Joseph Jr. received a revelation that the whole church should move

---

[49] Joseph Smith Jr. to Hyrum Smith, March 3-4, 1831, LDS archives; Jessee, *Personal Writings of Joseph Smith*, 257-58. Joseph Smith wrote to Martin Harris on Feb. 22, 1831: "see that Father Smiths family are taken care of and sent on. You will send to Colesville and have either Hiram [Smith] or Newel [Knight] to come immediately or both if they can be spared. You will not sell the books for less than 10 Shillings [$1.25]" (LDS archives, not in Jessee, *Personal Writings of Joseph Smith*).

[50] William G. Hartley, *Stand by My Servant Joseph: The Story of the Joseph Knight Family and the Restoration* (Provo, Utah: Joseph Fielding Smith Institute for LDS History and Salt Lake City: Deseret Book, 2003), 95. The letter termed Pratt "another servant and Apostle" and called the Colesville area "the seat of Satan." Compare an 1836 letter regarding the south part of Bainbridge, New York, in *History of Chenango and Madison Counties, New York*, 147. See also Elden J. Watson, comp., *The Orson Pratt Journals* (Salt Lake City: comp., 1975), 10.

to the state of Ohio.[51]

When Hyrum left Colesville for the last time in March 1831 the leadership of the branch transferred to Newel Knight. Hyrum and family probably went to Fayette to get his father, and then they moved to the new gathering place at Kirtland, Ohio, where the Smith family began anew.

Sometime after its publication Martin Harris visited Charles Anthon again in New York City and presented to him the printed Book of Mormon. Anthon declined receiving it.[52] A "List of Articles belonging to Martin Harris & left in the hands of Thomas Lakely for safe keeping not to be delivered to any person except by the written order of the said Harris Dated May 3. 1831" lists "300 Books of Mormon to be sold for $1.25 & account to the said Harris $1.00 for each copy, or deliver the said books to any person presenting the written order of the said Harris."[53]

In a letter to Reverend Ancil Beach dated January 1832, six leading citizens of Canandaigua wrote: "Martin Harris lately testified on a trial which related to the work of printing and publishing the Book that he had sent 2300 copies of it to the west."[54] Hyrum Smith's journal indicates that in 1832 he sold the Book of Mormon in Ohio for $1.25 a copy. The Book of Mormon was also used as an object of barter.[55] The next chapter will examine the Book of Mormon as a religious document.

---

[51] Marquardt, *Joseph Smith Revelations*, 98; BC 39:4; LDS D&C 37:3; RLDS D&C 37:2 (Dec. 1830).

[52] Vogel, *Early Mormon Documents* 4:380, 385-86. In his 1841 letter Anthon thought the visitor was Joseph Smith but it was Martin Harris.

[53] The list was signed by Harris and is located in the Palmyra Library Vertical files, Thomas Lakey's "Record of Court Proceedings 1827-1830," in the King's Daughters Library, Palmyra, New York.

[54] Nathaniel W. Howell, Walter Hubbell, Ansel D. Eddy, Henry Chapin, Jared Willson, and Lewis Jenkins to Ancil Beach, Jan. 1832, copy of letter in the Walter Hubbell Collection, Princeton University Library, Princeton, New Jersey. See Vogel, *Early Mormon Documents* 3:16.

[55] Jeffrey S. O'Driscoll, *Hyrum Smith: A Life of Integrity* (Salt Lake City: Deseret Book, 2003), 64.

9

Literary Dependence in the Book of Mormon: Two Studies

The Book of Mormon[1] contains fifteen books (one called Words of Mormon) that tell the religious and social history of the people it describes. The work is an abridgement of previous records. The main story takes place in Jerusalem near 600 B.C.E. and ends in America about 421 C.E.[2] It explains that God called Lehi to be a prophet and with his son Nephi they came by ship to the promise land. Two groups of the house of Israel are chiefly mentioned, the Lamanites and the Nephites. The record tells of their rulers, wars, and religious experiences covering to the time of Christ. A unique part of the book is the appearance of Jesus Christ among the natives after his crucifixion. The book 3 Nephi contains the teachings of Jesus including the establishment of his church.

The downfall of the Nephites is described with the records being written by Mormon and his son Moroni. The people remaining are the Lamanites, ancestors to the Native Americans. A short book is the Book of Ether telling about an earlier trip to America by ship (eight barges) shortly after the building of the biblical tower mentioned in Genesis. This other group is known as

---

[1] Since a number of churches use and publish the Book of Mormon, the edition used in this chapter is the 1981 edition published by the Church of Jesus Christ of Latter-day Saints, headquartered in Salt Lake City, Utah. In 1982 it was renamed and the title is now *The Book of Mormon: Another Testament of Jesus Christ*. The versification is the same as the 1879 Salt Lake edition and as used by the Church of Jesus Christ in Monongahela, Pennsylvania, and called "The Record of the Nephites" by the Church of Christ (with the Elijah Message) in Independence, Missouri. The edition of the Community of Christ (formerly the Reorganized Church of Jesus Christ of Latter Day Saints) also headquarters in Independence, Missouri, has different versification but the chapters numbers are the same as the 1830 first edition. The Church of Christ (Temple Lot) and other Latter Day Saint churches and groups use this latter versification.
[2] C.E. (Common Era) and B.C.E. (Before the Common Era) are alternate designations corresponding to A.D. and B.C. and is often used in scholarly literature.

the Jaredites. The last writing is the Book of Moroni giving a pattern to follow for church ordinances. The Book of Mormon is written in biblical style as a prophetic work to make things clearer than the Bible but in an American setting.

The abridgement was written to the descendents of the Lamanites, and also to Jew and Gentile. It was in essence a Native American book containing historical and religious writings of their ancestors. The title page tells its purpose—"to the convincing of the Jew and Gentile that JESUS is the CHRIST, the ETERNAL GOD."

Whether the Book of Mormon is an ancient record or a modern creation, it demands serious examination, since it is represented to be Judaeo-Christian scripture produced in the New World in pre-Columbian times. One such task is determining the extent to which the Bible, especially the New Testament, was used as a source in its production, and if so, what this may mean regarding the historicity of the Book of Mormon. Another task is weighing evidence of nineteenth century events reflected in the Book of Mormon and, again, considering the significance of this for the historicity of the Book of Mormon.

LITERARY DEPENDENCE ON THE BIBLE

The twenty-seven books of the New Testament were originally written between about 50-100 C.E. Yet numerous phrases from the New Testament appear in sections of the Book of Mormon ostensibly dating to hundreds of years before the birth of Jesus. This suggests that those sections are of much later composition. Consider a few of these New Testament phrases (written after 30 C.E.) which appear in 1 Nephi-Helaman (recorded 600 B.C.E.-1 C.E.): "ye must pray always, and not faint" (2 Ne. 32:9/Luke 18:1); some will go "into everlasting fire prepared for the devil and his angels" (Mosiah 26:27/Matt. 25:41); but "then shall the righteous shine forth in the kingdom of God" (Alma 40:25/Matt. 13:43). Believers should be "steadfast and immovable, always abounding in good works" (Mosiah 5:15/1 Cor. 15:58); ultimately this "mortal shall put on immortality" (Enos 27/1 Cor. 15:53), but until that day they need to grow "in the nurture and admonition of the Lord" (Enos 1/Eph. 6:4). Notice also that "Jew and Gentile, both bond and free, both male and female" (2 Ne. 10:16/Gal. 3:28), who fight against Zion shall perish. God is "the same, yesterday, today, and forever" (2 Ne. 2:4/Heb. 13 8); while believers "endured the crosses of the world, and despised the shame" (2 Ne. 9:18/Heb. 12:2). Finally, "if their works have been filthiness they must needs be filthy" (1 Ne. 15:33/Rev. 22:11).

The Book of Mormon asserts that ancient New World peoples possessed most of the Old Testament. However, Book of Mormon peoples would not have had access to the New Testament. Those who believe in the book's antiquity try to reconcile the presence of New Testament phrases by suggesting that in translating the book Joseph Smith was given an understanding of ideas on the golden plates but had to choose the words to express them. Consequently, where a thought was sufficiently close to biblical wording he adopted or adapted the biblical phrase. This does not sufficiently explain why he implemented the King James style throughout and not a "more original" style. It also ignores the fact that the adaptation of biblical texts is deeper than mere use of phrases from the New Testament in the Old Testament time period. The Book of Mormon does not simply introduce random New Testament phrases. It reflects on and expands New Testament meanings in an Old Testament context and creates Old Testament events that flow from these New Testament interpretations.

Alma 12 and 13 provide a good example of this in their use of the New Testament Epistle to the Hebrews. Hebrews employs Genesis 14:18-20 together with Psalm 2:7 and 110:4 to establish that the Messiah holds a priesthood higher than that of the Levitical priesthood, and that this priesthood "after the order of Melchisedec" superseded and abolished the Levitical one (Heb. 5:5-10; 6:20; 7:1-12). ("Melchizedek" is the spelling in Old Testament and contemporary LDS usage.) The Book of Mormon builds on this New Testament interpretation and adds its own misinterpretation to create an entire order of priests "after the order of the Son" (Alma 13:9), "being a type of his order" (v. 16), of whom Melchizedek is but the leading example (v. 19). Furthermore, Hebrew's interpretation of Melchizedek's name and title ("King of righteousness . . . King of peace") is expanded into an imaginary historical situation in which Melchizedek successfully calls his people to repentance and thus to righteousness and peace. This material is then worked together into a systematic doctrinal exposition that utilizes other New Testament phrases from such sources as the Gospels, 1 Corinthians, and Revelation. (Compare Alma 13:9, 13, 22 with parallel phrases in John 1:14; Matt. 3:8; Luke 2:10; and Alma 12:20; 13:28 with 1 Cor. 15:51-53; 10:13; also Alma 12:14, 16, 17, and 13:11 with Rev. 6:16; 20:5-6, 14-15; 19:20; 14:10-11; 20:10, and 7:14.)

The Book of Mormon's own theological statements, therefore, is drawn from, depend on, expand, and explain interpretations already present in the New Testament. In using New Testament interpretations and material as a basis for building such theological statements and exposition throughout the book, New Testament quotations become a part of the fabric of the Book of Mormon text and cannot be regarded as mere figures of speech employed in translating.

A second feature of the Book of Mormon's use of the Bible is how it presents prophecies about the New Testament time period. In 1 and 2 Nephi (600-545 B.C.E.) are prophecies of the coming of Jesus Christ. The prophecies in these two books use the language recorded in the New Testament, even the phasing of the King James Version. These events in the life and ministry of Jesus were recorded in the New Testament and written by the men then involved. Since the Book of Mormon did not appear until 1830, it is easy for the book to prophesy of events that had already occurred. Indeed, material in the Old Testament part of the Book of Mormon reads like a late Christian document, written after the New Testament was compiled.

Furthermore, the Book of Mormon preaches the "doctrine of Christ" nearly 600 years before Jesus initiated his ministry in Palestine. Notice the use of Christian terms and doctrine of "the Father, and of the Son, and of the Holy Ghost, which is one God" (2 Ne. 31:21) which comes from Matthew 28:19. This formula also occurs in Alma 11:44 (about 82 B.C.E.), but nowhere in the Hebrew Bible is anything of this type mentioned. The Book of Mormon throughout its Old Testament period material uses ideas and doctrines that come from the New Testament.

The Book of Mormon teaches that "many plain and precious things" were "taken away" from the Bible: "they have taken away from the gospel of the Lamb many parts which are plain and most precious" (1 Ne. 13:26, 28). The claim that writings were taken "from the gospel of the Lamb" is problematic. In fact, when one examines the New Testament manuscript material, which reaches back to the second century C.E., evidence that material was taken away is lacking.

There are, however, some places where material was added. One such example is Mark 16:9-20. This passage was probably added to Mark during the second century. Codex Sinaiticus and Codex Vaticanus, both written in the fourth century, along with a few other New Testament Greek manuscripts, do not contain this addition. Most New Testament scholars, after examining early manuscripts that contain Mark 16, find that the early writings of the church fathers support the view that verses 9-20 were originally not part of Mark.[3] Interestingly, passages in the King James Version of Mark 16:9-20 appear in three separate places in the Book of Mormon: 3 Ne. 11:33-34; Morm. 9:22-24 and Ether 4:18.

The Book of Mormon justifies this use of the Bible, and especially New Testament words and ideas, by suggesting that Christianity existed in Old Testament times: "Wherefore, I speak the same words unto one nation like unto another" (2 Ne. 29:8). Were these same words spoken to ancient Hebrew prophets? By examining Old Testament documents, we can see that the Book of Mormon has a gospel that was not taught and practiced in the Old Testament period. Rather, it was taught when Jesus and his apostles preached it as recorded only in the New Testament.

When Joseph Smith was in the process of dictating the religious text of the Book of Mormon he would at times read longer passages from the Old Testament to his scribe. A close examination indicates that chapters from Old Testament books were incorporated into the Book of Mormon. In these places Smith was dependent upon the Bible with the meaning essentially the same. An exception is the verses from Isaiah 29 added to 2 Nephi—it was expanded to make it fit Martin Harris' visit with the

---

[3] See, for example, George Eldon Ladd, *The New Testament and Criticism* (Grand Rapids, MI: Wm. B. Eerdmans, 1967), 72-74.

learned Professor Charles Anthon. The following chart contains examples of passages used:

Book of Mormon	Old Testament
1 Nephi chapters 20-21	Isaiah chapters 48-49
2 Nephi chapter 7	Isaiah chapter 50
2 Nephi 8:1-23	Isaiah chapter 51
2 Nephi chapters 12-24	Isaiah chapters 2-14
2 Nephi 20:24-34	Isaiah 10:24-34
2 Nephi 26:14-19	Isaiah 29:3-5
2 Nephi 27:1-35	Isaiah 29:6-24
2 Nephi 30:11-15	Isaiah 11:5-9
Mosiah 12:21-24	Isaiah 52:7-10
Mosiah 13:12-24	Exodus 20:4-17
Mosiah chapter 14	Isaiah chapter 53
3 Nephi 20:41-45	Isaiah 52:11-15
3 Nephi 21:12-18, 21	Micah 5:8-14, 15
2 Nephi chapter 22	Isaiah chapter 54
3 Nephi chapters 24-25	Malachi chapters 3-4

The majority of the chapters originate from the book of Isaiah. Since the printing of the 1830 edition of the Book of Mormon an earlier Hebrew text of Isaiah was discovered in 1947. Fragments and a large scroll of Isaiah (1QIsa[a]; copied circa 125 B.C.E.) were found in the Judean Desert caves near the Dead Sea and are part of the Dead Sea Scrolls. The variants in these manuscripts help understand the textual tradition when they were made. A basic comparison with the Isaiah in the Book of Mormon indicates that the King James Bible became the standard text when dictating the above texts for the Book of Mormon.[4]

---

[4] See David P. Wright, "Joseph Smith's Interpretation of Isaiah in the Book of Mormon," *Dialogue: A Journal of Mormon Thought* 31 (Winter 1998):181-206. See also *Scrolls from Qumrân Cave I: The Great Isaiah Scroll, The Order of the Community, The* Pesher *to Habakkuk*, From photographs by John C. Trever (Jerusalem: The Albright Institute of Archaeological Research and the Shrine of the Book, 1972); and Martin Abegg, Jr., Peter Flint and Eugene Ulrich, translated and with commentary, *The Dead Sea Scrolls Bible: The Oldest Known*

The Book of Mormon is part modern and part ancient, the ancient part coming from the Bible itself. Many familiar themes that are pre-Christian and contained in the earlier portion of the Book of Mormon are found in the Old Testament. Book of Mormon writers reportedly possessed these writings, and it would be natural for Israelite ideas to be in a book of Semitic origin.[5]

During the ministry of Jesus in Palestine, his disciples did not understand much of what he said to them. After his resurrection, they began to know what he meant, and a few wrote down accounts as they remembered them. A passage from John 12:16 emphasizes: "These things understood not his disciples at the first: but when Jesus was glorified, then remembered they that these things were written of him, and that they had done these things unto him" (see also Mark 9:32; Luke 9:45; 18:34).

By contrast, the Book of Mormon states that Nephite prophets already understood Jesus' mission, including the date of his birth, the name of his mother, his baptism, death, resurrection, and miracles. In relating these events, it uses later knowledge (written and recorded in the New Testament) and retroactively places them in a historical situation that predates Jesus' birth. These anachronisms mark the Book of Mormon as a work produced after Jesus was resurrected and the Christian church established.

The central book in the Book of Mormon is the book of Third Nephi.[6] It is represented as having been recorded upon plates of gold and abridged by the hand of a historian named Mormon. This book purports to give an account of Jesus Christ appearing in ancient America soon after His resurrection. This section will demonstrate that many passages from the New Testament were used for the Third Nephi account. What is being examined is the

---

Bible Translated for the First Time into English (New York: HarperSanFrancisco, 1999).

[5] For a theory that the Book of Mormon is part ancient and part modern with expansive commentary by Joseph Smith see Blake T. Ostler, "The Book of Mormon as a Modern Expansion of an Ancient Source," *Dialogue: A Journal of Mormon Thought* 20 (Spring 1987):66-123. This article contains numerous references to material in the Book of Mormon which has a close relationship to the biblical text. Ostler states, "The presence of the KJV [King James Version] in the book is, it seems to me, indisputable" (102).

[6] This book was first named "III Nephi" in the 1879 Salt Lake edition.

authenticity of the record of Third Nephi (i.e., its ancient character) and not the expression of Christ-like teaching.[7]

This reported visit is the climatic and central story in the Book of Mormon. Just prior to that supposed visitation, Third Nephi depicts vast destruction occurring on the American continent over a period of three hours, simultaneous with Jesus crucifixion (3 Nephi 8:19). Following this, thick darkness came upon the face of the land for the space of three days. The surviving American inhabitants heard a voice speaking words that in part were derived directly from the King James New Testament, and which are found exclusively in the Gospel of John.

> Behold, I am Jesus Christ the Son of God. ... *I am in the Father, and the Father in me* ... I *came unto* my *own, and* my *own received* me *not.* ... And *as many as* have *received* me, *to them* have I given to *become the sons of God*; and *even* so will I *to* as many as shall *believe on* my *name* ... in me is the law of Moses fulfilled (3 Nephi 9:15-17, emphasis added for similar words in John; compare John 14:11; 1:11-12).

Most of these words attributed to Jesus in this Third Nephi passage are found in John's Gospel, and they are actually John's words rather than the words spoken by Jesus himself. The account in Third Nephi has them spoken in America long before John penned them in the Old World circa 90 C.E. The voice continued with further words from John's Gospel as well as from the Book of Revelation.

I am the light and the life of the world (3 Ne. 9:18; compare John 8:12).

---

[7] The question of the wording of the Sermon on the Mount as recorded in Third Nephi is explored in Stan Larson, "The Historicity of the Matthean Sermon on the Mount in 3 Nephi," in Brent Lee Metcalfe, ed., *New Approaches to the Book of Mormon: Explorations in Critical Methodology* (Salt Lake City: Signature Books, 1993), 115-63). For the Third Nephi account, Nephi supposedly recorded the text soon after the reported visit of Jesus, and this record was later abridged by Mormon, after whom the Book of Mormon is named (see 3 Nephi 16:4; 23:4; 26:7, 11). See Ronald V. Huggins, "Did the Author of 3 Nephi Know the Gospel of Matthew?" *Dialogue: A Journal of Mormon Thought* 30 (Fall 1997):137-48.

I am Alpha and Omega, the beginning and the end (3 Ne. 9:19; compare Rev. 21:6; 22:13).

Alpha and *Omega* are the first and last letters of the Greek alphabet. Third Nephi opens with this Johannine-derived material, and depicts the purported post-resurrection visit of Christ to the Israelites of America. The account reports that a voice "as if it came out of heaven" (11:3) was soon heard in "the land Bountiful" (11:1). The voice echoed the words that opened Jesus' ministry in Palestine: "Behold *my Beloved Son, in whom I am well pleased*, in whom I have glorified my name—hear ye him" (11:7, emphasis added; compare Matt. 3:17; Mark 1:11; Luke 3:22; see also Matt. 17:5).[8]

The Gospel according to John records a time, after Christ's resurrection, when Thomas, one of Jesus' twelve apostles, expressed unbelief and wished to thrust his hand into the side of the resurrected Jesus to verify the resurrection. Jesus then appeared to the apostles with Thomas present and told him, "reach hither thy hand, and thrust it into my side." Thomas, now convinced, answered "My Lord and my God" (John 20:24-29). Third Nephi expands upon this event from John's Gospel, reporting that some twenty-five hundred people (3 Ne. 17:25) filed by "one by one" and touched the crucifixion wounds of Jesus' side, hands and feet and exclaimed, "Hosanna! Blessed be the name of the Most High God!" (11:17; see also 19:18).

Jesus gave power to baptize to the twelve disciples whom he commissioned on that day. Because Third Nephi presents Jesus as commanding that there should be no more disputations among the people, a baptismal prayer was given which reflects the words of Matthew's gospel: "Having authority given me of Jesus Christ, I baptize you *in the name of the Father, and of the Son, and of the Holy Ghost.* Amen" (11:25, emphasis added; compare Matt. 28:19). After clarifying that such baptism should be by immersion ("And then shall ye immerse them in the water, and come forth

---

[8] Other ideas from the New Testament appear earlier in Third Nephi, such as the "star" in the heavens (3 Ne. 1:21), which was used in telling about the birth of Christ (Helaman 14:5) to the people in the New World (see Matt. 2:2, 7, 9-10). And the day before Jesus was born it was claimed that Jesus had said "I come unto my own" (3 Ne. 1:14; compare John 1:11).

again out of the water" 11:26), Jesus again utters the words of John 14:11 "I am in the Father, and the Father in me" (11:27).

The doctrines that are reported to have been taught by Jesus to his twelve disciples in the New World are couched in the language of the New Testament, which had not as yet been written. They include the following:

1. Jesus "commandeth all men, everywhere, to repent" (11:32; compare Acts 17:30).
2. Repent and believe in Jesus, "And whoso believeth in me, and is baptized, the same shall be saved; ... And whoso believeth not in me, and is not baptized, shall be damned" (11:33-34; compare Mark 16:16). Here Third Nephi uses words from the ending of Mark that are recognized as not belonging in the original biblical text.
3. Whoever believes in Jesus believes in the Father and he will be visited "with fire and with the Holy Ghost" (11:35; compare Matt. 3:11; Luke 3:16).
4. Jesus declares "the Father, and I, and the Holy Ghost are one" (11:36, 27; compare John 10:30).
5. A person must "become as a little child, or ye can in nowise inherit the kingdom of God" (11:38; compare Luke 18:16-17; Mark 10:14-15; Matt. 18:3; 19:14).

In reporting the words of Jesus' commissioning of the disciples, the Book of Mormon again draws upon the wording of the as-yet-unwritten New Testament.

Verily, verily, I say unto you, that this is *my doctrine*, and whoso buildeth upon this buildeth *upon* my *rock*, and *the gates of hell shall not prevail against* them. And whoso shall declare more or less than this, and establish it for *my doctrine*, the same cometh of evil, and is not built *upon* my *rock*; but he buildeth *upon* a sandy foundation, and *the gates of hell* stand open to receive such when *the floods* come *and the winds beat upon* them (11:39-40, emphasis added; compare John 7:16-17; Matt. 7:24-27; 16:18; parallel text in Luke 6:47-49).

Jesus, after promising the multitude that he would baptize them "with fire and with the Holy Ghost" (12:1) says to the twelve disciples:

Yea, blessed are they who shall believe in your words, and come down into the depths of humility and be *baptized*, for they shall be visited *with fire* and *with the Holy Ghost*, and shall receive a *remission of* their *sins* (12:2, emphasis added; compare Matt. 3:11; Luke 3:16; Acts 2:38).

The Third Nephi text next moves to an even heavier dependence upon the New Testament material, attributing to Jesus a retelling of the discourse known as "The Sermon on the Mount" (as recorded in the Gospel according to Matthew). However, these words, which in Matthew belong in a pre-resurrection Jewish/Palestinian setting, are cast into a post-resurrection Nephite context in which the Law of Moses is considered already fulfilled. The sermon in Third Nephi has textual material in it (starting with Matthew, chapter 5, verse 3) which makes sense if Jesus is speaking to first century Jewish religious leaders in Palestine, but is incongruous when directed to a people who have a different culture and speak another language. Nevertheless, the material is presented with the same concepts and vocabulary as recorded in Matthew. Only the most obvious disparities were eliminated from the Third Nephi text, such as the deletion of the reference in Matthew 5:20 (3 Nephi 12:20) concerning scribes and Pharisees.[9] The time frame has also been altered to make the material fit into

---

[9] The Sermon on the Mount as recorded in the Gospel of Matthew was used in Third Nephi to document the teachings reportedly spoken by Jesus in America. See Richard P. Howard, *Restoration Scriptures: A Study of Their Textual Development* (Independence, Missouri: Herald House, 1969), 98; (2nd edition, 1995), 84. Krister Stendahl's analysis of "The Sermon on the Mount and Third Nephi" published in *Reflections on Mormonism, Judaeo-Christian Parallels* (Provo, Utah: Religious Studies Center, Brigham Young University, 1978), 139-54, argues that the Book of Mormon text of the Sermon on the Mount is not a genuine translation from an ancient language but is Joseph Smith's nineteenth century targumic expansion of the English King James text. Stendahl's study has been reprinted in *Meanings: The Bible as Document and as Guide* (Philadelphia: Fortress Press, 1984), 99-113.

the period after the resurrection of Jesus. Otherwise the text of Matthew has remained mostly unchanged.

In keeping with this shift, Third Nephi presents Jesus as adding that "the law is fulfilled," "Come unto me and be ye saved" and "except ye shall keep my commandments ... ye shall in no case enter into the kingdom of heaven" (12:19-20). To the text of Matthew 5:21, "Ye have heard that it was said by them of old time," is added "and it is also written before you" (12:21). The added words shift the meaning of Jesus' words away from the original sense they have in Matthew's gospel.

The next verse presents a similar problem of making words that have a distinctive Palestinian setting have any significant meaning to New World people. That verse, taken almost verbatim from the King James Version of Matthew except for the deletion of the words "without a cause," reads:

> But I say unto you, that whosoever is angry with his brother shall be in danger of his judgment. And whosoever shall say to his brother, Raca, shall be in danger of the council; and whosoever shall say, Thou fool, shall be in danger of hell fire (3 Ne. 12:22).

The use of the Aramaic word Raca (rêqa' or rêqâ), a term of opprobrium, would be meaningless to New World people who are depicted as speaking either Hebrew or reformed Egyptian. A further disparity lies in the phrase "shall be in danger of the council." In the Gospel account the reference is to the Jewish governing body, the Sanhedrin, but has no apparent point of reference in a New World context.

Finally, it is significant that the three words deleted from this verse in Third Nephi ("without a cause") are the same words that the commentaries of Joseph Smith's day had noted were lacking in some early Greek manuscripts. The questionable status of this phrase was therefore well known before work on the Book of Mormon had begun and may have influenced its deletion.[10] It is

---

[10] In the commentary on Matthew by Adam Clarke, published as early as 1818 (1825 edition used), comes the following regarding the words "without a cause" in Matt. 5:22: "without a cause, is wanting in the famous Vatican MS. and two others, the Ethiopic, latter Arabic, Saxon, Vulgate, two copies of the old Itala, J.

also possible that the deletion of the three words may have occurred since people normally would be angry with a cause.

The words of Matthew 5:27, "Ye have heard that it was said by them of old time, Thou shalt not commit adultery," is rendered in Third Nephi as "Behold, it is written by them of old time, that thou shalt not commit adultery" (12:27). The oldest Greek text of Matthew does not contain the words "by them of old time." New Testament papyrus fragment number 64, which includes this portion of the Sermon on the Mount and is dated about 200 C.E., contains no such words. Including these words in Third Nephi shows its dependence on the rendering of this text in the King James Bible rather than being an independent testament of Jesus Christ.[11]

The deletion of "neither by Jerusalem; for it is the city of the great King" from the following text removes it from its New Testament setting. This indicates that this was a change made on purpose to try to change the Gospel text and make it appear nearly the same in a New World context.

> But I say unto you, Swear not at all; neither by heaven; for it is God's throne: Nor by the earth; for it is his footstool: neither by Jerusalem; for it is the city of the great King (Matt. 5:34-35).

Martyr, Ptolomeus, Origen, Tertullian, and by all the ancient copies quoted by St. Jerom[e]. It was probably a marginal gloss originally, which in process of time crept into the text" (*Clarke's Commentary* 1:71). The phrase is also deleted in Joseph Smith's revision of Matthew in 1831. See New Testament MS 1, p. 10, RLDS Archives, in *The Holy Scriptures* (Independence, Missouri: Herald Publishing House, 1991), published by the Reorganized Church of Jesus Christ of Latter Day Saints (now Community of Christ), Matthew 5:24. This revision is referred to variously as the Inspired Version (I.V.) and the Joseph Smith Translation (cited hereafter as JST).

[11] In the manuscript of Joseph Smith's revision, New Testament MS 1, p. 10, the words "them of old time" were written and then crossed out in the manuscript and the text as printed in 3 Nephi 12:27 is written out. The Book of Mormon follows the King James Version and in his revision of the New Testament Joseph Smith used both the KJV and Third Nephi.

The revised text reads:

> But verily, verily, I say unto you, swear not at all; neither by heaven, for it is God's throne; Nor by the earth, for it is his footstool (3 Ne. 12:34-25)

For Third Nephi to have included the reference in Matthew 5:35 to Jerusalem, "the city of the great King" (wording derived apparently from Ps. 48:2), would have revealed the Old World setting of the passage.[12] After these departures from Matthew, the text in Third Nephi closely follows Matthew's wording in 5:39-42, 44, with but a few words different (compare 3 Ne. 12:39-42, 44). There is an omission of the words "and sendeth rain on the just and on the unjust" in verse 45, while Paul's words from 2 Corinthians, "Old things are done away, and all things have become new" are placed on Jesus' lips (12:47; compare 2 Cor. 5:17).

The main body of this material in Third Nephi is derived directly from the gospel of Matthew, since parallel texts in Mark or Luke are ignored for Matthews' wording. While it is true that, except for the words "should be cast into hell" (12:30), Matthew 5:29-30 is omitted from the Third Nephi account without any obvious reason, nevertheless the sequence found in Matthew is closely followed. These teachings of Jesus are found in the Gospels of Mark and Luke, but scattered throughout the narratives rather than grouped topically as Matthew records them. Several textual problems are contained within this chapter that makes these words out of place in a New World setting.[13]

Third Nephi 13 continues the presentation of the Sermon on the Mount taken from Matthew chapter 6, but places it upon the lips of Jesus as his teaching to the Nephites. This chapter is copied

---

[12] In 3 Nephi 12:23 the wording in Matthew 5:23 about bringing "thy gift to the altar" was also removed from the text of Matthew when placed in the Third Nephi record, possibly also to eliminate any Palestinian reference.

[13] As has been stated, many of the changes made in Third Nephi from the King James Matthew are also retained by Joseph Smith when he produced his Bible revision. The following verses in both texts are basically the same: 3 Nephi 12:3-13; compare with Matt. 5:5-15 (JST). When material was added which was not in the Matthew account to the Third Nephi version, these words were used in the Bible revision. See for example: 3 Nephi 12:2 with Matt. 5:4 (JST) and 3 Nephi 12:29-30 with Matt. 5:31 (JST).

into Third Nephi with very few textual differences from its printing in the King James Bible. Compare the following: 3 Nephi 13:3-9 with Matt. 6:3-9; 3 Nephi 13:11-24 with Matt. 6:12-24; 3 Nephi 13:25(part)-29 with Matt. 6:25-29 and 3 Nephi 13:33 with Matt. 6:33.

In this section, the familiar version of what is known as "The Lord's Prayer" is quoted from Matthew with two phrases deleted in the Third Nephi version. The phrases omitted are (1) "Thy kingdom come" (Matt. 6:10), and (2) "Give us this day our daily bread" (Matt. 6:11). The first phrase is also found in Luke 11:2 and the second phrase appears as "Give us day by day our daily bread" in Luke 11:3. It is not apparent on the surface just why these phrases were omitted since Joseph Smith later included them in his Bible revision.[14]

While the deletion of the two phrases may have no significance, it is of great importance to note that the closing of Matthew 6:13 (King James Version) – "For thine is the kingdom, and the power, and the glory, for ever. Amen" - is included in the Third Nephi text. This is widely recognized as an addition to the Matthean text, since the doxology is missing from the most reliable Greek manuscripts, such as the Codex Sinaiticus and Codex Vaticanus (both transcribed during the fourth century). Other manuscripts of Matthew give a variant form of doxology, indicating that this ending was an addition to the Lord's Prayer. Biblical scholars have concluded that the evidence indicates that the doxology became attached to the Matthean text from a liturgical use of the prayer in the early worship services of the Christian churches.[15] Various endings were added to the Lord's Prayer perhaps as early as the second century, and even where the doxology occurs it does so with several variations. It was not until

---

[14] The omission of the first phrase cannot be attributed to the theological terminology implied in "Thy kingdom come" for the exhortation of Jesus "But seek ye first the kingdom of God" (Matt. 6:33; compare Luke 12:31) is found in 3 Nephi 13:33.

[15] See Alfred Plummer, *An Exegetical Commentary on the Gospel According to S. Matthew* (Grand Rapids: Wm. B. Eerdmans, 1956), 103.

the fourth century that this doxology became fixed and standard in manuscripts of Matthew.[16]

Since this doxology was added to some New Testament manuscripts in the Old World in the fourth century, it is highly improbable that this identical wording was spoken by Christ in America shortly after His resurrection. A more plausible explanation is that Joseph Smith copied these words from the King James Bible, in ignorance of the textual history, rather than having been spoken by Jesus in the New World. This then would be but another example of the late textual material anachronistically placed into an earlier time-frame in Third Nephi.

One Latter-day Saint scholar has attempted to account for the obvious borrowing of the Third Nephi sermon from the Sermon on the Mount in Matthew:

> We recognize the fact that no two independent translators would be likely to translate a large portion of the Sermon word for word the same. That Joseph Smith used the King James version when he came to familiar scripture on the Gold Plates we shall not deny. As long as the Sermon in the familiar rendering of Matthew 5-7 agreed substantially with the Nephite version the prophet used it word for word; otherwise he corrected it to conform with the text before him on the metal plates. In this respect Joseph Smith did only what many translators would have done.[17]

However, this suggestion that the likeness of the text in Third Nephi was because the King James rendering of Matthew was used when it "agreed substantially with the Nephite version"

---

[16] In Joseph Smith's revision for the parallel text of the Lord's prayer recorded in Luke 11:4 (JST) he added (after "but deliver us from evil") a part of the doxology added to Matthew - namely, "for thine is the kingdom and power. Amen."

[17] Sidney B. Sperry, *Answers to Book of Mormon Questions* (Salt Lake City: Bookcraft, 1967), 112. The evidence does indicate that the sermons in Third Nephi are in part based upon the KJV New Testament. For a view of one who maintains that the King James Version was not used, see John W. Welch in *The Sermon at the Temple and the Sermon on the Mount* (Salt Lake City: Deseret Book and Provo: Foundation for Ancient Research and Mormon Studies, 1990), 148-63.

will not stand. There is no evidence to support this and including this late fourth century doxology in the Third Nephi text rules out such an explanation. To hold such a conclusion would mean that Jesus taught to the first century Nephites a doxology that would incorrectly be added in the fourth century to his words in Matthew.

In chapter 14 of Third Nephi the text again follows almost verbatim what is found in the Sermon on the Mount as recorded in the gospel of Matthew. Matthew 7:1-17 is here quoted from the King James New Testament (some of which had been previously paraphrased by Jesus in Third Nephi).

If there is still doubt that the author of Third Nephi has borrowed the text of the Matthean Sermon on the Mount, it should be dispelled when even words clearly composed by Matthew, and not attributable to Jesus, are brought over into the Third Nephi account. The Third Nephi text follows Matthew so closely that it even borrows Matthew's transitional phrase: "And it came to pass, when Jesus had ended these sayings" (Matt. 7:28; compare 3 Ne. 15:1). The Third Nephi text claims to have been written long before Matthew composed his account. The Third Nephi writings clearly are based upon a text written years after Jesus' resurrection.

Chapter 15 of Third Nephi presents Jesus as acknowledging that he was presenting the same material he had taught in Palestine, for it reports him saying, "Behold, ye have heard the things which I taught before I ascended to my Father" (15:1). However, the text understandably does not mention that this material was derived from the gospel of Matthew before Matthew had ever recorded it.

The Gospel of Matthew was not the only source for the words of Jesus in Third Nephi. Jesus opens chapter 15 explaining in Paul's words from 2 Corinthians that "old things had passed away, and that all things had become new" (a statement borrowed from 2 Cor. 5:17; compare 3 Ne. 12:47). He adds, "the law which was given unto Moses hath an end in me. Behold I am the law, and the light" (15:8-9). Next, Jesus tells the twelve American disciples that they are to be a light to these American Israelites "who are a remnant of the house of Joseph" (15:12), that America is to be the land of their inheritance (v. 13) and that their Jewish brothers at Jerusalem do not know of their existence (v. 14).

Furthermore, Jesus declares that he has not made known to the Jews in the Holy Land the existence of "the other tribes of the house of Israel, whom the Father hath led away out of the land" of Palestine (v. 15). Thus all ten tribes, including the segment descended from Joseph through Manasseh and Lehi (the original leader of the American colony, Alma 10:3), are depicted as completely lost and unknown to the Jews of Jesus' day.

At this point the Gospel of John provided another fruitful source for the words and prayers that are written in Third Nephi. Jesus is represented to have uttered words found in John's Gospel:

That other sheep I have which are not of this fold; them also I must bring, and they shall hear my voice; and there shall be one fold, and one shepherd (15:17; also 15:21; compare with John 10:16, John only).

The Third Nephi passage depends upon the King James Version of John. Third Nephi proceeds to give its own unique explanation of what Jesus meant by "other sheep," namely the Nephites and the lost tribes. It has Jesus saying that he hinted of the continued existence of this lost group of Israelites by telling the Jews in Palestine that he had "other sheep ... which are not of this fold," but the Jews thought he meant the Gentiles (verses 21-22). However, he explains the Gentiles will never personally "hear my voice" but will learn of Christ only "by the Holy Ghost" (v. 23). Rather than referring to the Israelites of America, this verse does not refer to any specific group other than non-Jews or Gentiles.

In the next chapter (chapter 16), Jesus adds that he is leaving to visit these "other sheep, which are not of this land [America], neither of the land of Jerusalem" so they may hear his voice, be numbered among his sheep and thus produce "one fold and one shepherd" (verses 1-3). These American Israelites are told that they are to jot down this information Jesus has shared with them just in case the Jews fail to inquire by the Holy Ghost about their existence and the existence of "the other tribes whom they know not of" (verse 4).

The knowledge given here is supposedly of importance since the Gentiles will later use it to reach the remnant of the American Hebrews who have been scattered over the continent because of their unbelief. Through this effort and knowledge, they may "be brought in, or may be brought to a knowledge of me, their

Redeemer" (verse 4). However, the Gentiles themselves should beware, or they will face rejection by God after they have scattered and mistreated these descendants of Israel so they have "become a hiss and a byword among them." If they fall into all kinds of sins and reject "the fulness of my gospel" (contained in the Book of Mormon), then the Lord will take that fulness from them and bring it to the house of Israel (Native Americans) and the Gentiles will no longer have power over them (verses 6-12). However, if the Gentiles repent, they will be numbered among the house of Israel. But if they remain stubborn, then the Native Americans will "tread them down," for "this land" (America) is divinely marked to be the inheritance of these sons of Israel (verses 13-16).

After expounding this unique eschatological interpretation of John 10:16, Jesus' words continue to pick up phrases from John's Gospel. In chapter 17, Jesus declares that he would "go unto the Father" (compare John 14:28) and also show himself "unto the lost tribes of Israel" (verse 4). The multitude "did look steadfastly upon him as if they would ask him to tarry a little longer with them" (verse 5). Then "the multitude, with one accord, did go forth with their sick and their afflicted, and their lame, and with their blind, and with their dumb, and with all them that were afflicted in any manner; and he did heal them every one as they were brought forth unto him" (verse 9). They did "bow down at his feet, and did worship him [Jesus]; and as many as could come for the multitude did kiss his feet, insomuch that they did bathe his feet with their tears" (verse 10). Their little children were brought to Jesus, reported Third Nephi, and "Jesus groaned within himself" (verse 14; compare John 11:33) and prayed great and marvelous things. Then he beheld the multitude and said: "Blessed are ye because of your faith. And now behold, my joy is full" (verse 20) then "he wept" (verse 21; compare John 11:35). Jesus next "took their little children, one by one, and blessed them" (verse 21) and prayed for them (see also Matt. 19:13-15; Mark 10:13-16 and Luke 18:15-17).

The disciples in chapter 18 were then commanded to bring the sacramental bread and wine to be blessed. For the bread, Jesus is reported to have said "this shall ye do in remembrance of my body, which I have shown unto you" (verse 7) and for the wine, "ye shall do it in remembrance of my blood, which I have shed for you" (verse 11; compare Luke 22:19-20; Matt. 26:26-28; Mark

14:22-24 and 1 Cor. 11:23-26). Third Nephi then continues by presenting Jesus as uttering the following words:

And if ye shall always do these things blessed are ye, for ye are built upon my rock. But whoso among you shall do more or less than these are not built upon my rock, but are built upon a sandy foundation; and when the rain descends, and the floods come, and the winds blow, and beat upon them, they shall fall, and the gates of hell are ready open to receive them (verses 12-13; compare Matt. 7:24-27; Luke 6:47-49; Matt. 16:18).

According to Third Nephi, Jesus reportedly said concerning prayer: "ye must watch and pray always lest ye enter into temptation; for Satan desireth to have you, that he may sift you as wheat" (verse 18; compare Luke 22:31). To the disciples he further is reported to have said that they should "not suffer any one knowingly to partake of my flesh and blood unworthily, when ye shall minister it" (verse 28). Jesus here is basically following the instructions which Paul some twenty years later would issue in his Epistle to the Corinthians, which state:

Wherefore whosoever shall eat this bread, and drink this cup of the Lord, unworthily, shall be guilty of the body and blood of the Lord. But let a man examine himself, and so let him eat of that bread, and drink of that cup. For he that eateth and drinketh unworthily, eateth and drinketh damnation to himself, not discerning the Lord's body (1 Cor. 11:27-29; compare 3 Ne. 18:28-29).

After further instructions, Jesus "touched with his hand the disciples whom he had chosen, one by one" (verse 36) and gave them power to give the Holy Ghost (verse 37).

In chapter 19 of Third Nephi, it is explained that Jesus ascended into heaven after His supposed first visit. Echoing the appointment of the twelve apostles in Palestine, the names of the twelve Nephite disciples are recorded in the Book of Mormon in the following manner:

And it came to pass that on the morrow, when the multitude was gathered together, behold, Nephi and his brother whom he had raised from the dead, whose name was Timothy, and also his son, whose name was Jonas, and also Mathoni, and Mathonihah, his brother, and Kumen, and Kumenonhi, and Jeremiah, and Shemnon, and Jonas, and Zedekiah, and Isaiah - now these were the names of the disciples whom Jesus had chosen (19:4)

The twelve disciples of Third Nephi, like the New Testament twelve apostles, were listed with two sets of brothers and with two disciples that have the same name, e.g., in Third Nephi, "Jonas" (see Matt. 10:2-4; Mark 3:16-19; Luke 6:13-16 and Acts 1:13).

Nephi, one of the twelve disciples, then "went down into the water and was baptized. And he came up out of the water and began to baptize. And he baptized all those whom Jesus had chosen" (verses 11-12). This, and other passages emphasizing immersion as the proper mode of baptism, seems to assume the existence of some conflicting mode such as pouring or sprinkling. The Nephite doctrinal disputes resemble those in Joseph Smith's day.

On Jesus' second visit, the multitude knelt down and the disciples "did pray unto Jesus, calling him their Lord and their God" (19:18; compare John 20:28). Jesus departed and went to pray by himself. The prayer recorded is very similar to the high-priestly prayer of Jesus in the Holy Land, recorded only in the Gospel of John. Compare the prayer in Third Nephi (19:20, 23, 28-29) and the one written in John's Gospel (17:1, 6, 9-10, 20-21). Even the ending is identical with the words written by John: "And *when Jesus had spoken these words*" (19:30, emphasis added)— "When Jesus had spoken these words" (John 18:1).

These prayers of Jesus in Third Nephi seem clearly to be based upon the Gospel of John. The Jesus presented in Third Nephi is not unique to the Third Nephi text, but is taken right out of the New Testament, even down to borrowing the gospel writers words and phrases. This use of John evidences still another example of textual borrowing in the Third Nephi account.

In chapter 20 of Third Nephi, it is related that Jesus gave all those assembled to hear him both bread and wine, but "there had been no bread, neither wine, brought by the disciples, neither by the multitude" (verse 6), a story that seems close to that of the feeding of the five thousand when there was a need for the sharing of food (Matt. 14:14-21; Mark 6:34-44; Luke 9:11-17 and John 6:5-14). That this is sacramental bread and wine is indicated in verse 8.

It is explained, as Jesus' discourse continues in chapter 21, that the Gentiles shall assist the Native Americans ("the remnant of Jacob") and any other Israelites that might be willing to join in ("as many of the house of Israel as shall come") to "build a city, which shall be called the New Jerusalem" (21:23) These Gentiles will also assist Native Americans scattered across the face of the land in coming to this "New Jerusalem" (verse 24). Then the power of heaven and Jesus himself will come down among them (verse 25). Earlier, the land of America itself was to be "a New Jerusalem" (20:22), but this now was to be a specific city. Third Nephi, however, had this New Jerusalem not "coming down from God out of the heaven" as predicted in the Book of Revelations (Rev. 21:2; see also Rev. 3:12), but simply that "the power of heaven come down" and Jesus promises to "be in the midst" (3 Ne. 21:25).

In chapter 23 Jesus adds to the Nephite record textual material from the New Testament about the graves opening at the time of Christ's resurrection—material that is otherwise found only in the Gospel according to Matthew. These words were reported to have been spoken years earlier by an American prophet named Samuel as a prediction of what would happen at the time of Christ's death. This resurrection event is supposed to have taken place in America, but it is like what is recorded in Matthew, even to the wording used (compare Helaman 14:25; 3 Nephi 23:9, 11 with Matt. 27:52-53).

As Jesus continued his discourse, other New Testament phrases appear. Reflecting Peter's words, Third Nephi related that Jesus "did expound all things ... yea, even all things which should come upon the face of the earth, even until the *elements* should *melt with fervent heat*" (26:3, emphasis added; compare 2 Peter 3:10, 12). In a paraphrase of John 5:29 the writer has Jesus saying: "If they be good, to the resurrection of everlasting life; and if they be evil, to the resurrection of damnation" (26:5; see also Mosiah 16:11 and Helaman 12:26).

Like the New Testament words of Jesus, the Third Nephi multitude even saw that their children "yea, even babes did open their mouths and utter marvelous things" (26:16; compare Matt. 11:25; Luke 10:21). Furthermore, the response to Jesus' discourse was impressive, for many were baptized and "they who were baptized in the name of Jesus were called the church of Christ" (verse 21).

During the third visit of Jesus in Third Nephi, the record claims that Christ came to settle a dispute among the people concerning the name of the church.

> Verily, verily, I say unto you, why is it that the people should murmur and dispute because of this thing? Have they not read the scriptures, which say ye must take upon you the name of Christ, which is my name? For by this name shall ye be called at the last day; And whoso taketh upon him my name, and endureth to the end, the same shall be saved at the last day. Therefore, whatsoever ye shall do, ye shall do it in my name; therefore ye shall call the church in my name (27:4-7)

This concern regarding the proper name of the church was an issue during the 1820s. This may have influenced its inclusion as words Christ would have said.

The remainder of Jesus' discourse during his third visit reflects the same dependence upon the language and thought of the New Testament. Jesus taught that he "had been lifted up upon the cross, that I might draw all men unto me" (27:14; compare John 12:32). After assuring them that "whatsoever things ye shall ask the Father in my name shall be given unto you" (verse 28; compare John 15:16), Jesus then exhorts them, drawing ideas and wording from Matthew chapter 7 (compare 3 Ne. 27:29 with Matt. 7:7-8 [identical wording also in Luke 11:9-10] and 27:33 with Matt. 7:13-14).

Jesus finally asked the twelve disciples, "What is it that ye desire of me, after that I am gone to the Father?" (28:1; compare John 21:20-23, only in John). Nine of the American disciples desired that they live "unto the age of man" (verse 2) and Jesus said to them "after that ye are seventy and two years old ye shall come unto me in my kingdom" (verse 3). To the remaining three disciples he said, borrowing language from 1 Corinthians:

Behold, I know your thoughts, and ye have desired the thing which John, my beloved, who was with me in my ministry, before that I was lifted up by the Jews, desired of me. Therefore, more blessed are ye, for ye shall never taste of death . . . but when I shall come in my glory ye shall be changed in the twinkling of an eye from mortality to immortality (verses 6-8; compare 1 Cor. 15:51-53).

The three disciples were to "bring the souls of men unto" Jesus "while the world shall stand" (verse 9). Then Jesus "touched every one of them with his finger save it were the three who were to tarry, and then he departed" from his third and final visit among the American Israelites (verse 12). Third Nephi records the following regarding the three disciples who were to tarry on the earth:

Behold, I was about to write the names of those who were never to taste of death, but the Lord forbade; therefore I write them not, for they are hid from the world (28:25).[18]

And they are as the angels of God, and if they shall pray unto the Father in the name of Jesus they can show themselves unto whatsoever man it seemeth them good (28:30).[19]

---

[18] Oliver B. Huntington recorded the names of those three Nephites in his journal: "February 16—1895 I am willing to state that the names of the 3 Nephites who do not sleep in the earth are Jeremiah, Zedekiah and Kumenonhi" (Oliver B. Huntington Journal, Book 17:173, L. Tom Perry Special Collections, Harold B. Lee Library, Brigham Young University, Provo, Utah).

[19] This later led to an extensive body of Mormon folklore about the sighting of these three immortal messengers in various Mormon communities. See Hector Lee, *The Three Nephites: The Substance and Significance of the Legend in Folklore* (New York: Arno Press, 1977) and William A. Wilson, "Freeways, Parking Lots, and Ice Cream Stands: The Three Nephites in Contemporary Society," *Dialogue: A Journal of Mormon Thought* 21 (Autumn 1988):13-26.

The clear conclusion of this examination is that the King James Version of the New Testament text was used extensively in the composition of the book of Third Nephi in the Book of Mormon. The Sermon on the Mount given by Jesus during his ministry in the Old World was used to flesh out the idea that Christ had appeared to the ancient inhabitants of America. Other teachings of Jesus were adapted from different texts in the New Testament to provide content for an appearance of Jesus during the three day period that Third Nephi claims for the visitation of the resurrected Jesus.

This documentation of extensive textual borrowing from the New Testament writings indicates there is a serious problem in accepting Third Nephi as an accurate account. If Jesus appeared in the New World as the Book of Mormon would have us believe, then the textual problems it contains would lead to the conclusion that it is not an accurate record of that event.

LITERARY DEPENDENCE ON NINETEENTH CENTURY EVENTS

Once one sees how the Book of Mormon draws on the King James Bible, it is not difficult to detect other contemporary material. For example, the Book of Mormon is clearly familiar with American history, particularly events that had occurred prior to 1830 such as the voyage of Columbus and the European settling of America. Anachronisms are present in the text, since for example the Revolutionary War had already occurred prior to the dictation of the Book of Mormon text. First Nephi, chapter 13 is represented to contain a prophetic vision of events in American history. Known historical happenings from the past are written as prophecy to make it appear that they were known in vision two thousand years earlier. This is evident from the following extracts, with interpretation in brackets:[20]

---

[20] Some of these identifications are contained in the footnotes of the 1879 Salt Lake edition of the Book of Mormon. Orson Pratt, apostle and official LDS church historian, prepared the references for that edition.

I looked and beheld many waters [Atlantic Ocean]; and they divided the Gentiles [in Europe] from the seed of my brethren [Native Americans] (1 Ne. 13:10).

And I looked and beheld a man [Columbus] among the Gentiles [in Europe] . . . and he went forth upon the many waters [Atlantic Ocean], even to the seed of my brethren [Native Americans], who were in the promised land [America] (1 Ne. 13:12).

And it came to pass that I beheld the Spirit of God, that it wrought upon other Gentiles [Pilgrim fathers]; and they went forth out of captivity, upon the many waters [Atlantic Ocean]. . . . I beheld many multitudes of the Gentiles [Pilgrim fathers] upon the land of promise [America]; and I beheld the wrath of God, that it was upon the seed of my brethren [the Indians (Native Americans)]; and they were scattered before the Gentiles and were smitten [judgment on Native Americans]. . . . And I beheld their mother Gentiles [the British] were gathered together upon the waters, and upon the land also, to battle against them [Thirteen Colonies] . . . the wrath of God was upon all those that were gathered together against them to battle [the Revolutionary War, 1776-1781] (1 Ne. 13:13-14, 17-18).

the Gentiles [the United States] that had gone out of captivity were delivered by the power of God out of the hands of all other nations [probably the War of 1812] (1 Ne. 13:19)

The Book of Mormon also refers to the Bible being brought to America:

I beheld a book [Bible], and it was carried forth among them [Native Americans] (1 Ne. 13:20).

Neither will he suffer that the Gentiles [United States] shall destroy the seed of thy brethren [the Indians (Native Americans)] (1 Ne. 13:31).

192

And it came to pass that I beheld the remnant of the seed of my brethren, and also the book of the Lamb of God, which had proceeded forth from the mouth of the Jew, that it came forth from the Gentiles unto the remnant of the seed of my brethren [bringing the Bible and doing missionary work among Native Americans[21]] (1 Ne. 13:38).

The Book of Mormon's religious and historical setting takes place not in the Old World but in the New and reflects the popular pride that most citizens of the day felt for their new nation.[22] The following are some major themes relating to the place of America as developed in the Book of Mormon making the book unique.

A Choice Land

that after the waters had receded from off the face of this land it became a choice land above all other lands, a chosen land of the Lord (Ether 13:2)

we have obtained a land of promise, a land which is choice above all other lands (2 Ne. 1:5)

Hid from Knowledge of Other Nations

And behold, it is wisdom that this land should be kept as yet from the knowledge of other nations; for behold, many nations would overrun the land, that there would be no place for an inheritance (2 Ne. 1:8).

---

[21] In 1663 the Bible was printed in the Algonquin Indian language in Massachusetts. It had been translated into their language by John Eliot. The first English New Testament was published in America in 1777 and the Holy Bible in 1782.

[22] Hans Kohn, *The Idea of Nationalism* (New York: Collier Books, 1969), 269-70.

A Land of Promise

be led to a land of promise; yea, even a land which I have prepared for you; yea, a land which is choice above all other lands (1 Ne. 2:20)

Land of Liberty

he named all the land which was south of the land Desolation, yea, and in fine, all the land, both on the north and on the south—A chosen land, and the land of liberty (Alma 46:17).

Free from Bondage

Behold, this is a choice land, and whatsoever nation shall possess it shall be free from bondage, and from captivity, and from all other nations under heaven (Ether 2:12).

No Kings on the Land

And this land shall be a land of liberty unto the Gentiles, and there shall be no kings upon the land, who shall raise up unto the Gentiles (2 Ne. 10:11).

America is Zion

And I will fortify this land against all other nations. And he that figheth against Zion shall perish, saith God (2 Ne. 10:12-13).

And all the nations that fight against Zion, and that distress her, shall be as a dream of a night vision . . . even so shall the multitude of all nations be that fight against Mount Zion (2 Ne. 27:3).

Visits of Christ to America after His Crucifixion

3 Nephi chapters 11-28 (3 days)

194

New Jerusalem to be Built in America

> And that it was the place of the New Jerusalem, which
> should come down out of heaven, and the holy sanctuary of
> the Lord. . . . And that a New Jerusalem should be built
> upon this land, unto the remnant of the seed of Joseph, for
> which things there has been a type (Ether 13:3, 6).

The third decade of the nineteenth century, when the Book
of Mormon appeared, was also a period of theological controversy.
The book takes sides on various issues under discussion, as the
following extracts demonstrate. The Book of Mormon's position is
quoted and a contemporary adherent of the same point of view is
given:

Baptism by Immersion

> On this wise shall ye baptize; and there shall be no
> disputations among you. . . . Behold, ye shall go down and
> stand in the water, and in my name shall ye baptize them. . .
> . And then shall ye immerse them in the water, and come
> forth again out of the water. . . . And according as I have
> commanded you thus shall ye baptize. And there shall be
> no disputations among you, as there have hitherto been (3
> Ne. 11:22, 23, 26, 28).

> We baptize by immersion, because we think from all the
> evidence we can obtain upon this subject, it was the way or
> mode by which the ordinance was administered when first
> administered when first instituted, and afterwards practiced
> by the ancient christians (David Millard, ed., *Gospel
> Luminary* 1 [Oct. 1825]:221, West Bloomfield, Ontario
> County, New York).

> But I am now to show that *christian immersion*, as
> instituted by Jesus Christ, (not as corrupted by men,) is the
> gospel in *water* (*The Christian Baptist*, 1955 reprint; 5
> [Feb. 5, 1828]:165, Bethany, Virginia, emphasis retained).

Name of the Church

And they who were baptized in the name of Jesus were called the church of Christ. . . . And they said unto him: Lord, we will that thou wouldst tell us the name whereby we shall call this church; for there are disputations among the people concerning this matter. And the Lord said unto them: Verily, verily, I say unto you, why is it that the people should murmur and dispute because of this thing? . . . ye must take upon you the name of Christ . . . therefore ye shall call the church in my name . . . And how be it my church save it be called in my name? For if a church be called in Moses' name then it be Moses' church; or if it be called in the name of a man then it be the church of a man; but if it be called in my name then it is my church, if it so be that they are built upon my gospel (3 Ne. 26:21; 27:3-5, 7-8).

When we give a *name* and a *creed* to a church, other than the name of *Christ*, or *Christian*, and *the New Testament*, or *the Gospel*, that church acquires in our *imaginations* and *feelings*, and in *fact*, a character altogether different from what the *Church of Christ* really possesses in the light of the New Testament (*The Christian Baptist* 2 [July 4, 1825]:237, emphasis retained).

We, however, choose to be known by the name of Christian to the exclusion of all other names not found in the scriptures, this bring the most significant appellation of the followers of Christ, and agreeably to our views, given by divine appointment (*Gospel Luminary* 3 [Aug. 1827]:188, West Bloomfield, Ontario County, New York).

Baptism of Children

for it grieveth me that there should disputations rise among you. For, if I have learned the truth, there have been disputations among you concerning the baptism of your little children . . . . I know that it is solemn mockery before

God, that ye should baptize little children. . . . For awful is the wickedness to suppose that God saveth one child because of baptism, and the other must perish because he hath no baptism (Moro. 8:4-5, 9, 15)

The question of *infant baptism* is now generally discussed all over the land, and immense has been the result (*The Christian Baptist* 5 [Jan. 7, 1828]:138, emphasis retained).

Freemasonry: A Topic of Discussion

The abduction and probable murder of William Morgan in September 1826 caused many Americans to view Freemasonry as a dangerous threat. George Washington's warning about "all combinations and associations" in his Farewell Address became the anti-Masonic motto, "Beware of Secret Combinations." Masons were regarded as shedding innocent blood, binding themselves with oaths, and bent on preventing just punishment from coming upon a fellow Mason. Whether this violent reaction to Masonry was justified, the controversy is reflected in the Book of Mormon.

According to the Book of Mormon, at the time the book was to appear there would be "secret combinations." The words "secret combinations" did not always refer to Masons. But the following quotations, from the many that are in the Book of Mormon, illustrate this unmistakable anti-Masonic influence.

Secret Combinations

And it shall come in a day when the blood of saints shall cry unto the Lord, because of secret combinations and the works of darkness (Morm. 8:27).

"BEWARE OF SECRET COMBINATIONS." These are the dying words of General George Washington. . . . Do not these words . . . point with an index that cannot be mistaken, to the Society of Freemasons? (*The Morgan Investigator* 1 [March 29, 1827]:1, Batavia, New York).

197

Masonic Rites

And there are also secret combinations, even as in times of old, according to the combinations of the devil, for he is the founder of all these things; yea, the founder of murder, and works of darkness; yea, and he leadeth them by the neck with a flaxen cord, until he bindeth them with his strong cords forever (2 Ne. 26:22).

The candidate is then blindfolded, his left foot bare, his right in a slipper, his left breast and arm naked, and a rope called a Cable-tow round his neck . . . (William Morgan, *Illustrations of Masonry by One of the Fraternity who has devoted Thirty Years to the Subject* [Batavia, New York: Printed for the Author, 1826], 18).

I fancy those men are fastening a "Cable Tow" about their necks, which will have a more uncomfortable set than those they have worn in the lodge and which they will in all probability wear to their graves (*The Morgan Investigator* 1 [March 29, 1827]:2).

The principles of masonry are confessedly ancient. They can be traced back to the time when the first deceiver said, "Ye shall not surely die, for God doth know that in the day ye eat thereof, ye shall be as God's knowing good and evil." . . . Freemasonry, without controversy, is the very master-piece of pandemonium. By means of these hidden mysteries, Satan has strangely outdone himself (*Republican Monitor* 6 [Nov. 23, 1828]:1, Cazenovia, New York).

Secret Signs and Words

And it came to pass that they did have their signs, yea, their secret signs, and their secret words; and this that they might distinguish a brother who had entered into the covenant, that whatsoever wickedness his brother should do he should not be injured by his brother, nor by those who did belong to his band, who had taken this covenant (Hel. 6:22).

As the signs, due-guards, grips, words, pass-words, and their several names comprise pretty much all the secrets of Masonry (William Morgan, *Illustrations of Masonry*, 55).

to protect their brethren from the lash of the civil laws . . . whether guilty or not guilty, treason and murder not excepted; and although they may be obliged to swear falsely to clear the guilty brother, they must do it, or incur the penalty of secret death (William W. Phelps, ed., *The Ontario Phoenix* 1 [Sept. 17, 1828]:2, Canandaigua, New York).

Masonic oaths were intended to screen criminal masons and enable them to elude public justice. The expectations of escaping the strong arm of the law, emboldens them to the commission of the most daring deeds of iniquity. The life of every Freemason is awfully pledged in defence [defense] of the brotherhood and the mysteries of the order. Hence it is extremely difficult to bring criminal masons to justice (*Republican Monitor* 6 [Nov. 23, 1828]:1).

Contrary to the Laws of God and Country

And thus they might murder, and plunder, and steal, and commit whoredoms and all manner of wickedness, contrary to the laws of their country and also the laws of their God (Hel. 6:23).

Masonry is a murderous institution. It is based on laws which require murder. Those laws which support the system, demand and take the life of a fellow creature, without any reference to the laws of God or the land . . . Who then does not see, that the very principles, spirit, and essence, of this ancient fraternity, are murderous! (John G. Stearns, *An Inquiry into the Nature and Tendency of Speculative Free-Masonry*, 1829 ed., 76).

that dark and treasonable plot, formed against the lives of our citizens and the laws of our country (*The Morgan Investigator* 1 [March 29, 1827]:2).

Native Americans of Hebrew Origin

The Book of Mormon asserts that Native Americans are of Hebrew descent, specifically from one of the lost tribes (Joseph), and uses the Old Testament to support this.[23] However, the idea that the American Indians were descendants of the Hebrews was a common one in early America before the Book of Mormon was published.

Since the discovery of America, many people had published various theories about the origins of the native Indians. The idea that their ancestors were of Hebrew origin was widely published in both Europe and America. This theory was not universally held but it was popular among religious leaders. The following works were among the most popular expressing the Hebrew origin of the Indians at the period before the publication of the Book of Mormon in 1830:

Thomas Thorowgood. *Jews in America, or, Probabilities that the Americans are of that Race*. London, 1650.

James Adair. *The History of the American Indians*. London, 1775.

---

[23] Those scholars who have studied the Solomon Spalding manuscript have noticed similarity in style and wording on some religious issues and sections relating to wars in that manuscript and in the Book of Mormon. See Vernal Holley, *Book of Mormon Authorship: A Closer Look* (Roy, Utah: author, 1989, 2nd ed.), which utilizes this material. Though of a different nature, Ethan Smith's *View of the Hebrews* includes topics that occur in the Book of Mormon. We should not be surprised that similar ideas are contained in a written document produced about the same time. At the time these writings were recorded it was widely believed that Indians were of the stock of Israel. Over the years we have learned that there is no solid evidence of Hebrew origin of Native Americans. The writings of B. H. Roberts are included in Brigham D. Madsen, ed., *Studies of the Book of Mormon* (Urbana: University of Illinois Press, 1985). See also David Persuitte, *Joseph Smith and the Origins of The Book of Mormon* (Jefferson, North Carolina: McFarland & Company, 2nd ed., 2000).

Charles Crawford. *An Essay upon the Propagation of the Gospel, in which there are facts to prove that many of the Indians in America are descended from the Ten Tribes.* Philadelphia, 1799.

Elias Boudinot. *A Star in the West; or, a Humble Attempt to Discover the Long Lost Tribes of Israel.* Trenton, New Jersey: Published by D. Fenton, S. Hutchinson, and J. Dunham, 1816.

Ethan Smith. *View of the Hebrews.* Poultney, Vermont: Printed and Published by Smith & Shute, 1823.

_____. *View of the Hebrews; or, the Tribes of Israel in America.* Poultney, Vermont: Published and Printed by Smith & Shute, 1825, 2d ed.

Josiah Priest. *The Wonders of Nature and Providence Displayed.* Albany, New York, 1825.

Some writers argued that Native Americans descended from the Ten Lost Tribes of Israel because of similarities between customs and languages. Others saw Christian ideas among the American Indians and believed that Christianity had been taught to them since the first century of the Christian era.[24] The idea was so important that writers of that period published lengthy books on the topic. Indeed, it was one of the most popular views at the time the Book of Mormon came off the press.[25]

---

[24] In 1816 Elias Boudinot claimed that the ancestors of the Native Americans had at least part of the Bible, "that the book which the white people have was once theirs" (Elias Boudinot, *A Star in the West*, 110). In this same year Boudinot founded the American Bible Society.

[25] On books published prior to 1830 on the origin of Native Americans, see George Weiner, "America's Jewish Braves," *Mankind* 4 (Oct. 1974):56-64; David A. Palmer, "A Survey of Pre-1830 Historical Sources Relating to the Book of Mormon," *Brigham Young University Studies* 17 (Autumn 1976):101-107; and Dan Vogel, *Indian Origins and the Book of Mormon* (Salt Lake City: Signature Books, 1986).

Events in life of Joseph Smith

Joseph Smith wrote the following about his youth: "by searching the scriptures I found that <mankind> did not come unto the Lord but that they had apostatised from the true and liveing faith and there was no society or denomination that built upon the gospel of Jesus Christ as recorded in the new testament."[26] This view finds expression in the Book of Mormon.

> And the Gentiles are lifted up in the pride of their eyes, and have stumbled, because of the greatness of their stumbling block, that they have built up many churches; nevertheless, they put down the power and miracles of God, and preach up unto themselves their own wisdom and their own learning, that they may get gain and grind upon the face of the poor. And there are many churches built up which cause envyings, and strifes, and malice (2 Ne. 26:20-21).

> For it shall come to pass in that day that the churches which are built up, and not unto the Lord, when the one shall say unto the other: Behold, I, I am the Lord's; and the others shall say: I, I am the Lord's; and thus shall every one say that hath built up churches, and not unto the Lord—And they shall contend one with another; and their priests shall contend one with another, and they shall teach with their learning, and deny the Holy Ghost, which giveth utterance. . . . Yea, they have all gone out of the way; they have become corrupted. Because of pride, and because of false teachers, and false doctrine, their churches have become corrupted, and their churches are lifted up; because of pride they are puffed up (2 Ne. 28:3-4, 11-12).

Joseph Smith was personally familiar with such religious controversies from his own active participation in his youth. His

---

[26] Jessee, *Papers of Joseph Smith*, 1:5. See Gordon S. Wood, "Evangelical America and Early Mormonism," *New York History* 61 (Oct. 1980):359-86.

early history mentions his quest for religious knowledge and "my intimate acquaintance with those different denominations."[27]

Also Joseph Smith believed in, and was a leading participant in, treasure seeking. His examination before Justice Albert Neely showed that this had been part of his early development in life. Jonathan Thompson testified in 1826 that Smith helped find a trunk full of treasure, but it kept "settling away" and they never could get it: "the board which he struck his spade upon was probably the chest, but on account of an enchantment the trunk kept settling away from under them while digging; that notwithstanding they continued constantly removing the dirt, yet the trunk kept about the same distance from them."[28] This idea of treasures slipping into the earth is reflected in the Book of Mormon.

> whoso shall hide up treasures in the earth shall find them again no more, because of the great curse of the land, save he be a righteous man and shall hide it up unto the Lord. For I will, saith the Lord, that they shall hide up their treasures unto me; and cursed be they who hide not up their treasures unto me; for none hideth up their treasures unto me save it be the righteous (Hel. 13:18-19)

> And behold, the time cometh that he curseth your riches, that they become slippery, that ye cannot hold them; and in the days of your poverty ye cannot retain them. . . . Yea, we have hid up our treasures and they have slipped away from us, because of the curse of the land. O that we had repented in the day that the word of the Lord came unto us; for behold the land is cursed, and all things are become slippery, and we cannot hold them. Behold, we are surrounded by demons, yea, we are encircled about by the angels of him who hath sought to destroy our souls (Hel. 13:31, 35-37).

---

[27] Jessee, *Papers of Joseph Smith* 1:5.

[28] Charles Marshall, "The Original Prophet. By a Visitor to Salt Lake City," *Fraser's Magazine* 7 (Feb. 1873):230. According to the Book of Mormon, Joseph Smith was instructed to hide up the book unto the Lord (see 2 Ne. 27:22; 30:3-5).

the inhabitants thereof began to hide up their treasures in the earth; and they became slippery, because the Lord had cursed the land, that they could not hold them, nor retain them again (Mormon 1:18).

Not only is Joseph Smith's treasure digging reflected in the Book of Mormon, but other events in which Joseph was involved show up there, after the events had already taken place. As discussed in chapter 7 the account of Martin Harris' visit to Charles Anthon of New York City was reportedly told by Harris to Joseph Smith. This trip occurred about February 1828. In the Book of Mormon this incident is mentioned but some of its features are different. This trip is discussed in the Book of Mormon. 2 Nephi 27:15-20 contains an expanded commentary on Isaiah 29, and in relation to this specific event expands Isaiah 29:11-12 as follows:

But behold, it shall come to pass that the Lord God shall say unto him to whom he shall deliver the book: Take these words which are not sealed and deliver them to another, that he may show them unto the learned, saying: Read this, I pray thee. And the learned shall say: Bring hither the book, and I will read them. . . . And the man shall say: I cannot bring the book, for it is sealed. Then shall the learned say: I cannot read it. Wherefore it shall come to pass, that the Lord God will deliver again the book and the words thereof to him that is not learned; and the man that is not learned shall say: I am not learned (2 Ne. 27:15, 17-19).

These changes in Isaiah 29 prophesy of an event that had already occurred to Martin Harris. There is no ancient text of Isaiah, either Hebrew (including the Dead Sea Scrolls) or in any ancient translation that supports Joseph Smith's changes that make the passage fit the incident that occurred early in 1828.[29] The

---

[29] For an examination of Isaiah 29 in the Book of Mormon, see Wesley P. Walters, *The Use of the Old Testament in the Book of Mormon* (Salt Lake City: Utah Lighthouse Ministry, 1990), 75-88. For a study on the use of Ezekiel 37, see Brian E. Keck, "Ezekiel 37, Sticks, and Babylonian Writing Boards: A Critical Reappraisal," *Dialogue: A Journal of Mormon Thought* 23 (Spring 1990):126-38.

above example shows Martin Harris' adventure being described in prophecy and was included in the Book of Mormon text. Professor Anthon wrote that he did not promise "to decipher the piece of writing in question—if the original records were brought to me."[30]

In March 1829, while working on the Book of Mormon, Joseph Smith stated there would be three special witnesses to the book. In a revelation for Joseph and Martin Harris received in Harmony, Pennsylvania, Smith was told:

> this Generation they shall have my word yea & the testimony of three of my servants shall go forth with my word unto this Generation yea three shall know of a surety that those things are true for I will give them power that they may Behold & view those things as they are & to none else will I grant this power among this Generation & the testimony of three Witnesses will I send forth[31]

When Joseph Smith recommenced his dictation he included in the text references to three witnesses who would testify of the Book of Mormon.

> Wherefore, at that day when the book shall be delivered unto the man of whom I have spoken, the book shall be hid from the eyes of the world, that the eyes of none shall behold it save it be that three witnesses shall behold it, by the power of God, besides him to whom the book shall be delivered; and they shall testify to the truth of the book and the things therein. And there is none other which shall view it, save it be a few according to the will of God (2 Ne. 27:12-13)

---

[30] Anthon to "Rev. and Dear Sir," Aug. 12, 1844, in *New-York Observer* 23 (May 3, 1845):69, New York.

[31] Marquardt, *Joseph Smith Revelations*, 27-28; BC 4:4; LDS D&C 5:11-15; RLDS D&C 5:3. Joseph Smith was further instructed, "when thou hast translated a few more pages, thou shalt stop for a season, even until I command thee again: then thou mayest translate again."

In one place instructions in the text inform him that he may "show the plates unto those who shall assist to bring forth this work."

And behold, ye may be privileged that ye may show the plates unto those who shall assist to bring forth this work; And unto three shall they be shown by the power of God; wherefore they shall know of a surety that these things are true. And in the mouth of three witnesses shall these things be established; and the testimony of three, and this work, in the which shall be shown forth the power of God and also his word, of which the Father, and the Son, and the Holy Ghost bear record—and all this shall stand as a testimony against the world at the last day (Ether 5:2-4).

The three witnesses chosen to view the gold plates were Oliver Cowdery, David Whitmer, and Martin Harris. Cowdery had seen the plates in a vision before meeting Joseph Smith.[32] In June 1829 they were told that by faith they would see them, even as Joseph Smith had seen them.[33] The testimony of the three witnesses, as published in the Book of Mormon, said that they saw an angel and engravings on the plates.

Martin Harris, the oldest witness, emphasized that his experience of seeing the plates was through the eye of faith as the 1829 revelation stated. John H. Gilbert recorded: "Martin was in the office when I finished setting up the testimony of the three witnesses,—(Harris—Cowdery and Whitmer) I said to him,—'Martin, did you see those plates with your naked eyes?' Martin looked down for an instant, raised his eyes up, and said, 'No, I saw them with a spiritual eye.'"[34]

---

[32] Jessee, *Papers of Joseph Smith* 1:10.

[33] Marquardt, *Joseph Smith Revelations*, 49; LDS D&C 17; RLDS D&C 15. This revelation, given previous to the three witnesses "having a view of the plates &c," was not included in the Book of Commandments but was published as sections 42 in the 1835 D&C. The "Manuscript History of Joseph Smith" mentions the circumstances of two visions relating to the three witnesses viewing the plates (Jessee, *Papers of Joseph Smith* 1:236-37, 295-97).

[34] Memorandum of John H. Gilbert, Sept. 8, 1892, introductory pages of *Joseph Smith Begins His Work*, Vol. 1 (Salt Lake City: Deseret News Press for Wilford C. Wood, 1958). In 1838 Martin Harris stated that he "never saw the plates with

David Whitmer wrote, "Of course we were in the spirit when we had the view, for no man can behold the face of an angel, except in a spiritual view, but we were in the body also, and everything was as natural to us, as it is at any time."[35] Oliver Cowdery reportedly handled the plates, "I beheld with my eyes And handled with my hands, the gold plates from which it was translated."[36]

Besides the three witnesses, eight other witnesses said Joseph Smith showed them the plates. Their statement records that they handled and lifted the plates. John Whitmer for instance wrote, "I have most assuredly seen the plates from whence the book of Mormon is translated, and that I have handled these plates."[37] Three years later he was reported as saying, "I handled those plates there was fine engravings on both sides. I handled them . . . they were shown to me by a supernatural power."[38] The testimonies of the witnesses to the Book of Mormon said that they saw an angel and viewed or handled the plates by faith.

The March 1829 revelation to Harris said of Joseph Smith, "he has a gift to translate the book, and I have commanded him that he shall pretend to no other gift, for I will grant him no other gift."[39] Smith's only gift was to translate the Book of Mormon. Like the previous examples, this restriction was made part of the Book of Mormon text:

---

his natural eyes only in vision or imagination" (Letter of Stephen Burnett to Lyman E. Johnson, April 15, 1838, Joseph Smith Letterbook 2:64, LDS archives).

[35] David Whitmer to Anthony Metcalf, April 2, 1887, in A. Metcalf, *Ten Years Before the Mast* (Malad City, Idaho, 1888), 74; also in Lyndon W. Cook, ed., *David Whitmer Interviews: A Restoration Witness* (Orem, Utah: Grandin Book, 1991), 247.

[36] Reuben Miller Journal, Oct. 21, 1848, LDS archives.

[37] *Latter Day Saints' Messenger and Advocate* 2 (March 1836):286-87, Kirtland, Ohio.

[38] Theodore Turley's memoranda, under date of April 4, 1839, handwriting of Thomas Bullock (1845), LDS archives; copied into Manuscript History Book C-1, 913, under date of April 5, 1839. See *History of the Church* 3:307.

[39] BC 4:2; LDS D&C 5:4; RLDS D&C 5:1. See Marquardt, *Joseph Smith Revelations*, 29-31 for commentary on this revelation.

And I will give unto him a commandment that he shall do none other work, save the work which I shall command him. And I will make him great in mine eyes; for he shall do my work (2 Ne. 3:8).

Joseph Smith was to "do none other work" but produce the Book of Mormon. After the publication of the Book of Mormon the young prophet commenced revising the Bible. This would be considered a gift going beyond his initial commandment.

Joseph Smith was named after his father and included his own name in the text of the Book of Mormon. In a prophecy attributed to the biblical Joseph, who was sold into Egypt, it reports that a choice seer would be called in the last days:

And thus prophesied Joseph, saying: Behold, that seer will the Lord bless; and they that seek to destroy him shall be confounded . . . And his name shall be called after me [Joseph of Egypt]; and it shall be after the name of his father [Joseph Smith Sr.] (2 Ne. 3:14-15).

Lucius Fenn wrote a letter in February 1830 and told what he had heard about the Book of Mormon and the man that is to find the book is to be named Joseph. Fenn stated:

[T]hey are a printing it in Palmyra it is expected that it <will> come out soon so that we can see it it speaks of the Millenniam [sic] day and tells when it is going to take plais [place] and it tells that the man that is to find this bible his name as [is] Joseph and his father[']s name is Joseph.[40]

The story of the gold plates was the vehicle that Joseph Smith used as a minister to preach his new emphasis on Jesus. Smith taught that at one time he had in his possession an ancient record of peoples who lived on the American continent more than

---

[40] Lucius Fenn to Birdseye Bronson, Feb. 12, 1830, William Robertson Coe Collection of Western Americana, Beinecke Rare Book and Manuscript Library, Yale University, New Haven, Connecticut. See William Mulder and A. Russell Mortensen, eds., *Among the Mormons: Historic Accounts by Contemporary Observers* (Lincoln: University of Nebraska Press, 1958), 28.

fifteenth hundred years earlier. Believers had faith that Smith was able to recover a record or set of gold plates. The purpose of Smith in his story was to make men and women believe as strong as gold in his role as God's minister of salvation. Whether Smith had visions about the gold plates, whether he at one time had them in his possession, or whether anyone saw the physical plates was not important as to what he was trying to accomplish. The message of the Book of Mormon, through the use of metal plates, was for others to believe in the Jesus who spoke to Native Americans and who speaks to Joseph Smith.

The Book of Mormon reflects events that had already occurred before the time of its publication, some of which Joseph Smith was directly involved in. Its stand on theological controversies of the 1820s made it an appealing bid as a revelation illuminating the Bible.[41] However, it also contains ideas on America, Masonry, the proper name of the Christian church, and events connected with Joseph Smith's life. These and other contemporary events and ideas prevalent at the time of its production are found in its pages.[42] The Book of Mormon evidences a nineteenth-century origin and can be identified as an example of early American religious fiction.

One of the ideas relating to the text of the Book of Mormon is saying that it is impossible for Joseph Smith to have written the book since he was unlearned at the time. This is not an accurate assessment of the education of the young prophet. Learning in the Smith home included Bible reading in addition to family and individual prayer. Lucy Mack Smith was an important influence on her family as they conducted family worship. Joseph Sr. led the family in singing and prayer as the head of the household. His

---

[41] See Timothy L. Smith, "The Book of Mormon in a Biblical Culture," *Journal of Mormon History* 7 (1980):3-21; Nathan O. Hatch, *The Democratization of American Christianity* (New Haven, Connecticut: Yale University Press, 1989), 113-22; and Alan Taylor, "The Free Seekers: Religious Culture in Upstate New York, 1790-1835," *Journal of Mormon History* 27 (Spring 2001):42-66.

[42] For additional pre-1830 published and contemporary ideas that are a background to the religious thoughts of this period, see Rick Grunder, *Mormon Parallels* (Ithaca, New York.: Rick Grunder Books, 1987).

experience as a school teacher would help as he instructed especially the male children in transacting farm business.

It should be remembers that Joseph Smith attended additional schooling when he was twenty years old. The narratives in the Book of Mormon are based upon how religion was reportedly practiced in ancient America. What is taught in the record is an indication of how Smith as a religious seer perceived the way the ancestors of Native Americans preached and battled. With the KJV Bible as his standard source text Joseph Smith projected his own religious beliefs into the Book of Mormon. This is an important clue to its authenticity as a nineteenth century work. It is what would be expected in a new book.

The Bible was an influential book in American life when Joseph Smith commenced his work. Joseph's gift was to incorporate his theological understanding into the material he was writing. He did not need the plates of gold to produce the Book of Mormon. He used Isaiah and Matthew to supplement his writing of the origin of Native Americans ending with two battles of heretofore unknown civilizations in Manchester, Ontario County, New York.

The published Book of Mormon projected Smith into a world that was skeptical of strange ideas and newly found religions. The majority of reviews about the Book of Mormon were negative. With religious freedom being one of the cornerstones of American democracy individuals could believe a new book as history even though it is a fictional book. What became important was not the book itself but the belief that Joseph Smith was a modern seer and prophet.

10

Restoring the Church of Christ

By March 26, 1830 5,000 copies of the Book of Mormon had been printed. Baptisms had been performed in May and June 1829, but no formal ecclesiastical organization had yet occurred.[1] In late March Joseph Knight drove Joseph Smith Jr. from Harmony, Pennsylvania, to the home of his father and brother Hyrum in Manchester. Knight later recalled that on the way Smith talked about anticipated success in selling the books and about organizing a church:

Now in the Spring of 1830 I went with my Team and took Joseph out to Manchester to his Fathers when we was on our way he told me that there must be a Church formed But Did not tell when. Now when we got near to his fathers we Saw a man Some Eighty Rods Before us run acros[s] the Street with a Bundle in his hand. there Says Joseph there is martin going a Cros [across] the road with Some thing in his hand Says I how Could you know him So far[?] Says he I Believe it is him and when we Came up it was Martin with a Bunch of morman [mormon] Books he Came to us and after Compliments he Says the Books will not sell[.] for no Body wants them Joseph Says I think they will Sell well Says he [Martin] l want a Commandment Why[?] Says Joseph fullfill what you have got But says he [Martin] I must have a Commandment Joseph put him off But he insisted three or four times he must have a Commandment . . . in the morning he got up and Said he must have a Commandment to Joseph and went home. and along in the after part of the Day Joseph and oliver Received a

---

[1] Marquardt, *Joseph Smith Revelations*, 41; BC 9:17; LDS D&C 10:67-68; RLDS D&C 3:16; see also BC 15:1.

[2] Joseph Knight Reminiscences, LDS archives. See Jessee, "Joseph Knight's Recollection," 36-37. The distance of eighty rods equals 1,320 feet or a quarter

Commandment[2]

The title of the revelation as printed stated: "A commandment of God and not of man to you, Martin, given (Manchester, New-York, March, 1830,) by him who is eternal."[3] Knight stayed at the Smiths' residence a few days waiting for more copies of the Book of Mormon to be bound.

As Joseph Smith had predicted to Knight, the "Church of Christ" was organized very soon thereafter—on April 6, 1830. Traditional accounts locate this meeting at the home of Peter Whitmer Sr. in Fayette, New York. No minutes of the meeting have survived, but the earliest accounts and supporting evidence suggest the event occurred not at Fayette but in the Smiths' log home in Manchester.

The Book of Commandments, published in 1833, contained a collection of six revelations dated April 6, 1830, given to six individuals who attended the organizational meeting: Oliver Cowdery, Hyrum Smith, Samuel H. Smith, Joseph Smith Sr., Joseph Knight Sr., and Joseph Smith Jr. himself. These revelations were received, according to their headings, at Manchester. A round trip between Manchester and Fayette being fifty miles, it is unlikely the same six men could have attended an organizational meeting in Fayette on the same day. The revelations were first arranged and copied by Joseph Smith with the assistance of John Whitmer in July 1830 at Harmony, Pennsylvania, and later became chapters 2-27 of the Book of Commandments. On July 20, 1833 the press printing the revelations in book form was destroyed, but several of the yet-to-be-completed Book of Commandments were put together and used by early ministers of the church.[4]

In addition, all references in *The Evening and the Morning Star* before 1834 refer to the township of Manchester as the location of the church's organization.[5] For example, the following account of church origins appeared in April 1833:

---

of a mile.

[3] Marquardt, *Joseph Smith Revelations*, 51; BC 16; LDS D&C 19; RLDS D&C 18 (March [26-31], 1830).

[4] Marquardt, *Joseph Smith Revelations*, 3-7.

[5] *The Evening and the Morning Star* 1 (March 1833):4 [p. 76] and 1 (April 1833):4 [p. 84], Independence, Missouri.

Soon after the book of Mormon came forth, containing the fulness of the gospel of Jesus Christ, the church was organized on the sixth of April, in Manchester; soon after, a branch was established in Fayette, and the June following, another in Colesville, New York. We shall not give, at this time, the particulars attending the organization of these branches of the church. . . . Twenty more [converts] were added to the church in Manchester and Fayette, in the month of April; and on the 28th of June, thirteen were baptized in Colesville. . . . In October, (1830) the number of disciples had increased to between seventy and eighty.[6]

As we have seen in previous chapters, the Smith home had become the center for many of the events associated with Joseph Smith's emerging religious vocation until the Smiths moved to Waterloo, New York, in the fall of 1830. William Smith remembered the organizational meeting being in Manchester. Although William seems to be incorrect in some of his recollections, he mentions that his family "went to my brother Hyrum's house" in 1829 and that "It was in this house that the first conference [sic] of the Church of Jesus Christ of Latter Day Saints [sic] was held, on the 6th day of April, 1830, at which I was present."[7]

Joseph Knight Sr. was staying with the Smiths when the church was organized. A neighbor and friend of the family, Benjamin Saunders, said the "<Smiths> held meetings at their house." Saunders mentioned that he was present at the baptisms and he probably would not have gone out of his way to travel to Fayette for the occasion.[8]

Early references refer to six founding members.[9] As to the identity of the six members present at the foundational meeting, two early lists made in 1842-43 exist. It is possible there may have

---

[6] Ibid., 1 (April 1833):4 [p. 84]; see also *Evening and Morning Star*, Kirtland, Ohio, reprint, April 1833 (published June 1836), 167.
[7] William Smith, *William Smith on Mormonism*, 14.
[8] Interview of Benjamin Saunders, 1884, 27, RLDS archives. See Vogel, *Early Mormon Documents* 2:138-39.
[9] *The Evening and the Morning Star* 1 (Jan. 1833):1 [p. 57]; and 1 (March 1833):4 [p. 76].

been no actual roll call made at the time and the names on the lists have slight variations. Brigham Young writing in 1843 identifies "The names of thouse [those] present at the organization" on April 6, 1830 as Joseph Smith Sr., Orrin Rockwell, Joseph Smith, Hyrum Smith, Samuel H. Smith, and Oliver Cowdery.[10] Jonathan Turner's *Mormonism in All Ages*, published in 1842, list is essentially the same as Young's except that Joseph Knight is mentioned rather than Orrin Rockwell.[11] By Knight's account, we know he was there, but he did not receive baptism on this day. The names mentioned in Joseph Smith's manuscript history of the church included Joseph Smith, Oliver Cowdery, Joseph Smith Sr., Lucy Smith, Martin Harris, and a member of the Rockwell family, Sarah Rockwell. It is unlikely that Lucy Smith or Sarah Rockwell would be counted as one of the original six though they were present. More likely, the six original members were Joseph Smith, Oliver Cowdery, Hyrum Smith, Samuel H. Smith, Joseph Smith Sr., and Martin Harris.[12] Years later, around 1858, several other lists were compiled reporting those baptized in May-June 1829 or having been present at the April 6 meeting.[13]

The revelation received by Joseph Smith during the founding organizational meeting itself (printed as chapter 22) was headed "A Revelation to Joseph, given in Manchester, New-York, April 6, 1830."[14] This was changed in later editions to Fayette. Hyrum Smith was told:

A Revelation to Hyrum, given in Manchester, New-York, April 6, 1830. Behold I speak unto you, Hyrum, a few words: For thou also art under no condemnation, and thy

---

[10] Brigham Young Journal, page with date of Oct. 7, 1843, LDS archives.

[11] J[onathan]. B. Turner, *Mormonism in All Ages* (New York: Published by Platt & Peters, 1842), 22.

[12] William E. McLellin, ed., *The Ensign of Liberty* 1 (March 1847):2, Kirtland, Ohio. William E. McLellin includes Lucy Smith and Martin Harris in his list.

[13] See Kenney, *Wilford Woodruff's Journal*, 5:239-40, entry for November 18, 1858; copy of a statement dated August 11, 1862 in Manuscript History of the Church, Book A-1, between pages 36 and 37; see *History of the Church* 1:76, note; Diary of Edward Stevenson, entries for Dec. 22, 1877 and Jan. 2, 1887, LDS archives; Cook, *David Whitmer Interviews*, 11, 214; *Ensign* 10 (June 1980):44-45 and (Oct. 1980):71.

[14] BC 22; LDS D&C 21; RLDS D&C 19 (April 6, 1830).

heart is opened, and thy tongue loosed; And thy calling is to exhortation, and to strengthen the church continually. Wherefore thy duty is unto the church forever; and this because of thy family. Amen.[15]

Circumstantial evidence places Hyrum Smith in the Palmyra-Manchester vicinity. He signed a note to Levi Daggett of Palmyra on April 7.[16] As mentioned others receiving revelations in Manchester the same day included Oliver Cowdery, Samuel Harrison Smith, and Joseph Smith Sr. Unlike the others, Joseph Knight's revelation exhorted him to "unite with the true church." He later wrote, "But I Should a felt Better if I had a gone forward But I went home and was Babtised in June with my wife and familey."[17] Knight later recalled details regarding the exhortations and instructions which were part of the activities:

On the sixth Day of April 1830 he Begun the Church with six members and received the following Revelation, Book of Covenants [1835 ed.] Page 177. They all kneeld down and prayed and Joseph gave them instructions how to B[u]ild up the Church and ex[h]orted them to Be faithful in all things for this is the work of God.[18]

The revelation to Smith instructed him to proceed with the first ordinations.[19] He ordained Oliver Cowdery an elder, and Cowdery ordained Smith a seer, translator, prophet, apostle, and first elder in the Church of Christ. Cowdery became the second elder. Joseph Smith's ordination as prophet and seer was the highlight ordinance on the day of the church's organization.

---

[15] BC 18:1-4; LDS D&C 23:3; RLDS D&C 21:2.

[16] Nathan Pierce Docket Book, 1827-30, June 8, 1830, facing page 77, located at Manchester Town Office.

[17] Joseph Knight Reminiscences.

[18] Ibid. The revelation was section 46 in the 1835 D&C; LDS D&C 21; RLDS D&C 19. When published in the 1835 D&C, this document did not indicate where it was received. In BC 22 the heading stated: "A Revelation to Joseph, given in Manchester, New-York, April 6, 1830" (45). The Manuscript History written in 1839 changes this for the first time to "Given at Fayette" (Jessee, *Papers of Joseph Smith* 1:303).

[19] BC 22:1, 13-14; LDS D&C 21:1, 10-11; RLDS D&C 19:1, 3 (April 6, 1830).

William E. McLellin, who visited Oliver Cowdery in July 1847, wrote: "While I was on a visit with O. Cowdery, during the past summer, I asked him, to what did you ordain Joseph on the 6th of April, 1830? He answered, I ordained him to be a Prophet, Seer, &c., just as the revelation says."[20]

It was within this context that the April 6 revelation gave directions to members of the new church regarding its preeminent leader: "Wherefore, meaning the church, thou shalt give heed unto all his [Joseph's] words, and commandments, which he shall give unto you, as he receiveth them, walking in all holiness before me: For his word ye shall receive, as if from mine own mouth, in all patience and faith."[21] Members were promised that if they obeyed, the gates of hell would not prevail against them, God would disperse the powers of darkness before them, and he would shake the heavens for their good.

At least four persons seem to have been baptized as part of the activities surrounding the organization. Knight describes two of the four baptisms, the baptisms of Joseph Smith Sr., and Martin Harris:

I had Be[e]n there Several Days Old Mr Smith and Martin Harris Come forrod [forward] to Be Babtise [Baptized] for the first they found a place in a Lot a Small Stream ran thro and they ware Baptized in the Evening Because of persecution they went forward and was Babtized [Baptized] Being the first I saw Babtized in the new and everlasting Covenant . . . there was one thing I will mention that evening that old Brother Smith and Martin Harris was Babtised Joseph was fild [filled] with the Spirrit to a grate [great] Degree to See his Father and Mr Harris that he had Bin [Been] with So much he Bast [burst] out with greaf [grief] and Joy and Seamed [Seemed] as tho the world Could not hold him he went out into the Lot and appear[e]d to want to git [get] out of Site [Sight] of every Body and would Sob and Crie [Cry] and Seamed [Seemed] to Be So full that he Could not Live oliver and I went after him and

---

[20] William E. McLellin, ed., *The Ensign of Liberty* 1 (Dec. 1847):42.
[21] BC 22:2-5; LDS D&C 21:2-4; RLDS D&C 19: 1-2.

Came to him and after a while he Came in But he was the most wrot [wrought] upon that I ever Saw any man But his Joy Seemed to Be full[22]

Lucy Smith's narrative is similar:

In the spring Joseph came up <and preached to us> after <Oliver got throu[g]h> with the Book. <My Husband and> and Martin H[a]rris was ba[p]tized. Joseph stood on the shore when his father came out of the water and as he took him by the hand, he cried out, Oh! my God I have lived to see my father baptized into the true church of Jesus Christ and <he> covered his face <in his father's bosom and wept aloud for joy as did> Joseph of old when he beheld his father coming up into the land of Egypt, this took pla<ace> on the sixth of April 1830, the d[a]y on which the church was organized.[23]

Lucy does not mention her own baptism. But a neighbor, Cornelius R. Stafford, recalled that as a young man he "saw old Jo Smith, his wife and Mrs. [Sarah W.] Rockwell baptized by prophet Jo Smith."[24] Benjamin Saunders also recollected: "I was there when they first baptized. Oliver Cowdery did the baptizing. Old brother <Smith> was baptized at that time and I think old Mrs. Rockwell."[25] Martin Harris years later recalled that he was not baptized "untill the church Was organised by Joseph Smith the Prophet then I Was Babtised by the Hands of Oliver Cowdery."[26]

---

[22] Joseph Knight Reminiscences.

[23] Anderson, *Lucy's Book*, 477. The 1853 edition of Lucy's book, but not the draft manuscript, reads: "On the morning of the sixth day of the same month, my husband and Martin Harris were baptized." Richard L. Bushman commented, "Lucy Smith said the baptism occurred in the morning, but Joseph Knight and Joseph Smith, Jr., placed it after the organizational meeting" (*Joseph Smith and the Beginnings of Mormonism*, 237n4).

[24] Statement by C. R. Stafford in *Naked Truths About Mormonism* 1 (Jan. 1888): 3. Mrs. Rockwell was forty-four years old. Her daughter Caroline (b. May 1, 1812 and baptized June 9, 1830) said, "My mother was one of the first Mormon converts" (Ibid. 1 [April 1888]:1).

[25] Interview of Benjamin Saunders, 1884, RLDS archives.

[26] Interview of Martin Harris by Edward Stevenson, Sept. 4, 1870, LDS

The place of these baptisms was no doubt Crooked Brook (now Hathaway Creek), a stream in the northwest corner of the township of Manchester. Crooked Brook ran north past the Smith residence toward Palmyra. Joseph Knight described it as a "Small Stream," which it still is.[27] According to a later newspaper account, the stream,

> not more than si[x]ty feet from the highway, is the first Mormon Jordan, a little creek which the Smith boys dammed at Joe's request and made a pool in which the first converts to Mormonism were baptized. It is a sing[i]n[g] meandering little brooklet about ten or fifte[e]n feet wide, with two or three feet of water standing in pools in the bends of the stream, but ordinarily the water is but a few inches deep.[28]

A history of Ontario County describes the stream in terms congruent with the accounts of those who claimed to be present at the church's organization: "Crooked brook, of Mormon fame, runs through the northwest part of the town[ship of Manchester], and it was in the waters of this stream that the Mormons baptized their early saints. Dr. [John] Stafford, an old resident of the village of Manchester, was present at the first baptism."[29] John Stafford, oldest son of William, "knew the Smith family well, and was present at the first baptism, when old Granny Smith and Sally Rockwell" were baptized.[30] The Stafford and Rockwell families were residents of the township of Manchester and lived within a mile of the Smith home.[31]

---

archives.

[27] Joseph Knight Reminiscences.

[28] *New York Herald*, June 25, 1893. A photograph of Crooked Brook was taken by George Edward Anderson in August 1907; see Richard Neitzel Holzapfel, T. Jeffery Cottle, and Ted D. Stoddard, eds., *Church History in Black and White: Geroge Edward Anderson's Photographic Mission to Latter-day Saint Historical Sites* (Provo, Utah: Religious Studies Center, Brigham Young University, 1995), 181.

[29] John H. Pratt, in Charles F. Milliken's *A History of Ontario County, New York and Its People* (New York: Lewis Historical Publishing Co., 1911), 1:418.

[30] *Shortsville Enterprise*, March 18, 1904.

[31] 1830 U.S. Census, Manchester, Ontario County, New York, 169-70.

In 1839, when Joseph Smith, with the help of scribe James Mulholland, compiled the opening portion of his history, he was more vague about chronology but seemed to confirm the other accounts: "Several persons who had attended the above meeting [April 6, 1830] and got convinced of the truth, came forward shortly after, and were received into the church, among the rest, my own father and mother were baptized to my great joy and consolation, and about the same time Martin Harris and A. [sic] Rockwell."[32] James Mulholland wrote at the bottom of what would be pages nine and ten of the 1839 draft: "Father Smith, Martin Harris baptized this evening 6th April. Mother Smith & Sister Rockwell 2 or 3 days afterward."[33] On the next page was recorded: "Several persons who attended this meeting, but who had <not> as yet been baptized, came forward shortly after. . . . Among the rest Father Smith, Martin Harris, Mother Smith."[34] The manuscript version behind the *Times and Seasons* edition added to the last phrase, "among the rest My own Father and Mother were baptized to my great joy and consolation, and about the same time, Martin Harris and a [blank] Rockwell."[35] Later the name "Orrin Porter" was mistakenly added in the blank space by someone other than James Mulholland.

Joseph Smith's 1839 history was not the first account to change the place of the church organization to Fayette, twenty-five miles away. The May 1834 edition of *The Evening and the Morning Star* contains probably the earliest error in the heading of the "MINUTES of a Conference of the Elders of the church of Christ, which church was organized in the township of Fayette, Seneca county, New-York, on the 6th of April, A.D. 1830." This conference of elders was held on May 3, 1834. Also, in the 1835 Doctrine and Covenants the texts of five of the six revelations received on April 6, 1830 and originally published in the 1833 Book of Commandments were amalgamated into a single revelation and the references to the location were deleted.[36]

---

[32] *Times and Seasons* 4 (Nov. 15, 1842):12, Nauvoo, Illinois. This and subsequent publications make Mrs. Sarah Rockwell's first initial an "A."

[33] Jessee, *Papers of Joseph Smith* 1:243n1.

[34] Ibid. 1:244.

[35] Manuscript History A-1:38; Jessee, *Papers of Joseph Smith* 1:303-304.

[36] See Preliminary Draft to History, 1839, and Manuscript History A-1:37, in

Not all official accounts after 1834 reflected the error in location. In 1840 Orson Pratt prepared the pamphlet *Remarkable Visions* in which he stated that the church was organized in Manchester. In 1842 Smith used Pratt's pamphlet for wording in a letter to John Wentworth. As published in the *Times and Seasons*, Smith's letter read: "On the 6th of April, 1830, the 'Church of Jesus Christ of Latter-Day Saints,' was first organized in the town of Manchester, Ontario co., state of New York."[37] In 1844 this letter was used as a source for a history published by Daniel Rupp.[38] However, in 1848 the Manchester reference in Pratt's pamphlet *Remarkable Visions* was changed to Fayette to agree with Smith's history.[39] Nearly thirty years later, in 1876, the LDS Doctrine and Covenants included Fayette as the site of the church's founding.[40] In 1880 the error was canonized.

It is difficult to support the argument that the early references to Manchester may have been mistaken and that on April 6 the church was in fact organized at Fayette. The question becomes, then, why the confusion and contradictions about the location. Joseph Smith's history betrays other anachronisms and conflations. After gathering "at the house of the above mentioned Mr [Peter] Whitmer" Sr., Smith recalled: "I then laid my hands upon Oliver Cowdery and ordained him an Elder of the 'Church of

---

Jessee, *Papers of Joseph Smith* 1:241-42, 302-303. See also BC 17-22; 1835 D&C 45-46; LDS D&C 21, 23; RLDS D&C 19, 21. For early references to the church being organized at Fayette, see Stanley R. Gunn, *Oliver Cowdery Second Elder and Scribe* (Salt Lake City: Bookcraft, 1962), 267, deed made on May 5, 1834; Nancy Clement Williams, *After One Hundred Years* (Independence, Missouri: Zion's Printing and Publishing Co., 1951), 228-30, deed of May 5, 1834; Deeds in Geauga Deed Records, Book 24:100, Geauga County, Ohio, microfilm #0020240, LDS Family History Library; see also Book 18:477-81, microfilm #0020237.

[37] *Times and Seasons* 3 (March 1, 1842):708. This was later changed to Fayette. See *History of the Church* 4:538.

[38] I Daniel Rupp, *He Pasa Ekklesia. An Original History of the Religious Denominations at Present Existing in the United States* (Philadelphia: Published by J. Y. Humphreys, 1844), 407. See *History of the Church* 6:428.

[39] O[rson]. Pratt, *Interesting Account of Several Remarkable Visions, and of the Late Discovery of Ancient American Records* (Edinburgh: Printed by Ballantyne and Hughes, 1840), 24. The change was made in one of the 1848 printings.

[40] See 1876 LDS D&C 21. The designation "at Fayette" first appeared in RLDS D&C 19 in 1952, probably based on the LDS D&C.

Jesus Christ of Latter Day Saints.'" In fact the official name of the church in 1830 was the Church of Christ. The name was changed to the Church of the Latter Day Saints in 1834 and finally to the Church of Jesus Christ of Latter-day Saints in 1838.[41]

Memory often conflates events which were once separate and distinct. Events which occurred within days of the April 6 meeting at Manchester, events which demonstrably occurred at the Whitmer house in Fayette, might have assumed greater importance in Smith's mind over time. In Fayette there was an increase in the number of baptisms, the Articles and Covenants of the new church were written and accepted, licenses for lay ministers to preach were issued, and the first three church conferences were convened.

One of the revelations given on April 6, 1830, a Tuesday, designated Oliver Cowdery to be "the first preacher of this church."[42] On April 11, the first Sunday after the organization of the church, Cowdery delivered "the first public discourse," the Fayette branch of the church was organized, and Cowdery performed six baptisms. A week later, on April 18, another baptismal service was held at Fayette, where Cowdery performed seven baptisms in Seneca Lake.[43] The manuscript history lists no one baptized at Fayette who lived in the Manchester/Palmyra area.

The next meeting mentioned in the history was the first conference of the church, which convened on June 9. For the first time the Manchester and Fayette branches came together. A copy of the minutes reads: "Minutes of the first Conference held in the Township of Fayette, Seneca County, State of New York."[44] Smith read "The Articles and Covenants of the church of Christ." They were "received by unanimous voice of the whole congregation."[45] The Articles and Covenants were then submitted as a confession of

[41] Manuscript History A-1:37; Jessee, *Papers of Joseph Smith* 1:302-303.
[42] Marquardt, *Joseph Smith Revelations*, 61; BC 22:15; LDS D&C 21:12; RLDS D&C 19:3.
[43] Manuscript History A-1: 39; Jessee, *Papers of Joseph Smith* 1:304.
[44] Donald Q. Cannon and Lyndon W. Cook, eds., *Far West Record: Minutes of The Church of Jesus Christ of Latter-day Saints, 1830-1844* (Salt Lake City: Deseret Book, 1983), 1-2. Manuscript History A-1:41, has the date of the conference as June 1 as does "History of Joseph Smith," *Times and Seasons* 4 (Dec. 1, 1842):22 and "Newel Knight's Journal," in *Scraps of Biography* (Salt Lake City: Juvenile Instructor Office, 1883), 52.
[45] Cannon and Cook, *Far West Record*, 1.

faith, members agreed that the statement reflected their beliefs, including the callings of Joseph Smith and Oliver Cowdery, the Book of Mormon, and what were to be the teachings and practices of the infant church.

At the Fayette conference prospective members from Manchester Township were baptized. They were Jerusha Smith (Hyrum Smith's wife), Katherine Smith, William Smith, Don Carlos Smith, Porter Rockwell, Caroline and Electa Rockwell (children of Sarah W. Rockwell).[46] Orrin Porter Rockwell was sixteen years old at the time of his baptism. In the 1820 Farmington and 1830 Manchester census records there is only one member of the Orin and Sarah Rockwell family in the age bracket of their son Porter. Consequently there is no "Peter" Rockwell who could have been baptized. These are the first baptisms of Manchester residents which can be documented as occurring in Fayette.

At the end of June, Smith and Cowdery were at Colesville, New York, to set up the church there. In the midst of opposition, Cowdery performed thirteen or fourteen baptisms and established the Colesville branch on Monday, June 28, 1830. Among those baptized were Joseph's wife Emma and Joseph and Polly Knight.[47]

Some historians have looked to David Whitmer, one of the three witnesses to the Book of Mormon, to substantiate the claim that the church was founded in Fayette, since he claimed to have been present at the meeting held on April 6.[48] However, a closer look makes clear that the events Whitmer describes as being in Fayette parallel most closely with what happened in meetings after

---

[46] Manuscript History A-1:42; *Times and Seasons* 4 (Dec. 1, 1842):23, spelling of Jerusha as "Jerushee" as in the manuscript. The name Porter Rockwell was written in the 1839 draft history. See Jessee, *Papers of Joseph Smith* 1:246, 250. The manuscript history has the reading "Peter" Rockwell. This is a scribal error made by James Mulholland when copying from his draft history and should read Porter (Ibid. 1:309). William Smith correctly list Porter Rockwell as being baptized on June 9, 1830. See *William Smith on Mormonism*, 16.

[47] *The Evening and the Morning Star* 1 (April 1833):4 [p. 84]; Manuscript History A-1:43; Jessee, *Papers of Joseph Smith* 1:311. "H. P. [Hezekiah Peck] and wife have been baptized, & are very strong in the faith" (Letter to the Editor, *Brattleboro' Messenger* 9 [Nov. 20, 1830]).

[48] John K. Carmack, "Fayette: The Place the Church was Organized," *Ensign* 19 (Feb. 1989):19; Jessee, *Papers of Joseph Smith* 1:242n2.

the organization of the church. In 1887 Whitmer wrote:

> Now, when April 6, 1830, had come, we had then
> established three branches of the "Church of Christ," in
> which three branches were about seventy members: One
> branch was at Fayette, N.Y.; one at Manchester, N.Y., and
> one at Colesville, Pa. [New York] It is all a mistake about
> the church being *organized* on April 6, 1830, as I will
> show. We were as fully *organized*—spiritually—before
> before April 6th as we were on that day. The reason why
> we met on that day was this; the world had been telling us
> that we were not a regularly organized church, and we had
> no right to officiate in the ordinance of marriage, hold
> church property, etc., and that we should organize
> according to the laws of the land. On this account we met at
> my father's house in Fayette, N.Y., on April 6, 1830, to
> attend to this matter of organizing according to the laws of
> the land. . . . Now brethren, how can it be that the church
> was any more organized--spiritually--on April 6th, than it
> was before that time? There were six elders and about
> seventy members before April 6th, and the same number of
> elders and members after that day.[49]

Whitmer's statement contains errors. He claims there were
seventy members in three branches of the church by April 6, 1830.
However, the "Far West Record" has the number at the time of the
first conference two months later, June 9, 1830, as only twenty-
seven.[50] Whitmer says there were three branches by April 6, but
the Fayette branch was not founded until April 11 and the
Colesville branch not until the latter part of June.

David Whitmer states that there were six elders. The only
time there were six elders was after the founding of the Fayette
branch. Two of these were Smith and Cowdery, who ordained each

---

[49] David Whitmer, *An Address to All Believers in Christ* (Richmond, Missouri:
author, 1887), 33; emphasis in original.

[50] Cannon and Cook, *Far West Record*, 3. The minutes state: "No. of the several
members uniting to this Church since the last Conference, thirty-five, making in
whole now belonging to this Church sixty-two." These minutes were copied
from the original in 1838.

other at Manchester on April 6, and the other four—Peter Whitmer, David Whitmer, John Whitmer, and Ziba Peterson—all from Fayette, were evidently ordained in April and received their licenses at the June conference, where Samuel H. Smith became the seventh elder of the church.[51]

Edward Stevenson recorded an interview with David Whitmer in January 1887 in which Whitmer told him, "on the 6th of April 1830, 6 Elders were at Peter Whitmers, David's Fathers. 2 Rooms were filled with members about 20 from Colesville, 15 from Manchester Church and about 20 from aro[u]nd about Father Whitmers. About 50 members & the 6 elders were presant [present]."[52] The earliest possible date when the Colesville church could have been represented at Fayette would have been the second conference in September.

Another indication that Whitmer was recalling a latter meeting is that J. W. Chatburn, who visited the Whitmers in the early 1880s, recorded that David Whitmer "said that he baptized fourteen in Seneca Lake, a few days before the Church was organized. I asked his wife [Julia Anne Jolly Whitmer] if she was present when the Church was organized on April 6th, 1830. She replied, Yes; and was a baptized member at that time."[53] The history of the church lists eleven people baptized on June 9, by David Whitmer, including his future wife Julia Jolly.[54]

Whitmer also declares that the organizational meeting was for legal purposes so the church could hold property and officiate in marriages. The cover of the Book of Commandments agrees that the Church of Christ was "Organized According to Law, on the 6th of April, 1830." However well-intentioned this event was, no records of incorporation have been found in the Fayette or Manchester/Palmyra area for April 6, 1830 or any other date.[55]

---

[51] Ibid. 1.

[52] Diary of Edward Stevenson, entry for Jan. 2, 1887, LDS archives, in Cook, *David Whitmer Interviews*, 214.

[53] *Saints Herald* 29 (June 15, 1882):189.

[54] Manuscript History A-1:42; *Papers of Joseph Smith* 1:309. The names of Julia Anne Jolly and Harriet Jolly were omitted when the history was published in 1842. See *Times and Seasons* 4 (Dec. 1, 1842):23. The history mentions that David Whitmer performed a baptism in May 1830.

[55] The records in the counties of Seneca, Ontario, and Wayne have been searched and no record has been found of incorporation of the Church of Christ

Ultimately, the meeting was more spiritual than legalistic.

A state law at the time specified how a church was to incorporate. The minister of a group was to post public notice of time and date for a meeting of the male members to elect trustees. The trustees were "to take charge of the estate and property belonging thereto, and to transact all affairs relative to the temporalities thereof." The congregation had to be notified "at least fifteen days before the day of election," and the notification was to be given for "two successive sabbaths or days on which such church, congregation or society, shall statedly meet for public worship" before the day of election.[56]

The Presbyterian congregation of West Bloomfield in Ontario County followed these specifications precisely: "Whereas at a meeting of the male members of the Presbyterian Congregation of West Bloomfield in the town of Bloomfield county of Ontario and state of New York convened agreeable to publick notice as directed by the statute in such cases made and provided at the Meeting House of said Congregation on the 31st day of May 1830."[57] Similar incorporations can be found in the Miscellaneous Records books of Wayne and Seneca counties.[58]

Joseph Smith was not at Manchester or Fayette long enough to give legal notice to incorporate. When he and Joseph Knight were on their way to Manchester, Knight says Smith told him "there must be a Church formed But did not tell when." This was at the most twelve days before April 6. Knight was still at Manchester when the baptisms occurred and Smith "Begun the

---

on April 6, 1830 or any other date (Correspondence from the Department of State, State of New York, Albany, Oct. 6, 1986 and Feb. 23, 1987 to H. Michael Marquardt; research trip to New York in October 1986).

[56] *Laws of the State of New-York, Revised and Passed at the Thirty-Sixth Session of the Legislature* (Albany: H. C. Southwick & Co., 1813), 2:214. For acts to amend "an act to provide for the incorporation of religious societies," passed April 5, 1813, see *Laws of the State of New-York* (Albany: J. Buel, 1819), 34, and *Laws of the State of New-York* (Albany: E. Croswell, 1826), 34-35.

[57] Recorded June 1, 1830, Miscellaneous Records, Book D:23-24, Ontario County Clerk's Office, Canandaigua, New York.

[58] See the incorporation of the First Baptist Church of Lodi, recorded Nov. 24, 1830, Miscellaneous Records Seneca County Book B:426-27, Seneca County Clerk's Office, Waterloo, New York; and of the First Congregational Society in Marion, signed March 16, 1829; filed March 28, 1829, Miscellaneous Docket 1:45, Lyons, Wayne County, New York.

Church with Six members."[59] Smith and Knight were not in Fayette at the end of March. David Marks, a Free-will Baptist evangelist, on March 29, 1830 "attended a meeting in Fayette, and tarried at the house of Mr. Whitmer." He saw two or three of Whitmer's sons, but Smith was not there.[60]

One early document states that the church was "regularly organized & established agreeable to the laws of our Country by the will & commandments of God." There are other early church licenses with similar wording.[61] This language might mean that the church was organized according to the freedom of religion clause amended to the United States Constitution in 1791. People were free to organize as a voluntary unincorporated religious society or church with no trustees. This is evidently what occurred on April 6, 1830. There were no known marriages performed in New York by ministers of the new church, no property that belonged to the church, and thus no compelling reason to organize according to the laws of New York State.

Certainly inaccuracies in both individual and community memory might account for the shift of the place of the church's organization from Manchester to Fayette. However, another intriguing possibility exists. The change in location may not have been inadvertent but part of a larger strategy for coping with the economic strains which plagued the church through the early years of its existence. As we have seen, what is probably the earliest reference to Fayette as the location of the April 6 events appears in

---

[59] Joseph Knight Reminiscences.

[60] *The Life of David Marks* (Limerick, ME: Printed at the Office of the Morning Star, 1831), 340-41. Marks wrote concerning selling the Book of Mormon, "Five thousand copies were published - and they said the angel told Smith to sell the book at a price which was one dollar and eight cents per copy more than the cost, that they '*might have the temporal profit*, as well as the spiritual'" (341, emphasis in original). In an 1830 account, published shortly after his visit in March, he stated, "we went to Fayette & held one meeting" (*Morning Star* 4 [April 28, 1830]:1, Limerick, Maine).

[61] MS Articles & Covenants, Zebedee Coltrin journal, LDS archives; compare BC 24:2; LDS D&C 20:2; RLDS D&C 17:19. Some of the early preaching licenses had wording such as the following: "this Church of Christ established & regularly organized" (licenses of John and Christian Whitmer, given June 9, 1830, original in the Coe Collection, Yale University Library; and the priest license for Joseph Smith Sr., also given June 9, 1830, in the Joseph Smith Collection, LDS archives).

a heading in *The Evening and Morning Star* to the minutes of a conference held in Kirtland, Ohio, on May 3, 1834. This conference was attended by Joseph Smith, Oliver Cowdery, Frederick G. Williams, Sidney Rigdon, and Newel K. Whitney, all leading elders of the church and members of the Kirtland United Firm. The minutes of that meeting report that it was decided that the church should be known by the name "The Church of the Latter Day Saints."[62] Perhaps after this conference the "Church of Christ" founded in Manchester, New York, became "The Church of the Latter Day Saints" founded in Fayette.

In the Book of Mormon, the simple title "Church of Christ" identifies the church as Jesus Christ's.[63] In 1829 Oliver Cowdery produced a document stating that the "Church shall be called The Church of Christ," and although other Christian churches before 1829 were similarly named, this name was confirmed in a revelation given on the day of its organization.[64]

Before the change in name, church leaders were concerned about obtaining donations to pay for the debts of the United Firm, to commence work on the Kirtland temple, and to provide funds for the forthcoming march of Zion's Camp to Missouri. In a letter from Kirtland on December 5, 1833, Smith wrote, "our means are already exhausted, and we are deeply in debt, and know of no means whereby we shall be able to extricate ourselves."[65] On January 11, 1834 Smith and his associates prayed "That the Lord would provide, in the order of his Providence, the bishop of this Church with means sufficient to discharge every debt that the Firm

---

[62] *The Evening and the Morning Star* 2 (May 1834):160. See *History of the Church* 2:62-63.

[63] See LDS Mosiah 18:17/RLDS 9:49; LDS 3 Ne. 26:21/RLDS 12:13; LDS 3 Ne. 28:23/RLDS 13:36; LDS 4 Ne. 1:1, 26, 29/RLDS 1:1, 28, 31; LDS//RLDS Moroni 6:4.

[64] "A commandment from God unto Oliver," LDS archives; BC 22:14; LDS D&C 21:11; RLDS D&C 19:3. For various arguments favoring the name change, see Oliver Cowdery, *The Evening and the Morning Star* 2 (May 1834):158-59; 2 (June 1834):164-65; Letter of John Smith to Elias Smith, Oct. 19, 1834, George Albert Smith Family Papers, Special Collections, Marriott Library, University of Utah, Salt Lake City; Thomas B. Marsh to Wilford Woodruff, *Elders' Journal* 1 (July 1838):37.

[65] In *History of the Church* 1:450. A copy of the letter is in Joseph Smith Letterbook 1:68, LDS archives.

owes, in due season, that the Church may not be braught [brought] into disrepute, and the saints be afflicted by the hands of their enemies."[66] Less than a month before the name and place changes, the United Firm was dissolved and separated into two firms, one in Missouri and one in Kirtland. Members of the firm in Kirtland were instructed to divide the properties among themselves.[67]

Additionally on May 5 the land designated for the Kirtland Temple was transferred to Smith and his successor in the office of the presidency of the church.[68] By 1835 the identities of United Firm members were obscured by pseudonyms.[69] In a revelation received by Smith on April 23, 1834, shortly before the name and location change, he was instructed: "Therefore, write speedily unto New York, and write according to that which shall be dictated by my spirit, and I will soften the hearts of those to whom you are in debt, that it shall be taken away out of <their> minds to bring afflictions upon you."[70]

All of these actions may well have been part of a larger attempt to frustrate church creditors or to avoid lawsuits. Unfortunately, there are no known letters extant written by Smith between April 23 and May 5, 1834, when he left Kirtland for Missouri. The evidence is too sketchy to reach a decisive conclusion, but this is an area of research worth pursuing and suggests a plausible motive for changing the church's name and relocating its place of organization to Fayette.

The Fayette location was unheard of until 1834. However, Fayette was important as the site of the first three church conferences, and the log home and farm of Peter Whitmer Sr.,

---

[66] Joseph Smith Journal, entry for Jan. 11, 1834, 45-46, LDS archives. Also in Jessee, *Papers of Joseph Smith* 2:19.

[67] "Kirtland Revelations" Book, 102-105, LDS archives; LDS D&C 104:19-59; RLDS D&C 101:3-10. See also "Kirtland Revelations" Book, 111, revelation dated Kirtland, April 28, 1834; Joseph Smith's diary, April 10, 1834, 71-72, also in Jessee, *Papers of Joseph Smith* 2:29.

[68] See, for example, the deed recorded in Geauga Deed Records, Book 18:478-79, Geauga County, Ohio; microfilm #0020237, LDS Family History Library. For some additional information on the Kirtland temple property, see *Restoration Studies IV* (Independence, Missouri: Herald Publishing House, 1988), 122n52.

[69] See 1835 D&C 75, 86, 93, 96, and 98.

[70] "Kirtland Revelations" Book, 107; LDS D&C 104:81; RLDS D&C 101:13d.

should retain a fundamental historical and sentimental position in Smith's Church of Christ.

As mentioned in June 1830 baptisms into the Church of Christ were performed in Colesville, New York, in a branch established there by Smith and Oliver Cowdery. The coming of the new church to the Colesville area occasioned a series of confrontations—between the state of New York and Joseph Smith, between the Presbyterian Church and the Church of Christ, and between the Coburn and Knight families.[71] These events were recorded by members of the newly founded church, by the minister of the Presbyterian Church, by one of the sisters involved, Emily Coburn, and by a judge at one of Joseph Smith's trials.

The family of Joseph Knight became the nucleus of the new church in Colesville just as the Smiths had been the nucleus in Manchester and the Whitmers in Fayette. And the Knights were at the center of difficulties erupting during the church's first summer in the area. The Knight family home and mill were located just across the Susquehanna River from the little village of Nineveh in Colesville Township. Joseph Smith had worked with Knight and others in the Colesville area while conducting his treasure-digging activities, and the Knights had helped Smith while he was working on the Book of Mormon.[72]

After the first church conference in Fayette, Smith and Cowdery made their way to Colesville.[73] Oliver Cowdery preached at the Knight home on Sunday, June 27. Baptisms were to be performed that Sunday, but antagonists destroyed the dam erected

---

[71] The church account is recorded in Manuscript History Book A-1:43; Jessee, *Papers of Joseph Smith* 1:310-11. The account in Book A-1 may have been based in part on Newel Knight's recollections. Joseph Smith's 1839 journal records for the dates July 4-5: "Thursday & Friday (assisted by Br Newel Knight) dictating History" (Joseph Smith Journal, kept by James Mulholland, LDS archives; Jessee, *Papers of Joseph Smith* 2:326). Newel Knight's published account is found in *Scraps of Biography* (Salt Lake City: Juvenile Instructor Office, 1883), 54. For the experience of Joseph Knight, see Jessee, "Joseph Knight's Recollection," 38.

[72] Albert L. Zobell, Jr., "Writing Paper for the Book of Mormon Manuscript," *Improvement Era* 72 (Feb. 1969):54-55.

[73] For problems in the Fayette area, see the letter of Rev. Diedrich Willers, June 18, 1830, Diedrich Willers Papers, Division of Rare and Manuscript Collections, Carl A. Kroch Library, Cornell University Library, Ithaca, New York. Published in Vogel, *Early Mormon Documents* 5:271-78.

for the purpose. On Monday, June 28, 1830, members of the Knight family and others were baptized near the Knight home, and the Colesville church began to take shape.[74]

Among those baptized was Newel Knight's wife Sarah Coburn (known as Sally).[75] Newel had been a Universalist and Sally a Presbyterian. Sally's father Amasa Coburn was an accomplished musician and earned part of his living by giving music and vocal lessons in the town of Guilford, Chenango County, where the Coburn family had established their residence sometime before 1820. Sally had grown up surrounded by music and had joined the local church choir.[76] The Presbyterian Church of Harpursville in 1827 was nearest to her home but was eventually absorbed into the church at Nineveh, just across the river from where they lived.[77]

A few days after Sally Knight's baptism, a young medical doctor, Abram W. Benton, a Presbyterian, swore out a warrant for Smith's arrest.[78] Smith's history records that "a young man named Benton, of the same religious [Presbyterian] faith, swore out the first warrant against me."[79] Constable Ebenezer Hatch was dispatched south to Colesville to arrest Joseph and return him to Bainbridge for trial. Joseph Knight Sr. provided lawyers for Smith's defense and later recalled:

they made a Catspaw of a young fellow By the name of

---

[74] Newel Knight, *Scraps of Biography*, 53-55.

[75] *Latter Day Saints' Messenger and Advocate* 1 (Oct. 1834):12, Kirtland, Ohio, has the date of Sally Knight's baptism as June 29, 1830. Since the day of baptisms was a Monday, the correct date is probably June 28. See *Utah Genealogical Magazine* 26 (Oct. 1935):147-48.

[76] Newel Knight, *Scraps of Biography*, 47.

[77] From 1824 to 1830 the work at Nineveh declined, being without a pastor. In 1830 it emerged as the Bainbridge and Ninevah Presbyterian church (J. S. Pattengill, *History of the Presbytery of Binghamton* [Binghamton, NY: Carl, Stoppard & Co., 1877], 16). None of the early records appear to have survived.

[78] According to records in the family Bible, Abram Willard Benton was "born July 16, 1805." He died on March 9, 1867 at Fulton, Illinois. His brief comments about Smith's 1830 Bainbridge trial appeared in "Mormonites," *Evangelical Magazine and Gospel Advocate*, New Series, 2 (April 9, 1831):120, Utica, New York, original periodical in Meadville Theological Seminary, Chicago, Illinois. See Vogel, *Early Mormon Documents* 4:94-99.

[79] Manuscript History Book A-1:48; Jessee, *Papers of Joseph Smith* 1:318.

Docter [Doctor] Benton in Chenengo County to Sware [Swear] out a warrent [warrant] against Joseph for as they Said pertending [pretending] to See under ground a little Clause they found in the [New] york Laws against Such things the of[f]icer Came to my house near knite [night] and took him I harnes[s]ed my horses and we all went up to the villie [village] But it was So Late they Could not try him that nite [night] and it was put of[f] till morning I asked Joseph if [he] wanted Counsell [Counsel] he Said he thot [thought] he Should. I went that nite [night] and Saw Mr James Davi[d]son a man I was acquainted with. the next morning ther[e] gather[e]d a multitude of peopel [people] that ware [were] against him [Smith] Mr Davi[d]son Said it Looked like a Squaley [Squally] Day he thot [thought] we had Better have John Read [Reed] a prety [pretty] good Speaker near by I told him we would So I imployed [employed] them Both. So after a trial all Day Jest [Just] at nite [night] he was Dismissed[80]

Smith's history describes how he was "visited by a constable" at Knight's home and "arrested by him on a warrant, on the charge of being a disorderly person." "On the day following," the history continues, "a court was convened for the purpose of investigating those charges," where there were "many witnesses called up against me."[81]

One of Smith's defense lawyers, John Reed, recalled that they "had him arraigned before Joseph Chamberlain, a justice of the peace, a man that was always ready to deal justice to all, and a man of great discernment of mind." The case started "about 10 o'clock, A.M.," and "closed about 12 o'clock at night."[82]

---

[80] Joseph Knight Reminiscences. The New York law Knight cited was part of the vagrancy law which regarded as a misdemeanor "pretending . . . to discover where lost goods may be found" (*Laws of the State of New York, Revised and Passed in the Thirty-Sixth Session of the Legislature* [1813], 1:114).

[81] Manuscript History A-1:44; Jessee, *Papers of Joseph Smith* 1:312-13.

[82] John Reed's speech was given on May 17, 1844 and appeared in *Times and Seasons* 5 (June 1, 1844):549-50; this quote is on page 550. See also footnote in *History of the Church* 1:94-96; 6:392-97. Our spelling of the name "Reed" comes from the 1839 draft of the Manuscript History (see Jessee, *Papers of Joseph Smith* 1:253, 257); *Times and Seasons*; and bills from Bainbridge, New

The bills submitted to the county by the constable and the justice at Smith's examination confirms the account in Smith's history. The bill of Constable Ebenezer Hatch "Dated at South Bainbridge July 4th 1830" reads:

To Serving warrant on Joseph Smith & keeping
him twenty four hours $2=00
3 meals Victuel & 1 Lodging   =50
Suppoenying 5 witness   62 1/2
                              $3=13 1/2
                                   75
                              $2.37 1/2

It is not evident why the costs were reduced by seventy five cents, but the $2.37 1/2 total, rounded off to $2.38, was recorded next to Hatch's name in the "Supervisor's Journal," confirming that Smith was in fact arrested one day, held over night, and tried the next day. It further shows that Hatch delivered five subpoenas to witnesses to take part in the hearing.

A second bill submitted by Justice Joseph Chamberlain for cases tried between June 1 and August 1830 includes the state of New York "vs Joseph Smith Jr a Disorderly person July 1st 1830," supplying the exact date of the trial, July 1, 1830, a Thursday.[83] That the examination in this case was lengthy is reflected in the itemized listing of Chamberlain's costs:

oath on Complaint   6 [cents]
filing Complaint   3
warrant   19
Examination 1 Day   1[.]00
10 Subpoenis   60
Swearing 12 witnesses   72

This bill shows there were actually twelve witnesses,

York, for the years 1826 and 1830.
[83] These bills were discovered in 1971 in the dead storage in the basement of the Norwich jail, with the 1826 bills. Chamberlain's bill is now in the Office of the Clerk of the Board of Supervisors, Chenango County Office Building, Norwich, New York.

indicating that another constable served seven additional subpoenas. Chamberlain's expenses for six cases totaled $11.74 for a three-month period. This amount was entered on the back of the bill and is recorded beside his name in the "Supervisor's Journal" under the Town of Bainbridge for the year 1830.[84]

The earliest printed account of this hearing appeared less than a year later in the April 9, 1831 issue of the *Evangelical Magazine and Gospel Advocate*. It was dated at South Bainbridge, March 1831, and signed A. W. B., identified by Dale L. Morgan, who uncovered this account, as Abram W. Benton who brought the complaint against Smith. Benton related the Bainbridge trial as follows:

> During the trial it was shown that the Book of Mormon was brought to light by the same magic power by which he pretended to tell fortunes, discover hidden treasures, &c. Oliver Cowd[e]ry, one of the three witnesses to the book [of Mormon], testified under oath, that said Smith found with the plates, from which he translated his book, two transparent stones, resembling glass, set in silver bows. That by looking through these, he was able to read in English, the reformed Egyptian characters, which were engraved on the plates.

Benton recalled an attempt to have Josiah Stowell admit that Smith had lied to him about his ability to locate buried treasure. Benton described the questioning of Stowell and his responses:

> Josiah Stowell, a Mormonite, being sworn, testified that he positively knew that said Smith never had lied to, or deceived him, and did not believe he ever tried to deceive any body else. The following questions were then asked him, to which he made the replies annexed.
> [Q] Did Smith ever tell you there was money hid in a certain place which he mentioned?

---

[84] If we could locate Justice Chamberlain's docket book, we might have a more complete record of the testimony of the witnesses, but the book's location, if it is still extant, is unknown to members of his family.

[A] Yes.

[Q] Did he tell you, you could find it by digging?

[A] Yes.

[Q] Did you dig?

[A] Yes.

[Q] Did you find any money?

[A] No.

[Q] Did he not lie to you then, and deceive you?

[A] No! the money was there, but we did not get quite to it!

[Q] How do you know it was there?

[A] Smith said it was![85]

The next witness, Addison Austin, testified that at the very same time that Stowell was digging for money, he, Austin was in company with said Smith alone, and asked him to tell him honestly whether he could see this money or not. Smith hesitated some time, but finally replied, "to be candid, between you and me, I cannot, any more than you or any body else; but any way to get a living."[86]

Joseph Smith's history adds the following testimony:

Among many witnesses called up against me [Joseph Smith], was Mr. Josiah Stoal [Stowell] (of whom I have made mention, as having worked for him some time) and examined to the following effect.

Q. Did not the prisoner Joseph Smith have a horse of you?

Ansr. Yes.

Q. Did not he go to you and tell you, that an angel had appeared unto him, and authorised him to get the horse from you?

Ansr. No, he told me no such story.

Q. Well; How had he the horse of you?

---

[85] A. W. Benton, "Mormonites," *Evangelical Magazine* 2 (April 9, 1831):120. Josiah Jones wrote that in the fall of 1830, "He [Oliver Cowdery] stated that Smith looked onto or through the transparent stones to translate what was on the plates" ("History of the Mormonites," *The Evangelist* 9 [June 1, 1841]:134, Carthage, Ohio). See LDS Mosiah 28:13; RLDS 12:18.

[86] Benton, "Mormonites," 120.

Ansr. He bought him of me, as an<other> man would do.

Q. Have you had your pay?

Ansr. That is not your business.

The question being again put, the witness replied, "I hold his note for the price of the horse, which I consider as good as the pay - for I am well acquainted with Joseph Smith Jr, and know him to be an honest man; and if he wishes I am ready to let him have another horse on the same terms".

Mr. Jonathan Thompson was next called up, and examined -

Q - Has not the prisoner, Joseph Smith Jr had a yoke of oxen of you?

Ansr. Yes.

Q. Did he not obtain them of you by telling you that he had a revelation to the effect that he was to have them?

Ansr. No, He did not mention a word of the kind concerning the oxen; he purchased them, the same as an<other> man would.[87]

Smith's account also adds Stowell's two daughters, probably Rhoda and Miriam, to the list of witnesses, and Benton included Joseph Knight and his son Newel.[88] Benton related that Newel "testified, under oath, that he positively had a devil cast out of himself by the instrumentality of Joseph Smith, jr., and that he saw the devil after it was out, but could not tell how it looked!"[89]

Smith's history indicated that he was "acquitted by this court."[90] According to John Reed, one of Smith's attorneys, "the court pronounced the words 'not guilty,' and the prisoner was

---

[87] Manuscript History Book A-1:44-45; Jessee, *Papers of Joseph Smith* 1:313-14. Smith wrote to Oliver Cowdery in 1829, "I have bought a horse of Mr. Stowell and want some one to come after it as soon as convenient" (Smith to Cowdery, Oct. 22, 1829, Joseph Smith Letterbook 1:9, LDS archives). See Jessee, *Personal Writings of Joseph Smith*, 252.

[88] On Josiah Stowell's family, see William H. H. Stowell, *Stowell Genealogy* (Rutland, Vermont: The Tuttle Co., 1922), 230.

[89] Benton, "Mormonites," 120.

[90] Manuscript History Book A-1:45; Jessee, *Papers of Joseph Smith* 1:314.

di[s]charged."[91]

According to Joel K. Noble of Colesville, before whom Smith was brought on a similar charge the next day, July 2, Smith won his dismissal by appealing to the statute of limitations. Noble wrote, "Jo. was arrested examination had Jo. plead in bar Statute of Limitations."[92] The limitation on a misdemeanor was set forth in the *Laws of the State of New York,* which read:

> all suits, informations and indictments which shall hereafter be brought or exhibited for any crime or misdemeanor, murder excepted, shall be brought or exhibited within three years next after the offence shall have been committed, and not after, and if brought or exhibited after the time hereby limited the same shall be void: *Provided however,* That if the person, against whom such suit, information or indictment shall be brought or exhibited, shall not have been an inhabitant or usually resident within this state during the said three years, then the same shall or may be brought or exhibited against such a person at anytime within three years, during which he shall be an inhabitant or usually resident within this state, after the offence committed.[93]

Joseph Smith's opponents may have felt that, due to his absence from New York while in Pennsylvania, the statue of limitations had not been violated. Since New York law limited misdemeanor charges to three years, and four years had elapsed since Smith was originally charged in Bainbridge, the case was dismissed.

However, the opposition did not give up that easily. No sooner had Smith stepped out of Justice Chamberlain's court in South Bainbridge, Chenango County, than he was served another warrant and taken a few miles south across the county line into

---

[91] *Times and Seasons* 5 (June 1, 1844):550; *History of the Church* 1:95n and 6:394.

[92] Joel K. Noble to Jonathan B. Turner, March 8, 1842, Jonathan B. Turner Collection, Illinois State Historical Library, Springfield.

[93] *Laws of the State of New York, Revised and Passed* (1813), 1:187, emphasis in original.

Colesville, Broome County, where he was arraigned before Justice Noble.

Joseph Knight recalled: "then thare [there] was a nother [another] of[f]icer was Re[a]dy and took him on the Same Case Down to Broom[e] County Below forth with. I hired Boath [Both] these Lawyers and took them Down home with me that nite [night] the next Day it Continued all Day till midnite [midnight] But they Could find no thing [nothing] against him therefore he was Dismist [Dismissed]."[94] Justice Noble expressed his disgust with the proceedings:

Jo was no Sooner Set on terifirma than arrested again, brought before me in a adjoining County only 6 miles Distant, trial protracted 23 hours the pros[e]cuti[on] was Cond[ucted] by a Gent[leman] well Skil[l]ed in [the] Science of Law, proof manifested by I think 43 Witnesses. . . . Jo. was asked by witness if he could see or tel[l] more than others Jo. said he could not and says any thing for a living. I now and then Get a Sh[i]lling.[95]

The well-skilled attorney who conducted the prosecution was probably William Seymour, another Presbyterian, the "Lawyer Seymour" mentioned in Smith's history. He pursued Smith's money-digging past.[96] Newel Knight was called as a witness and described his testimony during this trial:

As soon as I had been sworn, Mr. Seymour proceeded to

---

[94] Joseph Knight Reminiscences.

[95] Noble to Jonathan B. Turner, March 8, 1842. John Reed mentioned, "The prisoner was to be tried by three justices of the peace" (*Times and Seasons* 5 [June 1, 1844]:551). Since no bills for this trial in Colesville have yet been found we cannot verify this statement.

[96] Manuscript History Book A-1:46; Jessee, *Papers of Joseph Smith* 1:315. William Seymour had been a pioneer settler in Binghamton and after studying law moved to Windsor Township, next to Colesville. There he became an elder and clerk of session in the Presbyterian Church as well as a justice of the peace and town clerk. Returning to Binghamton, he became a county judge, a member of the U.S. Congress, and finally judge of the Court of Common Pleas. He died on December 28, 1848, highly commended by the Bar Association (*Binghamton Democrat*, Jan. 2, 1849, 3).

interrogate me as follows:

Question. - "Did the prisoner, Joseph Smith, Jun., cast the devil out of you?"

Answer. - "No, sir."

Q. - "Why, have you not had the devil cast out of you?"

A. - "Yes, sir."

Q. - "And had not Joseph Smith some hand in it being done?"

A. - "Yes, sir."

Q. - "And did he not cast him out of you?"

A. - "No, sir, it was done by the power of God, and Joseph Smith was the instrument in the hands of God on this occasion. He commanded him to come out of me in the name of Jesus Christ."

Q. - "And are you sure it was the devil?"

A. - "Yes, sir."

Q. - "Did you see him after he was cast out of you?"

A. - "Yes, sir, I saw him."

Q. - "Pray, what did he look like?"

(Here one of the lawyers on the part of the defense told me I need not answer that question.) I replied:

"I believe, I need not answer you that question, but I will do it if I am allowed to ask you one, and you can answer it. Do you, Mr. Seymour, understand the things of the Spirit?"

"No," answered Mr. Seymour, "I do not pretend to such big things."

"Well, then," I replied, "it will be of no use for me to tell you what the devil looked like, for it was a spiritual sight and spiritually discerned, and, of course, you would not understand it were I to tell you of it."

The lawyer dropped his head, while the loud laugh of the audience proclaimed his discomfiture.[97]

Joel Noble wrote, "a Mormon Swore in open court Jo. Smith cast a Devil out of him (M[ormo]n) and said how D[evi]l

---

[97] Knight, *Scraps of Biography*, 59-60, compare Manuscript History, Book A-1:46; Jessee, *Papers of Joseph Smith* 1:316. See also Vogel, *Early Mormon Documents* 4:32-33, 55-56.

Looked. Said Devil was a body of Light."[98] According to Smith's history, "The Court finding the charges against me, not sustained, I was accordingly acquitted."[99] Newel Knight also remembered that "he was discharged."[100]

George A. Smith, in a discourse given in 1855, repeated what he had heard from Emer Harris, an older brother of Martin Harris: "Forty-seven times he [Joseph Smith] was arraigned before the tribunals of law, and had to sustain all the expense of defending himself in those vexatious suits, and was every time acquitted. He was never found guilty but once. I have been told, by Patriarch Emer Harris, that on a certain occasion he was brought before a magistrate in the State of New York, and charged with having cast out devils; the magistrate, after hearing the witnesses, decided that he was guilty, but as the statutes of New York did not provide a punishment for casting out devils, he was acquitted."[101]

"[T]hrough the instrumentality of my new friend, the Constable," continued Smith's history, "I was enabled to escape them, and make my way in safety to my wifes sister's house, where I found my wife awaiting with much anxiety the issue of those ungodly proceedings: And with her in company next day arrived in safety at my house."[102]

Against this backdrop of dramatic public conflict, the Knight family played out parallel tensions within the more private arena of their extended family. When news reached Emily Coburn in Sandford that her sister Sally was interested in joining the church of which Joseph Smith the leader, she was doubtful of the report, "believing her to be of an unshaken mind and principle." Emily visited her sister "to try if possible to convince her of the error into which she had innocently been decoyed and

---

[98] Noble to Turner, March 8, 1842. A newspaper printed a portion of a letter written in 1830 which said, "we have seen none of their miracles here, except N.N. [Newel Knight] I heard say in meeting, that he had the devil cast out" (letter dated Oct. 8, 1830, in *Brattleboro' Messenger*, Nov. 20, 1830, as cited in Walker, *Dale Morgan on Early Mormonism*, 344).

[99] Manuscript History Book A-1:47; Jessee, *Papers of Joseph Smith* 1:317.

[100] Knight, *Scraps of Biography*, 61. W. R. Hine also reported that "Jo was discharged" (*Naked Truths About Mormonism* 1 [Jan. 1888]:2).

[101] *Journal of Discourses* 2:213, March 18, 1855.

[102] Manuscript History Book A-1:47; Jessee, *Papers of Joseph Smith* 1:317.

deceived."[103]

Emily, who had recently joined the Presbyterian Church in Sandford had a special concern about her sister. On Emily's several previous visits to her older sister's home in Colesville, she had become acquainted with young Smith and his treasure seeking activities which centered on Sally's father-in-law's farm. She recalled:

> I had seen him two or three times, while visiting at my sister's, but did not think it worth my while to take any notice of him. I never spoke to him, for he was a total stranger to me. However, I thought him odd looking and queer. He also told his friends that he could see money in pots, under the ground. He pretended to foretell people's future destiny, and, according to his prognostication, his friends agreed to suspend their avocations and dig for the treasures, which were hidden in the earth; a great share of which, he said, was on Joseph Knight's farm.

According to Emily's recollections, Sally's father-in-law, Joseph Knight, shared in the money-digging excursions on his own land:

> Old Uncle Joe, as we called him, was a wool carder, and a farmer; yet he abandoned all business, and joined with a number of others, to dig for money on his premises. While I was visiting my sister, we have walked out to see the places where they dug for money, and laughed to think of the absurdity of any people having common intellect to indulge in such a thought or action.

One story about the treasure-seekers' adventures stood out in Emily's mind:

---

[103] Emily Coburn's account is in her book under the name Emily M. Austin, *Mormonism; or, Life Among the Mormons* (Madison, WI: M. J. Cantwell, Book and Job Printers, 1882), 35-36 (hereafter as Austin, *Mormonism*). Emily's full name in 1882 was Emily Coburn Slade Austin. For the complete account see Vogel, *Early Mormon Documents* 4:164-76.

in the time of their digging for money and not finding it attainable, Joe Smith told them there was a charm on the pots of money, and if some animal was killed and the blood sprinkled around the place, then they could get it. So they killed a dog, and tried this method of obtaining the precious metal; but again money was scarce in those diggings. Still, they dug and dug, but never came to the precious treasure. Alas! how vivid was the expectation when the blood of poor Tray was used to take off the charm, and after all to find their mistake.[104]

In the years after these early encounters with Colesville folk life Emily lived with her brother Esick Lyon Coburn. He had married a milliner from Philadelphia and subsequently moved to Sandford. There he pursued his trade as a tanner, and his wife opened a millinery establishment. About 1828 Emily began a two-year apprentice with her sister-in-law. As Emily began her third year of residence she was caught up in a religious excitement in the neighborhood. She joined the newly organized Presbyterian Church in Sandford.

Sandford and Colesville had both been created in 1821 from the township of Windsor, which originally covered the entire eastern end of Broome County.[105] The Presbyterian Church had been in the Windsor area since 1800, but the separate Sandford church was organized in the winter of 1829-30.[106] On February 1,

---

[104] Ibid., 32-33. William G. Hartley wrote, "It is possible, although evidence is lacking, that the Knights had interest in money digging ventures, such as friend Stowell sponsored, and that their interest in Joseph's story about gold plates might have had a profit motive at first. But their devotion to Joseph Smith for the next two decades was religious, not commercial" (*"They Are My Friends": A History of the Joseph Knight Family, 1825-1850* [Provo, Utah: Grandin Book, 1986], 22).

[105] Thomas F. Gordon, *Gazetteer of the State of New York* (Philadelphia: T. K. and P. G. Collins, 1836), 362.

[106] The church was first organized as the North Branch of the Presbyterian Church of Windsor, and in 1812 it became a separate church known as the Colesville Presbyterian Church. It had its central meeting place on Cole's Hill, where Nathaniel Cole had built the tavern that gave the area its name. By 1820 there was a house of worship there (Pattengill, *History of the Presbytery of Binghamton*, 18-20). The General Assembly of the Presbyterian Church (U.S.A.) first listed the Sandford church in its May 1830 *Minutes*. The last time

1830, Reverend John Sherer was commissioned by the American Home Missionary Society to serve the Colesville and Sandford churches for a twelve-month period, with three months' salary in hand and the next three months pledged.[107] Sherer, then thirty-nine, was a graduate of Andover and had been ordained in 1825. He had served a pastorate in Litchfield, New Hampshire, and was a member of the Oneida Conference before being assigned to Broome County. He arrived on the field in February, and after completing six months of labor, he reported to the New York office on the status of his work.

At its organization the Sandford church consisted of five members and "As many more were examined and propounded for admission." By this he meant that five more were examined as to their personal experience of conversion and their understanding of the gospel message of repentance and faith in Jesus Christ for salvation. "These," he added, "have been received since. At another communion Three have been added, at another one <by letter>; and there now stand propounded, three others. A few more it is hoped will unite themselves." He adds, "Thus a vine has been planted, where a dreary moral waste has long <existed>. This little Flock of Christ appear to be 'steadfast, unmovable, always abounding in the work of the Lord,' though opposed on every side."

Concerning Colesville Reverend Sherer wrote: "In Colesville every good object seems to be opposed by some. Yet even here, hope seems to be lighting up. There have been a few cases of conversion, since I came here, and now there is an appearance of seriousness on the minds of several. In a distant part of the society where for a few sabbaths past I have appointed meetings at 5 o'Clock, there begins to be some favorable appearances."[108]

---

it appeared was in the May 1833 *Minutes*, after which it dissolved or was merged with another church.

[107] American Home Missionary Society (AHMS) archives, "Fourth Report," 34, #321. All papers and correspondence of AHMS are housed in the Amistad Research Center, Tilton Hall, Tulane University, New Orleans, Louisiana.

[108] John Sherer to Reverend Absalom Peters, Aug. 20, 1830, AHMS archives. Part of this letter was edited for publication and printed in *The Home Missionary, and American Pastor's Journal* 3 (Nov. 1, 1830):143.

Emily Coburn had been a new Presbyterian convert. She found her sister's religious enthusiasm more than a match for her own. "She was as firm as the everlasting hills in the belief of Mormonism," Emily wrote, "and seemed to have the whole Bible at her tongue's end. She was of the belief that God had again visited His People, and again set His hand, the second time, to recover the house of Israel." Sally warned Emily against condemning what she did not understand.

Emily had determined it was useless to try to change her sister's mind and she decided to return to her brother's in Sandford. Emily and the Knight family attended services at her sister's home on Sunday, June 27. Emily recalled, "The discourse was delivered by Oliver Cowd[e]ry, an elder of the Mormon church, and a witness to the gold plates."[109] A message came to Emily that her brother Esick wished to see her in the grove some distance from the house:

> I felt reluctant in granting his request, but through the advice of my sister I ventured to go. I at this time attempted to make plain to him the reason of my tarrying at my sister's, and I then believed he understood me perfectly. While in the midst of our conversation, who should come but the Rev. Mr. Sherer, pastor of our church in Sandford. He came and took my hand and holding it so long and firmly I thought it odd.[110]

Holding tightly to her hand, the pastor tried to move her down the lane to a spot where her uncle was waiting with a horse and buggy to take her back to Sandford. For some reason Sherer failed to mention this detail, and it was only gradually that she learned what their intent really was. At the time Emily felt Sherer's

---

[109] Austin, *Mormonism*, 36. Joseph Smith's history records, "The Sabbath arrived and we held our meeting, Oliver Cowdery preached" (Manuscript History A-1: 42; Jessee, *Papers of Joseph Smith* 1:309). This appears to be the Sabbath service that both Emily and Joseph Smith's history refers to when Oliver Cowdery preached. Cowdery and Smith returned to Colesville in July 1830 to confirm those who had been baptized but they were prevented and had to leave because of persecution (Ibid. 1:317-18).

[110] Austin, *Mormonism*, 40.

behavior seemed crazy, holding so tenaciously to her hand. She asked her brother to help her, but he refused, saying she would do well to listen to his advice.

At that point her sister, accompanied by other Mormons, arrived at the grove. Sally rushed up to Emily and wrenched Sherer's hand from hers, yelling, "What are you doing with my sister? What are you doing with my sister?" Emily remembered her white face as she repeated these words. The confrontation proved too much for Sherer and her brother, and Emily slipped into the house while the others argued for about half an hour. Finally Sally and her companions returned to the house and once more were seated and quietly talking and singing when, Emily remembered, her uncle Henry

> rode up to the door on a white, stately, beautiful horse, and as he drew up he exclaimed, "You are happy now you have accomplished your purpose, and I hope you enjoy it; but this will not be of long endurance, let me tell you." "O, yes," said one of the [Mormon] elders, "you are an attorney, probably you will take steps in this matter, but not to-day." "Sir," said another Mormon elder, "you are mad; you look as white as the horse you are riding; to-day is the holy Sabbath, and you are a deacon; don't indulge in such a passion." Many hard words were used on both sides; and here the subject ended, by putting spurs to the white steed, under a two hundred and twenty [pound] burden, which seemed light and easy for the noble animal.[111]

The matter did not end there. That evening, although it was dark and rainy, her brother-in-law spurred his horse on "through darkness, mud and rain, and dead of night" to her father's house in Guilford, some thirty miles away, where he obtained their permission to consult an attorney and seize Emily in her parents' name. Returning in the morning, he came to Emily and informed her that he now had authority to take her away. Emily replied that she would willingly have gone without all that trouble, if they had just asked her and provided some means of getting back. In fact,

---

[111] Ibid., 41-42.

she had on her own concluded to return to her brother's but Newel Knight had not yet found time or a team to take her. She returned to Sandford, where she was met with "sober faces and cold hands." Still she remembered that she managed to "choke down" her feelings. This incident appears in condensed form in Joseph Smith's history:

Amongst the many present at this meeting was one Emily Coburn sister to the wife of Newel Knight. The Revd. Mr. Shearer, a divine of the presbyterian faith, who had considered himself her pastor, came to understand that She was likely to believe our doctrine, and had a short <time> previous to this, our meeting, came to labor with her, but having spent some time with her without being able to persuade her against us, he endeavored to have her leave her sisters house, and go with him to her father's, who lived at a distance of at least some [blank] miles off: For this purpose he had recourse to stratagem, He told her that one of her brothers was waiting at a certain place, wishful to have her go home with him. He succeeded thus to get her a little distance from the house when, seeing that her brother was not in waiting for her, She refused to go any further with him; upon which he got hold of her by the arm to force her along; but her sister, was soon with them; the two women were too many for him and he was forced to sneak off without his errand, after all his labor and ingenuity. Nothing daunted however he went to her Father, represented to him something or other, which induced the Old Gentleman to give him a power of Attorney, which, as soon as our meeting was over, on the above named Sunday evening, he immediately served upon her and carried her off to her father's residence, by open violence, against her will. All his labor was in vain, however, for the said Emily Coburn, in a short time afterwards, was baptized and confirmed a member of "the Church of Jesus Christ of Latter Day Saints."[112]

---

[112] Manuscript History Book A-1: 43; Jessee, *Papers of Joseph Smith* 1:310-11, compare page 251. The name of the church at this time was the Church of Christ but by the time Smith's history was written it was called the Church of Jesus

After Emily returned home from Colesville, a rumor came to the attention of her family that she too was planning to join the new church Sally attended. "I received daily visits from the pastor of our church, who gave me a prayer book and wished me to learn some of the prayers," she reported, "but I returned the book, saying I wished to be led and taught by one who said, 'Take my yoke upon you, and learn of me.'"[113] Those words betray the pain and stubbornness of a strong-willed young woman.

In keeping with the Presbyterian procedures of church discipline, a course of gospel labor was commenced. Patterned on Matthew 18, the first step in such labor was for an individual privately to approach the offending party and seek to restore that person. If this failed one or two others were taken along for the second visit to assist in the settlement and to serve as witnesses in the event the matter had to be brought before the entire church.

The final stage in the process was lodging a formal complaint with the church and holding a public hearing. In Emily's case the complaint was lodged by officers of the church, including her own brother Esick Lyon Coburn.[114] The formal complaint read:

> *To the Church of Christ, in Sandford*:
> WHEREAS, E[mily]. M. [Coburn], a member of said church, embraces a most wicked and dangerous heresy; and whereas, we have taken with her the first and second steps of gospel labor, without obtaining satisfaction, we therefore make complaint to the church of which said E. M. [Emily Coburn] is a member, praying that the brethren of said church would bring her to an account for her unchristian conduct; and, as in duty bound, your servants will ever pray.
> H. M.
> E. L.

Christ of Latter Day Saints, which is what appears in the text. See Knight, *Sketches of Biography*, 54.

[113] Austin, *Mormonism*, 44.

[114] Ibid., 251. The initials E. L. on the complaint refer to her brother Esick Lyon [Coburn]. It is likely also that the initials H. M. represent the uncle she elsewhere (25) refers to as H. M. C., Hanry Cobourn listed in the 1830 census of Sandford as living just a few houses from Esek Cobourn (63). This is also probably the "Henry" Coburn recorded in the 1825 Sandford census.

B. S.[115]

Looking back on the affair, Emily acknowledged that her attitude could have been "more pleasing, cheerful, delightful." Yet each of the three separate times they visited her to labor with her, she affirms that

> I assured them I had no thought of joining them (the Mormons). This they did not seem to hear; and, to sum up the matter, their uncharitable actions drove me farther and still farther from believing in anything good. I was not yet eighteen years of age. My heart was stricken, and I could see no love manifested. In the advancement of time I perceived they still believed I intended joining that church, without listening to what I told them or trying to ascertain the truth in regard to it. They did not come to me in love and ask me to go with them to my brother's or my father's.[116]

The pastor continued to make his customary visits and eventually raised the matter of settling the complaint against her with the church. He informed her that there would be a meeting at the church the following day, and since the matter concerned her, he wished her to be present. "I did not intend to be obstinate," she recalled, "but my feelings revolted against it." Nevertheless she went and "as the meeting was expressly to the purpose of bringing me to an account," she stood before the church in her own defense. "I arose and told them the charges brought against me were incorrect," she reports, "and I was very sorry that so much hard labor had been done under false colors; but this I would say, for the satisfaction of the church, that inasmuch as I had been the means of so much dissatisfaction, I felt heartily sorry, and hoped that God and the church would pardon that mistake. This seemed to be all that was necessary, and they gave me the hand of fellowship, and here the trouble ended."[117]

Peace was short lived. Sometime in late September or early

---

[115] Ibid., 43, emphasis in original.
[116] Ibid., 39.
[117] Ibid., 47-48.

October, when the trees in New York take on a kaleidoscope of color, Emily returned to her father's home in Guilford. There she and her sister Jane braided straw bonnets, enjoyed the fall sunsets and the autumn-tinted trees. The painful events of the summer still lingered in her mind. "Why did not my father come or send after me when he heard of my intention to join the Mormon church? Why did they give a power of attorney to disgrace and ignominiously drag away this poor child[?]" Such unanswered questions flooded her mind and rendered her feelings peculiar.

Still her religious views remained the same, and she continued to pray that her life would be spent in the service of God and that her example would lead many to Christ. Then one day in autumn, when "the outward world seemed in slumber," a thought came into her mind that her sister Sally, whom she had not heard from for "several months" would come within two hours. Her mother refused to accept such a premonition. Yet within a short time Sally and her husband Newel arrived.

Even more startling than this presentiment was the willingness of her parents to let Emily return to the Knight farm in Colesville, where all the excitement had occurred. If this seemed inexplicable to Emily, it was even "more strange when, as if by some unknown power, I was baptized and confirmed in the Mormon church the next Sabbath after!" Such an intention had not entered her mind when she left her father's house, she confessed. All she could say in later reflection upon it is that she thought she was following her religious duty. Was it the utter confidence she had in her older sister's integrity, she wondered. She herself looked back on that day in surprise. Whatever the motivation that led her to unite with the new Church of Christ it profoundly altered the course of her young life.

The consternation and sorrow resulting from Emily Coburn's baptism into the new Church of Christ can be seen in the letter of Reverend John Sherer written in November describing the events of the summer:

> I will relate a circumstance that has given me pain. A member of the church in Sandford, a young female, has renounced her connexion with the church, and joined <another> in Colesville founded by Joseph Smith. This

man has been known, in these parts, for some time, as a kind of Juggler, who has pretended, through a glass, to see money under ground &c, &c. The book, on which he founds his new religion, is called the "Book of Mormon". It contains not much, and is rather calculated to suit the marvelous, and unthinking. No man in his right mind can think the Book or the doctrines it contains, worthy of the least notice; yet there are a number who profess to believe in it. Since the church was formed, which was some time in July [sic], about twenty have gathered around their standard, and have subscribed themselves to be the followers [of] Christ; for they call themselves a church of Christ, and the only church of Christ. All professing christians who do not adhere to their system, they consider as formalists; "having the form of Godliness, but denying the power." They have pretended to work miracles, such as casting out devils, and many other things, too blasphemous to mention. — It is believed, however, they have [atta]ined to about the zenith of their glory in this place. Their books remain unsold; <except> here and there an individual, none will buy them. It is thought the greatest speculation, which they probably anticipated, will prove a losing business. May the Lord speedily turn their counsels head long, and deliver those, whose feet have been taken in their snare.[118]

Meanwhile, at Fayette, in October 1830, the month after the second church conference, a minister named Peter Bauder spent a full day at the Peter Whitmer home. He spoke with Joseph Smith personally and published his recollection in 1834:

I called at P[eter]. Whitmer's house, for the purpose of

---

[118] Sherer to Rev. Absalom Peters, Nov. 18, 1830, AHMS archives. See Vogel, *Early Mormon Documents* 4:92-93. Smith's history reported Newel Knight's experience with the devil as occurring in April or May 1830, "he saw the devil leave him and vanish from his sight" (Manuscript History A-1:40; Jessee, *Papers of Joseph Smith* 1:306). Emily went with the Colesvlle church west to Ohio. From there she went on to the new Zion in western Missouri. She eventually settled in Nauvoo, Illinois, only to leave the church she had joined some ten years before.

seeing Smith, and searching into the mystery of his system of religion, and had the privilege of conversing with him alone, several hours, and of investigating his writings, church records, &c. I improved near four and twenty hours in close application with Smith and his followers: he could give me no christian experience, but told me that an angel told him he must go to a certain place in the town of Manchester, Ontario County, where was a secret treasure concealed, which he must reveal to the human family.[119]

While staying in Fayette in November, Joseph Smith met nineteen-year-old convert Orson Pratt who wrote, "By my request, on the 4th of Nov., the Prophet Joseph inquired of the Lord for me, and received the revelation published in the Doctrine and Covenants."[120] Pratt later added: "I went into that chamber [in the second story of the Peter Whitmer Sr.'s home] with the Prophet Joseph Smith, to inquire of the Lord; and he received a revelation for my benefit, which was written from the mouth of the Prophet by John Whitmer, one of the witnesses of the Book of Mormon."[121]

When Pratt and his traveling companion, Joseph F. Smith, visited David Whitmer on September 8, 1878, Pratt provided further insight into the way Smith obtained this revelation. In a letter written three weeks after their visit, James R. B. Vancleave reports asking Pratt about "his belief in the seer stone":

at Peter Whitmer Sr's residence he [Orson Pratt] asked Joseph whether he could not ascertain what his mission was, and Joseph answered him that he would see, & asked

---

[119] Peter Bauder, *The Kingdom and Gospel of Jesus Christ: Contrasted with that of Anti-Christ* (Canajohrie, New York: Printed by A. H. Calhoun, 1834), 36. One of the main focuses of Bauder's pamphlet was his understanding that Christian churches had throughout history lost the spirit of personal forgiveness and instead turned to domineering priestcraft. Therefore, he found it important that he could find no such experience of personal salvation in his conference with Smith.

[120] "History of Orson Pratt," *The Deseret News* 8 (June 2, 1858):62; also in Watson, *The Orson Pratt Journals*, 9. See Marquardt, *Joseph Smith Revelations*, 94; BC 36; LDS D&C 34; RLDS D&C 33.

[121] *Journal of Discourses* 7:311, Sept. 18, 1859. See also Ibid. 12:88, Aug. 11, 1867; and Ibid. 17:290, Feb. 7, 1875.

Pratt and John Whitmer to go upstairs with him, and on arriving there Joseph produced a small stone called a seer stone, and putting it into a Hat soon commenced speaking and asked Elder P[ratt]. to write as he would speak, but being too young and timid and feeling his unworthiness he asked whether Bro. John W[hitmer]. could not write it, and the Prophet said that he could: Then came the revelation to the Three named given Nov. 4th 1830.[122]

David Whitmer stated that many of Smith's early revelations were received through the seer stone. He wrote, "The revelations in the Book of Commnadments [sic] up to June, 1829, were given through the 'stone,' through which the Book of Mormon was translated."[123] Smith received many of his revelations from July 1828 to June 1829 (when he was dictating the text of the Book of Mormon) by a stone placed in his hat—the same method he used in hunting for lost treasure.[124]

Sidney Rigdon, a new convert from Ohio, met Joseph Smith the following month in December. He first heard about Mormonism early in November and received baptism on November 8, 1830.[125] He was ordained an Elder by Oliver Cowdery in Ohio. Rigdon, with Smith, visited the branch of the church in Colesville.[126] While there Rigdon evidently checked the docket books of both Joseph Chamberlain and Joel K. Noble. Reportedly when he returned to Ohio about February 1, 1831, he "with a great show of good nature, commenced a long detail of his

---

[122] James R. B. Vancleave to Joseph Smith III, Sept. 29, 1878, "Miscellaneous Letters and Papers," RLDS archives. See also Cook, *David Whitmer Interviews*, 239-40.

[123] David Whitmer, *An Address to All Believers in Christ*, 53.

[124] Joseph Smith's history records that eight revelations were received through the "Urim and Thummim" (seer stone in a hat) between July 1828 and June 1829. It is probable that all the revelations during this period were received through the stone as David Whitmer states.

[125] Copy of letter of Oliver Cowdery dated Nov. 12, 1830, in a Newel Knight Journal, private possession. See Vogel, *Early Mormon Documents* 2:415.

[126] The Book of John Whitmer as cited in Bruce N. Westergren, ed., *From Historian to Dissident: The Book of John Whitmer* (Salt Lake City: Signature Books, 1995), 8, 13, original in RLDS archives. Emily Coburn mentions a visit of Sidney Rigdon but places it at an earlier time frame in her account (Austin, *Mormonism*, 37).

researches after the character of Joseph Smith; he declared that even his enemies had nothing to say against his character; he had brought a transcript from the docket of two magistrates, where Smith had been tried as a disturber of the peace, which testified that he was honorably acquitted."[127]

During the early months of 1831 the Smith, Whitmer, and Knight families together with many converts from New York would join Rigdon and others in Kirtland, Ohio, now the gathering place of the Saints at their new church headquarters.

---

[127] "Mormonism," *The Telegraph* 2 (Feb. 15, 1831), Painesville, Ohio; reprinted in the David S. Burnet, ed., *Evangelical Inquirer* 1 (March 7, 1831):226, Dayton, Ohio; also published in Howe, *Mormonism Unvailed*, 113. Richard L. Anderson identified the article's author "M. S. C." as probably Matthew S. Clapp; see "The Impact of the First Preaching in Ohio," *Brigham Young University Studies* 11 (Summer 1971):480.

11

New Jerusalem in America

The Puritans who settled in America had a feeling of being the Chosen People, living in a land of promise as a new Israel. The idea of a western New Jerusalem was mentioned in the seventeenth century by Samuel Sewall when he asked "why the Heart of America may not be the seat of the New Jerusalem." Cotton Mather thought that the New Jerusalem would be westward, beyond the confines of New England.[1]

While some looked for a New Jerusalem in the state of New York, others spiritualized the idea and saw the cause of Zion in the revivals of the 1820s. Such expressions as "growing zeal for the prosperity of Zion," "enquiring the way to Zion" and "wishes well to the cause of Zion" were expressions of the revival movement and referred to the building up of the church.[2]

Out of this background came the Book of Mormon. According to this record Jesus Christ gave instructions to the forefathers of the Native Americans concerning the New Jerusalem to be built on this land. The Gentiles (who believe) "shall assist my people, the rem[n]ant of Jacob [Native Americans]; and also, as

---

[1] Alan Heimert, "Puritanism, the Wilderness, and the Frontier," *The New England Quarterly* 26 (Sept. 1953):380-81. See also Gustav H. Blanke with Karen Lynn, "God's Base of Operations: Mormon Variations on the American Sense of Mission," *Brigham Young University Studies* 20 (Fall 1979):83-92. James B. Allen and Glen M. Leonard wrote: "The Puritans saw themselves as a chosen people, commissioned by God to build a New Jerusalem, or a City of Zion, in America—an exemplary community that all could observe and emulate" (*The Story of the Latter-day Saints* [Salt Lake City: Deseret Book, 1976], 9).

[2] Rev. George Lane, "Revival of Religion on Ontario District," *The Methodist Magazine* (New York) 8 (April 1825):161, letter dated Jan. 25, 1825; *The Christian Herald* (Portsmouth) 8 (March 1825):7 and *Wayne Sentinel* 2 (March 2, 1825):4, Palmyra, New York. The minutes of the Geneva Presbytery states: "In the congregation of Palmyra, the Lord has appeared in his glory to build up Zion." (Geneva Presbytery Minutes, D:27, Presbyterian Historical Society, Philadelphia, Pennsylvania.

many of the house of Israel as shall come, that they may build a city, which shall be called the New Jerusalem."[3]

The development of this idea in the Book of Mormon occurs in the books of 3 Nephi and Ether. This land of America shall be a New Jerusalem with Jesus Christ being in the midst of the Native American people.[4] A city would be built "called the New Jerusalem" and this would become an earthly city that the Gentiles would assist the Native Americans to build.[5] In the book of Ether it is explained that America "became a choice land above all other lands, a chosen land of the Lord."[6]

> and that it was the place of the New Jerusalem, which should come down out of Heaven, and the Holy Sanctuary of the Lord. Behold, Ether saw the days of Christ, and he spake concerning a New Jerusalem upon this land . . . wherefore the remnant of the house of Joseph [Native Americans] shall be built upon this land; and it shall be a land of their inheritance; and they shall build up a holy city unto the Lord, like unto the Jerusalem of old[7]

Ether stated that after the earth passes away "there shall be a new heaven and a new earth" and then the New Jerusalem comes down out of heaven.[8] The New Jerusalem becomes identifiable with the heavenly city of Revelation chapter 21 coming down "out of heaven."[9]

In September 1830, five months after Joseph Smith Jr. organized the restoration Church of Christ, one of the eight witnesses to the Book of Mormon, Hiram Page claimed to receive revelations "concerning the upbuilding of Zion" and other matters through the medium of a seer stone. "Finding, however, that many especially the Whitmer family and Oliver Cowdery were believing

---

[3] 1830 BOM, 501; LDS 3 Nephi 21:23; RLDS 10:1.
[4] 1830 BOM, 497; LDS 3 Nephi 20:22 (see also 21:25); RLDS 9:58-59 (see also 10:4).
[5] 1830 BOM, 501; LDS 3 Nephi 21:23; RLDS 10:1.
[6] 1830 BOM, 566; LDS Ether 13:2; RLDS 6:2.
[7] 1830 BOM, 566; LDS Ether 13:3-4, 8; RLDS 6:3-4, 8.
[8] 1830 BOM, 566; LDS Ether 13:9, 10; RLDS 6:9, 10.
[9] Revelation 21:2, 10.

much in the things set forth by this stone" Joseph Smith inquired of God concerning this matter and Page was told that what had been written was not of him.[10] In a revelation originating at Fayette, New York, Oliver Cowdery, the second elder, was called to "go unto the Lamanites [Native Americans] and preach my gospel unto them, and cause my church to be established among them."[11] Concerning the city called New Jerusalem they were told that "it is not revealed, and no man knoweth where the city shall be built, but it shall be given hereafter. Behold I say unto you, that it shall be on the borders by the Lamanites."[12]

Later three others (including Peter Whitmer Jr.) were called to accompany Oliver Cowdery on this mission. In October, Parley P. Pratt and Ziba Peterson were called as well. The instructions stated that Pratt "shall go with my servant Oliver and Peter into the wilderness among the Lamanites and Ziba also shall go with them and I myself will go with them and be in their midst and I am their advocate with the Father and nothing shall prevail" against them.[13] On October 17, 1830 at Manchester, New York, Cowdery himself stated that he was going "to rear up a pillar as a witness to where the Temple of God shall be built, in the glorious New-Jerusalem."[14]

While there were Native Americans living in New York, the four elders "were appointed to go into the wilderness through the western States, and to the Indian territory."[15] The western states were those west of New York, including Ohio, Indiana, Illinois, and Missouri. The Indian country, where some of the woodland tribes had been relocated west of the Missouri River, was at that time unorganized. These missionaries knew the general location of

---

[10] Manuscript History, Book A-1:54; *History of the Church* 1:109-110; Jessee, *Papers of Joseph Smith* 1:263, 323. See also BC 30:11; LDS D&C 28:11; RLDS D&C 27:4.

[11] Marquardt, *Joseph Smith Revelations*, 84; BC 30:7; LDS D&C 28:8; RLDS D&C 27:3. "Lamanites" is a Book of Mormon term for the Native Americans.

[12] BC 30:8-9; LDS D&C 28:9; RLDS D&C 27:3.

[13] Marquardt, *Joseph Smith Revelations*, 92; LDS D&C 32:2-3; RLDS D&C 31:1. This revelation was not published in the BC.

[14] Statement signed by Oliver Cowdery and dated Oct. 17, 1830, cited in a letter of Ezra Booth to Rev. Ira Eddy, November 24, 1831 and published in the *Ohio Star* 2 (Dec. 8, 1831):3, Ravenna, Ohio..

[15] *Autobiography of Parley P. Pratt*, 35.

where they were going prior to their departure. Their destination would be outside the states in Indian Territory.

The missionaries traveled to what Pratt called the Cattaraugus Indians (actually the Seneca and Onondagas tribes) near Buffalo, New York.[16] They stayed a few hours and left two copies of the Book of Mormon. Then the Lamanite missionaries eventually traveled through the state of Ohio, to the Delaware Nation in the territory west of Missouri. But, lacking credentials, they were reduced to preaching to the white population in Jackson and Lafayette counties, Missouri. In essence, the mission failed— the Church of Christ was not established among the native population.

The missionaries arrived at Kirtland, Ohio, on October 29, 1830.[17] They preached and baptized seventeen people into the church on November 5. Pratt's former minister Sidney Rigdon was baptized a few days later. One of the converts, Frederick G. Williams, went with the missionaries on their journey. As they were preparing to depart, the Painesville *Telegraph* reported, "We understand that he [Cowdery] is bound for the regions beyond the Mississippi, where he contemplates founding a 'City of Refuge' for his followers, and converting the Indians, under his prophetic authority."[18] The five men traveled to Sandusky, Ohio, called upon the Wyandot Indians, and spent several days there. Then they continued on to Cincinnati on the Ohio River and walked to St. Louis, Missouri. From St. Louis they continued to Independence, Jackson County, Missouri, arriving about January 13, 1831. Of their arrival Peter Whitmer, Jr. wrote:

we came to independance on the twelfth [sic; first] month on the 13 d[ay] of the month on the 14 daye of the month I began to Labour with mine owne hands Brother Oliver & Parl[e]y and Frederick started to see the deleware tribe in a few dayes they came to see me & brother Ziba and they declared that the Lamanites received them with great joy

---

[16] "History of Parley P. Pratt," *Deseret News* 8 (May 19, 1858):53.
[17] Copy of Oliver Cowdery letter, dated Nov. 12, 1830, in a Newel Knight journal currently in private possession.
[18] *Telegraph* 2 (Nov. 16, 1830):3.

my brethren started againe to the deleweres- and also <to>
the Shayneye[19]

Parley Pratt mentioned that "Two of our number [Whitmer
and Peterson] now commenced work as tailors in the village of
Independence, while the others crossed the frontier line and
commenced a mission among the Lamanites, or Indians."[20] Oliver
Cowdery wrote that he

had two intervi<e>ws with the Chief of the delewares, who
is <a> very old & venerable looking man. after laying
before him & eighteen or twenty of the Council of that
nation the truth, he said that <he> he and they were very
glad for what I their Brother had told them and they had
received it in their hearts &c- But how the matter will go
with this tribe to me is uncirtain [uncertain] ne[i]ther Can I
at presen<t> Conclude mutch [much] about it[21]

Cowdery, Pratt, and Frederick G. Williams started to
preach and instruct the Shawnee and Delaware, but lacking a
government license, they were ordered off the reservation by
Indian agent Richard Cummins. They were told they could obtain a
permit from General Clark, who was in charge of Indian affairs in
St. Louis. General Clark was William Clark of the famed Lewis
and Clark expedition to the uncharted West.

Both Pratt and Cummins wrote to Clark in St. Louis. Clark
was not available from November 30, 1830 through March 31,
1831. Clark's business was being conducted by John Ruland, sub-
agent.[22] Cowdery's letter written on February 14 read:

---

[19] Statement of Peter Whitmer Jr., Dec. 13, 1831, LDS archives. That Whitmer
is incorrect as to their arrival in "the twelfth month" is clear from the writings of
Pratt and Cowdery. Pratt wrote that they were near St. Louis in "the beginning
of 1831" (*Autobiography of Parley P. Pratt*, 40). Cowdery reported on January
29, 1831 "we ar[r]ived at this place a few days since" (Jessee, *Personal Writings
of Joseph Smith*, 256).
[20] *Autobiography of Parley P. Pratt*, 41.
[21] Cowdery to "My dearly beloved bretheren [brethren]," Jan. 29, 1831, copy of
letter, see Jessee, *Personal Writings of Joseph Smith*, 256-57.
[22] Warren A. Jennings, "The First Mormon Mission to the Indians," *Kansas
Historical Quarterly* 37 (Autumn 1971):298.

As I have been appointed by a society of Christians in the State of New York to superintend the establishing Missions among the Indians I doubt not but I shall have the approbation of your honour and a permit for myself and all who may be recommended to me by that Society to have free intercourse with the several tribes in establishing schools for the instruction of their children and also teaching them the Christian religion without intruding or interfering with any other Mission now established.[23]

Cummins's letter to Clark of February 15 contained the following comments:

A few days agoe three Men all Strangers to me went among the Indians Shawanees & Delawares, they say for the purpose of preaching to and Instructing them in Religious Matters, they say they are sent by God and must proceed, they have a new Revelation with them, as there [their] Guide in teaching the Indians which they say was shown to one of their Sects in a miraculous way, and that an Angel from Heaven appeared to one of their Men and two others of their Sect, and shewed them that the work was from god and much more &c. I have refused to let them stay or, go among the Indians unless they first obtain permission from you or, some of the officers of the Genl. Government who I am bound to obey. I am informed that they intend to apply to you for permission to go among the Indians, if you refuse, then they will go to the Rocky Mountains.[24]

Pratt wrote in his autobiography: "Passing through the tribe of Shawnees we tarried one night with them, and the next day crossed the Kansas river and entered among the Delawares,"[25] where they met Chief William Anderson.

---

[23] "U.S. Superintendency of Indian Affairs," Vol. 6:103; William Clark Papers, MS 95, (microfilm edition), Manuscript Division, Kansas State Historical Society, Topeka, Kansas.

[24] Ibid. 6:113-14.

[25] *Autobiography of Parley P. Pratt*, 41.

We continued for several days to instruct the old chief and many of his tribe. . . . The excitement now reached the frontier settlements in Missouri, and stirred up the jealousy and envy of the Indian agents and sectarian missionaries to that degree that we were soon ordered out of the Indian country as disturbers of the peace; and even threatened with the military in case of non-compliance. We accordingly departed from the Indian country, and came over the line, and commenced laboring in Jackson County, Missouri, among the whites. We were well received and listened to by many; and some were baptized and added to the Church. Thus ended our first Indian Mission in which we had preached the gospel in its fulness, and distributed the record of their forefathers among three tribes, viz: the Catteraugus Indians [sic], near Buffalo, N.Y., the Wyandots of Ohio, and the Delawares west of Missouri.[26]

It was agreed that Pratt should travel to St. Louis. In a letter to Smith and others on April 8, Oliver Cowdery reported the following:

we had been long looking for [a] letter from you with the hope that the news we should received wou[l]d give our friend[s] who reside in this Land joy by confirming them in the belief that we were men of truth and the Lord God of hosts has not forsaken the earth but is in very deed about to redeem his ancien[t] covenant people & lead them with the fulness of the Gentiles to springs, yea, fountain of living waters to his holy hill of Zion[27]

Cowdery continued his letter:

the principl[e] chief says he believes ev[e]ry word of the Book [of Mormon] & there are many more in the Nation who believes & we understand there are many among the

---

[26] Ibid., 44.
[27] Cowdery to "My dearly beloved brethren and sisters in the Lord," April 8, 1831, copy of letter in Joseph Smith Letterbook 1:10, LDS archives.

Shawnees who also believe & we trust that when the Lord shall open our way we shall have glorious times . . . the agent for the Lamanites is very strict with us and we think some what strenuous respecting our having liberty to visit our brethren the Lamanites but we trust that when our brother Parley returns we shall have a permit from General Clark, who is the Superintendent of Indian affairs west of the Missi[ssi]ppi who must have a recommend or security before he can give a permit for any stranger or foreigner to go among them to teach or preach.

While Cowdery stated that his teachings were received with gladness, there was no mention of baptisms being performed. The Church of Christ was not established among the native population.

It is possible that Pratt carried Cowdery's letter to Clark personally. Another letter from Cowdery of April 16 is not extant. On May 7 Oliver wrote to Smith, "I have nothing particular to write as concerning the Lamanites."[28] Pratt left St. Louis and arrived in Kirtland, Ohio, near the end of March, and from there embarked on a mission to the Shakers.

Joseph Smith's history contains the following: "From P. P. Pratt, who had returned from the expedition of last fall, during the spring we had verbal information; and from letters from the still remaining elders we had written intelligence," and also that "this was the most important subject which then engrossed the attention of the saints."[29]

Two of the first converts among the white population in Jackson County were Joshua Lewis and his wife who lived in Kaw Township, west of Independence. They were baptized in early 1831.[30] Peter Whitmer Jr., stated, "then [we] resorted among the gentiles and declared the word and Babtized 7."[31]

---

[28] Cowdery to "Our dearly beloved Brethren," May 7, 1831, Ibid. 1:12.

[29] *Times and Seasons* 5 (Feb. 15, 1844):432. For a change in the manuscript history after the 1844 publication, see Jessee, *Papers of Joseph Smith,* 1:354 and *History of the Church*, 1:181-82.

[30] Jessee, "Joseph Knight's Recollection," 39; see also Journal History of the Church, Feb. 3, 1831, LDS archives.

[31] Statement of Peter Whitmer Jr., Dec. 13, 1831, LDS archives.

While the mission to the Native Americans was in progress Joseph Smith continued his revision of the Bible still working on the book of Genesis. During the month of December 1830 he dictated what was called the "Prophecy of Enoch" which contained a story about another holy city, know as the city of Enoch, built in Old Testament times and taken from the earth into heaven. The city was described in this way:

> And the Lord called his people, Zion, because they were of one heart and of one mind, and dwelt in righteousness; and there were no poor among them. And Enoch continued his preaching in righteousness unto the people of God. And it came to pass in his days, that he built a city that was called the city of Holiness, even Zion.[32]

Enoch beheld in vision that "Zion in [the] process of time was taken up into heaven." The elect were to be gathered "from the four quarters of the earth, unto a place which I shall prepare; an holy city, that my people may gird up their loins, and be looking forth for the time of my coming; for there shall be my tabernacle, and it shall be called Zion; a New Jerusalem."[33] In addition, the promise was made that in the last days Enoch's city of Zion "should again come on the earth."[34]

In January 1831 church leader Joseph Smith with others moved from Fayette, New York to Kirtland, Geauga County, Ohio and established church headquarters there. Within a week Smith revealed instructions on the laws of the church. Included in the

---

[32] Genesis 7:23-25 (JST); LDS Moses 7:18-19; RLDS D&C 36:2-3; Old Testament Dictated Manuscript, 16, RLDS archives; *The Evening and the Morning Star* 1 (Aug. 1832):2, Independence, Missouri.

[33] Genesis 7:27, 70 (JST); LDS Moses 7:21, 62; RLDS D&C 36:3, 12; compare with Book of Commandments 29:8-9; LDS D&C 29:7-8; RLDS D&C 28:2. "And it came to pass, that Zion [the city of Enoch] was not, for God received it up into his own bosom; and from thence went forth the saying, Zion is fled" (Genesis 7:78 [JST]; LDS Moses 7:69; RLDS D&C 36:14).

[34] Genesis 9:21 (JST). The coming together of the city of Enoch (Zion) and the New Jerusalem is further described in a revelation to Joseph Smith: "The Lord hath brought down Zion [of Enoch] from above. The Lord hath brought up Zion [the New Jerusalem] from beneath" (LDS D&C 84:100; RLDS D&C 83:17; *The Evening and the Morning Star* 1 [Jan. 1833]:3).

instructions the saints were told that what was left over from their consecrations to the church were to be used for:

> building up the New Jerusalem which is hereafter to be revealed that my Covenant people may be gathered in me in the day that I shall come to my Temple this do for the salvation of my people.[35]

After receiving a letter from Oliver Cowdery, Joseph received in March 1831 another revelation which instructed church members to gather their riches (money) so they could purchase an inheritance that would be designated later:

> it shall be called the New Jerusalem, a land of peace, a City of refuge, a place of safety for the saints of the most high God . . . & it shall come to pass that the righteous shall be gathered out from among all nations & shall come to Zion singing with songs of everlasting joy.[36]

Following a church conference in June 1831 at Kirtland, Ohio, certain men were instructed to convene the next conference in Missouri where missionaries to the Native Americans had gone. Missouri was "the land which I will consecrate unto my people, which are a remnant of Jacob [Native Americans], and them who are heirs according to the covenant. . . . if ye are faithful, ye shall assemble yourselves together to rejoice upon the land of Missouri, which is the land of your inheritance, which is now the land of your enemies. But behold I the Lord will hasten the city in its time."[37] The region westward unto the "borders of the Lamanites"

---

[35] Marquardt, *Joseph Smith Revelations*, 108; BC 44:29-30; LDS D&C 42:35-36; RLDS D&C 42:10 (9 Feb. 1831).

[36] Marquardt, *Joseph Smith Revelations*, 124; BC 48:59, 67; also published in *The Evening and the Morning Star* 1 (June 1832):2; see LDS D&C 45:66, 71; RLDS D&C 45:12, 14. On February 9 Joseph Smith mentioned the New Jerusalem that was to be built. See BC 44:9, 29, 47, 51; LDS D&C 42:9, 35, 62, 67; RLDS D&C 42:3, 10, 17, 18.

[37] Marquardt, *Joseph Smith Revelations*, 136, 138; BC 54:1, 43-44; LDS D&C 52:2, 42-43; RLDS D&C 52:1, 9 (June 6, 1831).

was where the saints were to obtain inheritance and the physical location of their city of Zion—the New Jerusalem.[38]

On June 19, 1831 Joseph Smith Jr., Sidney Rigdon, Martin Harris, Edward Partridge, William W. Phelps, Joseph Coe, A. Sidney Gilbert, and Elizabeth Gilbert left together for the cities of Cleveland, Cincinnati, and Louisville, Kentucky. The group arrived at St. Louis on July 1. They then divided into two groups with Smith, Harris, Phelps, Partridge, and Coe walking from St. Louis to Independence where they arrived on July 14. Members of the Colesville branch arrived in Independence eleven days later.

Ezra Booth gave a brief description of Independence when he arrived with Sidney Rigdon:

> It is a new Town, containing a courthouse built of brick, two or three merchant stores, and fifteen or twenty dwelling houses, built mostly of logs hewed on both sides; and is situated on a handsome rise of ground, about three miles south of the Missouri River, and about twelve miles east of the dividing line between the U. S. and the Indian Reserve, and is the County seat of Jackson County.[39]

Joseph Smith found no Lamanite church established among the natives. On July 20, 1831, Smith received the following revelation that mentioned the location of the temple to be built in the New Jerusalem:

> the land of Missouri which is the land which I have appointed and consecrated for the gathering of the saints Wherefore this is the land of promise and the place for the city of Zion yea and thus saith the Lord your God if ye will receive wisdom behold the place which is called Independence is the center place and the spot for the temple is lying westward upon a lot which is not far from the courthouse Wherefore it is wisdom that the Land should be

---

[38] Marquardt, *Joseph Smith Revelations*, 139; BC 56:9; LDS D&C 54:8; RLDS D&C 54:2. See revelation given in May 1831 which also mentions the "borders of the Lamanites" (Kirtland Revelations Book, 92, LDS archives).

[39] Booth to Rev. Ira Eddy, Nov. 14, 1831 in *Ohio Star* 2 (Nov. 17, 1831):3, Ravenna, Ohio.

purchased by the saints and also every tract lying westward even unto the line run[n]ing directly between Jew [Native Americans] and Gentile and also every tract bordering by the prairies inasmuch as my disciples are enabled to buy lands behold this is wisdom that they may obtain it for an everlasting inheritance[40]

Two manuscripts exist of the July 20, 1831 revelation regarding the gathering to Missouri, and also concerning A. Sidney Gilbert. This revelation pointed to Independence as "the place of the city of Zion and the gathering." The temple property was designated as "upon a lot which is not far from the courthouse," west of Independence.[41] The revelation also indicated that the gospel would be preached unto the Lamanites (Native Americans) by "clerks employed" in Gilbert's service at a future store, sending goods to the Lamanites under license.

Though there were no Indian converts when Joseph Smith and his associates arrived in Independence, it is evident that Smith was still planning to preach to the Native Americans. He could not have struck upon a doctrine more provocative on the frontier than his belief that the Lamanites would unite with the Mormons to prepare the way for Christ's return. Ezra Booth, one of the elders who arrived at Independence, wrote four months later as a former member:

Another method has been invented, in order to remove obstacles which hitherto have proved insurmountable. "The Lord's store-house," is to be furnished with goods suited to the Indian trade, and persons are to obtain license from the government to dispose of them to the Indians in their own territory; at the same time, they are to disseminate the principles of Mormonism among them. From this

---

[40] Marquardt, *Joseph Smith Revelations*, 142; LDS D&C 57:1-5; RLDS D&C 57:1.
[41] On the courthouse see Max H. Parkin, "The Courthouse mentioned in the Revelation on Zion," *Brigham Young University Studies* 14 (Summer 1974):451-57. On additional background see Pearl Wilcox, *The Latter Day Saints on the Missouri Frontier* (Independence: author, 1972), 15-42.

smug[g]ling method of preaching to the Indians, they anticipate a favorable result.

Booth also mentioned an alternate plan to get onto the Indian Territory:

In addition to this, and to co-operate with it, it has been made known by revelation, that it will be pleasing to the Lord, should they form a matrimonial alliance with the Natives; and by this means the Elders, who comply with the thing so pleasing to the Lord, and for which the Lord has promised to bless those who do it abundantly, gain a residence in the Indian territory, independent of the agent.[42]

Oliver Cowdery wrote an account of the dedication ceremony for the place where the temple was to be built:

The day following [August 3, 1831] eight Elders viz. Joseph Smith Jr., Oliver Cowdery, Sidney Rigdon, Peter Whitmer Jr., Frederick G. Williams, Wm. W. Phelps, Martin Harris, and Joseph Coe. assembled together where the temple is to be erected. Sidney Rigdon dedicated the ground where the city is to Stand: and Joseph Smith Jr. laid a stone at the North east corner of the contemplated Temple in the name of the Lord Jesus of Nazareth. After all present had rendered thanks to the great ruler of the universe. Sidney Rigdon pronounced this Spot of ground wholy [wholly] dedicated unto the Lord forever: Amen.[43]

The land and site of the temple was outside the Independence city boundary and at the time of the dedication the property was owned by the state of Missouri. Sidney Rigdon had been instructed previously to "consecrate and dedicate this land,

---

[42] Booth to Rev. Ira Eddy, Dec. 6, 1831, in *Ohio Star* 2 (Dec. 8, 1831):3.

[43] As copied into "The Book of John Whitmer Kept by Commandment," chapter 9, page 32, RLDS archives; published in *Journal of History* 1 (Jan. 1908):59-60; and Westergren, *From Historian to Dissident*, 86-87.

and the spot of the temple."[44] John Whitmer mentioned that the stone laid was the "cornerstone of the Temple."[45] Ezra Booth described the event three months later in a letter:

> Should the inhabitants of Independence, feel a desire to visit this place, destined at some future time to become celebrated, they will have only to walk one half of a mile out of the Town, to a rise of ground, a short distance south of the road. They will be able to ascertain the spot, by the means of a sappling [sapling], distinguished from others by the bark being taken off on the north and on the east side. – On the south side of the sappling [sapling] will be found the letter, T, which stands for Temple; and on the east side ZOM for Zomar; which Smith says is the original word for Zion. Near the foot of the sappling [sapling], they will find a small stone, covered over with bushes, which were cut for that purpose. This is the corner-stone for the Temple.[46]

On August 9, five days after the church conference held in the land of Zion, Joseph Smith and a number of elders left Independence and used canoes to travel on the Missouri River as they returned to Kirtland, Ohio. On the eleventh about a hundred miles from Independence the canoe in which Smith and Rigdon were riding in almost capsized as it ran into some wood and those aboard could have drown.[47] William Phelps "in an open vision, by daylight, saw the Destroyer [the devil], in his most horrible power, ride upon the face of the waters. Others heard the noise, but saw not the vision."[48] They stopped for the night at a location known as

---

[44] Marquardt, *Joseph Smith Revelations*, 148; BC 59:70; LDS D&C 58:57; RLDS D&C 58:13 (Aug. [1-2], 1831).

[45] Westergren, *From Historian to Dissident*, 85.

[46] Booth to Rev. Ira Eddy, Nov. 14, 1831 in *Ohio Star* 2 (Nov. 17, 1831):3. That Joseph Smith considered "Zomar" to be Zion see "Grammar & A[l]phabet of the Egyptian Language," 23, 1835 manuscript book located in LDS archives. See H. Michael Marquardt, comp., *The Joseph Smith Egyptian Papers* (Cullman, Alabama: Printing Service, 1981), 49-50.

[47] Booth to Edward Partridge, Sept. 20, 1831, copy of letter included in Booth to Rev. Ira Eddy, Nov. 21, 1831, *Ohio Star* 2 (Nov. 24, 1831):3.

[48] Manuscript History, A-1:142; Jessee, *Papers of Joseph Smith* 1:362.

McIlwaine's Bend. In the morning Joseph Smith received a revelation telling the group of the dangers of traveling on the river.

> But verily I say unto you, that it is not needful for this whole company of mine elders, to be moving swiftly upon the waters, whilst the inhabitants on either side are perishing in unbelief: Nevertheless, I suffered it that ye might bear record: Behold there are many dangers upon the waters and more especially hereafter, for I the Lord have decreed, in mine anger, many destructions upon the waters; Yea, and especially upon these waters; Nevertheless, all flesh is in mine hand, and he that is faithful among you, shall not perish by the waters. . . . Behold I the Lord in the beginning, blessed the waters, but in the last days by the mouth of my servant John, I cursed the waters: Wherefore, the days will come that no flesh shall be safe upon the waters, and it shall be said in days to come, that none is able to go up to the land of Zion, upon the waters, but he that is upright in heart.[49]

After these instructions were given Smith, Rigdon, and Oliver Cowdery went by land to St. Louis and then took a stage to Kirtland arriving there August 27. While in Jackson County Sidney Rigdon was commanded to "write a description of the land of Zion" in "an epistle and subscription, to be presented unto all the churches, to obtain moneys, to be put into the hands of the bishop, to purchase lands for the children of God."[50] In Kirtland Joseph was told in a revelation that Rigdon's initial writing was not acceptable to the Lord and he had one more chance to make another one or he could no longer hold church office.[51] Rigdon made another epistle and briefly described the area in Missouri for building the New Jerusalem:

---

[49] Marquardt, *Joseph Smith Revelations*, 152-53; BC 62:3-7, 16-17; LDS D&C 61:3-6, 14-16; RLDS D&C 61:1, 3 (Aug. 12, 1831).
[50] Marquardt, *Joseph Smith Revelations*, 147-48; BC 59:63; LDS D&C 58:50-51; RLDS D&C 58:11.
[51] Marquardt, *Joseph Smith Revelations*, 158; BC 64:62-63; LDS D&C 63:56; RLDS D&C 63:14.

This land being sittuated [situated] in the centre of the continent on which we dwell with an exceeding fertile soil & cleared ready for the hand of the cultivator bespeaks the goodness of our God in providing so goodly a heritage & its climate <suited> to persons from every quarter of this continent whether east west north or south yea I think I may say for all constitutions from every part of the world & its productions nearly all the verieties [varieties] of both grain & vegetables which are common to this coun[r]ty . . . I may say that the whole properties of the country invite the saints to come & partake in their blessings[52]

Oliver Cowdery and Newel K. Whitney were to take Sidney Rigdon's Epistle to the various churches or branches and solicit funds to purchase land in Jackson County, Missouri the land of their inheritance. Shortly afterwards Smith was told that the saints would be able to stay in Kirtland for at least five years:

for I the Lord willeth to retain a Strong hold in the Land of Kirtland for the space of five years in the which I will not overthrow the wicked that thereby I may save some.[53]

Joseph and Emma Smith moved to Hiram, Portage County, Ohio in September 1831. In the month of October William E. McLellin met Joseph for the first time. A revelation was given to McLellin calling him to repentance. In November a series of conference were held relating to publishing Joseph Smith's revelations. The appendix to the manuscript collection included instructions for church members to prepare, sanctify themselves, and gather together "upon the land of Zion, all you that have not been commanded to tarry. Go ye out from Babylon." The saints were told that the Savior shall reign over all flesh and about the return of the ten tribes with their prophets from countries north of Ohio:

---

[52] Sidney Rigdon's Epistle, Aug. 31, 1831, Sidney Rigdon Collection, LDS archives.
[53] Marquardt, *Joseph Smith Revelations*, 159; BC 65:27; LDS D&C 64:21; RLDS D&C 64:4 (Sept. 11, 1831).

And they who are in the north countries shall come in remembrance before the Lord, and their prophets shall hear his voice, and shall no longer stay themselves, and they shall smite the rocks, and the ice shall flow down at their presence. And an high way shall be cast up in the midst of the great deep. Their enemies shall become a prey unto them, and in the barren deserts there shall come forth pools of living water; and the parched ground shall no longer be a thirsty land. And they shall bring forth their rich treasures unto the children of Ephraim my servants. And the boundaries of the everlasting hills shall tremble at their presence.— And then shall they fall down and be crowned with glory, even in Zion, by the hands of the servants of the Lord, even the children of Ephraim; and they shall be filled with songs of everlasting joy.[54]

Church members consecrated and donated money to the church. With these funds Bishop Edward Partridge was able to purchase land in the area near Independence including the spot where the contemplated temple was to be erected. This purchase was made on December 19, 1831 and included a little over 63 acres.[55]

In September 1832 Joseph Smith and six elders gathered together in Kirtland where Smith received a revelation giving additional instructions for the gathering of the saints:

to stand upon mount Zion which shall be called the city New Jerusalem, which city shall be built begin[n]ing at the Temple lot which is appointed by the finger of the Lord in the western boundaries of the State of Misso[uri] and dedicated by the hand of Joseph [Smith, Jr.] and others with whom the Lord was well pleased, verily this is the word of

---

[54] Marquardt, *Joseph Smith Revelations*, 173-74; LDS D&C 133:4-5, 26-33; RLDS D&C 108:2, 6 (Nov. 3, 1831).
[55] Arthur M. Smith, *Temple Lot Deed*, 3rd ed., (Independence, Missouri: Board of Publications, Church of Christ, 1963), 5. See also Jackson County, Deed Record, Book B:1-3; *Deseret News*, Church Section, January 23, 1932, p. 1; Richard Price and Pamela Price, *The Temple of the Lord* (Independence, Missouri: authors, 1982), 32-38.

the Lord that the city New Jerusalem shall be built by the gath[e]ring of the saints begin[n]ing at this place, even the place of the Temple, which Temple shall be reared in this generation, for verely [verily] this generation shall not pass away untill an house shalt be built unto the Lord and a cloud shall rest upon it . . . which house shalt be built unto the Lord in this generation upon the consecrated spot as I have appointed.[56]

The saints in Missouri were not living the commandments given through Joseph Smith. Joseph rebuked them stating: "if Zion will not purify herself so as to be approved of in all things in his sight he will seek another people."[57]

During this period the thought was that only one temple would be built at the center place. But in June 1833 a draft containing a drawn plat of the city of Zion with explanations regarding the city center and plans for a number of houses called temples was sent to Missouri. This included a draft for "the house of the Lord which is to be built first in Zion."[58]

On the plat were marked numbers for twenty-four "temples," that were to be twenty-four buildings for the purpose of "houses of worship" and "schools." The twenty-four temples were divided into two groups, one set of twelve temples were for the high priesthood and the second group of twelve temples were for the lesser priesthood.

The draft of the temple to be built for the presidency of the high priesthood was in all essential features similar to the Kirtland Temple. It was to have two meeting rooms with pulpits at each end. Veils could be lowered whenever necessary and the congregation could view each series of pulpits by means of reversible seating just like the temple commanded to be built in

---

[56] Marquardt, *Joseph Smith Revelations*, 212-13; LDS D&C 84:2-5, 31; RLDS D&C 83:1-2, 6.
[57] Smith to William W. Phelps, Jan. 11, 1833, copy in Joseph Smith Letterbook 1:19, LDS archives; *History of the Church* 1:316. Compare with LDS D&C 84:56-59; RLDS D&C 83:8.
[58] Joseph Smith Letterbook 1:41; *History of the Church* 1:359.

Kirtland.[59] In the summer of 1833 a revelation was given which said in part:

> Verily I say unto you that it is my will that an house should be built unto me in the land of Zion, like unto the pattern which I have given you. Yea, let it be built speedily by the tithing of my people . . . for a place of instruction for all those who are called to the work of the ministry in all their several calling[s] and offices[60]

The saints were soon persecuted in Independence and were asked to leave Jackson County.[61] Oliver Cowdery hurried to Kirtland arriving on August 9, 1833. Cowdery and Frederick G. Williams, made corrections to the city plat of Zion and also the plan for the "house for the presidency" which was to be "built first in Zion." [62]

This temple for the presidency was to be ten feet longer that the previous draft indicated. Instead of five side windows for each story (level), these new plans added four more windows which made nine. The area for the storehouse in the earlier draft was removed, the lots for homes made smaller, changes in the location of the twelve temples for the lesser priesthood were made

---

[59] Joseph Smith Letterbook 1:38-41, LDS archives; Manuscript History, Book A-1:303-307; *History of the Church* 1:357-59. See Richard H. Jackson, "The Mormon Village: Genesis and Antecedents of the City of Zion," *Brigham Young University Studies* 17 (Winter 1977):223-40. This article is based upon the first draft of the City of Zion sent to Independence. For plans on the Kirtland Temple in Ohio, see Kirtland Revelations Book, 59-60; LDS D&C 95; RLDS D&C 92. See also Ronald E. Romig and John H. Siebert, "The Genesis of Zion and Kirtland and the Concept of Temples," *Restoration Studies IV* (Independence, Missouri: Herald Publishing House, 1988), 99-123.

[60] Marquardt, *Joseph Smith Revelations*, 242; LDS D&C 97:10-11, 13; RLDS D&C 94:3 (Aug. 2, 1833).

[61] On persecution in Jackson County, see Warren A. Jennings, "Zion is Fled: The Expulsion of the Mormons from Jackson County, Missouri" (PhD dissertation, University of Florida, 1962).

[62] Concerning modifications to the plans of the Independence Temple in Zion see T. Edgar Lyon, "The Sketches on the Papyri Backings," *Improvement Era* 71 (May 1968):18-23. Oliver Cowdery wrote: "Those patterns previously sent you per mail. by our brethren were incorrect in some respects being drawn in greta [great] haste."

and street names were added to the plat. The five named streets were: Zion, Jerusalem, Bethlehem, Chapel, and Kirtland.[63]

After settling in various locations in Jackson County, Missouri the saints were forced out of the county in November 1833. Their plans to establish the New Jerusalem were shattered but they hoped that eventually they would complete the vision of Joseph Smith in constructing the city of peace.

The gathering would have to take place temporary in other locations including Kirtland, Ohio and western Missouri. It was evident that the idea of building the New Jerusalem would have to be postponed. How long it would be until they could be on the land of their inheritance would depend on the saints. They were told that it was because of their transgression that Zion was lost for a little season.

Many saints were promised that if they lived faithfully they would live in the American New Jerusalem when Christ would appear. The dream of living and having an everlasting inheritance in the city of Zion upon the Missouri land of promise was never realized during their lifetime.

---

[63] The new sketch of the City of Zion "Drawn by F. G. Williams" is housed in the LDS archives. See Ronald E. Romig and John H. Siebert, "Jackson County, 1831-1833: A Look at the Development of Zion," *Restoration Studies III* (Independence, Missouri: Herald Publishing House), 286-304. Page 297 contains a photo of the revised plat of the City of Zion (August 1833).

12

Revelations through Joseph Smith

Revelation is usually thought of as the imparting of truth to men and women by Deity. How this wisdom has been communicated between heaven and earth and how it is different from ordinary human thought remains a mystery. For instance, Joseph Smith was accompanied by scribes who sometimes recorded his most casual observations. For Smith, revelation seemed to come from day-to-day experience, from interactions with other people, and from the study of biblical texts.

In the early years of his life, Smith was a treasure seer who divined where precious things were hidden. As he acquired a prophetic mantle, he used the same methods, including seer-stone gazing, to produce his church's foundational scripture, the Book of Mormon, and his first fifteen revelations.[1]

Smith began his ministry in 1828 at age twenty-two by dictating the content of the gold plates to his scribes Reuben Hale, his wife Emma Smith, and Martin Harris. The words of Joseph Smith's first revelation contain no first-person emphasis. The language is matter of fact and relates directly to the subject at hand: the lost manuscript pages of the dictated Book of Mormon text. However, in April 1829 one of Smith's revelations to another scribe, Oliver Cowdery, uses the first person: "Behold I am Jesus Christ" and "Verily, verily, I say unto you."[2]

While Smith did not comment on the manner in which he perceived God's mind, the linguistic idiosyncrasies are his own. Whether he believed that the ideas or the words themselves were God's is not completely known. Expressions that are borrowed from the King James Version (KJV) of the Bible seem to highlight the importance of the message.

---

[1] See Jessee, *Papers of Joseph Smith* 1:287, 289, 292, 294.

[2] Marquardt, *Joseph Smith Revelations*, 32. The words "Verily, verily, I say unto you" are in the Gospel of John (KJV) and in the Book of Mormon. The shorter wording "verily I say unto you" is in the New Testament Gospels.

Joseph Smith frequently revised the revelations in accordance with his developing theology. God's word, relayed through fallible prophets, was neither inerrant nor static in Smith's view—so as the need arose he revised the Bible and his own autobiography as well as the revelations.

On April 6, 1830, the day the church was organized, a revelation referred to Smith's authority as spokesman: "For his word ye shall receive, as if from mine own mouth."[3] One early disciple, Parley P. Pratt, wrote about the process of revelation:

After we had joined in prayer in his [Smith's] translating room, he dictated in our presence the following revelation:—(Each sentence was uttered slowly and very distinctly, and with a pause between each, sufficiently long for it to be recorded, by an ordinary writer, in long hand. This was the manner in which all of his written revelations were dictated and written. There was never any hesitation, reviewing, or reading back, in order to keep the run of the subject; neither did any of these communications undergo revisions, interlinings, or corrections. As he dictated them so they stood, so far as I have witnessed; and I was present to witness the dictation of several communications of several pages each. This inquiry was made and the answer given in May, 1831.)[4]

William E. McLellin was the scribe for Smith's October 1831 revelation and for David Whitmer's September 1847 illumination. McLellin wrote of the revelatory process:

I, as scribe, have written revelations from the mouth of both the Revelators, Joseph Smith and David Whitmer. And I have been present many times when others wrote for Joseph; therefore I speak as one having experience. The scribe seats himself at a desk or table, with pen, ink and paper. The subject of enquiry being understood, the Prophet

---

[3] Marquardt, *Joseph Smith Revelations*, 61; BC 22:5; LDS D&C 21:5; RLDS D&C 19:2.
[4] *Autobiography of Parley P. Pratt*, 48. See LDS and RLDS D&C 50.

and Revelator enquires of God. He spiritually sees, hears and feels, and then speaks as he is moved upon by the Holy Ghost, the "thus saith the Lord," sentence after sentence, and waits for his amanuenses to write and then read aloud each sentence. Thus they proceed until the revelator says Amen, at the close of what is then communicated.[5]

Note that McLellin has each sentence read aloud by the scribe while Pratt states that there was no reading back. Many of the manuscripts do not have punctuation marks, perhaps indicating they were dictated too rapidly to have been read back and corrected. In any case, the revelations were written as nearly as possible as Smith spoke them.

The early manuscripts have crossed-out words with substituted words above lines which appear to have been written near the time of the first composition. The orthography is unique for each particular scribe. Smith, on the other hand, was responsible for the content of every message. Many of the revelations are explicitly attributed to God, as illustrated by the following salutations:

> thus saith the Lord (OT; BOM; 1830-43)
> saith the Lord (OT; NT; BOM; 1830-43)
> Verily thus saith the Lord (1831-43)
> Behold thus saith the Lord (NT; BOM; 1831-38)
> verily I say unto you (NT; BOM; 1829-43)
> Verily, verily, I say unto you (NT; BOM; 1829-1843)
> I am God (OT; BOM; 1829-33)
> I am Alpha and Omega (NT; BOM; 1830-43)
> Listen to the voice (NT; 1830-32)
> I the Lord have spoken it (OT; 1831-33)
> Behold I am Jesus Christ (BOM; 1829-31)
> listen to the words of Jesus Christ (1829)
> give heed unto my word (1829)

In a revelation received on January 25, 1832, the wording commences: "Verily verily I say unto you I who speak even by the

---

[5] William E. McLellin, ed., *The Ensign of Liberty* 1 (Aug. 1849):98.

voice of my spirit even Alpha and Omega your Lord and your God" and continues "behold this is the will of the Lord your God concerning you even so Amen."[6] Joseph Smith stated this was a "commandment of Jesus Christ."[7] In another revelation he dictated, "these are the words of Alpha & Omega even Jesus Christ."[8] William W. Phelps underscored Smith's role as God's voice in a song, a portion of which reads: "The commandments to the church,/ Which the saints will always search,/ (Where the joys of heaven perch,)/ Came through him from Jesus Christ."[9]

A peculiarity in the revelations is that when there are minor differences between the original and subsequent versions, the meaning has usually remained the same. Theological and historical revisions are more apparent. The most drastic alterations were made in 1835, when the texts were amended, added to, excised, and in some cases assigned different historical settings. About a third of the texts from July 1828 to April 23, 1834 were revised. Among other emendations, the changes softened language, reinterpreted economic matters, added offices existing at the time of revision, and inserted references to priesthood restoration.

The earliest prophetic statements were addressed to individuals as a comfort or chastisement or to the church regarding organizational issues. Economic ideals, religious expectations, and millennial warnings were also prominent features. Missionaries were called to preach to the world for the last time.

The majority (51.7 percent) of the commandments, revelations, and instructions were received in Kirtland and Hiram, Ohio (1831-38), as doctrines, ordinances, and authority structures were solidified. From the revelations, it becomes clear that dissent was common and forgiveness was often offered to those who transgressed.

Some of the revelations were not only for a specific recipient, but were specifically withheld from the public. Martin

---

[6] Marquardt, *Joseph Smith Revelations*, 184; LDS D&C 75:1, 12; RLDS 75:1-2.
[7] Smith to W. W. Phelps, July 31, 1832, LDS archives. See Jessee, *Personal Writings of Joseph Smith*, 270.
[8] Marquardt, *Joseph Smith Revelations*, 201; LDS D&C 81; RLDS D&C 80 (March 15, 1832).
[9] *Latter Day Saints' Messenger and Advocate* 2 (Oct. 1835): 208; *A Collection of Sacred Hymns, for the Church of the Latter Day Saints*, 33-34.

Harris was instructed in March 1830: "And I command you, that you preach nought but repentance; and show not these things, neither speak these things unto the world, for they can not bear meat, but milk they must receive."[10] Almost a year later in March 1831 the church was told:

> & now I say unto you keep these things from going abroad unto the world that ye may accomplish this work in the eyes of the people & in the eyes of your enemies that they may not know your works untill ye have accomplished the thing which I have commanded you.[11]

At the November 1, 1831 church conference, a revelation authorized publication of the Book of Commandments: "What I the Lord have spoken, I have spoken, and I excuse not myself, and though the heavens and the earth pass away, my word shall not pass away, but shall all be fulfilled, whether by mine own voice, or by the voice of my servants, it is the same."[12] Originally the commandments were to be kept from the world—"And for this cause these commandments were given; they were commanded to be kept from the world in the d[a]y that they were given, but now [November 1831] are to go forth unto all flesh."[13] Realizing that some of the revelations were not intended for the world underscores the importance of the early texts. Joseph Smith

---

[10] Marquardt, *Joseph Smith Revelations*, 52; BC 16:22. For the 1835 D&C the instruction to Harris deleted "neither speak these things," while adding "until it is wisdom in me," to read: "show not these things unto the world until it is wisdom in me; for they cannot bear meat now, but milk they must receive" (1835 D&C 44:2). See LDS D&C 19:21-22; RLDS D&C 18:2.

[11] Marquardt, *Joseph Smith Revelations*, 124. After the words "keep these things from going abroad unto the world," six words were added for the BC: "until it is expedient in me" (BC 48:68; LDS D&C 45:72; RLDS D&C 45:15). The manuscript written by Edward Partridge does not contain these words nor does a copy made by William E. McLellin. See Jan Shipps and John W. Welch, eds., *The Journals of William E. McLellin 1831-1836* (Provo, Utah: BYU Studies/Urbana: University of Illinois Press, 1994), 240.

[12] Marquardt, *Joseph Smith Revelations*, 167; BC 1:7; LDS D&C 1:38; RLDS D&C 1:8.

[13] *The Evening and the Morning Star* 1 (May 1833): [2; whole page no. 90], Independence, Missouri; LDS D&C 133:60; RLDS D&C 108:11 (Nov. 3, 1831).

together with a few associates selected the revelations from the original handwritten manuscripts for canonization.

Individual followers of Joseph Smith's revelations believe them to be God's word but are often ignorant of the original text. The originals are not only generally the most authentic and uncontaminated, they also best represent the milieu of and open a window on human consciousness for that particular time and place. Yet so little thought is given today to the original texts because, in part, they are assumed to have been unchanged. They are considered sacrosanct—beyond scholarship. If church leaders made changes, they must have had good reason. This chapter outlines the history of the original texts. The details of this historical setting help explain how and why the texts were subsequently changed.

On April 6, 1830 at Manchester, New York, a revelation regarding Joseph Smith Jr., and the Church of Christ declared: "Wherefore, meaning the church, thou shalt give heed unto all his [Joseph Smith's] words, and commandments, which he shall give unto you, as he receiveth them, walking in all holiness before me."[14] This emphasis in heeding Smith's words "as he receiveth them" underscores the importance of understanding their historical context and original import. Unfortunately, for the majority of the documents there appears to be no extant original manuscripts of the revelations as they were first recorded. However, we have the next best thing: handwritten copies and early printed editions. By examining these texts, one can often reconstruct the original wording.

Many of these documents were printed by William W. Phelps and Company in 1832 and 1833 in Independence, Missouri. They appeared in the Mormon periodical *The Evening and the Morning Star*. Before that, in July 1830, at Harmony, Pennsylvania, the revelations were arranged and copied with the assistance of John Whitmer. These included what became Book of Commandments chapters 2-27.[15]

---

[14] Marquardt, *Joseph Smith Revelations*, 61; BC 22:4; also in LDS D&C 21:4; and RLDS D&C 19:2.

[15] See Manuscript History, Book A-1:50, written in 1839, LDS archives; Jessee, *Papers of Joseph Smith* 1:319.

In a revelation dictated at Fayette, New York, in September 1830, Joseph Smith was likened to Moses in his prophetic primacy: "no one shall be appointed to received commandments and revelations in this church, excepting my servant Joseph, for he receiveth them even as Moses."[16] Another revelation in June 1831, in Kirtland, stated that William W. Phelps, a recent convert but not yet baptized, should be "ordained to assist my servant Oliver [Cowdery] to do the work of printing."[17] The instructions for Phelps were: "let my servant William ... be established as a printer unto the church ... and let my servant Oliver assist him even as I have commanded in whatsoever place I shall appoint unto him to copy and to correct and select" the writings to be published.[18] Land was to be purchased at Independence, Missouri, the new Zion, "for the house of the printing."[19]

During the first half of November in Hiram, Ohio, a series of church conferences were held. Three of these dealt with printing the revelations. On November 1 it was voted that 10,000 copies of the revelations should be published in a book known as the Book of Commandments. As stated in the minutes: "br[other] Oliver Cowdery made a request desiring the mind of the Lord through this conference of Elders to know how many copies of the Book of commandments it was the will of the Lord should be published in the first edition of that work. Voted that there be ten thousand copies struck."[20] The preface to the manuscript was then received which began: "Behold, this is mine authority, and the authority of my servants, and my Preface unto the Book of my

---

[16] Marquardt, *Joseph Smith Revelations*, 83; BC 30:2; LDS D&C 28:2; RLDS D&C 27:2.

[17] Marquardt, *Joseph Smith Revelations*, 140; BC 57:5; LDS D&C 55:4; RLDS D&C 55:2.

[18] Marquardt, *Joseph Smith Revelations*, 143; LDS D&C 57:11, 13; RLDS D&C 57:5.

[19] Marquardt, *Joseph Smith Revelations*, 147; BC 59:49; LDS D&C 58:37; RLDS D&C 58:7.

[20] "The Conference Minutes and Record Book of Christ's Church of Latter Day Saints" (known as the "Far West Record"), 15, manuscript in possession of LDS church. See Cannon and Cook, *Far West Record*, 27.

Commandments, which I have given them to publish unto you, O inhabitants of the earth."[21]

In the afternoon "A number of the brethren arose and said that they were willing to testify to the world that they knew that they [the revelations] were of the Lord."[22] A revelation was received which said: "And now I the Lord give unto you a testimony of these commandments which are lying before you."[23] The next day "the brethren then arose in turn and bore witness to the truth of the Book of Commandments."[24] On November 3 Joseph Smith received a revelation designated as the "Appendix."[25] And at an November 8 meeting, it was "Resolved by this conference that Br[other] Joseph Smith Jr correct those errors or mistakes which he may discover by the holy Spirit while reviewing the revelations & commandments & also the fulness of the scriptures."[26]

On November 12 it was made known with regard to Oliver Cowdery's trip to Independence, Missouri, that: "it is not wisdom in me that he should be entrusted with the commandments and the moneys which he shall carry unto the land of Zion, except one go with him who will be true and faithful: wherefore I the Lord willeth that my servant John Whitmer, should go with my servant Oliver Cowdery."[27] Subsequently Cowdery and Whitmer were

---

[21] Marquardt, *Joseph Smith Revelations*, 166; BC 1:2; LDS D&C 1:6; RLDS D&C 1:2.

[22] Cannon and Cook, *Far West Record*, 27. David Whitmer wrote fifty-five years later that he objected to the printing of the revelations. See *An Address To All Believers in Christ*, 54-55. It appears that Whitmer went along with the consensus of the conference. Both Whitmer and William E. McLellin were present when the testimony to the revelations was given at the church conference.

[23] Marquardt, *Joseph Smith Revelations*, 168; 1835 D&C 25:2; LDS D&C 67:4; RLDS D&C 67:2.

[24] Cannon and Cook, *Far West Record*, 28. Compare Manuscript History, Book A-1:162-63; Jessee, *Papers of Joseph Smith* 1:367-68.

[25] "Having given, in a previous number, the Preface to the book of Commandments now in press, we give below the close, or as it has been called, the Appendix" (*The Evening and the Morning Star* 1 [May 1833]: 1 [89]). The manuscript of most of this revelation is in RLDS archives.

[26] Cannon and Cook, *Far West Record*, 29.

[27] Marquardt, *Joseph Smith Revelations*, 179; 1835 D&C 28:1; LDS D&C 69:1-2; RLDS D&C 69:1.

commissioned: "Voted that Joseph Smith jr. be appointed to dedicate & consecrate these brethren & the sacred writings & all they have entrusted to their care, to the Lord: done accordingly."[28]

On the same day Joseph Smith Jr., Martin Harris, Oliver Cowdery, John Whitmer, Sidney Rigdon, and William W. Phelps were made "stewards over the revelations and commandments which I have given unto them, and which I shall hereafter give unto them," to manage the publishing business and receive the benefits thereof.[29] Whitmer and Cowdery left Ohio on November 20 and arrived in Independence on January 5, 1832.[30] Cowdery wrote to Smith: "We expect soon to be ready to print and hope that brother Martin [Harris] can supply with paper."[31]

"Shall we procure the paper required of our breatheren [brethren] in thus [their] letter and carry it with us or not and if we do what moneys shall we use for that purpose[?]" Smith asked God in Hiram, Ohio, on March 20, 1832. The answer was:

> It is expedient saith the Lord unto you that the paper shall be purchased for the printing of the book of the Lord[']s commandments and it must needs be that you take it with [you] for it is not expedient that my servant Martin [Harris] should as yet go up unto the land of Zion. let the purchase be made by the Bishop of [if] it must needs be by hire; let whatsoever is done be done in the name of the Lord.[32]

The next month Smith and counselors Jesse Gause and Sidney Rigdon traveled to Independence and brought paper with them for publishing *The Evening and the Morning Star* and the Book of Commandments.

---

[28] Cannon and Cook, *Far West Record*, 32.

[29] Marquardt, *Joseph Smith Revelations*, 180; 1835 D&C 26:1; LDS D&C 70:3; RLDS D&C 70:1.

[30] Westergren, *From Historian to Dissident*, 102. Regarding the date of November 20, Richard P. Howard has written: "it appears to have been originally 20; but later was made into 10 by someone making a wide old 1 covering all but the presumed tail of the 2" (Howard to Marquardt, Feb. 6, 1981).

[31] Oliver Cowdery to Joseph Smith, Jan. 28, 1832, LDS archives. See Cannon and Cook, *Far West Record*, 238.

[32] Marquardt, *Joseph Smith Revelations*, 206-207.

At a council of the Literary Firm on April 30, it was "Ordered by the Council that three thousand copies of the book of Commandments be printed the first edition." Phelps, Cowdery, and Whitmer were "appointed to review the Book of Commandments & select for printing such as shall be deemed by them proper, as dictated by the Spirit & make all necessary verbal corrections."[33] Copies of revelations received since November 1831 were brought to Independence by the presidency of the High Priesthood. These included the vision of the three degrees of glory and a revelation to Jesse Gause as Smith's counselor which were copied by Whitmer for the Book of Commandments.[34]

The Evening and the Morning Star was published for the first time in June 1832. On the first page, under the title "Revelations" appeared "The Articles and Covenants of the Church of Christ." In the July issue Smith and Rigdon's "Vision" of the three degrees of glory was published. Each issue from June 1832 to July 1833 had either a complete revelation or a portion of a revelation, most of which were subsequently published in the Book of Commandments.[35] The printing of "A Book of Commandments, for the Government of the Church of Christ" commenced, but was a slow project.[36] Type was set on sheets of thirty-two pages each, sixteen pages per side, to be folded into signatures as follows:

Sheet A pages 1- 32	Title page and BC 1:1 to 12:5
Sheet B pages 33- 64	BC 12:5 to 29:40
Sheet C pages 65- 96	BC 29:40 to 45:6
Sheet D pages 97-128	BC 45:6 to 56:3
Sheet E pages 129-160	BC 56:4 to 65:47 [37]

---

[33] Cannon and Cook, *Far West Record*, 46.

[34] BC manuscript fragments (eight pages on four sheets) in RLDS archives. See Marquardt, *Joseph Smith Revelations*, 349-65.

[35] Peter Crawley, "A Bibliography of The Church of Jesus Christ of Latter-day Saints in New York, Ohio, and Missouri," *Brigham Young University Studies* 12 (Summer 1972):477-78; also Affidavit of W. W. Phelps, 28 Sept. 1832. On this same press, the *Upper Missouri Advertiser*, a weekly newspaper, was published.

[36] *The Evening and the Morning Star* 1 (Dec. 1832):8 [56] and 1 (May 1833):1 [89]. On December 1, 1832 Joseph Smith recorded in his journal: "wrote and corrected revelations &c" (Joseph Smith Journal, 3, LDS archives; Jessee, *Papers of Joseph Smith* 2:4).

[37] John McDonnell to the Editor, *Saints Herald* 124 (Dec. 1977):44.

On July 20, 1833 citizens of Jackson County, Missouri, met at the court house in Independence and formed a committee to ask the Mormons to shut down the printing office and leave the county.[38] When the latter proved unwilling to do so, the non-Mormon community voted to demolish the printing office. On that Saturday nearly four hundred individuals went to the residence and printing house of W. W. Phelps and Company, threw the press from the upper-story, scattered the type, and destroyed most of the building.[39]

The mob thus succeeded in stopping publication of the *Evening and the Morning Star*, the Book of Commandments, and the *Upper Missouri Advertiser* (published weekly by Phelps). The last verse on sheet E of the Book of Commandments read: "For verily I say that the rebellious are not of the blood of Ephraim."[40] The Mormons' press was later used when "Davis and Kelly" took it to Liberty, Missouri, to publish the *Upper Missouri Enquirer*.[41]

Sheets of the unfinished Book of Commandments were salvaged from the wreckage of the office and collected as they blew about the streets of Independence. From these sheets a small number of copies of the book were assembled, though the five printed sheets (160 pages) represented only a portion of the anticipated final work.[42] The few copies thus assembled were used by church members in reading and studying Smith's revelations.[43]

---

[38] Warren A. Jennings, "Factors in the Destruction of the Mormon Press in Missouri, 1833," *Utah Historical Quarterly* 35 (Winter 1967):57-76.

[39] Petition dated Sept. 28, 1833 in *The Evening and the Morning Star* (Kirtland, Ohio) 2 (Dec. 1833):114; *History of the Church* 1:412. See also *Times and Seasons* 1 (Dec. 1839):18; *History of the Church*, 1:390, footnote.

[40] BC 65:47 (page 160). For a photo of the last page used for Sheet E see Marquardt, *Joseph Smith Revelations*, 350. The surviving BC manuscript pages in RLDS archives were obtained with the David Whitmer papers in 1903. The retained pages included a few revelations brought to Independence by John Whitmer and Oliver Cowdery early in 1832.

[41] Manuscript History, Book A-1:412; *History of the Church* 1:470.

[42] Peter Crawley and Chad J. Flake, *Notable Mormon Books 1830-1857* (Provo, Utah: Friends of the Brigham Young University Library, 1974), 6. See also Peter Crawley, "Joseph Smith and A Book of Commandments," *The Princeton University Library Chronicle* 42 (Autumn 1980):18-32.

[43] Elden J. Watson, comp., *The Orson Pratt Journals*, 38, entry for April 2, 1834; *The Evening and the Morning Star* (Kirtland, Ohio) 2 (Aug. 1834):184, an

Though the books had different title pages and bindings, they constituted "the first book printed in the immense territory between St. Louis and the Pacific coast."[44]

By October plans were underway to get another press to publish the revelations at church headquarters in Kirtland. Frederick G. Williams wrote, "The book of commandments were nearly half finished at the time of the riot but were destroyed with the press and will probably be reprinted here as we have sent to New York for a press."[45] Although only a few Book of Commandments manuscript pages survived, the five printed sheets were an invaluable primary source used in preparing the Doctrine and Covenants along with the "Kirtland Revelations" book. This manuscript book contains documents recorded beginning in the fall of 1832.

Besides portions of the Book of Commandments manuscript, there are early manuscript copies of revelations in the papers of Newel K. Whitney, the "Bishop at Kirtland." These copies were written as early as 1831-32 and are among the earliest extant. It is possible that a number of the Whitney manuscripts were the original texts for some of the revelations.[46]

The Kirtland Revelations Book contains manuscript copies of revelations, as well. The book was begun in late 1832 with all but thirteen pages recorded by August 18, 1834. For many of the revelations, this is the only manuscript known to exist. The texts were copied months or years after they were first received onto this manuscript book. Some of these revelations were corrected at a later date in Smith's handwriting.[47]

Appeal dated July 1834; also Lectures on Theology, "Lecture Third," 1835 D&C, 36, 42. See also John Whitmer's Account Book, LDS archives.

[44] "Missouri History Not Found in Textbooks," *Missouri Historical Review* 44 (Oct. 1949):94; extract from an article by John Edward Hicks and published in the *Kansas City Star*, July 1, 1949.

[45] Williams to John Murdock, Kirtland, Ohio, Oct. 10, 1833, Joseph Smith Letterbook 1:62, LDS archives.

[46] Chad J. Flake, "The Newell K. Whitney Collection," *Brigham Young University Studies* 11 (Summer 1971):325.

[47] Frederick G. Williams [III], "Frederick Granger Williams of the First Presidency of the Church," *Brigham Young University Studies* 12 (Spring 1972): 250n21. At the end of the revelation of August 29, 1832, it states, "by Joseph the

Other manuscripts, books, or journals that contain copies of Smith's revelations and were written by early church members include William E. McLellin's journal and manuscripts, from 1831-32; Zebedee Coltrin's journal containing two documents copied in Independence on January 12, 1832; the "Book of Commandments, Laws and Covenants" designated "Book A," made in 1832; "Book B" containing revelations copied by June 12, 1833; and "Book C" made in 1834.[48]

The above works were evidently individual copies for personal use and not used for the 1835 Doctrine and Covenants. The Book of Commandments manuscript was a printer's manuscript for the forthcoming publication. The Kirtland Revelations Book with its handwritten changes in the texts was a church manuscript book and has notations that certain documents were to be included in the Doctrine and Covenants.

With the destruction of the church's press in Independence, a council of the United Firm met in Kirtland on September 11, 1833. Frederick G. Williams, Joseph Smith, Sidney Rigdon, and Newel K. Whitney, along with Oliver Cowdery (who was a "delegate to represent the residue of the said firm residing in Independence") conceived of having two publications printed by Williams. These were to be titled "The Latter day Saints messenger and advocate" and "the Star formerly published in Jackson County, Missouri." Cowdery was designated the editor of both. The expectation was that publication would eventually be transferred back to Independence.[49]

On April 19, 1834 in the "wilderness" at Norton, Ohio, Cowdery and Rigdon were commissioned to assist each other "in

---

seer and writ[t]en by F. G. Williams Scribe." Most of the copies of revelations up to March 15, 1833 are in Frederick G. Williams' handwriting.
[48] Earl E. Olson, "The Chronology of the Ohio Revelations," *Brigham Young University Studies* 11 (Summer 1971):332-35. See also Robert J. Woodford, "The Historical Development of the Doctrine and Covenants," (Ph.D. diss., Brigham Young University, 1974), 98-106.
[49] Kirtland Council Minute Book, 24, LDS archives. This book contains minutes of meetings, conferences, ordinations, and blessings for the period December 3, 1832 to November 27, 1837. See also Manuscript History, Book A-1:345; *History of the Church* 1:409; Lyndon W. Cook, *The Revelations of the Prophet Joseph Smith* (Provo, Utah: Seventy's Mission Bookstore, 1981), 114-15.

arranging the church covenants which are to be soon published."[50] A conference of elders would be held at Norton two days later. Soon afterwards a revelation dated April 23 called the United Firm's Kirtland printing office under Williams and Cowdery to print "the revelations which I have given unto you, & which I shall hereafter, fro[m] time to time, give unto you."[51] Also they were instructed to secure copyrights, "that others may not take the blessings away from you which I have confer[r]ed upon you."[52] At a high council meeting held on September 24:

> The council then proceeded to appoint a committee to arrange the items of the doctrine of Jesus Christ for the government of the church of Latter-Day Saints . . . Brother Samuel H. Smith then nominated brethren Joseph Smith Junr., Oliver Cowdery, Sidney Rigdon and Frederick G. Williams, to compose said committee which was seconded by brother Hyrum Smith. The Counsellors then gave their vote, which was also agreed to by the whole conference. The council then decided that said committee, after arranging and publishing said book of covenants, have the avails [royalties] of the same.[53]

The council thus sustained Cowdery and Rigdon who had been appointed four months previously at Norton.

In the September issue of the *Evening and the Morning Star*—printed in Kirtland—a "Prospectus for Re-printing the First and Second Volumes of The Evening and the Morning Star" appeared. According to the editor, the twenty-four numbers were to be reprinted with typographical corrections:

---

[50] Joseph Smith Journal, 76-79, handwriting of Oliver Cowdery; Jessee, *Papers of Joseph Smith* 2:31-32. See also Manuscript History, Book A-1:460; *History of the Church* 2:50-51.

[51] Marquardt, *Joseph Smith Revelations*, 258; 1835 D&C 98:10; LDS D&C 104:58; RLDS D&C 101:10. Compare LDS D&C 104:58 with LDS D&C 70:3; RLDS D&C 70:1.

[52] Marquardt, *Joseph Smith Revelations*, 258 from "Book of Commandments, Law and Covenants; Book C." See also Kirtland Revelations Book, 105, LDS archives. The copyright wording was not included in the 1835 D&C after 98:10.

[53] Kirtland Council Minute Book, 76. See also Manuscript History, Book B-1:556-57; *History of the Church* 2:165.

There are many typographical errors in both volumes, and especially in the last, which we shall endeavor carefully to correct, as well as principle, if we discover any.—It is also proper for us to say, that in the first 14 numbers, in the Revelations, are many errors, typographical, and others, occasioned by transcribing manuscript; but as we shall have access to originals, we shall endeavor to make proper corrections.[54]

Whether or not this was Cowdery's initial intent, careful study shows that if any original manuscripts (previous to 1835) were used, their exact wording was not adhered to. *The Evening and the Morning Star*, reprinted in Kirtland between January and June 1835 under the title *Evening and Morning Star*, altered the texts, deleted previously published material, and inserted editorial comments by Oliver Cowdery. For instance, in the January 1835 reissue for June 1832, the following remarks concerning Smith's revelations were added:

On the revelations we merely say, that we were not a little surprised to find the previous print so different from the original. We have given them a careful comparison, assisted by individuals whose known integrity and ability is uncensurable. Thus saying we cast no reflections upon those who were entrusted with the responsibility of publishing them in Missouri, as our own labors were included in that important service to the church, and it was our unceasing endeavor to have them correspond with the copy furnished us. We believe they are now correct. If not in every word, at least in principle. For the special good of the church we have also added a few items from other revelations.[55]

---

[54] Prospectus dated Sept. 26, 1834, Kirtland, Ohio, in *The Evening and the Morning Star* 2 (Sept. 1834):192. The prospectus was dated two days after the September 24, 1834 high council meeting.

[55] *Evening and Morning Star* (Kirtland reprint) 1 (June 1832):16, reprinted Jan. 1835.

Concerning these remarks, RLDS church historian Richard P. Howard wrote:

> It may be that Cowdery's surprise at the remarkable differences between the "original" and that which had been previously published arose from the fact that in late 1834 or early 1835, as he was beginning to republish the revelations, he was working from a *different* "original"— different, that is, from the one he and John Whitmer had copied from in 1831 in preparing the Book of Commandments manuscript for the Independence printer.[56]

The new copy was probably the manuscript being prepared for the 1835 Doctrine and Covenants. On February 4, 1835 Cowdery wrote to Bishop Newel K. Whitney requesting the original manuscript known as the Law of the Church:

> Bishop Whitney:
> Will you have the kindness to send us, by the bearer, the original copy of the Revelation given 12 elders Feb. 1831 called "The Law of the Church"? We are preparing the old Star for re-printing, and have no copy from which to correct, and kno[w] of no other beside yours.
> Your Ob't Serv't.
> Kirtland, Feb. 4, 1835.   Oliver Cowdery.[57]

It is not known if Cowdery received the original from Whitney. But the revised, expanded text contained material anachronistic to the original 1831 setting. Oliver Cowdery wrote in the March reprint: "Those who read this paper will see that it contains items of covenant of deep interest to the church of the saints, and as they have frequently been ridiculed in consequence of certain items contained in the one setting forth their faith on the

---

[56] Howard, *Restoration Scriptures* (1969), 202, emphasis retained; see also (2nd ed., 1995), 150.

[57] Newel K. Whitney Collection, L. Tom Perry Special Collections, Harold B. Lee Library, Brigham Young University. See photo of letter in Flake, "The Newell K. Whitney Collection," *Brigham Young University Studies* 11 (Summer 1971):325.

subject of bestowing temporal gifts for the benefit of the poor, it is a matter of joy to us to be able to present this document according to the original."[58] Cowdery's statement that he was presenting the February 9, 1831 revelation, "according to the original," makes sense only if by "original" he meant a new printer's manuscript prepared for the forthcoming Doctrine and Covenants.

The changes in many of the revelations reflected later theology, modifications in church government, recognition of former discrepancies, and sensitivity to criticism engendered by the originals. In reconstructing the events of 1835, it may be helpful to know something about the key players, specifically members of the First Presidency.

Joseph Smith Jr., was the prophet through whom the revelations came, and most of the Doctrine and Covenants, whether revelations or other documents, are believed to have been originally dictated by him. His own handwriting appears in the entry of a December 4, 1831 revelation copied into the Kirtland Revelations Book. Corrections for a number of sections previously recorded in 1832 are in his hand, as well. He blessed Sidney Rigdon and Oliver Cowdery for their work in arranging the revelations and was the presiding officer both of the Kirtland High Council and of the church.

Smith, and evidently Rigdon, assembled seven Lectures on Faith for use in the elders' school during the winter of 1834-35. These were "delivered before a Theological class" in Kirtland.[59] In January 1835 Smith was engaged "in preparing the Lectures on Theology for publication in the Book of Doctrine and covenants, which the committee appointed last September were now compiling."[60] The preface to the 1835 Doctrine and Covenants, drafted by the committee, said: "The first part of the book will be

---

[58] *Evening and Morning Star* (Kirtland reprint) 1 (Aug. 1832): 48, reprinted March 1835.

[59] Alan J. Phipps, "The Lectures on Faith: An Authorship Study," M.A. thesis, Brigham Young University, 1977 and Leland H. Gentry, "What of the Lectures on Faith?" *Brigham Young University Studies* 19 (Fall 1978):5-19. See also Richard S. Van Wagoner, Steven C. Walker, and Allen D. Roberts, "'The Lectures on Faith': A Case Study in Decanonization," *Dialogue: A Journal of Mormon Thought* 20 (Fall 1987):71-77.

[60] Manuscript History, Book B-1:563, written in 1843, LDS archives; *History of the Church* 2:180.

found to contain a series of Lectures as delivered before a Theological class in this place, and in consequence of their embracing the important doctrine of salvation, we have arranged them into the following work."[61]

Cowdery had been a close associate of Smith since April 1829 and a number of early revelations are in his handwriting. Although he was not in Ohio when many of the revelations were originally given, he copied a few of them into the Kirtland Revelations Book. He was set apart in April 1834 to assist Rigdon in compiling the book of covenants and was publicly selected for the committee on September 24. On December 5, 1834 he was ordained an assistant president to Smith and thus became a member of the First Presidency. As a member of the Doctrine and Covenants committee, his name appears on the preface to the 1835 edition. He edited the newspapers at Kirtland, including the *Messenger and Advocate*, until June 1835. At this time he relinquished the paper to church historian John Whitmer. Cowdery also edited the reprint of the *Evening and Morning Star* and, in February 1835, the short-lived community-oriented *Northern Times*. As one of the three witnesses to the Book of Mormon, he helped select the first twelve apostles of the church. In addition, he served on the Kirtland High Council.

Sidney Rigdon was a noted religious personality in his own right before joining with the Mormons. He became closely associated with Joseph Smith soon after they first met in December 1830. In March 1832 Sidney was ordained a counselor to Smith. Since he was one of Smith's scribes, his handwriting also appears in early manuscript revelations. Along with Cowdery, he was set apart to assist in compiling the book of covenants. He also worked on the Lectures on Faith, wrote theological articles for church publications, and, as a member of the First Presidency, attended Kirtland High Council meetings.

Frederick G. Williams was a scribe whose work started in July 1832 at a time when Rigdon for a short period was out of harmony with the church. In the winter of 1832-33, Williams was made a counselor to Smith. Most of the Kirtland Revelations Book

---

[61] 1835 D&C, [iii].

is in his handwriting. As a member of the First Presidency, he was also involved in Kirtland High Council meetings.

Although not a member of the revision committee, William W. Phelps, former editor of the *Evening and the Morning Star*, came to Kirtland in mid-May 1835 "and assisted the Committee in compiling the Book of Doctrine and Covenants."[62] The next month he copied revelations into his diary and compared documents for the Doctrine and Covenants. With his experience in operating a press, he also worked at the printing office on the Doctrine and Covenants and the *Northern Times*.

As members of the First Presidency of the church, and especially as members of the committee in whose charge the revelations were placed, these men were responsible for the 1835 publication. A preface prepared by this committee guaranteed that as presiding elders they had "carefully selected" and "compiled" the *Doctrine and Covenants of the Church of the Latter Day Saints*. The copyright was obtained on January 14, 1835.[63]

On August 17 a General Assembly was called in Kirtland. In this period of church history, the term "General Assembly" meant a gathering "of the several [priesthood] quorums which constitute the spiritual authorities of the church."[64] One of the purposes was to determine if the Doctrine and Covenants then in press would be approved by church authorities.

The minutes are recorded in the Kirtland Council Minute Book, and a printed version was published in the August 1835 issue of the *Messenger and Advocate* with an abbreviated version in the 1835 Doctrine and Covenants. Errors in the minutes were noticed too late to be corrected as they "escaped the eye of the proof reader" and were placed at the end of the book (xxv) as "Notes to the Reader."[65] The Kirtland Council Minute Book contains the following:

---

[62] Manuscript History, Book B-1:592; *History of the Church* 2:227.

[63] Woodford, "The Historical Development of the Doctrine and Covenants," 48.

[64] Marquardt, *Joseph Smith Revelations*, 269; 1835 D&C 3:11; LDS D&C 107:32; RLDS D&C 104:11 (April [28-30], 1835).

[65] The minutes were deleted from the 1844 Nauvoo edition of the D&C. The assembly minutes were first printed in RLDS D&C in the 1894 edition. In the 1911 RLDS edition, the minutes were numbered section "108A," and in the

This Committee having finished said Book according to the instructions given them, it was deemed necessary to call the general assembly of the Church to see whether the book be approved or not by the Authoroties [Authorities] of the church, that it may, if approved, become a law unto the church, and a rule of faith and practice unto the same.[66]

The presiding officers, Cowdery and Rigdon, were of course members of the committee that had prepared the Doctrine and Covenants. Smith and Williams were in Michigan, and all of the newly ordained apostles were absent on a mission.[67] Why such an important meeting did not occur previous to Smith's and Williams' departure is not known. Cowdery and Rigdon "proceeded to organize the whole assembly," including at least 118 priesthood members, into their respective quorums and non-priesthood groups.

Since not all twelve members of the Kirtland High Council could attend the assembly, eight substitutes stood in their place. In the Missouri High Council, as well, there were only three regular members present; four had been appointed apostles. Thus nine other priesthood holders served as substitutes for the Missouri council for the General Assembly. The seven presidents of the Seventy were represented by four regular members with three substitutes to fill this quorum. The bishop of Kirtland was present with his two counselors. Edward Partridge, bishop from Zion, was absent, but his position was represented by John Corrill. Other substitutes filled in for absentees among the elders, priests, teachers, and deacons presidencies.

In the morning session, ordinations and blessings took place. In the afternoon there was a vote on the Doctrine and

---

1970 RLDS D&C they were moved to the Introduction (9-12). They were subsequently removed and are not included in the 1990 RLDS edition.

[66] Kirtland Council Minute Book, 98.

[67] The manuscript history for the August 17, 1835 General Assembly states that Smith and Williams were "absent on a visit to the Saints in Michigan." The words "Joseph absent" are in the side margin (Manuscript History, Book B-1:600). Later the manuscript describes the Michigan trip as a "mission" (Book B-1:606). The printed version changes the word "mission" to "visit." See *History of the Church* 2:243, 253.

Covenants. President Cowdery "in behalf of the committee"[68] "arose with the Book of Doctrine and Covenants, (284 pages) contain[in]g the faith, articles and covenants of the Latter Day Saints."[69] President Rigdon then "explained the manner by which they intended to obtain the voice of the assembly for or against said book."[70] William W. Phelps commented on the book and said:

> he had examined it carefully, that it was well arranged and calculated to govern the church in righteousness, [and] if followed would bring the members to see eye to eye. And further that he had received the testimony from God, that the Revelations and commandments contained therein are true.

John Whitmer testified "that he was well acquainted with the work & knew it to be true and from God."[71] John Smith, "taking the lead of the high council in Kirtland," stated "that the lectures were judiciously arranged and compiled, and were profitable for doctrine."[72]

Voting took place as John Smith presented the following: "That they would receive the Book as the rule of theire [their] faith & practice and put themselves under the guidance of the same and also that they were satisfied with the committee that were chosen to compile it, as having discharged their duty faithfully." Levi Jackman "said that he had examined as many of the revelations contained in the book as were printed in Zion, & firmly believes them as he does the Book of Mormon or the Bible and also the whole contents of the Book." Neither set of minutes stated that Jackman actually compared the new document with the Book of Commandments or any other record. The First Presidency and two high councils voted in favor of the book and the committee.

---

[68] *Messenger and Advocate* 1 (Aug. 1835): 161.
[69] Kirtland Council Minute Book, 103. This 284-page book included articles on "Marriage" and "Of Governments and Laws in General," minutes of the General Assembly, Index, Contents, and Notes to the Reader.
[70] *Messenger and Advocate* 1 (Aug. 1835):161.
[71] Kirtland Council Minute Book, 103.
[72] *Messenger and Advocate* 1 (Aug. 1835):161.

William Phelps again arose and "read the written testimony of the 12 Apostles in favor of the Book and the Committee who compiled it."[73] Other leaders stated, as they passed the book to each other, that they knew the book was true and were satisfied with it and the committee that compiled it. Votes of the different priesthood quorums were taken, all in the affirmative. Thomas Gates "took the Book and expressed his satisfaction with it, and also called a vote of all the members present, both male & female, & They gave a decided voice in favor of it & also of the committee."[74] The *Messenger and Advocate* minutes stated: "The several authorities, and the general assembly, by a unanimous vote accepted of the labors of the committee."[75]

After this vote of confidence, Phelps read an article on marriage. It was voted upon and accepted. Cowdery then read an article on governments and laws in general. This was accepted as well. Both articles were "ordered to be printed in said book, by a unanimous vote."[76] After a hymn and prayer, the assembly was dismissed by Rigdon, having accepted the book as a whole but not having voted on the individual revelatory documents. Don H. Compier commented about this manner of canonizing the Doctrine and Covenants:

> It was the work of the committee—not the specific content of the Book of Doctrine and Covenants—that was considered by the quorums of the church on August 17, 1835. Their unanimous acceptance of the book that had not yet been published was in effect a decision to include the forthcoming publication in the church's canon of scripture. It is interesting to note that their action thus "canonized" not only Smith's revelations (selected and worded as he chose) but also non-revelatory material, namely the

---

[73] Kirtland Council Minute Book, 104.
[74] Ibid., 106.
[75] *Messenger and Advocate* 1 (Aug. 1835):162.
[76] Ibid. 1 (Aug. 1835):162-63.

"Lectures on Faith" and the articles on government and marriage." [77]

The following accounts reflect the attitudes of the people present at the General Assembly. Ira Ames wrote twenty-three years later: "I was present at a General Assembly of the Church on the 17th August 1835 to accept the Book of Doctrine & Covenants as our rule of faith. And gave my vote as president of the Priests Quorum. See D&C page 257 1st Edition."[78] Ebenezer Robinson, who worked in the printing office after his arrival in Kirtland in May 1835 (though was not a member of the church until October), recorded fifty-three years later:

On the 17th day of August, 1835, a general assembly of the church convened in the lower part of the temple, to hear the report of the compiling committee of said book, and determine, by vote, whether they "accepted and acknowledged it as the doctrine and covenants of their faith.["]

After the only two members of the committee, who were present, viz: Oliver Cowdery and Sidney Rigdon, had reported, several official members of the church, Presidents of quorums, arose, one after another, and testified to the truth of the book, and they and their quorums "accepted and acknowledged it as the doctrine and covenants of their faith." Afterwards the question was put to the whole assembly and carried, unanimously.

We attended that meeting, and noticed that a majority of those voting did so upon the testimony of those who bore record to the truth of the book, as they had neither time or opportunity to examine it for themselves. They had no means of knowing whether any alterations had been made in any of the revelations or not.

---

[77] "Canonization in the Reorganized Church of Jesus Christ of Latter Day Saints," *Restoration Studies III* (Independence, Missouri: Herald Publishing House, 1986), 179.

[78] Journal and Record of the Life & Family of Ira Ames, LDS archives.

Neither Joseph Smith jr. [n]or Frederick G. Williams, were present at this general assembly, as they had gone to Michigan.[79]

In September 1835 copies of the book arrived from the binder in Cleveland. William W. Phelps wrote: "We got some of the Commandments from Cleveland last week."[80] Wilford Woodruff received a copy on September 23 "as A Present from O[liver] Cowdery."[81]

There is no indication that anyone realized that the texts of some of the revelations had been revised, deleted, or enlarged. The revelations were accepted in their altered form without comment, apparently in the belief that they were identical to those originally given to the Saints. There was no explanation made by the committee, either in the preface or within the text of the revelations, as to why alterations had been made. Based on Oliver Cowdery's editorial comments, it seems that revelatory texts differing from those that had been previously published were changed without regard to the earlier documents.

Seven years later Joseph Smith read proof sheets with William W. Phelps in Nauvoo, Illinois, for a new edition of the Doctrine and Covenants.[82] In September 1844, two months after Smith's murder, the second edition was referenced in the *Times and Seasons* showing that it was available by that time.[83] This edition had eight additional sections, including two pre-1835 revelations; God's word to Smith in 1837, 1838, and 1841; two letters of 1842; and a testimonial regarding the martyrdom of the prophet and his brother Hyrum on June 27, 1844.

In the majority of church histories the primary source of Smith's revelations quoted and referred to is the 1835 Doctrine and

---

[79] Ebenezer Robinson, ed., "Items of Personal History of the Editor," *The Return* 1 (June 1889):88-89, Davis City, Iowa.

[80] Phelps to Sally Phelps, Sept. 16, 1835; as cited in Bruce A. Van Orden, ed., "Writing to Zion: The William W. Phelps Kirtland Letters (1835-1836)," *Brigham Young University Studies* 33 (1993):566.

[81] Kenney, *Wilford Woodruff's Journal* 1:43.

[82] Joseph Smith Journal, kept by Willard Richards, entry for 14 Feb. 1843, LDS archives. See *History of the Church* 5:273.

[83] *Times and Seasons* 5 (Sept. 2, 1844):636. The 1844 edition was printed in Nauvoo, church headquarters.

Covenants. The two major churches (LDS church and Community of Christ) have published their own retrospective updated editions of the Doctrine and Covenants. The texts of the revelations received prior to 1835 are based upon that publication.

It is a well-established canon of textual criticism that in order to uncover the original text one must follow the earliest and best manuscripts available.[84] In biblical textual criticism, the text critic works with versions from various scribes in attempting to determine which reading is closest to the original. Among the most significant conventions are assumptions that the shortest reading is probably closest to the original, since a scribe more often adds than takes away, and that the most difficult reading is probably nearest to the original wherever this rule can reasonably be applied. The possibility of transcription errors such as dittography must be kept in mind, as well.

In applying these principles to the revelations given by Joseph Smith, we must apply two distinctly different approaches to the texts themselves. The first involves comparing the various versions of the printed texts. Instead of peeling back layers of scribal variations, as one would do with biblical texts in an attempt to restore the original, the critic here peels back various layers of editing in an attempt to restore the original text of the revelation. The second approach is much like biblical text criticism. It involves examining the various extant scribal manuscripts of Joseph Smith's revelations and comparing them in an attempt to uncover the text of the revelation as Smith originally received it. Applying these principles to Smith's revelations allows us to re-establish the original text and to better understand the revelations in the context in which they were originally given.

The history of Joseph Smith, in a passage compiled in 1839, recalled a time in 1830 when Oliver Cowdery suggested a change in the Articles and Covenants of the church. Joseph Smith

---

[84] For text critical methods, see Kurt and Barbara Aland, *The Text of the New Testament, An Introduction to the Critical Edition and to the Theory and Practice of Modern Textual Criticism* (Grand Rapids, Michigan: Eerdmans/E.J. Brill, 1987); Bruce M. Metzger, *The Text of the New Testament, Its Transmission, Corruption, and Restoration*, 3rd ed. (New York: Oxford University Press, 1992); and Bruce M. Metzger, *A Textual Commentary on the Greek New Testament*, 2nd ed. (Stuttgart, Ger.: German Bible Society, 1994).

replied, asking Cowdery: "by what authority he [Cowdery] took upon him to command me [Smith] to alter, or erase, to add or diminish to or from a revelation or commandment from Almighty God."[85] Yet it appears that for the 1835 Doctrine and Covenants, Smith and Cowdery were both involved in this sort of editing.

On July 31, 1832 Smith wrote a letter to William W. Phelps concerning copies of the commandments and of the vision of three degrees of glory. Joseph Smith wrote:

I will send them to you as soon as possable [possible], but I will exhort you to be careful not to alter the sense of any of them for he that adds or diminishes to the prop[h]ecies must come under the condemnation writ[t]en therein.[86]

Indeed, this understanding of the unalterable nature of the revelatory text is found in the Book of Commandments. There it says concerning lost Book of Mormon manuscript pages: "I will confound those who have altered my words."[87]

In recent years there has been a growing willingness on the part of some writers to admit the existence of variant readings of the early revelations.[88] Some of this openness responds to the criticisms of some early rank-and-file members who harbored grievances against church leaders, including charges of textual revision. William Harris, for instance, who left the church, published a book in 1841, *Mormonism Portrayed*, in which he addressed textual changes: "Let me digress for one moment, and ask why this alteration? It does appear to have been done by

---

[85] Manuscript History, Book A-1:51. See Jessee, *Papers of Joseph Smith* 1:260, 320. See also *Times and Seasons* 4 (Feb. 15, 1843):108 and *History of the Church* 1:105.

[86] Smith to Phelps, July 31, 1832, LDS archives. See Jessee, *Personal Writings of Joseph Smith*, 273. The vision of three glories was published in the July 1832 issue of *The Evening and the Morning Star*, as Phelps already possessed a copy.

[87] Marquardt, *Joseph Smith Revelations*, 39-40; BC 9:10; LDS D&C 10:42; RLDS D&C 3:9.

[88] See, for example, Robert J. Woodford, "How the Revelations in the Doctrine and Covenants were Received and Compiled," *Ensign* 15 (Jan. 1985):27-33 and Melvin J. Petersen, "Preparing Early Revelations for Publication," Ibid. 15 (Feb. 1985):14-20.

command of God, but purports to be the same revelation as was first published."[89]

This important point has both historical and theological ramifications. Jonathan B. Turner in his 1842 book also dealt with changes in the 1835 Doctrine and Covenants:

> It would have been well for the world if Smith's divinity, instead of giving him a pair of stone spectacles, had given him a divine printer, and a divine press, and such types that he might have been enabled to fix the meaning of his inspired revelations, so that it would be possible to let them stand, at *least two years*, without abstracting, interpolating, altering, or garbling, to suit the times. But the ways of Smith's providence are indeed mysterious. We will not pretend to judge.[90]

Jonathan Turner further declared: "The revelations in the Book of Covenants cannot be understood without carefully comparing them with the history and position of the Mormon church at the time they were given."[91]

As far as is known, Joseph Smith made no response to these specific charges. He did state in Nauvoo that "there is no error in the revelations which I have taught."[92] It is not certain if he meant by this the original text, the 1835 revisions, or his teachings about the revelations. In any event, the earliest text is preferred over the revised 1835 text for clarity and historical consistency, and the earliest revelatory text is best understood when used in conjunction with contemporary letters and journals of the persons involved.[93]

---

[89] William Harris, *Mormonism Portrayed* (Warsaw, IL: Sharp & Gamble, Publishers, 1841), 29. Thomas C. Sharp helped prepare this work for publication.
[90] J[onathan]. B. Turner, *Mormonism in All Ages*, 226, emphasis in original.
[91] Ibid. 244.
[92] Report by Thomas Bullock of a discourse delivered on May 12, 1844, in Andrew F. Ehat and Lyndon W. Cook, eds., *The Words of Joseph Smith: The Contemporary Accounts of the Nauvoo Discourses of the Prophet Joseph* (Provo, Utah: Religious Studies Center, Brigham Young University, 1980), 369.
[93] For examples of textual revisions see Marquardt, *Joseph Smith Revelations*.

Some copies of revelations received by Joseph Smith after the publication of the 1835 Doctrine and Covenants were copied into three records kept of Smith's activities. The manuscript books include the Joseph Smith journal for part of 1835-36, the Scriptory Book of Joseph Smith for 1838, and the Book of the Law of the Lord containing revelatory documents of 1841-42.

As mentioned previously a second edition was being prepared before Smith's death. In 1876 a new edition of the LDS Doctrine and Covenants was expanded by adding twenty-five documents originating with Joseph Smith. In the 1981 edition a vision given to Smith in the Kirtland, Ohio was published. If need be there could be included about thirty-five additional revelations becoming part of the Doctrine and Covenants.

Even though some of the wording in Joseph Smith's revelatory documents claimed to be the words of Christ for Smith that did not mean that they were infallible. Since Joseph Smith was able to change his revelations he can change his story of the gold plates. New ideas can be incorporated always working on the religious tone of the narrative.

The alteration of revelations presents a historical problem for those trying to following the line of thought of Smith. As mentioned above as new wording was incorporated into the text there are some who consider these new ideas as originally given at the time of the reception rather than alterations made at a later time. Since the revelations imply that the words are given directly from Christ those documents that were changed indicate that Joseph Smith did not take them very seriously.

13

Missionary Work

The message of the Book of Mormon and the new covenant of the gospel preached by Joseph Smith were shared through missionary work. Early missionaries performed their duties and were usually men who had been ordained elders. They received official licenses to preach from the church. Some were called by special revelation through Smith while others had a desire to share the angel message. The angel story, the newly published Book of Mormon, along with the New Testament emphasis on baptism by immersion was preached in homes, courthouses, and churches.

The Articles and Covenants of the Church of Christ gave the general direction on what was to be preached. Essentially the Church of Christ was a new religious movement based on the Bible with an attempt to restore New Testament Christianity. There were many similarities with beliefs and church structure with churches of the day. A new book, proclaimed as an ancient record (the Book of Mormon), was considered a second Bible as it was a witnesses to the Holy Bible. With a current prophet, Joseph Smith Jr., individuals and the church would be guided by modern day revelation.

Like local Protestant churches emphasis on Jesus Christ, his life, death, and resurrection was foundational. The church structure of the infant church was led by two elders, Joseph Smith and Oliver Cowdery. Quarterly conferences were to be held similar to the Methodists. After faith and repentance the ordinance of baptism would need to be done by an ordained priest or elder who received his appointment from the church. Baptism by immersion was the only accepted way it could be performed. Church confirmation followed the laying on of hands with the promise of bestowal of the Holy Ghost.

As the church grew in membership more offices were added to administer its affairs both spiritual and temporal. Financial resources were need to further the work in the way of printing periodicals, latter day scriptures, support for full time leaders, assisting the poor, and eventually erecting buildings like the Kirtland Temple. Though it was envisioned that there would be twelve apostles in the church it was not until some years later that this was accomplished. A large majority of faithful men were ordained to offices in the priesthood and sent on short and long term missions to convert those who believed in their message of hope and salvation.

The revelations of Joseph Smith dealt with issues of consecrating money for the support of members and church programs. Inspired teachings intermingled temporal as well as the spirituality aspects for the benefit of individuals and families.

The start of missionary work in the Western Reserve around Kirtland, Ohio commenced with the arrival of the four Lamanite missionaries Oliver Cowdery, Peter Whitmer Jr., Ziba Peterson, and Parley P. Pratt. Pratt had recently been a preacher in the Reformed Baptist Church and was acquainted with Sidney Rigdon. He wanted to tell Rigdon about the new revelation of the Book of Mormon. The missionaries arrived in Kirtland, near Mentor on Friday, October 29 according to a letter written by Oliver Cowdery. They first went to see thirty-seven year old Rev. Sidney Rigdon at his home and Parley P. Pratt gave him a copy of the Book of Mormon. Rigdon was a Reformed Baptist pastor with a congregation in Mentor.

An early account mentioned that the missionaries asked the "brethren of the reformation . . . to receive their mission and book as from Heaven, which they said chiefly concerned the western Indians, as being an account of their origin, and a prophecy of their final conversion to [C]hristianity, and made them a white and delightsome people, and be reinstated in the possessing of their lands of which they have been despoiled by the whites."[1] The four missionaries mentioned that the aborigines "are a part of the tribe of Manasseh, and whose ancestors landed on the coast of Chili 600 years before the coming of Christ, and from them descended all the Indians of America."[2]

---

[1] "Mormonism," *Telegraph* 2 (Feb. 15, 1831), Painesville, Ohio.
[2] "The Golden Bible, or, Campbellism Improved," *Observer and Telegraph* 1 (Nov. 18, 1830), Hudson, Ohio.

Rigdon commenced reading the Book of Mormon but had a hard time becoming convinced of its authenticity. Parley Pratt recalled, "it was with much persuasion and argument, that he [Rigdon] was prevailed on to read it, and after he had read it, he had a great struggle of mind, before he fully believed and embraced it."[3]

Meetings were held at Isaac Morley's farm where there lived those who believed "it was necessary that there should be a community of goods among the brethren."[4] A few days later the four missionaries returned to the Morley farm and performed the first baptisms of their mission. Late on the night of Friday, November 5, seventeen individuals received the rite of baptism. Cowdery wrote that they "held a meeting with these brethren, and seventeen went immediately forward and were baptized, between eleven and twelve at night."[5]

Josiah Jones recalled that the missionaries preached in the Methodist meeting house and "exhorted the people to repent of their pride and priestcraft and all other sins, and be baptized by them for the remission of them, for they said that if they had been baptized it was of no avail, for there was no legal administer, neither had been for fourteen hundred years, until God had called them to the office, and had sent them into the world to publish it to this generation."[6]

The Painesville *Telegraph* of February 15, 1831 reported that after "seventeen persons were immersed by them in one night" that Rigdon "seemed much displeased" but shortly after "was convinced that Mormonism was true and divine." Sunday morning, November 7 Rigdon "had an appointment to preach in the Methodist chapel at Kirtland. He arose to address the congregation apparently much affected and deeply impressed. He seemed

---

[3] Parley P. Pratt, *Mormonism Unveiled* (New York, 1838), pamphlet dated March 24, 1838 on page 47; reprinted in *The Essential Parley P. Pratt* (Salt Lake City: Signature Books, 1990), 43.
[4] "History of the Mormonites," *The Evangelist* 9 (June 1, 1841):133, Carthage, Ohio. This account was written by Josiah Jones in 1831 but not published until 1841. See Milton V. Backman, Jr., ed., "A Non-Mormon View of the Birth of Mormonism in Ohio," *Brigham Young University Studies* 12 (Spring 1972):308.
[5] Cowdery to "Our beloved brethren," Nov. 12, 1830, Kirtland, Ohio, copy preserved in a Newel Knight Journal, private possession, typed copy.
[6] "History of the Mormonites," *The Evangelist* 9 (June 1, 1841):133.

exceedingly humble, confessed the sins of his former life, his great pride, ambition, vainglory, &c. &c." On that day twenty-eight more baptisms were performed.

Elder Pratt wrote, "At length Mr. Rigdon and many others became convinced that they had no authority to minister in the ordinances of God; and that they had not been legally baptized and ordained. They, therefore, came forward and were baptized by us, and received the gift of the Holy Ghost by the laying on of hands, and prayer in the name of Jesus Christ."[7]

The early accounts agree that Sidney Rigdon was baptized on a Monday. The baptism was performed by Oliver Cowdery and the date would have been November 8, 1830. Phebe, Sidney's wife was also baptized by Cowdery. The *Telegraph* reported, "The Monday following he was baptized."[8] Josiah Jones also mentions, "On Monday Elder Rigdon was *re-baptized*."[9] Ten days after the arrived of the four missionaries Rigdon received baptized.

As early as 1831 it has been published that Sidney Rigdon had some pre-1830 connection with Joseph Smith Jr. and the production of the text of the Book of Mormon. It appears that these accounts are not reliable. Parley P. Pratt recalled the visit to Rigdon in the fall of 1830, "We called on Elder S. Rigdon, and then for the first time, his eyes beheld the 'Book of Mormon; I, myself, had the happiness to present it to him in person."[10] A few days after Rigdon's conversion Oliver Cowdery wrote a letter telling about their success in having fifty-five baptisms:

> We arrived at this place two weeks this day, on our journey we called at the Buffalo tribe, but stayed a few hours only but left two books with them. We traveled directly to this place. On the fourth after attending a public meeting we came to the place where we had prophesied tarrying a few days. It is where several families had united themselves as a band of brethren and put all their property together determining to live separate from the world as much as

---

[7] *Autobiography of Parley P. Pratt*, 35.

[8] "Mormonism," *Telegraph* 2 (Feb. 15, 1831).

[9] "History of the Mormonites," *The Evangelist* 9 (June 1, 1841):134, emphasis in original.

[10] *Essential Parley P. Pratt*, 43, emphasis omitted.

possible and when we had returned we held a meeting with these brethren, and seventeen went immediately forward and were baptized, between eleven and twelve at night, and on the 6th there was one more, on the 7th nine in the daytime and at night nineteen, on the 8th three, on the 9th three, on the 10th at night one, on the 11th one, on this day another, making in the whole fifty five, among whom are brother Sidney Rigdon and wife.

Continuing his letter Cowdery wrote:

There is considerable call here for books, and I wish you would send five hundred immediately here, and when they are or a part of them are sold, one of these will fetch the money, and if our brother Rigdon does not come before that time, I think he will then. Be that sooner or later, receive him (as) if from my own bosom, for he is am [as] I am. I wish you without fail to communicate this to my aged parents. Do brethren if you respect me. We expect in a few days to pursue our journey to the Lamanites.[11]

Eber D. Howe editor of the *Telegraph* newspaper published in Painesville, north of Kirtland, wrote, "About two weeks since some persons came along here with the book, one [Oliver Cowdery] of whom pretends to have seen Angels , and assisted in translating the plates. He proclaims destruction upon the world within a few years, — holds forth that the ordinances of the gospel, have not been regularly administered since the days of the Apostles, till said Smith and himself commenced the work . . . We understand that he is bound for the regions beyond the Mississippi [River], where he contemplates founding a 'City of Refuge' for his followers, and converting the Indians under his prophetic authority."[12]

Parley P. Pratt summarized their labor, "we had baptized one hundred and twenty-seven souls."[13] Among those converted

---

[11] Cowdery to "Our beloved brethren," Nov. 12, 1830.
[12] "The Golden Bible," *Telegraph* 2 (Nov. 16, 1830):3.
[13] *Autobiography of Parley P. Pratt*, 36.

were Levi Hancock, Isaac Morley, John Murdock, Sidney Rigdon, Lyman Wight, and Frederick G. Williams. On November 22, 1830 the four missionaries departed the Kirtland region for Missouri with the addition of the newly converted Frederick Williams.

Joseph Smith arrived in Kirtland about February 1, 1831. He received the laws of the church a few days later. The revelation explained, in response to a number of questions, about assembling or gathering together. The document further mentioned preaching the gospel, repeated part of the Ten Commandments, and explained if you wanted to keep all of God's commandments you shall consecrate "all of thy property" to the church through the bishop. Other instructions gave directions to the elders of the church.[14]

Smith wrote a letter to Martin Harris on February 22 requesting him to "bring or cause to be brought all the books [of Mormon]" to Kirtland.[15] Harris made a brief trip with copies of the Book of Mormon. Martin arrived at Painesville on Saturday, March 12 bringing with him a large quantity of Books of Mormon. Harris's eccentric personality was immediately noted in the local paper:

He immediately planted himself in the bar-room of the hotel. . . . He told all about the gold plates, Angels, Spirits, and Jo Smith.—He had seen and handled them all, by the power of God!

The meeting was closed after Harris had declared to those in attendance "that all who believed the new Bible would see Christ within fifteen years, and all who did not would be absolutely be destroyed and dam'd [damned]."[16] A short time later, Martin Harris traveled back to Palmyra and sold his farm of 151 acres to Thomas Lakey for $3,000.[17] This amount covered the cost of printing the Book of Mormon.

---

[14] Marquardt, *Joseph Smith Revelations*, 107-110.
[15] Smith to Harris, Feb. 22, 1831, handwriting of Sidney Rigdon, signature of Joseph Smith, Jr., LDS archives.
[16] *Telegraph* 2 (March 15, 1831):3, emphasis omitted.
[17] Deed recorded in Deed Liber 10:515-16, Wayne County, Lyons, New York.

William E. McLellin, who was teaching school in Paris, Illinois, was twenty-five years old when he heard Harvey Whitlock and David Whitmer preach in July 1831. He rode on horseback to Jackson County arriving there on August 18. McLellin talked with Hyrum Smith and "inquired into the particulars of the coming forth of the record," the rise of the church and testimonies.[18] McLellin wrote a letter in 1832 to his relatives and explained what he had learned from the two elders:

> They said that in September 1827 an Angel appeared to Joseph Smith (in Ontario C. New-York) and showed to him the confusion on the earth respecting true religion. It also told him to go a few miles distant to a certain hill and there he should find some plates with engravings, which (if he was faithful) he should be enabled to translate. He went as directed and found plates (which had the appearance of fine Gold) about 8 inches long 5 or 6 [inches] wide and alltogether about 6 inches thick; each one about as thick as thin paste Board fastened together and opened in the form of a book containing engravings of reformed Egyptian Hieroglyphical characters, which he was inspired to translate and the record was published in 1830 and is called the book of Mormon. It is a record which was kept on this continent by the ancient inhabitants.[19]

William McLellin requested baptism from Hyrum Smith who baptized him on August 20 and four days later he was ordained an elder in the church. William left Jackson County with some elders. He accompanied Hyrum Smith as a companion and they traveled to Jacksonville, Illinois where McLellin preached in the courthouse on September 10. William explained in his letter, "We attended. the house though large was full of Judges, Lawyers, Doctors, Priests and People I think about 500. I spoke 3 hours."

McLellin wrote in his journal that in his discourse he "gave them a brief history of the book of Mormon, of its coming forth

---

[18] William E. McLelin Journal, LDS archives, in Shipps and Welch, *Journals of William E. McLellin*, 33.
[19] McLellin to "Beloved Relatives," Aug. 4, 1832, RLDS archives; Shipps and Welch, *Journals of William E. McLellin*, 79.

&c, Then reasoned upon and expounded prophecy after prophecy and scripture after scripture, which had reference to the book and to these days and after speaking with great liberty about 3 hours I concluded with a warning to them to flee from the wrath to come and gather themselves to Zion and prepare to meet the Lord at his second coming which was nigh at hand."[20] The local newspaper reported some of the discourse of William McLellin without naming him:

A Preacher of this sect visited us last Saturday. We heard a part of his lecture, which occupied more than two hours. From his account, this sect came into existence a little more than a year since in the following manner:—A young man about 23 years of age somewhere in Ontario county, N.Y. was visited by an angel! (here the preacher looked around him apparently to see if the credulity of the people in this enlightened age, could be thus imposed on) who informed him three times in one night that by visiting a certain place in that town he would have revealed to him something of importance.

McLellin said that, "At the place appointed he [Joseph Smith] found in the earth a box which contained a set of thin plates resembling gold, with Arabic characters inscribed on them." The newspaper article included probably the earliest printing of biblical passages used by missionaries to confirm the story line about the Book of Mormon. The book told of building a ship and coming to the western world. The article continued:

To prove this, the preacher referred us to Genesis, 49th chapter and 22d verse, and said the branches running over the wall was neither more nor less than the progeny of Joseph, leaving their own and coming to this country! He went into a detail of the reasons which induced him to join himself to this people—that on account of so many sects being in the world, and the discrepances in their opinions, he became sceptical—that hearing of these people in July

---

[20] Ibid., 39, entry for September 10, 1831.

last, he joined himself to them, believing them to constitute the true Church—and that he came this way to meet a convocation of elders in Jackson county, Missouri, which is to be their New Jerusalem, but was disappointed in not seeing them there. He insisted on the bible being joined with his book, by quoting the 16th and 17th verses of the 37th chapter of Ezekiel, and comparing the bible and Mormon's book to the two sticks there spoken of.[21]

In the middle of October 1831 at Kirtland a number of families were getting ready to move to the promised land of Missouri. Nancy Towle, an evangelist, and Elizabeth Venner came to town. The ladies were entertained by Elizabeth Godkin Marsh wife of Thomas B. Marsh. Towle wrote that she came to investigate the sect. After spending a day she considered it a deception though "they may be saved at last" by fire. At that time Nancy Towle conversed with William W. Phelps, Martin Harris, Sidney Rigdon, and Joseph Smith about the new religion.

Harris told her: "I have authority to say to you—You shall not enjoy, the comforts of God's grace, until you believe that book [the Book of Mormon]! . . . I should be willing to bear, all the sins of the human family, beyond the grave—if these things, are not so!" She had a question for Joseph Smith:

> Mr. Smith,—Can you, in the presence of Almighty God, give your word upon oath—that, an Angel from Heaven, shewed you the place, of those Plates:—and that, you took the things, contained in that Book, from those plates: and at the direction of the Angel, you returned the Plates, to the place, from whence you had taken them?

Joseph answered, "I will not swear at all!" He confirmed some women and children with the Holy Ghost. Nancy Towle asked Smith, "Are you not ashamed, of such pretensions?" and he replied, "The gift, has returned back again, as in former

---

[21] "Mormonism," *New-Hampshire Gazette* 76 (Oct. 25, 1831):4, Portsmouth, New Hampshire, emphasis omitted. Reprinted from the *Illinois Patriot* (Jacksonville, Illinois), issue of September 16, 1831, no known copy extant.

times, to illiterate fishermen." Nancy wrote, "So he got off, as quick as he could. . . . As we left the Mormonites, (for so they are called,) a number of families, started for the 'Promised-Land.' One turned to us, with much apparent animation, and said, 'We are now going to that Land, which is to be our dwelling-place, forever-more!'"[22]

Called by revelation Lyman E. Johnson and Orson Pratt were to preach in the eastern states. In Pennsylvania they preached in Franklin, Venango County, on February 11, 1832. Like other traveling elders they used the local courthouse as a good location for citizens to hear their message.

We of this place were visited on Saturday last by a couple of young men styling themselves Mormonites. They explained their doctrine to a large part of the citizens in the court house that evening. They commenced by reading the first chapter of Paul's Epistle to the Galatians: also by giving an account of their founder, Joseph Smith, then an inhabitant of the state of New-York, county of Ontario, and town of Manchester. Having repented of his sins, but not attached himself to any party of Christians, owing to the numerous divisions among them, and being in doubt what his duty was, he had recourse prayer. After retiring to bed one night, he was visited by an Angel and directed to proceed to a hill in the neighborhood where he would find a stone box containing a quantity of Gold plates. The plates were six or eight inches square, and as many of them as would make them six or eight inches thick, each as thick as a pane of glass.

The two preachers explained that Joseph Smith by divine aid produced the Mormon bible as a revelation to part of the house of Joseph. As reported in the newspaper the missionaries told about the Book of Mormon. They related to those attending:

---

[22] *Vicissitudes Illustrated, in the Experience of Nancy Towle, in Europe and America. Written by Herself* (Charleston: Printed for the Authoress by James L. Burges, 1832), 138, 143-146, emphasis omitted. The visit to Kirtland appears to have covered October 15-17, 1831.

about 600 years before Christ, with a prophet of the name of Lehi, of the tribe of Joseph, and a contemporary of the prophet Jeremiah, who had also warned the inhabitants of Jerusalem of their idolatry, & becoming unsafe in the city, was ordered by God to leave Jerusalem and journey toward the Red Sea. He with another family who accompanied him, built themselves a ship and landed on the coast of South America, where they increased very fast, and the Lord raised up a great many prophets among them. They built cities, and encouraged the arts and sciences.—Their prophecies foretold the appearance of the Messiah on the other continent, and gave as a sign that they should have two days without a night—also of his death, which was the cause of the terrible earthquakes, which rent all the rocks in our hills into the different shapes they now are. After our Savior's ascension to heaven, that he came down to this continent and appointed twelve disciples, and that Christianity flourished for three or four generations.—After that the inhabitants divided and wars ensued, in which the pagans prevailed.—The first battle was fought nigh to the straits of Darien, and the last at a hill called Comoro [Cumorah][23]

The missionaries besides discussing the contents of the Book of Mormon preached repentance, the return of the Jews to Palestine and "They insisted that our Savior would shortly appear, and that there were some present who would see him on the earth—that they knew it—that they were not deceiving their hearers; that it was all true."

At the church conference held on January 25, 1832 in Amherst, Lorain County, Ohio, Orson Hyde and Samuel H. Smith, were called as missionaries at the same time as Lyman Johnson and Orson Pratt. Hyde and Smith were also to preach in the eastern United States:

---

[23] "Mormonism," *The Fredonia Censor* 11 (March 7, 1832):4, Fredonia, New York; reprinted from the *Democrat*, circa Feb. 1832, Franklin, Pennsylvania. Lyman and Orson preached on February 8 in Mercer County. See "The Orators of Mormon," *Catholic Telegraph* 1 (April 14, 1832):204-205, Cincinnati, Ohio. Reprinted from *MercerPress*.

And again verily thus saith the Lord let my servent [servant] Orson Hyde and my servent [servant] Samuel take their journey into the eastern countries and proclaim the things which I have commanded them and inasmuch as they are faithfull lo I will be with them even unto the end[24]

Samuel H. Smith and Orson Hyde departed on their mission on February 1 and returned to Kirtland on December 22. This is one of the best documented proselyte mission performed by two stalwarts church representatives. Both Hyde and Smith kept journals while spreading the gospel in Ohio, Pennsylvania, New York, Massachusetts, New Hampshire, and Maine. They sold copies of the Book of Mormon and baptized converts. For example, on April 14, 1832 they held a meeting at the courthouse in Batavia, New York. The local newspaper did not look favorably upon them and reported, "Two Mormonites, last Saturday evening, attempted to give a history of their sect, and explain the principles of mormonism."[25] Orson Hyde recorded in his journal:

14[th] went on to Batavia 40 miles Preached once on the way publicly & from H[ouse] to house preached at the court House in Batavia to a large congregation & quite attentive

While Samuel H. Smith wrote about the meeting:

in Batavia in the Court house Warned them faithful[l]y of the Judgments that was Coming & the Court house was Crowded with people[26]

Though there was opposition to their preaching and many did not come forward to join the church they had a successful mission.

In April 1832 Joseph Smith with some other elders traveled to Missouri to accomplish church business. Joseph returned in June

---

[24] Marquardt, *Joseph Smith Revelations*, 184; LDS D&C 75:13; RLDS D&C 75:3.

[25] "Mormonism," *Republican Advocate* 1 (April 17, 1832):3, Batavia, New York.

[26] Orson Hyde Journal, entry for April 14, 1832 and Samuel H. Smith Journal, both in LDS archives.

to the Johnson home in Hiram, Ohio where his official residence was until September. Sidney Rigdon, one of two counselors to Joseph Smith, shook up the church at Kirtland when his spoke to members at one of their meetings. Lucy Mack Smith recorded that her husband discussed with Sidney and requested him to preach. Sidney "replied vehemently the keys of the kingdom <are> rent from the church and there shall not be a prayer put up in this place to day." Joseph Smith Sr. said I hope not. The saints were greatly excited over this and the sisters cried.

> Sister Howe[27] <particularly> was much terrified Oh! dear Me, said she, what shall we do[?] what shall we do[?] the keys of the Kingdom are taken from us - <and what shall we do>[?]
>
> I tell, repeated Syney [Sidney], with much apparent feeling, the keys of [the] Kingdom are <wrent> [rent] from <you> and you never will have them again untill you build me a new house.[28]

Hyrum Smith hearing this left Kirtland for Hiram to get Joseph to settle this issue of Sidney's claim. At a meeting held in Kirtland Smith "told the brethren to cast of[f] all their fear for they were under a great mistake that they were under no transgression and, said he, I myself hold the Keys of this last dispensation and I forever will hold them in time and eternity so set your hearts at rest for all is well."[29] Reynolds Cahoon recorded the following in his journal:

> thursday [July 5] 4 Ocloc[k] Met with some of the Br[ethren] for Me[e]ting and at the me[e]ting Br Sidney

---

[27] This may have been Sophia Hull Howe, wife of E. D. Howe, editor of the Painesville *Telegraph*, or his sister Harriet Howe, who according to Parley P. Pratt were both church members. See Pratt, *Mormonism Unveiled*, 40; reprinted in *Essential Parley P. Pratt*, 42.

[28] Lucy Mack Smith, draft manuscript, LDS archives. See Anderson, *Lucy's Book*, 561-62. Lucy Smith places this event before Joseph Smith's trip to Missouri rather than after his return. In 1843 this incident was not included in Manuscript History Book A-1.

[29] Anderson, *Lucy's Book*, 563.

remarked that he had a revelation from the Lord & said that the kingdo<m> was taken from <the> Church and left with him

    fryday [July 6] Br Hiram went after Joseph when he came he affirmed that the kingdom was ours & never Should be taking [taken] from the faithful[30]

Replacing Rigdon as Joseph's scribe at this time was Frederick G. Williams who was appointed on July 20. Eight days later "Brother Sidney was ordained to the hight [high] priesthood the second time."[31] In a letter written to William W. Phelps in Missouri Joseph Smith explaining:

for a moment he became frantick [frantic] & the advisary [adversary] taking the advantage, he spake unadvisedly with his lips after receiving a severe chastisement resigned his commis[s]ion and became a private member in the church, but has since repented like Peter of old and after a little suffering by the buffiting [buffeting] of Satan has been restored to his high standing in the church of God[32]

Joseph Smith after returning to Kirtland with Bishop Newel K. Whitney from their trip to the cities of New York, Albany, and Boston came home to an addition to his family, a son named Joseph Smith III. Emma and Joseph's son was born on November 6, 1832 in Kirtland.[33] Shortly after the birth of his son the prophet Joseph Smith commenced keeping a better account of himself and the councils in church government that had for the most part been neglected in the first two years of the church. Though separate minutes of meetings, some retained correspondence, and the original handwritten revelations had been kept it was now thought

---

[30] Reynolds Cahoon Journal, LDS archives, entries for July 5-6, 1832.
[31] Hyrum Smith Journal, entry for July 28, 1832, L. Tom Perry Special Collections, Harold B. Lee Library, Brigham Young University, Provo, Utah. See Jeffrey S. O'Driscoll, *Hyrum Smith: A Life of Integrity*, 68-69.
[32] Smith to Phelps, July 31, 1832, copy of letter, LDS archives. See Jessee, *Personal Writings of Joseph Smith*, 273.
[33] Jessee, *Papers of Joseph Smith* 1:18, 386.

proper for Smith to have a permanent record that would contain his and the church's acts for future generations.

In November Joseph Smith dictated and wrote his 1832 account of his early religious experiences, copied letters into what is known as Joseph Smith Letterbook 1, and started his personal journal. Soon after some of Joseph's revelations were copies into the Kirtland Revelations Book and minutes of meeting were recorded in the Kirtland Council Minute Book. These valuable records would be used in part to help compose the Manuscript History of Joseph Smith and the church.

Though missionaries described what they heard about how the Book of Mormon was obtained Joseph Smith had still not made a written record of the event for church members. At a conference held on October 25, 1831 at Orange, Ohio, the minutes recorded:

> Br. Hyrum Smith said that he thought best that the information of the coming forth of the Book of Mormon be related by Joseph himself to the Elders present that all might know for themselves. Br. Joseph Smith jr. said that it was not intended to tell the world all the particulars of the coming forth of the book of Mormon, & also said that it was not expedient for him to relate these things &c.[34]

A brief reference to Smith's early visions was included in the Articles and Covenants of the church: "For after that it was truly manifested unto this first Elder that he had received a remission of his Sins he was entangled again in the vanities of the world but after truly repenting [G]od ministered unto him by an Holy angel whose countenance was as lightening & whose garments were pure & white above all whiteness & gave unto commandments which inspired him from on high."[35]

Now Smith with his scribe Fredrick G. Williams wrote an account telling about his experiences and connecting them with the establishment of the church, "A History of the life of Joseph Smith Jr. an account of his marvilous experience and of all the mighty

---

[34] Cannon Cook, *Far West Record*, 23.
[35] Marquardt, *Joseph Smith Revelations*, 63; BC 24:6-7; LDS D&C 20:5-8; RLDS D&C 17:2 (June 1830).

acts which he doeth in the name of Jesus Ch[r]ist the son of the living God of whom he beareth record and also an account of the rise of the church of Christ in the eve of time according as the Lord brough<t> forth and established by his hand."

Next was written four occurrences that supported Smith's importance in the leadership of the church. First, Joseph Smith receiving the testimony from on high; second, the ministering of angels; third, the reception of the holy priesthood by the ministering of angels; and fourth, a confirmation and reception of the high priesthood with the keys of the Kingdom of God conferred upon him. Smith then recorded in his own hand the account of his first vision:

> therefore I cried unto the Lord for mercy for there was none else to whom I could go and obtain mercy and the Lord heard my cry in the wilderness and while in <the> attitude of calling upon the Lord <in the 16th year of my age> a piller of light above the brightness of the sun at noon day come down from above and rested upon me and I was filled with the spirit of god and the <Lord> opened the heavens upon me and I saw the Lord and he spake unto me saying Joseph <my son> thy sins are forgiven thee. go thy <way> walk in my statutes and keep my commandments behold I am the Lord of glory I was crucifyed for the world that all those who believe on my name may have Eternal life <behold> the world lieth in sin at this time and none doeth good no not one they have turned asside from the gospel and keep not <my> commandments they draw near to me with their lips while their hearts are far from me and mine anger is kindling against the inhabitants of the earth to visit them ac[c]ording to th[e]ir ungodliness and to bring to pass that which <hath> been spoken by the mouth of the prophets and Ap[o]stles behold and lo I come quickly as it [is] written of me in the cloud <clothed> in the glory of my Father[36]

---

[36] Joseph Smith Letterbook 1, LDS archives; Jessee, *Papers of Joseph Smith* 1:3, 6-7.

Frederick G. Williams taking down dictation recorded the second vision regarding an angel appearing to Joseph in a heavenly vision:

and it came to pass when I was seventeen years of age I called again upon the Lord and he shewed unto me a heavenly vision for behold an angel of the Lord came and stood before me and it was by night and he called me by name and he said the Lord had forgiven me my sins and he revealed unto me that in the Town of Manchester Ontario County N.Y. there was plates of gold upon which there was engravings which was engraven by Maroni [Moroni] & his fathers the servants of the living God in ancient days and deposited by the commandments of God and kept by the power thereof and that I should go and get them and he revealed unto me many things concerning the inhabitants of the earth which since have been revealed in commandments & revelations

and it was on the 22d day of Sept. AD 1822 and thus he appeared unto me three times in one night and once on the next day and then I immediately went to the place and found where the plates was deposited as the angel of the Lord had commanded me and straightway made three attempts to get them and then being exce[e]dingly frightened I supposed it had been a dreem [dream] of Vision but when I consid[e]red I knew it was not

therefore I cried unto the Lord in the agony of my soul why can I not obtain them behold the angel appeared unto me again and said unto me you have not kept the commandments of the Lord which I gave unto you therefore you cannot now obtain them for the time is not yet fulfilled therefore thou wast left unto temptation that thou mightest be made acquainted with the power of the advisary [adversary] therefore repent and call on the Lord thou shalt be forgiven and in his own due time thou shalt obtain them

for now I had been tempted of the advisary [adversary] and saught [sought] the Plates to obtain riches and kept not the commandment that I should have an eye single to the glory of God therefore I was chastened and saught [sought] diligently to obtain the plates and obtained them not untill I was twenty one years of age and in this year I was married to Emma Hale Daughter of Isaach [Isaac] Hale who lived in Harmony Susquehan[n]a County Pen[n]sylvania on the 18th January AD. 1827, on the 22d day of Sept of this same year I obtained the plates[37] .

Joseph Smith's personal journal is of interest since he recorded when he bought the blank book and includes his thoughts at the time. Smith wrote the following entries (with misspellings) in his own hand at the commencement of his journal:

Joseph Smith Jrs Book for Record Baught [Bought] on the 27[th] of November 1832 for the purpose to keep a minute ac[c]ount of all things that come under my obse[r]vation &c Oh may God grant that I may be directed in all my thaughts [thoughts] Oh bless thy Servent [Servant] Amen

November 28[th] this day I have [spent] in reading and writing this Evening my mind is calm and Serene for which I thank the Lord

November 29[th] this day road from Kirtland to Chardon to See my Sister Sop[h]ronia [Smith Stoddard] and also ca[lled] to See my Sister Catherine [Smith Salisbury] [and fou]nd them [well] this Evening Brother Frederic[k G. Williams] Prophecyed that next Spring I Should go to the city of PittsBurg to establish a Bishopwrick [Bishopric] and within one year I Should go to the city of New York the Lord Spare the life of thy Servent Amen[38]

Church members were forced to leave Jackson County, Missouri in November 1833. Bishop Edward Partridge wrote a letter to Joseph Smith that mentioned a prophecy of Parley P. Pratt: "br[other]. Parley has prophesied that we shall be enabled to return

---

[37] Ibid., 7-9. The date 1822 is recorded as 1823 in other accounts.

[38] Joseph Smith Journal, entries for November 27-29, 1832, LDS archives. See Jessee, *Papers of Joseph Smith* 2:2, 4. Smith did not make a trip to Pittsburgh or New York City within the year. These entries were not included in Manuscript History Book A-1.

to our houses by the first of next Jany [January] & enjoy the fruit of our labor & none to molest or make afraid. he says he was constrained to prophesy & if he ever spoke by the spirit of God he then did & if it does not come to pass we may call him a false prophet."[39]

With the disappointment of not being able to establish the city of the New Jerusalem Joseph Smith was told in a revelation to have armed young and middle aged men march to Missouri, replant the saints in their inheritances in Jackson County, and redeem the land of Zion. This army was known as Zion's Camp.

Smith recorded that on February 26, 1834 he "Started from home to obtain volenteers [volunteers] for Zion" traveling through Erie County, Pennsylvania to New York. The company arrived at Alvah Beeman's home in Avon, Livingston County, New York on March 15 and the next day "Brother Sidney [Rigdon] preached to a very large congregation in <Geneseo>."[40] Smith was interview on the same day at Geneva. The unnamed person who spoke with Joseph Smith did not have a high regard for him. His account of the short interview is as follows:

Embracing the opportunity thus thrown in my way, the following colloquy, substantially and almost verbatim, ensued between us.

Self: Sir, is your name Jo. Smith, Jun.?

Mormon Prophet. That is my name, Sir.

S. [Self] Have you a mission from God to this generation?

M. P. [Mormon Prophet] That question I shall leave you to answer, at present. You heard my testimony to-day.

S. [Self] But not being convinced of the truth of that testimony, I have embraced this opportunity to obtain more satisfactory evidence that your mission is from above; or more ample proof that you are an impostor. Ought you not to "be ready always to give me an answer" and "a reason to every man that asketh you"?

---

[39] Partridge to Smith, Nov. 1833, Joseph Smith Papers, LDS archives.

[40] Jessee, *Papers of Joseph Smith* 2:21, 25.

M. P. [Mormon Prophet] When put in a good spirit and at a proper time, I should be ready to answer. You commenced this conversation abruptly.

S. [Self] The questions were proposed in a spirit of candor. I do not reside in this neighborhood, and probably may never meet you again: I, therefore, have seized on such a time as circumstances have permitted. The importance of the subject matter to which my interrogatories had reference, must apologize for my abruptness of manner.[41]

The writer commented that Joseph Smith then "murmured out something which became inaudible in the distance, as he urged on his horse and was soon out of the reach of my voice." Parley P. Pratt wrote concerning the elders visit at the house of Alvah Beeman:

Among those whose hospitality we shared in that vicinity was old father Beeman and his amiable and interesting family. He was a good singer, and so were his three daughters; we were much edified and comforted in their society, and were deeply interested in hearing the old gentleman and brother Joseph converse on their early acquaintance and history. He had been intimate with Joseph long before the first organization of the Church; had assisted him to preserve the plates of the Book of Mormon from the enemy, and had at one time had them concealed under his own hearth.[42]

The three daughters of Sarah and Alvah Beeman were Mary Adeline, Louisa, and Artemisia. Twenty-three year old Mary wrote in her journal about the visit of Joseph Smith to her father's home:

---

[41] "Interview with the Mormon Prophet," *Evangelical Magazine and Gospel Advocate* 5 (April 5, 1834):107, Utica, New York. The interview was contained in a letter to the editors by "M. L. P.," of Henrietta, Monroe County, New York, March 17, 1834, emphasis omitted.
[42] *Autobiography of Parley P. Pratt*, 90. Alvah Beeman became president of the elders quorum in Kirtland on January 15, 1836. He died in November 1837.

this was the first time I ever beheld a Prophet of the Lord and I can truly say at the first sight that I had a testimony within my bosom that he was a man chosen to God to bring forth a great work in the last days.[43]

At the conference held on March 17 in Avon, Joseph Smith spoke of obtaining the men needed to assist in the redemption of Zion, gather funds to purchase land in Jackson County, and obtain $2,000 "for the relief of the brethren in Kirtland" from debt.[44] Parley P. Pratt mentioned in his journal an occurrence that happened after the Avon conference relating to a separate meeting held at Sackets Harbor, New York:

> While in Jefferson co. we held a meeting in the large village of Sacketsharbor and the house was filled to overflowing. After we were through preaching the Rev. Mr. More, a man noted for talents, learning and salary, arose and testified to the congregation that he had read the book of Mormon, and that there was no such thing written in it as Christ appearing to the Nephites, and teaching them his gospel and the mode of baptism. He also testified that there was no testimony of three witnesses written in the book, that they had seen an angel. The people then gave a shout and the whole house rang. With much ado I got their attention to hear one remark, which was this, I am happy, said I, to state that the book of Mormon is before the public, and if this congregation will take the trouble to examine it half an hour, they will have the satisfaction of proving to a demonstration, that the Rev. Mr. More is a willful liar. The house again resounded with the shouts of the multitude.[45]

---

[43] Journal of Mary A. Noble, LDS archives. See Vogel, *Early Mormon Documents* 3:309. Mary Adeline married Joseph Bates Noble later in 1834, Louisa was sealed to Joseph Smith in 1841 by Joseph Noble, and Artemisia married Erastus Fairbanks Snow in 1838.

[44] Kirtland Council Minute Book, 42-43, LDS archives.

[45] Journal of Parley P. Pratt, as published in *The Evening and the Morning Star* 2 (May 1834):157, Kirtland, Ohio.

Joseph Smith with his portion of Zion's Camp left Kirtland on May 5. In the middle of June they arrived in Clay County, the county north of Jackson County. Though Zion's Camp made the long journey to Clay County, Missouri they did not accomplish the plan of returning members to the land purchased for their settlements on the central land of Zion. Joseph Smith did set up a presidency of three men and a twelve man high council to administer the affairs of the church in Missouri.

At the meeting held on July 7 the ordinations took place. Smith ordained David Whitmer at this time as church president in Zion and as his successor as prophet in case he fell into transgression. Whitmer's assistants were his brother John Whitmer and William W. Phelps. The twelve counselors were also ordained.[46] The minutes fail to mention David Whitmer's ordination as Joseph Smith's successor.

Joseph Smith returned to Kirtland on August 1, 1834. On the sixteenth of August he set the date of the redemption of Zion to be September 11, 1836. In his letter he wrote, "in case the excitement continues to be allayed and peace prevails use every effort to prevail on the churches to gather to those regions and situate themselves to be in readiness to move into Jackson Co[unty]. in two years from the Eleventh of September next which is the appointed time for the redemption of Zion."[47]

Missionary work continued to be performed locally with short missions and to wider areas and longer duration like it had years earlier. Kirtland remained the center of church operations through 1837. Reports and letters from missionaries were published in the *Evening and the Morning Star* and later in the *Latter Day Saints' Messenger and Advocate*. The vast majority of journals kept by missionaries are preserved in the LDS Church Archives.

---

[46] Cannon and Cook, *Far West Record*, 71-72. The minutes were copied into the Far West Record at a later date.

[47] Smith to Lyman Wight et al., Aug. 16, 1834, Joseph Smith Letterbook, 1:86, LDS archives. See Jessee, *Personal Writings of Joseph Smith*, 349; *History of the Church* 2:145. The September 11 date refers to an earlier revelation that stated the land of Kirtland would be a stronghold for five years.

14

Bible Revision

The belief of Joseph Smith was that the gospel of Jesus Christ contained in the New Testament consisted of the same essential beliefs and ordinances practiced since the beginning of humankind. The sacred texts revealed through Joseph Smith explained that if it was necessary to believe in Jesus now, then Adam and other Old Testament patriarchs would have believed like the followers of Jesus in New Testament times. The same idea goes with the practice of the ordinances of Christian baptism, confirmation, and priesthood ordination.

As mentioned previously Joseph Smith was a student of the Bible. Smith was intensively interested in biblical themes. In his 1832 account he wrote about his search of the scriptures. Joseph recorded (spelling retained):

> At about the age of twelve years my mind become seriously imprest with regard to the all importent concerns for the wellfare of my immortal Soul which led me to searching the scriptures believeing as I was taught, that they contained the word of God[1]

The Book of Mormon commented on the plan of redemption:

> therefore he [God] sent angels to converse with them, which caused men to behold of his glory. And they began from that time forth to call on his name; therefore God conversed with men, and made known unto them the plan of redemption, which had been prepared from the foundation of the world; and this he made known unto

---

[1] "A History of the life of Joseph Smith Jr.," 1-2, LDS archives; Jessee, *Papers of Joseph Smith* 1:5.

them, according to their faith and repentance, and their holy works.[2]

Joseph Smith's additions to the early chapters of Genesis also illustrate the belief that the New Testament gospel was taught and practiced in Old Testament times. With additions to Genesis, such as the following, Smith in essence made that book a Christian document.

> & thus the Gospel began to be preached from the begin[n]ing being declared by Holy Angels sent forth from the presence of God & by his own voice & by the Gift of the Holy Ghost & thus all things were confirmed & the Gospel preached & a decree sent forth that it should be in the World until the end thereof & thus it was[3]

In 1832 Joseph Smith revised the first part of John 1:1 to read, "In the begin[n]ing was the gospel preached through the son. And the gospel was the word."[4] This was a constant theme throughout Smith's life. The Book of Mormon contains Christian ideas incorporated as prophetic insights into the life of Jesus such as his birth and baptism.[5] Joseph Smith dictated the text of a reported ancient vision that proclaimed that "many plain and precious things" had been removed from the Bible. As recorded in First Nephi an angel explained:

> Thou hast beheld that the Book proceeded forth from the mouth of a Jew; and when it proceeded forth from the mouth of a Jew, it contained the plainness of the Gospel of the Lord, of whom the twelve apostles bear record; and

---

[2] 1830 BOM, 257; LDS Alma 12:29-30; RLDS 9:48-50. The plan of redemption was faith, repentance, baptism, and the gift of the Holy Ghost.

[3] OT 1, 10, (Nov. 30, 1830), RLDS archives. At a later date the words "unto Adam by an holy ordinance" were added after the word "confirmed" onto OT 2, 14. See LDS Moses 5:58-59, Pearl of Great Price; and Genesis 5:44-45 (JST). Compare LDS D&C 29:42; RLDS D&C 28:12.

[4] NT 2, folio 4, 105, RLDS archives, revision of John 1:1, ca. Feb. 1832.

[5] 1830 BOM, 24-25; LDS 1 Nephi 11:13-27; RLDS 3:52-73.

they bear record according to the truth which is in the Lamb of God[6]

After the book is in the hands of the Gentiles the record of First Nephi stated the following:

thou seest the foundation of a great and abominable church, which is most abominable above all other churches; for behold, they have taken away from the Gospel of the Lamb, many parts which are plain and most precious; and also, many Covenants of the Lord have they taken away[7]

The Book of Mormon was to help recover the gospel—"I will manifest myself unto thy seed, that they shall write many things which I shall minister unto them, which shall be plain and precious." After being hidden the writings would come forth and contain "my Gospel, saith the Lamb, and my rock and my salvation."[8]

As anyone knows who has tried to accurately copy a text, it is very easy to omit a line or two in the copying process. When ancient scribes copied manuscripts they often accidentally omitted words. The revision made by Joseph Smith attempts to make the wording of the KJV English clearer. The additions by Smith are a reflection of his encounter with the text in the context of revelatory messages as the latter-day gospel was being restored in 1830-33. Smith's revision of the Bible was produced as a church text for those who accept the restored gospel.

Since Joseph Smith did not have knowledge of Hebrew or Greek during this period of Bible revision, we should not expect his revision to contain readings in ancient biblical manuscripts. Nor should we think that his revision is any kind of restoration of

---

[6] 1830 BOM, 30; LDS 1 Nephi 13:24; RLDS 3:165. The original BOM manuscript reads, "fulness of the Gospel" (LDS archives). The wording "planeness [plainness] of the Gospel" was written onto the Printer's manuscript (RLDS archives).

[7] 1830 BOM, 30; LDS 1 Nephi 13:26; RLDS 3:167-168. The original BOM manuscript reads, "formation of that great & abominable church." The Printer's manuscript has, "foundation of a great & abominable Church."

[8] 1830 BOM, 31; LDS 1 Nephi 13:35-36; RLDS 3:184, 186.

what was in the Hebrew Scriptures or in the Greek New Testament. Joseph Smith's work is a revision rather than a translation, since church members knew that Joseph Smith had not studied Hebrew or Greek to produce his manuscript. But church members also thought that Joseph did not have to know Hebrew or Greek because he got his corrections via revelation.

In October 1829 Oliver Cowdery purchased a large leather bound edition of the King James Version of the Bible (KJV) at Egbert B. Grandin's Bookstore in Palmyra, New York. At the time Smith was residing in Pennsylvania.[9] The Bible was published in Cooperstown, New York, by H. and E. Phinney Company in 1828. This printing included the Apocrypha. This KJV 1828 Bible became the textual basis for the revision. Inscribed on the fly leaf is the following:

> The Book of the Jews And the property of
> Joseph Smith Junior and Oliver Cowdery
> Bought October the 8th 1829 at Egbert B Grandins
> Book Store Palmyra Wayne County New York[10]

It had been asserted, prior to the time of Joseph Smith, by European biblical scholars that Moses could not have been the writer of Genesis. In June 1830 Joseph Smith received a new revelation originally given to Moses, previously unknown, that refuted this theory. This revelation began, "The words of God which he <spake> unto Moses."[11] In the revelation Smith said Moses was told:

> And now Moses my Son I will speak unto you concerning this Earth upon which thou standest & thou shalt write the things which I shall speak & in a day when the children of

---

[9] Joseph Smith arrived at Harmony, Pennsylvania on October 4, 1829 (Smith to Cowdery, Oct. 22, 1829, in Joseph Smith Letterbook 1:9, LDS archives. See Vogel, *Early Mormon Documents* 1:7. The Joseph Smith Bible has markings (including strike through of italic words) starting at OT Genesis chapter 25 and NT John chapter 6.

[10] The Joseph Smith Bible purchased by Oliver Cowdery is in the RLDS archives.

[11] OT 1, 1; LDS Moses 1:1; RLDS D&C 22:1.

men shall esteem my words as naught & take many of them
from the Book which thou shalt write behold I will raise up
another like unto thee [Moses] & they shall be had again
among the Children of men among even as many as shall
believe . . . And now they are also spoken unto you [Joseph
Smith] shew them not unto any except them that believe[12]

Joseph Smith's job was to recover the words that were
removed from the Bible. The opening portion of chapter one of
Genesis as revealed "to the Elders of the Church of Christ," circa
June 1830, was rendered:

And it came to pass that the Lord spake unto Moses saying
Behold I reveal unto you concerning this Heaven & this
Earth write the words which I speak I am the beginning &
the end the Almighty God by mine only begotten I created
these things yea in the beginning I created the Heaven &
the Earth upon which thou standest[13]

The underlining text is the KJV book of Genesis. This is
evident since the revision follows the order of that text except for
added material. Two examples of additional information are as
follows:

in that day the Holy Ghost fell upon Adam which bore
record of the Father & the Son saying I am Jesus Christ
from the beginning henceforth & forever[14]

---

[12] OT 1, 3; Compare LDS Moses 1:40-42; RLDS D&C 22:24-25.

[13] OT 1, 3; LDS Moses 2:1; Gen. 1:1-3 (JST). Though there is no first person
account such as "I Moses," like the Book of Mormon, there still is an indication
by Joseph Smith that Genesis had been dictated by inspiration in the words "I
God" or "I the Lord God" in the first five chapters of Genesis. Compare OT 1,
3-10; OT 2, 4-9; LDS Moses 2:1-5:40; Gen. 1:1-5:25 (JST) with Gen. 1:1-5:25
(KJV).

[14] OT 1, 8; LDS Moses 5:9; Gen. 4:9 (JST). Compare Gen. 3:24-4:1 (KJV). See
"The Gospel," *The Evening and the Morning Star* 1 (April 1833):1,
Independence, Missouri. This text was included when copied onto OT 2, 10 and
afterwards "Jesus Christ" was crossed out and "the only begotten of the father"
included above the line.

A revision that reflected some concern for the Masonic fraternity when Joseph Smith dictated the revealed words includes these words:

> satan saith unto Cain swear unto me by thy throat & if thou tell it thou shalt die & swear thy brethren by their heads & by the living God that they tell it not for if they tell it they shall surely die & this that thy father may not know it & this day I will deliver thy brother Abel into thine hands & Satan <swore> unto Cain that he would do according to his commands & all these things were done in secret & Cain saith truly I am Mahon the master of this great secret that I may murder & get gain Wherefore Cain was called master Mahon & he gloried in his wickedness[15]

When Peter Bauder visited the town of Fayette, New York in October 1830 he examined the ten page manuscript of the revision of Genesis:

> The manner in which it was written is as follows:—he [Joseph Smith] commenced at the first chapter of Genesis, he wrote a few verses of scripture, then added delusion, which he added every few verses of scripture, and so making a compound of scripture and delusion. On my interrogating him on the subject, he professed to be inspired by the Holy Ghost to write it.[16]

A revision with new material that included another reinterpretation of Genesis showed that baptism was being preached by Noah:

---

[15] OT 1, 9; LDS Moses 5:29-31; Gen. 5:14-16 (JST). When the text was copied "Mahon" was spelled "Mahan" (OT 2, 12). Compare Genesis 4:7-8 (KJV). See also OT 1, 10; Gen. 5:35 (JST); LDS Moses 5:49. On December 2, 1830 Joseph Smith wrote to his brother Hyrum, "beware of the freemasons" (as cited in Vogel, *Early Mormon Documents* 1:22).

[16] Peter Bauder, *The Kingdom and Gospel of Jesus Christ: Contrasted with that of Anti-Christ*, 37; Vogel, *Early Mormon Documents* 1:17-18.

And it came to pass that Noah continued his preaching unto
the people saying hearken and give heed unto my words
<beleive [believe]> and repent of your sins and be Baptized
in the name of Jesus christ the Son of God even as our
fathers did and ye shall receive the gift of the Holy Ghost[17]

The majority of Christian concepts and ordinances added to
the Old Testament of the Hebrew Scriptures occur in the first
seventeen chapters of Genesis. This stops after chapter 17 and with
no Christian material used for the remainder of Genesis or the rest
of the Old Testaments with one exception. There is a brief mention
of Christ in Isaiah 29:16 (JST).

Joseph Smith used the Book of Mormon text for part of
Genesis 50 (JST) to include a prophecy of Joseph of Egypt.[18] In
Isaiah 29 (JST) there is a prophecy regarding the coming forth of
the Book of Mormon from 2 Nephi that was incorporated into the
biblical text.[19] These textual additions are not supported by
Hebrew manuscripts of Genesis or Isaiah.

A December 1830 revelation considered the Bible revision
as a translation in the words—"it is not expedient in me that ye
should translate any more until ye go to the [state of] Ohio."[20] As
far as is known a Hebrew text was not consulted by Smith for
Genesis. The Bible revision is better understood as an inspired
correction, and where additions were made, as an expansion of the
biblical text.

The revision by Joseph Smith proceeded as follows. He
started with the OT book of Genesis (June 1830), then was
interrupted at Genesis 5:32 (KJV) in December 1830 by
preparations to move to Ohio. Smith briefly returned to OT and in
March 1831 he began revising of the NT. He revisited the OT
revision about July 1832. At Kirtland, Ohio, on February 9, 1831

---

[17] OT 1, 20; LDS Moses 8:23-24; Gen. 8:11 (JST). Compare Gen. 6:5-6 (KJV).
See "The Gospel," *The Evening and the Morning Star* 1 (April 1833):1.

[18] Gen. 50:24-35 (JST). Compare 1830 BOM, 66-67; LDS 2 Nephi 3:5-18;
RLDS 2 Nephi 2:6-37. See Gen. 50:24 (KJV) for traditional text.

[19] Isaiah 29:12-25 (JST). Compare 1830 BOM, 110-111; LDS 2 Nephi 27:7-23;
RLDS 2 Nephi 11:126-145. See Isaiah 29:11-13 (KJV).

[20] Marquardt, *Joseph Smith Revelations*, 97-98; LDS and RLDS D&C 37:1
(Dec. 1830).

Joseph Smith revealed the Laws of the Church which included this statement with regard to his revision of the scriptures:

> Thou shalt ask and my scriptures shall be given as I have appointed, and for thy salvation thou shalt hold thy peace concerning them till ye have rec[eive]d. them, and then I give unto you a Commandment that ye shall teach them unto all men & they also shall be taught unto all nations kindreds, tongues & people[21]

Two manuscripts have the earlier reading: "for thy salvation thou shalt hold thy peace concerning them." The Book of Commandments printed the text in a different form:

> Thou shalt ask and my scriptures shall be given as I have appointed; and for thy *safety it is expedient that* thou shouldst hold thy peace concerning them, until ye have received them: Then I give unto you a commandment that ye shall teach them unto all men; *for* they also shall be taught unto all nations, kindreds, tongues and people.[22]

In the 1835 D&C a further explanation appears in the revision of this revelation:

> Thou shalt ask, and my scriptures shall be given as I have appointed, and *they shall be preserved* in safety; *and* it is expedient that thou shouldst hold thy peace concerning them, *and not teach them* until ye have received them *in full. And* I give unto you a commandment, that *then* ye shall teach them unto all men; *for* they shall be taught unto all nations, kindreds, tongues and people.[23]

---

[21] Marquardt, *Joseph Smith Revelations*, 109, from manuscript designated "Book of Commandments, Law and Covenants; Book B" (LDS archives). Compare with LDS D&C 42:56-58; RLDS D&C 42:15.

[22] BC 44:43-44; italics added for emphasis on words not in manuscript Book B. The reading "for thy safety it is expedient that" appears in two post-November 1831 manuscripts and was evidently based upon the November 1831 Book of Commandments manuscript.

[23] 1835 D&C 13:15. Italics added for emphasis on wording not in BC 44:43-44.

At Kirtland during March 1831 Joseph Smith received a revelation to begin revising the New Testament. Concerning the teachings of Jesus in Matthew 24, he was instructed:

> & now behold I say unto you it shall not be given unto you to know any further than this [Matthew 24] untill the New Testament be translated & in it all these things shall be made known wherefore I give unto you that ye may now translate it that ye may be prepared for the things to come[24]

With this as a background Joseph Smith perceived that the text he supplied would give a broader view of the teachings of Jesus. It appears that Smith himself intended his revision to be for the most part an accurate form of the original meaning of the text and perceived it as such. On March 8 Joseph Smith dictated to his scribe Sidney Rigdon the beginning of the gospel according to Matthew. The heading of the manuscript read: "A Translation of the New Testament translated by the power of God."[25]

Like the Book of Mormon which was revealed "by the gift and power of God," the New Testament revision was a revealed text based upon the KJV Bible. Usually when working with the New Testament a person would use a standard text. In the case of revising Matthew 5 Smith used the KJV Bible and Third Nephi in the Book of Mormon.

Joseph Smith would read from the Bible purchased by Oliver Cowdery in 1829. Besides the Book of Mormon, Smith's work on the Bible was his next largest project. A manuscript was written for most of Matthew (NT 1). The text was then recopied to form another manuscript known as NT 2. This later manuscript was completely written out by Sidney Rigdon and John Whitmer for the revision for the synoptic gospels (Matthew, Mark, and Luke). Rigdon and Whitmer wrote out in full the text of NT 2 for Matthew 1:1 through John 5:47. Starting with John chapter 6 the gospel passages were revised by Joseph Smith with Sidney Rigdon recording what changes were to be made rather than having the

---

[24] Marquardt, *Joseph Smith Revelations*, 123. Compare LDS D&C 45:60-61; RLDS D&C 45:11 (March [6-7], 1831).

[25] NT 1, 1.

complete text being written out. Various markings were made in the Smith Bible for verses to be corrected and to indicate at what place the corrections for NT 2 were to be placed. This was a shorter method than having a scribe spend the time recording the complete text of John. Revisions for the remaining chapters (John six through twenty-one) were recorded on four pages by using this short method as were those for the remainder of the New Testament.[26]

Matthew 1:1-26:71 was recorded by scribe Sidney Rigdon as Joseph Smith dictated to Rigdon the words of the text during the months March through June 1831. The work was interrupted by a trip to Independence, Missouri, in the summer of 1831. John Whitmer served as a scribe for Matthew 26:1 through Mark 9:1 in the fall of 1831. Whitmer left Ohio in November 1831 and moved to Missouri.

After returning from a trip to Independence, Missouri, former elder Ezra Booth wrote with some sarcasm concerning the understanding of church members:

> the Bible is declared too defective to be trusted in its present form; and it is designed that it shall undergo a thorough alteration, or as they say, translation. This work is now in operation. The Gospel by St. Matthew has already received the purifying touch, and is prepared for the use of the church. It was intended to have kept this work a profound secret, and strict commandments were given for that purpose; and even the salvation of the church was said to depend upon it.[27]

The February 9, 1831 revelation corroborates parts of Booth's letter concerning the church's salvation and keeping the revision a secret. Nine months later the minutes of a general conference held on October 25, 1831 at Orange, Ohio, report that

---

[26] NT 2, f. 4, 115-18.
[27] Booth to Rev. Ira Eddy, Oct. 2, 1831, *The Ohio Star* 2 (Oct. 20, 1831):3, Ravenna, Ohio.

Joseph Smith said, "except the church recieve [receive] the fulness of the Scriptures that they would yet fall."[28]

A revelation given on January 10, 1832 explained concerning the New Testament that, "it is expedient to translate again . . . continue the work of translation untill it be finished."[29] In the next month, on February 16, 1832, Joseph Smith and his scribe Sidney Rigdon were working on John chapter 5 when they received what is termed the Vision; actually a series of visionary experiences relating to the afterlife. This is the Vision of three degrees of glory. They reported being in the Spirit when "our eyes were opened, and our understandings were enlightened." Smith and Rigdon give the following background:

> for as we sat doing the work of translation, which the Lord had appointed unto us, we came to the twenty ninth verse of the fifth chapter of John, which was given unto us thus: speaking of the resurrection of the dead who should hear the voice of the Son of man, and shall come forth; they who have done good in the resurrection of the just, and they who have done evil in the resurrection of the unjust. Now this caused us to marvel, for it was given us of the Spirit; and while we meditated upon these things, the Lord touched the eyes of our understanding, and they were opened[30]

Shortly afterwards, Joseph Smith and Sidney Rigdon finished revising John, and by March they were revising Revelation. On March 20, 1832 a question was asked by Rigdon and Smith on whether they should "finish the translation of the

---

[28] Minutes copied into the "Far West Record." See Cannon and Cook, *Far West Record*, 23. The phrase " fulness of the Scriptures" refers to Joseph Smith's Bible revision (See Marquardt, *Joseph Smith Revelations*, 108; LDS D&C 42:15; 104:58; RLDS D&C 42:5; 101:10; and the revision of Luke 11:52).

[29] Marquardt, *Joseph Smith Revelations*, 183; LDS D&C 73:3-4; RLDS D&C 73:2.

[30] Marquardt, *Joseph Smith Revelations*, 186-87. See LDS D&C 76:12, 15-19; RLDS D&C 76:3. If the words "speaking of the resurrection of the dead who should hear the voice of the Son of man" are considered a part of the revision of John, they were not added to the text of John 5:29 in NT 2, f. 4, 114. The words "and shall all be judged of the son of man" were added to the revision of John 5:29.

New Testament" before going to Independence, Missouri or wait until they return from the trip. The response was given: "It is expedient saith the Lord that there be no delays [in going] . . . Wherefore omit the translation for the present time."[31]

Smith wrote a letter on July 31, 1832 to William W. Phelps in Missouri telling him that the manuscripts of the revision would:

> not go from under my hand during my natural life for correction, revisal or printing and the will of [the] Lord be done therefore you need not expect them this fall, Broth[er] Frederick [G. Williams] is employed to be a scribe for me of the Lord—we have finished the translation of the New testament great and glorious things are revealed.[32]

During December 1832 and January 1833 Sidney Rigdon and Joseph Smith reviewed the New Testament manuscript revision. To Frederick G. Williams a revelation of January 5, 1833 stated, "my servant Joseph [Smith Jr.] is called to do a great work and hath needs that he may do the work of translation for the salvation of souls."[33] The review of the New Testament (going over the prior corrections) was finished on February 2, 1833 as recorded in the Kirtland Council Minute Book: "This day completed the translation and the reviewing of the New testament and sealed [it] up no more to be brokin [broken] till it goes to Zion [Independence, Missouri]."[34] NT 2 was completed and ready for publication. No lost writings were added to the New Testament during the nearly two year span when the revision was accomplished.

Work on the Old Testament continued and a revelatory message of March 8, 1833 said, "I give unto you a commandment that you continue in this ministry and presidency and when you have finished the translation of th[e] prophets you shall from

---

[31] Marquardt, *Joseph Smith Revelations*, 207.

[32] Smith to Phelps, July 31, 1832, LDS archives. The Bible manuscripts were kept by Joseph Smith at his home.

[33] Marquardt, *Joseph Smith Revelations*, 231. The correct date is January 5, rather than January 6. The year 1834 in the manuscript copy of the revelation is considered incorrect and should be the year 1833.

[34] Kirtland Council Minute Book, 8, LDS archives.

thenceforth preside over the affairs of the Church and school" of the prophets.[35]

On March 9, 1833 in answer to the question of whether to revise (translate) the Apocrypha Joseph Smith said the Lord told him that it was "mostly translated correct," and it contained "interpolation[s] by the hands of men," but there was no need to translate it.[36] The text of this revelation indicated there were "interpolations" (insertions into the text) by men rather than omissions. Joseph Smith did not identify any particular Apocrypha book as having this problem. The end result was that the Apocrypha was not read and revised. If there were additions to the Apocrypha, they were neither removed nor identified but left in the KJV.

In a letter written the following month (April 1833) Joseph Smith gave instructions that "it is not the will of the Lord to print any of the new translation in the Star but when it is published it will all go to the world together in a volum[e] by itself and the new Testament and the book of Mormon will be printed togeth[er]."[37] Though the *Evening and the Morning Star* had published extracts from Smith's revision of Genesis, the *Star* published in the July issue that "at no very distant period, we shall print the book of Mormon and the Testament, and bind them in one volume."[38]

In a revelation given on May 6, 1833 it was declared, "it is my will that y[ou] should hasten to translat[e] my script[ure]s."[39] When reading the Old Testament books Joseph Smith had his scribe write that seven books, viz., Obadiah, Micah, Nahum, Habakkuk, Zephaniah, Haggai, and Malachi were "correct" as recorded on OT 2.

Further communications were given to church members in Missouri: "In regard to the printing of the New Translation it

---

[35] Marquardt, *Joseph Smith Revelations*, 234-35; LDS D&C 90:12-13; RLDS D&C 87:5.

[36] Marquardt, *Joseph Smith Revelations*, 236; LDS D&C 91:1-3; RLDS D&C 88:1.

[37] Smith to "Dear breth[ren] in Zion," April 21, 1833, Joseph Smith Letterbook 1:35, LDS archives.

[38] "The Book of Mormon," *The Evening and the Morning Star* 2 (July 1833):109, Independence, Missouri.

[39] Marquardt, *Joseph Smith Revelations*, 239; LDS D&C 93:53; RLDS D&C 90:12.

cannot be done until we can attend to it ourselves, and this we will do as soon as the Lord permit[s]."[40]

The church presidency, then consisting of Joseph Smith, Sidney Rigdon, and Frederick G. Williams, wrote on July 2, 1833, "[W]e have finished the translating of the Scriptures."[41] Out of 929 chapters in the Old Testament 436 chapters (46.9%) were listed as "correct." Though Genesis had many corrections and additions, thirteen of its chapters were recorded as being correct on OT 2.

On August 2, 1833, the church presidency was instructed to dedicate a lot in Kirtland where a house would be built to print the translation of the scriptures.[42] Again the presidency wrote:

You will see by these revelations that we have to print the new translation here at Kirtland for which we will prepare as soon as possable [possible] . . . you are to print an Edition of the schriptures [scriptures] there at the same time we do here so that the two additions [editions] will be struck at the same time the one here and the other there."[43]

The church presidency was not aware that on July 20, 1833 the *Evening and the Morning Star* press had been destroyed in Independence, Missouri. Oliver Cowdery brought this sad news to church leaders when he arrived at Kirtland on August 9.

In an April 23, 1834 revelation Martin Harris, a member of the United Firm, was exhorted to "devote his moneys for the printing of my word as my servant Joseph [Smith, Jr.] shall direct." Firm members were told "for this purpose have I commanded you to organize yourselves, even to print my word, the fulness of my scriptures" and the revelations given to Joseph Smith. They were instructed to obtain copyrights for the Book of Mormon, Doctrine

---

[40] Joseph Smith Jr., Sidney Rigdon, Frederick G. Williams, and Martin Harris to "Brethren," June 25, 1833, LDS archives; copied into Joseph Smith Letterbook 1:48.

[41] Sidney Rigdon, Joseph Smith, and Frederick G. Williams to "Brethren," July 2, 1833, Joseph Smith Letterbook 1:51; OT 2, 119, has recorded "Finished on the 2d day of July 1833."

[42] Marquardt, *Joseph Smith Revelations*, 244; LDS D&C 94:10; RLDS D&C 91:3.

[43] Sidney Rigdon, Frederick G. Williams, and Joseph Smith to "Beloved Brethern [Brethren]," Aug. 6, 1833, LDS archives.

and Covenants, and one for the "new translation of the scriptures."[44]

A letter from Joseph Smith was written on June 15, 1835 appealed for money to print the New Translation:

> We are now commencing to prepare and print the New Translation, together with all the revelations which God has been pleased to give us in these last days, and as we are in want of funds to go on with so great and glorious a work, brethren <we> want you should donate and loan us all the means or money you can that we may be enable[d] to accomplish the work as a great means towards the salvation of men.[45]

Two years after Joseph Smith finished his NT revision and review of the manuscripts he commenced to study Hebrew and Greek. There is no evidence that his study of the Greek language led to changes in the NT 2. Warren Parrish recorded in Smith's journal:

> At Evening, President [Oliver] Cowdery returned from New York, bringing with him a quantity of Hebrew books for the benefit of the school, he presented me with a Hebrew bible, lexicon & grammar, also a Greek Lexicon and Webster['] s English Lexicon.[46]

On Joseph Smith's thirtieth birthday, December 23, 1835, he was "stud[y[ing the greek Language."[47]

---

[44] Marquardt, *Joseph Smith Revelations*, 256, 258; Compare LDS D&C 104:26, 58; RLDS D&C 101:4, 10. These instructions were obscured as printed in the 1835 D&C. The 1835 text has "Mahemson" [Martin Harris] to "devote his moneys for the proclaiming of my words" (1835 D&C 98:4).

[45] Smith to "Dear brethren in the Lord," June 15, 1835, LDS archives.

[46] Joseph Smith Journal, 47, entry for Nov. 20, 1835; Jessee, *Papers of Joseph Smith* 2:87. In a third person account recorded by Warren A. Cowdery part of the entry reads: "also a Greek & English lexicon." (Jessee, *Papers of Joseph Smith* 1:144) This was probably a Greek-English Lexicon of the New Testament.

[47] Jessee, *Papers of Joseph Smith* 2:120.

At Kirtland, besides printing the periodical the *Latter Day Saints' Messenger and Advocate*, the church published the *Northern Times*, the 1835 Doctrine and Covenants, *A Collection of Sacred Hymns* in 1836, and the 1837 (second edition) of the Book of Mormon.[48]

When settled at Nauvoo, Illinois, instructions regarding Smith's Bible revision were given on January 19, 1841 to the newly appointed second counselor in the church presidency William Law. He was told to support the poor and "publish the new translation of my holy word unto the inhabitants of the earth."[49]

After Joseph Smith's death in June 1844 the marked Joseph Smith Bible and the dictated and revised manuscripts of the New Translation were retained by his widow Emma Smith in Nauvoo. The beginning of an index for the revision of Genesis was kept among church records taken to Salt Lake City by historian Willard Richards.

In 1867, what became known as the Reorganized Church of Jesus Christ of Latter Day Saints (now Community of Christ), published in English (the only language edition) the revision by Joseph Smith. It was titled *The Holy Scriptures, Translated and Corrected by the Spirit of Revelation, by Joseph Smith, Jr., the Seer*. This Bible for over one hundred and thirty-five years has been used in a variety of ways.

In both LDS and RLDS tradition this Bible has endeared itself to believers in the mission of Joseph Smith. Comparing the latest manuscript (NT 2) with a number of printings shows that the printed text does not always follow the wording of the manuscript. Ten years later in September 1878 the RLDS church adopted a resolution affirming:

That this body, representing the Reorganized Church of Jesus Christ of Latter Day Saints, does hereby authoritatively indorse [endorse] the Holy Scriptures, as revised, corrected and translated by the Spirit of revelation,

---

[48] Peter Crawley, *A Descriptive Bibliography of the Mormon Church Volume One 1830-1847* (Provo, Utah: Religious Studies Center, Brigham Young University, 1997 [1998], 51-59, 66-68.
[49] Marquardt, *Joseph Smith Revelations*, 307; LDS D&C 124:89.

by Joseph Smith, Jr., the Seer, and as published by the church we represent.[50]

In October 1880 the LDS church accepted as canonical *The Pearl of Great Price* which included Joseph Smith's vision of Moses, together with the revisions and additions to Genesis 1:1-6:13 (KJV). For the New Testament, Matthew 23:39 and chapter 24 are the only textual revisions that have been canonized at present.[51] The *Pearl of Great Price* contains writings of Joseph Smith and was published posthumously as a church booklet in 1851, with subsequent revisions in 1878, 1902, 1921, and 1981.

In making corrections and additions there are places where Joseph Smith explains the text with the phrase "or in other words." Philip Barlow, Associate Professor of Theological Studies at Hanover College, explains:

A third category is "interpretive additions," often signaled by the phrase "or in other words," which the Prophet [Joseph Smith] appended to a passage he wished to clarify. Thus, to Jesus' counsel to turn one's other cheek if smitten (Luke 6:29), Smith added "or, in other words, it is better to offer the other [cheek], than to revile again." The interpretative phrase "or in other words" (often shortened to "in other words" or simply "or") is common in Smith's sermons as well as in the Book of Mormon, the Doctrine and Covenants, and the revisions of the Bible.[52]

---

[50] *World Conference Resolutions 2002 Edition Community of Christ* (Independence, Missouri: Herald Publishing House, 2003), 16.

[51] An undated broadside was published at Kirtland, Ohio, titled: "Extract from the new translation of the Bible, It being the 24th chapter of Matthew; but in order to show the connection we will commence with the last verse of the 23rd chapter, viz. [At end:] Published for the benefit of the Saints." The broadside mostly follows a text close to NT 1. See Crawley, *Descriptive Bibliography*, 60-61.

[52] Philip L. Barlow, *Mormons and the Bible: The Place of the Latter-day Saints in American Religion* (New York: Oxford University Press, 1991), 51-52. For the Old Testament revision see Gen. 14:34, 36 (JST).

Examples of such interpreted phrases are included in Joseph Smith's revision of the gospels. What follows was used by Joseph to interpret or clarify a particular passage:

> or whose place I am not able to fill (Matt. 3:11; John 1:27)
> or the destruction of the wicked (Matt. 13:39, 40; 24:3, 14; Mark 13:4, 10)
> or the messenger sent of heaven (Matt. 13:39)
> or in other words John the Baptist and Moses (Mark 9:4)
> or in other words it is better to offer the other [cheek] than to revile again (Luke 6:29)
> or in other words is afraid to lay down their life for my sake (Luke 14:26)
> or in other words whithersoever the saints are gathered (Luke 17:37)
> or thither will the remainder be gathered together (Luke 17:37)
> or in other words the Gentiles (Luke 23:31)

More than anything else the above listing shows Smith's involvement with the KJV revision process. One of the purposes in making the Bible revision was for Joseph Smith to clarify difficult English passages and make the gospel texts clearer for church members. This type of revision was similar to the revelations that he gave for church instruction.

Some interesting readings and omissions are included in the revision of Matthew. In Matthew 5:22 the KJV has "whosoever is angry with his brother without a cause shall be in danger of the judgment." Joseph Smith's revision omits "without a cause." The wording here is the same as the Book of Mormon. Some early Greek manuscripts support the exclusion of the phrase. John Wesley, founder theologian of the Methodist faith, commentated on this passage:

> *Whosoever is angry with his brother*—Some Copies add, *Without a cause*: But this is utterly foreign to the whole Scope and Tenor of our LORD's Discourse. If he had only forbidden, the being *angry without a Cause*, there was no manner of need of that solemn Declaration, *I say unto you*;

for the Scribes and Pharisees themselves said as much as this. Even they taught, Men ought not to be angry *without a Cause*. So that this *Righteousness* does not *exceed* theirs. But *Christ* teaches, That we ought not *for any cause* to be so *angry*, as to call any Man *Raca*, or *Fool*. We ought not for any Cause to be angry at the Person of the Sinner, but at his Sin only.[53]

New Testament scholars consider the ending of the Lord's Prayer to be an early addition to the gospel of Matthew. The text reads, "For thine is the kingdom, and the power, and the glory, for ever. Amen" (Matt. 6:13). That this was added is evident since the wording appears is various forms and is missing from the most reliable Greek manuscripts. The reading was retained by Joseph Smith in Matthew with after "and the glory, for ever" the addition of two words "and ever." Smith also rendered the Lord's Prayer in Luke 11:4 like Matthew with the added words "for thine is the kingdom, and power. Amen."[54]

Joseph Smith first retained the KJV wording of Matthew 13:30—"gather ye together first the tares and bind them in bundles to burn them."[55] During the review process a pinned note was made for the revision of Matthew 13:30: "gather ye together first the wheat into my barn, and the tares are bound in bundles to be burned."[56] The review of this verse reflects the wording of the revelation given to Joseph Smith on December 6, 1832 which states: "ye shall first gather out the wheat from the among the tears [tares] and after the gathering of the wheat, behold and lo the tears [tares] arc bound in bund[l]es, and the field remaineth to be burned."[57] Two passages, Matthew 18:11 and 23:14, which are not found in early Greek manuscripts, were retained in the revision of Matthew. Smith also added to the text of Matthew 18:11.

---

[53] John Wesley, *Explanatory Notes upon the New Testament* (Philadelphia: Joseph Crukshank, 1791), 1:29, emphasis retained; First American Edition. Brought to my attention by Ronald Huggins.

[54] NT 2, f. 3, 72.

[55] NT 1, 34. The same wording was copied onto NT 2, f. 1, 25.

[56] NT 2, f. 1, 25, pinned note to manuscript page.

[57] Marquardt, *Joseph Smith Revelations*, 221; LDS D&C 86:7; RLDS D&C 84:2.

Mark 9:44 and 46 are not part of the earliest Greek manuscripts. Joseph Smith omitted the reading of verse 46 while he retained verse 44. When Mark 13 was revised, verses 9, 11-12, 33-36 were omitted. The reason for these important omissions is because Smith substituted his previous revision of Matthew chapter 24 for Mark's text. Joseph Smith either presumed that Matthew preempted the writing of Mark or just wanted to use his prior revision of Matthew for the new text of Mark. This view is confirmed in the publication of the JST manuscripts:

> In the Bible, Matthew's account of Jesus' great discourse to the Twelve on the Mount of Olives (Matthew 24) is much longer and more detailed than Mark's (Mark 13). Both were changed significantly in the Joseph Smith Translation.
>
> A comparison of the Matthew and Mark accounts in the New Translation shows that when Joseph Smith and his scribe arrived at Mark 13, the Prophet decided to copy the corrected Matthew account from NT2.1 rather than to revise the existing verses in Mark.[58]

Besides short phrases or sentence additions to the gospels, large blocks of text of over fifty words each also appear in various places. These long texts appear to represent material that Joseph Smith believed were in the gospels anciently. For example, he added the following text to Luke 3:13:

> For it is well known unto you, Theophelus,[59] that after the manner of the Jews, and according to the custom of their law, in receiving money in the treasury, that out of the abundince [abundance] which was received was appointed unto the poor, every man his portion; and after this manner did the publicans also, wherefore John said unto them, exact no more than that which is appointed you.[60]

---

[58] Scott H. Faulring, Kent P. Jackson, and Robert J. Matthews, eds. *Joseph Smith's New Translation of the Bible: Original Manuscripts* (Provo, Utah: Religious Studies Center, Brigham Young University, 2004), 303-304.

[59] The name was spelled "Theophilus" in Luke 1:3 (KJV).

[60] NT 2, f. 3, 52. Robert J. Matthews wrote concerning this addition: "By inference, at least, the reader is led to believe that he is expected to regard this

This wording gives the impression that Joseph Smith is supplying a missing part to Luke. The wording shows that Smith is trying to present a better text rather than a commentary in this addition to Luke. The additional wording though represented to be in the text is not in Codex Vaticanus, Codex Sinaticus, or papyrus fragment P4 (ca. 200), nor in any other Greek manuscript. A longer insertion in Luke 3:4 is also an addition not paralleled by Greek manuscripts.[61]

The passage of John 7:53-8:11 about the woman taken in adultery was retained by Joseph Smith. Early Greek manuscripts do not include these verses. The reading in John 20:17 "Touch me not" was rendered "hold me not." Current versions of the New Testament read "Do not hold on to me."[62]

A good example of harmonization appears from the reading in John 20:12, "And seeth two angels in white." The gospel accounts of an angel, a man, two men, or two angels at the tomb was revised in an interesting way. The KJV text of John 20:12 provided an influence for the revisions of Matt. 28:2; Mark 16:5; Luke 24:2 and John 20:1.

KJV:	Revision:
the angel (Matt. 28:2)	two angels
a young man (Mark 16:5)	two angels
two men (Luke 24:4)	moved to revision of Luke 24:2 - two angels
John 20:1	two angels (addition)
two angels (John 20:12)	two angels (remained the same)

It is of interest that some revisions, from "James the less" to "James the younger" (revision of Mark 15:40), are the same as

---

information as a restoration of what Luke had originally written" (*"A Plainer Translation" Joseph Smith's Translation of the Bible: A History and Commentary* [Provo, Utah: Brigham Young University Press, 1975], 239).
[61] See Matt. 3:3 and Mark 1:2.
[62] See the New Revised Standard Version and the New International Version.

edited in Alexander Campbell's *The Sacred Writings of the Apostles and Evangelists of Jesus Christ* published in 1826.[63]

Campbell's New Testament also titled his gospels "The Testimony of . . ." This shows that others made similar changes in wording like Joseph Smith did. The changes involved correcting archaic English wording and at times omitting words printed in italics. These other revisions still retain wording similar to the KJV. They do not contain the additional words that Smith included.

The four gospels have a pattern like the revision of the Old Testament, of most of the text remaining the same as the KJV. Kurt and Barbara Aland, editors of the *Greek New Testament*, reported that they compared six printed editions of the Greek text with each other. Apart from the spelling of names and "Verses in which any one of the seven editions differs by a single word are not counted," many verses were found to be in general agreement with each other. Forty-five percent or more of the text is the same for each gospel. There is a difference of ten verses in the count of John. The following is their tabulation of verses that are variant-free:[64]

Gospels	Total Number of Verses	Variant-Free Verses Total	Percentage
Matthew	1071	642	59.9
Mark	678	306	45.1
Luke	1151	658	57.2
John	869	450	51.8

This is an average of 53.5 percent of the gospels being variant-free.

---

[63] Other readings like Smith's use of "imposture" in Matt. 27:64 and "empire" in Luke 2:1 use the same words as those employed in Campbell's 1826 publication.

[64] Kurt Aland and Barbara Aland, *The Text of the New Testament: An Introduction to the Critical Editions and to the Theory and Practice of Modern Textual Criticism.* Translated by Erroll F. Rhodes. (Grand Rapids, Michigan: William B. Eerdmans, 1987), 29.

Comparing Joseph Smith's revision with the KJV shows that over thirty-nine percent of the verses in the gospels that were retained are variant-free:

Gospels	Total Number of Verses	Verses with No Revisions	Verses Omitted	Verses with Minor Revisions	Total Percentage close to KJV
Matthew	1071	424 (39.6%)		479 (44.7%)	84.3%
Mark	678	262 (39.5%)	8	312 (46%)	85.5%
Luke	1151	463 (40.2%)	1	598 (51.9%)	92.1%
John	879	646 (73.4%)		183 (20.7%)	94.2%

Over forty-four percent of the revisions made to KJV verses have minor changes in upgrading the English or rearrangement of words in each verse. This comparison indicates that over eighty-four percent of the verses are identical or nearly identical to the KJV. This is the strongest evidence that the vast majority of corrections in the gospels are of little consequence.

The next chart shows the number of additions made by Joseph Smith to verses in the KJV gospels. Included are those additions of four or more words in a row (termed major additions).

Gospels	Total Number of Verses	Verses with Minor Revisions	Verses Omitted	Verses with Major Additions	Total Percentage Major Additions
Matthew	1071	479		168	15.6%
Mark	678	312	8	96	14%
Luke	1151	598	1	89	7.7%
John	879	183		50	5.6%

While the synoptic gospels have more changes than John, it will be noticed that the number of verses affected decreased as the revision progressed. The percentage of verses in Luke and John dropped over six percent. This chart indicates the small percentage of additions to the text. The following listing includes the major additions of words to KJV verses of fifty words or more:

Over 50 words	Over 100 words	Over 200 words
Matt. 2:23	Matt. 7:8	Mark 13:37
Matt. 3:7	Matt. 21:46	
Matt. 5:2	Mark 13:7	
Matt. 6:24	Mark 13:32	
Matt. 7:4	Luke 3:4	

Over 50 words	Over 100 words
Matt. 9:15	Luke 12:38
Matt. 27:37	Luke 16:17
Matt. 27:44	Luke 17:37
Mark 8:38	
Mark 9:45	
Luke 3:13	
Luke 12:9	
Luke 14:33	

Using a Greek-English interlinear translation of the Greek New Testament I have compared the above additions with the readings in Codex Vaticanus, Codex Sinaticus, and early papyri fragments. The Greek text shows no evidence that the added wording form a part of the manuscripts of the gospels. Passages that have added wording in blocks of text give the impression that they are recovered words from the lost original. These textual additions include words ascribed to Jesus.

An important revelation to Joseph Smith on July 20, 1831 included the early teaching of the gathering of the saints (church members) to the Independence, Missouri area. Especially significant is the interpretive phrase "or in other words whithersoever the saints are gathered." This interpretation follows Joseph Smith's teaching of the gathering which was a concept in the young church.[65] A portion of the revision of Luke 17:37 read (italic words are added to KJV text):

And they answered, and said unto him, Where, Lord, *shall they be taken?* And he said unto them, Wheresoever the body *is gathered; or, in other words, whithersoever the saints are gathered*, thither will the eagles be gathered together; *or, thither will the remainder be gathered together. This he spake signifying the gathering of his saints*[66]

---

[65] See Marquardt, *Joseph Smith Revelations*, 142; LDS and RLDS 57:1. Independence, Jackson County, Missouri was the center place for the gathering and where the city of Zion (New Jerusalem) would be built.
[66] NT 2, f. 3, 88-89.

The above interpretation shows Joseph Smith's concern for having the saints gather together in Jackson County as a group after his trip from the state of Missouri. Since this rendering reflects Smith's concept of a gathered church it is not surprising that it is not to be found in any Greek manuscript.

While some of the additional texts appear to be recovering what Jesus said, there are other places which give evidence of Joseph Smith's interpretive analysis such as when he used his earlier revision of Matthew 24 for the revision of Mark chapter 13.

Identify of "Elias" must have been of some concern to Joseph Smith. The proper name of Elijah is used in the Old Testament and in the Greek New Testament the name appears as Elias. They are the same person. The New Testament KJV records that John the Baptist was to go before the Lord in the spirit and power of Elias [Elijah].[67] Jesus explained that, for those who understood, John the Baptist was the Elijah they were waiting for.[68] John the Baptist was understood by Christ's disciples as the Elias (Elijah) who would "restore all things."[69]

Joseph Smith dictated his revision of Matthew 17 in the spring of 1831. It tells about Jesus being transfigured on a high mountain before Peter, James, and John. While Smith had the text refer to John the Baptist, he also had the name Elias used for "another which should come and restore all things." His scribe Sidney Rigdon wrote (italics are added words to the KJV):

> and his disciples asked him [Jesus] saying why then say the Scribes that Elias must first come[?] and Jesus answered and said unto them Elias truely [truly] shall first come and restore all things *as the prophets have written and again* I say unto you that Elias is come allready and they knew him not *and* have done unto him <whatsoever they> listed likewise shall also the son of man suffer of them
>
> *but I say unto you who is Elias[?] behold this is Elias who I send to prepare the way before me* Then the

---

[67] Luke 1:17.

[68] Matt. 11:14. This verse was revised in 1831 by Joseph Smith to have Jesus say that he was Elias.

[69] Compare Matt. 17:11-13; Mark 9:11-13.

Disciples understood that he spake unto them of John the Baptist *and also of another which should come and restore all things as they were written by the prophets*[70]

In August 1831 Joseph Smith was told about the "day of transfiguration shall come when the earth shall be transfigured even according to the pattern which was shown unto mine apostles upon the mount of which account the fulness ye have not yet received."[71] When Smith revised the gospel of Mark in the fall of 1831 concerning the transfiguration, Smith interpreted the Elias who appeared before the four men not as the prophet Elijah but as John the Baptist. The King James Version reads, "And there appeared unto them Elias with Moses: and they were talking with Jesus."[72] But Smith's revision, written by Sidney Rigdon, reads, "And there appeared unto them Elias with Moses, or in other words, John the baptist and Moses; and they were talking with Jesus."[73] The words "or in other words" help us to understand this is commentary by Smith. The mention of Moses and Elias in Matthew means Moses and Elijah, representative of the law and the prophets.[74]

When Joseph Smith first revised Matthew 11 in 1831, the manuscript had Jesus saying: "and if ye will receive me I am Elias which was for to come."[75] These words were afterwards copied onto NT 2. A number of changes were made to this manuscript and this reading was revised in December 1832 or January 1833 with the words "me I am Elias" crossed through and the passage now applying to John the Baptist.[76] Robert J. Matthews who has examined the manuscript wrote:

---

[70] Revision of Matt. 17:11-13; NT 1, 42. See NT 2, f. 1, 32 for additional revision to this passage.

[71] Marquardt, *Joseph Smith Revelations*, 156; LDS D&C 63:20-21; RLDS D&C 63:6 (Aug. [30-31], 1831).

[72] Mark 9:4; cf. Matt. 17:3 and Luke 9:30.

[73] NT 2, f. 2, 24; revision of Mark 9:3.

[74] Compare with modern translations of Mark 9:4.

[75] NT 1, 28; revision of Matt. 11:14.

[76] NT 2, f. 1, 21.

It is evident that the Prophet [Joseph Smith] was working with an idea that he developed and then discarded. He compared and contrasted John [the Baptist] with Jesus and then decided to speak only of John. He identified Jesus as Elias and then identified John as Elias. It is, however, interesting to note that the doctrinal ideas and identifications here introduced and then discarded were reintroduced in Matthew 17:9-14 on a partial basis and then more fully in John 1."[77]

John chapter 1 describes John the Baptist being questioned. Sidney Rigdon originally wrote in January or February 1832 the following:

and he [John the Baptist] confessed and denied [denied] not but confessed that I am not the christ and they asked <him> what then art thou Elias[?] and he saith I am not art thou that prophet[?] and he answered no . . . and they asked him and said unto him why baptisest thou then if thou be not the christ nor Elias neither that prophet[?] John answered ... he it is *of whom I bear record he is that Prophet, even Elias*[78]

This passage was further revised in December 1832 or January 1833 on a note pinned to the manuscript as follows:

And he [John the Baptist] confessed, and denied [denied] not *that he was Elias*; but confessed, *saying*: I am not the christ. And they asked him, *saying*; *How* then art thou Elias? And he sai<d>; I am not *that Elias who was to restore all things. And they asked him, saying*; Art thou that Prophet? And he answered; No ... And they asked him, and said unto him; why baptisest thou then, if thou be not *the* christ, nor Elias *who was to restore all things*, neither that prophet?[79]

---

[77] Matthews, *A Plainer Translation*, 217.

[78] NT 2, f. 4, 106, emphasis added. Compare John 1:20-21, 25-27.

[79] NT 2, f. 4, 106, emphasis of additional revision of John 1:20-21, 25.

Rather than a straightforward revision of the gospels we find many layers of working on a question that seemed to be of importance to Joseph Smith at the time.

In studying the four gospels I have placed emphasis first on a complete text for Matthew, Mark, Luke, and John. Codex Vaticanus and Codex Sinaiticus have been used as the base text. Earlier papyri fragments have also been utilized in comparing the additions to the KJV. The reason for this is that having one or more early manuscript helps establish a text at a certain point in time. After examining Greek manuscripts ranging from ca. 175 to 375 and considering the readings in Joseph Smith's revision of the gospels, it appears that the additions to KJV text (whether short phrases, sentences, or blocks of material) include no significant readings contained in these Greek manuscripts.

Passages that are omitted in Codex Vaticanus, Codex Sinaiticus, and early papyri show that Joseph Smith is correcting an English text and not a Greek text: For example, two recognized textual additions to New Testament manuscripts are the passages in Mark 16:9-20 and John 7:53-8:11. These long passages were retained by Joseph Smith in his KJV revision. At the end of John 8:11 Smith dictated the additional wording, "and the woman glorified God from that hour, and believed on his name."[80] Philip W. Comfort, Professor of Greek and New Testament at Trinity Episcopal Seminary, and senior editor of Bible Reference at Tyndale House Publishers, has written concerning the pericope of the woman caught in adultery printed in the KJV:

> The pericope about the adulteress woman (John 7:53-8:11) is not included in any of the earliest MSS (second-fourth century), including the two earliest, P66 and P75 . . . When this story is inserted in later MSS, it appears in different places: after John 7:52, after Luke 21:38, at the end of John; and when it does appear it is often marked off by asterisks or obeli to signal its probable spuriousness. The story is part of an oral tradition that was included in the Syriac Peshitta, circulated in the Western church, eventually finding its way into the Latin Vulgate, and from

---

[80] NT 2, f. 4, 116.

there into later Greek MSS, the like of which were used in formulating the Textus Receptus (Metzger).

The external evidence against the Johannine authorship of the periscope about the adulteress is overwhelming. The internal evidence against Johannine authorship is also impressive. . . . But there it stands—an obstacle to reading the true narrative of John's Gospel. Even worse, its presence in the text misrepresents the testimony of the earliest MSS, especially the papyri.[81]

Another such example of an addition is Mark 16:9-20. This passage was probably added to Mark during the second century. Codex Sinaiticus and Codex Vaticanus, both written in the fourth century, do not contain this addition. Most New Testament scholars, after examining early manuscripts that contain Mark 16, find that the early writings of the church fathers support the view that verses 9-20 were originally not part of Mark. George Eldon Ladd, Professor of New Testament at Fuller Theological Seminary, wrote concerning the ending of Mark:

The "long ending," consisting of verses 9-20 came into the text of the AV [King James Authorized Version] because it appears in the great majority of the minuscules and in most of the later uncials, and was therefore a part of the prevailing text known in the seventeenth century. It can be traced back to a very early date, for it appears in a Syriac harmony of the Gospels made in the second century by Tatian. Its earliest appearance in the Greek sources is from the fifth century. . . . the long ending is written in a non-Markan style. These facts, together with other considerations, have led most modern scholars to the conclusion that the long ending which appears in the AV is

---

[81] Philip Wesley Comfort, *Early Manuscripts & Modern Translations of the New Testament* (Grand Rapids, Michigan: Baker Books, 1996), 115-16. See Bruce M. Metzger, *A Textual Commentary on the Greek New Testament* (Stuttgart, Ger.: German Bible Society, 2nd ed., 1994), 187-89.

not authentic, but was produced by a copyist at an early date to smooth up the abrupt ending at 16:8. [82]

The results of the foregoing comparisons support the position that the textual variants added by Joseph Smith were independent of the Greek text. There is no manuscript evidence to support the additional words in the new translation of the gospels. This confirms the position that the word "translation" is not the proper term to designate what occurred during the dictation of the text by Smith based upon his textual changes.

Joseph Smith's "translation" for the most part does not reflect the early gospel text. Except for rearranged words in verses, omitting italic words, changing old spellings, and modernizing KJV English, the additions were a revelatory message relating to corrections of the KJV biblical text.

---

[82] George Eldon Ladd, *The New Testament and Criticism* (Grand Rapids, Michigan: Wm. B. Eerdmans, 1967), 72, 74. See Bruce M. Metzger, *The Text of the New Testament: Its Transmission, Corruption, and Restoration* (Oxford: Oxford University Press, Third, enlarged ed., 1992), 226-29. For the use of Mark 16:9-20 in other Restoration scriptures see 1830 BOM, 478, 537, 547; LDS 3 Nephi 11:33-34; RLDS 9:34-35; Mormon 9:22-24/RLDS 4:86-87; and Ether 4:18/RLDS 1:115. A part of Mark 16 was also incorporated in a revelation of September 1832 (Marquardt, *Joseph Smith Revelations*, 214-15; LDS D&C 84:62-74; RLDS D&C 83:10-12).

Priesthood Restoration

It was during February and the early days of March 1831 in Kirtland that Joseph Smith continued his revision of the Old Testament. For the book of Genesis he added a large amount of text to chapter 14 concerning Melchizedek, the king of Salem (known later as Jerusalem). The King James Version mentions that Melchizedek was "the priest of the most high God."[1] Smith stated that Melchizedek "was ordained a high Priest after the order of the covenant which God made with Enoch it being after the order of the Son of God."[2] The new text continues:

> for God having sworn unto Enoch and unto his seed with an oath by himself that every one being ordained after this order and calling should have power by faith to break Mountains to divide the seas to dry up watters [waters] to turn them out of their course to put at defience [defiance] the armies of nations to divide the earth to break every band to stand in the presence of God to do all things according to his will according to his command subdue principalities and powers[3]

These ideas relating to a High Priesthood in Old Testament times were similar to those written in 1829 in the Book of Mormon, where the high priesthood was related to the order of the Son of God. The following lengthy excerpt illustrates the importance of being called, obtaining the office of the high priesthood, and being a high priest forever:

> and thus being called by this holy calling, and ordained unto the High Priesthood of the holy order of God, to teach

---

[1] Gen. 14:18, KJV.
[2] Old Testament Dictated Manuscript (OT MS 1), 33-34, RLDS archives; Genesis 14:27-28 (JST); see also 14:37 (JST).
[3] OT MS 1, 34; Genesis 14:30-31 (JST).

his commandments unto the children of men, that they also might enter into his rest, this High Priesthood being after the order of his Son, which order was from the foundation of the world; or in other words, being without beginning of days or end of years, being prepared from eternity to all eternity . . . taking upon them the High Priesthood of the holy order, which calling, and ordinance, and High Priesthood, is without beginning or end . . .

yea, humble yourselves even as the people in the days of Melchizedek, who was also a High Priest after this same order which I have spoken, who also took upon him the High Priesthood forever. . . . Now these ordinances were given after this manner, that thereby the people might look forward on the Son of God, it being a type of his order, or it being his order . . . but Melchizedek having exercised mighty faith, and received the office of the High Priesthood, according to the holy order of God, did preach repentance unto his people. . . . Now there were many before him, and also there were many afterwards, but none were greater; therefore of him they have more particularly made mention.[4]

In a revelation received at the third conference held at Fayette, New York on January 2, 1831, church members were commanded to go to the state of Ohio. They were told "there I will give unto you my law, and there you shall be endowed with power from on high, and from thence, whomsoever I will shall go forth among all nations."[5] Another revelation given a few days later instructed, "And inasmuch as my people shall assemble themselves to the [state of] Ohio, I have kept in store a blessing such as is not known among the children of men, and it shall be poured forth upon their heads. And from thence men shall go forth into all

---

[4] 1830 BOM, 259-60; LDS Alma 13:6-8, 14, 16, 18-19; RLDS 9:69-72; 10:7, 9, 12, 15. Melchizedek is also mentioned in the Epistle to the Hebrews.
[5] Marquardt, *Joseph Smith Revelations*, 100; BC 40:28; LDS D&C 38:32-33; RLDS D&C 38:7.

nations."[6] Also a revelation received at Kirtland in February says "Sanctify yourselves and ye shall be endowed with power."[7]

Joseph Smith wrote to his brother Hyrum in March, "I think <you> had better Come into this Country immediately for the Lord has Commanded us that we should Call the Elders of this Church to gether unto this place as soon as possable."[8] And finally in May a revelation revealed, "let my servant Ezra [Thayer] humble himself and at the conference meeting he shall be ordained unto power from on high."[9]

The first general conference in Ohio was held early in June 1831. Various dates have been given for the conference meeting. In the recollections of those who attended the dates of June 3 (Friday), June 4 (Saturday), and June 6 (Monday) have been given as the conference dates. At a previous conference held on April 9 the minutes record the "Conference adjourned until the first Saturday in June next" which would be June 4. A church member named John Smith (not Joseph Smith's uncle) wrote, "friday June th[e] 3 went to Kirtland to attend Conference but did not reatch [reach] there till sat th[e] 4 & Conference was over & I Continued their [there] untill th[e] 6."[10] The conference was held on June 3 probably lasting the full day and into the night.[11] There appears to have been a number of meetings after the conference. A revelation was given on June 6 for those called to go on missions.

The conference was opened by Joseph Smith Jr. in exhortation and prayer. Sidney Rigdon also exhorted the congregation. John Whitmer in his history wrote:

---

[6] Marquardt, *Joseph Smith Revelations*, 101; BC 41:13-15; D&C 39:14-15; RLDS D&C 39:4.

[7] Marquardt, *Joseph Smith Revelations*, 116; BC 45:16, LDS D&C 43:16; RLDS D&C 43:4.

[8] Joseph Smith to Hyrum Smith, March 3-4, 1831, LDS archives; Jessee, *Personal Writings of Joseph Smith*, 257.

[9] Marquardt, *Joseph Smith Revelations*, 135.

[10] John Smith Journal, June 1831, LDS archives. John Smith was the father of Eden Smith.

[11] Cannon and Cook, *Far West Record*, 6-7. The minutes copied in the Far West Record has the date as June 3, 1831. John Whitmer was the clerk of the conference. Manuscript History A-1 has the date of the conference as June 6 with the revelation being received the next day, June 7. See Jessee, *Papers of Joseph Smith* 1:352-53.

The spirit of the Lord fell upon Joseph in an unusual manner. And prophecied that John the Revelator was then among the ten tribes of Israel who had been led away by Salmanaser King of israel [sic; Assyria], to prepare them for their return, from their Long dispersion, to again possess the land of their fathers.[12]

Joseph Smith laid his hands upon the head of Lyman Wight and ordained him to the High Priesthood after the Holy Order of God.[13] Lyman Wight then gave an exhortation to the saints. John Whitmer recorded:

And the Spirit fell upon Lyman, and he prophecied, concerning the coming of Christ, he said that there were some in this congregation that should live until the Savior shou[l]d de[s]cend from heaven, with a Shout, with all the holy angels with him. . . . He saw the hevans [heavens] opened, and the Son of man sitting on the right hand of the Father.[14]

Joseph Smith then ordained Harvey Whitlock. The devil bound Harvey Whitlock and he could not speak. Ezra Booth who had been ordained to the High Priesthood, but later left the church reported his comments in a letter written on October 31, 1831:

Another Elder [Harvey Whitlock], who had been ordained to the same office as Wite [Wight], at the bidding of Smith stept [stepped] upon the floor. Then ensued a scene, of which you can form no adequate conception; and which, I would forbear relating, did not truth require it. This Elder moved upon the floor, his legs inclining to a bend; one shoulder elevated above the other, upon which the head

---

[12] Westergren, *From Historian to Dissident*, 69-70. Whitmer recorded his history circa 1836-38.

[13] Ezra Booth who was in attendance wrote, "Wite [Wright] arose, and presented a pale countenance, a fierce look, with his arms extended, and his hands cramped backward, the whole system agitated, and a very unpleasant object to gaze upon" (*The Ohio Star* 2 [Nov. 3, 1831]:3, Ravenna, Ohio).

[14] Westergren, *From Historian to Dissident*, 70.

seemed disposed to recline, his arms partly extended; his hands half clenched; his mouth half open, and contracted in the shape of an italic O;[15] his eyes assumed a wild and ferocious cast, and his whole appearance presented a frightful object to the view of the beholder. "Speak, Brother Harvey" said [Joseph] Smith. But Harvey intimated by signs, that his power of articulation was in a state of suspense, and that he was unable to speak. Some conjectured that Harvey was possessed of the Devil, but Smith said, "The Lord binds in order to set at liberty." After different opinions had been given, and there had been much confusion, Smith learnt [learned] by the spirit, that Harvey was under a diabolical influence, and that Satan had bound him; and he commanded the unclean spirit to come out of him."[16]

Parley P. Pratt who attended the meeting wrote about the conference, "Here also were some strange manifestations of false spirits, which were immediately rebuked. Several were then selected by revelation, through President Smith, and ordained to the High Priesthood after the order of the Son of God; which is after the order of Melchizedek. This was the first occasion in which this priesthood had been revealed and conferred upon the Elders in this dispensation, although the office of an Elder is the same in a certain degree, but not in the fulness. On this occasion I was ordained to this holy ordinance and calling by President Smith."[17]

A copy of the minutes of the conference kept by John Whitmer shows that it contains an abbreviated version of the

---

[15] Zebedee Coltrin also mentioned that Whitlock's mouth "went into the shape of an italic O" (testimony of Coltrin, Feb. 5, 1878, as cited in Merle H. Graffam, ed., *Salt Lake School of the Prophets, Minute Book, 1883* [Palm Desert, CA: ULC Press, 1981], 70, original in LDS archives). Levi Hancock wrote about Whitlock: "his eyes was in the shape of Ovil [Oval] Oes [O's]" (Life of Levi W. Hancock, LDS archives).

[16] Booth to Rev. Ira Eddy, Oct. 31, 1831, *Ohio Star* 2 (Nov. 3, 1831):3, emphasis omitted.

[17] *Autobiography of Parley P. Pratt*, 53. Pratt dated the meeting as June 6, 1831.

events of the conference.[18] Whitmer, who had been appointed church historian, wrote his recollections of the June 3 conference:

> Joseph Smith Jr. Prophecied the day Previous that the man of Sin should be revealed. While the Lord poured out his spirit upon his servants, the Devil took occation [occasion], to make known his power, he bound Harvey Whitlock <and John Murdock> so that he could not speak and others were affected but the Lord showed to Joseph the Seer the design of this thing, he commanded the devil in the name of Christ and he departed to our joy and comfort.[19]

It was reported that there was an exhortation by Harvey Whitlock who "bore record of the opening of the heavens and of the coming of the Son of Man."[20]

Joseph Smith ordained three more elders to the High Priesthood. The devil entered Leman Copley and was cast out by Lyman Wight. Also Harvey Green was thrown to the floor.[21] Lyman Wight ordained an additional eighteen elders. Those included were Edward Partridge, Ezra Thayer, Joseph Smith Jr., and Sidney Rigdon. Joseph Smith and Lyman Wight performed all of the ordinations to the High Priesthood and Bishop Partridge blessed those ordained. Wight also ordained John Corrill and Isaac Morley as assistants to Bishop Partridge. An interesting account of the Kirtland conference is that recorded by Levi Hancock who attended the conference:

> The Fourth [sic] of June came and we all met in a little string of buildings under the hill near Isaac Morley[']s in Kirtland, Genoya [Geauga] County, Ohio. Then we all went to a school house on the hill about one fourth of a mile ascending nearly all the way. The building was built of logs. It was filled with slab benches. Here the Elders

---

[18] Cannon and Cook, *Far West Record*, 7.

[19] Westergren, *From Historian to Dissident*, 71.

[20] Philo Dibble, *Juvenile Instructor* 27 (May 15, 1892):303, Salt Lake City.

[21] Life of Levi W. Hancock, LDS archives. See also Zebedee Coltrin (Feb. 5, 1878) in Graffam, *Salt Lake School of the Prophets*, 69; Philo Dibble, *Juvenile Instructor* 27 (May 15, 1892):303.

were seated and the meeting was opened as usual. Joseph Smith began to speak, he said that the Kingdom of Christ that he spoke of that was like a grain of mustard seed was now before him and some should see it put forth its branches and the angels of heaven would some day come like birds to its branches just as the Saviour had said. Some of you shall live to see it come with great glory. Some of you must die for the testimony of this work and he looked at Lyman White [Wight] and said to him, "you shall see the Lord and meet him near the corner of the house and laid his hands upon him and blessed him with the visions of heaven. Joseph Smith then stepped out on the floor and said, "I now see God, and Jesus Christ at his right hand, let them kill me, I should not feel death as I am now."

Continuing his detailed account Hancock described the ordinations and other occurrences:

Joseph put his hands on Harvey Whitlock and ordained him to the high priesthood. He turned as black as Lyman was white. His fingers were set like claws. He went around the room and showed his hands and tried to speak, his eyes were in the shape of oval O's. Hyrum Smith said, "Joseph, that is not of God." Joseph said "do not speak against this." "I will not believe,["] said Hyrum, ["]unless you inquire of God and he ownes [owns] it." Joseph bowed his head, and in a short time got up and commanded Satan to leave Harvey, laying his hands upon his head at the same time. At that very instant an old man said to weigh two hundred and fourteen pounds sitting in the window turned a complete summersault in the house and came his back across a bench and lay helpless. Joseph told Lyman to cast Satan out. He did. The man's name was Leamon Coply [Leman Copley], formally a Quaker. The evil spirit left him and as quick as lightening Harvey Green fell bound and screamed like a panther. Satan was cast out of him. But immediately entered someone else. This continued all day and the greater part of the night.

Levi Hancock then wrote about the ordinations, John the Revelator, and what Whitlock and Green said:

But to return to the me[e]ting said Joseph now if you elders have sin[n]ed it will do you no good to preach if you have not repented Heamon [Heman]Basset you sit still the Devil wants to sift you and then ordained Jacob Scot[t] [22] and some others to the high priesthood he came to Zebidee [Zebedee] Coltrin and myself and told us that we had an other calling as high as any man in the house I was glad for that for I was so scared I would not stir without his liberty for all the <world> And I knew the things I had seen was not made

said Joseph John was to tarry untill Christ came he is now with the ten tribes a preaching and when we can git [get] ready for them they will come Joseph Smith called Lyman White [Wight] to Lay his hands on his head and say what God should tell him to say he did and the thing was so large I can not write them After this we went down to the house And he[a]rd Harv[e]y Whitlock say when Hyram Smith Said it was not God he disdained him in his h[e]art and when the Devil was Cast out he was convinced it was satan that was in him and he [k]new it I also he[a]rd Harv[e]y Green say that he could not describe the Auful [Awful] feelings he experienced while in the hands of Satan[23]

Ezra Booth mentioned, "Many of them [Mormonite preachers] have been ordained to the High Priesthood, or the order of Milchesidec [Melchisedec]; and profess to be endowed with the

---

[22] The minutes indicate that Jacob Scott was ordained by Lyman Wight (Cannon and Cook, *Far West Record*, 7).
[23] Life of Levi W. Hancock, LDS archives. Philo Dibble in his late recollection also indicated that Hyrum Smith had questions relating to the spirit that attended Harvey Whitlock (*Juvenile Instructor* 27 [May 15, 1892]:303). John Murdock wrote, "there was a great out po[u]ring of the Spirit manifested in that Conference" (John Murdock Autobiography, LDS archives).

same power as the ancient apostles were."[24] John Corrill wrote about the promise to receive an endowment at the conference. He stated, "The Melchesideck priesthood was then for the first time introduced and confer[r]ed on several of the elders. In this chiefly consisted the endowment, - It being a new order and bestowed <authority>. However, some doubting took place among the elders, and considerable conversation <was held> on the subject."[25]

The Manuscript History of the church written in 1842-43, records: "the Lord displayed his power in a manner that could not be mistaken. The man of sin was revealed, and the authority of the Melchisedec <priesthood> was manifested and conferred for the first time, upon several of the elders."[26] Levi Hancock recalled:

> June fifth [sic] we all assembled on the hill in a field whare [where] there was a larg[e] concours[e] of people collected. Lyman White [Wight] spoke. Joseph said from that from time the Elders would have large congregations to speak to and they must soon take there [their] departure into the Reagions [Regions] west. when the me[e]ting was out we went to [Sidney] Gilberts and Solomon [Hancock] sang some and we talk with brother Whitnier [Whitmer] and told him what hap[p]en[e]d at the conference He asked me if what Joseph had said was fulfilled about Some one seeing the Lord I told him I considered it so do you said he yes sir said I was you not there I understood him no[t] [27]

Brother Whitmer may have been David Whitmer who was listed as being present but not ordained to the High Priesthood at

---

[24] Booth to Rev. Ira Eddy, Oct. 2, 1831, *Ohio Star* 2 (Oct. 20, 1831):3. The spelling "Melchisedec" comes from King James Version of Hebrews 5-7 while that of "Melchizedek" is from Genesis 14.

[25] John Corrill, Brief History of the Church of Christ of Latter Day Saints, original in the Missouri Historical Society, St. Louis, Missouri. See *Brief History of the Church of Christ of Latter Day Saints* (St. Louis: Printed for the Author, 1839), 18.

[26] Manuscript History A-1:118, LDS archives. This was published in *Times and Seasons* 5 (Feb. 1, 1844):416 before handwritten changes in the text. See Jessee, *Papers of Joseph Smith* 1:353.

[27] Life of Levi W. Hancock, LDS archives.

the conference. From many accounts it can be determined that prior to June 1831 the elders in the church did not have conferred upon them the Melchizedek priesthood. The first ordinations to the high priesthood in June 1831 were the equivalent of those men being ordained to the office of high priest.

David Whitmer used his brother's history in explaining his view that the ordination of high priests in the church was a grievous error and that he was mistaken about it for many years. His position was that the true church under the New Covenant never had a high priest in it. He wrote in 1887:

In Kirtland, Ohio, in June, 1831, at a conference of the church, the first High Priests were ordained into the church. Brother Joseph ordained Lyman Wight, John Murdock, Harvey Whitlock, Hyrum Smith, Reynolds Cahoon and others to the office of a High Priest. When they were ordained, right there at the time, the devil caught and bound Harvey Whitlock so he could not speak, his face being twisted into demon-like shape. Also John Murdock and others were caught by the devil in a similar manner. Now brethren, do you not see that the displeasure of the Lord was upon their proceedings in ordaining High Priests? Of course it was. These facts were recorded in the History of the Church - written by my brother, John Whitmer, who was the regularly appointed church historian. I was not at that conference, being then in Hiram, which is near Kirtland, Ohio.[28]

The minutes kept by John Whitmer lists David Whitmer as being present. Whether he was present all the time is not known. David Whitmer was ordained to the high priesthood (a high priest) at the general conference held on October 25, 1831. William E. McLellin recorded in his journal for this date:

Here I first saw brother Joseph the Seer, also brothers Oliver [Cowdry], John [Whitmer] & Sidney [Rigdon] and a

---

[28] Whitmer, *An Address to All Believers in Christ*, 64-65. David Whitmer wrote that in 1848 he understood the ordinations were in error.

great many other Elders &c. This conference was attended by me with much spiritual edification & comfort to my heart. And Tuesday night in conference, a number of Elders were ordained to the High-Priesthood of the Holy order of God among whom though I felt unworthy I was ordained and took upon me the high responsibility of that office—A number of others present were ordained to the lesser Priest-Hood[29]

When the first baptisms were performed in May 1829, they were administered by Joseph Smith and his co-worker Oliver Cowdery. Both of these men claimed to have received the authorization through communication with God. How this was accomplished, when and where it occurred, and the words used have all been questions that need to be explored. Many writers and historians emphasized some of the documentation but have not taken into account the broader spectrum of what this may have meant to the early participants of the early church.

By June 1829 the text of the Book of Mormon was considered to be God's word, rock, church, and gospel. The authority of the forthcoming church was to be through that book.[30] Those who were called to be elders (apostles) waited until their ordination for the authorization to preach.[31] Hyrum Smith was instructed to wait until the Book of Mormon was printed for the doctrines of the gospel would be contained it.[32] Shortly after the printing of the book the Church of Christ was organized in Manchester, New York. Those previously called to preach were ordained to church offices in the new church.

The terms priesthood, authority, commission, power of God, called of God, and ordained are considered essentially the same. Since the organization of the church on April 6, 1830, the

---

[29] Shipps and Welch, *Journals of William E. McLellin*, 44-45.

[30] 1830 BOM, 31; LDS 1 Nephi 13:36; RLDS 3:186; Marquardt, *Joseph Smith Revelations*, 46; BC 15:3-4, the word "foundation" was added twice for the 1835 D&C. Compare with LDS D&C 18:4-5; RLDS D&C 16:1.

[31] Marquardt, *Joseph Smith Revelations*, 46; BC 15:10-11; LDS D&C 18:9; RLDS D&C 16:3. Also see Marquardt, *Joseph Smith Revelations*, 379 for a Commandment from God unto Oliver.

[32] Ibid., 42; BC 10:8; LDS D&C 11:15-17; RLDS D&C 10:8.

church recognized those who were to perform ordinances as representatives of the church and gave licenses to them. Except in a few instances where ordinations were considered void, or done without proper authorization, all ceremonies have been considered proper and recognized by the church.

During the dictation of the Book of Mormon, Joseph Smith and Oliver Cowdery contemplated a passage in Third Nephi relating to baptism for the remission of sins. They went to pray regarding their own baptism and received a response that baptism was needed and they should baptize each other. Their testimony is that they received from an angel authority to baptize and then ordain each other. By this authority they could baptize others. Samuel Harrison Smith received the ordinance of baptism in May 1829, and in June a few more baptisms were performed.

The Book of Mormon presents ministers and prophets who had received a call as high priests, elders, priests, and teachers as being ordained after the holy order of God. Melchizedek was the ideal person who had mighty faith and for whom those ordained should emulate.[33] In the account of Jesus Christ ministering in America, Nephi is given power to baptize.[34] The Book of Mormon reported Jesus saying:

On this wise shall ye baptize; and there shall be no disputations among you. Verily I say unto you, that whoso repenteth of his sins through your words, and desireth to be baptized in my name, on this wise shall ye baptize them: Behold, ye shall go down and stand in the water, and in my name shall ye baptize them. And now behold, these are the words which ye shall say, calling them by name, saying:

Having authority given me of Jesus Christ, I baptize you in the name of the Father, and of the Son, and of the Holy

---

[33] See G. St. John Stott, "Ordination and Ministry in the Book of Mormon," *Restoration Studies III* (Independence, Missouri: Herald Publishing House, 1986), 244-53. Melchizedek is described as having "received the office of the High Priesthood, according to the holy order of God" and became a high priest (1830 BOM, 260; LDS Alma 13:18, 14; RLDS 10:12, 7). Power to seal on earth and in heaven is mentioned in 1830 BOM, 435; LDS Helaman 10:7; RLDS 3:120.

[34] 1830 BOM, 477-78; LDS 3 Nephi 11:21; RLDS 5:21.

Ghost. Amen. And then shall ye immerse them in the water, and come forth again out of the water.[35]

It was after the dictation of Jesus' ministry to the Book of Mormon people that Joseph Smith and Oliver Cowdery enquired of the Lord concerning the authority to baptize. The story of the priesthood restoration gradually unfolded to the membership of the early church by Smith and Cowdery.[36] Early church members believed they had been baptized and ordained by those who were called of God but they did not refer to angel visitations to Joseph Smith and Oliver Cowdery for this authority.[37] Lucy Mack Smith described what she had heard about the events that led to Joseph being baptized:

> One morning, however, they sat down to their usual work when the first thing that presented itself to Joseph was a commandment from God that he and Oliver should repair to the water, [and] each of them be baptized. They immediately went down to the Susquehannah River and obeyed the mandate given them through the urim and Thum[m]im. . . . They had now received authority to baptize.[38]

How accurate Lucy Smith was in her recollection is difficult to ascertain because she was not with Joseph. The various telling by Joseph Smith and Oliver Cowdery need to be considered. The first printed account was written by Oliver Cowdery in a letter to William W. Phelps and his *Messenger and Advocate* audience. The language of Cowdery is flowery and in his writing the words of an angel are given. He states that it was in

---

[35] 1830 BOM, 478; LDS 3 Nephi 11:22-26; RLDS 5:23-26.

[36] See Mario S. DePillis, "The Quest for Religious Authority and the Rise of Mormonism," *Dialogue: A Journal of Mormon Thought* 1 (Spring 1966):68-88; William G. Hartley, "'Upon You My Fellow Servants': Restoration of the Priesthood," in Larry C. Porter and Susan Easton Black, eds., *The Prophet Joseph: Essays on the Life and Mission of Joseph Smith* (Salt Lake City: Deseret Book, 1988), 49-72; and Vogel, *Religious Seekers and the Advent of Mormonism*, 97-128.

[37] Palmer, *An Insider's View of Mormon Origins*, 215-34.

[38] Anderson, *Lucy's Book*, 439.

May when this occurred and that both of them were "wrapped in the vision of the Almighty":

> After writing the account given of the Savior's ministry to the remnant of the seed of Jacob, upon this continent . . .
>
> The Lord, who is rich in mercy, and ever willing to answer the consistent prayer of the humble, after we had called upon Him in a fervent manner, aside from the abodes of men, condescended to manifest to us His will. On a sudden, as from the midst of eternity, the voice of the Redeemer spake peace to us, while the veil was parted and the angel of God came down clothed with glory, and delivered the anxiously looked for message, and the keys of the Gospel of repentance. . . . our eyes beheld, our ears heard, as in the "blaze of day"; yes, more - above the glitter of the May sunbeam, which then shed its brilliancy over the face of nature! Then his voice, though mild, pierced to the center, and his words, "I am thy fellow-servant," dispelled every fear. We listened, we gazed, we admired! 'Twas the voice of an angel from glory, 'twas a message from the Most High! And as we heard we rejoiced, while His love enkindled upon our souls, and we were wrapped in the vision of the Almighty!
>
> Where was room for doubt? Nowhere; uncertainty had fled, doubt has sunk no more to rise, while fiction and deception had fled forever!
>
> But, dear brother, think, further think for a moment, what joy filled our hearts, and with what surprise we must have bowed, (for who would not have bowed the knee for such a blessing?) when we received under his hand the Holy Priesthood as he said,
>
> "Upon you my fellow-servants, in the name of Messiah, I confer this Priesthood and this authority, which shall remain upon earth, that the Sons of Levi may yet offer an offering unto the Lord in righteousness!"[39]

---

[39] Cowdery to Phelps, Sept. 7, 1834, *Messenger and Advocate* 1 (Oct. 1834):15-16.

In 1839 Joseph Smith dictated his own account and explained that a messenger (John the Baptist) appeared "in a cloud of light" to them:

> We still continued the <work of> translation, when in the ensuing month (May, Eighteen hundred and twenty nine) we on a certain day went into the woods to pray and inquire of the Lord respecting baptism for the remission of sins as we found mentioned in the translation of the plates. While we were thus employed praying and calling upon the Lord, a Messenger from heaven, descended in a cloud of light, and having laid his hands upon us, he ordained us, saying unto us;
>
> "Upon you my fellow servants in the name of Messiah I confer the priesthood of Aaron, which holds the keys of the minist[e]ring of angels and of the gospel of repentance, and of baptism by immersion for the remission of sins, and this shall never be taken again from the earth, untill the sons of Levi do offer again an offering unto the Lord in righteousness."
>
> He said this Aaronic priesthood had not the power of laying on of hands, for the gift of the Holy Ghost . . . Accordingly we went and were baptized, I baptized him first, and afterwards he baptized me, after which I laid my hands upon his head and ordained him to the Aaronick priesthood, and afterward he laid his hands on me and ordained me to the same priesthood, for so we were commanded. . . .
>
> It was on the fifteenth day of May, Eighteen hundred and twentynine that we were baptized; ~~under~~ and ordained under the hand of the Messenger.[40]

The italicized words in Oliver Cowdery's account are also in Joseph Smith's account:

---

[40] Manuscript History, Book A-1:17-18; Jessee, *Papers of Joseph Smith* 1:290-91; LDS D&C 13; and Joseph Smith-History 1:68-72, Pearl of Great Price.

Upon you my fellow-servants, in the name of Messiah, I confer this *Priesthood* and this authority, which *shall* remain upon *earth*, that *the Sons of Levi* may yet *offer an offering unto the Lord in righteousness.*[41]

The wording of Joseph Smith is similar to that of Oliver Cowdery. Smith's recollection has the words "of Aaron, which holds the keys of the ministering of angels, and the gospel of repentance, and of baptism by immersion for the remission of sins." This wording in similar to that of a revelation in the Doctrine and Covenants revealed in September 1832.[42] The priesthood of Aaron was not a term used in 1829.

The wording "the Sons of Levi may yet offer an offering unto the Lord in righteousness" is a text from Malachi 3:3. This passage states that the messenger (3:1) "shall purify the sons of Levi, and purge them as gold and silver, that they may offer unto the Lord an offering in righteousness." The New Testament refers to John the Baptist as the one to prepare the way before Jesus.[43]

In addition, the reference to the sons of Levi may also indicate that in the dictation process of the Book of Mormon that Smith and Cowdery had reached the end of 3 Nephi, since the Malachi text is used as a prophecy "unto future generations."[44] The meaning of Malachi 3:3 developed during Smith's lifetime.[45]

In November 1832 Joseph Smith dictated an account of his early life. In his introduction he stated, "thirdly the reception of the holy Priesthood by the minist[e]ring of Aangels [Angels] to admin[i]ster the letter of the Gospel - <-the Law and

---

[41] Here the angel, who is later identified as John the Baptist, ordains Joseph Smith and Oliver Cowdery to the priesthood and the authority is now to remain upon the earth. The New Testament does not indicate that John the Baptist ever performed ordinations.

[42] Marquardt, *Joseph Smith Revelations*, 213; LDS D&C 84:26-27; RLDS D&C 83:4.

[43] See Matthew 11:10; Mark 1:2 and Luke 7:27.

[44] 1830 BOM, 503-505; LDS 3 Nephi chapters 24-25; 26:2; RLDS chapter 11; 11:29.

[45] See LDS D&C 84:31; RLDS D&C 83:6 written nearly two years before the letter of Cowdery to Phelps. The revelation mentions "the sons of Aaron shall offer an acceptable offering and sacrifice in the house of the Lord" to be built in the city of New Jerusalem in the state of Missouri. See also LDS D&C 128:24.

commandments as they were given unto him-> and the ordinencs [ordinances]."[46] The reference to the "letter of the Gospel" and the ordinances evidently refers to having faith, repentance, and then receiving baptism and the reception of the Holy Ghost.

The 1832 account is the earliest written record of Joseph Smith receiving the priesthood. This account also mentions "fo[u]rthly a confirmation and reception of the high Priesthood after the holy order of the son of the living God power and ordinence [ordinance] from on high to preach the Gospel in the administration and demonstration of the spirit the Kees [Keys] of the Kingdom of God confer[r]ed upon him." The third item mentions angels, while the fourth item contains no reference to angels and could refer to the authority to preach the gospel or ordaining elders to the high priesthood, which commenced in June 1831. The similarities in the September 1832 revelation on priesthood makes it unclear as to what the words in the 1832 account would mean when put into an 1829 context.[47]

On February 12, 1834 Joseph Smith made a brief remark in a meeting held in Kirtland, "I shall now endeavor to set forth before this council, the dignity of the office which has been conferred upon me by the ministering of the Angel of God, by his own voice and by the voice of this Church."[48] Five days later Smith said, "Jerusalem was the seat of the Church Council in ancient days. The apostle, Peter, was the president of the Council and held the keys of the Kingdom of God on the earth was appointed to this office by the voice of the Savior and acknowledged in it by the voice of the Church."[49] This relates to Smith's position as President of the Church and President of the Kirtland High Council. The minutes do not name the angel, or what office was conferred. On April 21 at a conference held at Norton, Ohio, Oliver Cowdery recorded further remarks made by Joseph Smith:

---

[46] Jessee, *Papers of Joseph Smith* 1:3.

[47] Marquardt, *Joseph Smith Revelations*, 212-13; LDS D&C 84:6, 19, 26-27; RLDS D&C 83:2-4. See LDS D&C 78:1-2; RLDS D&C 77:1. See also LDS D&C 77:11.

[48] Kirtland Council Minute Book, 27, LDS archives.

[49] Ibid., 30, meeting of Feb. 17, 1834.

He then gave a relation of obtaining and translating the Book of Mormon, the revelation of the priesthood of Aaron, the organization of the Church in the year 1830, the revelation of the high priesthood, and the gift of the Holy Spirit poured out upon the Church, &c.[50]

These records of what Joseph Smith discussed show that prior to Cowdery's 1834 *Messenger and Advocate* account, there was no public description of the events relating to restoration of the authority to preach and administer the ordinances of the gospel. Missionaries did not relate having their authority by heavenly messengers but only that they had been called by God.

After publishing his statement of the vision of the angel, Oliver Cowdery became Assistant President of the High and Holy Priesthood in the Church of the Latter Day Saints on December 5, 1834. In explaining his position as being next to Joseph Smith, Cowdery wrote, "this promise was made by the angel while in company with President Smith, at the time they received the office of the lesser priesthood." The minutes in Cowdery's hand mentions his formal ordination and the "keys of this kingdom."[51] This ordination appears to have superseded the appointment of David Whitmer as Joseph Smith's successor.

In giving the general charge to the newly ordained Council of the Twelve Apostles on February 21, 1835, Cowdery told those Twelve in attendance, "You have been ordained to the Holy Priesthood. You have received it from those who had their power and authority from an angel."[52] The minutes are not clear as to who this angel was. The inference at this time was that the Holy Priesthood was the Apostleship the same authority given to Jesus' twelve apostles. In the instructions given by Joseph Smith in April 1835 details about priesthood offices are given but there is nothing included about receiving the priesthood through the ministering of angels.

When preparing the 1835 Doctrine and Covenants for publication, the presiding elders, including Cowdery and Smith,

---

[50] Ibid., 44.
[51] Jessee, *Papers of Joseph Smith* 1:21, 24. Compare with the journal of Joseph Smith, entry also by Oliver Cowdery for December 5, 1834 (Ibid., 2:36).
[52] Kirtland Council Minute Book, 159.

added wording not originally contained in revelations of 1829 and 1830. One of the early revelations dated September 1830, mentioned those who will drink wine on the earth with the Savior. The following are the additional words inserted into the text:

> and also John the son of Zacharias, which Zacharias he (Elias) visited and gave promise that he should have a son, and his name should be John, and he should be filled with the spirit of Elias; which John I have sent unto you, my servants, Joseph Smith, jr. and Oliver Cowdery, to ordain you unto this first priesthood which you have received, that you might be called and ordained even as Aaron . . .
>
> And also with Peter, James, and John, whom I have sent unto you, by whom I have ordained you and confirmed you to be apostles and especial witnesses of my name, and bear the keys of your ministry: and of the same things which I revealed unto them: unto whom I have committed the keys of my kingdom, and a dispensation of the gospel for the last times: and for the fulness of times[53]

This is probably the earliest reference to the angel being John the Baptist who appeared and ordained Smith and Cowdery to the first priesthood. Peter, James, and John were to have ordained Joseph Smith and Oliver Cowdery "to be apostles and especial witnesses of my name, and bear the keys of your ministry." The added text explains that biblical personages were sent to Smith and Cowdery. The text is silent on whether or not the conferring of authority or priesthood was performed by the laying on of hands or was by voice command.

No background information was provided by Joseph Smith in the Manuscript History as to how he and Cowdery experienced Peter, James, and John appearing to them. Oliver Cowdery, while not giving the words of the ordination, or the circumstances of this vision, mentioned two things relating to this event. The first is he said, "This priesthood is also to remain upon the earth untill the Last remnant of time." The second important item was "we then

---

[53] 1835 D&C 50:2-3. See Marquardt, *Joseph Smith Revelations*, 72-73; LDS D&C 27:7-8, 12-13; RLDS D&C 26:2-3.

confirmed [the priesthood] on each other by the will and commandment of god."[54] This conferral apparently refers to their ordination on April 6, 1830 at the church organization.

In the summer of 1835 some Egyptian papyri were purchased and Joseph Smith interpreted part of the material. He dictated to William Phelps information about priesthood in the lineage of the pharaohs of Egypt.[55] In September 1835, Oliver Cowdery wrote about the "heavenly vision" of the angel John. The following account is recorded in the Patriarchal Blessing Book of Joseph Smith Sr.:

he [Joseph Smith] was ordained by the angel John, unto the lesser or Aaronic priesthood, in company with myself, in the town of Harmony, Susquehannah County, Pennsylvania, on Fryday, the 15th day of May, 1829. after which we repaired to the water, even to the Susquehannah River, and were baptized, he first ministering unto me and after I to him. But before baptism, our souls were drawn out in mighty prayer to know how we might obtain the blessings of baptism and of the Holy Spirit, according to the order of God . . . we repaired to the woods . . . and called upon the name of the Lord, and he answered us out of the heavens, and while we were in the heavenly vision the angel came down and bestowed upon us this priesthood; and then, as I have said, we repaired to the water and were baptized. After this we received the high and holy priesthood: but an account of this will be given elsewhere, or in another place.[56]

The priesthood restoration by John the Baptist has enough background as to the place, date, and significance relating to Cowdery and Smith. But receiving additional priesthood from Peter, James, and John is very scarce. Oliver Cowdery refers to a

---

[54] Diary of Reuben Miller, October 21, 1848, LDS archives.
[55] Egyptian Grammar and Alphabet, manuscript, 1835, LDS archives. See Marquardt, *Joseph Smith Egyptian Papers.* See also LDS D&C 107:40-57; RLDS D&C 104:18-29 for a lineage of patriarchs from Adam to Noah "written in the book of Enoch."
[56] Patriarchal Blessing Book 1:8-9, LDS archives.

December 18, 1833 blessing he received from Joseph Smith. He then writes about a "Prophecy of Joseph," son of Jacob relating to the seer of the last days and the scribe. Oliver wrote that they received:

> the holy priesthood under the hands of those who had been held in reserve for a long season, even those who received it under the hand of the Messiah, while he should dwell in the flesh, upon the earth[57]

When Joseph Smith reported the conferral of priesthood from John the Baptist, he stated that the Baptist said he "acted under the direction <of> Peter, James, and John, who held the keys of the priesthood of Melchisedek, whi[c]h priesthood he said should in due time be conferred on us. And that I should be called the first Elder of the Church and he [Oliver Cowdery] the second [Elder]."[58] The wording "due time" is connected with Smith and Cowdery and is the promise of having the priesthood conferred upon them and being ordained first and second elders of the church. Cowdery's 1834 writing does not mention the angel (John the Baptist) acting under instructions of Peter, James, and John or of a future conferral of authority from them.

Though there were a few baptisms performed during June 1829, Joseph Smith's history tells about their being anxious about the promise of having the authority to bestow the Holy Ghost and receiving this additional authority. The first reference is a general statement:

> We now became anxious to have that promise realized to us, which the Angel that conferred upon us the Aaronick Priesthood had given us, viz: that provided we continued faithful; we should also have the Melchesidec Priesthood, which holds the authority of the laying on of hands for the gift of the Holy Ghost.

---

[57] Patriarchal Blessing Book 1:12, blessing for Oliver Cowdery by Joseph Smith Jr. This portion appears to be an 1835 addition to the original 1833 blessing. It was written and recorded by Oliver Cowdery on October 2, 1835.
[58] Jessee, *Papers of Joseph Smith* 1:291.

The Joseph Smith history then related that they prayed at Peter Whitmer Sr.'s house in Fayette Township:

> for we had not long been engaged in solemn and fervent prayer, when the word of the Lord, came unto us in the Chamber [upper story of the Whitmer home], commanding us; that I should ordain Oliver Cowdery to be an Elder in the Church of Jesus Christ, And that he also should ordain me to the same office, ~~accordin~~ and then <to> ordain others[59]

From this account is appears that neither Smith nor Cowdery had been ordained elders by June 1829 while they were staying at the Peter Whitmer home. Smith further stated that they were "to defer" their ordination.[60] The wording is clear that they were to wait and not ordain each other elders. Cowdery and Smith would not ordain each other until commanded of God.[61] On April 6, 1830 Oliver Cowdery ordained Joseph Smith the first elder, seer, prophet, and apostle in the church and Smith ordained Cowdery as the second elder, also an apostle of Jesus Christ.

No reference in Joseph Smith's history gives background to a visitation of the three apostles Peter, James, and John. Brigham H. Roberts, Assistant Church Historian, wrote, "there is no definite account of the event in the history of the Prophet Joseph, or, for matter of that, in any of our annals."[62] There is no account about Peter, James, and John extant, nor is there any location, date or ordination prayer relating to this experience by Smith.

Various individuals have proposed that the vision of the three ancient apostles to Joseph Smith and Oliver Cowdery occurred (1) in May or June 1829 before the church was organized; (2) about June-July 1830 after the establishment of the church; and (3) in June 1831, at the time that the high priesthood was conferred

---

[59] Ibid., 1:299.

[60] Ibid., 1:239, 299.

[61] Marquardt, *Joseph Smith Revelations*, 61; BC 22:13-14; LDS D&C 21:10-11; RLDS D&C 19:3.

[62] B. H. Roberts, ed., *History of the Church* 1:40, footnote. First edition published in 1902.

upon some of the church elders. These writings will be examined in reverse order.

In 1861 Brigham Young, who was baptized in April 1832, made the following comment, "When he [Joseph Smith] received the Melchisedek Priesthood, he had another revelation. Peter, James, and John came to him. You can read the revelation at your leisure. When he received this revelation in Kirtland, the Lord revealed to him that he should begin and ordain High Priests."[63] The appearance to Joseph Smith of Peter, James, and John is considered by Brigham Young to be a revelation. Smith received the high priesthood (high priest) on June 3, 1831.

A late recollection places the visitation of the three apostles in 1830. This comes from letters of Addison Everett. He wrote in 1881 that he had overheard a conversation thirty-five years earlier relating to a time when Joseph Smith and Oliver Cowdery were being persecuted for their religion in southern New York.[64] This would have been in July 1830 if the information is correct. Additional wording to a revelation, as discussed above, has also been used to indicate the appearance to 1830.[65] Addison Everett and Erastus Snow placed Peter, James, and John appearing to Joseph Smith and Oliver Cowdery after the organization of the church.

The more commonly held view is that the Peter, James, and John's appearance occurred in May or June 1829, prior to Smith and Cowdery arriving in Fayette, Seneca County to complete the writing of the Book of Mormon.[66] In 1842 Joseph Smith dictated a letter to William Clayton that contains a brief mention of a general location of where he heard the "voice" of the apostles. Smith wrote, "The voice of Peter, James & John, [came] in the wilderness, between Harmony, Susquehanna County,

---

[63] *Journal of Discourses*, 26 vols. (London and Liverpool: LDS Booksellers Depot, 1854-86), 9:89, discourse of May 7, 1861.

[64] Everett to Oliver B. Huntington, Feb. 17, 1881, Oliver B. Huntington Journal, L. Tom Perry Special Collections, Harold B. Lee Library. See Erastus Snow, *Journal of Discourses* 23:183, discourse of May 6, 1882.

[65] Bushman, *Joseph Smith and the Beginnings of Mormonism*, 163, 240-41n55.

[66] See Roberts, *History of the Church* 1:61, footnote; Joseph F. Smith, Jr., "Restoration of the Melchizedek Priesthood," *Improvement Era* 7 (Oct. 1904):938-43; and Larry C. Porter, "Dating the Restoration of the Melchizedek Priesthood," *Ensign* 9 (June 1979):5-10.

[Pennsylvania] and Colesville, Broom[e] County, [New York] on the [bank of the] Susquehanna river, declaring themselves as possessing the keys of the kingdom, and of the dispensation of the fulness of times."[67]

This letter gives no date on when the voice was heard. In this brief statement there is no mention of conferral of priesthood. Joseph Smith and Oliver Cowdery were together during the dictation process of the Book of Mormon prior to their move to Fayette in early June 1829. In 1844 Joseph Smith mentioned "the vision of his ordination to the priesthood of Aaron" but no mention of the vision of Peter, James and John.[68] Richard Bushman noted: "But the difficulties with both the proposed dates - summer 1829 or summer 1830 - means that we will not know for certain until more information is uncovered."[69]

A few members wrote that they had heard on different occasions that Joseph Smith mentioned the keys of the kingdom were given him by Peter, James, and John. Two late recollections are from Philo Dibble and Benjamin Winchester. Dibble said he remembered that in 1832 when Sidney Rigdon was making false pretensions that Joseph Smith said, "No power can pluck those keys from me, except the power that gave them to me; that was Peter, James and John."[70] Winchester mentions the meeting when David Whitmer was ordained successor to Joseph Smith in July 1834:

> Joseph said at that time that the keys of the kingdom had been given to him through the angels, Peter, James and John, and that he himself had finished his work so far as a complete organization of the church was concerned. He

---

[67] Jessee, *Papers of Joseph Smith* 2:474, letter dated Sept. 6, 1842. See LDS D&C 128:20. The original letter written by William Clayton is in the LDS archives.
[68] Franklin D. Richards, "Scriptural Items," March 10, 1844 in Ehat and Cook, *Words of Joseph Smith*, 334.
[69] Bushman, *Joseph Smith and the Beginnings of Mormonism*, 241n55.
[70] "Philo Dibble's Narrative," in *Early Scenes in Church History. Eighth Book of the Faith-Promoting Series* (Salt Lake City: Juvenile Instructor Office, 1882), 80.

then, in a conference, ordained David Whitmer to be his successor in case of accident to himself."[71]

Orson Pratt wrote about the early events of the church in which he was involved:

In that early day the prophet Joseph said to me that the Lord had revealed that twelve men were to be chosen as Apostles. A manuscript revelation to this effect, given in 1829 - before the rise of this Church - was laid before me, and I read it. Joseph said to me . . . that I should be one of this Twelve.[72]

The ordinations of those chosen for the quorum of the twelve apostles commenced in February 1835. This was during the time when textual additions were being made to the revelations of Joseph Smith.

Another consideration relating to problems of the priesthood restoration by Peter, James, and John is whether the event was by a physical ordination or by voice command.[73] In Joseph Smith's 1839 account, the appearance of John the Baptist has two ordinations occurring. The first ordination was from the angel and the second after Smith's and Cowdery's baptism when they ordained each other. It is of interest that John the Baptist did not baptize them. As there is no account of Peter, James, and John, we have no circumstances to judge it by.

---

[71] *Daily Tribune*, Sept. 22, 1889, Salt Lake City. See *History of the Church* 2:124 on Joseph Smith's statement that he had accomplished the great work the Lord had laid before him.

[72] *Journal of Discourses* 12:85-86, discourse of Aug. 11, 1867. Pratt was referring to a June 1829 revelation. See LDS D&C 18:27, 37; RLDS D&C 16:5-6.

[73] On the position that there was no physical ordination by Peter, James, and John, see RLDS writers Joseph Smith III and Heman C. Smith, in *The History of the Reorganized Church of Jesus Christ of Latter Day Saints* (Independence, MO: Herald Publishing House, 1897), 1:63-66; Richard P. Howard in *Saints Herald* 121 (Nov. 1974):53; 126 (May 1, 1979):29; 129 (May 1, 1982):28; and Howard, *The Church Through the Years* (Independence, Missouri: Herald Publishing House, 1992) 1:146n6 and Ibid., (1993) 2:481.

A very late recollection by David H. Cannon tells of an interview he had with David Whitmer in 1861. Whitmer recalled that prior to Oliver Cowdery's death in 1850, Cowdery bore his testimony to the Book of Mormon and then "laid his hands upon his own head, saying to the people assembled there, 'Peter, James, and John have laid their hands upon this head and conferred the Holy Melchizedek Priesthood.'"[74]

No Book of Mormon minister is recorded conferring priesthood on Joseph Smith and Oliver Cowdery only biblical personages. It appears that the power and authority that Smith and Cowdery received in their ordination as elders, gave them additional duties beyond the baptism authority. When they were ordained on April 6, 1830, they had authority to ordain other elders and confer the Holy Ghost like the Book of Mormon twelve Nephite disciples.

As mentioned previously, in June 1831, Joseph Smith (Oliver Cowdery was in Missouri at the time), commenced ordaining elders to the office of the high priesthood (high priests). When Smith was ordained President of the High Priesthood on January 25, 1832, Sidney Rigdon "sealed upon his head the blessings which he had formerly received."[75] All of the known statements concerning priesthood restoration by Smith and Cowdery were told after the Presidency of the High Priesthood had been established in March 1832 with Joseph Smith and his two counselors. This Presidency was to hold the keys of the kingdom of God on earth and the presidency of three was likened unto the three apostles of Jesus: Peter, James, and John.

The idea that Joseph Smith and Oliver Cowdery would develop the story of the visions of heavenly personages appearing to them is in line with other early embellishments. Examples of historical development of texts, location, name, and documents are as follows: (1) *Evening and Morning Star* reprint in Kirtland, with Oliver Cowdery as editor; (2) the change in the name of the church and the place it was organized; (3) significant revisions in some of

---

[74] Beatrice Cannon Evans and Janath Russell Cannon, eds., *Cannon Family Historical Treasury* (Salt Lake City: George Cannon Family Association, 1967), 251. This quote is from his brief autobiography written in 1922 at the age of eighty-four (240).

[75] Watson, *The Orson Pratt Journals*, 11.

the sacred texts of Joseph Smith's revelations permitted by the four members of Presidency for the 1835 Doctrine and Covenants; and (4) expansion of blessings given in December 1833 and their recording in the fall of 1835.[76]

For Joseph Smith and Oliver Cowdery to baptize and confer authority upon each other by an impression or voice command was like other ministers of the gospel at the time. No exclusive authority by the laying on of angelic hands was promoted when the church was organized in April 1830. The early revelations and missionaries did not say their authority could be traced from biblical personages in the first few years but they considered that they were called by inspiration and in some cases by Joseph Smith through a written revelation.

One short development was a conference or council of high priests where decisions could be made. On February 17, 1834 at Joseph Smith's home he "proceeded to organize the high council of the Church of Christ, which was to consist of twelve high priests, and one, or three presidents, as the case might require."[77] The council was basically a church court to settle important difficulties between members including church discipline. Cases could be appealed to the "high Council at the seat of the general government of the church" (presidency of the high priesthood or first presidency). If there was a question of doctrine the president of the church high council could inquire and obtain the mind of the Lord by revelation. It was voted by those present at the meeting that Joseph Smith make corrections by the spirit of revelation on the proceedings of the day.

Joseph Smith Sr. was chosen to be on the Kirtland high council as was his son Samuel H. Smith. The elder Smith blessed

---

[76] See (1) *Evening and Morning Star*, Kirtland reprint; (2) H. Michael Marquardt, "An Appraisal of Manchester as Location for the Organization of the Church," *Sunstone* 16 (Feb. 1992):49-57; (3) compare the texts between manuscript copies of certain revelations (appearing in the unfinished Book of Commandments and other revelatory documents not planned for publication in that book) with the 1835 Doctrine and Covenants; and (4) the recording of blessings in Joseph Smith's journal (Jessee, *Papers of Joseph Smith* 2:15-17) with Patriarchal Blessing Book 1 (LDS archives).

[77] Corrected minutes in Kirtland Council Minute Book, 32. See LDS D&C 102:1; RLDS D&C 99:1.

his sons on February 19. After putting his hands on the head of twenty-eight year old son Joseph he blessed him saying:

> Joseph, I lay my hands upon thy head, and pronounce the blessings of thy progenitors upon thee, that thou mayest hold the keys of the mysteries of the Kingdom of heaven until the coming of the Lord, Amen.[78]

Concerning the president of the high council the minutes of February 17 state:

> The president of the church, who is also the president of the Council, is appointed by the voice of the Saviour and acknowledged in his administration by the voice of the Church[79]

The minutes of this meeting were copied into the Kirtland Revelations Book. Sometime later the above sentence was revised with the words "the voice of the Savior" crossed out and "revelation" written above the line. The sentence now read for the 1835 Doctrine and Covenants:

> The president of the church who is also the president of the council, is appointed by revelation and acknowledged in his administration by the voice of the church.[80]

There is another place in the minutes where nothing is record for correction but a mention of the twelve apostles appears in the printed minutes in the Doctrine and Covenants as follows:

> There is a distinction between the high council of travelling high priests abroad, and the travelling high council composed of the twelve apostles, in their decisions: From the decision of the former there can be an appeal, but from the decision of the later there cannot. The later can only be

---

[78] Kirtland Council Minute Book, 37.

[79] Ibid.,, 33.

[80] Kirtland Revelations Book, 112-13, LDS archives; compare 1835 D&C 5:6; LDS D&C 102:9; RLDS D&C 99:6.

called in question by the general authorities of the church in case of transgression.[81]

A number of changes to the minutes were made by Joseph Smith in accordance to instructions of the high council: "The document was received by the unanimous voice of the Council, with this provision, that, if the president should hereafter discover any lack in the same he should be privileged to fill it up."[82]

According to a revelation given to Joseph Smith in June 1829 there were to be twelve disciples chosen by Oliver Cowdery and David Whitmer.[83] David Marks, who visited the Peter Whitmer home in March 1830 commented, "They further stated, that twelve apostles were to be appointed."[84] As mentioned earlier Orson Pratt an early convert to the church said:

In that early day the prophet Joseph said to me that the Lord had revealed that twelve men were to be chosen as Apostles. A manuscript revelation to this effect, given in 1829 - before the rise of this Church - was laid before me, and I read it. Joseph said to me . . . that I should be one of this Twelve. [85]

At a conference held at Orange, Ohio on October 26, 1831, Oliver Cowdery recorded "that the directions which himself & his br[other]. David Whitmer had received this morning respecting the choice of the twelve was that they would be ordained & sent forth from the Land of Zion [Missouri]."[86] Since the saints two years later had to abandon Jackson County other arrangements moved forward by adding Martin Harris and having the ordinations take place in Kirtland. This now would mean that the three witnesses to

---

[81] 1835 D&C 5:13; LDS D&C 102:30-32; RLDS D&C 99:13.

[82] Kirtland Council Minute Book, 36.

[83] Marquardt, *Joseph Smith Revelations*, 48; BC 15:42; LDS D&C 18:37; RLDS D&C 16:6.

[84] *The Life of David Marks* (Limerick, Maine: Printed at the Office of the Morning Star, 1831), 340.

[85] *Journal of Discourses* 12:85-86, discourse of Aug. 11, 1867. Pratt was referring to the June 1829 revelation.

[86] Cannon and Cook, *Far West Record*, 26.

the Book of Mormon would be the committee to choose the Twelve Apostles.

A meeting was held on February 14, 1835 and after prayer President Joseph Smith spoke regarding those men who had gone to Missouri in Zion's Camp. He said "it was the Will of God, that they should be ordained to the ministry and go forth to prune the vineyard for the last times, or the coming of the Lord which was nigh, even fifty six years, should wind up the scene." The minutes recorded Smith saying:

> The first business of the meeting was for the three witnesses of the Book of Mormon, to pray each one and then proceed to choose twelve men from the Church as Apostles to go to all nations, kindred, tounges [tongues] and people. The three Witnesses united in prayer (Viz.) Oliver Cowdery, David Whitmer & Martin Harris. These three Witnesses were then blessed by the laying on of the hands of the Presidency. They then according to a former commandment, proceeded to make choice of the twelve.[87]

As indicated by Joseph Smith's instructions the following sequence relating to the three witnesses were: (1) prayer, (2) blessed by the First Presidency, and (3) choose the Twelve. This committee was influenced by Smith in their choice of the only member of the Smith family to be in the quorum at their first organization. The minutes of the Quorum of the Twelve state:

> The Three Special witnesses of the Book of Mormon being present . . . it was ascertained that the time had come when they should be chosen: Consequently They proceeded by the spirit of prophecy and revelation to choose and set apart from among all the elders of the church the following persons to fill that high and responsible station[88]

---

[87] Kirtland Council Minute Book, 147, 149. On pruning the vineyard for the last time see LDS D&C 24:19; RLDS D&C 23:7 (July 1830) and LDS D&C 39:17; RLDS D&C 39:5 (Jan. 5, 1831).
[88] "A record of the transactions of the Twelve apostles," [1835], in Patriarchal Blessing Book 2, typed copy, LDS archives.

The following men were chosen to be among the twelve apostles: Luke S. Johnson (age 27), Lyman E. Johnson (age 23), Parley P. Pratt (age 27), Orson Pratt (age 23), Brigham Young (age 33), Heber C. Kimball (age 33), Orson Hyde (age 30), Thomas B. Marsh (age 34), David W. Patten (age 35; thought to be 34), John F. Boyington (age 23), William E. McLellin (age 29), and William Smith (age 23).

Statements by two of the committee, Oliver Cowdery and David Whitmer indicate that Phineas Young, brother to Brigham Young had originally been considered to be one of the twelve but that Joseph Smith requested they choose his brother William Smith. In a letter of Oliver Cowdery to Brigham Young, February 27, 1848, Cowdery wrote:

> At the time the Twelve were chosen in Kirtland, and I may say before, it had been manifested that brother Phineas [Young] was entitled to occupy the station as one of that number; but owing to brother Joseph's urgent request at the time, Brother David [Whitmer] and myself yielded to his wishing and consented for William [Smith] to be selected, contrary to our feelings and judgment, and to our deep mortification ever since. Brother Phineas occupied at that time a relation to myself [brother-in-law] that caused me to feel delicate about urging his name and besides Brother Joseph, about that time was bearing down heavily upon Brother Phineas. [89]

David Whitmer when interviewed in 1885 was asked "Do you know how the first Twelve was chosen?" The manuscript page is damaged that has Whitmer's answer (proposed reading in brackets):

> Yes. Cowdery and myself were appointed a com[mittee to choose] the Twelve but Jose[ph Smith] insisted that his brother William Smith should be put in as it was the only

---

[89] Cowdery to Brigham Young, Feb. 27, 1848, as cited in Stanley R. Gunn, *Oliver Cowdery Second Elder and Scribe* (Salt Lake City: Bookcraft, 1962), 268.

way by which he could be saved, otherwise we would not have chosen him.[90]

This would indicate that originally there were three sets of brothers chosen as apostles before two of the three witnesses were persuaded to replace the name of Phineas Young with William Smith.

A synopsis of the ordination blessings were later recorded in the Kirtland Council Minute Book. Three men were ordained on February 14 and six others on February 15. Lyman Johnson who was the youngest apostle received the following blessing on the fifteenth:

> in the name of Jesus Christ, that he should bear the tidings of salvation to nations, tongues and people, until the utmost corners of the earth shall hear the tidings, and that he shall be a witness of the things of God, to nations & tongues, and that Holy Angels shall administer to him occasionally and that no power of the enemy shall prevent him from going forth and doing the work of the Lord. And that he should live until the gathering was accomplished, according to the Holy Prophets. And that he should be like unto Enoch And your faith shall be like unto his, and he shall be called great among all the living and Satan shall tremble before thee, and that he shall see the Saviour come and stand on the Earth with power and great glory.[91]

William Smith whom Joseph Smith wanted to be in the quorum had the following apostolic blessing pronounced:

> That he may be purified in heart, that he may have communion with God. That he may be equal with his brethren in holding the keys of this ministry That he may be kept and be instrumental in leading Israel forth, that he may be delivered from the hands of those who seek to

---

[90] Interview of David Whitmer by Zenas H. Gurley Jr., Jan. 14, 1885, LDS archives. See Cook, *David Whitmer Interviews*, 157.

[91] Kirtland Council Minute Book, 149-50.

destroy him; that he may be enabled to bear testimony to the nations, that Jesus lives. That he may stand in the midst of pestilence and destruction, he shall be mighty in the hands of God, in bringing about the restoration of Israel. The nations shall rejoice at the greatness of the gifts which God has bestowed upon him, That his tongue shall be loosed, he shall have power to do great things in the name of Jesus. He shall be preserved and remain on the earth, until Christ shall come to take vengeance on the wicked.[92]

The record indicated that Parley P. Pratt was ordained on February 21 by Joseph Smith, David Whitmer, and Oliver Cowdery. This was because Martin Harris left Kirtland for New York. Thomas B. Marsh and Orson Pratt were ordained to the apostleship on April 26.

A meeting of the Council of the Twelve was held on April 28. The minutes state that the Twelve "Motioned and carried that we each forgive one another every wrong that has existed among us."[93] The twelve apostles were all present at this meeting and were preparing to go on their first mission. They wrote a letter to Joseph Smith asking, if possible, for a revelation that would contain their duty.[94]

Heber C. Kimball wrote concerning a meeting of the Twelve, "One evening when we were assembled to receive instruction, the revelation contained in the third section of the Book of Doctrine and Covenants, on Priesthood was given to Brother Joseph as he was instructing us, and we praised the Lord."[95] Joseph Smith commenced giving instructions to the Twelve Apostles:

---

[92] Ibid., 154.

[93] "A record of the transactions of the Twelve apostles," minutes for April 28, 1835.

[94] Orson Hyde and William E. McLellin to Smith, [April 28, 1835]. The date of the letter was recorded in the Kirtland Council Minutes (198) as March 28, 1836. The month should be April rather than March and the proper year is 1835 before the Twelve Apostles went on their mission.

[95] "Extracts from H. C. Kimball's Journal," *Times and Seasons* 6 (April 15, 1845):869. See 1835 D&C 3; LDS D&C 107; RLDS D&C 104.

There are, in the church, two priesthoods, namely: the Melchizedek, and the Aaronic, including the Levitical priesthood. Why the first is called the Melchizedek priesthood, is because Melchizedek was such a great high priest: before his day it was called *the holy priesthood, after the order of the Son of God*; but out of respect or reverence to the name of the Supreme Being, to avoid the too frequent repetition of his name, they, the church, in ancient days, called that priesthood after Melchizedek, or the Melchizedek priesthood.[96]

As printed the instructions included a number of separate items given at various times. This composite document contained instructions from Joseph Smith including a November 1831 revelation that had been enlarged, an extract from a patriarchal blessing given by Joseph Smith Sr., and a record of a vision relating to the new office of Seventy.

The duties of the Twelve included being "special witnesses of the name of Christ, in all the world," and being a quorum equal in authority to the First Presidency. They were told, "The twelve are a travelling, presiding high council, to officiate in the name of the Lord, under the direction of the presidency of the church." The Twelve can ordain evangelical ministers (patriarchs) in large branches of the church.[97] While the Twelve Apostles were on their first church mission a traveling showman arrived in Kirtland with four Egyptian mummies and some papyri as will be explained in the next chapter.

---

[96] Marquardt, *Joseph Smith Revelations*, 267, emphasis retained; LDS D&C 107:1-4; RLDS D&C 104:1 (April [28-30] 1835).

[97] Marquardt, *Joseph Smith Revelations*, 268-69; LDS D&C 107:23-24, 33, 39; RLDS D&C 104:11-12, 17. The jurisdiction of the Twelve was expanded in 1841.

16

Papyri and Writings of Abraham

Prior to 1823 a cache of mummies came into the possession of Antonio Lebolo. They were found in catacombs near Thebes in Egypt. Lebolo died at Castellamonte, Piedmont (now Italy) in February 1830. Later eleven mummies associated with Lebolo were transported to America. This appears to be the largest shipment to America up to that time. Only a few exhibits of mummies had been reported in major cities. A man named Michael H. Chandler said he secured the mummies and started exhibiting them in Philadelphia. To date there has been no independent confirmation of this. In April 1833 the mummies and papyri were put on display charging 25 cents for adults and 12½ cents for children to view them. During April through the first part of June they were shown at the Masonic Hall and the Philadelphia Arcade. One advertisement read:

The largest collection of EGYPTIAN MUMMIES ever exhibited in this city, is now to be seen at the Masonic Hall, in the [sic; on] Ches[t]nut Street above Seventh. They were found in the vicinity of Thebes, by the celebrated traveler Antonio Lebolo and Chevalier Drovetti, General Council of France in Egypt. Some writings on Papirus [Papyrus] with the Mummies, can also be seen, and will afford, no doubt, much satisfaction to Amateurs of Antiquities.[1]

It was reported that one of the mummies was stripped of its wrappings while in New York.[2] Two mummies were sold to the Academy of Natural Sciences of Philadelphia. In December 1833 Dr. Samuel George Morton dissected the mummies before academy members and others. This is confirmation that the

---

[1] *U.S. Gazette*, April 3, 1833, Philadelphia, as cited in H. Donl Peterson, *The Story of the Book of Abraham: Mummies, Manuscripts, and Mormonism* (Salt Lake City: Deseret Book, 1995), 89.

[2] Ibid., 92.

mummies and papyri were exhibited in Philadelphia that year. A certificate was made by a group of medical doctors:

> Having examined with considerable attention and deep interest, a number of Mummies from the catacombs, near Thebes, in Egypt, and now exhibited in the Arcade, we beg leave to recommend them to the observation of the curious inquirer on subjects of a period so long elapsed; probably not less than three thousand years ago. The features of some of these Mummies are in perfect expression. – The papyrus, covered with black or red ink, or paint, in excellent preservation, are very interesting. The undersigned, unsolicited by any person connected by interest with this exhibition, have voluntarily set their names hereunto, for the simple purpose of calling the attention of the public to an interesting collection, not sufficiently known in this city.
>
> JOHN REDMAN COXE, M.D.
> RICHARD HARLAN, M.D.
> J. PANCOAST, M.D.
> WILLIAM P.C. BARTON, M.D.
> E. F. RIVINUS, M.D.
> SAMUEL G. MORGAN [MORTON], M.D.
>
> I concur in the above sentiments, concerning the collection of Mummies in the Philadelphia Arcade, and consider them highly deserving the attention of the curious.
>
> W. E. HORNER, M.D.[3]

By March 1835 seven mummies had been sold before Chandler exhibited them in Cleveland, Ohio. A description of the mummies appeared in the Painesville *Telegraph*. There were three female mummies and one male mummy. Rolls of writings were with three of them. Of particular interest is the male mummy:

---

[3] "Egyptian Antiquities," in *Times and Seasons* 3 (May 2, 1842):774, Nauvoo, Illinois. See also *Latter Day Saints' Messenger and Advocate* 2 (Dec. 1835):235, Kirtland, Ohio.

No. 3.—Height 4 ft. 4½.—Male, very old, say 80; arms crossing on the breast, each hand on its opposite shoulder; had a roll of writing as No. 1 & 2; superior head, it will compare in the region of the sentiments with any in our land; passions mild.[4]

It should be pointed out that there were no scholars in America at the time who could give a good translation from the Egyptian writing. Books such as the one by J. G. H. Greppo, *Essay on the Hieroglyphic System of M. Champollion, Jun.* (Boston, 1830) contained some rudimentary ideas on the topic. Jean Francois Champollion, a young French scholar, helped decipher the Rosetta stone. But he died in 1832 leaving his important works to be published posthumously in Paris. His books *Grammaire égyptienne* (1836) and *Dictionnaire égyptienne* (1841) together with studies of other scholars led to the decipherment of the ancient Egyptian language.

Another Cleveland newspaper said the four mummies were three males and one female but this does not appear to be correct. The article described the writing found in "the arms of the old man" being in length about "10 or 12 inches, and 3 or 4 in width." Continuing it said, "The characters are the Egyptian hyeroglyphics; but of what it discourses none can tell."[5]

About June 30 Michael Chandler arrived with his exhibit of mummies at Kirtland, Ohio, church headquarters. Joseph Smith Jr., prophet-president of the Church of the Latter Day Saints was shown the mummies and papyri. Chandler had a placard which told of his showcase of four mummies. This handout said the mummies "may have lived in the days of Jacob, Moses, or David" and that figures and hieroglyphic characters upon papyrus "will be exhibited with the Mummies."[6]

Joseph Smith had more interest in the papyri than in the four Egyptian mummies. Smith took the records and went to his

---

[4] "Mummies," *Telegraph* 13 (March 27, 1835), Painesville, Ohio. See Jay M. Todd, *The Saga of the Book of Abraham* (Salt Lake City: Deseret Book, 1969), 134 and Peterson, *Story of the Book of Abraham*, 117.

[5] "A Rare Exhibition," *Cleveland Whig*, March 25, 1835, Cleveland, Ohio, as cited in Peterson, *Story of the Book of Abraham*, 112.

[6] "Egyptian Antiquities," *Times and Seasons* 3 (May 2, 1842):774.

translating room in his home. It was reported by William W. Phelps, a clerk and scribe for Joseph, that Smith considered one record to be of Joseph of Egypt and another roll as that of his great grandfather Abraham who lived for a time in Egypt. It was revealed that these papyri were related to the biblical Joseph and Abraham. Smith showed considerable interest in obtaining these ancient writings in order to work out a translation. Chandler said that previously "he obtained in a small degree, the translation of a few characters." Joseph Smith showed to Chandler some characters said to have been copied from the Book of Mormon plates. The following certificate was presented to Smith before any purchased was made:

> Kirtland, July 6th, 1835.
> This is to make known to all who may be desirous, concerning the knowledge of Mr. Joseph Smith, jr. in deciphering the ancient Egyptian hieroglyphic characters, in my possession, which I have, in many eminent cities, shown to the most learned: And, from the information that I could learn, or meet with, I find that of Mr. Joseph Smith, jr. to correspond in the most minute matters.
> (Signed)   Michael H. Chandler.
> Travelling with, and proprietor of Egyptian Mummies.[7]

Joseph Smith was very much interested in purchasing the records but they had to be sold with the four Egyptian mummies. The cost was to be $2400 a substantial amount especially considering the expenditures for building the Kirtland Temple. According to Joseph Coe arrangements were made to make the purchase before Chandler left Kirtland. Coe explained in 1844:

> Previous t[o] closing the contra[c]t with Chandler I made ar[r]angements with S[imeon]. Andrews for to take one third part and your self & Co. one third leaving one third to be borne by myself. . . . Chandler was only an agent acting

---

[7] Oliver Cowdery to William Frye, Dec. 22, 1835, Oliver Cowdery Letterbook, 72, Henry E. Huntington Library, San Marino, California. Published in *Messenger and Advocate* 2 (Dec. 1835):235.

for some men in Philadelphia, the mummies when delivered to him for exhibition wer[e] valued at some 2 or 300 dollars, but they sued him and was allowed the sum which he sold them to me for viz. $2400[8]

As mentioned when the papyri were shown to Joseph Smith he studied them for a short time and remarked that these records were that of the biblical Joseph in Egypt and of the patriarch Abraham. As told by Oliver Cowdery the better preserved papyrus was represented to be that of Joseph of the Hebrew Scriptures. The more damaged papyrus was represented to be that of Abraham, Father of the Hebrew nation.

Joseph Smith embarked on preparing an alphabet to help him translate and present an explanation of the Abraham papyrus to the church. Smith wrote and dictated his ideas to his scribes. William W. Phelps, one of the scribes, recorded the final version in the Egyptian Alphabet to Abraham's record. Eventually this included writing on thirty-four pages in a bound ledger book. William Phelps wrote in a letter to his wife Sally about the records and mummies purchased from Chandler:

Last evening we received your first letter after an absence of twelve weeks and twelve hours. . . . Brother Joseph remarked that it was as easy to shed tears while reading that letter as it was when reading the History of Joseph in Egypt. . . .

The last of June four Egyptian mummies were brought here; there were two papyrus rolls, besides some other ancient Egyptian writings with them. As no one could translate these writings, they were presented to President Smith. He soon knew what they were and said they, the "rolls of papyrus," contained the sacred record kept of Joseph in Pharaoh's Court in Egypt, and the teachings of Father Abraham. God has so ordered it that these mummies and writings have been brought in the Church, and the sacred writing I had just locked up in Brother Joseph's house when your letter came, so I had two consolations of

---

[8] Coe to Joseph Smith, Jan. 1, 1844, Joseph Smith Collection, LDS archives.

good things in one day. These records of old times, when we translate and print them in a book, will make a good witness for the Book of Mormon. There is nothing secret or hidden that shall not be revealed, and they come to the Saints.[9]

Shortly after purchasing the Egyptian artifacts Joseph Smith commenced working with Oliver Cowdery and William W. Phelps on what was described as an Egyptian "alphabet to the Book of Abraham."[10] Three preliminary manuscripts contain characters copied by Smith, Phelps and Cowdery. Some Egyptian characters were copied from the original vignette (illustration) of what became Facsimile No. 1 from the Book of Abraham. Written were Joseph Smith's explanations concerning Adam, the founding of Egypt, and astronomy. As they developed these ideas were arranged in a manuscript book labeled "Egyptian Alphabet." Though never completely finished, Joseph Smith worked on the Egyptian Alphabet with Phelps. Afterwards Warren Parrish was scribe for a small amount of material. While this is not a real Egyptian alphabet it is a helpful insight into the way Joseph Smith was working with the papyrus preparatory to his work on the Book of Abraham text.[11]

The English text of the majority of the Egyptian Alphabet manuscript book contains the writings of Joseph Smith dictated to his scribe and clerk William W. Phelps. On page one there is a mention "In translating this character" showing that Joseph Smith was rendering his interpretation to this work. There is not perfect harmony in the short work of thirty-four handwritten pages.

The book contains five divisions called "degrees." The following are some examples of how Joseph Smith was able to study the handwritten symbols. They were copied on the left side

---

[9] William W. Phelps to Sally Phelps, July 19-20, 1835, as cited in Leah Y. Phelps, "Letters of Faith from Kirtland," *Improvement Era* 45 (Aug. 1942):529. See Bruce A. Van Orden, ed., "Writing to Zion: The William W. Phelps Kirtland Letters (1835-1836)," *Brigham Young University Studies* 33:3 (1993):554-56.

[10] *History of the Church* 2:238, written in Manuscript History, Book B-1:597 in 1843, LDS archives.

[11] See Marquardt, *Joseph Smith Egyptian Papers*. Original in LDS archives.

of the page. Next appears in English the reported sound of the word, followed by Smith's English explanation to the right. In the examples that follow page numbers of the original "Grammar & A[l]phabet of the Egyptian Language" are given in parenthesis.

One interpretation from the third degree is the sound "Zub zool" meaning "pointing to the end of a fixed period. A road which leads to some particular place for instance: from Chaldea I travelled to dwell in the land of Canaan." (14) Another character would have different meanings in each of the five degrees was the sound "Ho-oop hah":

1st Degree: "Crown of a princess, or unmarried queen" (21)
2nd Degree: "Corwn [Crown] of a married Queen" (17)
3rd Degree: "Crown of a widowed queen" (13)
4th Degree: "Queen who has been married the second time" (9)
5th Degree: "Queen Kah tou mun, a distinction of Royal female lineage or descent, from her whom Egypt was discovered while it was under water, who was the daughter of Ham - a lineage with whom a record of the fathers was entrusted by the tradition of Ham and according to the tradition of their elders: by whom also the tradition of the art of embalming was kept" (3-4).

The story as Joseph Smith explained told about Abram (Abraham). Abraham's father was an idolater. A priest bound Abram attempting to have him as a human sacrifice. He was rescued by an angel. The King (Pharaoh) of Egypt descended from Ham and had Canaanite blood by birth. All the Egyptians came from this lineage. A story of the discovery of Egypt by Zeptah (or Egyptus) is told also about the government of Egypt. The rights of the priesthood are explained as coming from Noah.

In November 1835 Joseph Smith dictated to William W. Phelps such ideas about Father Abraham in the opening sentences of the Book of Abraham:

Translation of the Book of Abraham written by his own hand upon papyrus and found in the Catacombs of Egypt
In the land of the Chaldeans, at the residence of my fathers, I, Abraham, saw, that it was needful for me to obtain another place of residence, and seeing there was

greater happiness and peace and rest, for me, I sought for [the] blessings of the fathers, and the right whereunto I should be ordained to administer the same: Having been a follower of righteousness; desiring to be one who possessed great Knowledge; a greater follower of righteousness; <a possessor of greater knowledge;> a father of many nations; a prince of peace; one who keeps the commandments of God; a rightful heir; a high priest, holding the right belonging to the fathers, from the beginning of time; even from the beginning, or before the foundation of the earth, down to the present time; even the right of the first born, or the first man, who is Adam, or first father, through <the> fathers, unto me.[12]

There are three Translation Manuscripts of the Book of Abraham that represent Joseph Smith's dictation. The scribes for Joseph Smith were William W. Phelps, Frederick G. Williams, and Warren Parrish. A copy was made by Parrish and further dictation to him of the story. Smith represented the writings he was working on as Abraham's. The characters on the papyrus which are on the first column immediately to the left of the original Facsimile No. 1 were used (except the missing characters in the first three lines) in the three Translation Manuscripts. It appears that this section of the papyrus was considered the commencement of the Book of Abraham.

Line two has a lacuna (gap or break) in the papyrus fragment. Here restored characters were placed on the manuscript pages that are unnatural to the text. These incorrectly restored signs were then represented by Joseph Smith concerning the discovery of the land of Egypt and that from Ham, son of Noah, "sprang that race which preserved the curse in the land" (Abraham 1:24). It states that Pharaoh was of that lineage and that he could not have the right to the patriarchal priesthood (Abraham 1:27).[13] The text concerns itself with Abraham having written this record

---

[12] Translation Manuscript, No. 1, 1, LDS archives. See Marquardt, *Joseph Smith Egyptian Papers*, 147-48.

[13] This would be considered in Joseph Smith's day as the office of church patriarch. It was a hereditary office going from father to son. See LDS D&C 107:40; RLDS D&C 104:18.

(Abraham 1:1, 12, 14, 31), including the illustration (Facsimile No. 1) written at the beginning or commencement of the record.

Joseph Smith did not understand Egyptian so he could not actually translate from that language. The symbols inspired him with ideas. The text produced was represented by Joseph Smith as an inspired revelatory interpretation (translation). The saints knew Joseph Smith had no knowledge of Egyptian and that the contexts of the papyrus would have to be revealed by God.

As indicated earlier Smith employed scribes to help him write important records. These included the Book of Mormon, his revelations, his revision of the Bible, many of his letters, and his journal entries. While Joseph Smith's personal handwriting appears in texts produced by him, the majority of his writings were dictated to his appointed scribes. Because a document is not in Smith's hand does not mean that it was not produced by him. Several manuscripts termed as an "Egyptian Alphabet" likewise contain information that was dictated by Joseph Smith. One of these preliminary manuscripts contains his handwriting.

Joseph Smith Sr. was the first church patriarch and he was ordained to give blessings to members. The emphasis of priesthood authority was an important topic in the Latter-day Saint church in 1835. It was natural to want to trace the office of patriarch back to biblical times. Joseph Smith taught that the order of the patriarchal priesthood "was confirmed to be handed down from father to son, and rightly belongs to the literal descendants of the chosen seed, to whom the promises were made."[14] A listing, including the line of this authority from Adam to Noah was reportedly "written in the book of Enoch."[15]

In the month of June 1835 Joseph Smith wrote a letter which he dictated to his scribe William W. Phelps, wherein he stated: "We are now commencing to prepare and print the New Translation."[16] Smith already revised his dictated manuscript of Genesis in his Bible revision changing some of the ages of the

---

[14] Marquardt, *Joseph Smith Revelations*, 269; LDS D&C 107:40; RLDS D&C 104:18.

[15] Marquardt, *Joseph Smith Revelations*, 270; LDS D&C 107:39-57; RLDS D&C 104:17-29.

[16] Smith to "Dear brethren in the Lord," June 15, 1835, LDS archives. See Jessee, *Personal Writings of Joseph Smith*, 363.

patriarchs prior to Noah. That the subject of patriarchs was important to him is evident from his history where it mentions that on June 21 he "preached in Kirtland on the evangelical order."[17] This was prior to Michael Chandler coming to Kirtland with the four Egyptian mummies and rolls of papyrus.

The Manuscript History, known also as the History of Joseph Smith, was compiled in 1843 for the year 1835. It records the following two entries for the month of July 1835:

I, with W.W. Phelps and O. Cowdery, as scribes, commenced the translation of some of the characters or hieroglyphics[18]

The remainder of this month, I was continually engaged in translating an alphabet to the Book of Abraham, and arranging a grammar of the Egyptian language as practiced by the ancients.[19]

Joseph Smith did not work every day with these Egyptian records. In fact because of the small number of pages we can determine that only a short time period was involved. The preliminary alphabet manuscripts, as mentioned previously, are in the handwriting of Joseph Smith, William W. Phelps, and Oliver Cowdery. These three documents of four manuscript pages each contain characters written on the left side of the page with a few words for their meaning. These manuscripts were prepared in 1835 prior to and in connection with the bound Grammar and Alphabet.

The alphabet and grammar contained two sections. In the first section the symbols copied are interpreted in connection with ancient Egypt. The second section continued that topic and then goes into a type of astronomy which was reported to have been known to the Egyptians. Joseph Smith believed that the Christian gospel had been presented to the ancient Egyptians by the Old Testament patriarch Abraham. William Phelps wrote to his wife Sally on September 11, 1835:

---

[17] Manuscript History, Book B-1:595; LDS archives; *History of the Church* 2:234.

[18] Manuscript History, Book B-1:596; *History of the Church* 2:236.

[19] Manuscript History, Book B-1:597; *History of the Church* 2:238.

Nothing has been doing in translation of the Egyptian Record for a long time, and probably will not for some time to come.[20]

Joseph Smith's journal for 1835 was commenced on September 22. The first entry was recorded by Oliver Cowdery and entries for the next two days were written by Smith. Cowdery started again recording in the journal the entries from September 25 through October 2. For nine days no work with the Egyptian records was done. Oliver Cowdery recorded the following entry in Joseph's journal:

> October 1, 1835. This after noon labored on the Egyptian alphabet, in company with brsr. [brothers] O. Cowdery and W.W. Phelps: The system of astronomy was unfolded.[21]

Six days later on October 7 Frederick G. Williams recorded at the end of that entry, "this afternoon recommenced translating the ancient records."[22] This was Smith's first opportunity to work on the alphabet or other related pages since the afternoon of October first.

It was not until October 29 that an additional scribe, Warren Parrish, was appointed to assist Joseph Smith as his personal scribe. Parrish was also involved while Joseph Smith dictated the text to his Book of Abraham. Oliver Cowdery had departed Kirtland for the east and returned back on November 20 being gone about two weeks. There is no record that Smith did any work on the alphabet from October 8-31. A revelation was given on November 14 which mentioned the calling of Warren Parrish as a scribe for Joseph Smith stating in part:

> behold it shall come to pass in his day that he shall see much of my ancient records, and shall know of hid[d]en things, and shall be endowed with a knowledge of hid[d]en

---

[20] W. W. Phelps to Sally Phelps, Sept. 11, 1835, William Wines Phelps Papers, L. Tom Perry Special Collections, Brigham Young University. See Van Orden, "Writing to Zion," *Brigham Young University Studies* 33 (1993):563.

[21] Joseph Smith Journal, 3; Jessee, *Papers of Joseph Smith* 2:45.

[22] Ibid. 2:50.

languages, and if he desires and shall seek it at my hand, he shall be privileged with writing much of my word, as a scribe unto me for the benefit of my people, therefore this shall be his calling until I shall order it otherwise, in my wisdom and it shall be said of him in a time to come, behold Warren the Lord[']s Scribe, for the Lord[']s Seer whom he hath appointed in Israel[23]

The revelation states that Parrish should see "my ancient records." This revelation documents the call of Parrish in connection with the Egyptian records. Warren Parrish's handwriting appears on the last pages of the second part of the five degrees of the Egyptian Alphabet.

As an additional scribe to Joseph Smith, Parrish had the privilege to record entries in Smith's diary. Warren wrote entries for part of October, for the complete month of November 1835, and for December 1-18, except for part of a letter copied in the journal by Frederick G. Williams for the entry of November 16. Joseph Smith was attended the School of the Prophets from November 2-13. A revelation was given on November 8 stating that William Phelps and John Whitmer were "under condemnation before the Lord" which they were for a short time.[24] On November 17 Joseph "ex[h]ibited <the Alphabet> of the ancient records to Mr. Holmes and some others."[25] Smith's journal records the work on the translation of the text of the Book of Abraham in November during a four day period.

November 19: "I returned home and spent the day in translating the Egyptian records"
November 20: "we spent the day in translating, and made rapid progress"
November 24: "in the after-noon we translated some of the Egyptian records"
November 25: "spent the day in Translating"[26]

---

[23] Marquardt, *Joseph Smith Revelations*, 276; Jessee, *Papers of Joseph Smith* 2:79.
[24] Marquardt, *Joseph Smith Revelations*, 275; Jessee, *Papers of Joseph Smith* 2:68.
[25] Ibid., 2:85.
[26] Ibid., 2:87-88, 90.

From the above journal entries and from the manuscripts of the Book of Abraham text it appears that Joseph Smith on these days dictated the final text for what is now known as Abraham 1:1 to 2:18. The first half of page one of the dictated manuscripts is in the handwriting of William W. Phelps. This was the opening portion of the Book of Abraham. About this time Smith completed his astronomy section of the alphabet as dictated to Parrish. On November 19-20 Smith apparently dictated the text to both Warren Parrish and Frederick G. Williams at the same sitting.

Warren Parrish then copied the text of the Book of Abraham from the manuscript he had previously written onto the manuscript page where Phelps started the beginning of the Book of Abraham text. It was probably on November 24 or 25 that the remaining few pages were dictated by Smith to Parrish. The translation manuscripts of the Book of Abraham were produced by dictation from Joseph Smith in November 1835 as recorded in his journal.

On November 26 Parrish recorded, "we spent the day in transcribing Egyptian characters from the papyrus."[27] This entry mentions only copying characters. Smith and Parrish were both afflicted with a cold and no work was done in connection with the dictation of the Egyptian records for November 27. The diary entry of November 28 reads, "I am conciderably [considerably] recovered from my cold, & I think I shall be able in a few days to translate again, with the blessings of God."[28] Smith was not able to return to his work on the Book of Abraham until six years later in 1842 though he spoke to the saints concerning the work. The record of his activities in connection with his Egyptian Alphabet and the Book of Abraham had already been written by his scribes as is evident from the documents which were produced.

The Book of Abraham text contains ideas that were developed from the material in the bound Egyptian Alphabet manuscript book. This close relationship is clear since the characters are the same (including those not on the Egyptian papyrus) and many of the English explanations used are from the developed text of the fifth degree.

---

[27] Ibid., 2:90.
[28] Ibid., 2:91; not included in *History of the Church* 2:321.

The first chapter of the Book of Abraham contains ideas which are already developed from the previous existing text in the dictated Egyptian Alphabet. For example, the name Abraham came from a character with the sound "Ah broam" or "Ah brah-oam" which is interpreted starting with the first degree:

1st Degree: "The Father of the faithful. The first right - The elder" (20)
2nd Degree: "a follower of righteousness" (16)
3rd Degree: "one who possesses great knowle[d]ge" (13)
4th Degree: "a follower of righteousness a possessor of greater knowledge" (9)
5th Degree: "a father of many nations a prince of peace, one who keeps the commandments of God. A patriarch a rightful heir, a high priest" (2)[29]

The Book of Abraham contains these words:

> having been myself a follower of righteousness desiring also to be one who possessed great knowledge, and to be a greater follower of righteousness, and to possess a greater knowledge, and to be a father of many nations, a prince of peace, and desiring to receive instructions, and to keep the commandments of God, I became a rightful heir, a High Priest, holding the right belonging to the fathers.[30]

There was a gap in the papyrus and a character was placed on the page even though the papyrus was broken at this spot. Here Joseph Smith, besides adding a new character, continues his dictation from the explanation worked out in the Egyptian Alphabet. This character has the sound "Iota toues-Zip Zi." Here Smith dictated how Egypt was discovered:

1st Degree: "The land of Egypt" (21)
2nd Degree: "The land which was discovered under water by a woman" (18)

---

[29] See also in the fifth degree for "Kiah abran oam," Egyptian Alphabet, 3.
[30] LDS Abraham 1:2; wording is different than Translation MS No. 1, 1.

3rd Degree: "The woman sought to settle her sons in that land. She being the daughter of Ham" (14)
4th Degree: "The land of Egypt discovered by a woman who afterwards sett[l]ed her sons in it." (10)
5th Degree: "The land of Egypt which was first discovered by a woman whter [while?] under water, and afterwards settled by her sons she being a daughter of Ham" (5)

The Book of Abraham text reads:

The land of Egypt being first discovered by a woman, who was the daughter of Ham . . . When this woman discovered the land it was under water, who afterward settled her sons in it; and thus from Ham, sprang that race which preserved the curse in the land.[31]

For a character with the sound "Zub Zool eh" the meaning in the fifth degree was explained:

In the days of the first patr[i]archs In the reign of Adam; in the days of the first patriarchs; in the days of Noah; in the blessings of Noah; in the blessings of the children of Noah; in the first blessings of men; in the first blessings of the church. (6)

Like the other examples, the Book of Abraham explains:

in the days of the first patriarchal reign, even in the reign of Adam, and also of Noah, his [Ham's] father, who blessed him with the blessings of the earth, and with the blessings of wisdom, but cursed him as pertaining to the Priesthood.[32]

While this passage may not seem clear the theme was developed in the Egyptian Alphabet as meaning that Shem

---

[31] LDS Abraham 1:23-24. For using the reported curse by Noah for supporting slavery, see, Stephen R. Haynes, *Noah's Curse: The Biblical Justification of American Slavery* (New York: Oxford University Press, 2002).
[32] LDS Abraham 1:26.

obtained the priestly blessings (the patriarchal priesthood) from under the hand of his father Noah. Joseph Smith interpreted the character with the sound "Ho-e-oop" in the fifth degree as follows:

> A prince of the royal blood, a true des[c]endant from Ham, the son of Noah, and inheritor of the Kingly blessings from under the hand of Noah, but not according to the priestly blessing, because of the tran[s]gressions of Ham, which blessings fell upon Shem from under the hand of Noah (4)[33]

The Egyptian Alphabet was a step in the process by which Joseph Smith interpreted and explained the characters for the Book of Abraham. As shown above, some of the text was first interpreted in the Alphabet. Abraham 1:26 is more understandable when it is compared to what Smith dictated to William Phelps about the blessing of Ham in the bound alphabet book.

While dictating the Book of Abraham (what is now chapter 2) Joseph Smith used the KJV Genesis as a guide and text for part of his story. The actual wording in the story suggests the use of Genesis in composing this work. This would indicate that the wording dictated was basically a copying effort of a pre-established text. At times he revised the KJV text to make it an autobiographical account by Abraham. The wording as printed in the KJV was used as part of the text Abraham supposedly wrote by his own hand. It is clear that Joseph Smith had the Bible open to the book of Genesis as he dictated this section of the Book of Abraham.

The contents of part of Translation Manuscripts Nos. 1, 2 and 3 (written in 1835) have as a source two verses of Genesis chapter 11. Also Manuscripts Nos. 1 and 2 used chapter 12 from KJV Genesis for the new Abraham story. These Translation Manuscripts are part of the writings of Joseph Smith, written by his scribes William W. Phelps, Frederick G. Williams, and Warren

---

[33] The 1830 manuscript for the revised Genesis 9:26 (KJV) reads, "And he [Noah] said blessed be the Lord God of Shem and Canaan shall be his servent [servant] and a vail [veil] of darkness shall cover him that he shall be known among all men" (Old Testament Manuscript 1, 25, RLDS archives). See also *Messenger and Advocate* 2 (April 1836):290; in *The Essential Joseph Smith* (Salt Lake City: Signature Books, 1995), 87.

Parrish. Compare the Book of Abraham text to that recorded in Genesis:

Joseph Smith's story of Abraham   Genesis, Old Testament

Abraham 2:1-2   Genesis 11:28-29
Abraham 2:3   Genesis 12:1
Abraham 2:9   Genesis 12:2
Abraham 2:11   Genesis 12:3
Abraham 2:14-15, 18   Genesis 12:4-6

The text for Abraham 2:9, 11, 14-15, 18 is found only in Translation Manuscript No. 1 (pages 8-10) written from Joseph Smith's dictation by Warren Parrish. The actual Egyptian characters used to represents the text of the Book of Abraham when translated into English by Egyptologists does not correspond to the Abraham/Genesis text or subject matter.[34]

From close examination it is correct that Egyptian documents were once in the hands of Joseph Smith. Smith possessed no knowledge of the Egyptian language at any period of time while he was studying and producing his Egyptian papers. Joseph Smith was human, however considering his claim to correctly translate Egyptian into English it offers no more than a pretended translation from the Egyptian.

These primary historical documents are important because they show that the scribes were taking dictation from Joseph Smith. The Egyptian papers, including the Egyptian Alphabet, contain the record of Joseph Smith's efforts to work with ancient documents. One of the manuscripts of the "Egyptian alphabet" contains Joseph Smith's handwriting together with the handwriting of his scribe Oliver Cowdery. These 1835 documents help us

---

[34] See studies by Robert K. Ritner, "The 'Breathing Permit of Hôr' Thirty-four Years Later," *Dialogue: A Journal of Mormon Thought* 33 (Winter 2000):97-119; Ritner, "'The Breathing Permit of Hôr' among the Joseph Smith Papyri," *Journal of Near Eastern Studies* 62 (July 2003):161-80; and Michael D. Rhodes, *The Hor Book of Breathings: A Translation and Commentary* (Provo, Utah: Foundation for Ancient Research and Mormon Studies, Brigham Young University, 2002). See chapter 21 for additional information when the Book of Abraham was published in 1842.

understand how Smith dictated the text of the Book of Mormon six years earlier. The Egyptian Alphabet and related papers are preserved manuscript texts that show how Joseph Smith produced the ideas prior to and in connection with the Book of Abraham. These records have serious implications for the dictation process of the text of the Book of Mormon.

In his work on the Book of Mormon, before Joseph Smith commenced to dictate, he reportedly transcribed an Egyptian alphabet from the record of the Book of Mormon. Lucy Mack Smith, Joseph Smith's mother, described the importance of her son copying characters of an alphabet to show to the learned. The characters were claimed to have been in the Egyptian language and were to be shown to those who professed knowledge in languages other than English. Lucy wrote in her history (dictated in 1845), the following concerning the year 1827:

> It soon became necessary to take some measures to accomplish the translation of the record into English but he [Joseph Smith] was instructed to take off a fac simile of the ~~alphabet Egyptian~~ characters <composing the alphabet which were called reformed egyptian> Alphabetically and send them to all the learned men that he could find and ask them for the translation of the same.[35]

Lucy continued her narrative concerning the Egyptian alphabet:

> Joseph started [in] Dec[ember]. for Penn[sylvania] it was agreed that Martin Har[r]is should follow him as soon as ~~he~~ <Joseph> should have sufficient time to transcribe the Egyptian alphabet which Mr. Harris was to take to the east and through the country in every direction to all who professed linguists to give them an opertunity [opportunity] of showing their talents[36]

---

[35] Anderson, *Lucy's Book*, 393.
[36] Lucy Mack Smith, Manuscript Draft. See Anderson, *Lucy's Book*, 402.

That the characters were to be from an alphabet was clear when Lucy Smith addressed the church conference in October 1845. Lucy said that she had been called "upon by Joseph to go & tell Martin Harris & family that he [Joseph] had got the Plates & he wanted him [Martin] to take an a[l]phabet of the Characters & carry them to the learned men to decypher [decipher]."[37]

Joseph Smith's father understood that the last recorded plate of the Book of Mormon contained the alphabet as he explained to Fayette Lapham about 1830: "The remaining pages [of the gold plates] were closely written over in characters of some unknown tongue, the last containing the alphabet of this unknown language."[38]

One of the learned persons to whom Martin Harris visited in 1828 was Professor Charles Anthon of New York City. Harris took with him the characters which Joseph Smith had transcribed as a sample of what was contained on the record. In two of his letters Professor Anthon wrote about the sheet of paper which contained the characters of Smith's alphabet. The first extract is from Anthon's 1834 letter and the second one was written in 1841:

This paper was in fact a singular scrawl. It consisted of all kinds of crooked characters disposed in columns, and had evidently been prepared by some person who had before him at the time a book containing various alphabets.[39]

The import of what I wrote was, as far as I can now recollect, simply this, that the marks in the paper appeared to be merely an imitation of various alphabetic characters, and had in my opinion no meaning at all connected with them.[40]

---

[37] Norton Jacob Journal, entry for Oct. 8, 1845, LDS archives.
[38] "The Mormons," *Historical Magazine* 7 (May 1870):307. See Vogel, *Early Mormon Documents* 1:462-63.
[39] Charles Anthon to Eber D. Howe, Feb. 17, 1834, published in Howe, *Mormonism Unvailed*, 271; Vogel, *Early Mormon Documents* 4:380.
[40] Anthon to Rev. T. W. Coit, April 3, 1841, *The Church Record* 1 (1841):231; Vogel, *Early Mormon Documents* 4:384-85.

These references indicate that the first thing Joseph Smith did was to prepare an alphabet to the Book of Mormon. Professor Anthon commented that the characters appeared to be various alphabetical characters.

Joseph Smith's work on his Book of Abraham Egyptian alphabet, seven years later, shows that he could not understand or interpret documents written anciently. From examinations done by Egyptologists, their studies show that Smith had not the slightest idea what the Egyptian characters meant relating to names, places, and subject matter. These manuscript pages clearly show that Joseph Smith pretended to translate Egyptian records. The claim that they had been written by the biblical Abraham is without a solid foundation.

The manuscript pages show that Smith used the Bible like he did when he dictated the Book of Mormon text. In April 1829 Joseph Smith received a revelation for his scribe Oliver Cowdery. Cowdery evidently tried to dictate some words but could not. Smith explained in the revelation:

> But, behold, I say unto you, that you must study it out in your mind; then you must ask me if it be right, and if it is right I will cause that your bosom shall burn within you; therefore, you shall feel that it is right. But if it be not right you shall have no such feelings, but you shall have a stupor of thought that shall cause you to forget the thing which is wrong; therefore, you cannot write that which is sacred save it be given you from me.[41]

If the above is a correct description of how Joseph Smith produced the Book of Mormon text then it is an insight into the process of Joseph Smith's revelations, restoration of biblical texts, the Egyptian Alphabet, and the Book of Abraham. Whatever came into the bosom of Smith and was dictated was considered to be inspired. John Whitmer who had been another scribe when Joseph Smith dictated the Book of Mormon, and later some of his revision of the Bible, wrote in his history:

---

[41] Marquardt, *Joseph Smith Revelations*, 37; LDS D&C 9:8-9; RLDS D&C 9:3.

Joseph the Seer saw these Record[s] and by the revelation of Jesus Christ could translate these records, which gave an account of our forefathers, ~~even abraham~~ Much of which was written by Joseph of Egypt who was sold by his brethren Which when all translated will be a pleasing history and of great value to the saints.[42]

In 1829 when Joseph Smith dictated portions of the text of the Book of Mormon he read from the common Bible of the day, the King James Version. This became part of the process in which he composed the Book of Mormon. Passages in the Book of Mormon, when compared with the KJV, show that the Bible was used when it was being dictated and recorded by a scribe.

Only part of the original 1829 manuscript of the Book of Mormon pages of the dictated text is extent. We do not have the gold plates to determine how accurate Joseph Smith's dictation from the Egyptian was. But we do have the Egyptian papyri, Joseph Smith's Egyptian Alphabet, and the Book of Abraham Translation Manuscripts. These later manuscripts together with Joseph Smith's journal and knowing when his scribes worked with him all place the dictation process in the last half of 1835. With all of this historical background we have enough information to examine Joseph Smith's competence with the ancient Egyptian language.

None of Joseph Smith's scribes or witnesses to the plates of the Book of Mormon saw Joseph Smith consult the gold plates when he dictated the text. Just as no one said they saw Joseph Smith use the Bible when he dictated the Book of Mormon, no one said they saw him used the Bible as he dictated part of the text of the Book of Abraham. Warren Parrish described the time when he was taking dictation from Joseph:

> I have set [sic] by his [Joseph Smith's] side and penned down the translation of the Egyptian Hieroglyphicks [sic] as he claimed to receive it by direct inspiration from Heaven.[43]

---

[42] Westergren, *From Historian to Dissident*, 167.
[43] Parrish to the Editor, Feb. 5, 1838, *Painesville Republican* 2 (Feb. 15, 1838).

This clearly indicates that Parrish sat by Smith's side, took down the dictation from him as he interpreted the Egyptian writing by direct inspiration. This is the same way that Joseph Smith dictated the Book of Mormon text in 1829. It appears that the same method was used for both the Book of Mormon and the Book of Abraham. By making a transcript of an alphabet to the Egyptian language for these records it is clear that both books were to be in a form of ancient Egyptian. The manuscripts of the Book of Abraham and related papers serve as a good monitor to know how well Joseph Smith understood and interpreted ancient Egyptian characters.

The clear implication of a study of the Joseph Smith Egyptian Papers is that Joseph Smith had no knowledge of the ancient Egyptian language. Smith did not know how to translate ancient documents. If as John Whitmer and Warren Parrish suggests, Joseph Smith received a revelation regarding the contents of the Egyptian records then the revelation gave the wrong meaning. It does not matter how Joseph Smith arrived at his interpretation of Egyptian characters, his reading of the characters is at variance with the ancient text and is incorrect. The real value of the Egyptian Alphabet and the Translation Manuscripts of the Book of Abraham is that they show us that Joseph Smith can not get the interpretation of the Egyptian right through either linguist study or inspiration.

This places the question of how reliable his work on the Book of Mormon would be. The Book of Mormon is represented to have been written by the hand of a man named Mormon in a form of Egyptian. Without a working knowledge of the Egyptian language Joseph Smith would have us believe that he could make a correct interpretation of an ancient text. Whatever would come from his mouth as he dictated the Book of Mormon, Egyptian Alphabet, and Book of Abraham was considered inspired.

All indications are that since Smith did not really translate from an ancient language in his work on the Book of Abraham he could not be trusted in his earlier dictation, when he reportedly had a record written in the same basic language. The material he produced indicates that he had a vivid and creative imagination as the dictated text to his religious documents shows. David P. Wright, Associate Professor of Bible and Ancient Near East at

Brandeis University, Waltham, Massachusetts, wrote concerning Joseph Smith works including the Book of Abraham:

> this work is basically a reworking of the English biblical text (some Hebrew learning is exhibited as well, but not much). Consequently, in all his work [the Book of Mormon, Joseph Smith Revision of the Bible and the Book of Abraham] there is a consistency in approach and method: he is not working in any of them with ancient languages (except for the bit of Hebrew in Abraham) and in all of them there is attention (to a greater or lesser degree) to revising or responding to the KJV. (This common character of all the works shows, by the way, that Smith, and not some other nineteenth-century personage, is the author of the Book of Mormon.)[44]

Returning from a church mission on November 25, 1836 Wilford Woodruff went to the House of the Lord (Kirtland Temple) and viewed the records and mummies. He wrote in his journal, "we [Abraham Smoot and Woodruff] then visited the upper rooms & there viewed four Egyptian Mum[m]ies & also the Book of Abram [Abraham] Written by his own hand & not ownly [only] hieroglyphicks but also many figures that this precious treasure Contains are Calculated to make a lasting impression upon the mind which is not to be erased."[45]

William S. West of Braceville, Ohio, came to Kirtland to see what he could learn firsthand about the Mormons. After paying twenty-five cents for seeing the temple, Egyptian mummies and records, his curiosity was so much excited that he went again the next day to examine them once more. The following is his account:

> They say that the mummies were Egyptian, but the records are those of Abraham and Joseph . . . These records were

---

[44] David P. Wright, "'In Plain Terms that We May Understand': Joseph Smith's Transformation of Hebrews in Alma 12-13," in Brent Lee Metcalfe, ed., *New Approaches to the Book of Mormon: Explorations in Critical Methodology* (Salt Lake City, Signature Books, 1993), 211.
[45] Wilford Woodruff Journal, entry for Nov. 25, 1836, LDS archives; Kenney, *Wilford Woodruff's Journal* 1:107.

torn by being taken from the roll of embalming salve which contained them, and some parts entirely lost, but Smith is to translate the whole by divine inspiration, and that which is lost, like Nebuchadnezzar's dream, can be interpreted as well as that which is preserved; and a larger volume than the Bible will be required to contain them. Is it possible that a record written by Abraham, and another by Joseph, containing the most important revelation that God ever gave to man, should be entirely lost by the tenacious Israelites, and preserved by the unbelieving Egyptians, and by them embalmed and deposited in the catacombs with an Egyptian priest[?] . . . I venture to say no, it is not possible. It is more likely that the records are those of the Egyptians[46]

The portion of the Book of Abraham interpreted in 1835 was published in March 1842 at Nauvoo, Illinois.[47] Joseph Smith dictated additional information concerning Abraham. This included three illustrations from the Book of Abraham with its publication. Chapter 21 will contain a discussion of the facsimiles and text.

---

[46] Wm. S. West, *A Few Interesting Facts Respecting the Rise, Progress and Pretensions of the Mormons* (1837), 5-6.

[47] *Times and Seasons* 3 (March 1, 1842):704-706, Joseph Smith editor.

17

House of the Lord: The Kirtland Temple

In the latter part of September 1832 those who were to go out to preach were instructed: "he that receiveth you not, go away from him, alone by yourselves and cleanse your feet even with water, pure water, whether in heat or in cold and bare [bear] testamony [testimony] of it unto your father which is in heaven and return not again unto that man, and in whatsoever village or city ye enter do likewise."[1] The instruction relating to dusting and cleansing the feet was not something new but had been taught in July 1830.[2] This in a different way would become a ceremony for temple worship in Kirtland.

Eight days after the birth of his son, Joseph the third, Joseph Smith was speaking and singing in tongues according to Zebedee Coltrin. Coltrin wrote in his journal for November 14-18, 1832:

came to Kirtland to Brothers Joseph Smith and heard him Speak with Tongues and Sing in Tongues also 15 the 16 the Br Hyrum Smith was called to lay hands on Br Rigdon child with me and he was healed 17 the 18 the went to meating [meeting] the Lord blest [blessed] us much and in the Eaving [Evening] had meatig [meeting] Br Green Speak in tongs [tongues] and Br Joseph Smith with tongs [tongues] also by the Holy ghost[3]

The next month a two day conference of high priests was held in Joseph Smith's translating room. Smith commenced dictating a revelation which was finished on the second day. A commandment from the Lord was for the first laborers "in this last

---

[1] Marquardt, *Joseph Smith Revelations*, 216; LDS D&C 84:92-93; RLDS D&C 83:16 (Sept. 22-23, 1832).
[2] Marquardt, *Joseph Smith Revelations*, 70; LDS D&C 24:15; RLDS D&C 23:6. Dusting of feet is mentioned in Matthew 10:14; Mark 6:11.
[3] Zebedee Coltrin Journal, LDS archives.

kingdom" to organize and sanctify the priesthood leaders. They were to purify themselves and cleanse their hands and feet "that I may make you clean, that I may testify unto your father, and your God and my God, that you are clean from the blood of this wicked generation."

The high priests were to hold a special meeting called a "solemn assembly." They were to seek learning by study and faith. The revelatory message continued:

> establish an house, even an house of prayer, an house of fasting, an house of faith, an house of Learning, an house of glory, an house of orde[r] an house of God, that your incomings may be in the name of the Lord, that your outgoing[s] may be in the name of the Lord, that all your salutations may be in the name of the Lord, with uplifted hands unto the most high[4]

On January 3, 1833 instructions were given to establish what is termed a school of the prophets where those men in the ministry could learn their duties and share in spiritual experiences. There was to be a "house prepared for the presidency" for the school of the prophets where church officers could receive instructions. Upon entering the school the first minister was to "offer himself in prayer upon his knees before God, in token of the everlasting covenant." When subsequent members came into the meeting the teacher or first minister would say with uplifted hands:

> art thou a brother or brethren[?], I salute you in the name of the Lord Jesus Christ, in token of the everlasting covenant, in which covenant I receive you to fellowship, in a determination that is fixed, immovable, and unchang[e]able, to be your friend and brother through the grace of God in the bonds of Love, to walk in all the commandments of God blameless, in thanksgiving for ever and ever; Amen.[5]

---

[4] Marquardt, *Joseph Smith Revelations*, 225-26, 228; LDS D&C 88:70, 74-75, 117, 119-20; RLDS D&C 85:19-20, 36 (Dec. 27-28, 1832).
[5] Marquardt, *Joseph Smith Revelations*, 229; LDS D&C 88:127, 131, 133; RLDS D&C 85:39-41.

Samuel H. Smith who arrived in Kirtland with Orson Hyde in late December 1832 from their mission to the eastern states wrote in his journal, "thus the School of the Prophets was established & the School of the Prophetss [Prophets] continued a Short time & then it was a[d]journed for a season."[6] At that time the school of the prophets usually met in the second floor above the Newel K. Whitney store. Previous to building the House of the Lord the place where they met was considered a "house of God."[7]

On January 20 Hyrum Smith recorded that he "Baptised two in to the visible Church of Christ in <the> Beautiful waters of Kirtland the S[c]hool of Christ Began in Kirtland myself Spa[ke] with tounges [tongues] and many others."[8] A conference of high priests met on January 22 in the council room. Joseph Smith opened the meeting and "spake in an unknown Tongue he was followed by Br[other] Zebede[e] Coltrin and he by Bro William Smith after this the gift was poured out in a miraculou[s] manner until all the Elders obtained the gift together with several of the members of the Church both male& female. Great and glorious were the divine manifestation of the Holy Spirit, Praises were sang to God & the Lamb besides much speaking & praying all in tongues." The next morning after the conference opened the minutes stated that they:

> proce[e]ded to washing hands, faces, & feet in the name of the Lord as commanded of God each one washing his own after which the president [Joseph Smith] gurred [girded] himself with a towel and again washed the feet of all the Elders wiping them with the towel, his father [Joseph Smith Sr.] presenting himself. the President asked of him a blessing before he would wash his feet which he obtained by the laying on of his father['s] hands, pronouncing upon his head that he should continue in his Priest['s] office untill Christ come."[9]

---

[6] Samuel H. Smith Journal, winter 1832-33, LDS archives.
[7] Smith to Phelps, Jan. 1, 1833, Jessee, *Personal Writings of Joseph Smith*, 293.
[8] Hyrum Smith Journal, entry for Jan. 20, 1833, Hyrum Smith Papers, L. Tom Perry Special Collections, Harold B. Lee Library, Brigham Young University.
[9] Kirtland Council Minute Book, 7, LDS archives.

Afterwards President Smith told the elders that they were "all clean from the blood of this generation." At the end of the day they partook of the Lord's Supper. The school continued at various times and included secular education.

On February 27, 1833 Joseph Smith sang praises by the gift of tongues about Enoch of old and then interpreted it. Smith told of Enoch standing upon a mountain and gazing upon nature. The Kirtland Revelations Book recorded what Smith translated concerning ancient Enoch, which included:

he saw yea he saw and he glorif[i]ed God the salvation of his people his city caught up through the gospel of Christ he saw the begin[n]ing the ending of man he saw the time when Adam his fath[er] was made and he saw that he was in eternity before a grain of dust in the ballance [balance] was weighed[10]

The same day Smith received a revelation known as the word of wisdom given for the temporal salvation of the saints. Church members were told that wine or strong drink was not good but wine "of your own make" could be used for the sacrament of the Lord's Supper. Strong drinks could be used for "the washing of your bodies." Tobacco is not good "but is an herb for bruises," for sick cattle and to be used with judgment. Wholesome herbs were God ordained, also fruit, flesh of beasts, and fowls. They were to be used sparingly. The revelation continued:

all grain is good for the food of man as also the fruit of the vine that which yieldeth fruit whether in the ground or above the ground nevertheless wheat for man and corn for the ox and oats for the horse and rye for th[e] fowls & for swine and for all beasts of the field and barley for all useful animals and for mild drink[s] as also other grain

---

[10] Kirtland Revelations Book, 48, LDS archives. See Marquardt, *Joseph Smith Revelations*, 232; *The Evening and the Morning Star* 1 (May 1833):8 [p. 96]; and Michael Hicks, *Mormonism and Music: A History* (Urbana: University of Illinois Press, 1989), 36. Not included in 1835 D&C.

If the saints keep these sayings they were promised to "receive health in their naval and marrow to their bones," find wisdom and knowledge. The Lord also promised, "I the Lord give unto them a promise that the destroying angel shall pass them as the Children of Israel and not slay them."[11]

Early in June the word of the Lord said, "I gave unto you a commandment that you should build an hous[e] in the which house I design to endow those whom I have chosen with power from on high." The dimensions of the inside (inner court) were to be fifty-five feet wide and sixty-five feet long. The lower part of the inside court was to be dedicated for "your sacrament offering and for your preaching and your fasting and your praying and the offering up your most holy desires" to the Lord. The second floor of the inner court was to be dedicated for "the school of mine Apostles."[12] The conference appointed Joseph Smith, Sidney Rigdon, and Frederick G. Williams to work on a draft of the inner court of the house.[13]

Preparation for building the House of the Lord was being made by early June and the first stone was laid on July 23, 1833.[14] Other buildings were to be constructed such as a house for the church presidency and a building for printing. Only the building for printing was completed. The structure was used as an office for the presidency and for the printing establishment.

This religious edifice to be built in Kirtland was known by various names including the House of the Lord, stone house, chapel, and the Kirtland Temple. The first main floor was used for divine worship, the second main floor was intended to be used for the school of the prophets but was not completed, and the attic was divided into five rooms that could be used for the church presidency and priesthood quorums. Various classes were held in the attic floor included instructions in the Hebrew language.

---

[11] Marquardt, *Joseph Smith Revelations*, 233; LDS D&C 89:6-8, 16-18, 21; RLDS D&C 86:1, 3.

[12] Marquardt, *Joseph Smith Revelations*, 240; LDS D&C 95:8, 16-17; RLDS D&C 92:2-3 (June [1-3], 1833).

[13] Kirtland Council Minute Book, 12.

[14] "The House of God," *Messenger and Advocate* 1 (July 1835):147.

415

On January 16, 1836 a meeting was held preparing priesthood leaders for the forthcoming endowment. Oliver Cowdery wrote:

> Met in the evening with bro. Joseph Smith, jr. at his house, in company with bro. John Corrill, and after pure water was prepared, called upon the Lord and proceeded to wash each other's bodies, and bathe the same with whiskey, perfumed with cinnamon. This we did that we might be clean before the Lord for the Sabbath, confessing our sins and covenanting to be faithful to God.[15]

Another meeting was held on January 21 in the loft or office garret of the printing office behind the House of the Lord. At three o'clock in the afternoon Joseph Smith and others "attended to the ordinance of washing our bodies in pure water, we also perfumed our bodies and our heads, in the name of the Lord." In the evening Joseph Smith met with members of the church presidency in "the west school room in the Chapel [the Temple] to attend to the ordinance of annointing [anointing] our heads with holy oil" Joseph Smith consecrated the oil. Those in attendance anointed Joseph Smith Sr. with oil and blessed him as patriarch and that he would attend to his duties. Joseph Sr. anointed his son and sealed upon him "the blessings, of Moses, to lead Israel in the latter days."

Joseph Smith Jr. then obtained a vision of the celestial kingdom: "I saw the beautiful streets of that Kingdom, which had the appearance of being paved with gold — I saw father Adam, and Abraham and Michael and my father and mother, my brother Alvin that has long since slept, and marv[e]lled how it was that he had obtained an inheritance <in> that Kingdom, seeing that he had departed this life, before the Lord <had> set his hand to gather Israel <the second time> and had not been baptised for the remission of sins." Alvin Smith died twelve years earlier in November 1823. Smith said he heard the Lord say to him:

---

[15] Oliver Cowdery's Sketch Book, postscript to entry for Jan. 16, 1836, LDS archives, as cited in Leonard J. Arrington, "Oliver Cowdery's Kirtland, Ohio, 'Sketch Book,'" *Brigham Young University Studies* 12 (Summer 1972):416.

all who have died with[out] a knowledge of this gospel, who would have received it, if they had been permitted to tarry, shall be heirs of the celestial kingdom of God — also all that shall henseforth [henceforth], with<out> a knowledge of it, who would have received it, with all their hearts, shall be heirs of that kingdom, for I the Lord <will> judge all men according to their works according to the desires of their hearts[16]

Joseph then said "I also beheld that all children who die before they ar[r]ive to the years of accountability, are saved in the celestial kingdom of heaven."[17] Many of the brethren had glorious visions including seeing the Savior and holy angels. They prophesied and shouted hosannas to God.

As preparations was being made for the dedication of the House of the Lord a dedicatory prayer was written out. This occurred on March 26 when the following brethren assisted in writing the prayer: Joseph Smith, Oliver Cowdery, Sidney Rigdon, Warren A. Cowdery, and Warren Parrish.[18] For the dedication service the Melchizedek pulpits located on the west side of chapel, from the top or highest pulpit (first pulpit) to the lowest, were assigned to the church presidents in the following manner:

First Pulpit: Frederick G. Williams; Joseph Smith Sr., and William W. Phelps
Second Pulpit: Sidney Rigdon, Joseph Smith Jr., and Hyrum Smith
Third Pulpit: David Whitmer, Oliver Cowdery, and John Whitmer[19]

---

[16] Marquardt, *Joseph Smith Revelations*, 278. LDS D&C 137:4-9 omitted the words "and Michael."

[17] Marquardt, *Joseph Smith Revelations*, 278; LDS D&C 137:10. The age of eight years for children being accountable was designated in February-March 1831 (Old Testament Dictated Manuscript, OT 1, 41; Gen. 17:11 [JST]); and LDS D&C 68:25, 27; RLDS D&C 68:4 (Nov. [1-3], 1831).

[18] Arrington, "Oliver Cowdery's Kirtland, Ohio, 'Sketch Book,'" *Brigham Young University Studies* 12 (Summer 1972):426

[19] See Jessee, *Papers of Joseph Smith* 2:192-93.

The first dedicatory meeting was held on Sunday, March 27, 1836 in the House of the Lord. "The congregation began to assemble before 8 o'clock A. M. and thronged the doors until 9, when the Presidents of the church who assisted in seating the congregation were reluctantly compelled to order the door-keepers to close the doors; every seat and aisle were crowed."[20] It was estimated that about one thousand persons were in attendance. Donations were accepted at the door.

The service commenced by reading scripture, singing by the choir, and prayer. Sidney Rigdon, first counselor in the First Presidency, gave a lengthy two and a half hour discourse. Afterwards Joseph Smith was accepted by vote as a prophet and seer. A hymn was sung and then Smith "presented the several Presidents of the church" to be vote upon as "being equal with himself, acknowledging them to be Prophets and Seers." Each priesthood quorums voted separately and then the congregation voted. The vote was unanimous in each instance.

President Joseph Smith spoke and prophesied. The Lord's anointed bore testimony "to this generation, if they receive it, they shall be blessed, but if not, the judgments of God will follow close upon them, until that city or that house, that rejects them, shall be left desolate." After another hymn was sung the dedicatory prayer was read by Joseph Smith. The prayer included a supplication of empowerment to church ministers that their anointing might be sealed upon them with power from on high. Joseph asked: "let the gift of tongues be poured out upon thy people, even cloven tongues as of fire, and the interpretation thereof. And let thy house be filled, as with a rushing mighty wind, with thy glory." The choir then sung the hymn "The Spirit of God like a fire is burning" to the tune Hosanna. The following verse was included:

> We'll wash, and be wash'd, and with oil be anointed
> Withal not omitting the washing of feet:
> For he that receiveth his PENNY appointed,
> Must surely be clean at the harvest of wheat.[21]

---

[20] The proceedings were printed in *Messenger and Advocate* 2 (March 1836):274-81, emphasis omitted.

[21] *A Collection of Sacred Hymns, for the Church of the Latter Day Saints*, 121; also in *Messenger and Advocate* 2 (March 1836):280. See Crawley, *A*

The Eucharist (Sacrament or Lord's Supper) was administered. Don Carlos Smith blessed the bread and wine which was then distributed to the members in the congregation. A few brethren bore their testimony including Frederick G. Williams who said "that a Holy Angel of God, came and set between him and J[oseph]. Smith sen. while the house was being dedicated." Sidney Rigdon made some closing remarks and ended the meeting with prayer. Afterwards the Hosanna shout was given with uplifted hands:

Hosanna! Hosanna! Hosanna to God and the Lamb
Amen, Amen, Amen!
Hosanna! Hosanna! Hosanna to God and the Lamb
Amen, Amen, Amen!
Hosanna! Hosanna! Hosanna to God and the Lamb
Amen, Amen, Amen!

The amount of donations collected to help defray the expensive of building the house was nine hundred sixty-three dollars. That evening a meeting was held with the official members. Oliver Cowdery wrote about the meeting: "I saw the glory of God, like a great cloud, come down and rest upon the house, and fill the same like a mighty rushing wind. I also saw cloven tongues, like as of fire rest upon many, (for there were 316 present,) while they spake with other tongues and prophesied."[22]

Three days later on the evening of March 30, after a day of fasting, the bread and wine was brought in and blessed. Joseph Smith made some remarks, "I want to enter into the following covenant, that if any more of our brethren are slain or driven from their lands in Missouri by the mob that we will give ourselves no rest until we are avenged of our enimies [enemies] to the uttermost." This was "sealed unanimously by a hosanna and Amen."[23]

Descriptive Bibliography of the Mormon Church Volume One 1830-1847, 59. Stephen Post purchased his copy of the hymnal on April 1, 1836.

[22] Arrington, "Oliver Cowdery's Kirtland, Ohio, 'Sketch Book,'" *Brigham Young University Studies* 12 (Summer 1972):426.

[23] Jessee, *Papers of Joseph Smith* 2:206.

John Whitmer explained that the ordinance of washing of feet "belongs only to ordained members and not the whole church."[24] Stephen Post wrote in his journal the events of the evening, "the ordained members met in the house of the Lord to attend to the last ordinance of the endowment viz: the ordinance of the washing of feet this ordinance is administered to none but those who are clear from the blood of the generation in which they live."[25]

The brethren of the different quorums stayed overnight experiencing visions of the Savior and angels. The members of the quorums, Post recorded, were told not to leave the building unless necessary:

after the washing the Brethren commenced prophesying for the spirit of prophecy was poured out upon the congregation: the house was divided into 4 parts by the curtains & they prophesied, spake and sang in tongues in each room. we fasted until even[ing] when we partook of bread & wine in commemoration of the marriage supper of the Lamb. Now having attended through the endowment I could form an idea of the endowment anciently for God[']s ordinances change not.

The next Sunday, April 3, the saints again met in the House of the Lord. Stephen Post recorded in his journal:

P.M. partook of the sacrament confirmed a large number & blessed those little children that had not been blessed. the curtains were unfolded & confirmation, sacrament &c was attended to in 4 parts at the sa[me] time, the presidency took the pulpit during the confirmation & blessing of the children after which the curtains were raised & the people dismissed.[26]

---

[24] Westergren, *From Historian to Dissident*, 174.

[25] Stephen Post Journal, entry for March 30, 1836, LDS archives.

[26] Ibid., entry for April 3, 1836.

Joseph Smith's journal recorded in third person, probably from a first person account, a number of visionary experiences by Smith and Oliver Cowdery by their spiritual eyes. After rising from prayer a vision was opened to them:

> The vail [veil] was taken from their minds and the eyes of their understandings were opened. They saw the Lord standing upon the breast work of the pulpit before them, and under his feet was a paved work of pure gold, in color like amber: his eyes were as a flame of fire; the hair of his head was like the pure snow, his countenance shone above the brightness of the sun, and his voice was as the sound of the rushing of great waters, even the voice of Jehovah, saying. I am the first and the last, I am he who liveth, I am he who was slain. I am your Advocate with the Father.[27]

Jesus told them that their sins were forgiven and that he accepted this house and his name would be here. This vision closed and Moses appeared and gave them "the keys of the gathering of Israel from the four parts of the Earth and the leading of the ten tribes from the Land of the North" Next Elias appeared "and committed the dispensation of the gospel of Abraham."[28] Finally Elijah, the Prophet, stood before Smith and Cowdery in fulfillment of the promise of Malachi of turning the hearts of fathers and children to each other. They were told, "Therefore, the keys of this dispensation are committed into your hands, and by this ye may know that the great and dreadful day of the Lord is near, even at the doors."[29]

This is the last known group vision Oliver Cowdery and Joseph Smith received together. A few days later a non-member wrote a letter telling about the Mormons at Kirtland and their spiritual experiences in the temple:

---

[27] For a similar description see Revelation 1:14-16.

[28] The mention of "Elias" appearing is curious since in a subsequent vision "Elijah" stood in their view. Elias is used for Elijah in the Greek New Testament. Whether this is a scribal error made in the journal is not known.

[29] Marquardt, *Joseph Smith Revelations*, 279-80. See Malachi 4:5-6.

Do you know anything about the Mormons, if not I will inform you a little about them they are a sect who believe in the book of Mormon as a part of the Bible the author and proprietor of which is Joseph Smith Jun who is their Prophet and Seer

They have lately had what they term a solemn assembly this was at the completion of the lower story of the Temple which is finished in a very singular order having four Pulpits on each end of the House and curtains between each also curtains dividing the house in the centre They have had wonderful manifestations there of late behind the curtains this was in the night their meeting held for several nights in succession none but the Prophets and Elders were admitted the number of the Prophets now amount to twelve some can see angels and others cannot they report that the Savior appeared personly [personally] <with angels> and endowed the Elders with power to work Miracles[30]

The building of the house or temple cost more than $30,000. Meetings were continually held in the temple. As explained in the *Messenger and Advocate* in 1837:

On Thursday P.M. a prayer meeting is held in the lower part of the house where any and all persons may assemble and pray and praise the Lord. This meeting, though free for all, is conducted more particularly by J[oseph]. Smith senior, the patriarch of the church.[31]

A visitor, William West, came to Kirtland in 1837 and inquired about the Kirtland Temple and some of the beliefs of the saints. The inscription located high on the front of the temple read:

HOUSE OF THE LORD
BUILT BY THE CHURCH OF THE
LATTER DAY SAINTS. A. D. 1834.

---

[30] Lucius Pomeroy Parsons to "Dear Sister" [Pamelia Parsons], April 10, 1836. Courtesy of the Western Reserve Historical Society, Cleveland, Ohio.
[31] "Our Village," *Messenger and Advocate* 3 (Jan. 1837):444.

On the lower floor of the temple were bench seats which could be moved so that an individual could face either the west or east end of the building where the presiding officer was officiating. William West describes the appearance of the inside of the sacred House of the Lord:

> The vails [veils] by which the house is divided into quarters, are of canvass, painted white, and are rolled up or drawn at pleasure, by means of cords which come down the pillars concealed, and are worked with cranks; also each official seat is completely vailed [veiled], both sides and front; these are also worked with cords which come to the seats concealed. The second story is not finished; but is to be of the same pattern except the official seats which are not so much elevated.[32]

Spiritual gifts continued to be exercised by the saints. Wilford Woodruff wrote in early January, "I repaired to the house of the Lord for a Prayer meeting at 2 o[']clock PM. We had a good time. One man gave us an account of the general gathering of Israel in the gift of tongues. I interpreted the Substance of the same."[33] The next day he visited the office of the Kirtland Safety Society Bank which issued the first money to Jacob Bump. Wilford was present when Joseph Smith spoke upon the subject of the bank:

> I also he[a]rd President Joseph Smith jr. declare in the presence of F[rederick G.] Williams, D[avid]. Whitmer, S[ylvester?]. Smith, W[arren]. Parrish, & others in the Deposit Office that he had received that morning the Word of the Lord upon the Subject of the Kirtland Safety Society. He was alone in a room by himself & he had not ownly [only] the voice of the Spirit upon the Subject but even an audable [audible] voice. He did not tell us at that time what the LORD said upon the subject but remarked that if we

---

[32] Wm. S. West, *A Few Interesting Facts Respecting the Rise, Progress and Pretensions of the Mormons*, 4-5.
[33] Kenney, *Wilford Woodruff's Journal* 1:120, entry for Jan. 5, 1837.

would give heed to the Commandments the Lord had given this morning all would be well.

Woodruff then recorded in his journal this prayer: "May the Lord bless Joseph with all the Saints & support the above named institution & Protect it so that every weapen [weapon] formed against it may be broaken [broken] & come to nought [naught] while the Kirtland Safety Society shall become the greatest of all institutions on EARTH."[34] On January 31 Wilford Woodruff recorded another meeting in the house where he heard addresses from Joseph Smith and Sidney Rigdon:

> on the temporal business of the Church & Petitioned for a Charter to the Assembly of the State for the Kirtland Safety Society & the presidency of the Church bought the Monroe [Bank] Charter & we all lent a hand in esstablishing [establishing] it that it might be benifical [beneficial] to us in forwarding the building of the temporal Kingdom.[35]

Other visitors to Kirtland included S. A. Davis, a Universalist minister and editor of *The Glad Tidings, and Ohio Christian Telescope* published in Pittsburgh, Pennsylvania. He wrote: "On the whole, our visit to Kirtland, was a pleasant one, notwithstanding I am far from believing their doctrine as any person can be, yet I must say that they manifested a spirit of liberality, and Christianity, which many of their bitterest persecutors would do well to imitate."[36]

William West discussed one of the printed revelations that included the heading: "Revelation given to Enoch, concerning the order of the church for the benefit of the poor." There was no location, date, or indication that the revelation related to appointing members of the Kirtland United Firm their stewardship or property. Some of the saints believed that it was a revelation given to ancient Enoch while others knew it was a revelation given to

---

[34] Ibid., 1:120, entry for Jan. 6, 1837.

[35] Ibid., 1:124, entry for Jan. 31, 1837. The Monroe Bank was located in the state of Michigan.

[36] "From the Glad Tidings, of March 14," as cited in *Messenger and Advocate* 3 (April 1837):491.

Joseph Smith but disguised with pseudonyms. That West found out some of the pseudonyms for a contemporary situation shows his diligence in determining for himself the context of this revelation.

West reported, "I conversed with two men in particular, who were very free to instruct me in the way of their belief, so I asked them the meaning of these names: one of them began to tell me that they were the names of certain persons who lived in the days of Enoch: I asked him if Pelagoram did not mean Sidney Rigdon, upon which the other advised me to learn things of less importance before I sought into such deep matters, said he was in haste, and they both left me."[37] One paragraph published in the 1835 Doctrine and Covenants (with known meanings included in brackets) is as follows:

> And again, let my servant Ahashdah [Newel K. Whitney] have appointed unto him, the houses and lot where he now resides, and the lot and building on which the Ozondah [store] stands; and also the lot which is on the corner south of the Ozondah [store]; and also the lot on which the Shule [ashery] is situated: And all this I have appointed unto my servant Ahashdah [Newel K. Whitney], for his stewardship, for a blessing upon him and his seed after him, for the benefit of the Ozondah [mercantile establishment] of my order [firm], which I have established for my stake in the land of Shinehah [Kirtland]; yea, verily this is the stewardship which I have appointed unto my servant Ahashdah [Newel K. Whitney]; even this whole Ozondah [mercantile] establishment, him and his agent, and his seed after him, and inasmuch as he is faithful in keeping my commandments, which I have given unto him, I will multiply blessings upon him, and his seed after him, even a multiplicity of blessings.[38]

---

[37] West, *A Few Interesting Facts Respecting the Rise, Progress and Pretensions of the Mormons*, 13.

[38] 1835 D&C 98:7; LDS D&C 104:39-42, pseudonyms omitted in 1981 LDS edition; RLDS 101:7, pseudonyms retained in RLDS text and explained in the introduction to that section. See Marquardt, *Joseph Smith Revelations*, 257. The revelation is dated April 23, 1834.

William West discussed the revelation with Ebenezer Barr and wrote about the conversation:

> Ebenezer Barr, of whom I requested an explanation of this revelation, read it in full, and then handed me the book, saying there it is.
> I told him that I wanted to know the meaning of those words.
> "O! said he that is another thing."
> Can't you tell me what they mean?
> "I shall not."
> Are they the names of men who live in Kirtland, or did they live in the days of Enoch?
> "They are names of certain persons who live in Kirtland."
> Who are they?
> "I shall not tell you."
> Why?
> "Because if I should you would sound it to the four winds: it is not to be made known to the world."[39]

In preparation for another Solemn Assembly to be held on April 6, 1837 in the House of the Lord members of priesthood quorums who were not in Kirtland in the spring of 1836 would received their endowment. Wilford Woodruff's wrote about his experience with others in his quorum, "After washing our bodies from head to foot in soap & watter [water] we then washed ourselves in clear watter [water] next in perfumed spirits."[40]

The quorums of priesthood repeated this ordinance the next day and then they were anointed with oil and received a blessing by the laying on of hands which was sealed upon their heads. On the day of the assembly Joseph Smith addressed the priesthood holders. Speaking concerning the seventies Smith said:

> The seventies are also members of the same priesthood, are a sort of traveling council, or priesthood, and may preside

---

[39] West, *A Few Interesting Facts Respecting the Rise, Progress and Pretensions of the Mormons*, 14.
[40] Kenney, *Wilford Woodruff's Journal* 1:128, entry for April 3, 1837.

over a church or churches until a high priest can be had. The seventies are to be taken from the quorum of elders and are not to be high priests. They are subject to the direction and dictation of the twelve, who have the keys of the ministry.[41]

There were five presidents of the first quorum of seventies who had previously been ordained high priests but were ordained seventies in early 1835. Joseph Smith released the presidents who were already high priests and replaced them in 1837. Hazen Aldrich, one of the presidents released, wrote: "Joseph first charged us to ordain the Seventies Highpriests & afterwards dropped 5 of us that was presidants [presidents] becaus[e] we were Highpriests or in otherwords ordained 5 others and left us; without giving any explination [explanation] why he done so."[42]

President Smith mentioned the temporal affairs of the church "stating the causes of the embarrassments of a pecuniary nature that were now pressing upon the heads of the church." He said that more houses must be built and "observed that large contracts had been entered into for land on all sides where our enemies had signed away their right." Continuing he said:

> We are indebted to them to be sure, but our brethren abroad have only to come with their money, take these contracts, relieve their brethren of the pecuniary embarrassments under which they now labor, and procure for themselves a peaceful place of rest among us. He then closed at about 4 P. M. by uttering a prophesy saying this place must be built up, and would be built up, and that every brother that would take hold and help secure and discharge those contracts that had been made, should be rich."[43]

---

[41] "Anniversary of the Church of Latter Day Saints," *Messenger and Advocate* 3 (April 1837):487.

[42] Aldrich to James J. Strang, April 1846, James Jesse Strang Collection, Beinecke Rare Book and Manuscript Library, Yale University, New Haven, Connecticut. Aldrich wrote about why he discontinued attending church, "I stopped becaus[e] the Gentiles conducted [t]hemselves better than the church."

[43] "Anniversary of the Church of the Later Day Saints," *Messenger and Advocate* 3 (April 1837):487-88.

Church debts included $6,000 relating to persecutions in Jackson County, Missouri; nearly $13,000 for provisions for the building of the House of the Lord; and an unpublished amount for the purchase of land in the Kirtland area. The amount of indebtedness would have been well over $20,000. Rigdon "uttered a prediction, that if all would exert themselves as they might, three months should not pass away before we can shout victory over the adversary."[44]

The next day Wilford Woodruff went to the House of the Lord with Milton Holmes and Joseph B. Noble to worship. Woodruff recorded: "We entered one of the stands within the veils & fell upon our knees & Satan appeared also but not to worship God but to deprive us of the privilege. Satan strove against us with great power by tempting & otherwis[e]. He at one time drove me from my stand while I was striving with my brethren to enter into the visions of heaven." Freeman Nickerson joined the group in prayer and "Satan departed, temp[t]ation found no place is our h[e]arts The power of God rested upon us & we were baptized with the Holy Ghost & the Spirit of God was like fire shut up in our bones."[45]

In 1838 most of the saints departed Kirtland for Missouri. Those who stayed worshiped in the Lord's house intermittently. Churches under various leaders used the temple as a meeting place, for conferences, and at times tried to obtain possession of the structure.[46] Today the House of the Lord (Kirtland Temple) is open, by appointment, to all churches and factions of the Restoration movement originating with Joseph Smith.

---

[44] Ibid., 3 (April 1837):488-89.

[45] Kenney, *Wilford Woodruff's Journal* 1:136-37, entry for April 7, 1837.

[46] Christin Craft Mackay and Lachlan Mackay, "A Time of Transition: The Kirtland Temple, 1838-1880," *John Whitmer Historical Association Journal* 18 (1998):133-48.

18

Problems at Kirtland

The redemption of Zion was the important object of Joseph Smith since the expulsion of church members from Jackson County in the fall of 1833. In preparation to put the saints back upon their own lands Smith set up a War Department consisting of church leaders. On September 22, 1835, eight years after going to the Manchester, New York hill with his wife Emma, Joseph Smith received a prophetic blessing for David Whitmer. Oliver Cowdery recorded, "This day Joseph Smith, jr. labored with Oliver Cowdery, in obtaining and writing blessings." There is no indication that David Whitmer was present when Smith had Cowdery write David's blessing. The wording of the blessing included, "for behold, he it is, whom the Lord hath appointed to be captain of his host."[1] Two days later, on September 24 Joseph Smith wrote in his journal:

This day the High Council met at my house to take into conside[r]ation the redeemtion [redemption] of Zion and it was the voice of the spirit of the Lord that we petition to the Governer [Governor][2] that is, those who have been driven out <should> do so to be set back on their Lands next spring and we go next season to live or dy [die] in Jackson County we truly had a good time and Covena[n]ted to strug[g]le for this thing u[n]till death shall desolve [dissolve] this union and if one falls that the rest be not discouraged but pesue [pursue] this object untill it is ac[c]omplished which may God grant u[n]to us in the name of Christ our Lord

---

[1] Patriarchal Blessing Book 1:13, LDS archives. See "David Whitmer's Blessing," *The Return* 2 (Feb. 1890):212-13, Davis City, Iowa and Cook, *David Whitmer Interviews*, 261. The commandment to meet and organize a war department was given about this time.

[2] Daniel Dunklin was the governor of Missouri.

This day drew up an Arti<c>le of inrollment [enrollment] for the redem[p]tion of Zion that we may obtain volenteers [volunteers] to go next Spring to <Mo> I ask in the name of Jesus that we may obtain Eight hundred men <or one thousand> well armed and that they may ac[c]omplish this great work even so Amen[3]

John Whitmer wrote of this meeting in his history:

And it came to pass on the 24 day of Sept 1835, on which day we met in course at the house of J[oseph]. Smith Jr. the Seer, where we according to a previous commandment given, appointed David Whitmer Capt[ain] of the Lord[']s host and Prs. F. G. Williams and Sidney Rigdon his assistants. And Pres. W. W. Phelps, myself, and John Corrill as an assistant quorum, and Joseph Smith Jr. the seer to stand at the head and be assisted by Hyrum Smith and Oliver Cowd[e]ry. This much for the war department by revelation.[4]

There were organized two quorums presided over by Joseph Smith, assisted by Hyrum Smith and Oliver Cowdery. The first one was with David Whitmer, as captain, with Williams and Rigdon as assistants. The second quorum consisted of William Phelps, John Whitmer, and John Corrill. Though no formal army was in place this did prepare the leadership, like Zion's Camp in 1834, for possible military confrontation if a need existed.

The redemption of Zion, set for September 11, 1836, was still being looked forward to at this time. On March 13, 1836 it was the resolution of the presidency and members of the twelve "to emigrate on or before the 15 of May next, if kind providence smiles, upon us and openes [opens] the way before us."[5]

In July 1836 members of the church presidency took a trip east to New York and Massachusetts. Loans had previously been

---

[3] Jessee, *Papers of Joseph Smith* 2:41-42, entry for September 24, 1835. It appears that the twelve high counselors did not meet with the presidency. There are no minutes recorded in the Kirtland Council Minute Book for this date.
[4] Westergren, *From Historian to Dissident*, 173.
[5] Jessee, *Papers of Joseph Smith* 2:188.

made by church leaders and this created a large debt owed to creditors. The reason for the trip east has been variously described as for business, for health, to locate a treasure (money), for missionary work, or that included a few of these motives. The importance of this journey is indicated by who went, by the time away from church headquarters, and by the expense it took to traveled from Kirtland to New York City, then to Boston, and finally to Salem, Massachusetts. Oliver Cowdery, Joseph Smith, Sidney Rigdon, and Hyrum Smith made the trip. Cowdery wrote two letters that were published in the *Messenger and Advocate* which told what cities the four visited.

Two documents originating from Joseph Smith were written in August and help us understand the primary reason for the month long trip. One is a revelation Smith received at Salem; the other is a personal letter to Emma written thirteen days later. Both of these documents told about the object Joseph Smith was seeking. There was plenty of time to tour interesting sites, look into possible church business ventures or loans, and even take out a loan.

Oliver Cowdery wrote to his brother Warren the nature of the trip and said it was for his health. This is indicated in the introduction to the first letter, "that his former degree of health may be restored." The following extracts from Oliver's letters indicate the public reason for Sidney Rigdon and himself going on the trip, "Brother R's and my own health," "my ill health," "ill state of my health," "recess from business, has so far been to my health."[6] Brother "R" is Sidney Rigdon.

In Oliver Cowdery's letters he describes visiting some sites of interest but he does not discuss things beyond making the trip for health reasons. Once he described his traveling companions as "Our other brethren." According to Cowdery the leading brethren left on the evening of July 25 from Fairport Harbor on a steamer for Buffalo, New York. On board some of the brethren discussed religion or as Cowdery wrote they contended for the faith. They traveled to Rochester, Utica, Albany, and finally to New York City

---

[6] Cowdery to "Dear Brother" [Warren A. Cowdery], 3 [4] Aug. 1836 in *Messenger and Advocate* 2 (Sept. 1836):372-73, 375; Cowdery to "Dear Brother," 24 Aug. 1836, Ibid., 3 (Oct. 1836):388.

where they spent about a week. Cowdery wrote, "The great exchange, once the pride and boast of the sellers and buyers of cash, is a heap. There is money yet in Wall street, and 'Draper, Underwood,' and others, ready to help incorporated bodies to plates and dyes, to make more" money.[7] The two companies mentioned did engravings.

From New York City the group took a boat to Providence, Rhode Island and then took the railroad to Boston, Massachusetts. Oliver was enjoying himself:

> It would be altogether uninteresting to lead you all the round of scouting to, and bathing in the sea, and how beneficial a change of climate, as well as a recess from business, has so far been to my health.

From Boston they traveled a short distance to Salem but Cowdery does not state what the group did in that town but does quote material relating to some history dealing with the alleged crime of witchcraft in that city. The reason why the church leaders were in Salem was explained many years later by Ebenezer Robinson who worked with Don Carlos Smith in the Kirtland printing office. Robinson wrote in his personal recollection:

> A brother in the church, by the name of Burgess, had come to Kirtland and stated that a large amount of money had been secreted in a cellar of a certain house in Salem, Massachusetts, which had belonged to a widow, and he thought he was the only person now living, who had knowledge of it, or to the location of the house. We saw the brother Burgess, but Don Carlos Smith told us with regard to the hidden treasure.[8]

Arriving in Salem Joseph Smith received a revelation concerning their destination. The word received was shrouded in mystery since the initial object and reason for being in Salem was

---

[7] Ibid., 2 (Sept. 1836):375, emphasis omitted..

[8] Ebenezer Robinson, ed., "Items of Personal History of the Editor," *The Return* 1 (July 1889):105.

the hope to secure needed money. The revelatory document commenced:

I the Lord your God am not displeased with your coming this Journey, notwithstandi[n]g your follies I have much treasure in this city for you, for the benefit of Zion; and many people in this city whom I will gather out in due time for the benefit of Zion, through your instrumentality. Therefore it is expedient that you should form acquaintance with men in this city, as you shall be led, and as it shall be given you.

Smith was told not to worry about his debts or about Zion which date of redemption was drawing closer:

And it shall come to pass, in due time, that I will give this city into your hands, that you shall have power over it, insomuch that they shall not discover your secret parts; and its wealth, pertaining to gold and silver, shall be yours. Concern not yourselves about your debts, for I will give you power to pay them. Concern not yourselves about Zion, for I will deal merciful[ly] with her.

Tarry in this place and in the regions round about, and the place where it is my will that you should tarry, for the main, shall be signalized unto you by the peace and the power of my Spirit, that shall flow unto you.

This place you may obtain by hire &c. And inquire diligently concerning the more ancient inhabitants and founders of this city, for there are more treasures than one for you, in this city: Therefore, be ye as wise as serpents and yet without sin, and I will order all things for your good as fast as ye are able to receive them: Amen.[9]

It appears that Joseph Smith considered the report he heard from brother Burgess credible enough to make the trip to Salem. The church was in serious debt and this seemed to be a quick venture to obtain money with not a lot of effort. Whether Joseph

---

[9] Marquardt, *Joseph Smith Revelations*, 281; LDS D&C 111 (Aug. 6, 1836).

considered, if they found any money, it would be theirs to keep is not known. It would appear that Burgess came to Kirtland and discussed the matter with Joseph Smith with the intent that if they actually found the money they would keep it. Otherwise Burgess could have told someone else about the money and ask if there was a reward for turning it in to the proper authorities.

While in Salem one of the places visited was the East India Marine Society Museum (now Peabody Museum). Oliver Cowdery and Sidney Rigdon viewed the museum on August 6 while Joseph Smith visited it three days later.[10] Hyrum Smith and Oliver Cowdery went to Boston and were there on August 8 according to Brigham Young.[11]

A week later on August 17 Cowdery and Rigdon signed a promissory note for one hundred dollars from Jonathan Burgess: "For value received we promise to pay Jonathan Burgess one hundred dollars, one year from date with use."[12]

Two days later, on August 19, Joseph wrote a letter to Emma that was hand carried by Hyrum Smith to her. Joseph wrote about the "great object of our mission" and having "found the house since Bro[ther]. Burgess left us." The letter shows how important it was to locate the house:

> Bro. Hyrum is about to start for home before the rest of us, which seems wisdom in God, as our business here can not be determined as soon as we could wish to have it. . . . With regard to the great object of our mission, you will be anxious to know. We have found the house since Bro. Burgess left us, very luckily and providentially, as we had one spell been most discouraged. The house is occupied, and it will require much care and patience to rent or buy it. We think we shall be able to effect [affect] it; if not now within the course of a few months. We think we shall be at

---

[10] They signed their names in the "Album, for the Use of Visitors," under Aug. 6 and 9, 1836, Peabody Museum, Salem, Massachusetts.

[11] Brigham Young Journal, Aug. 8, 1836, LDS archives.

[12] Promissory note of August 17, 1836, Joseph Smith Collection, LDS archives.

within the course of a few months. We think we shall be at home about the middle of September.[13]

Joseph Smith did not preach in Salem during the two weeks he was there. Rather forty-three years old Sidney Rigdon delivered a lecture at the Lyceum on Saturday, August 20. One of the local newspapers, the *Essex Register*, reported:

MORMONISM. Notices were sent round on Saturday, that Mr. Rigdon, of Ohio, would preach at the Lyceum that afternoon, on the subject of the Christian religion. Having understood that he was a *Mormonite*, we went to the Lyceum, expecting to hear something on the subject of the peculiar doctrines of that sect, and perhaps to get a view of the "Mormon Bible," translated from the Golden Plates said to have been discovered by Jo. Smith, their prophet! The preacher was a man of very respectable appearance, apparently about 40 years of age, and very fluent in his language. He commenced by reading the 1st chapter of the Epistle to the Galatians—then followed a prayer—he then began his discourse, founded upon Galatians i. 8; "Though we, or an angel from heaven, should preach any other gospel than that which we have preached to you, let him be accursed." He said we hear a great deal of want of charity, he thought the Saviour and his apostles were the most uncharitable persons he ever heard of.[14]

A few days later it was reported in the same newspaper that the group left Salem:

MR. RIGDON, the Mormon preacher, who introduced himself at our Lyceum last week, has since left the city, with his three or four associates. It is said they retain possession of the tenement leased by them in Union street,

---

[13] Smith to "My beloved wife," Aug. 19, 1836, Salem, Massachusetts, as cited in "Letters of Joseph Smith, The Martyr," *Saints Herald* 26 (Dec. 1, 1879):357; Jessee, *Personal Writings of Joseph Smith*, 389-90.

[14] *Essex Register* 36 (Aug. 22, 1836):3, Salem, Massachusetts, emphasis retained.

and intent to return to this city next spring. None knew the names, character, or object of these men, until the day RIGDON held forth, although they had been for a week or two in the city.[15]

While in Salem for about seventeen days Joseph Smith did not locate the cache of money but considered returning in the spring of 1837 if necessary. This expectation never materialized. Since Hyrum Smith departed the three remaining members of the party spent a number of days in Boston. The *Boston Daily Times* told about a meeting held on August 24 where Rigdon was answered. Unlike Salem Joseph Smith was recognized: "Joe Smith, the original founder of the sect and the high priest and prophet of his tribe of impostors, was also present, and was obliged to undergo the "searching operation" of divers questions which were propounded to him by those who knew more of his history than he was aware.[16]

Oliver Cowdery told of "Having just returned from a visit to the navy yard, Bunker hill monument and the burnt convent, in company with bro. R[igdon]."[17] The three men arrived back at Kirtland in September. Later in 1841 elder Erastus Snow commenced missionary work in Salem having received a copy of the revelation from Hyrum Smith.

In November 1836 Oliver Cowdery went to Philadelphia to obtain printing plates for the bank while Orson Hyde was to travel to Columbus to petition the Ohio legislature for an act of incorporation. A meeting of the stockholders of the Kirtland Safety Society Bank was held on November 2 where the preamble and articles of the society were read three times and adopted. The first article stated, "The capital stock of said Bank shall not be less than four millions of dollars; to be divided into shares of fifty dollars each; and may be increased to any amount, at the discretion of the directors."[18]

---

[15] Ibid., 36 (Aug. 25, 1836):2.

[16] *Boston Daily Times* 2 (Aug. 26, 1836):2, Boston.

[17] Cowdery to "Dear Brother" [Warren A. Cowdery], Aug. 24, 1836, *Messenger and Advocate* 3 (Oct. 1836):392.

[18] *Latter Day Saints' Messenger and Advocate. Extra*, Dec. 1836, LDS archives.

Orson Hyde did not return from Columbus with a charter for the bank and a special meeting was held on January 2, 1837. Members of the society met and voted to annul the old constitution and adopted new articles of agreement. The wording of article one was changed to read in part, "The capital stock of said society or firm shall not be less than four million of dollars."[19] The bank was changed in the new articles to "society or firm." On February 10 an amendment was added to a legislative banking bill but was defeated.

It is of interest that for the period June 17, 1836 to May 10, 1837 there are no minutes kept of meetings in the Kirtland Council Minute Book. Scribes kept no journal for Joseph Smith from April 4, 1836 to January 1838 when Joseph left Kirtland. Three months after Smith, Rigdon, and Cowdery returned from Salem church members were reminded to repent of their sins and backslidings so that the judgment of God would not fall upon them.[20] This warning was given while the second edition of the Book of Mormon was being printed.

On January 10, 1837, Brigham Young, one of the twelve apostles, "gave us an interesting exhortation & warned us not to murmer [murmur] against Moses (or) Joseph or the heads of the Church." The next week Wilford Woodruff attended a meeting of the seventies where President David Whitmer gave a lecture:

He warned us to humble ourselves before God lest his hand rest upon us in anger for our pride & many sins that we were run[n]ing into in our days of prosperity as the ancient Nephites did & it does now appear evident that a scourge awates [awaits] this stake of Zion even Kirtland if their [there] is not great repentance immediately

At the House of the Lord on Sunday the twenty-second Parley P. Pratt warned the saints to humble themselves before God, feed the poor, cloth the needy, and put away all their sins.[21] In February another meeting was held in the sacred building. Wilford

---

[19]*Messenger, Extra.—March, 1837*, LDS archives; also in *Messenger and Advocate* 3 (March 1837):475.
[20] Kenney, *Wilford Woodruff's Journal* 1:111, entry for Dec. 11, 1836.
[21] Ibid., 1:121-22, entries for Jan. 10, 17, and 22, 1837.

Woodruff wrote that Joseph Smith spoke to the saints for several hours. He wrote, "Joseph had been absent from Kirtland on business for the Church, though not half as long as Moses was in the mount, & many were stir'd up in their hearts & some were against him as the Israelites were against Moses."[22]

Internal strife arose in the church early in 1837, stemming from problems with the church's financial institution, the "Kirtland Safety Society Anti-Banking Company." Stanley B. Kimball explained the situation:

The bank had difficulties from the beginning. The State of Ohio refused the Mormons a charter, and the bank was poorly underwritten. Heber [C. Kimball], for example, subscribed to $50,000 worth of shares for only $15 in cash. In all, 200 church members subscribed to 79,420 shares, worth at face value approximately $3,854,000 at $50 par value, which was backed up with only $20,725 cash. The bank, furthermore, was weakened by speculation, mismanagement, and dishonesty.[23]

While in the Kirtland Temple, Joseph Smith "proclaimed that Severe Judgment awaited those Characters that professed to be his friends & friends to humanity & the Kirtland Safety Society But had turned tr[a]itors & opposed the Currency & its friends which has given power in to the hands of the enemy & oppressed the poor Saints."[24] Even visitors to Kirtland noticed the dissatisfaction among the saints. William S. West wrote:

When I was in Kirtland, I ascertained from a variety of sources, too numerous to mention, that the Mormons had been in serious difficulty, many had been dissatisfied with their leaders, and wanted a new prophet, but the majority adhered to Smith. One day, when I went to the Temple, I

---

[22] Ibid., 1:125, entry for 19 Feb. 1837.
[23] Stanley B. Kimball, *Heber C. Kimball: Mormon Patriarch and Pioneer* (Urbana: University of Illinois Press, 1981), 40. See also Kimball, "Sources on the History of the Mormons in Ohio: 1830-1838," *Brigham Young University Studies* 11 (Summer 1971):531-33.
[24] Kenney, *Wilford Woodruff's Journal* 1:138, entry for April 9, 1837.

saw a number of men about it, busy in conversation, Smith was among them, and the topics of discussion were the bank, money, the steam saw mill, etc.; the prophet was kept very busy, but at last he started toward the bank, when a man said to him, "brother Joseph, I want to speak with you a minute," upon which he exclaimed, "my God, I wish I was translated!" He did not stop to speak with him, but went on grumbling that every one wanted to speak with him a minute, etc.[25]

On July 23, 1837, Joseph Smith received a revelation for Thomas B. Marsh, president of the Quorum of the Twelve Apostles:

Exalt not yourselves; rebel not against my servant Joseph [Smith, Jr.] . . . Behold vengeance cometh speedily upon the inhabitants of the earth . . . And upon my house [Kirtland Temple] shall it begin and from my house shall it go forth saith the Lord. First among those among you saith the Lord; who have professed to know my name and have not known me and have blasphemed against me in the midst of my house saith the Lord.[26]

A church conference met on September 3, 1837 in the Kirtland Temple, where objections were made to the high council positions of John Johnson, Joseph Coe, Martin Harris, and Joseph Kingsbury.[27] John Corrill wrote about these events:

During their mercantile and banking operations they not only indulged in pride, but also suffered jealousies to arise among them, and several persons dissented from the church, and accused the leaders of the church with bad

---

[25] West, A *Few Interesting Facts, Respecting the Rise, Progress and Pretensions of the Mormons*, 14.
[26] Marquardt, *Joseph Smith Revelations*, 282-83; LDS D&C 112:15, 24-26; RLDS D&C 105:6, 9-10.
[27] Kirtland Council Minute Book, 234-38. See also letter copied into the Scriptory Book of Joseph Smith in Jessee, *Papers of Joseph Smith* 2:217-19. It appears that Joseph C. Kingsbury made reconciliation with the church.

management, selfishness, seeking for riches, honor, and dominion, tyranising [tyrannizing] over the people, and striving constantly after power and property.

On the other hand, the leaders of the church accused the dissenters with dishonesty, want of faith, and righteousness, wicked in their intentions, guilty of crimes, such as stealing, lying, encouraging the making of counterfeit money, &c.; and this strife or opposition arose to a great height, so that, instead of pulling together as brethren, they tried every way in their power, seemingly, to destroy each other; their enemies from without rejoiced at this, and assisted the dissenters what they could, until [Joseph] Smith and Rigden [Sidney Rigdon] finally were obliged to leave Kirtland, and, with their families, came to Far West, in March or April 1838.[28]

Thomas B. Marsh wrote a letter to Wilford Woodruff telling about the split in the church:

it seems that [Warren] Parrish, J[ohn]. F. Boynton, Luke Johnson, Joseph Coe, and some others, united together for the overthrow of the church. President [Joseph] Smith, and his company, returned [to Kirtland], on, or about the 10th of December [1837]; soon after which this dissenting band, openly, and publicly, renounced the church of Christ, of Latter Day Saints, and claimed themselves to be the old standard; called themselves the church of Christ, excluded that of Saints, and set at naught Br[other]. Joseph [Smith], and the whole church, denounced them as heretics.[29]

During the week of December 24-30, 1837, twenty-eight members were cut off from the church or excluded (excommunicated) by the High Council of Kirtland. It is not known if any of these church members were present at this

---

[28] John Corrill, *A Brief History of the Church of Christ of Latter Day* Saints, 27. Smith arrived in Far West, Missouri on March 14, 1838 (Jessee, *Papers of Joseph Smith* 2:213).

[29] Marsh to Woodruff, no date, in *Elders' Journal of the Church of Jesus Christ of Latter Day Saints* 1 (July 1838):36-37, Far West, Missouri.

meeting. John Smith, in a letter to his son George A. Smith, explained:

> the spiritual condition at this time is gloomy also. I called the High Council together last week and laid Before <them> the case of a compan<y> of Decenters [Dissenters] 28 persons where [were] upon after mature Discussion proceeded to cut them off from the chh [church]; the Leaders were Cyrus Smalling[,] Joseph Coe[,] Martin Harris[,] Luke Johnson[,] John Boynton and W[arren] W Parrish. we have cut off Between 40 & 50 from the Chh [Church] Since you Left[30]

Vilate Kimball wrote to her husband Heber in England: "the leaders of this band is Martin Harris, Warren Parrish, Joseph Coe, Luke Jo[h]nson, and John Boynton. (I have no doubt but it will pain your heart to read these two last names; but so it is.) They have by their stratagem drawn away many and some whom I believe are honest (but such I think will soon return)."[31]

On January 7, 1838, Joseph Smith received a revelation for Edward Partridge instructing: "let my people be aware of dissentiors [dissenters] among them, lest the enemy have power over them; Awake my shepherds and warn my people! for behold the wolf[32] cometh to destroy them,—receive him not."[33]

Five days later (January 12), a revelation to the church presidency said: "Thus Saith the Lord Let the presidency of my Church take their families as soon as it is practicable and a door is open for them and moove [move] unto the west [Far West] as fast as the way is made pla[in] before their faces and let their hearts be comforted for I will be with them."[34] Joseph Smith left Kirtland about 10 o'clock that night.[35]

---

[30] John and Clarissa Smith to George A. Smith, Jan. 1, 1838, George A. Smith Papers, LDS archives. Added material to letter by Andrew Jenson not included.

[31] Vilate Kimball to Heber C. Kimball, January 19-29, 1838, LDS archives.

[32] David W. Patten stated on February 5, 1838 that the wolf "was the dissenters in Kirtland" (Cannon and Cook, *Far West Record*, 138).

[33] Marquardt, *Joseph Smith Revelations*, 284.

[34] Ibid., 286.

[35] Manuscript History B-1:780; *History of the Church* 3:1.

Shortly after the departure of Smith a notice was posted on the outside of the Kirtland Temple by these dissenters, calling for a meeting of the "Church of Christ." In accordance with Ohio law, trustees were chosen and the original church name was incorporated, with Joseph Coe, Martin Harris, and Cyrus Smalling as trustees. The records of Geauga County reported the action:[36]

State of Ohio} Be it known that before me Warren Geauga County ss. } A. Cowdery a Justice of the Peace in and for Kirtland Township in said County personally appeared Joseph Coe, Martin Harris & Cyrus Smalling and took the following oath to wit; You and each of you do swear in the presence of Almighty God, that you will support the Constitution of the United States and the constitution of the state of Ohio, and will faithfully discharge your duties as Trustees of the Church of Christ in Kirtland township in said County to the best of your abilities
Kirtland Jany 18th. 1838. W.A. Cowdery J.P.

State of Ohio } ss. To the Clerk of the Court of Common
    Geauga County } Pleas in said County.
We the undersigned Trustees of the Church of Christ do certify under our hands & seals that we do recognize the name of the Church of Christ and that the above proceedings, have been had, and said Church is situated in Kirtland Township in said County.

Joseph Coe   [Seal]
Martin Harris   [Seal]
Cyrus Smalling [Seal]

Kirtland Jany 18. 1838.

Hepzibah (Hepsy) Richards wrote her brother, Willard Richards, concerning the events that recently occurred at Kirtland:

---

[36] Geauga County, Ohio, Execution Docket 1831-1835, microfilm # 1,289,257, item 1, Family History Library. This entry was located by Lachlan Mackay, Director of the Kirtland Temple Historic Center, Kirtland, Ohio in 1996.

A large number have dissented from the body of the church and are very violent in their opposition to the President [presidency, viz., Joseph Smith, Jr., Sidney Rigdon, and Hyrum Smith] and all who uphold them. They have organized a church and appointed a meeting in the house [Kirtland Temple] next sabbath. Say they will have it, if it is by the shedding of blood. They have the keys already.

The printing-office has been attached on a judgment that [Grandison] Newel held against the Presidents of K[irtland] money. Last monday it was sold at auction into the hands of Mr. Millican [Nathaniel Milliken], one of the dissenters. At one o[']clock the night following cousin Mary waked me, and said that Kirtland was all in flames. It proved to be the Printing-office—the fire was then in its height and in one hour it was consumed with all its contents. The Temple and other buildings badly scorched. Tuesday eve a meeting was held and a patrol consisting of 21 men, 3 for each night in the week, chosen to guard the city to prevent further destruction by fire. A part of these men are members of the church—a part dissenters.[37]

Benjamin F. Johnson explained who burned the facility:

The printing office and material which our enemies thought to use to bolster up a church organization opposed to the Prophet was set on fire by Bro Lyman R. Sherman and destroyed.[38]

Lyman Sherman and others were brought before Warren A. Cowdery, justice of the peace, for setting the fire that destroyed the

---

[37] Hepzibah Richards to Willard Richards, Jan. 18-19, 1838, original LDS archives, as cited in Kenneth W. Godfrey, Audrey M. Godfrey, and Jill Mulvay Derr, eds., *Women's Voices: An Untold History of the Latter-day Saints, 1830-1900* (Salt Lake City: Deseret Book, 1982), 71.

[38] "A Life Review," Benjamin Franklin Johnson Papers, 24, LDS archives. The top of the manuscript page noted "Printing office burned by L R Sherman." See Benjamin F. Johnson, *My Life's Review* (Independence, Missouri: Zion's Printing and Publishing Co., 1947), 29-30.

printing office and bookbindery. They were discharged because "no facts were elicited that went too [to] convict the prisoners of the crime charged in the complaint, either as principle or accessories."[39]

Parley P. Pratt, one of the Council of the Twelve Apostles, was married to Thankful Halsey for nine years and they were expecting the birth of another child. While giving birth to a baby boy Thankful died. This was on March 24, 1837 and Parley named the child after himself.[40] After returning from a trip to Canada Pratt married Mary Ann Frost Stearns on May 14, 1837.[41] Parley Pratt wrote years later:

> About this time, after I had returned from Canada, there were jarrings and discords in the Church at Kirtland, and many fell away and became enemies and apostates. There were also envyings, lyings, strifes and divisions, which caused much trouble and sorrow. By such spirits I was also accused, misrepresented and abused. And at one time, I also was overcome by the same spirit in a great measure, and it seemed as if the very powers of darkness which war against the Saints were let loose upon me. But the Lord knew my faith, my zeal, my integrity of purpose, and he gave me the victory.[42]

But at the time Parley P. Pratt was upset with the church leadership. On May 23 Pratt wrote a letter to Joseph Smith expressing his disapproval of how Smith and Sidney Rigdon were conducting business affairs. Parley started his letter: "As it is difficult to obtain a personal interview with you at all times, by reason of the multitude of business in which you are engaged, you will excuse my saying in writing what I would otherwise say by word of mouth." He wrote sharply to Joseph that he believed that the whole scheme of "speculation in which we have been engaged, is of the devil." He was convinced that Joseph and Sidney "both by

---

[39] Oliver Cowdery's Docket Book, January 17-19, 1838, typed copy, original in Huntington Library.

[40] "Obituary," *Messenger and Advocate* 3 (April 1837):496.

[41] "Hymeneal," Ibid., 3 (May 1837):512.

[42] *Autobiography of Parley P. Pratt*, 144.

precept and example, have been the principa[l] means in leading this people astray."

Parley said he was upset that Joseph had sold to him and others three lots of land at the extraordinary "price of $2000 dollars, which never cost you 100 dollars." Parley was concerned because this action would ruin him and his family. The personal notes of indebtedness were turned over by Smith to "the mercy of the bank." Parley considered this "taking advantage of your brother by an undue religious influence."[43] Pratt's letter closed with a post script: "Do not suppose for a moment that I Lack any Confidence in the Book of Mormon or Doctrine and Covenants Nay It is my firm belief in those Records that hinders my Belief In the course we have Been Led of Late."[44]

Later at Far West, Missouri, Pratt after his reconciliation with Joseph Smith wrote an explanation of his earlier May 1837 letter and said that it was published without his permission. He wrote that the letter was not a true copy and had been altered. He admitted that he had written the letter yet he had expressed his "entire confidence in the faith of the church." He stated that the leaders were liable to errors and mistakes "in things which were not inspired from heaven; but managed by their own judgement." He concluded, "I no longer censure them [Smith and Rigdon] for any thing that is past."[45]

The same spirit of murmuring since February was reaching a heightened state by the end of May. At the worship service of May 28 Joseph Smith spoke in his defense and Sidney Rigdon, as Joseph's spokesman, spoke in favor of Smith's integrity. In addition to Parley P. Pratt, charges were filed against Frederick G. Williams of the First Presidency, David Whitmer of the extended church presidency, Lyman E. Johnson of the Quorum of the Twelve, and Warren Parrish a seventy and former scribe of Joseph Smith.

---

[43] Pratt to "Dear Brother" [Joseph Smith Jr.], May 23, 1837, as cited in *Zion's Watchman*, March 24, 1838, New York City. The letter was handwritten and some words misspelled or hard to read. *Naked Truths About Mormonism* 1 (April 1888):4, stated that Pratt's original letter or a copy of it was in the Lake County Historical Society. Present location unknown.

[44] The post script was not included in the printing of Pratt's letter in *Zion's Watchman*. It was included in *Naked Truths About Mormonism* 1 (April 1888):4.

[45] "To the Public," *Elders' Journal* 1 (Aug. 1838):50.

Wilford Woodruff wrote the following in his journal about the high council meeting. The part in angled brackets for this particular journal entry was written in Taylor shorthand:

> May 29th I met in the house of the Lord to attend an important Conference or meeting of the high Councel [Council] to attend to some important business of the Church. Let memory speak upon this subject. Two <of the presidency> two <of the Twelve and> one <of the seventy were stood before the Council for [agression?]>. It was considered not <lawful to> try <the president> before the high Council but before the Bishop. The Presidents withdrew. The council closed without transacting business.[46]

The High Council of Kirtland met in the Lord's House with Sidney Rigdon presiding. The charge made by five church members against Frederick G. Williams, David Whitmer, Parley P. Pratt, Lyman Johnson, and Warren Parrish stated they believed "their course for some time past has been injurious to the Church of God in which they are high officers."[47] Presidents Williams and Whitmer asked whether they should be tried before the present council.

One of the high counselors, John P. Greene, gave "his opinion that the present council was not the proper authority to try Presidents Williams & Whitmer." It was decided by a majority of the council that they could not conscientiously proceed to try Frederick G. Williams and David Whitmer. They were then discharged.[48]

In the afternoon with Sidney Rigdon and Oliver Cowdery presiding, high counselor Martin Harris "motioned that Prest. F G Williams take a seat with the Presidents." Williams took his seat and now presided with Rigdon and Cowdery. The minutes state the following concerning Parley P. Pratt:

---

[46] Kenney, *Wilford Woodruff's Journal* 1:147-48, entries for May 28-29, 1837. It is possible that the word "agression" should be "transgression."
[47] Kirtland Council Minute Book, 226, LDS archives.
[48] Ibid., 228.

Eld[er]. P. P. Pratt then arose and objected to being tried by President Rigdon or Joseph Smith Jr. in consequence of their having previously expressed their opinion against him, stating also that he could bring evidence to prove what he then said

Sidney Rigdon finally said "he could not conscientiously proceed to try the case and after a few remarks left the stand." After some remarks, Oliver Cowdery also left the stand. Frederick Williams, the remaining president, said he "should be unwilling to preside in the case and left the stand." The minutes kept by Warren Cowdery read, "The council and assembly then dispersed in confusion."[49] There was no judgment against any of the persons who were brought to trial. On the same day Orson Pratt, Parley's brother, together with Lyman E. Johnson (both members of the twelve) preferred charges to Bishop Newel K. Whitney against Joseph Smith. The document reads:

To the Bishop & his council in Kirtland the Stake of Zion
We prefer the following charges against Pres. Joseph Smith Jr. viz. for lying & misrepresentation – also for extortion – and for speaking disrespectfully against his brethren behind their backs.

Lyman E. Johnson

Kirtland May 29th 1837   Orson Pratt

Warren Parrish also preferred charges the same day against Sidney Rigdon "for expressing an unbelief in the revelations of God, both old and new, also an unbelief in the agency of man and his accountability to God, or that there is Such a principle existing as Sin. – and also for lying & declaring that God required it at his hands." In addition another Apostle, Luke S. Johnson, preferred charges against Joseph Smith Sr. "for closing the doors of the House of the Lord against the high council."[50]

---

[49] The High Council Minutes for May 29, 1837 are contained in Kirtland Council Minute Book, 226-30.
[50] The three statements are in Newel K. Whitney Collection, L. Tom Perry Special Collections, Harold B. Lee Library, Brigham Young University.

Mary Fielding wrote to her sister about going "to the house of the Lord and found that Elder P P Pratt had taken upon himself the Services of the morning. we sat and heard him deliver a very plausable [plausible] decourse [discourse] he labored throughout two hour[s] that nearly all the Church had departed from God and that Brother J. S [Joseph Smith] had committed great sins." Mary said that when Orson Pratt began to speak "I and a great many more left the House." She reported that she heard that Elder Warren Parrish addressed the people and that the meeting broke up "for the first time since the House of <the> Lord was built without commemorating the Lord[']s Supper. many tears ware [were] <that> day shed by those who had come up here to worship God <in> his <house> but could not have the priviledge [privilege]."[51] In her July letter Mary Fielding wrote that Orson Pratt withdrew his charge and did not know anything personally against Joseph Smith.[52]

Parley P. Pratt explained that he went privately to President Smith and asked forgiveness:

I went to brother Joseph Smith in tears, and, with a broken heart and contrite spirit, confessed wherein I had erred in spirit, murmured, or done or said amiss. He frankly forgave me, prayed for me and blessed me. Thus, by experience, I learned more fully to discern and to contrast the two spirits, and to resist the one and cleave to the other.[53]

Leaving Kirtland Parley P. Pratt went to New York City and during August and September he wrote what became an important missionary booklet titled *A Voice of Warning and Instruction to All People.*[54]

---

[51] Mary Fielding to Mercy Fielding Thompson, circa June 15, 1837, Mary Fielding Smith Collection, LDS archives.

[52] Mary Fielding to Mercy Fielding Thompson, letter commencing July 8, 1837, LDS archives. This section of the damaged letter reads: "Orson Pratt who express[ed] [lacuna] for what he had sa[id] [lacuna] Spirit, he withdrew the ch[arge?] [lacuna] did not know personal[l]y that [lacuna] Brother Joseph and believed [lacuna] quite satisfyd [satisfied], he said more [lacuna]."

[53] *Autobiography of Parley Parker Pratt*, 144.

[54] Pratt to Don Carlos Smith, Oct. 3, 1837, *Elders' Journal* 1 (Oct. 1837):8, Kirtland.

At the church conference held in Kirtland on September 4, 1837 Luke S. Johnson, his brother Lyman, and John F. Boynton were not sustained in their station as apostles.[55] Joseph Smith considered Oliver Cowdery, David Whitmer, John Whitmer, and William W. Phelps, church leaders in Missouri, to be in transgression. In Kirtland Leonard Rich was singled out. Paraphrasing Galatians 1:8, Smith wrote:

> Though we or an Angel from Heaven preach any other gospel or introduce [any] order of things <than> those things which ye have received and are authorised to receive from the first Presidency let him be accursed[56]

Six days later on September 10 the three apostles, Luke and Lyman Johnson and John F. Boynton made a confession to the church and they retained their apostleship. All of the apostles were reconciled and the Quorum of the Twelve was together again. Afterwards Joseph left Kirtland on September 27 with Vinson Knight and his brother William Smith for Far West, Missouri to settle difficulties in the church.[57] Joseph Smith returned from Missouri on December 10.

Luman Shurtliff (also spelled Shirtliff) who heard missionaries preach the gospel a few years earlier came to Kirtland to investigate Mormonism. Shurtliff talked with David Whitmer and wrote years afterwards about his discussion:

> I told him [David Whitmer] briefly in as few words as possible my belief and unbelief and that I did believe the Gospel they preached as far as I read it in the Bible But I could not say that I believed that Joseph Smith Jun was a true Prophet of God for I did not neither do I believe the Book of Mormon is a Revelation from God. Then facing him I said, now you know what I believe and what I do not believe And if you think I am a fit subject for Baptism I am read to go to the water if not I intend to start holm [home]

---

[55] Kirtland Council Minute Book, 235; Jessee, *Papers of Joseph Smith* 2:218.
[56] Smith to "Dear Brotheren [Brethren]," letter to John Corrill, et al, Sept. 4, 1837, Jessee, *Papers of Joseph Smith*, 2:220.
[57] *Elders' Journal* 1 (Nov. 1837):27, Kirtland.

to morrow and neaver [never] trouble my head any more about Mormonism. Mr Whitmer was silant [silent] a few seconds the<n> replide [replied] I will go to the <water> and baptise you or get one of my Quorum to do it. On our way to the River he called on Sylvester Smith and he Baptised me

This baptism occurred on August 21, 1836. Going home he prayed and heard a voice saying: "Joseph Smith Jun Is a Prophet of the Most High God raised up for the restoration of Israel in these last Days And the Book of Mormon which you hold under your arm is true and brought forth for the Restitution of the scattered remnants of Jacob."[58] William E. McLellin maintained that he left the church about this time and sent in his elder's license to church headquarters thereby leaving his apostolic ministry.

In January 1837 McLellin received a letter from fellow apostles dated December 18, 1836 asking him to come back to Kirtland. William McLellin wrote back: "My course I know has been novel in the history of the transactions of the anointed." He indicated he was sorry of what he had done and asked forgiveness. "If so write to me immediately and let me *know* it. And please to obtain from President Smith my licence [license] and send it to me, so that I may again feel that I have authority to lift up *my* voice in the midst of this generation."[59] McLellin was issued another minister's license and returned to fellowship with the apostles.

At Kirtland, Joseph Smith's name was associated with a couple of young women. While the church had a code of morality members at times did not strictly follow it. According to William E. McLellin (see below) the first incident involved a Miss Hill. Nothing is known about her besides working at the Smith residence. The time period is not certain since Oliver Cowdery's name is mentioned as being at Kirtland when Joseph Smith III was born. In fact Cowdery left for Independence, Missouri in

---

[58] Luman Andros Shurtliff Autobiography, original in LDS archives, 72-73. In the autobiography his name is spelled Shirtliff. See also *Messenger and Advocate* 3 (March 1837):472.

[59] McLellin to "My dear old Friends," Jan. 24, 1837, copy of original letter, LDS archives, emphasis retained. See Shipps and Welch, *Journals of William E. McLellin*, 230.

November 1831 and did not return until August 1833. It is possible that the incident occurred near the birth of Frederick Granger Williams Smith (born on June 20, 1836) rather than the birth of Joseph Smith III.

The second female was a teenager and her name was Fanny Alger. Oliver Cowdery mentioned her name in early 1838 as the girl he was referring to whereas statements and church records do not name her. Fanny was born to Samuel and Clarissa Hancock Alger in September 1816. It appears that Joseph Smith had sexual contact with her.

Exactly what year this occurred has been a subject of controversy since it was not until 1837-38 when a disagreement between Oliver Cowdery and Joseph Smith reappeared and for a number of reasons Cowdery resigned from the church. After moving away from church headquarters Fanny Ward Alger married Solomon Custer on November 16, 1836 at Dublin, Indiana.[60] It is apparent that whatever happened between Fanny and Joseph occurred prior to the fall of 1836. Joseph would have been thirty years old and Fanny would have been nineteen years old.

At a church trial on the conduct of Oliver Cowdery held on April 12, 1838, at Far West, Missouri, Ebenezer Robinson recorded, "Joseph Smith jr testifies that Oliver Cowdery had been his bosom friend, therefore he intrusted [entrusted] him with many things. He then gave a history respecting the girl business."[61] It was not until three years after Joseph Smith's death that William E. McLellin visited Emma Smith in Nauvoo, Illinois. McLellin discussed the events concerning her husband Joseph. Their conversation took place in August 1847.[62]

McLellin's talk with Emma Smith was during the time when she talked to others about Joseph Smith's involvement with polygamy. In a letter to Joseph Smith III who at this time was

---

[60] Richard S. Van Wagoner, *Mormon Polygamy: A History* (Salt Lake City: Signature Books, 2nd ed., 1989), 9.

[61] Cannon and Cook, *Far West Record*, 168.

[62] McLellin wrote, "I had many hours conversation with Mrs. Smith, and learned many particulars from her, relative to the history of her husband from her first acquaintance with him, until the time of his cruel death" (*The Ensign of Liberty* 1 [Dec. 1847]:34).

president of the Reorganized Church of Jesus Christ of Latter Day Saints which had a church position that Joseph Smith was not involved with women other than his wife Emma. The letter mentioned the incidents about which McLellin had heard and not what he witnessed. There were two known letters from William McLellin to Joseph Smith III. The first letter was written in 1861 but does not give any names, and the second letter written in 1872, twenty-four years after talking to Emma. If McLellin was making up the story of what Emma Smith had confirmed to him in 1847 then Joseph Smith III would only need to see Emma and discuss the matter with her and she could point out any errors in McLellin's 1872 letter. William E. McLellin wrote:

Now Joseph [Smith III] I will relate to you some history, and refer you to your own dear Mother for the truth. You will probably remember that I visited your Mother and family in 1847, and held a lengthy conversation with her, retired in the Mansion House in Nauvoo. I did not ask her to tell, but I told her some stories I had heard. And she told me whether I was properly informed.

Dr. F[rederick]. G. Williams practiced with me in Clay Co. Mo. during the latter part of 1838. And he told me that at your birth your father committed an act with a Miss Hill - a hired girl. Emma saw him, and spoke to him. He desisted, but Mrs. Smith refused to be satisfied. He called in Dr. Williams, O[liver]. Cowdery, and S[idney]. Rigdon to reconcile Emma. But she told them just as the circumstances took place. He found he was caught. He confessed humbly, and begged forgiveness. Emma and all forgave him. She told me this story was true!!

Again I told her I heard that one night she missed Joseph and Fanny Alger. she went to the barn and saw him and Fanny in the barn together alone. She looked through a crack and saw the transaction!!! She told me this story too was verily true.[63]

---

[63] McLellin to Joseph Smith III, commenced in July 1872, RLDS archives.

There is a late recollection by Mosiah Hancock, son of Levi Hancock, written fourteen years after his father's death. Mosiah Hancock was born in 1834 and his autobiography was written about 1896, sixty-two years after his birth. His information may have been obtained through family tradition. In his account he has his father Levi perform a marriage ceremony between Joseph Smith and Fanny Alger near the date of March 29, 1833 when Levi Hancock was married. There are historical problems with the text that does not make it a reliable source as far as this marriage is concern.[64]

As far as the Fanny Alger incident there is selective screening of what was discussed between Joseph Smith and Oliver Cowdery. David W. Patten talked to Cowdery in the summer of 1837 while Thomas B. Marsh talked to him in November 1837 at Far West. One of the issues was whether Joseph Smith confessed to the act of adultery with Fanny Alger. A second issue is whether Cowdery lied about Joseph Smith committing adultery with Fanny. At the church trial Patten gave his testimony:

David W. Patten testifies, that he went to Oliver Cowdery to enquire of him if a certain story was true respecting J. Smith's committing adultery with a certain girl, when he [Cowdery] turned on his heel and insinuated as though he was guilty; he [Cowdery] then went on and gave a history of some circumstances respecting the adultery scrape stating that no doubt it was true. Also said that Joseph told him [Cowdery], he had confessed to Emma, Also that he [Cowdery] has used his influence to urge on lawsuits.[65]

Another witness at the trial was Thomas B. Marsh, president of the Twelve Apostles, who told about the Patten/Cowdery conversation in Kirtland and the Smith/Cowdery discussion at Far West in November 1837:

Thomas B. Marsh testifies that while in Kirtland last summer, David W. Patten asked Oliver Cowdery if he,

---

[64] Autobiography of Mosiah Hancock, LDS archives.
[65] Cannon and Cook, *Far West Record*, 167, meeting of April 12, 1838.

Joseph Smith jr, had confessed to his wife that he was guilty of adultery with a certain girl, when Oliver Cowdery cocked up his eye very knowingly and hesitated to answer the question, saying he did not know as he was bound to answer the question yet conveyed the idea that it was true.

Last fall after Oliver came to this place he heard a conversation take place between Joseph Smith and Oliver Cowdery when J. Smith asked him if he had ever confessed to him that he was guilty of adultery, when after a considerable winking &c. he said *No*. Joseph then asked him if he ever told him that he confessed to any body, when he answered *No*.[66]

All of the details of what they discussed are not known but they shook hands and agreed to let the matter drop. Warren and Lyman Cowdery, Oliver's brothers, inquired of the rumors they heard. In a letter Oliver Cowdery explained his position on the matter relating to Joseph Smith:

You will see from the other page that your own and Brother Lyman's requests concerning the *Stated* confession made to Mr. Smith, is, if I am to be credited, not so. From what he pretended to have made it, is to me unaccountable. I can assure you and bro. Lyman, that as God is to judge my soul in the world to come, I never confessed, intimated <or admitted> that I ever willfully lied about him. When he was here we had some conversation in which in every instance I did not fail to affirm that what I had said was strictly true. A dirty, nasty, filthy affair of his and Fanny Alger's was talked over in which I strictly declared that I never deviated from the truth on the matters, and as I supposed was admitted by himself.

Oliver continued his letter to his brothers in Kirtland:

---

[66] Ibid., 167-68, emphasis retained. A council met on November 6, 1837 and the minutes state, "All difficulties were satisfactorily settled except a matter between J. Smith jr., Oliver Cowdery and T. B. Marsh which was referred to themselves with the agreement that their settlement of the affair should be sufficient for the Council" (Ibid., 120).

At any rate, just before leaving, he [Joseph Smith] wanted to drop every past thing, in which had been a difficulty or difference - he called witnesses to the fact, gave me his hand in their presence, and I might have supposed of an honest man, calculated to say nothing of former matters. Never believe that Oliver will disgrace the gray hairs of his father, or the high sense of honor in the bosom of his brothers, so much as to acknowledge to Joseph Smith, Jr. that he has lied about him. There is something to[o] damning in the thought.[67]

Oliver Cowdery received correspondence from Kirtland saying that Joseph Smith was publicly talking about their private meeting and that Oliver lied:

I learn from Kirtland, by the last letters, that you have publickly [publicly] said, that when you were here I confessed to you that I had willfully lied about you - this compels me to ask you to correct that statement, and give me an explanation - until which you and myself are two.[68]

From the above discussion it appears that Joseph Smith had a sexual encounter with Fanny Alger. Emma saw Fanny with Smith in a barn and Joseph later discussed it with Emma. Oliver Cowdery knew about the event but Joseph Smith does not appear willing to define this as adultery. After Cowdery and Smith agreed to left matters drop it was Smith who brought it up publicly in Kirtland since his return from Far West in December and said that Cowdery lied about him. This caused the split between them as Cowdery explained in his letter.

The second edition of the Book of Mormon was published at the church printing office in Kirtland and included the date 1837 on the title page. It is generally known as the 1837 edition. It is not

---

[67] Oliver Cowdery to Warren A. Cowdery, Jan. 21, 1838, Oliver Cowdery Letterbook, 81, Huntington Library, emphasis retained.

[68] Cowdery to Smith, Jan. 21, 1838, a copy of letter in Oliver Cowdery to Warren A. Cowdery, Jan. 21, 1838, Oliver Cowdery Letterbook, 80. It is not known if Joseph Smith received the letter as he left Kirtland on January 12, 1838.

known when the type was first set for the galleries but it was probably in the fall of 1836. Joseph Smith made some corrections on the pages of the Printer's Manuscript of the Book of Mormon. It appears that this edition was funded by John Goodman, who was a recent convert from Canada, and that Parley P. Pratt assisted since the title pages states it was "Printed by O. Cowdery & Co. for P. P. Pratt and J. Goodson." The *Messenger and Advocate* printed a notice in its February 1837 issue stating that Oliver Cowdery's interest the printing company was now owned by Joseph Smith Jr. and Sidney Rigdon.[69]

The preface to the 1837 edition of the Book of Mormon presented to the reader an explanation indicating "manuscript editions" (i.e. the 1830 Book of Mormon) contained typographical errors but they had been compared with the original. The preface stated:

> Individuals acquainted with book printing, are aware of the numerous typographical errors which always occur in manuscript editions. It is only necessary to say, that the whole has been carefully re-examined and compared with the original manuscripts, by elder Joseph Smith, Jr. the translator of the book of Mormon, assisted by the present printer, brother O. Cowdery, who formerly wrote the greatest portion of the same, as dictated by brother Smith.

For the second edition Joseph Smith, Oliver Cowdery, and the typesetters made refinements in the text. About 2,000 were recorded onto the pages of the Printer's Manuscript with another 1,000 not indicated on that document. The largest number of changes was to the book's grammar that needed updating. Contrary to the preface the majority of the textual changes were not typographical in nature. For example, the word "which" was corrected to "who" over 700 times, "was" to "were," "is" to "are," "are" to "is," and "were" to "was." While these clarifications upgraded the grammar and made the book clearer they should not

---

[69] "Notice," *Messenger and Advocate* 3 (Feb. 1837):458, dated Feb 1.

be regarded as the words dictated in 1829 and used for the first edition.[70]

Though some errors in the type were made in the 1830 Book of Mormon (BOM), many of the corrections made by Joseph Smith were changes he made on the Printer's Manuscript for the 1837 edition. A couple of passages were clarified relating to God and Christ. The following five examples are theologically significant and clarify texts found only in chapter 3 of the First Book of Nephi. Both the original manuscript (O MS), where available, and the printer's manuscript (P MS) are used for these passages. The 1830 edition is printed first, with a note on the reading of the manuscripts, and then followed by the revised text of the 1837 edition. Emphasis indicates the changed text.

[1] 1830 BOM, 25
And he said unto me, Behold, the virgin which thou seest, is the mother of God, after the manner of the flesh.

P MS, 16 "the son of" inserted [O MS, 16-17 same as 1830 BOM]
1837 BOM, 27 (LDS 1 Nephi 11:18; RLDS 3:58)
And he said unto me, behold, the virgin *whom* thou seest, is the mother of *the Son of* God, after the manner of the flesh.

[2] 1830 BOM, 25
And the angel said unto me, behold the Lamb of God, yea, even the Eternal Father!

P MS, p. 17 no insertion [O MS, 17 same as 1830 BOM]
1837 BOM, p. 27-28 (LDS 1 Nephi 11:21; RLDS 3:62)
And the angel said unto me, behold the Lamb of God, yea, even the *Son of the* Eternal Father!

[3] 1830 BOM, 26
And I looked and beheld the Lamb of God, that he was taken by the people; yea, the Everlasting God, was judged of the world; and I saw and bear record.

---

[70] Richard P. Howard, *Restoration Scriptures: A Study of Their Textual Development*, second ed., 27.

P MS, 17 no insertion [O MS, 17-18 same as 1830 BOM]
1837 BOM, p. 28-29 (LDS 1 Nephi 11:32; RLDS 3:86)
And I looked and beheld the Lamb of God, that he was taken by the people; yea, the *Son of the* everlasting God was judged of the world; and I saw and bear record.

[4] 1830 BOM, 28
And a great and a terrible gulf divideth them; yea, even the word of the justice of the Eternal God, and Jesus Christ, which is the Lamb of God

P MS, 19 "Mosiah who" inserted ("Mosiah" should have been spelled "Messiah")
[O MS, 19 same as 1830 BOM except "sword" is written which was copied as "word"]
1837 BOM, 30 (LDS 1 Nephi 12:18; RLDS 3:127)
And a great and a terrible gulf divideth them; yea, even the word of the justice of the eternal God, and *the Messiah who* is the Lamb of God

[5] 1830 BOM, 32
and shall make known to all kindreds, tongues, and people, that the Lamb of God is the Eternal Father and the Saviour of the world

P MS, 22 "son of the" inserted [O MS not extant]
1837 BOM, p. 35 (LDS 1 Nephi 13:40; RLDS 3:193)
and shall make known to all kindreds, tongues and people, that the Lamb of God is the *Son of the* eternal Father, and the Savior of the world

The above examples indicate that there were changes that were more than typographical errors. Comparisons between the first and second editions of the Book of Mormon show that in the later edition many of the changes corrected the grammar of Joseph Smith. The 3,000 changes in grammar and orthography were made to overcome objections of the book relating to the poor wording in the first edition. The publishers, Pratt and Goodman, hoped to have published the Book of Mormon together with the Doctrine and

Covenants in one volume but it was finally considered that the volume would be too large for a pocket companion.

In June preparations were made for members of the Quorum of the Twelve Apostles to travel to England and preach the gospel. Heber C. Kimball was called to head this mission.[71] John Goodman also went to England bringing copies of the 1837 Book of Mormon with him.

As mentioned by December 1837 there were still tensions in the church. For those remaining in Kirtland religious worship was still important. Of the three witnesses to the Book of Mormon Martin Harris was the only one residing in Kirtland. Stephen Burnett, one of the early Ohio converts, wrote a letter to Lyman E. Johnson in April 1838 explaining his change in attitude after hearing Martin Harris speak:

> I have reflected long and deliberately upon the history of this church & weighed the evidence for & against it — loth to give it up — but when I came to hear Martin Harris state in a public ~~congregation~~ that he never saw the plates with his natural eyes only in vision or imagination, neither Oliver [Cowdery] nor David [Whitmer] & also that the eight witnesses never saw them & hesitated to sign that instrument for that reason, but were persuaded to do it, the last pedestal gave way, in my view our foundations was sapped & the entire superstructure fell a heap of ruins, I therefore three weeks since in the Stone Chapel gave a full history of the church since I became acquainted with it, the false preaching & prophecying [prophesying] of Joseph [Smith] together with the reasons why I took the course which I was resolved to do, and renounced the Book of Mormon with the whole scene of lying and deception practiced by J[oseph]. S[mith] & S[idney]. R[igdon] in this church, believing as I verily do, that it is all a wicked deception palmed upon us unawares

---

[71] Marquardt, *Joseph Smith Revelations*, 377.

Burnett said that after he spoke he was followed by Warren Parrish, Luke Johnson, and John Boynton all of who concurred with him. When they were finished speaking:

> M[artin] Harris arose & said he was sorry for any man who rejected the Book of Mormon for he knew it was true, he said he had hefted the plates repeatedly in a box with only a tablecloth or a handkerchief over them, but he never saw them only as he saw a city throught [through] a mountain. And said that he never should have told that the testimony of the eight [witnesses] was false, if it had not been picked out of [h]im but should have let it passed as it was[72]

This debate broke up the newly established Church of Christ headed by the three trustees, Martin Harris, Joseph Coe, and Cyrus Smalling. Many members of the larger Church of the Latter Day Saints (also known as the Church of Christ of Latter Day Saints) left the Kirtland area for Missouri. There were some saints who continued to build up the church after the Kirtland apostasy. Dissatisfaction left many wondering where their faith was in Mormonism. About fifteen percent of the local membership in the Kirtland area disassociated themselves from the church. "Almost half of those who were excommunicate, disfellowshipped, or dropped from their positions of responsibility in 1837 or 1838 later repented and returned to the Church."[73]

This was a sad state of affairs. Many saints left their homes to gather to Kirtland and to be at church headquarters. With all the prophetic promises, bickering among church leaders and financial considerations church members were put in a delicate position. Soon many members chose to leave Kirtland and travel west to Missouri to join others at a new gathering center.

---

[72] Burnett to Johnson, April 15, 1838. On May 24, 1838 a copy of the original was made. This copy was then recopied in 1839 into a letterbook. The above extract is from the 1839 copy, located in Joseph Smith Letterbook 2:64-66, LDS archives. This letterbook contains copies of letters from April 20, 1837 to Feb. 8, 1843 with a few letters of other years.

[73] Milton V. Backman, Jr., *The Heavens Resound: A History of the Latter-day Saints in Ohio 1830-1838* (Salt Lake City: Deseret Book, 1983), 328. See also Jessee, *Papers of Joseph Smith* 2:217n2.

19

Dissenters and Danites

Dissent not only occurred at Kirtland, Ohio but in the city of Far West, Missouri. Various saints had a hard time following church directives. For example, in Far West a meeting was held on January 30, 1838 at the home of Oliver Cowdery. Those in attendance were Frederick G. Williams, David Whitmer, William W. Phelps, John Whitmer, Jacob Whitmer, Lyman E. Johnson, and Oliver Cowdery. They were concerned because some of the church leaders were "endeavoring to unite ecclesiastical with civil authority and force men under a pretense of incurring the displeasure of heaven to use their earthly substance contrary to their own interest." Also according to those in the meeting these same authorities were "endeavoring to make it a rule of faith for said church to uphold a certain man or men right or wrong."[1]

A church general assembly was held in February where the Missouri presidency (David Whitmer, John Whitmer, and William W. Phelps) were rejected from holding their position of leadership. In a High Council meeting the former presidency were removed from signing ministerial licenses. Apostles Thomas B. Marsh and David W. Patten were voted in as presidents pro tem of the church in Missouri until Joseph Smith and Sidney Rigdon should arrive.[2] On March 10 the High Council of Zion met to consider the conduct of William W. Phelps and John Whitmer. The following letter was written on that day:

Far West, March 10, 1838.

SIR:

It is contrary to the principles of the revelations of Jesus Christ, and his gospel, and the laws of the land, to try a person for an offense, by an illegal tribunal, or by men

---

[1] Minutes of Jan. 30, 1838 contained in letter of Oliver Cowdery to Warren and Lyman Cowdery, Feb. 4, 1838, Oliver Cowdery Letterbook, 85, Huntington Library, emphasis omitted.

[2] Cannon and Cook, *Far West Record*, 137-41.

prejudiced against him, or by authority that has given an opinion, or descision [decision] beforehand, or in his absence.

Very Respectfully
we have the honor to be,
David Whitmer,
W. W. Phelps,
John Whitmer;
Presidents of the church of Christ in Mo.
To T. B. MARSH.
One of the travelling Counsellors.
Attest:
Oliver Cowdery,
Clerk of the High Council of the church of Christ in Missouri.
I certify the foregoing to be a true copy from the original.
Oliver Cowdery, Clerk
of High Council.[3]

After discussing the case against Phelps and John Whitmer the council voted that they be excommunicated from the church.[4] In April three members wrote letters of resignation. On April 12 Cowdery wrote, "This attempt to controll [control] me in my temporal interests, I conceive to be a disposition to take from me a portion of my Constitutional privileges and inherent rights. I only, respectfully, ask leave, therefore to withdraw from a society assuming they have such a right." Lyman E. Johnson questioned one of the charges against him about a civil suit and stated that until the charge was removed he "shall withdraw my self from your society and fellowship." David Whitmer expressed himself in a letter written on April 13. Whitmer wrote that he did not consider certain councils legal, ending his letter:

Believing as I verily do, that you and the leaders of the Councils have a determination to persue [pursue] your

---

[3] "Minutes of High Council," *Elders' Journal* 1 (July 1838):46. See also Cannon and Cook, *Far West Record*, 146-47.
[4] Ibid., 149.

unlawful course at all hazards, and bring others to your standard in violating of the revelations, to spare you any further trouble I hereby withdraw from your fellowship and communion—choosing to seek a place among the meek and humble, where the revelations of Heaven will be observed and the rights of men regarded."[5]

After reading each of their letters of resignations they were excommunicated from the church. For the period from about September 1837 to May 1838 the crisis within church leadership lead to resignations, withdrawals of participation, or excommunications by church courts of the following members with location in parenthesis:

Associate President; member of First Presidency:
Oliver Cowdery (Far West)
Frederick G. Williams (Far West)

Presidency of the Church in Missouri:
David Whitmer (Far West)
John Whitmer (Far West)
William W. Phelps (Far West)

Quorum of Twelve Apostles:
John F. Boynton (Kirtland & Far West) Lyman E. Johnson (Far West)
Luke S. Johnson (Kirtland & Far West) William E. McLellin (Far West)

Book of Mormon Witnesses:
Oliver Cowdery (Far West)   John Whitmer (Far West)
David Whitmer (Far West)   Jacob Whitmer (Far West)
Martin Harris (Kirtland)   Hiram Page (Far West)

Some of these individuals came back into fellowship at different times. For example, Frederick G. Williams was rebaptized in the summer of 1838. Luke S. Johnson subsequently rejoined the church in 1846 and Oliver Cowdery in 1848.

---

[5] Ibid., 165, 173, 177.

After Joseph Smith and family arrived at Far West in March 1838 George W. Robinson recorded for Smith—"the following sentiments occur[r]ed to my mind":

> Motto of the Church of Christ of Latterday Saints.
> The Constitution of our country formed by the Fathers of Liberty.
> Peace and good order in society Love to God and good will to man.
> All good and wholesome law's; And virtue and truth above all things
> And Aristarchy live forever!!!
> But Wo, to tyrants, Mobs, Aristocracy, Anarchy and Toryism: And all those who invent or seek out unrighteous and vexatious lawsuits under the pretext or color of law or office, either religious or political.
> Exalt the standard of Democracy! Down with that of Priestcraft, and let all the people say Amen! that the blood of our Fathers may not cry from the ground against us.
> Sacred is the Memory of that Blood which baught [bought] for us our liberty.

Signed	Joseph Smith Jr
Geo, W. Robinson	Thomas B. Marsh
	D. W. Patten
	Brigham Young
	Samuel H. Smith
	George M. Hinkle
	John Corrill.[6]

Sidney Rigdon of the First Presidency gave a speech on Sunday, June 17 against church dissenters. John Corrill, who recently left the church, wrote his recollection of the sermon in 1839:

President Rigden [Rigdon] delivered from the pulpit what I call the salt sermon; "If the salt have lost its savour, it is

---

[6] Copied into Scriptory Book of Joseph Smith Jr., in Jessee, *Papers of Joseph Smith* 2:213-14, emphasis omitted.

thenceforth good for nothing, but to be cast out and trodden under the feet of men," was his text, and although he did not call names in his sermon, yet it was plainly understood that he meant the dissenters, or those who denied the faith, ought to be cast out, and literally trodden under foot. He, indirectly, accused some of them with crime.[7]

George W. Robinson made the following record of the salt sermon in these words, "Prest Rigdon preached one Sabbath upon the salt that had lost its savour, that it is henceforth good for nothing but to be cast out, and trod[d]en under foot of men."[8] The church presidency was concerned with the Far West dissenters and it was felt there was a need to rid the church of them. To this end a long letter was composed and signed by eighty-three church members warning Oliver Cowdery, David Whitmer, John Whitmer, William W. Phelps, and Lyman E. Johnson to leave Caldwell County. Knowing the animosity of a large number of the brethren it appears that all of them left except for Phelps.

Also in June a secret order was established at church headquarters in Far West, though it went by various names, the group was generally known as the Danites. In July additional members were organized at Adam-ondi-Ahman in Daviess County. This organization will be discussed later in this chapter.

At a gathering held on the sixty-second anniversary of the Declaration of Independence a recommencement of the laying of the cornerstone of the Far West temple occurred. The year previous on July 3, 1837 the ground was broken for building a House of the Lord in that city. William W. Phelps wrote about the event:

Monday the 3d of July, was a great and glorious day in Far West; more than fifteen hundred saints assembled in this place, and, at ½ past 8 in the morning, after a prayer, singing, and an address, proceeded to break the ground for the Lord's House; the day was beautiful, the Spirit of the

---

[7] John Corrill, *A Brief History of the Church of Christ of Latter Day Saints*, 30. The text is similar to Matthew 5:13. See also LDS D&C 101:40; RLDS D&C 98:5; and LDS D&C 103:10; RLDS D&C 100:2.

[8] Jessee, *Papers of Joseph Smith* 2:249.

Lord was with us, a cellar for this great edifice, 110 long by 80 broad was nearly finished: on Tuesday the fourth, we had a large meeting and several of the Missourians were baptized[9]

Later at the November 6, 1837 conference it was voted "that the building of the house of the Lord in this place be postponed till the Lord shall reveal it to be his will to be commenced."[10] The next year on April 26, 1838 a revelation explained that on the fourth of July the foundation would be laid again. The saints received the following instructions for the temple for the next year (1839):

let them recommence laying the foundation of my house; thus let them from that time forth laibour [labor] diligently untill it shall be finished, from the Corner Stone thereof unto the top thereof, untill there shall not any thing remain that is not finished.[11]

Thomas B. Marsh, President of the Twelve Apostles wrote concerning the 1837 commencement of building a house for the Lord, "Thus we see that the Lord is more wise than men, for Phelps and Whitmer thought to commence it long before this, but it was not the Lord's time, therefore, he overthrew it, and has appointed his own time."[12] On the fourth of July 1838 the day was a day spent in celebration, and the saints made a declaration of Independence "from all mobs and persecutions, which have been inflicted upon us time after time <un>till we could bear it no longer," and the corner stones for the Far West temple were laid.[13] Sidney Rigdon gave an oration talking about it being another anniversary of the independence of the United States, and described the plans for the Far West temple:

---

[9] Phelps to "Dear Brother in the Lord," July 7, 1837, *Messenger and Advocate* 3 (July 1837):529; (Aug. 1837):560.

[10] Cannon and Cook, *Far West Record*, 120.

[11] Marquardt, *Joseph Smith Revelations*, 291; LDS D&C 115:11-12.

[12] Marsh to Wilford Woodruff, no date, *Elders' Journal* 1 (July 1838):38.

[13] Jessee, *Papers of Joseph Smith* 2:248.

The first floor will be for sacred devotion, and the two others, for the purpose of education. The building to be one hundred and ten feet by eighty, with three floors, and not far from thirty feet between the floors: all to be finished, according to the best stile [style] of such buildings in our country.

Rigdon related the persecution church members had endured for such a long time and issued the following warning:

We take God and all the holy angels to witness this day, that we warn all men in the name of Jesus Christ, to come on us no more forever, for from this hour, we will bear it no more, our rights shall no more be trampled on with impunity. The man or the set of men, who attempts it, does it at the expense of their lives. And that mob that comes on us to disturb us; it shall be between us and them a war of extermination, for we will follow them, till the last drop of their blood is spilled, or else they will have to exterminate us: for we will carry the seat of war to their own houses, and their own families, and one party or the other shall be utterly destroyed.—Remember it then all MEN.

Sidney Rigdon ended his oration with this proclamation:

We therefore, take all men to record this day, that we proclaim our liberty on this day, as did our fathers. And we pledge this day to one another, our fortunes, our lives, and our sacred honors, to be delivered from the persecutions which we have had to endure, for the last nine years, or nearly that. Neither will we indulge any man, or set of men, in instituting vexatious law suits against us, to cheat us our of our rights, if they attempt it we say wo be unto them. We this day then proclaim ourselves free, with a purpose and a determination, that never can be broken, "no never! no never!! NO NEVER."!!![14]

---

[14] *Oration Delivered by Mr. S. Rigdon, on the 4th of July, 1838* (Far West: Printed at the Journal Office, 1838), 8, 12.

After the oration was delivered the saints gave a shout of hosanna. The *Elders' Journal* published the speech as a pamphlet. It was recommended that the saints obtain a copy of it. The *Elders' Journal* expressed its approval in making Sidney Rigdon's speech available in the following words:

The oration delivered on the occasion, is now published in pamphlet form: those of our friends wishing to have one, can get it, by calling on Ebenezer Robinson, by whom they were printed. We would recommend to all the saints to get one, to be had in their families, as it contains an outline of the suffering and persecutions of the Church from its rise. As also the fixed determinations of the saints, in relation to the persecutors, who are, and have been, continually, not only threatening us with mobs, but actually have been putting their threats into execution; with which we are absolutely determined no longer to bear, come life or come death, for to be mob[b]ed any more without taking vengeance, we will not.[15]

Ebenezer Robinson wrote about the publishing of the Rigdon's speech:

A copy of the oration was furnished the editor, and printed in "The Far West," a weekly newspaper printed in Liberty, the county seat of Clay county. It was also printed in pamphlet form, by the writer of this, in the printing office of the Elders' Journal, in the city of Far West, a copy of which we have preserved.

This oration, and the stand taken by the church in endorsing it, and its publication, undoubtedly exerted a powerful influence in arousing the people of the whole upper Missouri country.[16]

---

[15] *Elders' Journal* 1 (Aug. 1838):54.
[16] Ebenezer Robinson, ed., "Items of Personal History of the Editor," *The Return* 1 (Nov. 1889):170-71, Davis City, Iowa.

In the month of June the beginning of the organization known by such names as the "daughter of Zion," or "Danites" commenced at Far West. The leading officers were at the events held on July fourth. The order of the day for the celebration included a procession headed first by the First Presidency, then by the marshals of the day and then by Generals Jared Carter, Sampson Avard, and Cornelius P. Lott who were the three leading Danites at the time.[17] This was the day for the laying of the corner stones of the temple.

The Danities was an extra-legal group of church members who pledged to support Joseph Smith and joined together in extreme activities working to further their goals. The organization was not directed by the state of Missouri but was composed of male church members. They believed that certain dissenters had to leave Caldwell County to save the church from further fractures. They were to protect the homes and lives of members from any adverse action from those they perceived as mob like or enemies of the church. They agreed to assist each other if necessary. Organized like regular troops this Mormon force was acting under the direction of their own leaders. In Missouri history this period is known as the Mormon War.

It appears that Joseph Smith, Sidney Rigdon, and Hyrum Smith, members of the First Presidency, did not take the Danite oath as the Danites were to support their program. Rigdon mentioned in 1843 that the Danites were formed for mutual protection and they "had certain signs and words by which they could know one another, either by day or night."[18] In July the order of Danites was organized at Adam-ondi-Ahman headed by Lyman Wight. The total number who joined the Danite organization at the two locations numbered in the hundreds. The leaders had military titles. There are no known minutes of the secret meetings where members were initiated. Reed Peck, who had been an Adjutant with the Danites mentioned the names of the leading officers of the band of Danites.[19] The following is a listing of these officers:

---

[17] "Celebration of the 4th of July," *Elders' Journal* 1 (Aug. 1838):60.

[18] *Times and Seasons* 4 (15 July 1843):271, Nauvoo, Illinois.

[19] Missouri General Assembly, *Document Containing the Correspondence, Orders, &c. in Relation to the Disturbances with the Mormons; and the Evidence Given before the Hon. Austin A. King, Judge of the Fifth Judicial*

Captain General – Jared Carter (replaced after July 4 by Elias Higbee)
Brigadier General – Sampson Avard
Major General – Cornelius P. Lott
Colonel - George W. Robinson
Lieutenant Colonel – Philo Dibble
Major – Seymour Brunson

George W. Robinson recorded under the date of July 27 the following concerning the Danite order:

> Some time past the bretheren [brethren] or saints have come up day after day to consecrate, and to bring their offerings into the store house of the lord, to prove him now herewith and se[e] if he will not pour us out a blessing that there will not be room enough to contain it, They have come up hither
>
> Thus far, according to the <Revelat[o]r> order of the Danites, we have a company of Danites in these times, to put to right physically that which is not right, and to cleanse the Church of verry [very] great evils which hath hitherto existed among us inasmuch as they cannot be put to right by teachings & persuasyons [persuasions], This company or a part of them exhibited on the fourth day of July They come up to consecrate, by companies of tens, commanded by their captain over ten.[20]

John Corrill wrote concerning the Danites, "They said they

Circuit of the State of Missouri, at the Court-House in Richmond, in a Criminal Court of Inquiry, begun November 12, 1838, on the trial of Joseph Smith, Jr., and others, for High Treason and Other Crimes Against the State (Fayette, Missouri: Printed at the office of the Boon's Lick Democrat, 1841), 116-17, 120. Reed Peck in his 1839 manuscript mentioned the leaders and has Avard holding the office of Major General and Lot as Brigadier General. Peck was an Adjutant, and the Danites had captains of fifties and tens (Peck to "Dear Friends," Sept. 18, 1839, 45-46, Huntington Library, copy in Manuscripts Division, Marriott Library, University of Utah).

[20] Scriptory Book of Joseph Smith, 60-61, original wording. The portion of the entry on manuscript page 61 starting at "Thus far, according to the" and ending with "commanded by their captain over ten" was at a later date crossed out. See Jessee, *Joseph Smith Papers* 2:262.

meant to cleanse their own members first, and then the church. In order to carry on their operations, they organised themselves into companies of fifties and tens, with a captain to each company, that they might be ready to act in concert on any occasion."[21]

Reed Peck wrote, "In July the law of consecration took effect which required every person to give up to the bishop all surplus property of every description not necessary for their present support."[22] When George Robinson wrote, "This company or a part of them exhibited on the fourth day of July" he meant the Danite company exhibited itself at the Fourth of July activities.

On August 6 at Gallatin an election was to be held. Some Latter Day Saints were prevented from voting and a fight broke out between Missourians and Mormons that resulted in injuries. On the morning of the next day church leaders at Far West heard a report that at the election two or three brethren were killed and other rumors. No one was killed but at the time this they followed the oral report. Robinson wrote in the Scriptory Book that the First Presidency rode with the Far West Danite chiefs to the settlement at Adam-ondi-Ahman:

> before we arrived at Col. Wights we had a large company Prests Smith and Rigdon and H[yrum] Smith, all the first presidency, General [Elias] Higbee, Gen. [Sampson] Avard[,] myself [Colonel George W. Robinson] and ma<n>y others to[o] tedious to mention at this time or in this record, were in the company.

Luman Shurtliff mentioned that near the beginning of August 1838 he joined the Danites. Luman, who was thirty-one years old when he joined, wrote the following regarding the Danites:

> About this time I received an invitation to unite with a Society called the Danite society and to meet with them at their next meeting which I did. And found <it> was got up

---

[21] Corrill, *A Brief History of the Church of Christ of Latter Day Saints*, 31.
[22] Peck to "Dear Friends, Sept. 18, 1839, 50. The law of consecration mentioned by Peck was one of the revelations given on July 8, 1838. See Marquardt, *Joseph Smith Revelations*, 293; LDS D&C 119; RLDS D&C 106.

for our personal defense also of Our Families[,] Proper<ty> and our Religeon [Religion,] Sighns [Signs] and pass-words given which each member could know the Other whare [where] ever they met night or day[.] Each person to settle all difficulty if he had any <with a member> of the Society before he could be received. I considered this a go<o>d institution for the benefit of society and a blessing for this people[.] But it Braok [Broke] up on our leaveing [leaving] the State of Missouri.[23]

Of interest in Shirtliff's recollection is the time when he was on guard duty showing that Joseph and Hyrum Smith knew the Danite secret countersign, "I he[a]rd two Men Comeing from towa[r]d Camp I knew by their voicees [voices] it was our Prophet and his Br Hyrum when they came in hailing distance I hailed them enquired who they ware [were] the answer was friends I bade them advance and give the Countersign which they did." At another time Shurtliff felt he could not "use any sighn [sign] or password" since he learned that John Taylor was not a Danite.[24]

Missourians were scared by the activities of Mormon forces. Correspondence was sent to Governor Boggs by citizens and government officials telling him of the fear of the Mormons by events that had recently occurred. This helped necessitate Boggs to issue a dreadful executive order to expel or even to exterminate the Mormons from Missouri. Whatever actions good or bad that both sides were involve in the action of the governor was enough to get the attention of the saints. Their stay in Missouri as a group was over and they needed to depart. Both sides contributed to the events that caused anger and hardships which continued for many years afterwards.

In 1841 the Missouri General Assembly published a lengthy compilation of one hundred sixty-three pages of printed material. This was printed in Fayette under the title *Document Containing the Correspondence, Orders, &c. in Relation to the Disturbances with the Mormons; and the Evidence Given before the Hon. Austin A. King, Judge of the Fifth Judicial Circuit of the*

---

[23] Luman Andrus Shurtliff Autobiography, 120, LDS archives.
[24] Ibid., 122, 125.

State of Missouri, at the Court-House in Richmond, in a Criminal Court of Inquiry, begun November 12, 1838, on the trial of Joseph Smith, Jr., and others, for High Treason and Other Crimes Against the State.[25]

The publication contained an index, Missouri Legislative Proceedings, correspondence, affidavits, testimonies, summaries by Judge King, and certificates. The testimonies of witnesses mainly for the prosecution and a few for the defense are contained under the heading "evidence" covering pages 97 through 149. Judge Austin Augustus King was born in Tennessee in 1802 being appointed as a circuit judge of the fifth circuit in 1837. At the time of the Mormon Inquest hearing he was thirty-six years old.

The printed text at times has different wording than the signed statements in the manuscript.[26] A few corrections may have been made on the pages during the printing process. In a couple of places the order of the testimony was changed. There are variants in how the names are spelled of those who gave testimony. Three testimonies of Mormons were not published in the 1841 printing. The important aspect of this document is that it contains the original signatures of those who testified before Judge King. What is presented hereafter is a short summary from that document.

One of the rumors heard prior to the court hearing was that there was a group of Mormons called Danites. On September 4, 1838 John N. Sapp made an affidavit saying he left the Mormons on August 15 and was a member of the Danites (1841, 17). There was also a statement made by Philip Covington, an acting justice of the peace in Daviess County, which adjoined Caldwell County, who said that on the October 18 Mormons went to Gallatin and robbed a store and told the citizens to leave the county (1841,

---

[25] Missouri General Assembly, *Document Containing the Correspondence, Orders. . .* (Fayette, Missouri: Printed at the office of the Boon's Lick Democrat, 1841). This work will hereafter be cited in the text as 1841 followed by the page number.

[26] The original testimony is located in the Eugene Morrow Violette Collection, Collection Number 1033,Western Historical Manuscript Collection-Columbia, 23 Ellis Library, University of Missouri, Columbia, Missouri. The first number cited in parenthesis is from my page by page transcription of this manuscript titled "Mormon Inquest Testimony, 1838," (excluding crossed through words), and the second reference is from the 1841 printing. This transcription is in the possession of the author.

43).[27] Another letter of October 23 to the governor also mentioned the store of Jacob Stollings being robbed and burned including the post office that was located in the structure (1841, 49).

George M. Hinkle was a colonel in Caldwell County militia and for a time in charge of the local militia. The majority of citizens living in the county were Mormons. The church high council on March 10, 1838 resolved that those holding preaching licenses, between eighteen and forty-five years old, who were not officiating in their office "be subject to military duty."[28] How many Mormons were involved in unlawful activities in the Caldwell County militia or in the Far West or Adam-ondi-Ahman companies of Danites is not a part of our examination. Every Mormon male was not a Danite. The Mormon town Adam-ondi-Ahman was called Diahman (spelled Diahmon in the record of the hearing),

It appears that Joseph Smith in part directed Mormon troops. John Cleminson recalled that Lyman Wight believed that the Mormons could settle the difficulties themselves (53; 1841, 116). Whether armed Mormon men were considered under the banner of Danites, the Army of Israel, being part of a militia, or defending their families, what we have here are Mormon troops who considered their actions as defending their rights. It is not a question of whether these troops were legal or not. To the Mormons they were going to retaliate and take revenge upon the enemies of the kingdom of God.

These courses of events lead to leadership problems in the organizational history of the church apostles. In October 1838 David W. Patten (who was known as Captain Fearnaught) commanded a company of soldiers and went to Gallatin and committed acts of destruction. He was later killed in a battle with Captain Samuel Bogart at Crooked River. Two apostles left the church over activities that at the time were sanctioned by church leaders. Thomas B. Marsh, President of the Quorum of the Twelve Apostles made an affidavit on October 24, 1838 discussing what church members had done and their threats against Mormon

---

[27] The date of the statement was printed as September 22, 1838 rather than the correct month of October.

[28] Cannon and Cook, *Far West Record*, 146.

dissenters. Apostle Orson Hyde concurred with what Marsh wrote (1841, 57-59).[29]

Charges and counter charges have been told about who did acts of aggression towards citizens of Missouri and also to the Mormons. These recollections before Judge King were given closer to the events than later published explanations. It appears from my examination that most of the testimony came from those who were still church members with the exception of John Whitmer who had been excommunicated eight months prior to the hearing.

This was a court of inquiry or preliminary hearing sometime called a trial. The hearing was held over a period of eighteen days, from November 12-29, 1838. If there was enough evidence against the defendants they were to be brought to trial. In this case evidence was to be presented before a grand jury. This hearing related to the purported guilt on the Mormon side of the question and not on the side of wrong doings of local residents upon the Latter Day Saints. For example, no hearing was held relating to Missourians killing Mormons at Haun's Mill.

The inquiry represented only one side of the recent disturbances. It was the State of Missouri verses Joseph Smith and the Mormons. The examination started with fifty-three defendants charged "with the several crimes of high treason against the State, Murder, burglary, arson, robbery & larceny" (1; 1841, 97). During the days of the hearing; eleven more Mormons were added making a total of sixty-four defendants. Some of these individuals were later released. Some persons who gave testimony remembered the dates of events that took place while most did not. What the witnesses affirmed appear to be genuinely believed by each individual.[30]

A large part of testimony told about the Mormon troops making raids on small towns in Daviess County. The number of

---

[29] See also Marsh to "Brother and Sister Abbot," October 25, 1838, copy in Joseph Smith Letterbook 2:18, LDS archives. Orson Hyde added to the letter that he left the church.

[30] This observation is contrary to what Hyrum Smith and Sidney Rigdon, members of the First Presidency, stated in 1843. See *Times and Seasons* 4 (1 July 1843):253; (Aug. 1, 1843):278; and Firmage and Mangrum, *Zion in the Courts*, 75.

troops mentioned in testimony appears to be an estimate based upon the perception of each individual. On October 18, 1838 Lyman Wight led about eighty men to Millport and burned some houses while David W. Patten commanded another eighty troops (some estimated they were from one hundred to one hundred fifty) to Gallatin. The battle at Crooked River was between the forces led by David W. Patten and the state troops commanded by Captain Samuel Bogart.

The testimonies given at the examination can be broken down as follows: of the forty-two witnesses twenty-two were or had been Latter Day Saints. This included seven who had been Danites. The longest testimonies of those who were members of the Danites were that of Sampson Avard, Reed Peck, and Burr Riggs. Those men who had never been Danites and who gave lengthy testimony were William W. Phelps, George M. Hinckle, and John Corrill. In addition near the end of the examination seven witnesses testified in behalf of the defense including fifteen-year-old Nancy Rigdon, daughter of Sidney Rigdon. The state had twenty non-Mormon witnesses who testified.

Witnesses were examined concerning the activity of Mormon troops led by David Patten to Gallatin. Some testimony was given relative to the settlement of Millport and to a lesser degree to Grindstone Fork. The hearing concerned itself mainly with the events that took place at Gallatin and Millport in Daviess County, the Danite band, the fight with state troops led by Captain Bogart, and the reported intentions of church leaders. Justice Austin King certified "that the several witnesses herein before examined, were severally sworn by me according to law, and their examination taken by me, in the presence of the prisoners, and reduced to writing under my direction, and signed by said witnesses respectively, after the same was read over to them" (1841, 150-51).

Ebenezer Robinson, who was one of the defendants, gave a description of the building where the court of inquiry was held. His recollection, given fifty-one years later, gives us an insight into the conditions under which these testimonies were heard:

> At Richmond we were taken into the court house, which was a new unfinished brick building, with no inside work done except a floor laid across one end, some 16 or 20 feet

wide. There were two large fire places built in the wall where the floor was laid. A railing was built across the room at the edge of the floor, and we were quartered inside the railing as our prison, with a strong guard inside and outside the building.

Two 3 pail iron kettles for boiling our meat, and two or more iron bake kettles, or dutch ovens, for baking our corn bread in, were furnished us, together with sacks of corn meal and meat in the bulk. We did our own cooking. This arrangement suited us very well, and we enjoyed ourselves as well as men could under similar circumstances. We spread our blankets upon the floor at night for our beds, and before retiring, we sang an hymn and had prayers, and practiced the same each morning before breakfast. . . .

Tuesday, Nov. 13, A space on the south end of the floor in the court house was appropriated for the use of the court, which convened on that day, with Austin A. King on the bench, and Thomas C. Burch, state's attorney, when the prisoners named above, together with those confined in the court house, were arraigned for trial, viz: . . .

All the above named prisoners were severally charged with high treason against the state, murder, burglary, arson, robbery and larceny.

The charge of murder was made on account of the man that was killed in the Bogart battle, wherein one Missourian and three of our men were killed. Fortunately, most of our brethren who had participated in that battle had left the state, consequently only a few of our fellow prisoners had anything to do with that unfortunate affair.[31]

George M. Hinkle wrote to William W. Phelps (both were witnesses before Judge King): "When the Court of Enquiry held its session in Richmond, I did not turn State's evidence, but was

---

[31] Robinson, "Items of Personal History of the Editor" *The Return* 2 (March 1890):234.

legally subpoenaed, as you know."[32] One such subpoena made out by Judge King near the end of the examination reads:[33]

> The State of Missouri to James
> Blakely Nathaniel Blakely, James B.
> Turner, Laburn Marion, John Lockard
> Timothey Lewiss
> Greeting, you are hereby comman-
> did that setting aside all ex-
> cuse, and delay you be and
> appear forthwith before me at
> the Court House in the town
> of Richmond there and there to
> give evidence and the truth to
> say on a certain examination
> & inquiry there and there pending
> before me wherein the State of
> Missouri is plaintiff and Joseph
> Smith Jr and others are defendants
> on behalf of the state. Herein
> fail not at your peril. Given un-
> der my hand this 21st day of
> November 1838.
>
> Austin A King
Judge &C

First and foremost in the court of inquiry was the examination of Sampson Avard. Avard was baptism into the church and ordained an elder in 1835 by Orson Pratt.[34] Later Avard was ordained a high priest and participated at one June 1838 high council meeting in the city of Far West. Avard held the rank of

---

[32] Hinkle to Phelps, Aug. 14, 1844, *The Ensign* 1 (Aug. 1844):31, Buffalo, Iowa Territory.

[33] Greg and MarJane Christofferson Collection, Irvine, California. Used by permission. Of those commanded to appear before the court James B. Turner, John Lockhart (spelled Lockard on document), and Timothy Lewis gave testimony before Judge King circa November 26, 1838.

[34] Orson Pratt to "Dear Brother" [John Whitmer], Nov. 18, 1835, *Messenger and Advocate* 2 (Nov. 1835):224.

Brigadier General and was one of the leaders in the Danite order but not the individual in charge of the organization. In July he was present when Joseph Smith received a revelation for the Twelve Apostles.[35] At the hearing Avard produced a copy of a reported Constitution and also a copy of a warning to dissenters that was signed by eighty-three individuals. This last document as has been stated warned Oliver Cowdery, David Whitmer, John Whitmer, William W. Phelps, and Lyman E. Johnson to depart out of Caldwell County. Of those warned only William W. Phelps, postmaster of the town, became repentant and stayed in Far West while the others fled. Sampson Avard indicated in his testimony that those becoming Danites entered into a covenant. After raising their right hand they repeated:

> In the name of Jesus Christ the son of God, I do solemnly obligate myself ever to conceal & never to reveal the secret purposes of this society called the daughter of Zion; Should I ever do the same I hold my life as the forfeiture (3; 1841, 97).[36]

At a meeting held in the schoolhouse the church presidency, Joseph Smith, Sidney Rigdon, and Hyrum Smith blessed the officers of the Danites.[37] Avard mentioned that Joseph Smith said "it was necessary this band should be bound together by a covenant that those who revealed the secrets of the society should be put to death" (2-3; 1841, 97). Avard recalled, "At the Election last August a report came to Far West that some of the brethren in Davis [Daviess County] were killed. I called for 20 volunteers to accompany me to Davis [Daviess] to see into this matter.- I went and about 120 mormons accompanied me to Adam Ondi Ahman. Mr Joseph Smith Jr in company, when we arrived there I found the report exag[g]erated, none were killed" (3; 1841, 98). At a later date Joseph Smith dropped Avard from his position.

---

[35] Marquardt, *Joseph Smith Revelations*, 292; LDS D&C 118 (July 8, 1838).

[36] John Corrill said he was at one of the meetings "where an oath in substance the same as testified <to> by Dr Avard was administered" (30; 1841, 110).

[37] Based upon the testimonies of Avard (2; 1841, 97); John Corrill (30; 1841, 111); and Reed Peck (55; 1841, 117).

Avard said he did not know if the members of the first presidency ever took the Danite oath. He also mentioned an anecdote that Joseph Smith gave about the Duchman's potatoes:

about a captain who applied to a Dutchman to purchase potates [potatoes], who refused to sell, the Capt[ain] then charged his company several different times not to touch the Dutchmans potatoes. In the morning the Dutchman <had> not a potatoe left in his patch (5; 1841, 98-99).

Further in his testimony Sampson Avard said that Captain David W. Patten with about 100 men went to Gallatin, removed goods out of the store of Jacob Stollings and took them to the storehouse in Diahman in the care of Bishop Vincent (Vinson) Knight.

Those who opposed the operations of the Danites included John Corrill, William W. Phelps, and former member John Whitmer. What started out as secret society to cleanse the church of undesirables afterwards turned into an organization of defense and retaliation against nonmember Missourians. Most nonmembers including the governor were considered being part of a mob bent on having the Mormons leave the state.

John Corrill said he was at a Danite meeting where the officers of the society were blessed by the first presidency in their calling.[38] Joseph Smith said "he wished to do nothing unlawful" and told them to obey the presidency (30; 1841, 111).

George M. Hinkle talked with Joseph Smith and "told him that this course of things of burning houses & plundering by the mormon troops would ruin us, that it could not be kept hid and would bring the force of the State upon us, that houses would be searched & stolen property found." Hinkle said that Smith replied in a rough manner "to keep still, that I should say nothing about it, that it would discourage the men & he would <not> suffer me to say any thing about it" (38-39; 1841, 126).

---

[38] On John Corrill see Kenneth H. Winn, "'Such Republicanism as This': John Corrill's Rejection of Prophetic Rule," in Roger D. Launius and Linda Thatcher, eds., *Differing Visions: Dissenters in Mormon History* (Urbana: University of Illinois Press, 1994), 45-75.

Hinkle received an order from Judge Elias Higbee to order out the militia of Caldwell County. Joseph Smith reduced Hinkle's command and took charge of the forces. George Hinkle recalled:

I have heard Jos[eph] Smith Jr say that he believed Mahommet [Mahomet] was a good man, that the Koran was not a true thing, but the world believed Mahommet [Mahomet] as they beli[e]ved him. & that he believed Mahommet [Mahomet] a true prophet (42; 1841, 128).

James C. Owens testified Joseph Smith "observed that he didn't intend to obey the laws any longer, that he had had a great many writs served on him, & that he was of age, and did not intend to have another served on him" (47; 1841, 113).

Jeremiah Myers said he was in the last expedition to Daviess County (in October 1838) and was "summoned from my home in the east part of Caldwell county, by my militia officer to go to Far West" (67; 1841, 131). He went and Captain Fearnaught [David W. Patten] took a company of men and went to Gallatin. Myers was told there was a mob there. That evening he saw the goods that had been removed from the store in Gallatin and they were at the bishop's storehouse. The goods were called consecrated property.

Samuel Kimble gave testimony that he heard Joseph Smith say in a speech to a large company under arms:

It was impossible to please a mob, that he had applied to the Governor, and he understood the governor said he could do nothing for us, he said that the whole state was a mob, and that the governor was nothing but a mob, & if he come upon them he would make war upon him. he cursed the state as a damn mob & that God would damn them. he observed that the people might think he was swearing, but that the Lord would not take notice of it (82; 1841, 138).

Addison Greene mentioned that he was in the spy company. He was taken prisoner and then released before the fight with Bogart (108; 1841, 144).[39] William W. Phelps, who recently rejoined the church after being excommunicated, remembered at one time attending a meeting held in the spring of 1838 where Sidney Rigdon spoke:

> as early as April last, at a meeting, in Far West, of 8 or 12 persons, Mr Rigdon, arose and made an address to them in which he spoke of having bo<u>rne persecutions & law suits & other privations, and did not intend to bear them any longer. that they meant to resist the law, and if a sheriff came after them with writs they would kill <him>. and if any body opposed them they would take off their heads. Geo W Harris who was present observed, you mean the head of their influence I suppose. Rigdon answered, he meant, that lump of flesh & bones called the skull or scalp (83; 1841, 121)

Abner Scovel, whose testimony was not published in 1841, said he heard Joseph Smith say he would conquer the people by the sword of the Spirit; also "what do we care for the laws of the land <is> so long as there is no person to put them in force." Scovel said the following concerning the rebaptisms of William W. Phelps and Frederick G. Williams:

> Soon after the time that Phelps & Williams was baptized, (about the last of June <or July> last) I heard Sidney Rigdon say, in Far West, that if Phelps or Williams apostatised again, or <set up against the government or kingdom>, the Lord would kill them in half an hour, or would put it into the hearts of his saints to kill them (49).

The testimony of Scovel helps us determine when the rebaptism of these men occurred. Both Phelps and Williams lost their office in the church. They were told in a revelation to Joseph Smith, "in consequence of their transgressions, their former

---

[39] Compare with a short statement made by Greene on March 17, 1840 in Clark V. Johnson, *Mormon Redress Petitions: Documents of the 1833-1838 Missouri Conflict* (Provo, Utah: Religious Studies Center, Brigham Young University, 1992), 220.

standing has been taken away from them And now if they will be saved, Let them be ordained as Elders, in my Church, to preach my gospel."[40] On July 26 Phelps was called upon to draw up a petition to remove the county seat to Far West.[41] The Scriptory Book of Joseph Smith recorded for August 5, "Br. F. G. Williams was among the number, who being rebaptized a few days since was this day confirmed."[42]

In his testimony Phelps said he attended a meeting where Rigdon and Smith "meant to have the words of the presidency to be as good, and as undisputed as the words of God. and that no one should speak against what they said" (84; 1841, 121). It was told at another meeting that if anyone spoke against the presidency they would be turned over into the hands of the "brother of Gideon."

William Phelps said he heard from David Patten "that Rigdon was writing a declaration, to declare the Church independent." Phelps said he replied to Patten, "I thought such a thing treasonable, to set up a government within a government. he [Patten] answered it would not be treasonable if they could maintain it" (87; 1841, 122). Phelps heard Joseph Smith tell the anecdote of the Dutchman's potatoes. Phelps said he also heard Joseph Smith remark that there was a store at Gallatin and a grocery at Millport. Phelps understood that Captain Fearnaught (David W. Patten) should take a company of men and go to Gallatin and take the goods out of the store and bring them to Diahman and burn the store. Also Lyman Wight to take a company to Millport and Seymour Brunson take a company to Grindstone Fork.

The other two testimonies given during the examination that were not published in 1841 were those of Robert Snodgrass and George Walter. Snodgrass said he heard Joseph Smith say in Far West a number of months previously "That the time had now come that the Saints should <rise &> take the kingdom, <and they should> do it by the <sword of the> Spirit, and if not, by the sword of power" (35).

---

[40] Marquardt, *Joseph Smith Revelations*, 293. The revelation was given on July 8, 1838.
[41] Jessee, *Papers of Joseph Smith* 2:262.
[42] Ibid. 2:264.

George Walter, who was examined at length, said he heard Joseph Smith say in Far West that he believed that Mahomet "was an inspired man, and had done a great deal of good." Walter gave bail for Lyman E. Johnson, a dissenter and former apostle, who had been driven from Far West. On leaving town Johnson was fired upon. "Jos[eph] Smith Jr accused me of lying, of harbouring the mob, of being too intimate with the dissenters" and also carrying news to Richmond and other places. Smith said "it was a time of war, and to permit persons who are right in among them to go out and carry news, would never do and it should be stop[p]ed, if not in any other way, they would do it by taking their lives." (36). Joseph Smith further said, "the militia was nothing but a mob, <that> the state of Missouri was a mob. & that the Governor himself was a mob character." Smith also said, according to Walter, "that it was time to lay religion aside and take up <their> guns" (37-38).

In addition to Sampson Avard six other Danites were examined at the hearing. Reed Peck said in June 1838 George W. Robinson and Philo Dibble "invited me to a danite meeting, I went. The only speaker was Dr Avard who explained the object of the meeting, and said that its object was that they might be perfectly organized, to defend <them>selves against mobs. that we were all to be govern[e]d by the presidency, & do whatever they required. and uphold them that we were not to judge for ourselves whether it were right or [w]rong that God had raised us a prophet who would judge for us, & that it was proper we should stand by each other in all cases" (54; 1841, 116).

Peck learned that "Jared Carter was captain General of the band." Reed Peck was present when the officers were introduced and blessed by the presidency and indicated that Avard did not explain what he was teaching to the church presidency probably because it was a secret society. Peck said he heard Avard "say that the danites were to consecrate their surplus property, and to come in by tens to do so." Peck also said that in October:

I heard Jos[eph] Smith Jr in a speech say, in refference [reference] to stealing, that in a general way he did not approve of it, but that on one occasion our Saviour & his disciples stole corn in passing thro' the corn fields for the reason that they could not otherwise procure any thing to eat. He told an anecdote of a Dutchmans potatoes, and said in substance that a colonel or captain was quarter[e]d near a Dutchman from whom he wished to purchase some potatoes, who refused to sell them. the officer then charged his men, not to be cau<gh>t stealing the dutchmans potatoes but next morning he found his potatoes all dug (56; 1841, 117).

Morris Phelps told about attending two Danite meetings. At the second meeting he took objection to taking spoils or plunder and said he never attended a Danite meeting since. He also heard Joseph Smith talk about the Dutchman's potatoes (28-29; 1841, 110).

Witness Burr Riggs discussed the time he was at Diahman when he "saw a great deal of plunder brought in, consisting of beds. & bed cloths, I also saw one clock, and I saw 36 head of cattle drove up & put in a pen. all the above property was called consecrated property." Riggs heard from John L. Butler "that they had taken the cattle from the citizens of the Grindstone fork, and said he had made a valuable expedition" (73; 1841, 134). Burr Riggs also mentioned, "When Patten was raising his company to go against Bogart. he remarked that it (Bogarts company) was said to be militia, but it was a cursed mob, and that in the name of the Lord he would go and disperse them" (76; 1841, 135).

Finally Ezra Williams (son of Frederick G. Williams), who had just turned fifteen years old since the start of the hearing, testified and said he was in Captain Patten's company "when he took Gallatin, and rob[b]ed the store, the goods were packed off a great many of them before the men on their horses, my Captain often gave me some, which I packed off before me to Diahmon, they were deposited in a house on the river bank" (107; 1841, 144).

The non-Mormons who gave testimony during the examination discussed events that occurred in Millport and being taken prisoners by the Mormons. They also told about the attack upon Captain Bogart, and the taking of goods from the store of Jacob Stollings at Gallatin. Charles Bleckley and James Cobb were both examined and said they observed Joseph Smith, Lyman

Wight, and George Robinson on horse back looking at the burning of a house at Millport (77-78; 1841, 136).

James B. Turner said the day after Millport was burned he saw Joseph Smith, Hyrum Smith, Lyman Wight along with two others. Mr. Cobb the mail rider said, "see what the damn Mormons, have done," referring to the burning and Hyrum Smith asked how he knew it was the Mormons. "Lyman Wight said their cause was just" and they were acting on the defensive (97; 1841, 139-40).

Elisha Camron said he was taken prisoner and informed Lyman Wight they were raising a militia in Clay County and there was no mob out there (77; 1841, 136). A rebuttal witness, Asa Cook, said he told a man who said he was a Mormon that "we were no mob, but militia" (120; 1841, 149). Andrew Job said he was taken prisoner by Captain Fearnaught (David Patten). While traveling Job saw ten houses on fire between Millport and Diahman. Job also said Ebenezer Page told him that the mob was burning their own houses and would blame the Mormons. The next morning Lyman Wight told the prisoners that they had four hours to leave the county. Afterwards Job found various articles taken from the residence of his stepmother at the house of Lyman Wight (69-70; 1841, 132-33).

Jesse Kelley testified that a company of Mormons led by Alexander McRay took him and Addison Price prisoners. McRay told them if they did not wish to flight they needed to leave the state. They were released soon after (79-80; 1841, 137). Addison Price concurred with Kelly's testimony as being taken prisoner and said that McRay, captain of the company, raised his right hand and warned him in the name of God to leave the county and he had better leave the state. The company said they were militia and bore a white flag (80-82; 1841, 137-38).

Captain Samuel Bogart said that on the evening of October 24 he met with several Mormons and read to them his order of General Atchison. Bogart supposed that they would inform the Mormons of Caldwell County the character of his company (27; 1841, 108). Wiatt Craven, who was in Captain Bogart's company, mentioned that Parley P. Pratt and David Patten made an attack upon them and Craven was wounded. Craven said the Mormons approached and both parties commenced firing about the same time and he was taken prisoner. Moses Rowland and several Mormons were killed during this battle (24-25; 1841, 109).

Testifying also was John Lockhart who was in Bogart's company being one of two picket guards. The guards hailed the other company, that was the Mormon company, and told them to lay down their arms but they did not (102-104; 1841, 142). Nehemiah Odle Sr. was also in the battle of October 25 between Captain Bogart and the Mormons. Odle said Parley P. Pratt participated but he did not know who fired first (26; 1841, 108).

A number of witnesses told about the stolen goods taken from the store of Jacob Stollings in Gallatin. Patrick Lynch mentioned that he was a clerk in the store. Lynch said he saw the Mormons at a distance and he locked the door of the store. He saw the Mormon troops taking goods from the store. Later the merchandise was found in Diahman. Among the items taken were a ledger, three daybooks, and notes of hand. The books were not recovered "but the notes I found in the house of bishop Knight, at Diahmon, in the possession of his wife, except the notes on mormons." Later Lynch returned and found the storehouse burnt which housed the post office and the treasurer's office (110-11; 1841, 145).

Joseph H. McGee said it was on Thursday, October 18 when the Mormons came to Gallatin. His shop was broken open and George Worthington's saddlebags were taken, also two quilts, a coat, and other clothing that belonged to McGee. Items belonging to other individuals were also removed. McGee saw the Mormons removing goods out of the storehouse and packing articles on their horses. A short time later he saw the place in smoke and flames. McGee said he heard Parley P. Pratt order the men to take the goods prior to the house being set on fire (101-102; 1841, 141).

Another witness, Thomas M. Odle, stated that on Saturday (October 20), after Gallatin was burned, a company of twelve men came to John Raglin's house in Daviess County where he lived. They said their object was to drive the mob from the county and that he must go. He was told to be gone next morning or they would take his life. Mrs. Raglin was also told to leave. The men said they had been driven long enough and would defend themselves and they intended to make it a war of extermination (64-65; 1841, 130).

George W. Worthington testified that it was about Thursday, October 18 that the Mormons troops took Gallatin. About 100 Mormons, he later learned under the command of Captain Patten, rushed the town. Worthington lived about a half mile from Gallatin. He said the Mormons took a horse, saddle, and bridle that belonged to John A. Williams. They did not take his mare but took his gun. Later Worthington looked toward the storehouse and saw smoke in the roof and soon after flames burst out from the top. He left his home that evening leaving his property in the house. His home was burned and property gone. At a subsequent time he saw his property in a storehouse and some in a house said to be bishop Knight's in Diahman (98-100; 1841, 140-41).

Porter Yale said he was at Gallatin when the Mormons made an attack upon it and burned it. They took some guns from his father's house. He went with the Mormons to Diahman and they kept him there two or three days. There were about 100 Mormons there. He saw a great deal of plunder brought into Diahman and it was called consecrated property (104-105; 1841, 142-43).

After Judge Austin A. King heard the testimony of the witnesses he discharged twenty-nine of the defendants because of the lack of sufficient evidence. Twenty-four Mormon prisoners were considered guilty of arson, burglary, robbery, and larceny in Daviess County and as the offences were bailable they could post bail until the next term of the Daviess County Circuit Court. But the court believed that Joseph Smith and four other Mormons were guilty of overt acts of treason in Daviess County. Smith together with Lyman Wight, Hyrum Smith, Alexander McRay, and Caleb Baldwin were to answer the charge in March 1839. Sidney Rigdon was charged with treason committed in Caldwell County. They were committed to Liberty Jail in Clay County. Since the death of Moses Rowland occurred in Ray County it was believed that Parley P. Pratt, Norman Shearer, Darwin Chase, Luman Gibbs, and Morris Phelps were guilty and they were to be held in the Ray County jail.

In January 1839 Sidney Rigdon represented himself in his plea of habeas corpus. He said he was innocent of high treason. He was able to give bail and was released but he stayed in Liberty Jail for protection for ten days before leaving the state.[43]   The other petitioners remained confined as prisoners.

At a March 1839 conference individual names were presented for excommunication from the church. This included six men who testified at the hearing.[44] A few months later Joseph Smith and his fellow Mormons prisoners were allowed to escape from custody and fled to Quincy, Illinois. This was one reason why further legal processes were made in an effort to get Joseph Smith extradited back to Missouri.

What occurred in Missouri during those trying times was a sad state of affairs. There was no restoration of homes and property for either the Mormons or the Missourians. The insurrection surely assisted Governor Boggs to help the early settlers in their efforts to get rid of the Mormons. Petitions for help from the local citizens resulted in the extreme measure of Executive Order number forty-four issued by Boggs on October 27, 1838. It took another executive order, issued 137 years later in 1976 by Missouri Governor Christopher S. Bond to heal the wounds made in 1838.

In New York City Parley P. Pratt wrote a response to La Roy Sunderland editor of *Zion's Watchman* a Methodist periodical. The pamphlet refers to Book of Mormon passages from the second (1837) edition. It contains a prophecy by Apostle Pratt regarding the Book of Mormon:

> Also, p. 527, where all who will not hearken to the Book of Mormon, shall be cut off from among the people; and that too, in the day it comes forth to the Gentiles and is rejected by them. And not only does this page set the time for the overthrow of our government and all other Gentile governments on the American continent, but the way and means of this utter destruction are clearly foretold, namely, the remnant of Jacob [Native Americans] will go through among the Gentiles and tear them in pieces, like a lion among the flocks of sheep. Their hand shall be lifted up

---

[43] Richard S. Van Wagoner, *Sidney Rigdon: A Portrait of Religious Excess* (Salt Lake City: Signature Books, 1994), 254.

[44] "Extracts of the Minutes of Conferences," *Times and Seasons* 1 (July 1839): 15, Commerce, Illinois, conference held on March 17, 1839 at Quincy, Illinois; republished in Ibid., 1 (Nov. 1839):15.

upon their adversaries, and all their enemies shall be cut off. This destruction includes an utter overthrow, and desolation of all our Cities, Forts, and Strong Holds—an entire annihilation of our race, except such as embrace the Covenant, and are numbered with Israel.

Now, Mr. Sunderland, you have something definite and tangible, the time, the manner, the means, the names, the dates; and I will state as a prophesy, that there will not be an unbelieving Gentile upon this continent 50 years hence; and if they are not greatly scourged, and in a great measure overthrown, within five or ten years from this date, then the Book of Mormon will have proved itself false.[45]

This theological statement by Apostle Parley P. Pratt regarding the primary founding book of the church presents an interesting situation as he defended his beliefs. The next chapter will concern itself with development in church theology.

---

[45] P. P. Pratt, *Mormonism Unveiled: Zion's Watchman Unmasked, and Its Editor, Mr. L. R. Sunderland, Exposed: Truth Vindicated: The Devil Mad, and Priestcraft in Danger!* (New York: Printed for the Publisher, 1838), 15, dated March 24, 1838 (47). See *The Essential Parley P. Pratt* (Salt Lake City: Signature Books, 1990), 23-24. The text Pratt refers to is in LDS 3 Nephi 21:6-17; RLDS 9:92-103.

20

Development in Theology

The development discussed in this chapter concerns that of Joseph Smith. Previous to the events in Missouri Smith made textual changes to his revision of the Bible, revised some of his revelations, and discussed his early religious experiences that led to the organization of the church. With the excommunication of church historian John Whitmer it was determined that Joseph Smith would compile a history of what he considered important for church members. Whitmer would not give up his history to church leaders. On April 27, 1838 Joseph Smith and Sidney Rigdon together with George W. Robinson as scribe spent the day in "writing a history of this Church from the earliest period of its existance [existence] up to this date."[1]

The initial 1838 draft of this history was written during a four-day period by George W. Robinson and most of it is not extant. In 1839 it was copied by James Mulholland, another of Joseph Smith's scribes, into what is known as the Manuscript History of the Church, Book A-1. The A-1 book was revised before and after its first publication and is now considered to be Smith's official narrative. It incorporates an account of Joseph's early religious calling and has served as the basis for virtually all later official and semi-official histories of the church.

The earliest part of this history was published in installments in the Mormon newspaper *Times and Seasons* in Nauvoo, Illinois, between March and May 1842.[2] Later it was reprinted in *The Latter Day Saints' Millennial Star* in England. In 1851 it was included in a pamphlet, *The Pearl of Great Price*. This was presented in revised form at a general conference of the church in Salt Lake City on October 10, 1880 and accepted as scripture. It has since been widely circulated and is regarded by

---

[1] Jessee, *Papers of Joseph Smith* 2:233.
[2] Joseph Smith started publishing his history in the March 15, 1842 issue, stating that it was an "extract from my journal" (*Times and Seasons* 3:726).

Mormons as an essential introduction in any investigation of the history of Mormonism. The following extract is from the Manuscript History written in 1839 by Mulholland before it was edited for publication:

> Owing to the many reports which have been put in circulation by evil disposed and designing persons in relation to the rise and progress of the Church of Latter day Saints, all of which have been designed by the authors thereof to militate against its character as a church, and its progress in the world; I have been induced to write this history so as to disabuse the publick mind, and put all enquirers after truth into possession of the facts as they have transpired in relation both to myself and the Church as far as I have such facts in [my] possession.
>
> In this history I will present the various events in relation to this Church in truth and righteousness as they have transpired, or as they at present exist, being now the eighth year since the organization of said Church.[3]

The history then gives the date of Smith's birth and mentions the family's move to New York. As discussed in chapter two the Palmyra excitement or revival is the backdrop for Joseph Smith's first vision. This history is a theological or faith account telling the events "as they have transpired, or as they at present exist." David Thelen wrote concerning memory, "What is important is that the memory be authentic for the person at the moment of construction, not that it be an accurate depiction of a past moment."[4] Another historian, Marvin S. Hill, concluded that the 1838-39 account was "streamlined for publication," making the story "more logical and compelling."[5]

Joseph Smith's history leaves much to be desired since it leaves out events known from other sources. For example, there is no mention of the use by Smith of a peep stone (known as a seer

---

[3] Jessee, *Papers of Joseph Smith* 1:267-68.
[4] David Thelen, "Memory and American History," *Journal of American History* 75 (March 1989):1,123.
[5] Marvin S. Hill, "The First Vision Controversy: A Critique and Reconciliation," *Dialogue: A Journal of Mormon Thought* 15 (Summer 1982):39.

stone) placed in a hat, the times spent helping others search for hidden treasures that were illusive, or the importance to the treasure guardian for Joseph to bring another individual with him to the hill where the plates were said to be deposited. That the telling of the first vision is theological is known when compared with the historical event that Smith associated with it.

As Joseph Smith explained there was an "excitement on the subject of religion" that preceded his visionary experience. Since the Palmyra revival occurred during the period 1824-25 it creates a problem by including the first vision at a period of time after the revival occurred. Since Lucy Mack Smith and three of her children joined the Palmyra Presbyterian Church during the excitement this brings into question whether the message in Joseph Smith's first vision included the information about the churches being an abomination. From Joseph's 1832 and 1835 accounts it appears that his quest was for a forgiveness of sins and that he received mercy and was forgiven.

The history states, "But in the process of time my mind became somewhat partial to the Methodist sect, and I felt some desire to be united with them." This is of interest since Joseph Smith had previously been an exhorter for the Methodist class in Palmyra. Smith said he prayed in the spring of 1820 and he saw two personages one of them pointing to the other and said "This is my beloved Son, Hear him" indicating that Joseph Smith should listen to the Son meaning Jesus Christ. The history says that it had never entered into Joseph's heart that all sects were wrong so he inquired which of the sects or churches was right and which he should join. The account included the following information:

> I was answered that I must join none of them, for they were all wrong, and the Personage who addressed me said that all their Creeds were an abomination in his sight, that those professors were all corrupt, that "they draw near to me with their lips but their hearts are far from me, They teach for doctrines the commandments of men, having a form of Godliness but they deny the power thereof."[6]

---

[6] Jessee, *Papers of Joseph Smith* 1:273; Joseph Smith-History 1:19, Pearl of Great Price. See Isaiah 29:13; Mark 7:6-7; 2 Timothy 3:5.

Rather than the question concerning whether the churches followed the New Testament this recollection presents Joseph with a clear and straight forward answer. Smith's earlier statement in 1832 was about knowing the churches did not adorn their profession and had apostatized. In answer to his prayer the Lord told him "they have turned asside [aside] from the gospel and keep not <my> commandments they draw near to me with their lips while their hearts are far from me and mine anger is kindling against the inhabitants of the earth to visit them ac[c]ording to th[e]ir ungodliness." In his 1835 telling Smith told of seeing many angels in the vision. These previous incidents were not as important to include this time. Receiving the forgiveness of sins was not included because the central message was not forgiveness. Joseph Smith's first vision was his call to be God's prophet.

How much of his 1838-39 account recalls his feelings near the time of Joseph's vision is hard to determine. But when other events are taken into consideration it appears that using the word "abomination" in reference to the creeds is too strong of language to use especially since members of Smith's family joined the local Presbyterian Church after 1820. As has been pointed out Lucy Mack Smith and three children joined with the Palmyra Presbyterians after the excitement of religion (revival) that commenced four year later.

When it comes to Smith's second vision telling about gold plates and providing the wording of the messenger it is clear that the words are post 1823. Using Joseph's story as a guide we can see clearer into how the words in his history fit closer to 1838 rather than prior to 1827. The reason for this is that in 1836 Joseph Smith and Oliver Cowdery reported they had a vision of the Old Testament prophet Elijah. Since the words spoken to Smith are quoted a comparison shows that they would not have been spoken in the context of 1823. This indicates that the retelling of the historical context and wording of the angel of the second vision does not have to coincide with history. This is a sure sign that we are dealing with a theological issue and not a historical event.

Joseph Smith dictated his longest 1838 account of what he said he had repeated many times to family and friends. Joseph stated that in September 1823 a personage appear to him at night in his bedroom. This personage (named Nephi in the history) told him that there was a book deposited in a nearby hill written in an unreadable language upon gold plates and this record contained an account of the former inhabitants of America. A vision opened to his mind and he saw where the plates were deposited.

The messenger repeated his message to Smith two additional times that night. These visions led Joseph to finding the gold plates in the morning and removing them from the ground four years later in September 1827. Joseph Smith then dictated the contents of the gold record to his scribes. This personage is represented to have quoted Old Testament passages in instructing Joseph. The messenger quoted Malachi chapter 4, verse 5, in the following words:

> Behold I will reveal unto you the Priesthood by the hand of Elijah the prophet before the coming of the great and dreadful day of the Lord.[7]

Is it correct that the personage would have spoken these words in 1823? If these words were not spoken in the vision then this would confirm that we are dealing with a theological story. It means that those actual words were not spoken during the visionary experience. It is a story of faith to those who embrace it.

A simple examination makes it clear that the words of the angel would not have been used as early as 1823 but at a time beyond the publication of the Book of Mormon. The textual variant relates to revealing "the Priesthood by the hand of" Elijah. The biblical text reads:

> Behold, I will send you Elijah the prophet before the coming of the great and dreadful day of the Lord: And he shall turn the heart of the fathers to the children, and the heart of the children to their fathers, lest I come and smite the earth with a curse.[8]

---

[7] Jessee, *Papers of Joseph Smith* 1:278; LDS D&C 2; Joseph Smith-History 1:38.
[8] Malachi 4:5-6 (KJV); quoted the same in 1830 BOM, 505; LDS 3 Nephi 25:5-6; RLDS 3 11:26-27.

When Joseph Smith made his revision of Malachi in July 1833 he considered the book "Correct."[9] In explaining the importance of renouncing war and proclaiming peace Joseph revealed the next month to seek diligently "to turn the hearts of the children to their fathers and the hearts of the fathers to the children and again the hearts of [the] Jews to the prophets and the prophets unto the Jews lest I come and smite the whole earth with a curse."[10] Though the order is reversed the message is the same as Malachi. In 1823 there would have been no reason to quote the passage differently. Sidney Rigdon in 1830 was looked upon as a preparer like John the Baptist to prepare the way "before Elijah which should come."[11]

When one of the early commandments received on September 4, 1830 was prepared for the 1835 Doctrine and Covenants wording was added relating to biblical individuals who will drink wine with the Savior indicating that Elijah held priesthood keys in the words, "and also Elijah, unto whom I have committed the keys of the power of turning the hearts of the fathers to the children and the hearts of the children to the fathers, that the whole earth may not be smitten with a curse"[12]

On April 3, 1836 it is recorded that Elijah the prophet appeared in a glorious vision to Joseph Smith and Oliver Cowdery and committed to them "the keys of this dispensation." Elijah was sent "to turn the hearts of the Fathers to the children, and the children to the fathers, lest the whole earth be smitten with a curse."[13] The understanding of the text in Malachi departed in some of its wording as it developed. By 1838 when Joseph Smith started dictated his Manuscript History, later recopied by James Mulholland, this following portion of the passage from Malachi was quoted by the angel in the wording:

---

[9] OT 2, 119, RLDS archives.

[10] Marquardt, *Joseph Smith Revelations*, 245; LDS D&C 98:16-17; RLDS D&C 95:3 (Aug. 6, 1833).

[11] Marquardt, *Joseph Smith Revelations*, 95; LDS D&C 35:4; RLDS D&C 34:2 (Dec. 1830).

[12] 1835 D&C 50:2; LDS D&C 27:9; RLDS D&C 26:2. For commentary on the textual revision see Marquardt, *Joseph Smith Revelations*, 72-80.

[13] Ibid., 280; LDS D&C 110:13-16.

And he shall plant in the hearts of the children the promises made to the fathers, and the hearts of the children shall turn to their fathers, if it were not so the whole earth would be utterly wasted at his coming.

Looking back to 1836 Smith explained that the promise of Elijah coming to reveal priesthood keys was a fulfillment of a promise made in connection to the time he first learned about the Book of Mormon plates. The added words relating to the future promise of obtaining from the hand of Elijah the Priesthood are an anachronism. This makes Smith's story suspect since it brings into question the accuracy of what he recalled as the words revealed to him in a vision.

The earliest version of Smith's story about the plates of gold being buried in the ground was told in a treasure seeking content with the plates or record being protected by a guardian. Joseph Smith's revision of how he first heard about the plates and that he received religious instructions from an angel show we are dealing with a faith story. By 1838 the recounting of the 1823 vision became more impressive with theological significance.

Another problem with the story is that there is no evidence that gold plates were used in the dictation of the text of the forthcoming Book of Mormon. Since Joseph Smith did not use the gold plates to produce the Book of Mormon text then the story of having them revealed in 1823 and going to their depository in a hill on a certain day once each year for five years (1823, 1824, 1825, 1826, 1827) is suspect. Smith indicated that after his September 1823 visit to the hill there was a four year waiting period and then he would obtain the plates. Joseph Smith's credibility becomes shaken when after he tells about obtaining possession of the plates, it is discovered that they were not used for the purpose for which they were reportedly preserved, revealed, and secured. It is pretty hard to believe a man who did not have or use what he said he obtained.

Problems occur when taking Joseph Smith's official 1838-39 story as historical fact rather than a faith account of religious significance. A helpful insight into understanding Smith is how he regards the confusion among the churches. Joseph by having the

Palmyra revival take place before the vision it creates an additional indication of how this story is being told.

If it is maintained that the 1838-39 history should be read literally one additional problem needs to be addressed. The story of the second vision, occurring after the excitement of religion in the neighborhood, which has been shown to have ended in 1825, would mean that the earliest time this vision of the angel would have occurred would be in September 1825. There would be one additional trip to the hill in September 1826 with Joseph going to the hill with Emma Hale Smith in 1827 It is of interest that John Corrill, an early church member, gave a shorter time period before Joseph Smith's first introduction to the gold plates. Corrill wrote in 1839:

> The simple story as related by others was this. Sometime in A.D. 1825, as nearly as I can recollect, Smith was informed by an angel, that there was a valuable record concealed in the earth, and the time had now arrived for it to be brought forth and published to the world.[14]

This would fit if the vision happened after Rev. Lane and Rev. Stockton preached in Palmyra during the revival. Whether the second vision happened in 1823 or 1825 may not be important since Joseph Smith said he did not take the record out of the ground until September 22, 1827. The correct dating cannot be known for sure because the vision of the angel is an issue for theologians in the telling of a religious saga.

Another development related to where the Garden of Eden was located. Biblical readers and scholars have placed the story of a garden in the Persian Gulf region in the historical setting as outlined in Genesis. Joseph Smith followed this reasoning until his arrival in Missouri. Joseph now taught that Adam lived in the present state of Missouri in America.

About July 1838 George W. Robinson recorded in the Scriptory Book the events that occurred earlier in May during a trip taken by Joseph Smith. On May 18 Joseph Smith, Sidney Rigdon, Thomas B. Marsh, David W. Patten, Alanson Ripley, and

---

[14] John Corrill, *A Brief History of the Church of Christ of Latter Day Saints*, 12.

George W. Robinson among others went north of Far West looking for a location for the gathering of the saints. The next day the group crossed Grand River and arrived at Lyman Wight's home. Robinson wrote, "we came to Col. Lyman Wights who lives at the foot of Tower Hill, a name appropriated by Prest Smith, in consequence of the remains of an old Nephitish Alter [Altar] an[d] Tower." Smith, Rigdon, and George Robinson came to a place where there was a spring and a small hill. After giving the range numbers of the area Robinson recorded:

which was called Spring Hill a name appropriated by the brethren present, But afterwards named by the mouth of [the] Lord and was called Adam Ondi Awmen [Ahman], because, said he, it is the place where Adam shall come to visit his people, or the Ancient of days shall sit as spoken of by Daniel the Prophet.[15]

The next month William Swartzell worked on walling in the spring. He prayed by the side of the spring that it might produce good water. Rather than keeping the name of the city Spring Hill Joseph Smith renamed it Adam-ondi-Ahman as recorded by Swartzell for June:

I observed to Joseph Smith that this city should have a new name. Brother Joseph placed his back against a small shady tree near the spring, and then said, "We shall alter the name of this stake," (every city being called a stake,) and looking towards heaven for short time, said, "It does not take me long to get a revelation from heaven, and this stake, or city, shall be called Adam-on-Diammon [Adam-ondi-Ahman]."[16]

---

[15] Jessee, *Papers of Joseph Smith* 2:244-45. See LDS D&C 116. See Daniel 7:13.

[16] William Swartzell, *Mormonism Exposed, Being a Journal of a Residence in Missouri from the 28th of May to the 20th of August, 1838* (Pekin, Ohio: Published by the Author, 1840), 11, entry for June 11, 1838. The journal was expanded for publication including the wording "in two or three days the spring began to fail, and in about one week it went entirely dry." The name was given by Smith about June 11-16 and not in May.

On July 8 Joseph Smith received a revelation that contained the following question:

> Is there not room enough upon the mountains of Adam Ondi Awmen [Ahman], and upon the plains of Olah[a] Shinehah, or in the land where Adam dwelt[17]

The surveying was completed for town lots and the brethren continued traveling north looking for possible settlements for church members. The area was known by the shortened name Diahman. Church members wrote in their recollections that Joseph Smith discovered what was believed to be the remains of an altar on which Adam offered sacrifices. There may have been a number of altars shown by Smith at Adam-ondi-Ahman. Twenty year old Benjamin F. Johnson, who arrived in late October and was not married, chose a lot with a view of Grand River. Johnson recalled:

> So I chose the upper [area] which at first appeared rocky; which made the other lots appear almost enviable. But when, after a few days, the Prophet [Joseph Smith] accompanied us to this spot, and pointed out those rocks as the ones of which Adam built an altar and offered sacrifice upon this spot, where he stood up and blessed the multitude of his children, when they called him Michael, and where he will again sit as the Ancient of Days, — then I was not envious of any one's choice for a city lot in Adam-ondi-Ahman.[18]

The name Adam-ondi-Ahman was used prior to 1838 as the place of the residence of Adam. It was used in Kirtland and a hymn was composed by William W. Phelps with the same title. The location was considered to be in the Near East until 1838.[19] With

---

[17] Marquardt, *Joseph Smith Revelations*, 294; LDS D&C 117:8.

[18] Benjamin Franklin Johnson Papers, "My Life Review," 30, LDS archives. See *My Life's Review*, 36.

[19] Ronald K. Harrison, Professor of Old Testament, Wycliffe College, University of Toronto, wrote the following concerning the location of the Garden of Eden: "On the basis of currently available information it would appear that the one that locates Eden near the head of the Persian Gulf combines

new insight Joseph Smith reported that the Garden of Eden was located in what is now Missouri.[20]

Adam was a central role model for Joseph Smith in his salvation theology. The 1835 Doctrine and Covenants presents additional wording to a March 1832 revelation. The added section included the words "who hath established the foundations of Adam-ondi-Ahman; who hath appointed Michael, your prince, and established his feet, and set him upon high; and given unto him the keys of salvation under the counsel and direction of the Holy One, who is without beginning of days or end of life."[21] This addition indicates that Michael or Adam has the "keys of salvation" under the Holy One.

Joseph Smith responded to the question "If the Mormon doctrine is true what has become of all those who have died since the days of the apostles" and he answered:

> All those who have not had an opportunity of hearing the gospel, and being administered to by an inspired man in the flesh, must have it hereafter, before they can be finally judged.[22]

The possibility of the gospel being preached to deceased individuals involved priesthood keys or presidency. Since Adam according to Joseph Smith held the priesthood it was important to rely in part to biblical passages in interpreting the relationship of Adam to the human family. In the summer of 1839 Joseph Smith explained:

---

the greatest number of probabilities of every kind" (in Geoffrey W. Bromiley, general ed., *The International Standard Bible Encyclopedia* [Grand Rapids, Michigan: William B. Eerdmans Publishing Co., 1982], 2:17).

[20] Brigham Young said he heard about the location of the biblical Garden of Eden from Joseph Smith. Wilford Woodruff reported Young saying, "Now Jackson County is the garden of Eden Joseph has declaired [declared] this & I am as much bound to believe it as much as I am to believe Joseph is a prophet of God" (*Wilford Woodruff's Journal* 5:33, entry for March 15, 1857; see also 7:129).

[21] Marquardt, *Joseph Smith Revelations*, 197-98; 1835 D&C 75:3; LDS D&C 78:15-16; RLDS D&C 77:3 (1 March 1832). See Daniel 10:13, 21, and 12:1.

[22] *Elders' Journal* 1 (July 1838):43.

The Priesthood was. first given to Adam: he obtained the first Presidency & held the Keys of it, from generation to Generation; he obtained it in the creation before the world was formed . . . the Keys have to be brought from heaven whenever the Gospel is sent. = When they are revealed from Heaven it is by Adam[']s Authority.

Dan[iel] VII Speaks of the Ancient of days, he means the oldest man, our Father Adam, Michael; he will call his children together. & hold a council with them to prepare them for the coming of the Son of Man. He, (Adam) is the Father of the human family & presides over the Spirits of all men, & all that have had the Keys must Stand before him in this grand Council.[23]

Continuing Smith gave instructions on salvation for the dead. He quoted in part from Hebrews 11:40 that they without us should or cannot be made perfect. Joseph Smith explained, "These men are in heaven, but their children are on Earth. . . . We cannot be made perfect without them, nor they without us. . . . The hearts of the children will have to be turned to the fathers, & the fathers to the children living or dead to prepare them for the coming of the Son of Man. If Elijah did not come the whole earth would be smitten."[24]

This comment developed into the necessity of having performed on behalf of the fathers (deceased men and women) by living proxies perform the ordinance of baptism for the dead that the individual could not have done while living. In the summer of 1840 proxy baptisms were performed in the Mississippi River where the wording for the baptismal ceremony was similar to how regular baptism into the church was done. But in this case the ceremony was performed with a church member standing in the place of the deceased person. The living saints now had a need to work for the salvation of the dead. According to Joseph Smith this

---

[23] "Willard Richards Pocket Companion, written in England," 63-64, emphasis omitted, LDS archives. See Ehat and Cook, *Words of Joseph Smith*, 8-9.

[24] Ibid., 10-11. In Joseph Smith's revision of Hebrews he changed the wording in Hebrews 11:40 to read, "for without sufferings they could not be made perfect" (NT MS 2, folio 4, 141).

could not be passed over lightly "for their salvation is necessary and essential to our salvation."[25]

The following comments were made by Joseph Smith pertaining to his key to detect evil spirits, the devil and others when they are to appear to mortals. These teachings were developed in Missouri, Iowa, and Illinois. In July 1839 President Smith explained to the members of the Quorum of the Twelve some of the keys of the kingdom of God. Wilford Woodruff recorded Smith giving instructions on detecting the devil and the necessity of shaking hands with an angel:

> In order to detect the devel [devil] when he transforms himself nigh unto an angel of light. When an angel of God appears unto man face to face in personage & reaches out his hand unto the man & he takes hold of the angels hand & feels a substance the same as one man would in Shaking hands with another he may then know that it is an angel of God, & he should place all Confidence in him. Such personages or angels are Saints with there [their] resurrected Bodies. But if a personage appears unto man & offers him his hand & the man takes told of it & feels nothing or does not sens[e] any substance he may know it is the devel [devil]

Then Smith continued with how to detect a non-resurrected saint when he appears:

> for when a Saint whose body is not resurrected appears unto man in the flesh he will not offer him his hand for this is against the law given him & in keeping in mind these things we may detec[t] the devil that he decieved [deceive] us not.[26]

That summer Joseph Smith mentioned that an angel of God does not have wings but "has flesh and bones, we see not their

---

[25] Marquardt, *Joseph Smith Revelations*, 320; LDS D&C 128:15 (Sept. 6, 1842).
[26] *Wilford Woodruff's Journal* 1:341, entry for June 27, 1839; Ehat and Cook, *Words of Joseph Smith*, 6.

glory."[27] An editorial in the *Times and Seasons* discussed trying the spirits and told of a sister in New York State to whom an angel appeared with sandy colored hair. It was asked how "was this known to be a bad angel? by the color of his hair; that is one of the signs that he can be known by, and by his contradicting a former revelation."[28]

Joseph Smith gave a discourse in Nauvoo on May 1, 1842. He explained other signs and words to detect false appearances. Willard Richards recorded that Joseph preached in the grove and said: "The keys are certain signs & words by which false spirits & personages may be detected from true.—which cannot be revealed to the Elders till the Temple is completed.—The rich can only get them in the Temple. The poor may get them on the mountain top as did Moses."[29]

The next year, on February 9, 1843, Joseph Smith explained that "There are two kinds of beings in heaven viz: Angels who are resurrected personages having bodies of flesh and bones, for instance Jesus said 'handle me and see for a spirit hath not flesh and bones as ye see me have.['] 2nd The spirits of just men made perfect, they who are not resurrected but inherit the same glory." He gave three keys on how to detect whether a messenger (angel, spirit, or devil) came from God.

First, "When a messenger comes saying he has a message from God offer him your hand and request him to shake hands with you. If he be an angel he will do so and you will feel his hand." Second, "If he be the spirit of a just man made perfect he will come in his glory for that is the only way he can appear. Ask him to shake hands with you, but he will not move, because it is contrary to the order of Heaven for a just man to deceive but he will still deliver his message." And third, "If it be the devil as an angel of light when you ask him to shake hands he will offer you his hand and you will not feel anything, you may there fore detect him." As

---

[27] Willard Richards Pocket Companion, 72. See Ehat and Cook, *Words of Joseph Smith*, 12.

[28] "Try the Spirits," *Times and Seasons* 3 (April 1, 1842):747.

[29] Jessee, *Papers of Joseph Smith* 2:379.

Smith indicated, "These are the three grand keys whereby you may know w[h]ether any administration is from God."[30]

There were a number of ways that church members could use to detect a spirit, angel, or devil appearing. They included the discerning by those appointed to watch over the church, by prayer, by shaking hands, by the color of hair, and by comparing the message with previous revelations for agreement.[31]

While in Liberty Jail, Clay County, Missouri, Joseph Smith agonized over his situation being held for months on reported crimes. He reflected and gave instructions to the church that included moving from a belief in monotheism (one God) to polytheism (many Gods). God, explained Smith, would reveal knowledge not previous revealed. There would be "a time to come in the which nothing shall be with held whither [whether] there be one god or many gods they shall be manifest all thrones and dominions, principalities and powers shall be revealed and set forth upon all who have indured [endured] valiently [valiantly] for the gospel of Jesus Christ." Joseph Smith told the saints:

> if there be bounds set to the heavens or to the seas or to the dry land or to the sun, moon or starrs [stars] all the times of their revolutions all their appointed days, month[s] and years and all the Days of their days, months and years, and all their glories, laws and set times shall be reveal[e]d in the days of the dispensation of the fullness of times according to that which was ordained in the midst of the councyl [council] of the eternal God of all other Gods before this world was[32]

---

[30] James B. Allen, *No Toil nor Labor Fear: The Story of William Clayton* (Provo, Utah: Brigham Young University Press, 2002), 388 from William Clayton Journal, entry for February 9, 1843; LDS D&C 129.

[31] For teachings relating to prayer and the discerning of spirits, see LDS D&C 46:15-16, 23, 27; RLDS D&C 46:6 (March 8, 1831) and LDS D&C 50:30-35; RLDS D&C 50:6-7 (May 9, 1831).

[32] Marquardt, *Joseph Smith Revelations*, 297, epistle of Joseph Smith Jr., et al., to the church at Quincy, Illinois, and scattered abroad, and to Bishop Edward Partridge, March 20, 1839; LDS D&C 121:28-32.

By the beginning of 1841 Joseph Smith was teaching, "That which is without body or parts is nothing. There is no other God in heaven but that God who has flesh and bones."[33] In 1842 Joseph published his Book of Abraham and indicated that the earth was planned by a council of Gods. Two years later in 1844 Smith stated that "God himself, who sits enthroned in yonder heavens, is a man like unto one of yourselves, that is the great secret."[34] In June of the same year Smith said that he had always preached a plurality of Gods since 1829. Thomas Bullock wrote what was said using short abbreviations that are filled out with brackets:

> I wish to declare I have allways—& in all congregat[ion]s. when I have preached it has been the plurality of Gods it has been preached 15 years—I have always decl[are]d. God to be a distinct personage—J[esus]. C[hrist]. a sep[arate]. & distinct pers[onage] from God the Fa[the]r. the H[oly]. G[host]. was a distinct personage & or Sp[irit] & these 3 constit[ute]. 3 distinct personages & 3 Gods[35]

Joseph Smith like other individuals developed in his ideas. Smith's recollection of events in his early life took on more of a theological nature than historical reality and his story grew in the telling. The words that he said the angel spoke to him in 1823 about Elijah became of importance significance as he looked back to his early life. Placing the Garden of Eden and Adam-ondi-Ahman in Missouri was accepted by church members since it was spoken by Joseph. His theology about the nature of God became clear to him as he expounded the idea of a plurality of Gods. The question to him was not if any of his ideas changed or contradicted what he had said at an earlier time. Joseph was able to express his interpretation of events as he presented new ideas in a revelatory manner. As an oracle to his followers his theological development became the word of God.

---

[33] "Extracts from Wm Clayton's Private Book," LDS archives, Jan. 5, 1841; Ehat and Cook, *Words of Joseph Smith*, 60.

[34] "Conference Minutes," *Times and Seasons* 5 (Aug. 15, 1844):613.

[35] Thomas Bullock Report, June 16, 1844, as cited in Ehat and Cook, *Words of Joseph Smith*, 378.

21

Building Nauvoo

With the exodus from Missouri many church members traveled east to the state of Illinois. One of the first actions was at a church conference held at Quincy, Illinois on March 17, 1839 where some members who testified at Justice Austin King's preliminary hearing were excommunicated from the church. It appears that they were not present at the meeting. Those excommunicated included Sampson Avard, John Corrill, George M. Hinkle, Reed Peck, William W. Phelps, and Burr Riggs.[1]

Joseph Smith arrived in Quincy on April 22 and shortly afterwards church leaders purchased land at Commerce (later named Nauvoo). Dimick B. Huntington recalled when Joseph Smith came to town on the Quincy ferry boat. Huntington said that Smith was dressed "in an old Pair of Boots full of Holes, Pants Torn, Tucked Inside of boots, Blue Cloak with collar Turned up, wide Brimd Black hat, Rim S[l]oped Down, not been Shaved for Some time <Looked Pale & Hag[g]ard>." Dimick recognize Joseph:

> when I got within about 16 ft of him he Raised his head. I Exclaimed My God it is you Bro Jos[eph] he Raised his hand & Stop[p]ed me Saying Hush Hush. He then asked where is my family. I told him they were 4 miles East at Judge Clevelands in a Room I had Provided for them. I asked him if he wished to see his father & mother as they were in Quincy. he said no it would be to[o] Great a Shock they are old & cannot bear it. take me to my family as Quick as you can. in Passing Through the Back Streets of Quincy a number of men Knew him, an[d] arivind [arrived] At the House where his family was Emma Knew him as he was Dismounting from his Horse. She met him Half way to

---

[1] "Extracts of the Minutes of Conferences," *Times and Seasons* 1 (Nov. 1839):15, Commerce, Illinois.

the Gate. Joseph not [k]nowing the universal frienaly [friendly] feelings that Existed, in Quincy, was fearfull he might be ar[r]ested again.[2]

Six months later on October 29 Joseph Smith and his fellow companions left Nauvoo for Washington, D.C. seeking redress for wrongs that occurred against church members in Missouri. Part of the time Smith and Sidney Rigdon traveled incognito for fear of enemies.[3] Joseph Smith met with President Martin Van Buren a month later. The President told Smith in essence, "What can I do? I can do nothing for you! If I do anything, I shall come in contact with the whole state of Missouri."[4] While waiting for the Saints' petition to be presented to Congress Joseph Smith visited Philadelphia on December 21. A few months previously in September Benjamin Winchester came to Philadelphia and preached in the city. On October 1 baptisms were performed in the Delaware River. Among those baptized was William Small "the first candidate baptized in Philadelphia" and Samuel Bennett who became the first branch president.[5] The Philadelphia Branch was organized on December 23, 1839 by Joseph Smith.[6] Apostle Orson Pratt wrote to his wife Sarah:

I went to Philadelphia on Saturday the 21st of December, there I found President J[oseph]. Smith jr.; he had just arrived from Washington city, where he had been about 3 weeks - 4 or 5 days after, Judge Higbee, with Porter Rockwell, came to Philadelphia; they are well. . . . I staid [stayed] with brother Smith, in Philadelphia, about 8 days; we then took the rail road, and went some 35 or 40 miles, to a large branch of the church in Monmouth co. N[ew]. J[ersey]. Which numbers 90 members: there I left him on

---

[2] Statement of Dimick B. Huntington, circa 1855, LDS archives.
[3] Robert D. Foster to Joseph Smith III, Feb. 14, 1874 in *True Latter Day Saints' Herald* 22 (April 15, 1875):226.
[4] Joseph Smith Jr. and Elias Higbee to Hyrum Smith, Dec. 5, 1839 as cited in *History of the Church* 4:40.
[5] Walter W. Smith, "The History of the Philadelphia, Pennsylvania Branch," *Journal of History* 11 (July 1918):362.
[6] Philadelphia Branch Minutes, 2, typed copy, RLDS archives.

new year's day . . . Elder Winchester had when I left Philadelphia, baptized 45 in that city[7]

Sidney Rigdon and Dr. Robert Foster arrived in the city by the time of the January 13, 1840 Philadelphia Branch Conference. Benjamin Winchester mentioned the conference held in the city, "We had a conference here the first [part] of Jan. 1840, J[oseph]. Smith, Jr. S[idney]. Rigdon, Orson, P[arley]. P. Pratt, and many other elders, were present. . . . J[oseph]. Smith, jr. bore testimony to the coming forth of the book of mormon which was the means of doing much good."[8] At the conference Parley P. Pratt spoke about the possibility of printing an edition of the Book of Mormon in New York. The minutes state that in the afternoon:

Brother Joseph Smith Jr dilated [expanded] at some length on the offices of the Priesthood and on the duties of Elders, Bishops, Priests, &c and directed it should be intered [entered] on the minutes as the injunction of the Presidency that travelling Elders should be especially cautious of incroaching [encroaching] on the ground of stationed & presiding Elders and rather direct their efforts to breaking up and occupying new ground and that the Churches generally refuse to be burthened [burdened] with the support of unprofitable and dilatory labourers. It was unanimously resolved that this be received as the will and wish of the Conference.[9]

Evidently the day after the branch conference Joseph Smith preached at the pulpit of the Universalist Church at Fourth and Lombard Streets.[10] Apostle Parley P. Pratt recalled about this

[7] Extract from letter of Orson Pratt to Sarah Pratt, Jan. 6, 1840, *Times and Seasons* 1 (Feb. 1840):61, Nauvoo.

[8] Benjamin Winchester to "Dear Brother in the Lord," Feb. 10, 1840, *Times and Seasons* 1 (May 1840):104. Winchester listed Orson Pratt as being present but he was probably not in Philadelphia at the time.

[9] Philadelphia Branch Minutes, Jan. 13, 1840, 3-4. See Richard P. Howard, "Values in Old Minute Books," *Saints Herald* 123 (Dec. 1976):48.

[10] Smith, "The History of the Philadelphia, Pennsylvania Branch," *Journal of History* 11 (July 1918):363. The First Independent Church of Christ (Universalist) treasurer's book contains the entry on renting the building, "1840

meeting, "a very large church was opened for him to preach in . . . Brother Rigdon spoke first, and dwelt on the Gospel, illustrating his doctrine by the Bible." Parley Pratt wrote that Smith bore "testimony of the visions he had seen, the ministering of angels which he had enjoyed; and how he had found the plates of the Book of Mormon, and translated them by the gift and power of God."[11] Parley wrote afterwards: "While in Philadelphia, I had the happiness of meeting with Elders J. Smith, Jun., and S. Rigdon, who had come from the west [Nauvoo] on a mission to the seat of government, to lay before Congress and the President of the United States, the facts of the Missouri persecution. From them I received much precious instruction, in which I shall always rejoice."[12] Smith traveled back to Washington, D.C. and was back in Nauvoo by the first of March 1840.

In April, near the end of the month, two individuals visited Joseph Smith and had an interview with him. Smith showed them "several frames, covered with glass, under which were numerous fragments of Egyptian papyrus, on which, as usual, a great variety of hieroglyphical characters had been imprinted." They talked about his visit to President Martin Van Buren:

> the conversation turned upon his recent visit to Washington, and his talk with the President of the United States. He gave us distinctly to understand that his political views had undergone an entire change; and his description of the reception given him at the executive mansion was any thing but flattering to the distinguished individual who presides over its hospitalities.
>
> Before he had heard the story of our wrongs, said the indignant Prophet, Mr. Van Buren gave us to understand

---

January 14 For use of the Church from Rev. J. Smith by G. H. McCully $13.63." See John Shiffert, "Site of Joseph Smith's 1839 [sic; 1840] Philadelphia Sermon Identified," *Ensign* 23 (May 1993):101. This article quotes from Parley P. Pratt and says that he refers to the last week in December 1839. This is incorrect since the meeting was in January 1840. The building is currently used by the Jewish Yaron Chapel of Congregation Kesher Israel, 412 Lombard Street.

[11] *Autobiography of Parley P. Pratt*, 260.

[12] Editor, "Sketch of Travels in America, and Voyage to England," *Latter-Day Saints' Millennial Star* 1 (July 1840):51, Manchester, England.

that he could do nothing for the redress of our grievances lest it should interfere with his political prospects in Missouri. He is not as fit said he, as my dog, for the chair of state; for my dog will make an effort to protect his abused and insulted master, while the present chief magistrate will not so much as lift his finger to relieve an oppressed and persecuted community of freemen, whose glory it has been that they were citizens of the United States.[13]

John Cook Bennett an ambitious man, who was at the time Quarter Master General of the state of Illinois, wrote a series of letters to Joseph Smith and Sidney Rigdon. Bennett seemed obsessed with joining the church. Near the end of August 1840 he arrived in Nauvoo to lend a hand in its establishment as a city. Shortly afterwards Bennett was baptized into the church and probably received the first patriarchal blessing given under the hands of Hyrum Smith the new patriarch on September 21.

At the church conference held in October John C. Bennett together with Joseph Smith and Robert B. Thompson were appointed to a committee to draw up a bill for the incorporation of Nauvoo and other purposes. It was resolved "that Dr. J. C. Bennett, be appointed delegate to Springfield, to urge the passage of said bill through the legislature." The published conference minutes mentioned:

Dr. Bennett then, made some very appropriate remarks on the duty of the saints in regard to those, who had, under circumstances of affliction, held out the hand of friendship, and that it was their duty to uphold such men and give them the[i]r suffrages, and support.[14]

In December Bennett writing under the pseudonym "Joab, General in Israel" explained that the act for incorporation the City of Nauvoo passed the Illinois State Legislature with provisions to establish a Nauvoo Legion and a University of the City of

---

[13] *Quincy Whig* 3 (Oct. 17, 1840):1, Quincy.
[14] *Times and Seasons* 1 (Oct. 1840):186.

Nauvoo.[15] Most but not all of the articles contained in the charter were patterned after the Springfield, Illinois city charter. The act was signed by Governor Thomas Carlin. Election for the city government was held on February 1, 1841 when John C. Bennett was voted mayor. Vilate Kimball told of one happy event that occurred at the end of 1840:

> our people had bought a boat; they have named her Nauvoo. the last trip she made up the river, President Smith went with her, and when he returned who should accompany him but John F Boynton and his wife, and Lymon [Lyman] Johnson. they made it there [their] home to Joseph Smiths all the time they were here.
>
> I never saw Joseph appear more happy; said he, I am a going to have all my old friends around me again; they both bought lots and calculate to build and move here the ensuing Season. as to their faith, I have not heard much about it, but I conclude they have got some, or they [would?] have no object in comeing [coming] here. I never saw any body that appeared glader to see me than John[']s wife, they all called brother, and sister, and appeared as friendly as I ever saw them![16]

Religiously Joseph Smith's longest revelation was given on January 19, 1841. This document referred to projected church projects such as building a temple and constructing a boarding house for the Smith family and visitors to the city. Joseph's older brother Hyrum who had been ordained by his father in September 1840 was confirmed as church patriarch. Sidney Rigdon was to continue to be a counselor and William Law was appointed to the first presidency to receive the oracles for the church. The Quorum of the Twelve, a church high council, and various priesthood quorums composed the central organization.[17]

---

[15] Ibid. 2 (Jan. 1, 1841):266-67.

[16] Vilate Kimball to Heber C. Kimball, Dec. 8, 1840, LDS archives.

[17] Marquardt, *Joseph Smith Revelations*, 309-310; LDS D&C 124:125-145.

As mentioned previously John C. Bennett was able to obtain the charter for the city of Nauvoo. In January 1841 the first presidency wrote concerning Bennett:

he addressed us a letter, tendering to us his assistance in delivering us out of the hands of our enemies, and restoring us again to our privileges, and only required at our hands to point out the way, and he would be forthcoming, with all the forces he could raise for that purpose—He has been one of the principal instruments, in effecting our safety and deliverance from the unjust persecutions and demands of the authorities of Missouri, and also in procuring the city charter—He is a man of enterprize [enterprise], extensive acquirements, and of independant [independent] mind, and is calculated to be a great blessing to our community.[18]

The saints were told in the revelation of January 19:

Again, let my servant John C. Bennett, help you in your labor in sending my word to the kings and people of the earth, and stand by you, even you my servant Joseph Smith, in the hour of affliction, and his reward shall not fail, if he receive counsel; and for his love he shall be great; for he shall be mine if he do[es] this, saith the Lord. I have seen the work which he hath done, which I accept, if he continue, and will crown him with blessings and great glory.[19]

A third edition of the Book of Mormon was published in 1840. In one of the passages in 1 Nephi Joseph Smith gave additional clarification by adding the words "or out of the waters of baptism" to the text of Isaiah 48:1:

Hearken and hear this, O house of Jacob, who are called by the name of Israel, and are come forth out of the waters of

---

[18] "A Proclamation, To the Saints Scattered Abroad," *Times and Seasons* 2 (Jan. 15, 1841):275.
[19] Marquardt, *Joseph Smith Revelations*, 301; LDS D&C 124:16-17.

Judah, (or out of the waters of baptism,) who swear by the name of the Lord, and make mention of the God of Israel[20]

Ebenezer Robinson recalled that Joseph made this change in the text.[21] The 1840 edition (third edition) of the Book of Mormon contained some textual revisions. The title page included the words "Carefully revised by the translator." Robinson was involved in having stereotyped plates made. The Book of Mormon was printed by Shepard and Stearns in Cincinnati, Ohio. The first run of 2,000 copies was finished in October.[22] A number of items including the original manuscript of the Book of Mormon were placed in the southeast cornerstone of the Nauvoo House on October 2, 1841. Warren Foote wrote, "Joseph Smith came up with the manuscript of the Book of Mormon and said that he wanted to put that in there, as he had had trouble enough with it."[23]

A preacher from St. Louis in company with a friend told of his visit to Nauvoo and his interview with Joseph Smith on November 3 and mentioned, "The Prophet was asleep, in his rocking chair, when we entered. His wife and children were busy about the room, ironing, &c., and one or two Mormon preachers, lately returned from England, were sitting by the large log fire." Concerning the influence Smith had in Nauvoo, Joseph replied:

I bought 900 acres here, a few years ago, and they all have their lands of me. My influence, however, is ecclesiastical

---

[20] 1840 BOM, 53; LDS 1 Nephi 20:1; not in RLDS 1 Nephi 6:8. This reading is not reflected in the Isaiah Dead Sea scroll 1QIs^a which would not be expected since this is an interpretation of a text. See *The Dead Sea Scroll Bible: The Oldest Known Bible Translated for the First Time into English*, Translated and with Commentary by Martin Abegg, Jr., Peter Flint, and Eugene Ulrich (New York: HarperSanFrancisco, 1999), 349.

[21] Robinson, "A Historical Reminiscence," *Saints Herald* 30 (March 10, 1883):146.

[22] Robinson, "Testimony on the Book of Mormon," *Saints Herald* 33 (Dec. 11, 1886):778-81.

[23] Autobiography of Warren Foote, LDS archives. The list of items placed in the cornerstone was recorded in the Book of the Law of the Lord. See a photograph published in Joseph F. Smith Jr., "The Original Manuscript of the Book of Mormon," *Improvement Era* 10 (June 1907):575 and "Book of Mormon Manuscript Put In Nauvoo House Corner Stone," Church Section, *Deseret News*, Aug. 8, 1931.

only; in civil affairs, I am but a common citizen. To be sure, I am a member of the City Council, and Lieutenant General of the Nauvoo Legion. I can command a thousand men to the field, at any moment, to support the laws. I had hard work to make them turn out and form the 'Legion,' until I shouldered my musket, and entered the ranks myself. Now, they have nearly all provided themselves with a good uniform, poor as they are.[24]

It was at Nauvoo that Joseph Smith published the Book of Abraham. In early 1842 Joseph Smith and Reuben Hedlock worked on restoring three illustrations. They are known as Facsimile Numbers 1, 2, and 3. From the Egyptian Alphabet and Smith's explanations we know that he considered they represented teachings relating to astronomy. For Facsimile No. 1 the hieroglyphics in the columns on the original document were omitted and the damaged papyrus restored. Facsimile No. 3 which would have been on the inside of the roll was better preserved. The head of Figure 6 "a slave belonging to the prince" was altered and included the preserved Egyptian characters. Facsimile No. 2 the round object was now a complete circle with restored portions including characters from the Egyptian papyrus used in the Translation Manuscripts. These reproductions were included with the printing of the Book of Abraham.

Joseph Smith spent additional time working on the Book of Abraham and preparing his explanations of the three restored Facsimiles. These were published in the church paper the *Times and Seasons*. Apostle Wilford Woodruff set some of the type for the Book of Abraham. He wrote a summary statement in his journal:

Joseph the Seer has presented us some of the Book of Abraham which was written by his own hand but hid from the knowledge of man for the last four thousand years but has now come to light through the mercy of God. Joseph

---

[24] "Mormons and Mormonism," *St. Louis Republican* 20 (Nov. 25, 1841), St. Louis, Missouri. On the military uniforms of the Nauvoo Legion see Glen M. Leonard, "Picturing the Nauvoo Legion," *Brigham Young University Studies* 35, no. 2 (1995):95-135.

has had these records in his possession for several years but has never presented them before the world untill now. But he is now about to publish it to the world or parts of it by publishing it in the Times & Seasons, for Joseph the Seer is now the Editor of that paper & Elder [John] Taylor assists him in writing while it has fallen to my lot to take charge of the Business part of the esstablishment [establishment].[25]

The March 1 issue of the *Times and Seasons* states, "This paper commences my [Joseph Smith's] editorial career, I alone stand responsible for it." The manuscript draft of the editorial contains the following, "In the present no. will be found the commencement of the Records discovered in Egypt. Some time since. as penned by the hand of Father Abraham. which I shall continue to translate & publish as fast as possible till the whole is completed."[26]

Facsimile No. 1

In ancient Egypt there was the belief in many deities. The vignette (or illustration) drawn on this papyrus was for Horus who was deceased. This illustration shows the deceased (identified with Osiris, god of the underworld) lying on a lion-shaped funerary bier while Anubis (the jackal-headed god of embalming) ready for the mummification process. Below the bier are four conopic jars which held the vital organs of the deceased. This papyrus is known as the Book of Breathings or Breathing Permit. It was a late rendition and condensed version of what is called the Book of the Dead.

Sometime after the papyrus was purchased it was glued to the backing paper and the standing figure (number 3) was given a head and a knife. It is possible that this was done prior to moving

---

[25] Kenney, *Wilford Woodruff's Journal* 2:155, entry for Feb. 19, 1842. The text of the Book of Abraham was published in *Times and Seasons* 3, no. 9 (March 1, 1842):704-706, paragraphs 1-13 (LDS Abraham 1:1-2:18, written in November 1835) and ibid., 3, no. 10 (March 15, 1842):719-22, paragraphs 14-32 (LDS Abraham 2:19-5:21, written in March 1842).

[26] *Times and Seasons* 3 (March 1, 1842):710. The draft editorial is in the handwriting of Willard Richards (Joseph Smith Collection, LDS archives). A portion of this editorial (first paragraph reworded) was published.

to Nauvoo. With preparation for the publication of the illustration the final result was that figure 3 had a head similar to figure 2. Joseph Smith's explanation of figure 3 is: "The idolatrous priest of Elkenah attempting to offer up Abraham as a sacrifice."

First vignette of Breathing Permit of Horus (Original in LDS archives). Original papyrus of Facsimile No. 1. Damage continued in the writing to the left of this drawing. Joseph Smith represented this as a complete picture when published.

The characters on the side of the illustration were omitted in order to fit the page without turning the page sideways. Though the original was damaged the cut was prepared by Reuben Hedlock under the direction of Joseph Smith and printed as though the illustration was complete and not damaged.

Various newspapers reproduced Facsimile 1 from the published illustration in the *Times and Seasons*. While there was interest in what Smith was doing the newspapers did not take him seriously. Joseph Smith regarded the illustration as representing Abraham on an altar about to be sacrificed by a standing black figure with a white face like Abraham's.

Joseph Smith in his explanation said the bird (Figure 1) was the angel of the Lord with the "Idolatrous Priest of Elkenah attempting to offer up Abraham as a sacrifice" (Figure 3) before five idolatrous gods. The original vignette was damaged in the area of the body of the lying figure. As indicated the head of the standing figure was filled in after the papyrus was glued to the backing paper. The proposed reconstruction had the head facing sideways and a knife in the hand of the priest. When printed in the *Times and Seasons* the illustration appeared to be complete.

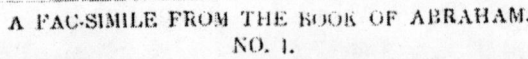

Times and Seasons 3, no. 9 (March 1, 1842):703, first page of issue. The head of figure 3 was added. Compare with original. The black figure is Anubus. Columns on both sides were omitted when published. The size of Facsimile 1 is close to the size of Facsimile 3 being from the same scroll.

Facsimile No. 2

In publishing Facsimile No. 2 careful attention was made to fill in the missing areas on the round illustration or Egyptian hypocephalus (meaning under the head, where the object was to be placed for the deceased). The damaged parts were filled in from papyri in order to make the round object appear whole or complete in its recovered state. The hypocephalus contains elements that are Egyptian but from various sources. To the common person it would appear as a complete picture and not damaged, though persons who saw the original would have seen it fragmented.

The Book of the Law of the Lord kept in Nauvoo by Willard Richards recorded for March 4, 1842 the following activity of Joseph Smith: "Exhibeting [Exhibiting] the Book of Abraham, in the original, To Bro[ther] Reuben Hadlock [Hedlock]. . . . also gave instruction concerning the arrangement of the writing on the Large cut. illustrating the principles of Astronomy."[27] This was Facsimile No. 2 and appeared in the *Times and Seasons* as a large fold out page. Though it was represented to be "A Fac-simile from the Book of Abraham" the illustration was larger in size and not from the same scroll as Facsimiles 1 and 3, as it is an Egyptian hypocephalus not a breathing permit. Also the name of deceased is not Horus.

Figure 3 at the top right of the reconstructed illustration, filled in from another papyrus, was explained by Joseph Smith:

Is made to represent God, sitting upon his throne, clothed with power and authority; with a crown of eternal light upon his head; representing, also, the grand Key words of the Holy Priesthood, as revealed to Adam in the Garden of Eden, as also to Seth, Noah, Melchisedek [Melchizedek], Abraham and all to whom the Priesthood was revealed.

Another drawing that has a throne is interpreted as "Representing God sitting upon his throne, revealing, through the heavens, the grand Keys words of the Pricsthood; as, also the sign of the Holy Ghost unto Abraham, in the form of a dove." The facsimile was to help present sacred information that was to be revealed in the priesthood endowment ceremony. In May Joseph Smith initiated his brother Hyrum and a few close friends into the Holy Order of the Priesthood or Quorum of the Anointed.

---

[27] Jessee, *Papers of Joseph Smith* 2:366. Regarding Facsimile No. 1 Richards recorded that Joseph Smith was at "the printing office correcting the first plate or cut. of the Records of father Abraham. prepared by Reuben Hadlock [Hedlock] for the Times & Seasons" (Ibid., 2:363-64, entry for March 1, 1842). The next day Smith "Read the Proof of the 'Times and Seasons' as Editor for the first time, No.9-Vol 3d in which is the commencement of the Book of Abraham" (Ibid., 2:364).

Joseph spent two days on the Book of Abraham text. Willard Richards recorded for March 8 that Smith, "Commenced Translating from the Book of Abraham, for the 10 No of the Times and Seasons." The next day Joseph "continued the Translation of the Book of Abraham . . . with the Recorder [Willard Richards]. & continued translating & revising."[28] The same day, March 9, Joseph wrote, "I am now very busily engaged in Translating"[29] and Richards told his brother Levi he was "writing the translation of the Book of Abraham in which I am engaged today."[30]

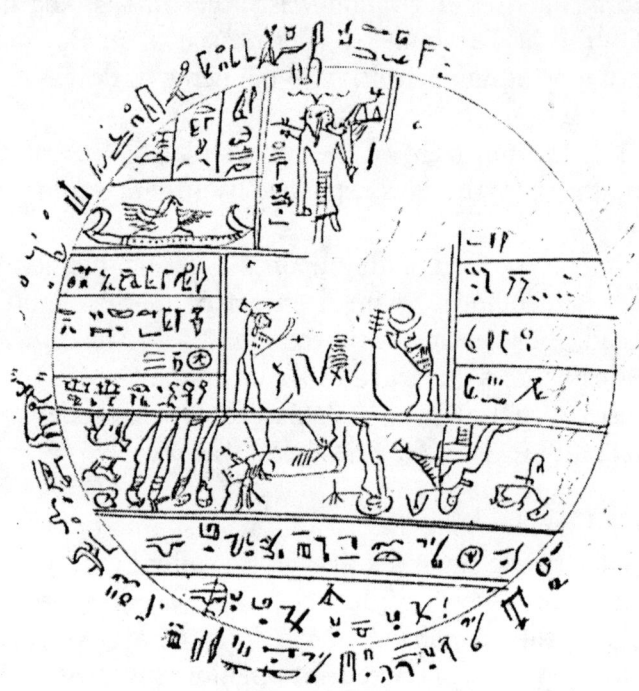

The above drawing came from the lost original. It was damaged in certain areas. (Original sketch in LDS archives).

---

[28] Ibid., 2:367.

[29] Smith to Edward Hunter, March 9-11, 1842 in Jessee, *Personal Writings of Joseph Smith*, 550.

[30] Willard Richards to Levi Richards, March 7-25, 1842, as cited in Joseph Grant Stevenson, ed., *Richards Family History* (Provo, Utah: Stevenson's Genealogical Center, 1991), 3:88. This part of letter was written on March 9.

A FAC-SIMILE FROM THE BOOK OF ABRAHAM, NO. 2.

Times and Seasons 3, no. 10 (March 15, 1842): foldout page between pages 720 and 721. Compare with the drawing on the opposite page. Notice the filled in parts. Facsimile No. 2 is larger in size and is round. It was made for a different individual than Facsimiles 1 and 3 and would not be considered from the same record.

Facsimile No. 3

Joseph Smith's explanation of Facsimile No. 3 indicated that for figures 2, 4, and 5 the written characters told who the individuals were.

Times and Seasons 3, no. 14 (May 16, 1842):783, first page of issue. The head of figure 6 is small and not the head of a jackal. The black figure is Anubus with an ear showing. The size of the facsimile is close to Facsimile 1. This is from the same scroll and is less damaged because it was on the inside of the roll.

Times and Seasons volume 3, number 14 for May 16, 1842 contained Joseph Smith's explanation of Facsimile 3 on page 784:

1. Abraham sitting upon Pharaoh's throne, by the politeness of the king; with a crown upon his head, representing the priesthood; as emblematical of the grand presidency in heaven; with the sceptre [scepter] of justice, and judgment in his hand.

2. King Pharaoh; whose name is given in the characters above his head.

3. Signifies Abraham, in Egypt; referring to Abraham, as given in the 9th No. of the Times & Seasons.

4. Prince of Pharaoh, King of Egypt; as written above the hand.
5. Shulem; one of the king[']s principle waiters; as represented by the characters above his hand.
6. Olimlah; a slave belonging to the prince.
Abraham is reasoning upon the principles of astronomy, in the king[']s Court.

With Genesis 12:7-13 as a base text Smith told about Abram's journey toward Egypt.[31] The story has Abram learning about the stars (the great one is called Kolob), the moon (the lesser light), and the sun (the greater light). The text mentions spirits that are intelligent and have no beginning and no end. The intelligences were organized before the creation of the world. Materials were used to make the earth.

Using the Genesis account of the creation story for a backdrop Joseph Smith mentioned in his Book of Abraham that there was a council of Gods who were involved in the planning and creation of the earth.[32] This concept was advanced from when he dictated the writings of Moses. When correcting the Bible in June 1830 he used God (singular) in the act of creation.[33] Joseph believed in 1830 that there was one God. Genesis 2:11-14 which named the four rivers coming out of Eden (retained in the 1830 revision of Genesis) was not included in the Abraham account because Smith indicated in 1838 that the Garden of Eden was in what is known as Jackson County, Missouri.

The ancient Egyptians had there own ideas concerning their gods that made sense to them. Joseph Smith's view in the Book of Abraham is different in the context of the Judaeo-Christian and Islamic belief in one God. One way to understand this is to know that Smith's religious beliefs changed over time and that he taught that there were many gods and that believers could become gods as there were Gods who had direction over the creation of this earth.[34]

---

[31] Compare Genesis 12:7-13 with LDS Abraham 2:19-25.
[32] Compare Genesis 1:1-2:10, 15-18, 21-25, 19-20 with LDS Abraham 4:1-5:21.
[33] Old Testament Manuscript No. 1, 3, RLDS archives.
[34] Marquardt, *Joseph Smith Revelations*, 297, 325; LDS D&C 121:32 (March 20, 1839); LDS D&C 132:19-20 (July 12, 1843).

The monotheism in the Book of Mormon and Smith's corrections in the writings of Moses in Genesis made it clear that there is only one God. The oneness of God was worked on in the lectures on theology (known as the Lectures on Faith). The ideas relating to God developed in the church and moved toward two separate members of the Godhead though there was varying degrees of this teaching. By 1839 Joseph Smith's idea of a governing council of Gods (polytheism) started to formulate. So when Smith worked on the latter portion of the text of the Book of Abraham in Nauvoo he already accepted polytheism, though in LDS terms it is known as plurality of Gods.[35]

The concept of a council of creation Gods was incorporated into Latter-day Saint temple worship in Nauvoo. The endowment ceremony contained the idea of a council of Gods giving direction for the creation of the world. It followed, in part, the Abraham text:

And then the Lord said, let us go down; and they went down at the beginning, and they organized and formed, (that is, the Gods,) the heavens and the earth. And the earth, after it was formed, was empty and desolate; because they had not formed anything but the earth: and darkness reigned upon the face of the deep, and the spirit of the Gods was brooding upon the faces of the water.

And they said, the Gods, let there be light, and there was light. And they, the Gods, comprehended the light, for it was bright; and they divided the light, or caused it to be divided from the darkness, and the Gods called the light day, and the darkness they called night. And it came to pass that from the evening until morning, they called day: and this was the first, or the beginning of that which they called day and night.

And the Gods also said let there be an expanse in the midst of the waters, and it shall divide the waters from the waters. And the Gods ordered the expanse, so that it divided the waters which were under the expanse, from the

---

[35] For essays on the Mormon concept of God consult Gary James Bergera, ed., *Line Upon Line: Essays on Mormon Doctrine* (Salt Lake City: Signature Books, 1990).

waters which were above the expanse: and it was so, even as they ordered. And the Gods called the expanse, heaven. And it came to pass that it was from the evening until morning, that they called night; and it came to pass that it was from morning until evening, that they called day: and this was the second time, that they called night and day.

And the Gods ordered, saying, let the waters under the heaven be gathered together unto one place, and let the earth come up dry, and it was so, as they ordered; and the gods pronounced the earth dry, and the gathering together of the waters, pronounced they great waters: and the Gods saw that they were obeyed. And the Gods said, let us prepare the earth to bring forth grass; the herb yielding seed; the fruit tree yielding fruit, after his kind, whose seed in itself yieldeth its own likeness upon the earth; and it was so even as they ordered.[36]

Joseph Smith's famous King Follett discourse expands upon the topic of many Gods.[37] Joseph's understanding while in Nauvoo was different than his revelatory pronouncements in New York and early teachings in Ohio.

After Joseph Smith's death Lucy Mack Smith continued to show the records and mummies to visitors at Nauvoo. She died in May 1856 and they were purchased by Abel Combs, "From translations by Mr. [Joseph] Smith of the Records, these Mummies were found to be the family of Pharo [Pharaoh] King of Egypt." The bill of sale was signed by Louis Bidamon, his wife Emma Hale Smith Bidamon and her eldest son Joseph Smith III.[38] Abel Combs died in Philadelphia in 1892. The records were eventually obtained by the Metropolitan Museum of Art in New York City

---

[36] *Times and Seasons* 3 (March 15, 1842):720-21; LDS Abraham 4:1-11.

[37] See Donald Q. Cannon, "The King Follett Discourse: Joseph Smith's Greatest Sermon in Historical Perspective," *Brigham Young University Studies* 18 (Winter 1978):179-92. See accounts of the April 7, 1844 discourse on plurality of Gods in Ehat and Cook, *Words of Joseph Smith*, 340-62.

[38] The bill of sale is dated May 25, 1856, LDS archives. See Todd, *Saga of the Book of Abraham*, 290; Peterson, *Story of the Book of Abraham*, 203. The bill was printed in "The Mormon Prophet's Mummies," *Daily Missouri Democrat*, June 12, 1857, St. Louis, Missouri.

and transferred to the Church of Jesus Christ of Latter-day Saints in November 1967.

Since the time of rediscovery Egyptologists have translated the meaning of the three facsimiles and the papyrus used in preparing the Book of Abraham Translation Manuscripts.[39] What follows is the basic reading of the documents in question with restorations of text not in the original included in brackets. Egyptologists interpret the writing and illustrations based upon their experience. The words chosen to explain what the Egyptians meant are not always the same and sometimes names are spelled differently.

The owner of the papyrus was a priest named Horus (or Hôr) who was deceased. His mother, also deceased, was named Taykhebyt (or Taikhibit). The papyrus dates to about the second century B.C.E. The text below is a composite and does not depend on one translation.

Original of Facsimile No. 1

The writing in four columns along the side of the original Facsimile No. 1 reads:

. . . god's servant of Amon-Re, king of the gods, god's servant of Min, who massacres his enemies, priest of Khonsu . . . Horus, justified, son of one of like titles, master of secrets . . . Taykhebyt. May your soul live in their midst. May you be buried [in] the West . . . on the West [of Thebes] . . .

---

[39] See Klaus Baer, "The Breathing Permit of Hôr," *Dialogue: A Journal of Mormon Thought* 3 (Autumn 1968):109-134; Robert K. Ritner, "The 'Breathing Permit of Hôr' Thirty-four Years Later," Ibid., 33 (Winter 2000):97-119; Ritner, "'The Breathing Permit of Hôr' Among the Joseph Smith Papyri," *Journal of Near Eastern Studies* 62 (July 2003):161-80. For a Latter-day Saint translation of the papyrus see Michael D. Rhodes, *The Hor Book of Breathings: A Translation and Commentary* (Provo, Utah: Foundation for Ancient Research and Mormon Studies, Brigham Young University, 2002), 21, 23 (original of Facsimile No. 1); 24-25 (Facsimile No. 3), and 27-28 (papyrus used for Translation Manuscripts).

The wrapping instructions of the priest Horus (column 1, previously attached to original of Facsimile No. 1) include the following:

. . . pool of Khonsu [Orisis Horus, justified], born of Taykhebyt, justified after his two arms are put over his heart the Breathing Permit which is made with writings inside and outside, is fastened in royal linen, and placed at left arm near his heart. This having been done at his outer wrapping. If this is made for him, then he will breath like the souls of the gods forever and ever

Egyptologists agree that this is the basic wording from the Egyptian characters contained in the column 1 of the writings next to the original of Facsimile No. 1. The commencement of the Breathing Permit begins in the next column to the left of the wrapping instructions and is badly damaged.

Restored Facsimile No. 2

As mentioned, the large round illustration published in the *Times and Seasons* was represented as a complete picture (facsimile) with an explanation. Part of the writing was explained by Joseph Smith as follows—

Figure 8: "Contains writings that cannot be revealed unto the world; but is to be had in the Holy Temple of God." Figure 9: "Ought not to be revealed at the present time." Figure 10: "Also." Figure 11: "Also. If the world can find out these numbers, so let it be. Amen."

The Egyptian hieroglyphics as published are read in reversed order for Figures 11, 10, 9 and 8. They read something like: "O God of the Sleeping Ones from the time of the creation. O mighty God, Lord of Heaven and Earth, the Neatherworld and his Great Waters, grant that the soul of Osiris Sheshonk may live."[40]

---

[40] Michael D. Rhodes, "A Translation and Commentary of the Joseph Smith Hypocephalus," *Brigham Young University Studies* 17 (Spring 1977):265. In an

In Figure 8 the name of person for whom this hypocephalus was prepared for is named Sheshonk (or Shishaq).

On the top right side of the round disk near one o'clock appears in hieratic characters part of Horus's mother name (Taykhebyt) repeated twice — hebyt, hebyt. What this means is that the Horus Papyrus was used to restore the damaged hypocephalus made for a different person. Horus's mother's name was used in preparing the Book of Abraham Translation Manuscripts. A portion of the Horus Papyrus was not lost but has remained on the printed facsimile since 1842.

To further show that the Horus Papyrus was used to fill in a missing area on the hypocephalus is the word sensen on the fourth line. It appears at the place labeled Figure 14. These hieratic characters are upside down and backward in comparison to the hieroglyphic text. So we can conclude that the Horus Papyrus was used for the published restored Facsimile No. 2. Joseph Smith's study of Hebrew is also indicated in his explanations of a few of the figures.[41]

Facsimile No. 3 (ending scene of Horus papyrus)

This facsimile is represented to be from the Book of Abraham. At the bottom of this illustration in Egyptian is the following prayer:

> gods of the Caverns, gods of the south, north, west, and east, grant well-being to Osiris Horus, justified, born of Taykhebyt

---

update Rhodes translates it: "O God of the Sleeping Ones from the time of the creation. O mighty God, Lord of heaven and earth, of the hereafter, and his great waters, grant the soul of the Osiris Shishaq be granted life." (*The Joseph Smith Hypocephalus . . . Seventeen Years Later* (Provo, Utah: Foundation for Ancient Research and Mormon Studies, 1994), 5.

[41] In Kirtland Joseph Smith studied the Hebrew language. See Louis Zucker, "Joseph Smith as a Student of Hebrew," *Dialogue: A Journal of Mormon Thought* 3 (Summer 1968):41-55 and Michael T. Walton, "Professor Seixas, the Hebrew Bible, and the Book of Abraham," *Sunstone* 6:2 (March 1981):41-43.

The characters above the hand of Figure Number 5 are explained by Joseph Smith as "Shulem, one of the king's principle waiters, as represented by the characters above his hand." The Egyptian characters read: Osiris Horus. Rather than being a waiter in Pharaoh's court at a time when Abraham is sitting upon the throne, the characters tell about the deceased priest Horus. The figures in the illustration are as follows:

Figure 1 is Osiris
Figure 2 is Isis
Figure 3 is an offering stand
Figure 4 is Maat
Figure 5 is Horus (deceased, for who the papyrus was written)
Figure 6 (black figure) is Anubis.

Joseph Smith did not know Egyptian but believed he could translate Egyptian through inspiration. Smith promised to produce more of the Book of Abraham text but did not prior to his death. The *Times and Seasons* stated: "We would further state that we have the promise of Br. Joseph, to furnish us with further extracts from the Book of Abraham."[42] Some have faith that Smith had an insight into Abraham's teachings, while others have faith in knowing his limited work in this area of his ministry.[43]

In April 1842 Henry Caswall, a clergyman in his early thirties, visited Nauvoo with a manuscript of a Greek Psalter written on parchment intending to test the prophetic abilities of Joseph Smith. As Caswall described his visit there was much interest in the manuscript book he brought with him. In his account Caswall wrote that he stayed at Montrose across the Mississippi River from Nauvoo. On April 19 Henry Caswall crossed the river on his third visit to Nauvoo when he had an interview with the prophet. Caswall reported:

I handed the book to the prophet, and begged him to explain its contents. He asked me if I had any idea of its

---

[42] *Times and Seasons* 4 (Feb. 1, 1843):95, John Taylor, editor.
[43] See Stephen E. Thompson, "Egyptology and the Book of Abraham," *Dialogue: A Journal of Mormon Thought* 28 (Spring 1995):143-60.

meaning. I replied, that I believed it to be a Greek Psalter; but that I should like to hear his opinion. "No," he said; "it ain't [isn't] Greek at all; except, perhaps, a few words. What ain't [isn't] Greek, is Egyptian; and what ain't [isn't] Egyptian, is Greek. This book is very valuable. *It is a dictionary of Egyptian Hieroglyphics.*" Pointing to the capital letters at the commencement of each verse, he said, "Them figures is Egyptian hieroglyphics; and them which follows, is the interpretation of the hieroglyphics, written in the reformed Egyptian. Them characters is like the letters that was engraved on the gold plates."[44]

Being asked at what price he would like to sell the manuscript Caswall declined to sell or lend the manuscript. Caswall told Smith he wanted to see the papyrus which he had previously seen and was interested in Smith's explanations first hand. Caswall wrote: "I pointed to a particular hieroglyphic, and requested him to expound its meaning. No answer being returned, I looked up, and behold! the prophet had disappeared. The Mormons told me that he had just stepped out, and would probably soon return. I waited some time, but in vain: and at length descended to the street in front of the store. Here I heard the noise of wheels, and presently I saw the prophet in his waggon [wagon], flourishing his whip and driving away as fast as two fine horses could draw him."[45] Some religious discussion followed the departure of Smith and finally Caswall said:

["]Your prophet has committed himself to-day, and I will make the fact known to the world. Would you believe a man calling himself a prophet, who should say that black is white?" "No," they replied. "Would you believe him if he should say that English is French?" "Certainly not." "But you heard your prophet declare, that this book of mine is a Dictionary of Egyptian hieroglyphics, written in characters

---

[44] Henry Caswall, *The City of the Mormons; or, Three Days at Nauvoo, in 1842* (London: Printed for J. G. F. & J. Rivington, 1842), 35-36, emphasis in original. It is hard to determine if all of the poor grammar was that of Joseph Smith or Henry Caswall.

[45] Ibid., 37.

like those of the original Book of Mormon. I know it most positively to be the Psalms of David, written in ancient Greek. Now what shall I think of your prophet?"

Willard Richards replied to Henry Caswall, "Sometimes Mr. Smith speaks as a prophet, and sometimes as a mere man. If he gave a wrong opinion respecting the book, he spoke as a mere man." Caswall responded:

Whether he spoke as a prophet or as a mere man, he has committed himself, for he has said what is not true. If he spoke as a prophet, therefore, he is a false prophet. If he spoke as a mere man, he cannot be trusted, for he spoke positively and like an oracle respecting that of which he knew nothing.[46]

In June George Moore a Unitarian minister from Quincy had a short visit with Joseph Smith. He recorded in his journal:

We conversed about the *gold plates*, wh[ich] he professes to have dug up and translated into the Book of Mormon. "Those plates are not now in this country," he said - "they were exhibited to a few at first for the sake of obtaining their testimony - no others have ever seen them - and they will never again be exhibited." He showed me some specimens of the hieroglyphics, such as, he says, were on the gold plates.

Smith expounded: "We believe in three Gods, equal in power and glory. There are three persons in heaven, but those three are not one." Rev. Moore described Smith at this time as being "a man of large frame - tending to corpulency - has blue eyes, light

---

[46] Ibid., 43. Willard Richards recorded Joseph Smith saying in 1843, "'A Prophet is not always a Prophet' only when he is acting as such" (Joseph Smith Journal, entry for Feb. 8, 1843, LDS archives).

complexion, one or two of his front teeth gone - he has a rather benevolent expression of countenance."[47]

In December 1842 Rev. Moore related that a deacon in his church joined the Mormon faith by baptism while in Nauvoo. This individual was Joseph L. Heywood. George Moore recorded in his journal his visit with Heywood:

> In the course of conversation, he professed to believe that Jo. Smith is the best & purest being on earth, a perfect human being, the prophet of the Almighty. – I asked him what evidence he had of this. He said he had seen & conversed with Mr. Smith, and had heard the testimony of his friends and family who ought to know him best.

Not being impressed Rev. Moore asked for stronger evidence and Joseph Haywood mentioned a couple of miracles. Moore thought that Heywood would regret the step he had taken.[48]

It was during the Nauvoo period that Joseph Smith developed additional concepts relating to God, priesthood, and temple. In his public sermons that are preserved Smith gave new emphasis to salvation theology. The doctrines and teachings were expounded with special emphasis on obedience to authority.

Like in Kirtland and Far West internal division was festering. The organization had its ups and downs. In the church there were growing problems relating to church leadership especially that of John C. Bennett who was a friend of Smith. New doctrines and ordinances were expounded to close associates and friends. Joseph Smith became endeared to many at church headquarters. Chapter 22 will look at a number these priesthood ordinances.

---

[47] George Moore Journal, entry for June 3, 1842, emphasis retained, American Antiquarian Society, Worcester, Massachusetts. See also "A Visit to Joe Smith," *Times and Seasons* 3 (Sept. 15, 1842):926.
[48] George Moore Journal, entry for Dec. 20, 1842.

22

Priesthood Ordinances

When the Book of Mormon was printed in 1830 it contained a simple prayer for ordination to the priesthood. Instructions were given for the basic form and the words to be used for the ordination prayer for the offices of elder, priest, and teacher. Those having authority would lay their hands upon individuals and in the name of Jesus Christ ordain them:

> to preach repentance and remission of sins through Jesus Christ, by the endurance of faith on his name to the end. Amen.[1]

In this way the authority or priesthood was conferred on male church members. Though this form was not used all the time it was the pattern to be used for ordination. The conferral of office was done before the church was organized when Joseph Smith and Oliver Cowdery were baptized in the Susquehanna River in May 1829. After the church was established those ordained to authority were called to go on missions for the church. They were to preach using the Bible and Book of Mormon and preach repentance, baptize men and women into the church, administer the bread and wine, perform healings, set up branches for the church, and other duties necessary to carry on the work.

One of Joseph Smith's early revelations explained that converts would be entering into a new covenant when they joined the church:

> Behold I say unto you that all old covenants have I caused to be done away in this thing and this is a new and an everlasting covenant even the same which was from the beginning[2]

---

[1] 1830 BOM, 575; LDS Moroni 3:3; RLDS 3:2.
[2] Marquardt, *Joseph Smith Revelations*, 62; LDS D&C 22:1; RLDS D&C 20:1.

The Book of Mormon teaches that the time we are living is the time to prepare for the afterlife. This is one of the basic beliefs of the book. Those who never knew the gospel law are innocent according to the word:

> For behold, this life is the time for men to prepare to meet God; yea, behold the day of this life is the day for men to perform their labors. And now, as I said unto you before, as ye have had so many witnesses, therefore, I beseech of you that ye do not procrastinate the day of your repentance until the end; for after this day of life, which is given us to prepare for eternity, behold, if we do not improve our time while in this life, then cometh the night of darkness wherein there can be no labor performed.[3]

As explained in the Book of Mormon "where there is no law given there is no punishment; and where there is no punishment there is no condemnation; and where there is no condemnation the mercies of the Holy One of Israel have claim upon them, because of the atonement."[4] Near the end of the book it is explained that those individuals who died without knowing the law or gospel are in the same category as little children:

> For behold that all little children are alive in Christ, and also all they that are without the law. For the power of redemption cometh on all them that have no law; wherefore, he that is not condemned, or he that is under no condemnation, cannot repent; and unto such baptism availeth nothing— But it is mockery before God, denying the mercies of Christ, and the power of his Holy Spirit, and putting trust in dead works.[5]

Joseph Smith added text to the early portion of Genesis concerning Enoch. This reflected Smith's insight concerning

---

[3] 1830 BOM, 320-21; LDS Alma 34:32-33; RLDS 16:228-30. See also LDS 3 Nephi 27:33; RLDS 13:11; and John 9:4.
[4] 1830 BOM, 81; LDS 2 Nephi 9:25; RLDS 6:51.
[5] 1830 BOM, 582; LDS Moroni 8:22-23; RLDS 8:25-27. See also LDS D&C 45:54; RLDS D&C 45:10.

sinners who were to perish in the flood in the days of Noah. It was said that the Lord prepared a prison for them. Also that after the resurrection of the Son of Man "as many of the spirits as were in prison came forth, and stood on the right hand of God; and the remainder were reserved in chains of darkness until the judgment of the great day."[6]

In February 1832 Joseph Smith and Sidney Rigdon were revising the gospel of John and had a visionary experience. Rather than retaining the belief in two destinies—a place for the just (heaven) and the unjust (hell)—they perceived three degrees of glory after the judgment. These destinations are known as the celestial (the highest), terrestrial, and telestial kingdoms. This became a demarcation in the thinking of church members. The vision was interpreted for the terrestrial kingdom as follows:

And again, we saw the Terrestrial world, and behold and lo! these are they who are of the terrestrial, whose glory differeth from that of the church of the first born who have received of the fulness of the Father, even as that of the Moon differeth from the Sun in the firmament. Behold, these are they who died without law; and also they who are the spirits of men kept in prison, whom the Son visited and preached the Gospel unto them, that they might be judged according to men in the flesh, who received not the testimony of Jesus in the flesh, but afterwards received it[7]

Almost four years later in the west room on the third floor of the Kirtland Temple Joseph Smith saw in vision the celestial kingdom. Among others he saw his brother Alvin who died in 1823 and had not been baptized. Joseph said he heard the voice of the Lord saying:

all who have died with[out] a knowledge of this gospel, who would have received it, if they had been permitted to tarry, shall be heirs of the celestial kingdom of God—also

---

[6] OT MS 1, 17-18; LDS Moses 7:38, 57; Genesis 7:44, 64 (JST). See 1 Peter 3:18-20.
[7] Marquardt, *Joseph Smith Revelations*, 189; LDS D&C 76:71–74; RLDS 76:6. See also LDS D&C 88:99; RLDS D&C 85:28 (Feb. 16, 1832).

all that shall die henseforth [henceforth], without a knowledge of it, who would have received it, with all their hearts, shall be heirs of that kingdom, for I the Lord will judge all men according to their works according to the desire of their hearts

Smith also saw "that all children who die before they ar[r]ive to the years of accountability are saved in the celestial kingdom of heaven."[8] In 1840 this would change with the introduction of a new doctrine — baptism for the dead.

Living in Nauvoo Vilate Kimball wrote to her husband Heber in England, "Semor [Seymour] Brunson is dead. . . . a short time before he died he told Joseph not to hold him any longer, for said he, I have see[n] David Patten and he wants me and the Lord wants me, and I want to go."[9] Joseph Smith preached the funeral sermon of Brunson and presented the topic of baptism for the dead on August 15, 1840. There is no known contemporary report of the discourse but Smith used one verse from 1 Corinthians 15:29 to explain the basis behind this new doctrine and practice for Latter-day Saints. The words from Paul's letter to the Corinthians were used to support the practice:

Else what shall they do which are baptized for the dead, if the dead rise not at all? why are they then baptized for the dead?

Paul mentioned the practice of Christians at Corinth performing baptism on behalf of the dead. Those who did the ritual did not understanding that they were affirming a belief in the resurrection of the body after death. There were some Christians who performed ceremonies relating to baptizing for deceased relatives who had not obtained a Christian baptism. To Joseph Smith it invited a new and exciting exploration into saving the kindred dead of church members and others who did not hear the gospel of Christ in this life.

---

[8] Marquardt, *Joseph Smith Revelations*, 278; LDS D&C 137:7-10 (Jan. 21, 1836).

[9] Vilate Kimball to Heber C. Kimball, Sept. 6, 1840, LDS archives.

Members could be baptized for and in behalf of either sex. These baptisms were first performed in the Mississippi River and later in a temporary wooden font on the backs of twelve carved oxen in the basement of the Nauvoo Temple. This font was replaced by a more permanent one for the saints to enter and perform this rite. In another letter Sister Vilate Kimball wrote after a church conference:

> President Smith has open[e]d a new and glorious subject of late which has caused quite a revival in the church. that is, being baptised for the dead. Paul speaks of it, in first Corinthians 15th chapter 29th vers[e]. Joseph has received a more full explaination of it by Revelation. he says it is the privilege of this church to be baptised for all their kinsfolks that have died before this Gospel came forth; even back to their great Gran[d]father and Mother if they have be[e]n personally acquainted with them. by so doing we act as agents for them, and give them the privilege of comeing forth in the first resur[r]ection. he says they will have the Gospel preached [to] them in Prison, but there is no such thing as spirrits [spirits] being baptised.

Explaining what she had observed and understood Vilate mentioned to Heber:

> Since this order has be[e]n preached here, the waters have be[e]n continually troubled. During conference there were sometimes from eight to ten Elders in the river at a time baptiseing. . . . I want to be baptised for my Mother. I calculated to wate [wait] until you come home but the last time Joseph spoke upon the subject he advised every one to be up and a doing and liberate their friends from bondage as quick as posable [possible]. so I think I shall go forward this week, as there is a number of the neighbors going forward. Some have alre[a]dy be[e]n baptised a number of times over. they have to be baptised and confirmed for one person before they can be baptis[e]d for another. Those that have no friends on the earth to be baptised for them can [se]nd ministering spirits to whom so ever they will, and

make known their request. thus you see there is a chance for all. Is not this a glorious doctrine[?] Surely the Gentiles will mock; but we will rejoice in it.[10]

Joseph Smith's clerk at the time, Robert B. Thompson, also wrote a letter to Heber C. Kimball explaining the doctrine of baptism for the dead and said it was introduced by President Joseph Smith "So that the Saints have the priviledge [privilege] of being baptized for their relatives and friends who have not had the priviledge of hearing the gospel while in the flesh but who probably receive it while in the spirit in prison. so that they can claim them at the ressurrection [resurrection] of the just."[11]

The first president of the United States, George Washington, was an early deceased candidate for proxy baptism. Church members were ready to release from the spirit prison those who they felt would accept the gospel message through ministers in the spirit world. The space after death and before the resurrection was called the spirit world. Some spirits would be separated and go to paradise and others to a spirit prison before being having their body join with their spirit and be resurrected. Joseph Smith in December wrote a letter to the members of the Council of the Twelve and Elders serving in England. The letter included more information on the doctrine of baptism for the dead:

The saints have the priviledge [privilege] of being baptised for those of their relatives who are dead, who they feel to believe would have embraced the gospel if they had been priviledged [privileged] with hearing it, and who have received the gospel in the spirit through the instrumentality of those who may have been commissioned to preach to them in prison.[12]

---

[10] Vilate Kimball to Heber C. Kimball, Oct. 11-13, 1840, LDS archives.

[11] Robert B. Thompson to Heber C. Kimball, Nov. 5, 1840, LDS archives.

[12] Joseph Smith to "Beloved Brethren," Dec. 15, 1840, LDS archives. This letter, in the handwriting of Robert B. Thompson and signed by Joseph Smith, was written to the Traveling High Council (Twelve Apostles) and Elders in Great Britain.

One portion of the longest revelation of Joseph Smith gave instructions for the saints to build a temple at Nauvoo including a font where baptisms for the dead could be performed. The importance of erecting a temple was emphasized:

> For, for this cause I commanded Moses that he should build a tabernacle, that they should bear it with them in the wilderness, and to build a house in the land of promise, that those ordinances might be revealed, which had been hid from before the world was; therefore, verily I say unto you, that your anointings and your washings, and your baptisms for the dead, and your solemn assemblies, and your memorials for your sacrifices, by the sons of Levi, and for your oracles in your most holy places, wherein you receive conversations, and your statutes and judgments, for the beginning of the revelations and foundation of Zion, and for the glory, honor and endowment of all her municipals, are ordained by the ordinance of my holy house which my people are always commanded to build unto my holy name.[13]

At the October 1841 church conference Joseph Smith "presented 'Baptism for the Dead' as the only way that men can appear as saviors on mount Zion." The doctrine showed "the wisdom and mercy of God, in preparing an ordinance for the salvation of the dead, being baptised by proxy, their names recorded in heaven, and they judged according to the deeds done in the body. This doctrine was the burden of the scriptures. Those saints who neglect it, in behalf of their deceased relatives, do it at the peril of their own salvation."[14]

In his first epistle on baptism for the dead Smith wrote, "when any of you are baptised for your dead let there be a recorder." He reiterated that the Lord was "about to restore many

---

[13] Marquardt, *Joseph Smith Revelations*, 302-303; LDS D&C 124:38-39 (Jan. 19, 1841).

[14] "Minutes of a Conference of the Church of Jesus Christ of Latter Day Saints, held in Nauvoo, Ill, commencing Oct. 1st, 1841," *Times and Seasons* 2 (Oct. 15, 1841):577-78.

things to the Earth, pertaining to the Priesthood."[15] The second epistle written in less than a week Joseph Smith told about the importance of making a proper record on earth which will be recorded in heaven. Smith said that the relationship between the dead and the living "cannot be lightly passed over, as pertaining to our salvation: for their salvation is necessary and essential to our salvation; as Paul says concerning the fathers, 'That they without us, cannot be made perfect;' neither can we without our dead, be made perfect." Continuing Smith exclaimed, "Let the dead speak forth anthems of eternal praise to the king Immanuel, who hath ordain'd before the world was, that which would enable us to redeem them out of their prisons; for the prisoner[s] shall go free."[16]

On May 12, 1844 Joseph Smith explained in a discourse reported by Thomas Bullock:

> every man that has been baptized and belongs to the Kingdom, has a right to be baptized for those who are gone before, and, as soon as the Law of the Gospel is obeyed here by their friends, who act as proxy for them, the Lord has administrators there to set them free—a man may act as proxy for his own relatives—the ordinances of the Gospel which was laid out before the foundation of the world has been thus fulfilled, by them, and we may be baptized for those who we have much friendship for, but it must be revealed to the man of God, lest we should run too far[17]

In early September 1842 a report came that Adams County Sheriff James Pittman was coming to Nauvoo to arrest Joseph Smith. On September 3 the sheriff with two assistants arrived in Nauvoo. William Clayton recorded in the Book of the Law of the Lord that former apostle John F. Boynton was at the Smith residence. At the time the family was eating dinner when the

---

[15] Marquardt, *Joseph Smith Revelations*, 317; LDS D&C 127:6, 8 (Sept. 1, 1842).
[16] Marquardt, *Joseph Smith Revelations*, 320, 322; LDS D&C 128:15, 22 (Sept. 6, 1842).
[17] Thomas Bullock Report, May 12, 1844, as cited in Ehat and Cook, *Words of Joseph Smith*, 368.

authorities came to the house. "John Boynton happened to be the first person discovered by the Sheriffs and they began to ask him where Mr Smith was. He answered that he saw him early in the morning; but did not say that he had seen him since. While this conversation was passing, president Joseph passed out at the back door and through the corn in his garden to brother Newel K. Whitney's."[18]

Not too much is known about the introduction of the sealing of husband and wife for time and all eternity. Some men were sealed to plural wives before they were sealed to their legal wife. It is believed that Heber and Vilate Kimball were sealed together in early 1842. Newel and Elizabeth Whitney were sealed in August 1842. This was months before the general practice of time and eternity sealings for other church members. Joseph and Emma Smith were not sealed until May 1843. Proxy sealings with one spouse living and the other deceased were performed by men holding the priesthood. This was performed so the spouses would be together for all eternity in the afterlife. Thus projecting what was done on earth to everlasting life in the celestial kingdom.

Other ordinances that were performed at Nauvoo include rebaptism for the remission of sins and baptism for health (church members who were sick and believed that having another baptism would assist in restoring them to good health). The practice continued of members receiving a patriarchal blessing from an ordained church patriarch. This was a priesthood blessing sometimes foretelling what may occur in the individual's lifetime and in many cases pronouncing the lineage or Israelite tribe they descended from or whom they would receive blessings through.

The Book of Mormon indicated in its perspective for the future that there would be a great and last sacrifice that would stop the shedding of blood through animal sacrifice. This would be brought about by the sacrifice of Christ, the Son of God:

> therefore it is expedient that there should be a great and last sacrifice; and then shall there be, or it is expedient there should be, a stop to the shedding of blood; then shall the law of Moses be fulfilled; yea, it shall be all fulfilled; every

---

[18] Jessee, *Papers of Joseph Smith*, 448-49, entry for Sept. 3, 1842.

jot and tittle, and none shall have passed away. And behold, this is the whole meaning of the law; every whit a pointing to that great and last sacrifice; and that great and last sacrifice will be the Son of God; yea, Infinite and Eternal[19]

Joseph Smith taught that performing animal sacrifice was still a duty of the priesthood. Smith said that Elijah held these priesthood keys. It may be remembered that in April 1836 Smith and Oliver Cowdery had a vision wherein they received keys from Elijah the prophet. At the October 1840 conference Joseph Smith said in his prepared remarks on priesthood, read by his scribe Robert B. Thompson, the following:

As it is generally supposed that Sacrifice was entirely done away when the great sacrifi[c]e was offered up—and that there will be no necessity for the ordinance of Sacrifice in [the] future, but those who assert this, are certainly not a[c]quainted with the duties, privileges and authority of the priesthood. or with the prophets. The offering of Sacrifice has ever been connected and forms a part of the duties of the priesthood. It began with the priesthood and will be continued untill after the coming of Christ from generation to generation

Smith went on to explain that the offering of sacrifice "will be continued when the priesthood is restored with all its authority, power and blessings. Elijah was the last prophet that held the keys of this priesthood, and who will, before the last dispensation, restore the authority and delive[r] the Keys of this priesthood in order that all the ordinances may be attended to in righteousness."[20] In Joseph Smith's 1842 interpretation of Malachi 4:5-6 he considers this to be "the restoration of the Priesthood" and the "most glorious of all subjects belonging to the everlasting gospel, viz. the baptism for the dead."[21]

---

[19] BOM 1830, 319; LDS Alma 34:13-14; RLDS 16:213-15.
[20] Manuscript in LDS archives, Oct. 5, 1840, as cited in Ehat and Cook, *Words of Joseph Smith*, 43. See LDS D&C 124:39.
[21] Marquardt, *Joseph Smith Revelations*, 320-21; LDS D&C 128:17 (Sept. 6, 1842).

When the saints settled in Nauvoo further instructions dealing with the building of this new city were recorded as a revelation to the church. At the April 1841 conference the revelation was read by John C. Bennett from the manuscript volume titled "Book of the Law of the Lord." Concerning those who hinder the saints from performing their work God would "require that work no more" but accept their offering.[22] As it related to the work that was commanded prior to the establishment of the Nauvoo Stake of Zion the revelation stated: "I have accepted the offering of those men who I commanded to build up a city and a house unto my name in Jackson county, Missouri."[23]

Though the Nauvoo Masonic Lodge was not a church organization it did introduce into Mormon culture the idea to keep secrets from the uninitiated. This would make a division between church members who were knowledgeable of certain doctrines or practices and keep them from other church members. Those who have been given secrets do not need to share them with others who know nothing about them. This brings with it a culture of secrets. To protect the secrets it was permissible to lie in order to help the cause of the gospel.

Priesthood ordinances were performed in a group known as the Holy Order of the Holy Priesthood (also known as the Quorum of the Anointed). An individual would have his body washed and then anointed in preparation of what is known as the endowment. He would receive an undergarment known as the garment of the holy priesthood together with a new name. The endowment contained religious instructions by the priesthood on the creation of the world, covenants of obedience, signs and tokens together with keys of the priesthood. There were penalties associated with receiving the signs and tokens. Under various ways in which life could be taken the person who receive the endowment could lose

---

[22] "Gen. Bennett then read the revelations from 'The Book of the Law of the Lord,' which had been received since the last general conference" (*Times and Seasons* 2 [April 15, 1841]:346).

[23] Ibid., 2 (June 1, 1841):427; LDS D&C 124:51. Lyndon W. Cook commenting on LDS D&C 84; RLDS D&C 83 wrote: "Verses 1-5 concern themselves with the building of the New Jerusalem in Jackson County, Missouri (particularly the construction of a temple). This divine injunction was rescinded in 1841. (See [LDS] D&C 124:49 and 51)" (*Revelations of the Prophet Joseph Smith*, 176).

his or her life if they revealed what they learned. Covenants of consecration to the church and kingdom of God were taken. The outline was given by Joseph Smith and expanded after his death.

Joseph explained that there are "certain key words & signs belonging to the priesthood which must be observed in order to obtaine [obtain] the Blessings."[24] These keys were shared in the endowment ceremony. The instructions started in May 1842 and recommenced in May 1843. Four months later the leading men holding the Melchizedek priesthood invited women to participate in the holy order of the anointed quorum.

Besides being sealed to their legal husband certain women obtained an anointing with their husband. The husband was anointed a king and priest unto God and his wife was anointed a queen and priestess unto her husband. This ordinance is known as the second anointing. A special part is preserved for a private setting where the wife will anoint the feet of her husband so she can be called forth in the first resurrection.

Joseph Smith's salvation theology was developing into a theology of exaltation. At the head of this was Michael one of the creation Gods who became the first man Adam in Mormon theology. In the endowment ceremony inaugurated by Smith the ideas he followed were inline with the published text of the Book of Abraham. After relating in ceremonial form the creation of the earth the candidates were to follow the first parents mentioned in the Bible. Adam and Eve were considered the ideal parents of the human race and as such those initiated into the higher mysteries of the kingdom were to follow their example. If they followed them they could be exalted as they had been. The religious instruction of the priesthood given in the ceremony of the endowment was to be available to all saints who were prepared to receive it.

The small group who received the first endowments in May 1842 included Joseph Smith and William Law of the first presidency; apostles Brigham Young, Heber C. Kimball, and Willard Richards; patriarchs Hyrum Smith and James Adams; bishop Newel K. Whitney, Nauvoo stake president William Marks; and president of the high priest quorum George Miller. It did not include Sidney Rigdon or John C. Bennett who were associated

---

[24] Kenney, *Wilford Woodruff's Journal*, 2:162, entry for March 20, 1842.

with the church presidency. The Book of the Law of the Lord recorded that those in attendance were "given certain instructions concerning the priesthood."[25] At a later date Heber C. Kimball wrote that he was initiated into the ancient order and was washed, anointed, sealed, and ordained to be a priest.[26] Apostle Kimball wrote in June 1842:

> thare [there] is a similarity. of preast Hood [priesthood] in masonary [masonry]. Br Joseph Ses [says] Masonary [Masonry] was taken from preastHood [priesthood] but has become degen[e]rated. but menny [many] things are perfect.[27]

As explained by Heber Kimball there was a relationship between the special instructions he received from Joseph Smith and those given through Masonry. Many of the signs, tokens (hand claps), and penalties were the same in each fraternity. The Nauvoo Lodge Under Dispensation initiated many male church member into its ranks. In March 1842 Willard Richards wrote a letter to his brother Levi:

> March 15th. This day the Masonic lodge of Nauvoo was installed on the hill near the Temple, in the grove. Thousands of people present. 16th. President Joseph and Sidney are initiated by Grand Master Jonas, of the Grand Lodge of Illinois. Masonry had its origin in the Priesthood. A hint to the wise is sufficient.[28]

---

[25] Jessee, *Papers of Joseph Smith*, 380, entry for May 4, 1842. Endowments in behalf of the dead were not commenced until after the completion and dedication of the LDS St. George Temple in 1877.

[26] Heber C. Kimball Journal, June 10-October 19, 1843, LDS archives, in Stanley B. Kimball, ed., *On the Potter's Wheel: The Diaries of Heber C. Kimball* (Salt Lake City: Signature Books in association with Smith Research Associates, 1987), 55. The entries at the end of this journal were written circa 1847. The event was dated June 1842 but the actual month was May.

[27] Heber C. Kimball to Parley P. Pratt, June 17, 1842, LDS archives.

[28] Willard Richards to Levi Richards, 7-25 March 1842, as cited in Stevenson, *Richards Family History* 3:90.

Joseph Smith as the church president, holding the keys of the dispensation of the fullness of times, was looked upon as a prophet and seer to whom artifacts could be brought to and obtain an interpretation. It was in this setting that three men, about April 1843, unknown to others beside themselves, manufactured a set of six bell-shaped brass plates. The plates were small about 2 7/8 high by 2 1/4 inches. These they hid in the ground and later several men dug in an ancient burial mound near Kinderhook, Pike County, Illinois. Here the men "discovered" these ancient looking artifacts. With the plates were the remains of a man. The plates were cleaned and on them it was found that they contained hieroglyphics. Some men made a statement about the discovery and the plates were publicly displayed in the town of Quincy.

The public was interested in the meaning and whether the writing on the plates told anything about the person with whom they were found with. The *Quincy Whig* printed the following:

By whom these plates were deposited there, must ever remain a secret, unless some one skilled in deciphering hieroglyphics, may be found to unravel the mystery. Some pretend to say, that Smith the Mormon leader, has the ability to read them. If he has, he will confer a great favor on the public by removing the mystery which hangs over them. We learn there was a Mormon present when the plates were found, who it is said, leaped for joy at the discovery, and remarked that it would go to prove the authenticity of the Book of Mormon . . . if Smith can decipher the hieroglyphics on the plates, he will do more towards throwing light on the early history of this continent, than any man now living.[29]

These plates were brought to Nauvoo and shown to Joseph Smith. He had previously claimed to have translated an earlier set of gold plates. Smith examined the ancient characters and commented that the writing was like those on the Book of Mormon

---

[29] *Quincy Whig* 6 (May 3, 1843). Reprinted in *Times and Seasons* 4 (May 1, 1843):186-87. An editorial in the church paper stated, "We have no doubt however, but Mr. Smith will be able to translate them" (186).

plates. He said they contained a history of the person with whom they were found. That person was said to be a Jaredite (the earliest race of ancient Americans) who descended from a Pharaoh of Egypt through Ham, one of the sons of Noah.

This linked the bell shaped plates to the Book of Mormon and the Book of Abraham both dictated by Joseph Smith. The script was compared with a copy of Egyptian characters said be from the gold plates. It was claimed that the contents of the newly found Kinderhook Plates told something about the race of the person with whom they were found. His descent was through Pharaoh, a topic of the Book of Abraham.[30]

On May 1, 1843, William Clayton, one of Joseph Smith's secretaries, took supper with Smith. Clayton made a tracing of one plate in his journal and recorded the following about the plates and Smith's comments relating to the translation of part of the writings:

> I have seen 6 brass plates which were found in Adams [sic; Pike] County by some persons who were digging in a mound They found a skeleton about 6 feet from the surface of the earth which was 9 foot high [tracing of plate] The plates were on the breast of the skeleton - This diagram shows the size of the plates being drawn on the edge of one of them. They are covered with ancient characters of language containing from 30 to 40 on each side of the plates. Prest J[oseph]. has translated a portion and says they contain the history of the person with whom they were found & he was a descendant of Ham through the loins of Pharaoh king of Egypt, and that he received his kingdom from the ruler of heaven & earth[31]

In the morning of that day Clayton sealed Lucy Walker to Joseph Smith as a plural wife. The next day, May 2, non-member

---

[30] On the Book of Abraham see H. Michael Marquardt, "The Book of Abraham Revisited," *Journal of Pastoral Practice* 5 (1982):101-12.

[31] William Clayton Journal, entry for May 1, 1843, as cited in James B. Allen, *No Toil Nor Labor Fear: The Story of William Clayton* (Provo, Utah: Brigham Young University Press, 2002), 393. The Clayton journal was used in compiling some of the Nauvoo portion of the Manuscript History (Ibid., 385-413). See also *History of the Church* 5:372.

Charlotte Haven wrote a letter that mentioned the plates. She stated that Mr. Joshua Moore showed the six bell shaped plates to Joseph Smith. Moore reported to her that Smith

> said that the figures or writing on them was similar to that in which the Book of Mormon was written, and if Mr. Moore could leave them, he thought that by the help of revelation he would be able to translate them.[32]

Brigham Young, President of the Twelve Apostles, like William Clayton also traced one of the plates in his journal and put the following brief comment inside the outline:

> May 3th 1843
> I took this at
> Joseph Smiths
> house
> found near
> Quincy [33]

Four days later on May 7 Parley P. Pratt, one of the Twelve Apostles, included the following comments in a letter:

> I have no further news except that six plates having the appearance of Brass have lately been dug out of a mound by a gentleman in Pike Co. Illinois. They are small and filled with engravings in Egyptian language and contain the genealogy of one of the ancient Jaredites back to Ham the son of Noah . . . The gentlemen who found them were unconnected with this church but have brought them to Joseph Smith for examination & translation a large number of Citizens here have seen them and compared the characters with those on the Egyptian papyrus which is now in this city.[34]

---

[32] Haven to "My dear home friends," May 2, 1843, as quoted in "A Girl's Letters from Nauvoo," *Overland Monthly* 16 (Dec. 1890):630, San Francisco.

[33] Brigham Young Journal, entry for May 3, 1843, LDS archives.

[34] Parley P. Pratt to John Van Cott, May 7, 1843, LDS archives.

Both William Clayton and Parley P. Pratt indicated that the brass plates contained information on this individual who descended from the biblical Ham, son of Noah. The Kinderhook Plates were at Joseph Smith's home for a brief time. Elder Reuben Hedlock, who in 1842 assisted Smith in making the three facsimiles of the Book of Abraham, now prepared facsimiles of the Kinderhook Plates for the saints. There were twelve facsimiles of the strange looking characters and a broadside was published and sold. The broadside stated:

The contents of the Plates, together with a Fac-Simile of the same, will be published in the "Times & Seasons," as soon as the translation is completed. [35]

In 1981 Stanley B. Kimball published an article in the *Ensign* magazine that stated the plates were produced in the nineteenth century and were not ancient as originally thought. He tried to down play the contemporary sources showing that Joseph believed that the characters could be translated and giving an explanation of what information they contained. The bell shaped plates were not an ancient American relic.[36] From 1843 until 1981 (138 years) it had been repeatedly asserted that these newly found brass plates were genuine.[37] Smith's comments should be looked at concerning his ability to correctly decipher ancient appearing characters.

Joseph Smith's important secret in Nauvoo was keeping secret the practice of certain priesthood members who married and cohabited with plural wives. By the authority of Joseph Smith certain men were given priesthood keys to perform a marital sealing. This period of church history remains controversial especially because of the character of John C. Bennett who was closely associated with Joseph Smith.

---

[35] Broadside titled "Discovery of the Brass Plates," published at Nauvoo, Illinois, June 24, 1843. Copy in LDS Archives.

[36] Stanley B. Kimball, "Kinderhook Plates Brought to Joseph Smith Appear to be a Nineteenth-Century Hoax," *Ensign* 11 (Aug. 1981):66-74.

[37] See *History of the Church* 5:372-78 and Jason Frederick Peters, "The Kinderhook Plates: Examining a Nineteenth-Century Hoax," *Journal of the Illinois State Historical Society* 96, no. 2 (Summer 2003):130-45.

With the commencement of building the Nauvoo Temple and of Smith's boarding house (Nauvoo House) the saints sacrificed their money and time to complete them in a timely fashion. Their dedication is evident as Nauvoo became the largest Mississippi River city in Illinois. Joseph Smith continued in the central role of the faith.

The saints were especially interested in Joseph Smith's public preaching and attended meetings and conferences whenever opportunity presented itself. Priesthood ordinances were now going to include a higher law of the marriage covenant for those chosen. The following four chapters examine the secret doctrine and practice of a plurality of wives in Nauvoo.

23

Plural Wives in Nauvoo

There was a gradual development in regard to the belief in men holding the Melchizedek Priesthood being married to an additional wife or wives by priesthood authority. This is in one sense was known as polygamy (though technically the word would include women having more than one husband). It was also known as spiritual wifery, celestial (heavenly) marriage, plural marriage, or the principle. Various religious beliefs regarding marriage of individuals and groups had been around for years. The Latter-day Saint version of having more than one wife marriage was taught and practiced in Nauvoo.

This chapter will explore what is currently known about the marriages or priesthood sealings of wives to Joseph Smith. It also includes an attempt by Brigham Young to obtain a plural wife. Some background is needed to understand how this system of marriage was introduced to believers in the prophetic ministry of Smith. Many questions remain unanswered because of the secret nature of the practice. When unauthorized discussion of marriage beliefs was made public those involved denied the practice so as to not reveal the true nature of what was going on secretly. Some church members knew nothing about the plural marriage in Nauvoo.

The text of the Book of Mormon explains that it is an abomination to have many wives and concubines. The command was for a man to have one wife. In explaining the story the Lamanites were said to be more righteous than the Nephites in regard to marital relations. The instructions gave the bad example of David and Solomon:

> But the word of God burdens me because of your grosser crimes. For behold, thus saith the Lord: This People begin to wax in iniquity; they understand not the Scriptures: for they seek to excuse themselves in committing whoredoms,

because of the things which were written concerning David, and Solomon his son. Behold, David and Solomon truly had many wives and concubines, which thing was abominable before me, saith the Lord[1]

So essential was the Book of Mormon text that there is a large section that explains that "whoredoms are an abomination." God's command should be kept "in all the lands of my people." While the wording "otherwise they shall hearken unto these things" may not be clear what is definite is the command to have one wife. Expressed in Book of Mormon terms the words in Jacob gave important direction:

Wherefore, my brethren, hear me, and hearken to the word of the Lord: for there shall not any man among you have save it be one wife; and concubines he shall have none: For I, the Lord God, delighteth in the chastity of women. And whoredoms is an abomination before me: thus saith the Lord of Hosts. Wherefore, this people shall keep my commandments, saith the Lord of Hosts, or cursed be the land for their sakes. For if I will, saith the Lord of Hosts, raise up seed unto me, I will command my people: otherwise, they shall hearken unto these things. For behold, I, the Lord, have seen the sorrow, and heard the mourning of the daughters of my people in the land of Jerusalem; yea, and in all the lands of my people, because of the wickedness and abominations of their husbands.[2]

Men in biblical times, such as Abram (Abraham) and Jacob, had wives or concubines. As discussed in the book of Genesis there were problems and long time blessings associated with their individual lives and in their households. Before his death Jacob (Israel) blessed his twelve sons with a father's blessing. These blessings are recorded in Genesis 49.

---

[1] 1830 BOM, 126-27; LDS Jacob 2:23-24; RLDS 2:31-33.
[2] 1830 BOM, 127; LDS Jacob 2:27-31; RLDS 2:36-40. See also LDS Jacob 3:5; RLDS 2:54-55.

Many years afterwards laws were instituted for Israelites to regulate how men could add to their households. In a list of prohibitions that were regarded as abominations the writings in Leviticus recorded a command to Moses that included not uncovering a mother and her daughter: "Thou shalt not uncover the nakedness of a woman and her daughter" or marrying sisters while they are both alive, "Neither shalt thou take a wife to her sister, to vex her, to uncover her nakedness, beside the other in her life time."[3] Added to this were instructions that if Israel had a king, "Neither shall he multiply wives to himself, that his heart turn not away."[4] But it was permitted that if a man died, having no child (son), then that man's brother could take her as a wife.[5]

A concubine could be added to a man's family in addition to his recognized wife. The husband was obliged to feed, clothe, and have marital rights with his additional wife.[6] Though men in biblical times were allowed to have more than one wife there was an obligation of the husband for additional support of that wife.

While polygamy for men was practiced in ancient times it was required of wealthy men to support and maintain those women who were additions to their household. A king would usually have resources to maintain his wives and concubines. Such is the situation of David and Solomon who are given as an example of how women can lead kings astray from God. Solomon was reported to have "seven hundred wives, princesses, and three hundred concubines."[7]

The Book of Mormon also described what can happen. It tells about one king Noah who was disobedient to God and "had many wives and concubines." The people did sin and he laid a heavy burden of taxes upon them. The text reads: "And all this did he take, to support himself, and his wives, and his concubines, and also, his priests, and their wives, and their concubines; thus he had changed the affairs of the kingdom."[8]

---

[3] Leviticus 18:17-18. On marrying a daughter and her mother see 20:14.
[4] Deuteronomy 17:17.
[5] Ibid., 25:5.
[6] Exodus 21:10.
[7] 1 Kings 11:3.
[8] 1830 BOM, 178; LDS Mosiah 11:2, 4; RLDS 7:3, 7.

One of the first revelations given by Joseph Smith on February 9, 1831, after he arrived in Kirtland, Ohio, was relating to church law:

Thou shalt love thy wife with all thy heart and cleave unto her & none else, and he that looketh upon a woman to lust after her shall deny the faith & shall not have the spirit & if he repent not he shall be cast out. Thou shalt not Commit adultery and he that committeth adultery & repenteth not shall be cast out and he that committeth adultery and repenteth with all his heart and forsaketh & doeth it no more, thou shalt forgive him, but if he do it again he shall not be forgiven, but shall be cast out.[9]

The next month a revelation was received by Smith telling those going to preach to the Shakers: "marriage is ordained of God unto man: Wherefore it is lawful that he should have one wife, and they twain [two] shall be one flesh, and all this that the earth might answer the end of its creation; and that it might be filled with the measure of man, according to his creation before the world was made."[10] This instruction followed the early Christian church which taught that elders, deacons, or a bishop were to be "the husband of one wife."[11]

In 1833 when Joseph Smith was revising the Old Testament he considered the Song of Solomon as uninspired. This writing mentioned sexual love. The marriage of Solomon is mentioned in chapter three verse eleven. When Smith revised 1 Kings chapter three he added the wording, "the Lord was not pleased with" Solomon.[12] Smith's revision reflects his concern of Solomon being like David his father (see 1 Kings 11:4, 6). The following biblical text tells about Solomon:

---

[9] Marquardt, *Joseph Smith Revelations*, 108; LDS D&C 42:22-26; RLDS D&C 42:7.

[10] Marquardt, *Joseph Smith Revelations*, 129; LDS D&C 49:15-17; RLDS D&C 49:3; (March 1831).

[11] See Titus 1:5-6; 1 Timothy 3:12; 3:2.

[12] OT MS 2, 75, RLDS archives, revised in 1832; revision of 1 Kings 3:1.

But king Solomon loved many strange women . . . Solomon clave unto these in love. And he had seven hundred wives, princesses, and three hundred concubines: and his wives turned away his heart. For it came to pass, when Solomon was old, that his wives turned away his heart after other gods[13]

This problem of love and women was a concern for Smith as he reviewed David and his son Solomon having many wives and concubines continuing his objection found in the Book of Mormon. By the time Joseph recommenced revising the Old Testament in 1833 he had his scribe write, "The Songs of Solomon are not Inspired writings."[14]

As discussed in chapter 18 it appears that Joseph Smith had an affair with Fanny Alger about 1836 before she left Kirtland. Luman A. Shirtliff married Eunice Bagg Gaylord, sister of Lester Gaylord. Elder Shirtliff described a conversation he had with his brother-in-law Lester Gaylord about March 1838 in Ohio before he departed for Missouri:

> While I and Br Leister [Lester Gaylord] was going from Kirtland to Sullivan to see about getting our Teems [Teams] In our conversation on the advancement of the Kingdom of God on the Earth I told him I believed that the time would come when men <in this Church> would have more than <one> Wife. Br Gaylord told his Wife and she told Sister [Rebecca] Williams and Sister Williams had told Br [Frederick G.] Williams and They had talked it over and concluded it was redicalous [ridiculous] for an Elder to believe such an awfull [awful] doctrin<e>

Luman said he defended his position with brother Williams. Rebecca Williams said, "I tell you br Shirtliff if such things are ever practiced in this Church I will leave it before Night that I will." Shirtliff continued his narrative telling when he was in the Nauvoo Temple in 1846:

---

[13] 1 Kings 11:1-4.
[14] OT MS 2, 97, RLDS archives.

I think no other word of that nature passed between us for over six years. while sitting near her in one of the upper Rooms of the Temple in Nauvoo while a Br[other] was passing through the Room with two women to the Sealing Room to be Sealed I said to Sister Williams, what do you think of that[?] she replied, O that is all right. I then said, then you don[']t think of leaveing to night[?] O no I am perfectly Satesfied [Satisfied].[15]

Joseph Smith was sexually active with Emma his wife for thirteen years before he taught others the importance of being married to additional wives not only in this life but for eternity. As prophet Smith's word was regarded by church members as the word of God. It appears that he would teach individual members the principle of plural marriage in secret and have them ask God for confirmation that it was a correct teaching. Joseph and Emma prior to moving to Nauvoo had six children; three of them died the day they were born. The couple was also raising an adopted daughter Julia. The three children that lived prior to the birth of Don Carlos in June 1840 were young Joseph, known as Joseph III, (born November 6, 1832), Frederick Granger Williams (born June 20, 1836), and Alexander Hale (born June 2, 1838).

The law of Illinois was clear on the status of matrimony: "Bigamy consists in the having of two wives or two husbands at one and the same time, knowing that the former husband or wife is still alive." Conviction could lead to a thousand dollar fine and send the guilty to the penitentiary for up to two years. For an unmarried woman, if convicted, she could be fined up to five hundred dollars and be imprisoned not more than a year.[16]

The religious ceremony of celestial marriage included the possibility of widowed, married, or single women being sealed in a

---

[15] Luman Andrus Shurtliff Autobiography, 116-118, LDS archives. Rebecca Williams was sealed for time and all eternity to her deceased husband Frederick (Heber C. Kimball was proxy) in the Nauvoo Temple on February 7, 1846 (Stanley B. Kimball, *Heber C. Kimball: Mormon Patriarch and Pioneer*, 314). Prior to the temple sealing Rebecca was sealed to Heber for time (this life) on September 2, 1844.

[16] *The Revised Laws of Illinois* (Vandalia: Printed by Greiner & Sherman, 1833), 198.

priesthood rite to Joseph Smith with the promise, if faithful, to enter the celestial kingdom of heaven with themselves, their families, and be associated with Smith for eternity.

Documentation of the secret nature of this ordinance like other priesthood related practices was secret for many reasons. Publicly in Nauvoo the practice of being married or sealed to more than one wife was denied. After Joseph Smith's death some of the women made notarized affidavits which gave the date and named the person who performed the ceremony. Other women told about it in their life story. Some women believed that Smith's advances were too much for their comfort. A few plural wives died before making any statement. Joseph Bates Noble recalled that as early as 1840 he was told about celestial marriage:

> in the fall of the year A.D. 1840 Joseph Smith taught him [Noble] the principle of Celestial marriage or a "plurality of wives", and that the said Joseph Smith declaired [declared] that he had received a Revelation from God on the subject, and that the Angel of the Lord had commanded him, (Joseph Smith) to move forward in the said order of marriage[17]

Louisa Beeman was sealed to Joseph Smith by Joseph Noble. According to Noble he performed the sealing on April 5, 1841. This was "according to the order of Celestial Marriage revealed to the Said Joseph Smith."[18] In early 1842 rumors circulated that certain unnamed men had "debauch the innocent" stating they had authority from church leaders. At the third meeting of the Relief Society held on March 30, 1842 Emma Smith, society president, read an Epistle prepared for the sisters which would be a test in keeping secrets:

> A knowledge of some such things having come to our ears, we improve this favorable opportunity, wherein so goodly a

---

[17] Affidavit of Joseph B. Noble, June 26, 1869, Joseph F. Smith Affidavit Book 1:38, original in LDS archives. See also Andrew Jenson, "Plural Marriage," *Historical Record* 6 (May 1887):221, Salt Lake City.

[18] Affidavit of Joseph B. Noble, June 26, 1869, separate affidavit from one noted in footnote 17, Joseph F. Smith Affidavit Book 1:3.

number of you may be inform'd that no such authority ever has, ever can, or ever will be given to any man, and if any man has been guilty of any such thing, let him be treated with utter contempt, and let the curse of God fall on his head, and let him be turned out of Society as unworthy of a place among men, & denounced as the blackest & the most unprincipled wretch; and finally let him be damned!

The Epistle further stated:

We do not mention their names, not knowing but what there may be some among you who are not sufficiently skill'd in Masonry as to keep a secret, therefore, suffice it to say, there are those, and we therefore warn you, & forewarn you, in the name of the Lord, to check & destroy any faith that any innocent person may have in any such character; for we do not want any one to believe *any thing* as coming from us, contrary to the old established morals & virtues & scriptural laws, regulating the habits, customs & conduct of society; and all persons pretending to be authoriz'd by us, or having any permit, or sanction from us, are & will be *liars & base impostors*, & you are authoriz'd on the very first intimation of the kind, to denounce them as such, & shun them as the flying fiery serpent, whether they are prophets, Seers, or revelators; Patriarchs, twelve Apostles, Elders, Priests, Mayors, Generals, City Councillors, Aldermen, Marshalls, Police, Lord Mayors or the Devil, are alike culpable & shall be damned for such evil practices; and if you yourselves adhere to anything of the kind, you also shall be damned. . . . Let this Epistle be had as a private matter in your Society, and then we shall learn whether you are good masons.[19]

This Epistle was signed by church president Joseph Smith, Apostles Brigham Young, Heber C. Kimball, and Willard

---

[19] A Book of Records, Containing the proceedings of The Female Relief Society of Nauvoo, 86-88, LDS archives, emphasis retained. The epistle was recorded at the end of the September 28, 1842 meeting.

Richards; also church patriarch Hyrum Smith, and bishop Vinson Knight.

It appears that women were sealed to the prophet Joseph Smith to secure their salvation. At times these sealings were to also assist the parents of the wife to have a family relationship and eternal glory with Smith. In 1842 the sealing of women to Joseph Smith was accelerated. Smith made advances toward females some of whom objected. Most accepted his doctrine and were united by a priesthood sealing ceremony. As far as known these women were secretly sealed to Joseph Smith without courtship. Many of the single women because of their commitment to Smith in a plural relationship would not be able to marry a man near their own age.

The following is a listing of women who obtained the sealing rite with the date and person who performed the ceremony if known.[20] Some of the sealings of single women are not as well documented as others. The dates are based on statements made in 1869 by over a dozen women and on other recollections of the women or the men who attended the sealing. Included were a couple of wives who were biological sisters. While the charts presented on the following pages may not include all of Smith plural wives it does give an indication of the variety of situations involved in plural marriage at Nauvoo.

SINGLE WOMEN SEALED TO JOSEPH SMITH

Spiritual Wives	Age	Sealing Date	By Whom
Louisa Beeman	26	April 5, 1841	Joseph B. Noble
Eliza Roxey Snow	38	June 29, 1842	Brigham Young
Sarah Ann Whitney	17	July 27, 1842	Newel K. Whitney
Desdemona W. Fullmer	32-33	1842-43	Brigham Young
Emily Dow Partridge	19	March 4, 1843	Heber C. Kimball
sealed a second time		May [23], 1843	James Adams
Eliza Maria Partridge	22	March 8, 1843	Heber C. Kimball
sealed a second time		May [23], 1843	James Adams
Flora Ann Woodworth	16	circa April 1843	unknown
Lucy Walker	17	May 1, 1843	William Clayton

---

[20] Andrew Jenson printed in the *Historical Record* 6 (May 1887):233-34 a list of twenty-seven reported wives of Joseph Smith. The article included some biographical sketches of a few of the women. Apostle Wilford Woodruff wrote to Jenson, "We do not think it a wise step to give these names to the world, at the present time, in the manner which you have done in this 'Historical Record'" (Woodruff to Jenson, Aug. 6, 1887, typed copy, LDS archives).

SINGLE WOMEN SEALED TO JOSEPH SMITH

Spiritual Wives	Age	Sealing Date	By Whom
Maria Lawrence	19	circa May 1843	unknown
Sarah Lawrence	17	circa May 1843	unknown
Rhoda Richards	58	June 12, 1843	Willard Richards
Helen Mar Kimball	14	circa June 1843	unknown
Almera W. Johnson	29-30	circa June-Aug. 1843	Hyrum Smith
Melissa Lott	19	Sept. 20, 1843	Hyrum Smith
Hannah S. Ells	29-30	1843	unknown

Accounts vary as to the character of Joseph Smith and women at Nauvoo. John C. Bennett indicated in his book that he considered Smith being licentious. The same type of charge was made against Bennett. These two men became good friends and then had a bitter relationship and exposé of each other after their falling out in May 1842. [21] Among the earliest exposés of plural marriage was that of John Cook Bennett,[22] who lived in the prophet's home for nine months.[23] Statements on spiritual wifeism made by the opportunist Bennett were countered by Joseph Smith and friends in the Nauvoo press. Rather than get into the politics of their debate we intend to document a couple of instances relating to attempts to obtain wives in Nauvoo before Bennett left Nauvoo.

The pressure was enormous not to discuss details of how individual men attempted to secure plural wives. In order to talk to a woman a man would have to teach her ideas or doctrines that the church had opposed for years. Two women who were approached were Nancy Rigdon, daughter of Sidney Rigdon, and Martha Brotherton, a convert from England.

Women who were sealed to Smith considered him to be a prophet and rarely said anything about the sexual nature of their marriage. Most of the sealings in private sealing ceremonies were kept from the knowledge of his legal wife Emma. Whatever Joseph Smith's reasoning for celestial marriage he knew that Emma would

---

[21] See Andrew F. Smith, *The Saintly Scoundrel: The Life and Times of Dr. John Cook Bennett* (Urbana: University of Illinois Press, 1997).

[22] John C. Bennett's book length exposé was *The History of the Saints; or, An Exposé of Joe Smith and Mormonism* (Boston: Leland & Whiting, 1842).

[23] "Autobiography of Emily D. P. Young," *Woman's Exponent* 14 (Aug. 1, 1885):37. Emily wrote, "John C. Bennett made his home at the Prophet's house at this time." See Smith, *The Saintly Scoundrel*, 214n10.

probably not approve of having women sealed to her husband. The priesthood ordinance was withheld from his wife for two years. It was not until May 1843 that Joseph was able to convince Emma to be a part of this process. She did consent to some sealings in 1843.

Besides the few single women sealed to Smith in 1841-42 there were married women who received the sealing ordinance to Joseph. This type of sealing commenced late in 1841. Included is the sealing of a daughter and her mother (Silvia Sessions Lyon and Patty Sessions) to Smith. Exactly what arrangement was made between those women who had a living husband and were sealed to Joseph Smith is not known. Smith evidently offered them association with himself in the celestial kingdom. The following charts list some of the married and widow sisters who went forward and were sealed to President Smith.

MARRIED WOMEN SEALED TO JOSEPH SMITH

Spiritual Wives	Age	Sealing Date	By Whom
Zina D. Huntington Jacobs	20	Oct. 27, 1841	Dimick Huntington
Prescenda Huntington Buell	31	Dec. 11, 1841	Dimick Huntington
Sylvia Sessions Lyon	23	Feb. 8, 1842	unknown
Mary Rollins Lightner	23	circa Feb. 1842	Brigham Young
Patty Bartlett Sessions	47	March 9, 1842	Willard Richards
Marinda Johnson Hyde	27	May 1843	Brigham Young
Elvira Cowles Holmes	29	June 1, 1843	Heber C. Kimball
Ruth Vose Sayers	35-36	1843-44	Hyrum Smith

WIDOWED WOMEN SEALED TO JOSEPH SMITH

Spiritual Wives	Age	Sealing Date	By Whom
Agnes Coolbrith Smith	33	Jan. 6, 1842	Brigham Young
Martha McBride Knight	37	circa Aug. 1842	Heber C. Kimball
Fanny Young Carr Murray	56	Nov. 2, 1843	Brigham Young

Publicly these women were not known as Smith's spiritual wife as Emma was the only legal wife of Joseph. It appears that Emma did not give Joseph permission to be sealed to married women or widows. What Emma's knowledge was is not known. A number of females who did domestic work in Joseph Smith's homestead

THE RISE OF MORMONISM

became Smith's wives. Three of these women were Desdemona Fullmer, Eliza and her sister Emily Partridge.[24]

Those sealed to Smith were not publicly known as spiritual wives of Joseph Smith. For example, they did not go with him to public meetings or social activities. They had no legal status as Smith's wives. There is no indication how the sealings of married wives were to be worked out temporally or spiritually. On the other hand John C. Bennett and other male members approached females to obtain sexual intercourse with their intended victims.[25]

Only a few church members knew about the command to practice plural marriage and there were some honest denials of the practice. Stake president William Marks said he knew "of no Order in the Church which admits of a plurality of wives, and do not believe that Joseph Smith ever taught such a doctrine."[26]

Of the seven spiritual wives that John C. Bennett listed (with asterisks for their last names) some have been identified. Bennett wrote, "Joe Smith was privately married to his spiritual wives" and mentioned "Mrs. A**** S****, by Apostle Brigham Young" this was Mrs. Agnes Smith (widow of Don Carlos Smith) being sealed to Joseph Smith in January 1842. "Miss L***** B*****, by Elder Joseph Bates Noble" was Louisa Beeman sealed to Smith in April 1841. "Mrs. B****" who was Mrs. Prescenda Huntington Buell having been also sealed in 1841. Bennett listed a "Mrs. S*******" which was for Mrs. Sylvia Sessions or Mrs. Patty Sessions.[27]

Seventeen year old Martha Brotherton, her older sister Elizabeth, and their parents Thomas and Sarah left Liverpool, England on the ship *Tyrian* and arrived at New Orleans on November 9, 1841.[28] Later the family moved to Nauvoo and

---

[24] Nauvoo Stake, Ward Census 1842, Fourth Ward, LDS archives. The church census was taken in February 1842.

[25] See Gary James Bergera, "'Illicit Intercourse,' Plural Marriage and the Nauvoo Stake High Council, 1840-1844," *John Whitmer Historical Association Journal* 23 (2003):59-90.

[26] *Times and Seasons* 3 (Aug. 1, 1842):875.

[27] Bennett, *History of the Saints*, 256.

[28] Conway B. Soone, *Ships, Saints, and Mariners: A Maritime Encyclopedia of Mormon Migration 1830-1890* (Salt Lake City: University of Utah Press, 1987), 190. See Paul B. Pixton, "The *Tyrian* and Its Mormon Passengers," *Mormon Historical Studies* 5 (Spring 2004):29-52.

Martha received a patriarchal blessing from Hyrum Smith on February 23, 1842.

John C. Bennett requested Martha to make a public statement. She did on July 13. Martha gave some background of her meeting with Brigham Young and Heber C. Kimball at Joseph Smith's red brick store. At the store Martha saw William Clayton who she recognized in the tithing office.[29] The following conversation is based upon Martha's affidavit written in July 1842.[30] Brigham Young wanted Martha as a plural wife. This exchange probably took place in March of that year. Her affidavit is one of the earliest published documents concerning the belief in a plurality of wives by leaders of the church. Martha said she sat down and wrote about her experience shortly after it took place.

Going upstairs with Heber C. Kimball to the second floor of the red brick store she found Brigham Young and Joseph Smith alone. Martha was introduced to the Prophet Joseph Smith (JS) by Brigham Young. Joseph offered Martha his seat after which Smith and Heber Kimball left the room leaving Martha alone with Apostle Young. Brigham Young (BY) arose, locked the door, closed the window, and drew the curtain. He then came and sat before Martha Brotherton (MB). The following is based on her memory of what took place that day:

BY: This is our private room, Martha.

MB: Indeed, sir, I must be highly honored to be permitted to enter it.

BY: Sister Martha, I want to ask you a few questions; will you answer them?

MB: Yes, sir.

BY: And will you promise not to mention them to anyone?

MB: If it is your desire, sir, I will not.

---

[29] Clayton began to enter the amounts of tithes on February 10, 1842 (William Clayton Journal, L. Tom Perry Special Collections, Harold B. Lee Library, Brigham Young University).

[30] Brotherton to Bennett, July 13, 1842, *Native American Bulletin* 1 (July 16, 1842), St. Louis, Missouri, emphasis omitted. Martha Brotherton's affidavit appeared in a number of Illinois newspapers and was published twice in New York City. See *New York Herald* 8 (July 25 and 27, 1842).

BY: And you will not think any the worse of me for it, will you, Martha?"

MB: No sir.

BY: Well, what are your feelings toward me?

MB: My feelings are just the same towards you that they ever were, sir.

BY: But, to come to the point more closely, have not you an affection for me, that, were it lawful and right, you could accept of me for your husband and companion?

MB: If it was lawful and right perhaps I might; but you know, sir, it is not.

BY: Well, brother Joseph has had a revelation from God that it is lawful and right for a man to have two wives; for as it was in the days of Abraham, so it shall be in these last days, and whoever is the first that is willing to take up the cross will receive the greatest blessings; and if you will accept of me I will take you straight to the celestial kingdom; and if you will have me in this world, I will have you in that which is to come, and brother Joseph will marry us here today, and you can go home this evening, and your parents will not know any thing about it.

MB: Sir, I should not like to do anything of the kind without the permission of my parents.

BY: Well, you are of age, are you not?

MB: No, sir, I shall not be until the 24th of May.

BY: Well, that does not make any difference. You will be of age before they know, and you need not fear. If you will take my counsel it will be well with you, for I know it to be right before God, and if there is any sin in it, I will answer for it. But brother Joseph wishes to have some talk with you on the subject, he will explain things, will you hear him?

MB: I do not mind.

BY: Well, I want you to say something.

MB: I want time to think about it.

BY: Well, I will have a kiss any how.

Brigham Young said he would bring Joseph Smith. Brigham unlocked the door, and took the key and relocked Martha in the room alone for about ten minutes and returned with Joseph. The interview continued:

BY to JS: Well, sister Martha would be willing if she knew if was lawful and right before God.

JS: Well, Martha, it is lawful and right before God. I know it is. Look here, don't you believe in me? Well Martha, just go ahead and do as Brigham wants you to, he is the best man in the world except me.

BY: Oh then you are as good.

JS: Yes.

BY: Well, we believe Joseph to be a Prophet. I have known him near eight years, and always found him the same.

JS: Yes, and I know that this is lawful and right before God, and if there is any sin in it I will answer for it before God, and I have the keys of the kingdom, and whatever I bind on earth is bound in heaven, and whatever I loose on earth is loosed in heaven; and if you will accept of Brigham, you shall be blessed. God shall bless you, and my blessing shall rest upon you, and if you will be led by him you will do well; for I know Brigham will take care of you, and if he don't do his duty to you, come to me and I will make him; and if you do not like it in a month or two, come to me and I will make you free again; and if he turns you off I will take you on.

MB: Sir, it will be too late to think in a month or two after. I want time to think first.

JS: Well, the old proverb is, "Nothing ventured, nothing gained;" and it would be the greatest blessing that was ever bestowed upon you.

BY: Yes, and you will never have reason to repent it, that is, if I do not turn from righteousness, and that I trust I never shall, for I believe God who has kept me so long will continue to keep me faithful. Did you ever see me act in any way wrong in England, Martha?

MB: No, sir.

BY: No, neither can any one else lay any thing to my charge.

JS: Well, then, what are you afraid of? Come let me do the business for you.

MB: Sir, do let me have a little time to think about it, and I will promise not to mention it to any one.

BY: Well, look here, you know a fellow will never be damned for doing the best he knows how.

MB: Well, then, the best way I know of, is to go home and think and pray about it.

BY: Well, I shall leave it with brother Joseph, whether it would be best for you to have time or not.

JS: Well, I see no harm in her having time to think, if she will not fall into temptation.

MB: O, sir, there is no fear of my falling into temptation.

BY: Well, you must promise me you will never mention it to any one.

MB: I do promise it.

JS: Well, you must promise me the same.

MB: I promise.

JS: Upon your honor, you will not tell.

MB: No, sir, I will lose my life first.

JS: Well, that will do, that is the principle we go upon. I think I can trust you, Martha.

MB: Yes, I think you ought.

JS: She looks as if she could keep a secret.

Martha left the store and he next day being Sunday she sat down and wrote the conversation. She shared it with her sister. Later rumor went around relating to the incident. At a special conference held on April 7, Hyrum Smith "spoke in contradiction of a report in circulation about Elder Kimball, B. Young, himself, and others of the Twelve, alledging [alleging] that a sister had been shut in a room for several days, and that they had endeavored to induce her to believe in having two wives."[31] How accurate the rumor was we do not know. It did mention Brigham Young and the idea to believe that men could have two wives. That the sister was to have been "shut in a room for several days" was certainly an exaggeration.

Later Martha Brotherton's July statement would bring denials from both Brigham Young and Heber C. Kimball. Martha wrote to her relatives in England. The church periodical, not knowing the private teachings in Nauvoo, wrote:

---

[31] "Conference Minutes," *Times and Seasons* 3 (April 15, 1842):763.

But, for the information of those who may be assailed by those foolish tales about the two wives, we would say that no such principle ever existed among the Latter-day Saints, and never will; this is well known to all who are acquainted with our books, the Book of Mormon, Doctrine and Covenants; and also all our periodicals are very strict and explicit on that subject, indeed far more so than the Bible.[32]

Reaction in the church from Martha's published recollection was negative against her integrity. Martha's brother-in-law John McIlwrick made a statement that Martha "is a deliberate liar." Her two sisters, Elizabeth and Mary, concurred. Brigham Young also made an affidavit stating, "I do hereby testify that the affidavit of Miss Martha Brotherton that is going the rounds in the politics and religious papers, is a base falsehood, with regard to any private intercourse or unlawful conduct or conversation with me."[33]

Shortly afterwards it was rumored that Joseph Smith privately asked Nancy Rigdon, a daughter of Sidney Rigdon, to become his (Smith's) spiritual wife. She declined but Smith dictated a letter to her of a doctrinal nature. The letter by Joseph Smith contained ideas that were conducive to persuading a person to accept a religious principle though it may be contrary to the accepted norm. Smith indicated:

Happiness is the object and design of our existence, and will be the end thereof, if we pursue the path that leads to it, and this path is virtue, uprightness, faithfulness, holiness, and keeping all the commandments of God. . . . Whatever God requires is right, no matter what it is, although we may

---

[32] "Apostacy," *Millennial Star* 3 (Aug. 1842):74.

[33] Affidavit of Brigham Young, Aug. 25, 1842, sworn and subscribed to on August 27, 1842, published in the broadside *Affidavits and Certificates, Disproving the Statements and Affidavits Contained in John C. Bennett's Letters. Nauvoo. Aug. 31, 1842.* Subsequently Brigham Young had Martha Brotherton sealed to him after her death. Her younger sister Elizabeth being proxy for her, in the Endowment House in Salt Lake City. Apostle Joseph F. Smith performed the sealing (Salt Lake Temple and Endowment House Records, under date of August 1, 1870, Family History Library).

not see the reason thereof till long after the events transpire. If we seek first the kingdom of God, all good things will be added. So with Solomon—first he asked wisdom, and God gave it him, and with it every Desire of his heart, even things which might be considered abominable to all who understand the order of heaven only in part, but which, in reality, were right, because God gave and sanctioned by special revelation.[34]

George W. Robinson, son-in-law of Sidney Rigdon, wrote that Nancy told her story in front of her family and Joseph Smith. Robinson wrote about the meeting:

I was present. Smith attempted to deny it at first, and face her down with the lie; but she told the facts with so much earnestness, and the fact of a letter being present, which he had caused to be written to her, on the same subject, the day after the attempt made on her virtue, breathing the same spirit, and which he had fondly hoped was destroyed,—all came with such force that he could not withstand the testimony; and he then and there acknowledged that every word of Miss Rigdon's testimony was true. Now for his excuse, which he made for such a base attempt, and for using the name of the Lord in vain, on that occasion. He wished to ascertain whether she was virtuous or not, and took that course to learn the facts!!![35]

While Smith's confession was private Nancy did not make a public statement. The letter dictated by Smith and written by Willard Richards was still in her possession. The public position taken in the Nauvoo newspaper *The Wasp* was denial that Joseph Smith was its author.

---

[34] Smith to Nancy Rigdon, circa April 11, 1842, original letter in the handwriting of Willard Richards not extant. Published in the *Sangamo Journal* 10 (Aug. 19, 1842):2, Springfield, Illinois. Quotation marks and emphasis are omitted. See Jessee, *Personal Writings of Joseph Smith*, 538-39.

[35] Robinson to James Arlington Bennet, July 27, 1842, as cited in John C. Bennett, *History of the Saints*, 246, emphasis omitted.

To further complicate the matter Stephen Markham wrote despairing comments about Bennett and Nancy insinuating that they "were guilty of unlawful and illicit intercourse with each other."[36] Sidney Rigdon countered this by stating that "Markham is not to be believed, that his word for truth and veracity is not good."[37] The statement by Markham was so unreliable that the *Wasp* reported, "We are authorized to say, by Gen. Joseph Smith, that the affidavit of Stephen Markham, relative to Miss Nancy Rigdon, as published in the handbill of affidavits, was unauthorized by him: the certificate of Elder Rigdon relative to the letter, being satisfactory."[38] The handbill was authorized by Smith who made no affidavit regarding his conduct with Nancy Rigdon. Concerning the letter to his daughter Sidney Rigdon made his own statement:

I am fully authorized by my daughter, Nancy, to say to the public through the medium of your paper, that the letter which has appeared in the Sangamo Journal, making part of General Bennett's letters to said paper, purporting to have been written by Mr. Joseph Smith to her, was unauthorized by her, and that she never said to Gen. Bennett or any other person, that said letter was written by said Mr. Smith, nor in his hand writing, but by another person, and in another persons' hand writing. . . . I would further state that Mr. Smith denied to me the authorship of that letter.[39]

The date when Heber C. and Vilate Kimball were sealed together for time and all eternity is not known. According to family tradition thirty year old Sarah Peak Noon was "abandoned in Nauvoo by her husband [William Spencer Noon] when he returned

---

[36] Affidavit of Stephen Markham, Aug. 29, 1842, published in the broadside *Affidavits and Certificates, Disproving the Statements and Affidavits Contained in John C. Bennett's Letters. Nauvoo. Aug. 31, 1842.*

[37] Certificate of Sidney Rigdon, Sept. 3, 1842, *Sangamo Journal* 10 (Sept. 23, 1842).

[38] *The Wasp* 1 (Sept. 3, 1842):2, Nauvoo.

[39] Rigdon to Editor, Aug. 27, 1842, Ibid., 1 (Sept. 3, 1842):3. Also printed in *Affidavits and Certificates.*

to England."[40] Shortly after, about January 1842, Sarah Peak was sealed to Apostle Heber C. Kimball as a plural wife. Sarah entered into the plural relationship with two children. In July Heber wrote to Vilate from Pittsburgh, "give my kind love to sister S[arah]. fore [for] she is not forgot[t]en."[41] In October Vilate wrote a letter to Heber when she and Sarah Moon were both pregnant:

Our good friend S[arah]. is as ever, and we are one. You said I must tell you all my feelings; but if I were to tell you that I sometimes felt tempted and tried and feel as though my burden was greater that I could bear, it would only be a source of sorrow to you, and the Lord knows that I do not wish to add one sorrow to your heart, for be assured my dear Heber, that I do not love you any less for what has transpired, neither do I believe that you do me; therefore I will keep my bad feelings to myself, as much as possible; and tell you the good. I can say with propriety that the most of my time I feel comfortable in my mind, and feel that I have much to be thankful for. I realize that the scenes we are called to pass through are calculated to wean us from the world, and prepare us for a better one. . . . I must leave room for Sister S[arah]. to write you a few lines.

Vilate ended her portion of the letter and left room for Sarah Moon, Heber's first plural wife, to add her thoughts in the same letter:

My very dear friend: Inasmuch as I have listened to your counsel hitherto I have prospered, therefore I hope that I shall ever adhere to it strictly in future. Your kind letter was joyfully received. I never read it but I receive some comfort and feel strengthened, and thank you for it. You may depend upon my moving as soon as the house is ready. I feel anxious as I perceive my infirmities increasing daily. Your request with regard to Sister Kimball I will attend to. Nothing gives me more pleasure than to add to the

---

[40] Kimball, *Heber C. Kimball: Mormon Patriarch and Pioneer*, 95.
[41] Heber C. Kimball to Vilate Kimball, July 25, 1842, LDS archives.

happiness of my friends; I only wish that I had more ability to do so. I am very glad we are likely to see you soon, and pray that nothing may occur to disappoint us. When you request Vilate to meet you, perhaps you forget that I shall then stand in jeopardy every hour, and would not have her absent for worlds. My mind is fixed and I am rather particular, but still, for your comfort, I will submit.[42]

The first known child born to a plural wife in Nauvoo was a son Adelmon (Adelbert) who was born October or November 1842 to Heber and Sarah. Six months later little Adelmon died. His obituary reads: "Adelmon H. Noon, 6 months; fit of Appoplexy" having died the week ending April 24, 1843.[43]

On January 2, 1843 Charles S. Kimball was born to Vilate and Heber. If Heber and Vilate were sealed for time and eternity by this time then the birth of Charles would be the first child born in the new eternal covenant of marriage. Helen Mar Kimball, fourteen years old at the time, recalled many years later, "I remember the birth of another son of my father's wife Sarah which happened not far from the time that that my mother's was born."[44]

In another letter Vilate told Heber about Parley and Mary Ann Pratt coming to their home and mentioned to Heber that one (plural wife) had been appointed for Parley. The next month Elizabeth Brotherton was sealed to Parley P. Pratt on July 24, 1843 by Hyrum Smith. Vilate wrote:

> June 29th since writing the above I have had a visit from brother Pa<r>ley and his wife they are truly converted it appears that J....h [Joseph] has taught him some principles

[42] Vilate Kimball to Heber C. Kimball, Oct. 16, 1842, as cited in Helen Mar [Kimball] Whitney, "Scenes and Incidents in Nauvoo," *Woman's Exponent* 11 (June 1, 1882):1-2. The words "(Sarah, father's other wife)" after "friend S." are omitted.

[43] *The Wasp* 1 (April 26, 1843):3. Also recorded in "Record of Deaths in the City of Nauvoo," LDS archives. See Fred E. Woods, "The Cemetery Record of William D. Huntington, Nauvoo Sexton," *Mormon Historical Studies* 3, no. 1 (2002):138.

[44] Helen Mar [Kimball] Whitney, "Scenes and Incidents in Nauvoo," *Woman's Exponent* 11 (July 15, 1882):26. Charles Spalding Kimball died Dec. 2, 1925 and is buried in the Salt Lake City Cemetery.

and told him his privilege, and even appointed one for him, I dare not tell you who it is, you would be astonished and I guess some tried. she has be[e]n to me for counsel, I told her I did not wish to advise in such matters. sister Pratt has be[e]n rageing against these things, she told me her self that the devel [devil] had be[e]n in her until within a few days past, she said the Lord had shown her it was all right. she wants Parley to go ahead, says she will do all in her power to help him; they are so ingagued [engaged] I feer [fear] they will run to[o] fast. they asked me many questions on principle I told them I did not know much and I rather they would go to those that had authority to teach. Parley said he and J[oseph] were interrupted before he got what instruction he had wanted, and now he did not know when he should have an opportunity. he seamed [seemed] unwilling to wate [wait]. I told him these were sacred things and he better not make a moove [move] until he got more instruction.[45]

There are gaps in our knowledge of plural marriage because of the scarcity of written records. Some letters written at Nauvoo asks the recipient to burn the letter after reading it because of the nature of the content. But there are enough documents retained through the years that help us establish the basic nature of the plural relationships. The next chapter will discuss the marriage of Sarah Ann Whitney to Joseph Smith in July 1842.

---

[45] Vilate Kimball to Heber C. Kimball, June 27-29, 1843, LDS archives. The letter ended: "I think you had better burn this, as soon as yuo [you] can after reading it. I should not dare to send it by mail, but I trust it will go safe."

24

Sarah Ann Whitney

At Nauvoo in 1842 the Joseph Smith store was the headquarters of the Church of Jesus Christ of Latter Day Saints.[1] Working at the store was Newel K. Whitney, church bishop, and his brother-in-law, Joseph C. Kingsbury. Also helping Joseph Smith was Willard Richards, apostle and clerk, assisting in keeping records such as the Book of the Law of the Lord. For the date of March 22, 1842 Richards wrote that Smith was "At the General Business office (Sarah Ann Whitney's Birth day, celebration, at the Lodge Room, co[mpany]. waited upon by the Recr [Recorder]) home in the eve[ning]."[2] Helen Mar Kimball Whitney recalled being at Sarah Ann's seventeenth birthday celebration:

> My first introduction into her circle was at a party given in honor of her seventeenth birthday, in March, 1842, in the Masonic room above Joseph Smith's store. The latter her father had charge of, and his family occupied a small house adjoining it. . . . The Prophet spent a little time with them, but took no part. I believe that I was the youngest and I know that I was the most bashful, so much so that I declined nearly every invitation to take part in their various games.[3]

There was a close relationship between Joseph Smith, Prophet and President of the Church, and Bishop Newel K. Whitney.

This bond of affection was strengthened and intensified by the giving in marriage to the former of the Bishop's eldest

---

[1] Richard P. Howard, "The Joseph Smith Store: Church Headquarters at Nauvoo?" *Saints Herald* 118 (Oct. 1971):34.

[2] Jessee, *Papers of Joseph Smith* 2:372, original reading of entry.

[3] Helen Mar [Kimball] Whitney, "Scenes in Nauvoo after the Martyrdom of the Prophet and Patriarch," *Woman's Exponent* 11 (March 1, 1883):146.

daughter, Sarah, in obedience to a revelation from God. This girl was but seventeen years of age, but she had implicit faith in the doctrine of plural marriage, as revealed to and practiced by the Prophet, was of celestial origin. She was the first woman, in this dispensation, who was given in plural marriage by and with the consent of both parents. Her father himself officiated in the ceremony. The revelation commanding and consecrating this union, is in existence, though it has never been published. It bears the date of July 27, 1842, and was given through the Prophet to the writer's grandfather, Newel K. Whitney, whose daughter Sarah, on that day, became the wedded wife of Joseph Smith for time and all eternity.[4]

Sarah Ann Whitney was the eldest daughter of Newel and Elizabeth Ann Whitney and was born on March 22, 1825. At the age of seventeen she was married to the Prophet Joseph Smith in a priesthood sealing ceremony on July 27, 1842, by her father. She died in Salt Lake City on September 4, 1873, thirty-one years after her marriage with Joseph Smith.

Joseph Smith had first seen Sarah Ann Whitney when he arrived in Kirtland, Ohio, about the first of February 1831; she was then almost six years old. Eleven years later they were married by her father as husband and wife for time and for all eternity. Besides their prayers it appears that it took a special revelation to Joseph Smith to help win the parents consent. Years later Sarah Ann and Elizabeth Whitney made affidavits concerning this matter. Sarah Ann [Whitney] Kimball maintained that "on the twenty Seventh day of July A.D. 1842 at the City of Nauvoo, County of Hancock, State of Illinois, She was married or Sealed to Joseph Smith, President of the Church of Jesus Christ of Latterday Saints, by Newel K. Whitney, Presiding Bishop of Said Church"[5] Elizabeth Ann Whitney said "She was present and witnessed the marrying or

---

[4] O[rson]. F. Whitney, "The Aaronic Priesthood," *The Contributor* 6 (Jan. 1885):131, Salt Lake City; also found in the Andrew Jenson, *Latter-Day Saints Biographical Encyclopaedia* (Salt Lake City: A. Jenson History Company, and Printed by the Deseret News, 1901), 1:226.
[5] Affidavit of Sarah A. [Whitney] Kimball, June 19, 1869, Joseph F. Smith Affidavit Book 1:36, LDS archives.

Sealing of her daughter Sarah Ann Whitney to the Prophet Joseph Smith, for time and all eternity, by her husband Newel K. Whitney."[6]

Elizabeth Ann Whitney mentioned that Joseph Smith "had been strictly charged, by the angel who committed these precious things in his keeping, that he should only reveal them to such ones as were pure, and full of integrity to the truth, and worthy and capable of being entrusted with divine messages." Elizabeth and Newel prayed that "the Lord would grant us some special manifestation concerning this new and strange doctrine. The Lord was very merciful to us, revealing unto us his power and glory. We were seemingly wrapt in a heavenly vision; a halo of light encircled us, and we were convinced in our own bosoms that God heard and approved our prayers and intercedings before him." Continuing her account Elizabeth Whitney remarked:

Our hearts were comforted, and our faith made so perfect that we were willing to give our eldest daughter, then only seventeen years of age, to Joseph, in the holy order of plural marriage. . . . Yet, laying aside all our traditions and former notions in regard to marriage, we gave her with our mutual consent. She was the first woman ever given in plural marriage by or with the consent of both parents. Of course these things had to be kept an inviolate secret[7]

William Clayton knew that Sarah Ann was one plural wife among others who was sealed to Joseph Smith. Clayton recalled:

During this period [1842-43] the Prophet Joseph took several other wives. Amongst the number I well remember Eliza Partridge, Emily Partridge, Sarah Ann Whitney, Helen Kimball and Flora Woodworth. These all, he

---

[6] Affidavit of E[lizabeth]. A. Whitney, Aug. 30, 1869, Joseph F. Smith Affidavit Book titled "40 Affidavits on Celestial Marriage," 74.

[7] Edward W. Tullidge, *The Women of Mormondom* (New York: Tullidge and Crandall, 1877), 368-69; [Elizabeth Ann Whitney] "A Leaf from an Autobiography," *Woman's Exponent* 7 (Dec. 15, 1878):105. See also Helen Mar [Kimball] Whitney, "Scenes in Nauvoo after the Martyrdom of the Prophet and Patriarch," Ibid., 11 (March 1, 1883):146.

acknowledged to me, were his lawful, wedded wives, according to the celestial order.[8]

Joseph Smith received a revelation at Nauvoo on July 27, 1842 that gave instructions for Bishop Newel K. Whitney to perform the agreed upon ceremony to join in marriage his daughter Sarah Ann to Joseph Smith. The revelation contained the wording of the marriage ceremony to be used by Bishop Whitney.

Verily thus saith the Lord unto my se[r]vant N[ewel]. K. Whitney the thing that my se[r]vant Joseph Smith has made known unto you and your Famely [Family] and which you have agreed upon is right in mine eyes and shall be rewarded upon your heads with honor and immortality and eternal life to all your house both old & young because of the lineage of my Preast [Priest] Hood saith the Lord it shall be upon you and upon your children after you from generation to generation By virtue of the Holy promise which I now make unto you saith the Lord.

these are the words which you shall pronounce upon my se[r]vant Joseph [Smith] and your Daughter S. A. [Sarah Ann] Whitney they shall take each other by the hand and you shall say

you both mutu[al]ly agree calling them by name to be each others companion so long as you both shall live preser[v]ing yourselv[es] for each other and from all others[9] and also through [o]ut eternity reserving only those rights which have been given to my servant Joseph [Smith] by revelation and commandment and by legal Authority in times passed [past]

If you both agree to covenant and do this then I give you S. A. [Sarah Ann] Whitney my Daughter to Joseph Smith

---

[8] Affidavit of William Clayton, Feb. 16, 1874, LDS archives; in Andrew Jenson, *Historical Record* 6 (May 1887):225.

[9] The 1835 D&C contains the following question as part of the marriage ceremony: "You both mutually agree to be each other's companion, husband and wife, observing the legal rights belonging to this condition; that is, keeping yourselves wholly for each other, and from all others, during your lives?" (1835 D&C 101).

to be his wife to observe all the rights betwe[e]n you both that belong to that condition I do it in my own name and in the name of my wife your mother and in the name of my Holy Progenitors by the right of birth which is of Priest Hood vested in me by revelation and commandment and promise of the liveing God obtained by the Holy Melchesdick[10] Gethrow[11] and other of the Holy Fathers commanding in the name of the Lord all those Powers to concentrate in you and through [you] to your po[s]terity for ever

all these things I do in the name of the Lord Jesus Christ that through this order he may be gloryfied [glorified] and [that] through the power of anointing Davied [David] may reign King over Iseral [Israel] which shall hereafter be revealed let immortality and eternal life henc[e]forth be sealed upon your heads forever and ever.

Following the text of the revelation was recorded events that occurred to Newel and Elizabeth Whitney in August:

Part in the first reserection [resurrection] together with other blessings now added sunday 27st [21st] [12] day of augt [august] [18]42 myself[13] and wife I now also bless[ed] with part in the first reserrection [resurrection] also with many other blessings together with the promise to all of my house the same day & of the same time

27 augt [august] [18]42 saturday evening myself and wife to[o] were Baptised for remission of sins[14]

Sunday in fore part of the day we were all confirmed & b[l]essed again[15] with all good things & eternal life in first

---

[10] Melchizedek.
[11] Jethro.
[12] Another manuscript has the date as August "21st" which was the third Sunday of the month. August 21 was when Newel and Elizabeth Whitney were sealed and received the blessings of the resurrection as they pertain to the new and everlasting covenant of marriage.
[13] Newel K. Whitney.
[14] Newel and Elizabeth Whitney were rebaptized on August 27, 1842.
[15] On Sunday morning, August 28, 1842, Newel and Elizabeth Whitney received their confirmation blessings.

reserrection [resurrection] I was blessed above others with long life the Keys of the Priest Hood a double portion of t[he] spirit heretofore confer[r]ed upon my fellows with all gifts posses[s]ed by my prog[e]nitors who held the Priest Hood before me anciently.[16]

In August 1842 the activities of Joseph Smith were given as follows:

Mon. 8. - Joseph Smith was arrested by a deputy sheriff at Nauvoo, by requisition from Gov. Thos. Reynolds, of Missouri, falsely accused of being accessory to the shooting of ex-Governor Boggs. O. Porter Rockwell was also arrested as principal. A writ of *habeas corpus* was issued by the municipal court of Nauvoo, by which the prisoners were released for the time being. Wed. 10. - The deputy sheriff returned to Nauvoo to re-arrest Joseph Smith and O. Porter Rockwell, but they could not be found. To escape imprisonment the Prophet had to keep concealed for some time.[17]

While Joseph Smith concealed himself in the house of Edward Sayer, he wrote a letter to Emma, to whom he had been married for more than fifteen years. He was considering leaving Nauvoo with her and twenty or thirty men and travel up the Mississippi River. At the close of this letter to Emma Smith, dated August 16, 1842, he wrote: "Yours in haste, your affectionate husband until death, through all eternity forevermore."[18] On the same day Joseph dictated his sentiments to William Clayton, who was keeping the Law of the Lord, concerning Sarah Ann's father Newel K. Whitney:

---

[16] Marquardt, *Joseph Smith Revelations*, 315-16; revelation not in LDS D&C. There are two copies of the revelation and notations in LDS archives.

[17] Andrew Jenson, comp., *Church Chronology* (Salt Lake City: Printed at the Deseret News, 1886), 21, emphasis retained. See also *The Wasp* 1 (Aug. 13, 1842):3 and the *Times and Seasons* 3 (Aug. 15, 1842):887-88.

[18] Joseph Smith to Emma Smith, Aug. 16, 1842, in Jessee, *Papers of Joseph Smith* 2:431-32.

here is brother Newel K. Whitney also, how many scenes of sorrow, have strewed our paths together; and yet we meet once more to share again. Thou art a faithful friend in whom the afflicted sons of men can confide, with the most perfect safety. Let the blessings of the eternal be crowned also upon his head; how warm that heart! how anxious that soul! for the welfare of one who has been cast out, and hated of almost all men. Brother Whitney, thou knowest not how strong those ties are, that bind my soul and heart to thee.[19]

It was reported that Joseph Smith then "went to Carlos Granger's."[20] While he was hiding at the home of Carlos Granger, who although not a Mormon was friendly to them,[21] Joseph wrote a very revealing letter to three of his closest friends. They were Bishop Newel K. Whitney, his wife Elizabeth Ann and the person whom he refers to as "and &c" — Sarah Ann whom he had been married to for twenty-two days. The letter refers to this event in his life in the words "Since what has pas[s]ed lately between us."[22]

From reading this letter one can gain an insight into the thought pattern of Joseph Smith, especially what he thought of his wife Emma. The letter was written in Smith's own hand on August 18, 1842. Joseph wrote the following remarks concerning Emma: "the only thing to be careful of, is to find out when Emma comes then you cannot be Safe, but when She is not here, there is the most perfect *Safty*" also "I think Emma wont come tonight if she dont dont fail to come to night."

The following is the letter by Joseph Smith to Newel K. Whitney, his wife and daughter, spelling retained as in original.

---

[19] Ibid., 2:416.

[20] Manuscript History Book D-1:1,378, LDS archives, written in the summer of 1845 in the handwriting of Thomas Bullock. See *History of the Church* 5:118.

[21] *Times and Seasons* 3 (Aug. 1, 1842):878.

[22] Photographs of both sides of the original letter in the handwriting of Joseph Smith are in the George Albert Smith Family Papers, Manuscript 36, Box 1, Early Smith Documents, 1731-1849, Manuscripts Division, Western Americana, J. Willard Marriott Library, University of Utah, Salt Lake City. See Jessee, *Personal Writings of Joseph Smith*, 566-69.

They were to "burn this letter as soon as you read it," this instruction they did not keep.

Nauvoo August 18th 1842
Dear, and Beloved, Brother and Sister, Whitney, and &
c.—

I take this oppertunity to communi[c]ate, Some of my feelings, privetely at this time, which I want you three Eternaly to keep in your own bosams; for my feelings are so Strong for you Since what has pas[s]ed lately between us, that the time of my abscence from you Seems so long, and dreary, that it Seems, as if I could not live long in this way: and <if you> three would come and See me in this my lonely retreat, it would afford me great relief, of mind, if those with whom I am al[l]ied, do love me, now is the time to afford me succour, in the days of exile, for you know I foretold you of these things.

I am now at Carlos Graingers, Just back of Brother Hyram[']s farm, it is only one mile from town, the nights are very pleasant, indeed, all three of you <can> come and See me in the fore part of the night, let Brother Whitney come a little a head, and [k]nock at the south East corner of the house at <the> window; it is next to the cornfield; I have a room intirely by myself, the whole matter can be attended to with most perfect Safty,[23] I <know> it is the will of God that you should comfort <me> now in this time of affliction, or not at all now is the time or never, but I hav[e] no kneed of saying any such thing, to you, for I know the goodness of your hearts, and that you will do the will of the Lord, when it is made known to you; the only thing to be careful of, is to find out when Emma comes then you cannot be Safe, but when She is not here, there is the most perfect Safty:[24]

only be careful to escape observation, as much as possible, I know it is a heroick undertaking; but so much the greater friendship, and the more Joy, when I see you I

---

[23] Another sealing ceremony.

[24] Not to let Emma Smith know that they are going to visit Joseph.

<will> tell you all my plans, I cannot write them on paper, burn this letter as soon as you read it, keep all locked up in your breasts, my life depends upon it, one thing I want to see you for is <to> git [get] the fulness of my blessing Sealed upon our heads, &c. you will pardon me for my ernestness on <this subject> when you consider how lonesome I must be, your good feelings know how to <make> every allowance for me, I close my letter. I think Emma wont come tonight if she dont dont fail to come to night. I subscribe myself your most obedient, <and> affectionate, companion, and friend. Joseph Smith

What is included in this letter was to make sure that Emma knew nothing about the meeting. The letter indicated the relationship with the Whitney family on what occurred the previous month. It also emphasized the importance of keeping the secret from Emma. Joseph Smith wrote about his most secret desire to give a priesthood blessing to the Whitneys as "the whole matter can be attended to with most perfect Saf[e]ty." It appears that the Whitneys did not visit Joseph Smith that evening. Three days later on August 21 Newel and Elizabeth were sealed as husband and wife for time and all eternity. It is not known if Sarah Ann accompanied them.

On September 6 for consideration of "one thousand dollars" Joseph Smith as Trustee-in-Trust conveyed lot 2 in block 139 of the City of Nauvoo to Sarah Ann Whitney. The deed was signed by Smith before Sarah Ann's father, Justice of the Peace Newel K. Whitney, in the presence of William Clayton.[25]

In October two statements were signed mostly by church members who did not know about the new order that had been introduced by Joseph Smith. These statements said that there was one marriage ceremony in the church and that they "know of no other rule or system of marriage than the one published from the Book of Doctrine and Covenants." The following certificates were published in the *Times and Seasons*:[26]

---

[25] Deed dated Sept. 6, 1842, Joseph Smith Collection, LDS archives.
[26] *Times and Seasons* 3 (Oct. 1, 1842):939-40. Eliza R. Snow had been sealed to Joseph Smith for three months.

We the undersigned members of the church of Jesus Christ of Latter-Day Saints and residents of the city of Nauvoo, persons of families do hereby certify and declare that we know of no other rule or system of marriage than the one published from the Book of Doctrine and Covenants, and we give this certificate to show that Dr. J. C. Bennett's "secret wife system" is a creature of his own make as we know of no such society in this place nor never did.

S[amuel]. Bennett,	N. K. Whitney,
George Miller,	Albert Pettey,
Alpheus Cutler,	Elias Higbee,
Reynolds Cahoon,	John Taylor,
Wilson Law,	E. Robinson,
W. Woodruff,	Aaron Johnson.

———

We the undersigned members of the ladies' relief society, and married females do certify and declare that we know of no system of marriage being practiced in the church of Jesus Christ of Latter Day Saints save the one contained in the Book of Doctrine and Covenants, and we give this certificate to the public to show that J. C. Bennett's "secret wife system" is a disclosure of his own make.

Emma Smith, President,
Elizabeth Ann Whitney, Counsellor,
Sarah M. Cleveland, Counsellor,
Eliza R. Snow Secretary,

Mary C. Miller,	Catherine Pettey,
Lois Cutler,	Sarah Higbee,
Thirza Cahoon,	Phebe Woodruff,
Ann Hunter,	Leonora Taylor,
Jane Law,	Sarah Hillman,
Sophia R. Marks,	Rosannah Marks
Polly Z. Johnson,	Angeline Robinson,
Abigail Works.	

Ebenezer Robinson, one of the men whose name appears on the first certificate, wrote concerning the statement he signed as follows:

> In October, 1842, a statement was written out, and signed by a large number of the brethren and sisters, including myself and wife, setting forth the fact that we *knew of* no other form of marriage ceremony in the church except the one published in the book of Doctrine and Covenants, which statement was true at *that time*, as we had no *knowledge* of such a ceremony, or that "spiritual wifery," or "polygamy," was taught by the *heads* of the church, as *they* had not up to that time taught it to us.[27]

Among the other names of persons which appeared upon the certificates were Bishop Newel K. Whitney, the father of Sarah Ann Whitney and the one who performed the marriage ceremony between Sarah Ann and Joseph Smith. Elizabeth Ann, who was a counselor in the Relief Society, was a witness to the marriage of her daughter. Elizabeth's name was on the certificate of the ladies who belonged to the Nauvoo Relief Society. Eliza R. Snow, as has been indicated, was sealed to Smith in June 1842 put her name on the statement.

Nine months after Joseph's marriage to Sarah Ann, she was married to Joseph C. Kingsbury. Kingsbury said he knew that Sarah was married to President Smith:

> I will add that I also knew that the Prophet Joseph Smith had married other women besides his first wife - Emma; I was well aware of the fact of his having married Sarah Ann Whitney, the eldest daughter of Bishop Newel K. Whitney and Elizabeth Ann Whitney, his wife.[28]

A pretended marriage was performed for the glory of Joseph Smith and Sarah Ann and to shield the fact that they were

---

[27] Ebenezer Robinson, ed., "Items of Personal History of the Editor," *The Return* 3 (Feb. 1891):28, emphasis retained.
[28] Affidavit of Joseph C. Kingsbury, May 22, 1886, LDS archives; in Jenson, *Historical Record* 6 (May 1887):226.

husband and wife. When Joseph C. Kingsbury wrote his history[29] he commenced it by writing, "A Record of Joseph Corrodon Kingsbury giving a Sketch of his life, or in the first place his desent [decent] & C[h]ronology as far back & he has any Knowledg[e] or information And I Joseph C Kingsbury write this Record with my own hands."[30]

Then Kingsbury told of the death of his wife: "on the 16[th] day of Oct. Caroline My Wife Died after Severe Sickniss [Sickness] of three Months & being deliver[e]d of A Son the Same day of her death Which Lived Thirteen Hours (his Name is Newel)."[31] Joseph Kingsbury mentioned that he acted as a proxy husband for Sarah Ann Whitney and that Joseph Smith performed the civil marriage ceremony:

on 29[th] of April 1843 I according to President Joseph Smith Council & others agreed to Stand by Sarah <Ann> Whitney as Supposed to be her husband & had a pretended marriage for the purpose of Bringing about the purposes of God in these last days as Spoken by the mouth of the prophits [prophets] Is[a]iah Jeremiah Ezekiel and also Joseph Smith, & Sarah Ann Should Recd. a Great Glory Honner [Honor] & Eternal Lives and I Also Should Recd. a Great Glory Honner & Eternal lives to the full desire of my heart in having my Companion Carolin[e] in the first Reserection [Resurrection] to kain [claim] her & no one to have power

---

[29] "The History of Joseph C. Kingsbury," Manuscript Division, Marriott Library, University of Utah. This portion of the journal was written between 1846 and 1848. The following sentence shows that the material quoted concerning Joseph Smith was written by 1848: "We are now in a fort, comfortable & are doing all we can to Raise our living in tilling the Earth June 25th 1848,)." Minor word additions not included.

[30] For a biographical sketch of Joseph C. Kingsbury see Orson F. Whitney, *History of Utah* (Salt Lake City: George Q. Cannon & Sons, 1904), 4:114-15. See also Lyndon W. Cook, *Joseph C. Kingsbury: A Biography* (Provo, Utah: Grandin Book, 1985).

[31] Joseph C. Kingsbury's wife Caroline was the sister of Bishop Newel K. Whitney. They were married on February 3, 1836, at Kirtland, Ohio. See "Oliver Cowdery's Sketch Book," *Brigham Young University Studies* 12 (Summer 1972):421. Documentation for her death can be found in *The Wasp* 1 (Oct. 22, 1842):3 and 1 (Oct. 29, 1842):3. She died at the age of 26 years and 7 months.

to take her from me & We Both Shall be Crowned & Enthrowned togeather in the Celestial Kingdom of God Enjoying Each others Society in all of th[e] fullness of the Gospel of Jesus Christ & our little ones with us as is Recorded in the blessing that President Joseph Smith Sealed upon my head on the Twenty third day of March 1843 as follows-[32]

Here Kingsbury copied a patriarchal blessing received from Joseph Smith on March 23, 1843. This is significant since those who witnessed the blessing were Newel, Elizabeth, and Sarah Ann Whitney.

Brother Joseph I Lay My hands upon thy head in the name of Jesus Christ to bestow upon the[e] a Patriarkle [Patriarchal] Blessing according to the Power and authority of the Holy Priesthood vested in me. I Say unto thee thou Shalt Be Blessed with Good things of this wourld [world] abundently in thy Life time and I Seal the[e] up to Come forth in the first reserection [resurrection] unto Eternal Life - And thy Companion Caroline who is now dead thou Shalt have in the first Reserection for I Seal thee up for and in her behalf to Come forth in the first Reserection unto Eternal lives (and it Shall be as though She was present her Self) and thou Shalt hail her and She Shall be thine and no one Shall have power to take her from thee,

And you both Shall be crowned and enthroned to dwell together in a Kingdom in the Celestial Glory in the presents [presence] of God, And you Shall Enjoy each other Society & Embraces in all the fulness of the Gospell of Jesus Christ Wourls [Worlds] with out End And I Seal these blessings upon thee and for thy Companion in the Name of Jesus Christ for thou Shalt receive the holy anointing & Endowment in this Life to prepare you for all these blessings even So Amen [Witnesses to above Blessing

---

[32] Chronologically the paragraph which follows precedes the one above.

Newel K Whitney Elizabeth Ann Whitney and Sarah Ann Whitney][33]

On the same day Joseph Smith gave a written blessing for Sarah Ann that invoked promises for her and the Whitney household:

Oh Lord my God thou that dwellest on high bless I beseach [beseech] of thee the one into whose hands this may fall and crown her with a diadem of glory in the Eternal worlds Oh let <it> be sealed this day on high that she shall come forth in the first reserrection [resurrection] to recieve [receive] the same and verily it shall be so saith the Lord if she remain in the Everlasting covenant to the end as also all her Father['s] house shall be saved in the same Eternal glory and if any of them shall wander from the fo<a>ld [fold] of the Lord they shall not perish but shall return saith the Lord and be saived [saved] and by repentance be crowned with all the fullness of the glory of the Everlasting Gospel These promises I seal upon all of their heads in the name of Jesus Christ by the Law of the Holy Priesthood even so Amen[34]

To give a summary, on April 29, 1843 Joseph Smith performed a civil marriage between his plural wife Sarah Ann Whitney and Joseph C. Kingsbury who he blessed the previous month. Kingsbury's wife died the previous October six months earlier. This occurred while Emma Smith was on a trip to St. Louis. Emma and Lorin Walker returned to Nauvoo on May 2. That Joseph Smith performed the ceremony that joined Joseph Kingsbury and Sarah Ann Whitney together in mock marriage is known from a record of marriages performed in Nauvoo. The following is from a slip of paper signed by Joseph Smith as an Elder wherein he stated that he performed this marriage ceremony:

[33] Brackets in original. The blessing was also recorded in Patriarchal Blessing Book 1:145 in 1860, LDS archives.
[34] "Blessing Given to Sarah Ann Whitney by Joseph Smith. Nauvoo City, 23 March 1843," typed copy, LDS archives.

I hereby certify, that I have upon this the 29th day of April 1843, joined together in Marriage Joseph C. Kingsbury and Sarah Ann Whitney, in the City of Nauvoo, Illinois.[35]

The marriage was then recorded in "A Record of Marriages, in the City of Nauvoo, Illinois" from which the following is taken: "Joseph C. Kingsbury and Sarah Ann Whitney were joined together in marriage, in the City of Nauvoo, Ills, upon the 29th day of April 1843, by Joseph Smith, Elder."[36]

Helen Mar Kimball Whitney recollected that after she heard about the plural order of marriage her father, Heber C. Kimball, "took the first opportunity to introduce Sarah Ann to me as Joseph's wife." Helen wrote about not being able to tell her brother Horace about Sarah's sealing to Joseph Smith:

Sarah Ann took this step of her own free will, but had to do it unbeknown to her brother, which greived [grieved] her most, and also her mother, that they could not open their hearts to him. But Joseph feared to disclose it, believing that the Higbee boys would embitter Horace against him, as they had already caused serious trouble, and for this reason he favored his going East, which Horace was not slow to accept. He had had some slight suspicions that the stories about Joseph were not all without foundation, but had never told them, nor did he know the facts till after his return to Nauvoo, when Sarah hastened to tell him all.[37]

Helen Kimball continued her account and mentioned that it was not until the summer of 1843 after Horace left to go east that she learned of the plural order of marriage. Her father Heber "was the first to introduce it to me; which had a similar effect to a

---

[35] "Civil Marriages Performed, Nauvoo, Hancock County, Illinois, 1842-1843," Family History Library, Salt Lake City.

[36] "A Record of Marriages, in the City of Nauvoo, Illinois" (1842-1845), 12, Family History Library.

[37] Helen Mar [Kimball] Whitney, "Scenes in Nauvoo after the Martyrdom of the Prophet and Patriarch," *Woman's Exponent* 11 (March 1, 1883):146. Helen Mar was sealed to Joseph Smith (proxy sealing) and married Horace Whitney for time on February 3, 1846 in the Nauvoo Temple.

sudden shock of a small earthquake. When he found (after the first outburst of displeasure for supposed injury) that I received it meekly, he took the first opportunity to introduce Sarah Ann to me as Joseph's wife."

After Joseph Smith's death in June 1844 Sarah Ann continued to live with Kingsbury. She was sealed on March 17, 1845 to Apostle Heber C. Kimball.[38] Though Sarah Ann became pregnant with her and Heber Kimball's child she remained known as Joseph C. Kingsbury's wife, under the name Sarah Ann Kingsbury while residing in Nauvoo. In the Nauvoo Temple Sarah Ann had her marriage to Joseph Smith sealed by proxy and she was sealed again for time (this life) to Kimball. Later in 1846 she started living with members of the Kimball family.

---

[38] In the Whitney account book is recorded: "monday evening March 17 1845 Sarah was LAV to HCK" (Newel K. Whitney 1841-45 Account Book & Diary, L. Tom Perry Special Collections, Harold B. Lee Library, Brigham Young University).

25

Emily Dow Partridge

Emily Dow Partridge was born February 28, 1824 in Painesville, Geauga County, Ohio. She was the daughter of Edward Partridge who became the first church bishop and her mother Lydia. After being expelled from Missouri the Edward Partridge family moved to Commerce (later named Nauvoo). Here Edward became the bishop of the Upper Ward.[1]

Emily was sixteen years old when her older sister Harriet died of an unknown illness at the age of eighteen on May 16, 1840. Then tragedy struck again when her father Edward died eleven days later on May 27. He was only forty-six years old.[2] Emily wrote, "After father's death Brother [William] Law took our whole family and administered to our wants and with such good and kind care we began to improve in health, and when we had sufficiently regained our health we went back into our little hut once more."[3] Four months after the death of her husband Lydia married William Huntington Sr. who was a widower of fourteen months.[4]

Just short of being seventeen, Emily received her first patriarchal blessing from Isaac Morley. In the blessing she was told "if thou wilt listen to the voice of wisdom length of days shalt be given unto thee, and thou shalt have the blessing to see the winding up scene of this generation; peace and tranquility restored to man."[5] Contemplating their situation, Emily's sister Eliza, who

---

[1] *Times and Seasons* 1 (Dec. 1839):30, Commerce.
[2] Ibid. 1 (June 1840):127-28, Nauvoo.
[3] "Autobiography of Emily D. P. Young," *Woman's Exponent* 14 (July 15, 1885):26.
[4] William Huntington's wife Zina died on July 8, 1839, *Times and Seasons* 1 (Dec. 1839):32 and William married Lydia Partridge on September 27, 1840, Ibid. 1 (Oct. 1840):191. See Martha Sonntag Bradley and Mary Brown Firmage Woodward, *Four Zinas: A Story of Mothers and Daughters on the Mormon Frontier* (Salt Lake City: Signature Books, 2000), 105 where the date of the marriage is given as September 29, 1840.
[5] Patriarchal Blessing given by Isaac Morley on February 3, 1841, cited in "Autobiography of Emily D. P. Young," *Woman's Exponent* 14 (Aug. 1, 1885):

was a good seamstress, went to work to earn income for the family. Younger Emily, though she had a little schooling, says that she knew only basic household duties such as washing dishes, sweeping, and scrubbing floors. Emily wrote of these times:

> Sister Emma [Smith] sent for me to come and live with her and nurse her baby. It seemed as if the Lord had opened up my way, it was so unexpected, and nothing could have suited me better, for tending babies was my delight. My sister Eliza, also, went there to live, which made it pleasanter for me and more home-like. Joseph and Emma were very kind to us; they were almost like a father and mother, and I loved Emma and the children, especially the baby, little Don Carlos.[6]

Living in the Smith home made Emily and Eliza available to be taught that it was a revealed rite to be sealed to a married man and become a plural wife. Emily was also attending school at Robert B. Thompson's house. Lessons were taught by Howard and Martha Coray during the summer of 1841.[7] Emma and Joseph had a son born on February 6, 1842 and he died the same day. The next month Emma Smith was appointed president of the Female Relief Society of Nauvoo of which Emily was made a member on April 28.[8] In her autobiography Emily mentioned only briefly being married to Joseph Smith:

> I was married to him on the 11th of May [1843], by Elder James Adams. Emma was present. She gave her free and full consent. She had always, up to this time, been very kind to me and my sister Eliza, who was also married to the Prophet Joseph with Emma's consent, but ever after she

---

37.

[6] Ibid. Don Carlos Smith, son of Emma and Joseph Smith, was born on June 13, 1840 and died on August 15, 1841 (*Times and Seasons* 2 [Sept 1, 1841]:533).

[7] Charles D. Tate Jr., "Howard and Martha Jane Knowlton Coray of Nauvoo," in H. Dean Garrett, ed., *Regional Studies in Latter-day Saint Church History: Illinois* (Provo, Utah: Department of Church History and Doctrine, Brigham Young University, 1995), 339.

[8] A Book of Records Containing the proceedings of The Female Relief Society of Nauvoo, 34, LDS archives.

was our enemy.[9]

What is not mentioned is the activity that led up to the first marriage in Emily's life. While she made an affidavit of an earlier March marriage, her published autobiography is silent. This may have been because after the death of Emma Smith in 1879 more emphasis was given to Emma as approving plural wives for her prophet-husband. Emily's assessment of Emma Smith was negative. An account written eight years earlier titled "Incidents of the early life of Emily Dow Partridge" gives more details of the beginnings of her life in plural marriage.

One day in the spring of 1842 eighteen-year-old Emily was doing her household duties in the Smith family home. Joseph Smith said to her, "Emily if you will not betray me, I will tell you something for your benefit" but he did not give a hint what it might be.[10] The secret alluded to by Smith was the new doctrine of plural marriage that he taught privately to only a limited number of church members.

Approximately a year after Emily declined to share Joseph's secret Elizabeth Durfee, wife of Jabez Durfee, invited Eliza and Emily to her home. Emily wrote, "She introduced the subject of spiritual wives as they called it in that day. She wondered if there was any truth in the report she heard." Some time later Mrs. Durfee came to Emily one day and as Emily later related it said, "Joseph would like an opportunity to talk with me. I asked her if she knew what he wanted. She said she thought he wanted me for a wife. . . . I was to meet him in the evening at Mr. Kimballs." After Emily finished the washing she left the Smith home in the evening, still wearing her wash dress, and went to see her mother Lydia and then walked to the place appointed — the house of Heber C. Kimball. Heber told Emily that his wife Vilate was not at home. Emily met Joseph Smith:

I cannot tell all Joseph said, but he said the Lord had

---

[9] "Autobiography of Emily D. P. Young," *Woman's Exponent* 14 (Aug. 1, 1885):38.
[10] Emily Dow Partridge Young, "Incidents of the early life of Emily Dow Partridge," 4, typed copy, Emily Dow Partridge Smith Young Papers, Manuscripts Division, Marriott Library, University of Utah.

commanded [him] to enter into plural marriage and had given me to him and although I had got badly frightened he knew I would yet have him. So he waited till the Lord told him. My mind was now prepared and would receive the principles. . . . Well I was married there and then. Joseph went home his way and I going my way alone. A strange way of getting married wasent [wasn't] it. Brother Kimball married us, the 4th of March 1843.[11]

Joseph was eighteen years older than Emily at the time of their marriage. Smith was thirty-seven years old and Emily became nineteen in February. She had a firm faith in the prophet. The Nauvoo journal of Joseph Smith kept by Willard Richards recorded for the date of March 4 in shorthand that Joseph went to the Kimball home.[12] Four days afterwards Eliza Partridge also became a plural wife of Joseph Smith.[13]

Unaware of the Partridge sealings to her husband, Emma Smith briefly converted to the principle of plural marriage two months later. Joseph explained to Emma and Brigham Young to Joseph's older brother Hyrum that the marriage relationship was an important part of the restored gospel.[14] Emma chose Emily and Eliza to be sealed to Joseph. In a religious ceremony Emma placed in Joseph's hand each woman's hand and they were sealed by James Adams, a high priest. As Emily explained, in May 1843 Emma told Joseph that she would permit him to have two wives:

Emma told Joseph she would give him two wives if he would let her choose them for him. She chose my sister and I and helped explain the principles to us. We did not make much trouble, but were sealed in her presence with her full and free consent. It was the 11th [sic] of May but before the

---

[11] Ibid.

[12] Joseph Smith Journal, entry for March 4, 1843, LDS archives. It includes in Taylor shorthand "and Kimballs." See Scott H. Faulring, ed., *An American Prophet's Record: The Diaries and Journals of Joseph Smith* (Salt Lake City: Signature Books in association with Smith Research Associates, 1987), 327.

[13] Affidavit of Eliza Maria Partridge Lyman, July 1, 1869, LDS archives. The ceremony was performed by Apostle Heber C. Kimball.

[14] Linda King Newell and Valeen Tippetts Avery, *Mormon Enigma: Emma Hale Smith,* 2nd ed. (Urbana: University of Illinois Press, 1994), 141-43.

day was over she turned around, or repented what she had done and kept Joseph up till very late in the night talking to him. She kept close watch of us."[15]

Twenty-six years after her first sealing to Joseph, during a time when the sons of prophet-founder Joseph Smith questioned his involvement in polygamy, Emily signed two affidavits concerning her marriage to Smith. Emily's two affidavits were made on the same day. The first affidavit concerns her first sealing on March 4, 1843 and the second affidavit concerns the repeated ceremony which she thought occurred on May 11, 1843. Emily's testimony maintained this later date until she was questioned during the Temple Lot Case in 1892.

<u>Affidavit of Emily D. P. Young on first sealing</u>

> Territory of Utah
>
> SS.
>
> County of Salt Lake
> Be it remembered that on this first day of May A.D. 1869, personally appeared before me, Elias Smith Probate Judge for Said County, Emily Dow Partridge Young, who was by me Sworn in due form of law and upon her oath Saith, that on the fourth day of March A.D. 1843 at the City of Nauvoo, County of Hancock State of Illinois, She was married or Sealed to Joseph Smith, President of the Church of Jesus Christ of Latter Day Saints by Heber C. Kimball, one of the Twelve Apostles of Said Church, according to the laws of the Same regulating marriage, in the presence of [blank space].
>
> Emily D. P. Young
>
> Subscribed and Sworn to by the
> said Emily D. P. Young, the day
> and year first above written,

---

[15] Emily Dow Partridge Young, "Incidents of the early life of Emily Dow Partridge," 4-5. Ten years later Emily wrote, "To save the [Smith] family trouble Brother Joseph thought it best to have another ceremony performed" (*Historical Record* 6 [May 1887]:240). The May 11, 1843 date is in error. James Adams made his May trip from Springfield arriving in Nauvoo on May 21.

E. Smith

Probate Judge[16]

Affidavit of Emily D. P. Young on repeated sealing

Territory of Utah

SS.

County of Salt Lake

Be it remembered that on this first day of May A.D. 1869, personally appeared before me, Elias Smith, Probate Judge for Said County, Emily Dow Partridge Young, who was by me Sworn in due form of law, and upon her oath Saith that on the eleventh day of May A.D. 1843 at the City of Nauvoo, County of Hancock State of Illinois, She was married or Sealed to Joseph Smith, President of the Church of Jesus Christ of Latter Day Saints, by James Adams, a High-Priest in said Church; according to the laws of the Same regulating marriage, in [the] presence of Emma (Hale) Smith, and Eliza Maria Partridge (Lyman).

Emily D. P. Young

Subscribed and Sworn to by
the Said Emily D. P. Young, the day
and year first above written

E. Smith

Probate Judge[17]

Emily mentioned that after her second marriage/sealing Emma Smith kept a careful watch over where she and Eliza were in the Smith home. There finally came a time when Emma put a halt to this sealing. Emily wrote in her account that sister Smith asked the sisters to come to her room:

---

[16] Affidavit of Emily D[ow]. P[artridge]. Young, May 1, 1869, Joseph F. Smith Affidavit Book 1:11, LDS archives.

[17] Affidavit of Emily D. P. Young, May 1, 1869, Joseph F. Smith Affidavit Book 1:13. This affidavit is a separate one from the one mentioned in footnote 16. The affidavit when published in the "Joseph the Seer's Plural Marriages," *Deseret Evening News* 12 (Oct. 18, 1879):2 omitted the words "according to the laws of the Same regulating marriage."

When we went in Joseph was there, his countenance was the perfect picture of despair. I cannot remember all that passed at that time bur [but] she insisted that we should promise to break our covenants, that we had made before God. Joseph asked her if we made her the promises she required, if she would cease to trouble us, and not persist in our marrying someone else. She made the promise. Joseph came to us and shook hands with us and the understanding was that all was ended between us. I for one meant to keep the promise I was forced to make.[18]

After going downstairs, Emily continues, "Joseph soon came into the room where I was, said, how do you feel Emily. My heart being still hard, I answered him rather short that I expected I felt as anybody would under the circumstance. He said you know my hands are tied."[19]

William Clayton kept a journal which records not only his own problems with the principle of plural marriage but also some private moments with the prophet. Though his complete Nauvoo journals are not available to scholars the brief extracts that have been published show his personal struggle and the secret nature of the practice. Clayton recorded in his journal for the date of August 16, 1843 a passage concerning Emma Smith:

This A.M. J[oseph]. told me that since E[mma]. came back from St Louis she had resisted the P. [priesthood principle of plural marriage] in toto & he had to tell her he would relinquish all for her sake. She said she would given him E. & E. P [Emily and Eliza Partridge] but he knew if he took them she would pitch on him & obtain a divorce & leave him. He however told me he should not relinquish any thing.[20]

---

[18] Emily Dow Partridge Young, "Incidents of the early life of Emily Dow Partridge," 5.

[19] Ibid. Emily says they "remained in the [Smith] family several months after this" (*Historical Record* 6 [May 1887]:240).

[20] William Clayton Journal, entry for August 16, 1843, typed copy. Original Nauvoo journals located in the Office of the First Presidency, Church of Jesus Christ of Latter-day Saints, Salt Lake City. See George D. Smith, ed., *An*

This entry is difficult to understand since Emma had already given Eliza and Emily to Joseph as wives. But what Clayton wrote may be a combined account of more than one occasion when Joseph Smith confided in him some family matters. In summary, Emma had returned from another trip to St. Louis on August 12. Joseph said to Clayton that he was not going to relinquish them. It may have been soon after this when Joseph in front of Emma shook Emily's and Eliza's hands and released them from their priesthood sealing. When Emily left the Smith home she mentions not "seeing Joseph but once to speak to after I left the Mansion house and that was just before he started for Carthage" where he was murdered.[21]

Granville Hedrick, a leader of a separate church from that led by Brigham Young, said he received a revelation on April 24, 1864 appointing the year 1867 as the time to return to Jackson County, Missouri.[22] His followers were interested in purchasing the land where the temple would be built. It was on land purchased near Independence, Missouri where the New Jerusalem mentioned in Joseph Smith's revelations and in the Book of Mormon was to be located. The purchase of a little over sixty-three acres was made on December 19, 1831.[23]

One small portion of acreage is considered where Joseph Smith laid the stone for the single temple in 1831 and which had become in time part of the Woodson and Maxwell Addition to the City of Independence. Lots numbered fifteen through twenty-two, that included where the temple had been planned, were eventually purchased and obtained by Granville Hedrick, president and trustee-in-trust for what became the Church of Christ, known as the Temple Lot church.[24]

Intimate Chronicle: The Journals of William Clayton (Salt Lake City: Signature Books in association with Smith Research Associates, 1991), 117.

[21] Emily Dow Partridge Young, "Incidents of the early life of Emily Dow Partridge," 6.

[22] "Revelation," *The Truth Teller* 1 (July 1864):4, Bloomington, Illinois.

[23] Arthur M. Smith, *Temple Lot Deed*, 3rd ed., (Independence: Board of Publications, Church of Christ, 1963), 5; see also Jackson County, Deed Record, Book B:1-3; *Deseret News*, Church Section, January 23, 1932, p. 1; and Richard Price and Pamela Price, *The Temple of the Lord* (Independence: authors, 1982), 32-38.

[24] Smith, *Temple Lot Deed*, 7-12; B. C. Flint, *An Outline History of the Church*

The RLDS church in August 1891 brought suit in U. S. Circuit Court, Western District of Missouri, by filing a bill of equity against the Church of Christ (Temple Lot) for possession of what was known as the Temple Lots or Lot. This became known as the Temple Lot Case.[25] Among those who gave depositions in the Temple Lot Case were three plural wives of Joseph Smith, viz. Emily Dow Partridge Young, Lucy Walker Kimball, and Melissa Lott Willis.

Emily Partridge gave two depositions at the Templeton Hotel in Salt Lake City. The first deposition of March 14, 1892 related to the deed to the sixty-three acres in Independence. Emily said that her mother and sisters went to a town in Missouri and executed the deed in 1848. She said, "Neither myself, nor any of my brothers and sisters, nor my mother while she was living ever made any claim to the property."[26] The second deposition was concerned her claim of being a plural wife of Joseph Smith.

Over forty pages of testimony by Emily Partridge as a plural wife were omitted when her testimony was printed by the RLDS church publishing firm. In her second deposition Emily said she was a plural wife of Joseph Smith. The leading question relating to plural marriage was: "I will ask you to state what you know in regard to the principle of plural marriage, or what is some times called polygamy, as to its being taught or practiced in the Church of Jesus Christ of Latter Day Saints, before the death of Joseph Smith, at Nauvoo, Illinois?" Emily answered, "Do I have to answer the question?" When Emily was told yes, she said, "personally I think he taught the doctrine, for he taught it to me with his own lips."[27] Then she explained that while living in Joseph Smith's home:

---

of Christ Temple Lot (Independence: Board of Publications, Church of Christ, Temple Lot, 1953), 111.

[25] Transcripts of the entire Temple Lot suit are located in LDS and RLDS archives.

[26] *The Reorganized Church of Jesus Christ of Latter Day Saints, Complaint. Vs. The Church of Christ at Independence; Richard Hill, Trustee . . . Respondents. In Equity. Complainant's Abstract of Pleading and Evidence* (Lamoni, Iowa: Herald Publishing House and Bindery, 1893), 177.

[27] Deposition of Emily D. Partridge Young in Salt Lake City on March 19, 1892, Respondents Testimony, 349 (hereafter cited as Respondents Testimony).

he came there into the room where I was one day, when I was in the room alone, and he asked me if I could keep a secret. I was about eighteen years of age then I think, - at any rate I was quite young. He asked me if I could keep a secret, and I told him I thought I could, and then he told me that he would some time if he had an opportunity, - he would tell me some thing that would be for my benefit, if I would not betray him, and I told him I wouldn't.[28]

On another occasion when Joseph Smith was sitting in a room he spoke to Emily and said to her "he would write me a letter, if I would agree to burn it as soon as I had read it." She initially thought something was not right about it and told him so. Emily said she prayed to know what it was for she was "greatly troubled over it." As she prayed for guidance, "I became convinced that there was nothing wrong about it, and that it would be right for me to hear what he had to say." In Emily's previously account she wrote that Smith "asked me if I would burn it if he would write me a letter." She "promised to do as he wished" and prayed about the matter asking to be directed. Then Emily returned and told Smith that she "could not take a private letter from him." Smith asked her if she I wished the matter ended and Emily said she did.[29]

A few months later Joseph Smith taught her the principle of plural marriage, "he told me that this principle had been revealed to him but it was not generally known; and he went on and said that the Lord had given me to him, and he wanted to know if I would consent to a marriage, and I consented." Emily stated, "I was married to him on the 4th day of March 1843, and after that in the same year, I think it was in May" Emma consented.[30]

In her testimony Emily emphasized that Emma "had chosen myself and my sister, and we were married in her presence again because we thought [it] proper to say nothing about the former marriage, and it was done over again on the 11th of May 1843 in her presence, and she gave her consent fully and freely and voluntarily." Asked for the reason why the ceremony was

---

[28] Respondents Testimony, 350.
[29] Emily Dow Partridge Young, "Incidents of the early life of Emily Dow Partridge," 4.
[30] Respondents Testimony, 350.

performed for a second time Emily testified, "Well Emma had a good many feelings we supposed, - she was a rather high strung woman of a very nervous organization, and we thought that she had her feelings, and so we thought there was no use in saying any thing about it, so long as she had chosen us herself, - there was no use of having another ceremony only for that reason. That is the only reason I know for not saying anything about it."[31]

When asked regarding what she knew concerning a revelation to Joseph Smith being given on plural marriage she responded there was a revelation given "that was not printed or generally known" and after Eliza and herself were married "there was one given that was made more public." On being asked more specific, "How do you know that there was any revelation at all?" Emily said "he told me himself that he had had a revelation." And then she said, "Joseph Smith told me himself that the angel had appeared to him and had given him that revelation."[32]

The prophet Joseph Smith conveyed to only a few persons in private that an angel had appeared to him and commanded him to enter into plural marriage.[33] Lorenzo Snow returned from his mission to England on April 12, 1843. A few days later Joseph Smith explained to him "the doctrine of plurality of wives. He said that the Lord had revealed it unto him, and commanded him to have women Sealed to him as wives. — that he foresaw the trouble that would follow, and Sought to turn away from the Commandment—that an Angel from Heaven appeared before him with a drawn Sword, threatening him with destruction unless he went forward and obeyed the Commandment."[34] The revelation on

---

[31] Ibid., 351. Previously Emily explained on obtaining Emma Smith's permission, "it would have been the same with or without her consent" (Emily Dow Partridge Smith Young, "Testimony That Cannot Be Refuted," (*Woman's Exponent* 12 [April 1, 1884]:165).

[32] Respondents Testimony, 352.

[33] Affidavit of Joseph B. Noble, June 26, 1869, Joseph F. Smith Affidavit Book 1:38, LDS archives. See also Jenson, *Historical Record* 6 (May 1887):221. Helen Mar Whitney, one of Smith's wives wrote, "Joseph's own testimony was, that an angel was sent to command him to teach and to enter into this order. This angel, he states, stood over him with a drawn sword prepared to inflict the penalty of death if he should be disobedient" (*Plural Marriage as Taught by the Prophet Joseph* [Salt Lake City: Juvenile Instructor Office, 1882], 13).

[34] Affidavit of Lorenzo Snow, Aug. 28, 1869, copy in Joseph F. Smith Affidavit

plural marriage was not read to the High Council in 1840 or 1841. But it appears that the commandment was told to Apostles Brigham Young and Heber C. Kimball after returning from their English mission in 1841.

Under cross examination Emily mentioned she went to live in Joseph's and Emma's home "as a nurse girl, for they had a young baby and they wanted me to tend it for them. That is what I delighted in, - attending babies, and that is what they got me there to do more particularly."[35] Joseph spoke to Emily about writing the letter in 1842 and the next time he spoke to her was in March 1843 at the home of Heber C. Kimball. Questions were asked Emily such as:

> Q:- Did he offer to take your hand then? A;- No sir.
> Q:- Or put his hand around you? A;- No sir.
> Q:- He never did any such a thing as that? A;- No sir.
> Q:- At any time or place? A;- No sir, - not before we were married.
> Q:- Now did he tell you there about the principle of sealing? A;- Yes sir.
> Q:- He did? A;- Yes sir.
> Q:- He told you all about the doctrine or principle of sealing? A;- Yes sir.
> Q:- Was it sealing for eternity? A;- Yes sir, - time and eternity.[36]

Before being told by Joseph Smith about plural marriage Emily recalled that there were "reports around that made me think, - that gave me an idea of what it was he wanted to say to me but I did not know what it was about, or had no idea what it was that he wanted to speak to me about any more than that I had heard, which gave me a suspicion of what it was. . . . there was so many reports flying around there in Nauvoo, that I did not pay much attention to it until he spoke to me about it, and then I found out that the reports I had heard were connected with what he had to tell me. I did not think so much about it until he told me himself." When

---

Book 2:19; also in Jenson, *Historical Record* 6 (May 1887):222.
[35] Respondents Testimony, 356.
[36] Ibid., 358.

asked if she had seen the revelation, Emily responded, "No sir."
She was further questioned:

Q:- How did you come to marry him without seeing it? A;-
Well he told me it was all right and I just took his word for
it.
Q:- Well did you go and get married without ever knowing
it was the law of the church? A;- I got married on his own
teachings, - he was the prophet of the church and he told
me it was all right and I took his word for it.
Q:- You took his word for it and got married to him in that
way on his own teachings? A;- Yes sir, and on my own
convictions, for I believed it was all right or he would not
have taught me and told me what he did.
Q:- Now did he teach you that a man could have more
women then one? A;- Yes sir.
Q:- As wives? A;- Yes sir.[37]

Questions were asked relating to the second marriage in
May 1843. Emily could not remember whether the ceremony took
place in the forenoon or afternoon. At this point in her testimony
she was still sure of the marriage date. Next, specific questions
were asked her:

Q:- Who roomed with Joseph Smith that night, - the night
of that day the 11th of May 1843 when you say you and
your sister were married to Joseph Smith? A;- Well I don't
want to answer that question.
[By Mr. Hall, -] Q:- Well answer it if you can, if you
know? A;- Well it was myself.
Q:- Now you have answered it, and that will do?
[By Mr. Kelley, -] Q:- You roomed with Joseph Smith that
night? A;- Yes sir.[38]

An affidavit made by William Clayton in 1874 was read
concerning Hyrum Smith's report that Emma was "very bitter and

---

[37] Ibid., 360.
[38] Ibid., 363-64.

full of disappointment and anger" after Hyrum read the July 12, 1843 revelation to her. When asked about her comment that Emma turned bitter from the minute she was married, Emily replied, "Well I might have said that, but I meant from a short time after we were married, - It might have been from the hour we were married. I know she was bitter soon after that, but I can't say how long it was afterwards that she got that way, but I know it was very soon after that. . . . Well after the next day you might say that she was bitter." On asking Emily if she left the house right away after this, Emily said, speaking of herself and her sister Eliza, "We did not leave the house for several months after that.[39]

Emily wrote in 1887, "from that very hour, however, Emma was our bitter enemy" and that they remained in the family several months after this.[40] Whether this perception was one of 1843 is hard to determine. Emma was hot and cold regarding polygamy. On the day the revelation of July 12, 1843 was received it told Emma to "receive all those that have been given unto my Servent [Servant] Joseph, and who are virtuous and pure before me; and those who are not pure, and have Said they ware [were] pure Shall be destroyed."[41] Emma according to Clayton's source "said she did not believe a word of it and appeared very rebellious."[42]

The next day July 13 Clayton recorded that Joseph sent for him and he met with Joseph and Emma in a private room where Emma and Joseph made an agreement between them and "stated their feelings on many subjects & wept considerable." Willard Richards recorded in Smith's journal, "In conversation with Emma most of the day."[43]

In taking the deposition of Emily in 1892 the entry from the "History of Joseph Smith" as published in the *Millennial Star* for May 11 was read. The activities for that day included baptisms at six in the morning, Emma Smith traveling to Quincy in a new carriage, and Joseph riding onto the prairie outside of Nauvoo. Emily was told "Now that is the private journal of Joseph Smith

---

[39] Ibid., 366.

[40] *Historical Record* 6 (May 1887):240.

[41] Marquardt, *Joseph Smith Revelations*, 327; LDS D&C 132:52.

[42] William Clayton Journal, entry for July 12, 1843, typed copy.

[43] Joseph Smith Journal, entry for July 13, 1843, LDS archives.

for the 11th of May 1843, the day that you say you were married to him." She was asked, "What do you say to that?" She responded, "Well it is possible that I have made a mistake in the dates, but I haven't made any mistake in the facts." She was then asked if she was married before or after the May 11 date. She said, "Well it must have been before that."[44] It appears that it was afterwards. A probable date is May 23, 1843.

On the date Emily remembered there were rebaptisms performed. The ordinance of rebaptism was common in Nauvoo since 1841. At the April 1841 conference President Joseph Smith requested those who wished to be baptized to go to the water.[45] Smith and his counselor Sidney Rigdon went into the water for rebaptism.[46] On another Sunday in 1842 Wilford Woodruff wrote, "Joseph the seer went into the river & Baptized all that Came unto him & I considered it my privilege to be Baptized for the remission of my sins for I had not been since I first Joined the Church in 1833. . . . I went forth into the river & was Baptized under the hands of JOSEPH THE SEER & likewise did Elder J[ohn] Taylor & many others."[47] Willard Richards made the following entry in Smith's journal for May 1843: "Thursday May 11th 6 A.M. baptized [blank space] Snow. Louisa Beman. Sarah Alley &c"[48] Louisa Beeman (plural wife of Joseph Smith) and Sarah Alley (plural wife of Joseph B. Noble) received the ordinance of rebaptism early that morning.

It is possible that Emily and Eliza Partridge may have been rebaptized on this morning though there is no clear record. The date of May 11 stuck in their minds as the date of their second sealing to Joseph Smith. Neither woman kept a journal at the time. So Emily's various accounts were oral histories. That the date Emily considered through the years as being the day she was married to Joseph the second time is in error is because James

---

[44] Respondents Testimony, 367.

[45] "Minutes of the general conference," *Times and Seasons* 2 (April 15, 1841):388.

[46] William Huntington recorded: "Joseph and Sidney baptised each other for the remission of their Sins as this order was then Instituted in the church" (William Huntington Journal, entry for April 11, 1841, typed copy, L. Tom Perry Special Collections, Harold B. Lee Library).

[47] Kenney, *Wilford Woodruff's Journal*, 2:165, entry for March 27, 1842.

[48] Joseph Smith Journal, entry for May 11, 1843, LDS archives.

Adams arrived in Nauvoo from Springfield on May 21.[49] Sometime later, probably on May 23, Adams sealed the Partridge sisters to the prophet Joseph Smith with Emma participating.[50] Emily was asked regarding her marriage to Smith:

> Q:- Have you got a marriage certificate? A;- No sir.
> Q:- Did you ever have one? A;- No sir.
> Q:- Why did you not get one? A;- Well it was not thought necessary in those days.[51]

While a marriage certificate was not given, it was an important part of the revealed order of a plural sealing for the first (legal) wife to place the new wife's hand in the right hand of her husband. When asked "Did Emma take your hand and place it in Joseph Smith's hand?" She said "I think she did." Then she replied "I could not swear to it at all" maybe not wanting to tell about an important part of her second marriage ceremony.[52] Orson Pratt published in 1853 a portion of a plural marriage sealing. A question is asked by the person holding the sealing authority to the legal wife, "Are you willing to give this woman to your husband to be his lawful and wedded wife for time and for all eternity? If you are, you will manifest it by placing her right hand within the right hand of your husband."[53] James Whitehead, a clerk who worked in Joseph Smith's store and an assistant to William Clayton, talked to William W. Blair in 1874. To make the diary passage clearer the few letters intended for words in Blair's diary are included in brackets for easier reading:

> [Whitehead] Says J[oseph] did te[ach]- p[olygamy]- and pr[actice]- too. That E[mma]- knows it too that She put h[a]nd of Wives in Jos[eph] ha[n]d W[hitehead]. Says Alex

---

[49] "Judge Adams arrived in Town," Joseph Smith Journal, entry for May 21, 1843. See Faulring, *An American Prophet's Record*, 380.

[50] "At home in conversation with Judge Adams and others" (Joseph Smith Journal, entry for May 23, 1843, LDS archives).

[51] Respondents Testimony, 367.

[52] Ibid., 371.

[53] Orson Pratt, "Celestial Marriage," *The Seer* 1 (Feb. 1853):31, Washington, D.C.

H Smith asked him when sleeping with him at his house in Alton [Illinois on May 14, 1864], if J[oseph] - did p[ractice] & tea[ch]. p[olygamy], and he, W[hitehead]. told him he did.[54]

On the church law regulating marriage Emily was asked if she knew "that the section on marriage was there, and you knew what it contained, - you knew what it was as it was printed in the book of Doctrine and Covenants?" She responded, "Yes sir, at that time I did." The following was asked with her answers:

Q:- And you knew at the time that you married him that he had a wife named Emma? A;- Yes sir I knew that too, - but if Joseph Smith had one revelation he could have others too. He had a revelation permitting, -
Q:- Well never mind about the revelation he had, - You say you knew that Joseph Smith had a wife named Emma at that time? A;- Yes sir I knew that.
Q:- And still in the face of that knowledge, - of the knowledge of what the law of the church was on the question of marriage as printed in the book of Doctrine and Covenants at that time, and the further knowledge that he had a wife living, you married him? A;- Yes sir.[55]

Emily was also asked important intimate questions about her sleeping with the prophet Joseph Smith:

Q:- Well do you make the declaration now that you ever roomed with him at any time? A;- Yes sir.
Q:- Do you make the declaration that you ever slept with him in the same bed? A;- Yes sir.
Q:- How many nights? A;- One.
Q:- Only one night? A; Yes sir.

---

[54] William W. Blair Diary, entry for June 17, 1874, RLDS archives. In his diary Blair wrote that the day before James Whitehead "Says J did te- p- and pr- too. That E- knows it too that She put hnd of Wives in Jos hnd W. Says Alex H. Smith asked him when sleeping with him at his house in Atlon, if J- did p & tea. p, and he, W. told him he did."
[55] Respondents Testimony, 374-75.

Q:- Then you only slept with him in the same bed one night? A;- Yes sir.

Q:- Did you ever have carnal intercourse with Joseph Smith? A;- Yes sir.

Q:- How many nights? A;- I could not tell you.

Q:- Do you make the declaration that you never [sic] slept with him one night? A; Yes sir.

Q:- And that was the only time and place that you ever were in bed with him? A;- No sir.

Q;- Were you in bed with him at any place before that time? A;- Before what time?

Q:- Before you were married? A;- No sir, not before I was married to him I never was.

Q:- Do you mean that you were in bed with him after the 4th of March 1843? A;- Yes sir, but that was after I was first married to him.[56]

Emily was asked under what revelation she was married to Joseph Smith. She replied that Smith told her "in so many words that he had a revelation, and that was the revelation we were married under. I just took his word for it, and I believed he had it."[57] The ceremony they were married under included time and eternity. Being asked what they agreed to when they were married, Emily responded, "we agreed to be each others companions, - husband and wife."[58]

Though Emily's testimony in the Temple Lot Case is a late recollection, for the most part, it summarized her writings relating to her plural marriage to Joseph Smith. As indicated in this chapter there was no marriage certificates made for this sealing.

The March 1894 verdict was given by Justice John F. Phillips whereby the RLDS church obtained judgment on the temple lot. This decision was appealed and on September 30, 1895 the U. S. Circuit Court of Appeal, Eighth Circuit reversed the decision. This granted the Church of Christ (Temple Lot) possession of this important spot in Latter-day Saint history.

---

[56] Ibid., 384.
[57] Ibid., 385.
[58] Ibid., 387.

26

More on Nauvoo Plural Wives

Another young woman who lived in the home of Emma and Joseph Smith in 1842 was Lucy Walker. Lucy recalled when Joseph spoke to her about becoming a wife:

In the year 1842 President Joseph Smith Sought an interview with me, and said: "I have a message for you. I have been com[m]anded of God to take another wife, and you are the woman." My astonishment knew no bounds. This announcement was indeed a thunderbolt to me. He asked me if I believed him to be a Prophet of God. "Most assuredly, I do I replied."

Smith explained to her that the principle of plural or celestial marriage was to be restored and "it would prove an everlasting blessing to my father's house. and form a chain that could never be broken, worlds without end." Smith said, "If you will pray sincerely for light and understanding in relation thereto, you shall receive a testimony of the correctness of this principle." Lucy prayed for guidance as her mother Lydia was deceased and her father was not in Nauvoo. Joseph seeing her sorrow told Lucy, "I have no f[l]attering words to offer. it is a command of God to you. I will give you untill tomorrow to decide this matter. If you reject this message the gate will be closed forever against you."

Lucy Walker expressed to Smith her desire to find out if God approved of this course. Joseph promised her that she would receive a testimony. She prayed again when her room "became filled with a holy influence" and she received an irresistible testimony of the truth of plural marriage. Lucy recalled that morning:

As I descended the stairs, Pres. Smith opened the door below, took me by the hand and said: "Thank God, you have the testimony. I too, have prayed." he led me to a chair, placed his hands upon my head, and blessed me with every blessing my heart could possibly desire. On the first day of May, 1843, I consented to become the wife of the Prophet Joseph Smith. and was Sealed to him for time and all eternity, at his own house by Elder Wm Clayton, on whom he confer[r]ed that authority.[1]

Lucy's father John Walker was at the time on a church mission so Joseph asked her twenty-two years old brother William for consent to marry Lucy. William Walker replied that it was her choice and he had no objection.[2] Lucy was seventeen years old at the time she was sealed to Joseph Smith by William Clayton.

Helen Mar Kimball, daughter of Vilate and Heber C. Kimball, was fourteen years old when Joseph Smith approached her. Helen told how her father, Apostle Kimball, in the summer of 1843 asked her if she would believe him "that it was right for married men to take other wives." Her "first impulse was anger, for I thought he had only said it to test my virtue, as I had heard that tales of this kind had been published by such characters as the Higbees, Foster and Bennett, but which I supposed were without any foundation." Helen continued:

I replied to him, short and emphatically, No, I wouldn't! I had always been taught to believe it a heinous crime, improper and unnatural, and I indignantly resented it. This was the first time that I ever openly manifested anger towards him; but I was somewhat surprised at his countenance, as he seemed rather pleased than otherwise. Then he commenced talking seriously and reasoned and explained the principle, and why it was again to be established upon the earth, etc., but did not tell me then that

---

[1] A Brief Biographical Sketch of the Life & Labors of Lucy Walker Kimball Smith, LDS archives. The account with a few words different is in Rodney Wilson Walker and Noel Stevenson, comp., *The Second Edition of Ancestry and Descendants of John Walker 1794-1869* ([Salt Lake City:] John Walker Family Organization, 1985), 17-19.
[2] *The Life Incidents and Travels of Elder William Holmes Walker, and His Association with Joseph Smith, the Prophet* (Bountiful, Utah: John Walker Family Organization, printed by Horizon Publishers, 3rd ed., 1975), 22.

anyone had yet practiced it, but left me to reflect upon it for the next twenty-four hours, during which time I was filled with various and conflicting ideas.[3]

      Heber had "a great desire to be connected with the Prophet" and asked Helen if she would be sealed to Joseph Smith. The next day Joseph Smith came to the Kimball home and they heard Smith teach and explain the principle of celestial marriage to them. Helen believed because of the testimony of her father and Joseph. She thought that was sufficient. Smith said to her: "If you will take this step, it will ensure your eternal salvation & exaltation and that of your father's household & all of your kindred." Joseph then asked Vilate is she would be willing to have Helen sealed to him she replied, "If Helen is willing I have nothing more to say."[4]

      Helen Kimball's sealing to Joseph Smith was a spiritual one unlike other wives who had sexual relations with the prophet. She wrote, "At that time spiritual wife was the title by which every woman who entered into this order [of marriage] was called, for it was taught and practiced as a spiritual order and not a temporal one . . . The Prophet Joseph revealed the plural order to but few of the honest and pure in heart, who accepted it in the true spirit in which it was taught, as a celestial law that would eventually redeem and exalt the human family. He charged them not to divulge it, as he was harassed by day and by night by his enemies, and on their sacrecy [secrecy] depended his life."[5]

PLURAL WIVES, 1842-1844

Name	Plural Wives	Sealing Date	By Whom
Heber C. Kimball	Sarah Peak Noon	circa Jan. 1842	Joseph Smith
Brigham Young	Lucy Decker Seeley	June 14, 1842	Joseph Smith
	Augusta Adams Cobb	Nov. 2, 1843	Joseph Smith
	Harriet E. Cook	Nov. 2, 1843	Joseph Smith
	Clarissa Decker	May 8, 1844	Willard Richards

---

[3] "Scenes and Incidents in Nauvoo," *Woman's Exponent* 11 (Aug. 1, 1882):39-40, emphasis omitted.

[4] Helen Mar Kimball Whitney Autobiography, March 30, 1881, LDS archives, as cited in Holzapfel and Holzapfel, *A Woman's View: Helen Mar Whitney's Reminiscences of Early Church History*, 482-86.

[5] Whitney, *Plural Marriage as Taught by the Prophet Joseph*, 15-16.

PLURAL WIVES, 1842-1844

Name	Plural Wives	Sealing Date	By Whom
Orson Hyde	Martha R. Browett	Feb. /Mar. 1843	Joseph Smith
	Mary Ann Price	April 1843	Joseph Smith
Joseph B. Noble	Sarah B. Alley	April 5, 1843	Joseph Smith
	Mary Ann Washburn	1843	unknown
William Clayton	Margaret Moon	April 27, 1843	Joseph Smith
Willard Richards	Susannah Liptrot	June 12, 1843	Joseph Smith
James Adams	Roxena Repshire	July 11, 1843	Joseph Smith
Parley P. Pratt	Elizabeth Brotherton	July 24, 1843	Hyrum Smith
Hyrum Smith	Mercy F. Thompson	Aug. 11, 1843	Joseph Smith
	Catherine Phillips	Aug. 1843	Joseph Smith
John Smith	Mary Aikens Smith	Aug. 13, 1843	Joseph Smith
John Taylor	Elizabeth Kaighin	Dec. 12, 1843	unknown
	Jane Ballantyne	Feb. 25, 1844	unknown
Isaac Morley	Leonora S. Leavitt	1843	unknown
Erastus Snow	Minerva White	circa March 1844	Hyrum Smith
Ezra T. Benson	Adeline B. Andrus	April 27, 1844	Hyrum Smith
Howard Egan	Catherine Clawson	1844	Hyrum Smith

As indicated in the chapter 25 Emma Smith gave permission for the Partridge sisters to be Joseph Smith's plural wives. Emma was not really enthusiastic about sharing her husband with other women. It was probably for this reason that Joseph did not bring this issue to Emma until May 1843. This was risky business of having some of their closest friends being secretly associated in spiritual marriage. For Joseph to perform the pretended marriage of Sarah Ann Whitney and Joseph C. Kingsbury in April 1843 shows how desperate he was in keeping this sealing in confidence.

As the Nauvoo Relief Society president, Emma had followed church procedures relating to the regulation of marriage. She opposed any attempt to alter the commonly accepted norm of marriage in Christian fellowship. Whether she suspected that an authorized system of plural marriage was going on under Joseph Smith's direction is not known. The secretary in the Relief Society, Eliza R. Snow had been sealed to Smith in celestial marriage since June 1842.

Another individual who was a close associate of Joseph Smith was William Clayton. Clayton had been clerking for President Joseph Smith since February 1842 and he was invited into the new order of marriage. William kept a detailed journal and was taught this doctrine in March 1843 by Brigham Young. Ruth Moon and William Clayton had been married since 1836. But on April 27, 1843 Clayton had Margaret Moon sealed to himself as a plural wife by Joseph Smith. In his journal William Clayton recorded his family's experiences and struggles as he tried to practice the principle of plural marriage. The journal records the ups and down in his priesthood sealing to Margaret Moon.

Clayton's journal contains private discussions with his own family plus those of Joseph and Emma. The journal also records activities occurring in Nauvoo from Clayton's perspective. Because of its importance the following extracts from his lengthy journal gives us some insights into plural marriage at Nauvoo. Dates have been added in brackets. A number of journals were kept by William Clayton while living in Nauvoo. Since the handwritten journals at times contain more than one entry for the same date the term journal is used.[6]

[March 7, 1843] Er [Elder] B[righam]. Young called me on one side & said he wants to give me some instructions on the priesthood the first opportunity. He said the prophet had told him to do so & to give me a favor which I have long desired. For this again I feel grateful to God & his servant, and the desire of my heart is to do right and be saved.[7]

[April 24, 1843] sister Marg[are]t Moon went with me [to Carthage, Illinois] she is a lovely woman and desires to do right in all things and will submit to council with all her heart. Got back at dark conversed some with President[8]

[April 27, 1843]. At the Temple A.M. went to prests. who rode with me to bro. H.C. Kimballs where sister Marg[are]t. Moon was sealed up by the priesthood, by the president - and M[arried] to me. . . . evening told Mother in law [Lydia Moon] concerning the priesthood

---

[6] William Clayton Journal, typed copy.
[7] The favor probably relates to Sarah Crooks a church member living in England whom Clayton liked.
[8] Margaret Moon was engaged to Aaron Farr who was on a church mission. This presented a delicate situation as discussed under other dates in Clayton's journal.

In another Nauvoo journal Clayton recorded a shorter version for this date: "At the Temple A.M. at 10 bro Kimballs was M[arried] to M. M. [Margaret Moon] . . . evening told Mother in law concerning the priesthood."

[May 1, 1843] May 1st. A.M. at the Temple. at 10. m[arried] J[oseph] to L.W. [Lucy Walker][9]

[May 14, 1843] Walked out with Mt [Margaret] who promises to be true.

[May 23, 1843] Conversed with H C. K. [Heber C. Kimball] concerning a plot that is being laid to entrap the brethren of the secret priesthood by bro H[yrum Smith]. and others.

[May 26, 1843] Prest. in meeting with the Twelve & Judge Adams. Hyrum [Smith] received the doctrine of priesthood.

[October 19, 1843] at 11 W[illiam]. Walker came & said Prest. J[oseph] wanted me to go to Macedonia I went immediately to see him & he requested me to go with him. I went home & got dinner & got ready he soon came up and we started out After we had got on the road he [Joseph] began to tell me that E[mma]. was turned quite friendly & kind. she had been anointed & he also had been a[nointed]. K[ing]. He said that it was her [Emma's] advice that I should keep M[argaret] at home and it was also his council. Says he just keep her [Margaret] at home and brook it and if they raise trouble about it and bring you before me I will give you an awful scourging & probably cut you off from the church and then I will baptise you & set you ahead as good as ever.[10]

---

[9] In a letter William Clayton wrote, "I had the honor to seal one woman to Joseph under his direction" (Clayton to Madison M. Scott, Nov. 11, 1871, copy of letter in LDS archives).

[10] William Clayton's plural wife Margaret Moon was about five months pregnant at this time. Joseph Smith told Clayton about their second anointing that occurred three weeks earlier. This was recorded by Willard Richards:

[February 18, 1844] About 12 A.M. M[argaret] began to be sick and continued to grow worse until 5 o clock when she was delivered of a son. She did remarkably well for which I thank my heavenly father. Mother [in law Lydia Moon] attended her. I was at home all day. M[argaret] seems to do very well[11]

Ebenezer and Angeline Robinson stated: "in the fall of 1843 Hyrum Smith, brother of Joseph Smith came to our house in Nauvoo, Ill. and taught us the doctrine of polygamy. And I, the said Ebenezer Robinson, hereby further state that he gave me special instructions how I could manage the matter so as not to have it known to the public. He also told us that while he had heretofore opposed the doctrine, he was wrong, and his brother Joseph was right; referring to his teaching it."[12] Levi Richards recorded in his journal a sermon Hyrum Smith gave on Sunday, May 14, 1843:

attended meeting at the Temple A.M. Hyrum Smith addressed the people – subjects from the Book of Mormon 2[d] Chap. Jacob – remember that – the Book [of] Mormon was a mirror, & key, to the Bible - spoke of persecution as being one of the means of salvation when persecution ceased, oft to forget the first commandment – said there were many that had a great deal to say about the ancient order of things as Solomon & David having many wifes [wives] & concubine[s] - but its an abomination in the sight of God — If an angel from heaven should come & preach such doctrine would be sure to See his cloven foot & cloud of blackness over his head, - though his garments might shine as white as snow – a <man> might have one wife –

"anointed and ord[ained] to the highest and holiest order of the priesthood (and companion)" (Joseph Smith Journal, entry for Sept. 28, 1843).

[11] The son born to William and Margaret was named Daniel Adebert (or Adelbert). Their son died six months later on August 27, 1844.

[12] Affidavit of Ebenezer and Angeline E. Robinson, Dec. 29, 1873, copy in RLDS archives. See also *Biographical and Historical Record of Ringold and Decatur Counties, Iowa* (Chicago: Lewis Publishing Co., 1887), 543-44.

Concubines he should have none – observed, that, the idea was that this was given to Jacob for a perpetual principle[13]

The year previous Hyrum wrote an address on behalf of the First Presidency to Parley P. Pratt, the elders of the church in England and Europe, and to the saints. It emphasized the topic of gathering to Nauvoo and that families should not be broken up. In the words of Hyrum:

And we also forbid that a woman leave her husband because he is an unbeliever. We also forbid that a man shall leave his wife because she is an unbeliever. If he be a bad man (i.e. the unbeliever) there is a law to remedy that evil. And if she be a bad woman, there is a law to remedy that evil. And if the law divorce them, then they are at liberty; otherwise they are bound as long as they two shall live, and it is not our prerogative to go beyond this; if we do it, it will be at the expense of our reputation.[14]

Twelve days after Hyrum Smith's pubic discourse and opposition to the doctrine of men having many wives and concubines he was converted and received the principle as doctrine. The following are excerpts from Joseph Smith's journal kept by Willard Richards who recorded meetings of the Holy Order of the Holy Priesthood. The entries include notations made in Taylor shorthand regarding the sacred ordinance of sealing with the meaning noted in brackets:

[May 26, 1843] 5 P.M. J[oseph]. and Hiram. & Judge Adams & Bishop Whitney. B. Young. H. C. Kimball. W[illard]. Richards & Wm Law, in council in upper room, receiving instructions on the priesthood. the new and everlasting covenant. &c. &c. adjourned to Sunday P.M. 5

---

[13] Levi Richards Journal, entry for May 14, 1843, LDS archives.

[14] "Address from the First Presidency," *Millennial Star* 3 (Nov. 1842):115. The document concluded: "Written by Hyrum Smith, patriarch, by the order of Joseph Smith, president over the whole church of Jesus Christ of Latter-day Saints."

[May 28, 1843] 5 P.M. - adjourned council met in the upper Room. Atten[d]ed to ordinances and counselled . . . Joseph - & J. Adams [Taylor shorthand meaning: were married][15]

[June 12, 1843] . . . [Taylor shorthand meaning: married to Rhoda Richards and Willard Richards married to Susan Liptrot][16]

Joseph Smith preached on May 21 the doctrine of eternal marriage in a public setting. In his sermon he indicated that many people think that a prophet "must be a great deal better than any body else." But Joseph told them, "I don[']t want you to think I am righteous, for I am not very righteous." Continuing he said: "we have no claim in our eternal comfort, in relation to Eternal things unless our actions, & contracts & all things tend to this end."[17]

In July Joseph Smith continued to teach about the covenant of eternal marriage. William Clayton wrote, "He [Smith] showed that a man must enter into an everlasting covenant with his wife in this world or he will have no claim on her in the next. He said that he could not reveal the fulness of these things untill the Temple is completed."[18] Willard Richards wrote in Joseph Smith's journal:

Wednesday July 12 Received a Revelation in the office in presence of Hyrum & Wm Clayton

The majority of women who were sealed to Joseph Smith had the ordinance performed before this revelation on marriage was dictated to William Clayton. For example, nineteen year old Melissa Lott was sealed to Smith in September and Fanny Young, a fifty-six year old widow, was

---

[15] Taylor shorthand "wr mrd" meant were married. This appears to be the date when Emma and Joseph Smith and also Harriet and James Adams were sealed as husband and wife for time and all eternity.

[16] This entry means that on June 12, 1843 Joseph Smith was married to Rhoda Richards, a sister of Willard Richards and Willard was married to Susannah Lee Liptrot.

[17] Joseph Smith Journal kept by Willard Richards, entry for May 21, 1843. See Ehat and Cook, *Words of Joseph Smith*, 204-205.

[18] William Clayton Journal, entry for July 16, 1843.

sealed in November 1843. The July 12, 1843 revelation was not the first instruction for Smith to take other wives. As mentioned by Joseph Smith to Joseph B. Noble and others an angel gave the commandment to take plural wives. The written revelation was given over a year after John C. Bennett's expose of Joseph Smith spiritual wife system. Some of the text deals with taking virgins for wives. There is no mention of how the marriage covenant applied to married or widowed women who were probably not virgins.

As quoted Willard Richards recorded that William Clayton was present with Hyrum and Joseph Smith when the revelation was received. Clayton wrote in his personal journal:

This A.M. I wrote a Revelation - consisting of 10 pages on the order of the Priesthood, showing the designs in Moses, Abraham, David and Solomon having many wives & concubines &c. After it was wrote Prests Joseph & Hyrum presented it and read it to E[mma]. who said she did not believe a word of it and appeared very rebellious. J[oseph]. told me to Deed all the unincumbered lots to E[mma]. & the children He appears much troubled about E[mma].[19]

Joseph C. Kingsbury mentioned that shortly afterwards he "wrote the Revelation on C[e]lestial or plural marriage from the mouth of Bishop Newel K. Whitney as he read from the original, which was in his possession."[20] It was the Kingsbury copy that was preserved after the original was destroyed by either Emma or Joseph. The revelation gives Joseph Smith's role as the one who holds the keys to the eternity of the marriage covenant. The revelation commenced:

Verily thus Saith the Lord, unto you my Servant Joseph, that inasmuch as you have inquired of my hand to know

---

[19] William Clayton Journal, entry for July 12, 1843.

[20] Affidavit of Joseph C. Kingsbury, March 7, 1870, Joseph F. Smith Affidavit Book 2:18, LDS archives. This copy of the revelation was read in Salt Lake City on August 29, 1852. It was added to the 1876 edition of the LDS D&C (section 132) and the 1878 edition of the Pearl of Great Price (PGP). The document was removed and not included in the 1902 revision of the PGP.

and understand wherein I the Lord justified my Servants, Abraham Isaac and Jacob; as also Moses, David and Solomon, my Servants, as touching the principle and doctrin[e] of their having many wives and concubines: Behold and lo, I am the Lord thy God, and will answer thee as touching this matter[21]

The revelation then goes into the basic law of the priesthood. Whoever enters into the new and everlasting covenant of marriage are told they must obey the law or be damned. If the marriage is not by one who holds priesthood keys it would not be in force after death. But those sealed by proper authority, if faithful, can in the resurrection obtain their exaltation and be Gods.

Joseph is told that Abraham has received his exaltation (Godhood) and sits upon his throne. Smith holds the keys and power of the priesthood and can seal on earth and it would be eternally bound in the heavens. He can remit or retain sins of individuals and it would be recognized in heaven. Now Joseph received the ultimate blessing:

> For Verily, I seal upon you, your exaltation, and prepare a throne for you in the Kingdom of my Father, with Abraham your Father.[22]

Emma was told to forgive her husband his trespasses and she would be forgiven hers. Smith imparted these words of warning concerning Satan:

> let not my Servant Joseph put his property out of his hands, lest an enemy come and distroy [destroy] him, for Satan seeketh to distroy [destroy]; For I am the Lord thy God, and he is my Servent [Servant]; and behold! and lo, I am with him as I was with Abraham, thy Father, even unto his exaltation and glory.[23]

[21] Marquardt, *Joseph Smith Revelations*, 323; LDS D&C 132:1-2.
[22] Ibid., 327; LDS D&C 132:49.
[23] Ibid., 327-28; LDS D&C 132:57.

Joseph Smith indicated that when anyone having the keys of the priesthood does anything in and by God's name, law, or word he will not commit sin but will be justified. The revelation mentions being espoused to virgins. Evidently referring to Emma, since Joseph holds the priesthood keys, the revelation said:

> if any man have a wife who holds the Keys of this power, & he teaches unto her the Law of my priesthood as pertaining to these things, then Shall She believe & administer unto him; or She Shall be distroy [destroyed], Saith the Lord your God[24]

As indicated this revelation gives justification for plural wives by referring to the Old Testament where some men had wives and concubines in ancient times. It provides little information on how this priesthood law was to be practiced in current society. It appears that the revelation was given for the benefit of Emma Smith and maybe even Hyrum Smith. The next month Hyrum read the revelation to Nauvoo High Council. It was probably on August 12 when this occurred though the minutes do not record that a revelation was read or discussed at the meeting. The brief minutes of the Nauvoo High Council state:

> August 12th 1843 Council met according to adjt [adjournment] at H. Smith's office No business before the Council. Teaching by Prest Hiram Smith & William Marks. Adjd till next Saturday at 2 o'clock P.M. Hosea Stout, Clerk[25]

Hosea Stout explained in an 1883 letter to Joseph F. Smith that he was at the meeting and "At that very time I had another appoint[ment] to meet, and was excused by the council, supposing it [the revelation] would be filed there and come into my hands as clerk, I could then peruse it at my leasure [leisure]. When I returned the Council had adjourned, and your father [Hyrum

---

[24] Ibid., 328; LDS D&C 132:64.
[25] Minutes of the Nauvoo High Council, Aug. 12, 1843, typed copy, original in LDS archives.

Smith] had gone, taking the revelation with him. But I saw several of the counsellors, who informed me as to the purport of the revelation which corresponded to what is published and now in the book of Doctrine and Covenants."[26]

Of those in attendance it is understood that two members of the stake presidency, viz. William Marks and Austin A. Coles did not accept the revelation. Evidently referring to this meeting Franklin D. Richards wrote:

> Hiram [Hyrum Smith] said before the High council that no prophet ever did transgress but was directed by the impulse of the spirit involuntarily Also The Law that a man shall take his brothers wife and raise up seed unto him as it was in israel must be again established[27]

Because plural or celestial marriage was secretly practiced and against Illinois state law the practice was denied. This would create mixed signals to regular church members who did not know the teachings of priesthood leaders. Willard Richards recorded that on October 15 Joseph Smith mentioned in a discourse, "stop this spinning [of] street yarn and talking about spiritual wives."[28] Four days later is when Smith told William Clayton that if there was trouble brought against Clayton he would probably cut him off from the church and then "set you ahead as good as ever."[29] Hyrum Smith who had been performing sealings of plural marriages since his conversion to the principle spoke to the elders at conference on April 8, 1844 about reports from abroad:

> almost every man runs to here [Nauvoo] to enquire if things are true how many sp [spiritual] wives a man may have – I know nothing abt. [about] it . . . I am authd [authorized] to

---

[26] Hosea Stout to Joseph F. Smith, July 24, 1883, LDS archives. The July 12, 1843 revelation appeared in the 1876 edition of the LDS Doctrine and Covenants.

[27] Franklin D. Richards Notebook with "Words of the Prophets / Scriptural Items" on the title page, LDS archives.

[28] Joseph Smith Journal, entry for Oct. 15, 1843. See Ehat and Cook, *Words of Joseph Smith*, 257.

[29] William Clayton Journal, entry for Oct. 19, 1843.

tell you from henceforth that any man who comes in c [and] tell any such dn [damn] fool doctrine to come in – to take away his license. none but a fool teaches such stuff

Hyrum continued his discourse:

I wish the El [Elders] of Israel to understand it is lawful for a man to marry a wife But it is unlawful to have more. c [and] God has not comd [commanded] any one to have more – c [and] if any of you dare to presume to do any such thing it will spoil your fun for you will never preach the gospel

Then Hyrum told about his own experience as his first wife Jerusha died on October 13, 1837 and he then married Mary Fielding. Hyrum discussed the doctrine of sealing for eternity:

I married me a wife c [and] was the only one who had any write [right] to her – till we had 5 chd. [children] the covt. [covenant] was made for our lives – she fell in the grave bef[ore] God shewed us his will God has shewn me the covt. [covenant] is dead c [and] had no more force neither could I have her in the resn. [ressurrection] but we shod [should] be as the angels – it troubled me. Bro Jsh [Joseph said] you can be sealed to her upon the same prin[ciple] as you can be bap[tized] for the dead what can I do for mine 2nd wife[?] – you can make a cov. [covenant] with her for etern[ity] c [and] sealed to her – c [and] she sd [said] I will act as proxy for the one that is dead and I will be seal[e]d to you for eternity – if there is any man that has no sense c [and] will make any story of such a fact – his name shall be pubd. [published] – it is a doctrine not to be taught to the world[30]

---

[30] Minutes of Conference held at Nauvoo on April 8, 1844, Thomas Bullock, clerk, LDS archives. Willard Richards wrote, "a large collection of Elders assembled at the stand address by patriarch Hyrum Smith on Spiritual wife system – The first one we heard refuting such stories" (Joseph Smith Journal, entry for April 8, 1844).

Joseph's wife Emma did not have a full knowledge of the involvement of her husband in all maters pertaining to the principle of celestial marriage. She was both hot and cold on this priesthood ordinance. This is understandable since there had been public denials to both those inside and outside the church. It is not known if Emma knew about Joseph's practice of having married and widowed women sealed to him. Further whether she knew which women were married to Joseph prior to May 1843 is not known. Emma and Joseph receive their second anointing in September 1843 so she would have received her endowment by that date.

In the period 1846-47 Emma mentioned to a few saints about giving her consent for Joseph to have plural wives including two sets of sisters. Women who were biological sisters were known as sister wives. Lucy Walker Kimball wrote about Emma giving consent at the time of the sealing of the Partridge and Lawrence sisters to her husband:

> I can also state that Emma Smith was present and did consent to Eliza and Emily Partridge, also Maria and Sarah Lawrence being sealed to her husband. This I had from the Prophet's own mouth; also the testimony of her own niece, Hyrum Smith's eldest daughter, (my brother Lorin's wife), as well as that of the young ladies named themselves, with whom I was on most intimate terms, and was glad that they too, had accepted that order of marriage.[31]

Emma left Nauvoo and resided in Fulton City for a short time.[32] Lovina Smith Walker, who was the daughter of Hyrum Smith, said she talked with Emma at that location. Lovina was nineteen years old at the time she was at Fulton City and affirmed, "while I was living with Aunt Emma Smith, in Fulton City, Fulton Co. Illinois, in the year 1846, that She told me that She, Emma

---

[31] A Brief Biographical Sketch of the Life and Labor of Lucy Walker Kimball Smith, LDS archives. See Walker and Stevenson, *The Second Edition of Ancestry and Descendants of John Walker 1794-1869*, 19.

[32] Buddy Youngreen wrote, "Emma left with her children for Fulton City, Whiteside County, Illinois, on 12 September 1846 . . . she and her family returned posthaste to Nauvoo by land, arriving 19 February 1847" (*Reflections of Emma*, [Orem, Utah: Grandin Book, 1982], 119n63).

Smith was present and witnessed the marrying or Sealing of Eliza Partridge, Emily Partridge[,] Maria Lawrence, and Sarah Lawrence to her husband, Joseph Smith, and that She gave her concent [consent] thereto."[33]

Other associates said that Emma knew plural marriage (polygamy) was practiced by Joseph. James Whitehead told about activities that occurred in Nauvoo. Alexander Hale Smith wrote in his journal about an 1864 visit: "went to see Old Bro Whitehead stayed all night with him he gave me some useful information told me some things that I did not know and can not understand."[34] Ten years later in 1874 William W. Blair recorded in his journal that he also talked to James Whitehead who confirmed that Smith practiced polygamy and Emma put the hand of wives in Joseph's hand.[35]

In 1848 Joseph Smith III indicated to his cousin John Smith that he did not believe his father or Uncle Hyrum upheld or practiced spiritual wifery and other institutions. In his letter Joseph III wrote, "I do not now nor shall I ever countenance such iniquity so help me heaven."[36] Even though he heard from acquaintances of Joseph Smith that plural marriage was practiced at Nauvoo he maintained this stance throughout his life. When Joseph Smith III did interview his mother in February 1879 (over thirty years after she talked to Lovina Smith) the questions on polygamy were carefully asked to Emma and it produced negative responses by her.[37]

---

[33] Certificate of Lovina [Smith] Walker, June 16, 1869, Joseph F. Smith Affidavit Book titled "40 Affidavits on Celestial Marriage," 30, LDS archives.

[34] Alexander Hale Smith Journal, entry for May 14, 1864, RLDS archives.

[35] William W. Blair Journal, entry for June 17, 1874, RLDS archives.

[36] Joseph Smith III to John Smith, March 21, 1848, L. Tom Perry Special Collections, Harold B. Lee Library, Brigham Young University.

[37] See "Last Testimony of Sister Emma," *The Saints Herald* 26 (Oct. 1, 1879):290. For the struggles of David Hyrum Smith, another son of Joseph Smith, born in November 1844, see Valeen Tippetts Avery, *From Mission to Madness: Last Son of the Mormon Prophet* (Urbana: University of Illinois Press, 1998), 176-77.

27

Tragedy: Death of a Prophet

As the church's prophet and leader Joseph Smith gave instructions in other ways beside written revelations. A few of his remarks and predictions are given below to show some of the topics of the times. Building the Nauvoo House and the Nauvoo Temple was indicated in a revelation received in January 1841. Three years later Joseph Smith still spoke "on the importance of building the Nauvoo House stressing that the time had come to build it. and the church must either do it or suffer the condemnation of not fulfilling the commandments of God."[1]

Joseph Smith would at times prophesy about political opponents and the nation as a whole. On June 30, 1843 Smith made comments about Illinois state governor Thomas Ford and in December Joseph believed that if a petition to congress was not successful the government would be broken up. Willard Richards the prophet's secretary and church historian recorded the following in the journal he kept for Joseph Smith:

> I prophecy in the name of the Lord God that Governor Ford by granting the write [writ] against me has damned himself politically and his carcase [carcass] will stink on the face of the earth food for the cairion [carrion] crow & Turkey buzzard[2]

> I prophecy by virtue of the holy Priesthood, vested in me, in the name of Jesus Christ that if congress will not hear

---

[1] William Clayton Journal, entry for April 6, 1843. On the Nauvoo House see *Times and Seasons* 4 (Nov. 15, 1842):11. Later in March 1844 Joseph Smith said "he did not know but it was best to let the Nauvoo house be till the temple is completed. – we need the temple more than any thing else. . . . we will let the Nauvoo house stand till the temple is done and we will put all our forces on the temple" (Joseph Smith Journal, entry for March 4, 1844).

[2] Joseph Smith Journal, entry for June 30, 1843.

our petition, and grant us protection, they shall be broken up as a government and God shall damn them, and there shall nothing be left of them, not even a grease spot.[3]

The year 1844 saw significant developments as Joseph Smith's name was put forth at the lower end of the political process as a candidate for the office of president of the United States. Smith as Lieutenant General of the Nauvoo Legion military force was known throughout Illinois and was a widely published individual.

Since the middle of 1842 William W. Phelps, a former confidant came to Nauvoo from Ohio; he became the political advisor to Joseph Smith. As a close friend of the prophet Phelps composed letters for President Smith. Phelps was the main person behind the writing of the political views to which Smith attached his name.[4]

On January 29, 1844 it was "Moved by Willard Richards and voted unanimously that we have independent electors and that Joseph Smith be a candidate for the next presidency [of the United States] and that we use all honorable means to secure his election."[5] Smith's journal shows the involvement of William Phelps in writing *General Smith's Views of the Powers and Policy of the Government of the United States.*[6] In the latter part of February 1,500 copies of the *General Smith's Views* were published. Missionaries were sent to preach the gospel and also support Joseph Smith's candidacy for the United States presidency. This was known as electioneering.

---

[3] Ibid., entry for Dec 16, 1843. In April 1844 Joseph prophesied "the entire overthrow of this nation in a few years" (William Clayton Journal, entry for April 13, 1844).

[4] Bruce A. Van Orden, "William W. Phelps's Service in Nauvoo as Joseph Smith's Political Clerk," *Brigham Young University Studies* 32 (Winter/Spring 1992):81-94. Phelps assisted Willard Richards in continuing the compilation of the "History of Joseph Smith" which was being published in the *Times and Seasons.* By March 1844 the history was written to the middle of 1838 and printed to August 1831.

[5] Joseph Smith Journal, entry for Jan. 29, 1844.

[6] John Taylor, Printer: Nauvoo, Illinois, 1844. This was a twelve page printed work.

The publication gave positions on domestic issues such as abolishing slavery with Congress paying for slaves that are freed by revenue from the sale of public lands and the deduction of pay from members of Congress. Other ideas included having a national bank, set prisoners free, and confinement or death for murders. On foreign issues there was the idea of taking into the United States the territory of Oregon and if Texas asks for admission as a state accept her. Included was an interesting religious comment:

> Like the good Samaritan, send every lawyer as soon as he repents and obeys the ordinances of heaven, to preach the gospel to the destitute, without purse or scrip, pouring in the oil and the wine: a learned priesthood is certainly more honorable than a *"hireling clergy"*.

In March Willard Richards learned that the chosen vice presidential candidate, fifty-five year old James Arlington Bennet, baptized by Brigham Young in August 1843, reported that he was born in Ireland. But this not the case since he was actually born in New York. James Bennet wrote to Richards in April:

> If you can by any supernatural means elect Brother Joseph [Smith] President of the U. States, I have not a doubt but that he would govern the people and administer the laws in good faith, and with righteous intentions, but I can see no natural means by what he has the slightest chance of receiving the votes even of one state. If the object of his friends be to aid the cause of Mormonism in foreign lands, or in this country among a certain class of persons, by holding its chief up for the highest office in the gift of the people, then I think they are somewhat in the right track, but if they are aiming in reality at that high office then I must say that at present they, in my opinion, are on a wild goose chase.[7]

---

[7] James Arlington Bennet to "Dear Doctor" [Willard Richards], April 14, 1844, typed copy, emphasis omitted, LDS archives. Bennet wrote in the letter, "I wish for no nomination for Vice President of the U. States, or other civil station, yet the *idea* of my not being a naive born citizen would not exclude me from the office."

A letter was written to Solomon Copeland of Tennessee on being the Vice President with Joseph Smith. By May 6 Sidney Rigdon was chosen to be the candidate for the Vice Presidency as the running mate with Smith. On May 17 the Illinois state convention was held in the assembly room of Joseph's store. This convention then made General Joseph Smith their choice for President of the United States with Sidney Rigdon as Vice President. A convention was planned to be held in Baltimore in July. John S. Reed gave a speech supporting Smith. He was Joseph's lawyer in the summer of 1830. Reed recalled, "I early discovered that his mind was constantly in search of truth, expressing an anxious desire to know the will of God concerning his children here below, often speaking of those things which professed christians believe in."[8] The *Times and Seasons* announced in the June 1 issue:

FOR PRESIDENT,
GEN. JOSEPH SMITH,
NAUVOO, ILLINOIS.

FOR VICE PRESIDENT,
Sidney Rigdon, Esq:
OF PENNSYLVANIA.

Prior to this Joseph Smith organized what is known as the Council of Fifty (though there were more than fifty members). Smith based this upon a revelation of April 7, 1842 which stated: "Verily thus saith the Lord, this is the name by which you shall be called, the kingdom of God and his law with the keys and power thereof and judgments in the hands of his servants Ahman Christ."[9] Almost two years later on March 11, 1844 the Council of Fifty (Kingdom of God) was organized. On the thirteenth Brigham Young recorded in his journal that a number of persons organized themselves "into a compacked [compacted] Boddy [Body] for the further advenment [advancement] of the gospel of Christ."[10]

---

[8] "Some of the remarks of John S. Reed, Esq., as delivered before the State Convention," *Times and Seasons* 5 (June 1, 1844):549.
[9] Marquardt, *Joseph Smith Revelations*, 314.
[10] Brigham Young Journal, entry for March 13, 1844, typed copy, LDS archives.

William Clayton reflected on the Council of Fifty in which he was clerk nine months after the formal organization:

> In this council was the plan arranged for supporting president Joseph Smith as a candidate for the presidency of the U.S. Prest. Joseph was the standing chairman of the council and myself the clerk. In this council was also devised the plan of establishing an immigration to Texas and plans laid for the exaltation of a standard and ensign of truths for the nations of the earth.

Clayton continued his summary of the activities of the Kingdom of God:

> In this council was the plan devised to restore the Ancients [Native Americans] to the knowledge of the truth and the restoration of union and peace among ourselves. In this council was Prest. Joseph chosen as our prophet, Priest, & King by Hosannas. In this council was the principles of eternal truths rolled forth to the hearers without reserve and the hearts of the servants of God made to rejoice exceedingly.[11]

It was on April 11 as mentioned by William Clayton that Joseph Smith "was voted our P[rophet]. P[riest]. & K[ing]. with loud Hosannas."[12] The council of the Kingdom of God held over a dozen meetings by the end of May.

Sidney Rigdon spoke at length at the April church conference. Joseph Smith preached a funeral discourse for King Follett who died before conference was held. A report from the clerks of the conference, Thomas Bullock and William Clayton, was published in *Times and Seasons*. Smith remarks included his teachings of a plurality of Gods.[13]

As events unfolded the second counselor to Joseph Smith, William Law, presented another internal problem. Some of the

---

[11] William Clayton Journal, entry for Jan. 1, 1845.

[12] Ibid., entry for April 11, 1844.

[13] "Conference Minutes," *Times and Seasons* 5 (Aug. 15, 1844):612-17.

advanced teachings of the prophet Law could not accept. William had been appointed to the First Presidency in January 1841 and initiated into the Masonic Lodge in April 1842. He received his endowment in the Holy Order in May, and again a year later but now rejected Smith's teaching regarding the practice of plural marriage. William Law and associates were excommunicated from the church as recorded by William Clayton: "I also attended in council with the Twelve & High Council on the case of the Laws & R[obert]. D. Foster – when Wm Law & his wife Jane Law – Wilson Law and R. D. Foster were cut off from the church by unanimous vote."[14]

This led to the accusation by William Law that the proceedings held were illegal and they were not notified of any charges. Shortly afterwards Law started a new reformed church with himself as president. The complaint relating to their excommunication appeared in the *Nauvoo Expositor*:

On thursday evening, the 18th of April, there was a council called, unknown to the Church, which tried, condemned, and cut off brothers Wm. Law, Wilson Law, and sister Law, (Wm's. wife,) brother R. D. Foster, and one brother Smith, with whom we are unacquainted; which we contend is contrary to the book of Doctrine and Covenants, for our law condemnest no man untill he is heard.[15]

Curtis Edwin Bolton, who saw Joseph Smith for the last time in May, wrote concerning Joseph, "he was Standing with his youngest boy in his arms, at the brow of the hill on the west side of the Nauvoo House in the middle of the Street. No one was near him. He was a most beautiful formed man. And was laughing pleasantly to the brethren on board the Steamboat who were leaving to go a preaching."[16]

That same month Willard Richards recorded that "A son of John Quincy Adams [Charles Francis Adams], Mr [Josiah] Quincy,

---

[14] William Clayton Journal, entry for April 18, 1844. Howard Smith was also excommunicated at the same time. The minutes of this meeting were not recorded in the high council minutes.

[15] *Nauvoo Expositor* 1 (7 June 1844):2, Nauvoo, Illinois.

[16] Curtis Edwin Bolton Journal, LDS archives.

& Dr Goforth visited at the Mansion."[17] Charles Adams wrote of his visit to Nauvoo. He said that Smith took them into his mother's chamber where Joseph Smith:

> showed us four Egyptian mummies stripped and then undertook to explain the contents of a chart or manuscript which he said had been taken from the bosom of one of them. The cool impudence of this imposture amused me very much. 'This,['] said he, [']was written by the hand of Abraham and means so and so. If any one denies it, let him prove the contrary. *I* say it.' Of course, we were too polite to prove the negative, against a man fortified by revelation. His mother looked on with attention and aided in the explanation whenever the prophet hesitated, from which I inferred that she was usually made the exponent of the writing to strangers. At the close, he notified us that for this instruction, his mother was in the habit of receiving a quarter of a dollar a piece from them, which sum we paid forthwith.[18]

The *Nauvoo Expositor*, a four page local newspaper, was issued on June 7. It contained criticism of local events that related to church president Joseph Smith and political issues that he was mostly involved in. The paper called for the unconditional repeal of the Nauvoo Charter, an important topic that was being called into serious question in Illinois. The editor Sylvester Emmons stated on page one:

> We give place this week to the following Preamble, Resolutions and Affidavits, of the Seceders from the Church at Nauvoo.—The request is compiled with on account of their deeming it very important that the public should know the true cause of their dissenting, as all manner of falsehood is spread abroad in relation to the schism in the Church. In our subsequent numbers several

---

[17] Joseph Smith Journal, entry for May 15, 1844.
[18] Diary of Charles Francis Adams, entry for May 15, 1844, emphasis retained, Adams Papers, Massachusetts Historical Society, Boston.

affidavits will be published, to substantiate the facts alleged. Hereafter, no further Church proceedings will appear in our columns, except in the form of brief communications.[19]

The Preamble contained the conviction that they knew the "religion of the Latter Day Saints, as originally taught by Joseph Smith, which is contained in the Old and New Testaments, Book of Covenants, and Book of Mormon, is verily true." But they condemned "Joseph Smith's pretensions to righteousness." Complaints included among other things the doctrines of a woman becoming a spiritual wife and the belief in many Gods. The paper reported on two meetings of church leaders relating to the fellowship of certain dissenters.

Included in the publication was a listed of fifteen strongly worded resolutions relating to the church and the abuses that were considered objectionable. Most importantly were three affidavits giving a brief summary of the July 12, 1843 revelation. One of the affidavits was by William Law, one by Jane Law, and another by Austin Cowles a member of the Nauvoo High Council until he withdrew from that calling.

I hereby certify that Hyrum Smith did, (in his office,) read to me a certain written document, which he said was a revelation from God, he said that he was with Joseph when it was received. He afterwards gave me the document to read, and I took it to my house, and read it, and showed it to my wife, and returned it next day. The revelation (so called) authorized certain men to have more wives than one at a time, in this world and in the world to come. It said this was the law, and commanded Joseph to enter into the law.—And also that he should administer to others. Several other items were in the revelation, supporting the above doctrines.

WM. LAW.

---

[19] *Nauvoo Expositor* 1 (June 7, 1844):1.

Austin Cowles, who on September 23, 1843 resigned his seat on the Nauvoo High Council as a councilor to Stake President William Marks, made an affidavit that included:

> In the latter part of the summer, 1843, the Patriarch, Hyrum Smith, did in the High Council, of which I was a member, introduce what he said was a revelation given through the Prophet; that the said Hyrum Smith did essay to read the said revelation in the said Council, that according to his reading here was contained the following doctrines; 1st, the sealing up of persons to eternal life, against all sins, save that of shed[d]ing innocent blood or of consenting thereto; 2nd, the doctrine of a plurality of wives, or marrying virgins; that "David and Solomon had many wives, yet in this they sinned not save in the matter of Uriah.["][20]

The fourth page contained an article from the *Quincy Whig* which told about two representatives of the dissenters who mentioned the spiritual wife doctrine. The paper reported that Elder John P. Greene, the city marshal of Nauvoo, responded in defense of the Joseph Smith. Greene was reported to have said "he had been a Mormon for the last twelve years—and had always been intimate with Smith, and that such doctrines as were ascribed to Smith by his enemies, had never been taught to him. He further said that Smith was like a diamond, the more he was rubbed, the brighter he appeared." The *Quincy Whig* explained the position of most of the non-members in the area:

> It is not so much the particular doctrines, which Smith upholds and practices, however abominable they may be in themselves, that our citizens care about—as it is the anti-republican nature of the organization, over which he has almost supreme control—and which is trained and disciplined to act in accordance with his selfish will. The spectacle presented in Smith's case of a civil, ecclesiastical and military leader, united in one and the same person, with

---

[20] Ibid. 1 (June 7, 1844):2. The affidavits of Law and Cowles were subscribed to on May 4, 1844. On Uriah see LDS D&C 132:39.

power over life and liberty, can never find favor in the minds of sound and thinking Republicans.[21]

On June 8 the Nauvoo City Council met to discuss the situation regarding the *Expositor* newspaper. One of the charges printed in the *Expositor* was concerning the doctrine of plural wives. Both Hyrum and Joseph Smith discussed this at the council meeting. The published minutes state that Hyrum "referred to the revelation, read to the High Council of the Church, which has caused so much talk about a multiplicity of wives; that said Revelation was in answer to a question concerning things which transpired in former days, and had no reference to the present time." Hyrum Smith replied to Austin Cowles's affidavit saying "it was in reference to *former* days, and not the present time as related by Cowles."

Mayor Joseph Smith said the revelation was given in view of eternity and "he received for answer, men in this life must marry in view of eternity, otherwise they must remain as angels, or be single in heaven, which was the amount of the revelation referred to, and the Mayor spoke in considerable length in explanation of this principle."[22] This was an attempt by the Smith brothers to obscure the real intend of the revelatory message. It was trying to give no credit to the statements printed in the *Expositor*.

Joseph Smith on June 10 commanded the city marshal to destroy the printing press, pi the type in the street, and burn all the *Expositor* papers. William Clayton reported: "The City council passed a resolution declaring the Printing press on the hill a 'nuisance' and ordered it destroyed if not moved in 3 hours notice. About sun down The police gathered at the Temple about sundown and after organizing proceeded to the office and demolished the press & scattered the Type."[23] Vilate Kimball wrote to her husband Heber about the activities of that day:

Nauvoo was a scene of confusion last night, some hundred of the Brethren turned out and burned the printing press,

---

[21] The *Expositor* took the article from "The Mormons," *Quincy Whig* 7 (May 22, 1844), Quincy.

[22] *Nauvoo Neighbor* 2 (June 19, 1844):2-3, emphasis retained.

[23] William Clayton Journal, entry for June 10, 1844.

and all the ap[p]aratus pertaining to the office of the op[p]osite party; this was done by order of the City Councel [Council]. they had only published one Paper, which is concidered [considered] a public nucence [nuisance]. but I do not know whether it will be concidered [considered] so in the eyes of the Law or not. they have sworn revenge, and no doubt they will have it.[24]

On June 18 about two o'clock Joseph Smith declared Nauvoo under martial law. John and Patrick Calhoun, sons of John C. Calhoun a well know politician of South Carolina, visited Nauvoo on June 22 and conversed with President Smith. John wrote almost a month later that Smith "invited us to the drawing room, where he soon joined us, he gave us a full description of his difficulties, and also an exposition of his faith, frequently calling himself the Prophet, in the course of conversation."[25] The same day William Clayton wrote that "Joseph whispered and told me either to put the r[ecord]. of K[ingdom]. into the hands of some faithful man and send them away, or burn them, or bury them. I concluded to bury them, which I did immediately on my return home."[26] Vilate Kimball continued her letter to Heber:

Joseph went over the river out of the united states, and there stop[p]ed and composed his mind, and got the will of the Lord concerning him, and that was, that he should return and give himself up for trial; he sent a messenger amediately [immediately] to Carthage to tell the Governor he would meet his staff at the big mound at eight oclock

---

[24] Vilate Kimball to Heber C. Kimball, June 9-24, 1844, LDS archives. This part of the letter was written on June 11. Joseph Smith's journal records, "about 8 o'clock the Marshall reported that he had removed the press, type, and printed papers and fixtures into the street and fired them" (Joseph Smith Journal, entry for June 10, 1844).

[25] John C. Calhoun Jr. to "My dear brother" [James Edward Calhoun], July 19, 1844, as cited in Brian Q. Cannon, "John C. Calhoun, Jr., Meets the Prophet Joseph Smith Shortly before the Departure for Carthage," *Brigham Young University Studies* 33, no. 4 (1993):777. See also *History of the Church* 6:540, 545 footnote; 7:78.

[26] William Clayton Journal, entry for June 22, 1844. Clayton retrieved the records on July 3 but they were water damaged. He then recopied the record.

this morning in company with all that the ritt [writ]
demanded. they have just passed by here, on their way
thare [there]. my heart said Lord bless those dear men, and
presurve [preserve] them from those that thirst for their
blood. their giveing themselves up, is all that will save our
city from destruction.[27]

Visiting Carthage Jail Cyrus H. Wheelock gave Joseph
Smith a pistol (a pepper-box). Smith put it in his pocket. Shortly
after five o'clock in the afternoon on June 27 many armed men
stormed the jail and started going up the stairs where the prisoners
were located. In the jailor's room at the time were Joseph Smith,
Hyrum Smith and two apostles, Willard Richards and John Taylor.
The assaulting party were shouting and shooting their arms at the
four men who had a wooden door as protection. Willard Richards
who was in the jail with Joseph wrote the following soon after:

Dr [Willard] glanced an eye by the curtain - saw a 100
armed men around the door. – Joseph, Hyrum & Taylor
coat[s] were of off – Josep[h] sprang to his coat for his 6.
shooter, Hyrum for his single barrel - Taylor for Markhams
cane - & Dr for Taylors cane - - all sprung against the door
- the balls whistled up the stair way - & in an instant. one
came through the door - - Joseph, Taylor & Richards -
sprang to the left. Hyrum back in front of the door - &
snapped his pistol. - when a ball struck him in the left side
of his nose. fell back on floor saying - *I am a dead man*
Joseph discharged his 6 shooter - in the entry reaching
round - the door casing continual discharges came in the
room. - 6 shooter missed fire 2 or 3 times. - Taylor sprang
to leap from the east window - was shot in the window[28]

---

[27] Kimball to Kimball, June 9-24, 1844. Vilate wrote this under the June 24
portion of the letter. The next day Joseph and Hyrum Smith were charged with
treason.

[28] Willard Richards Journal, entry for June 27, 1844, LDS archives, emphasis
retained. Some words made complete from handwriting. See Richards, "Two
Minutes in Jail," *Times and Seasons* 5 (Aug. 1, 1844):598-99. See also "The
Murder," Ibid. 5 (July 15, 1844):584-86 and John Taylor's account in

Jennetta Richards, wife of Willard, wrote concerning her husband, "Mr Richards was not wounded <only> a ball Passed under his left ear scared <his necke [neck]> and took a little of the tip of his ear."[29] John Taylor's watch gave the approximate time when he was shot – five o'clock, sixteen minutes, and twenty-six seconds when it was hit by a ball from a weapon. The mob killed Joseph and Hyrum Smith, Prophet and Patriarch, and sent shock waves to the residents of Carthage, Nauvoo and surrounding towns. Their bodies were transported to Nauvoo. Wooden canes were reportedly made from the coffin in which the prophet's body was brought to Nauvoo.[30] The actual bodies of Hyrum and Joseph were then secretly buried.[31]

As to who would be Joseph Smith's successor there were various rumors on that topic. One was that Joseph Smith blessed his son Joseph Smith III who was eleven years old at the time of the death of his father. Emma Smith was expecting a child at the time. William Clayton reported talk wherein Joseph Smith "said that if he and Hyrum were taken away Samuel H. Smith would be his successor."[32] But Samuel died two weeks later on July 30.

At Joseph Smith's death the 1844 edition (second edition) of the Doctrine and Covenants was not published.[33] Neither was Joseph Smith's revision of the Bible. Smith work on the Book of

---

"Martyrdom of Joseph Smith and his Brother Hyrum" (1844 D&C, 444-45; LDS D&C 135).

[29] Jennetta Richards to "My dearly beloved Parents, Sister and Brother," July 8, 1844, L. Tom Perry Special Collections, Harold B. Lee Library, Brigham Young University.

[30] Steven G. Barnett, "The Canes of the Martyrdom," *Brigham Young University Studies* 21 (Spring 1981):205-211. A newspaper in Ohio reprinted an article from the *Cleveland Herald* that reported the "box in which the body of the Prophet Joseph was conveyed from Carthage to Nauvoo has been manufactured into walking sticks for the faithful" (*Telegraph* 10 [Aug. 28, 1844]:2, Painesville, Ohio).

[31] See Shannon M. Tracy, *In Search for Joseph* (Orem, Utah: KenningHouse, 1995) and Lachlan Mackay, "A Brief History of the Smith Family Nauvoo Cemetery," *Mormon Historical Studies* 3 (Fall 2002):241-52.

[32] William Clayton Journal, entry for July 12, 1844.

[33] "The Book of *Doctrine and Covenants* will be published in about one month from this time" ("Notice," *Nauvoo Neighbor* 2 [June 12, 1844]:3, emphasis retained). By September the new edition was being used. See *Times and Seasons* 5 (Sept. 2, 1844):636.

Abraham was not completed nor was his forthcoming text of the Kinderhook Plates. While he gave priesthood endowments this was not generally known to the church at large.

A certain body of men in connection with the Quorum of the Twelve Apostles, with Brigham Young as president of that quorum, was among those who held priesthood keys. They were involved with the Quorum of the Anointed (Holy Order), the second anointing, eternal, and plural marriage. Given their known rank in the church the Quorum of the Twelve were chosen on August 8, 1844 to lead the church. William Clayton wrote in his journal:

> P.M. attended conference. The Church universally voted to sustain the Twelve in their calling as next in presidency and to sustain Er [Elder] Rigdon and A[masa] Lyman as councillors [counselors] to the Twelve as they had been to the First Presidency. The church also voted to leave the regulation of all the church matters in the hands of the Twelve.[34]

As has been mentioned some of the apostles were practicing polygamists. It is only natural that the principles espoused by Joseph Smith would continue to be followed by those committed to his teachings whether known by the church at large or practiced in secret in selected homes in Nauvoo.

The majority of Joseph Smith's personal correspondence and journals remained with the church under the direction and leadership of the Council of the Twelve. Some writings remained with the Smith family. The prophet's mother, Lucy Mack Smith, retained in her possession the Egyptian papyri, the four mummies, and the longest Translation Manuscript of the Book of Abraham written years earlier in Kirtland. Emma Smith kept in her possession the manuscripts of Joseph's Bible revision together with the marked King James Bible.

---

[34] William Clayton Journal, entry for August 8, 1844. See *Wilford Woodruff's Journal* 2:440. See also "Special Meeting," *Times and Seasons* 5 (Sept. 2, 1844):637-38.

Conclusion – Progress of Mormonism

In the early years of development the church looked toward the imminent second coming of Jesus Christ. By 1835 when Joseph Smith planned to organize a quorum of twelve apostles he said that Christ's return would not occur for sixty-five years. Later in Nauvoo Smith indicated that he was not sure of the meaning of the words spoken to him except that some event would occur forty years in the future.

As has been shown prior revelatory texts were codified to reflect the changing times in the early Mormonism. Certain ideas were modified because of new insights and events did not turn out as anticipated since the time of the original revelations. The alterations did not occur all at once. It was a gradual and slow process. It appears that no one complained at the time and the record of the modifications appeared in the 1835 Doctrine and Covenants. Many histories of Mormonism continue to use the 1835 revisions in their individual publications.

There are various Restoration churches that believe and teach from the Book of Mormon. They include the Church of Jesus Christ of Latter-day Saints, the Community of Christ, the Church of Jesus Christ, the Church of Christ (Temple Lot), churches of Christ (with the Elijah Message), the Remnant Church of Jesus Christ of Latter Day Saints, the Fundamentalist Church of Jesus Christ of Latter-day Saints, other organizations, branches, and groups.

The largest church is the Church of Jesus Christ of Latter-day Saints with world headquarters in Salt Lake City, Utah. They are known for the Mormon Tabernacle Choir, Temple Square, Family History Library, and Conference Center. Congregations meet in Ward meeting houses worldwide. A number of wards are part of a geographical unit known as a stake.

Looking at the restoration movement as a whole provides a broad expanse of how things have operated. In the Church of Jesus Christ of Latter-day Saints, Community of Christ, and the Church of Christ (Temple Lot) doctrines and practices throughout the years have been downgraded, omitted, or rejected.

Some members have tried to produce a denial of historical facts in the prior lived out history of the saints. This has created a division among those seeking the mysteries of the kingdom. One of the best known examples is in regard to individuals known in LDS circles as fundamentalist Mormons. That is, those who profess to follow teachings that were taught by priesthood leaders in prior generations. Doctrines such as Adam-God (Adam being God the Father), blood atonement, and plural marriage are examples of both denials and affirmations.

The LDS endowment ceremony itself is another example. The endowment has been modified throughout the years by removal of portions of the ceremony considered by prior generations as sacred. The church after much story has omitted parts of the ceremony. In this way the ceremony has been streamlined and thereby takes away public criticism.

The LDS church as a world wide religious organization has realized the growing problem of inactivity in wards, stakes, and missions. Guidance to church members can be less authoritarian and more inclusive. Old ideas need to be brought up to date with openness and less critical of others. Religion is personal and when certain ideas are promoted members can become extremists. This has happened in the past and is occurring in many countries in the world. Hate crimes, whether produced by the written word or spoken from the pulpit by religious leaders, have no place in today's society.

Certain patterns mentioned in this book have emerged that are important. For example, Joseph Smith said an angel told him about gold plates before going to the hill. While in Nauvoo he spoke about the angel who commanded him to enter into plural marriage. In 1828 Smith worked on an alphabet for the Book of Mormon and seven years later commenced an alphabet to the Book of Abraham. When questioned in 1834 he mounted his horse and rode away and likewise in 1842 when in conversation at Nauvoo he again departed on a horse without responding.

When religious texts were produced Joseph Smith used the KJV Bible as the standard text and incorporated its words into the Book of Mormon and the Book of Abraham. Also when times got tough we find that in Kirtland and in Nauvoo a printing press was destroyed. Freedom of the press was infringed upon through questionable methods. The surprising thing is that many newspaper articles and books reported statements and historical events with striking accuracy. Of course there were inaccurate claims and theories about Mormonism then as now.

People do not live in isolation from their historical and cultural situation. They are influenced by their own time and place. The origins of Mormonism are closely tied to the Joseph Smith Sr. family. It also includes other individuals who came in contact with representatives of the fledging movement. Even though we have moved far away from that day, Latter-day Saint heritage is linked to the America of the early decades of the 1820s, 1830s, and 1840s.

Some of Joseph Smith's ideas were wrong and some of his religious writings were inaccurate, but his influence has made a permanent impact on believers in his mission. He is revered as a prophet by modern church leaders and members. They regard the Book of Mormon and Smith's prophetic ministry as a guide to obtain heavenly treasures.

With the growth of the Church of Jesus Christ of Latter-day Saints in the past thirty years the future still holds a period of growth. With people seeking a religion with a stable organization, preaching family values and friendship it is only proper that they welcome an organization that gives many directives from the top. By joining the church an individual joins a society. People take on the image of pioneers, a persecuted people, and the idea that they have found the truth.

It takes many years for an organization that believes in modern revelation to accept historical facts. Some examples follow. The Kinderhook Plates for many years was believed to be genuine (1843-1981) but is now known to be a hoax. The Horus Papyrus (Breathing Permit) is an Egyptian document rather than a record written by Abraham. The Facsimiles of the Book of Abraham are funerary documents as indicated in 1861. Joseph Smith was a glass looker and treasure seer as mentioned in articles and books.

There is room for improvement such as acknowledging that the excitement of religion that Joseph Smith mentioned in his official account was the Palmyra revival of 1824-25. Another historical event to affirm is that the original Church of Christ organized by Joseph Smith occurred in Manchester, Ontario County, New York on April 6, 1830.

Joseph Smith believed that he spoke with supernatural beings, whether he did is ultimately left to each person as a matter of faith. It is hoped that those studying Mormonism will keep an open mind as they advance to a deeper understanding of the early days of the movement.

One of the earliest principles for church membership was that of obedience to leadership. This is stated in a revelatory message delivered on the day the church was organized concerning what Joseph Smith would reveal to them.

> Wherefore, meaning the church, thou shalt give heed unto all his words, and commandments, which he shall give unto you, as he receiveth them, walking in all holiness before me: For his word ye shall receive, as if from mine own mouth, in all patience and faith; For by doing these things, the gates of hell shall not prevail against you: Yea, and the Lord God will disperse the powers of darkness from before you; and cause the heavens to shake for your good, and his name's glory (LDS D&C 21:4-6; RLDS D&C 19:2).

As mentioned after Smith's death the majority of church members followed the leadership of senior apostle Brigham Young and the Quorum of the Twelve Apostles. Young presided over the affairs of the church for thirty-three years (1844-77) and made a permanent mark on the movement.

Young was succeeded in church leadership by individuals who were members of the Quorum of the Twelve. Tradition holds that after the death of a church president a member of the Quorum of the Twelve will become church president.

Though a corporation sole was established for the Presiding Bishop in the State of Utah it was considered needful to establish a Corporation of the President. This was accomplished in 1923 by church president Heber J. Grant. Two important sections of the Articles of Incorporation of the Corporation of the President of the Church of Jesus Christ of Latter-day Saints are cited below:

The object of this corporation shall be to acquire, hold and dispose of such real and personal property as may be conveyed to or acquired by said corporation for the benefit of the members of the Church of Jesus Christ of Latter-day Saints, a religious society, for the benefit of religion, for works of charity and for public worship. Such real and personal property may be situated, either within the State of Utah, or elsewhere, and this corporation shall have power, without any authority or authorization from the members of said Church or religious society, to grant, sell, convey, rent, mortgage, exchange, or otherwise dispose of any part or all of such property.

Sixteen years later in 1940 Heber J. Grant made an amendment to the Fourth Article of Incorporation that included wording which related to succession:

But in the event of death or resignation from office of the President of the Church of Jesus Christ of Latter-day Saints, or in the event of a vacancy in that office from any cause, the President or Acting President of the Quorum of the Twelve Apostles of said Church, or one of the members of said Quorum thereunto designated by that Quorum, shall, pending the installation of a successor President of the Church of Jesus Christ of Latter-day Saints, be the corporation sole under these articles, and the laws pursuant to which they are made, and shall be and is authorized in his official capacity to execute in the name of the corporation all documents or other writings necessary to the carrying on of its purposes, business and objects, and to do all things in the name of the corporation which the original signer of the articles of incorporation might do; it being the purpose of these articles that there shall be no failure in succession in the office of such corporation sole (Original in State of Utah Archives, Salt Lake City).

When a new church president is ordained and set apart to his office the president or acting president of the Quorum of the

Twelve certifies the ordination to the state for the new president to continue the office of corporation sole.

Missionaries are called to perform service in many countries throughout the world. The program is to perform baptisms of those who accept the message of the restored gospel. After faith and repentance the convert is baptized by immersion and confirmed a church member with the reception of the gift of the Holy Ghost. Male members can be ordained to either the Aaronic or Melchizedek Priesthood. The sacrament (Lord's Supper) of break and water is usually served each Sunday. Various activities and services are attended to during the week.

For some young members missionary work becomes their rite of passage being away from home for the first time. A number of individuals figure they will obtain a testimony on their mission. The same principles as taught in 1830s are expounded with additional emphasis on prophetic leadership, the word of wisdom, tithing, and church service. One problem area has been converts who drop out of activity shortly after baptism.

Besides missionary work to obtain converts the LDS church builds temples for higher ordinances for faithful church members. For example, missionaries prior to going on their mission receive a ceremonial washing and anointing, they are officially clothed in the garment of the holy priesthood and progress through what is known as the endowment. They make promises and covenants thereby receiving certain signs and handclasps that are necessary to enter the celestial kingdom. Another ceremony is marriage in the new and everlasting covenant for time and all eternity. This is known as temple marriage where a man and a woman are sealed together. An even higher sealing, though limited in number, is the second anointing where as couple are promised, if faithful, their eternal reward.

A unique aspect of ordinances performed in Latter-day Saint temples is work for and in behalf of the dead. To become a savior on Mount Zion the saints are told they must perform by proxy a baptism, washing, anointing, clothing with a new name, (if for a deceased male then priesthood ordination), listen and go through the endowment ceremony for the named deceased person. Marriages (sealings) are also performed for couples who have died.

When LDS temples are open you may see faithful church members bringing their suitcases to the temple. In the suitcase is white clothing including temple robes. Temples are located throughout the world. Since the salvation of church members is linked to those who have died there is special interest in genealogy. Not only do non-members compile family histories but church members are admonished to do their own. Name extraction from various civil and religious records is another way to obtain names for proxy temple work.

One of the special interest of Latter-day Saints is the spiritual confirmation that the church is true. Missionaries maintain the truthfulness of the church as they seek for converts by telling them to pray about their message. If the Book of Mormon is true then Joseph Smith is a prophet, the church represented is true and for the larger churches their current president is a prophet.

Once a month a fast and testimony meeting is held in wards. Testimonies are given relating to individual's life, that the church is true, that Joseph Smith is a prophet of God, and that the church president is also God's prophet. Having a testimony that one knows certain church related things is reinforced over and over again.

The importance of the role of Joseph Smith is overwhelming. The church has emphasized that Smith is a prophet and if that is not so there is no truth to it. This is constantly expresses at church conferences and meetings. Many church members put explicit trust in Joseph's story of finding and obtaining the gold plates for translation purposes. To some members if Joseph Smith did not procure the plates from the Manchester, New York "Hill Cumorah" then there is no truth in Mormonism.

One thing is certain the story of the plates was believed by Smith's family and close friends. Since Joseph Smith did not use the plates while dictating the Book of Mormon there may need to be a new emphasis relating to Smith's story. The story may have been told to get people to believe who had religious questions and looked forward to a restoration of the New Testament church in their own lifetime. Since parts of Joseph Smith's history of his religious experiences have been canonized any change is a difficult process.

The role of Joseph Smith in Latter-day Saint history and theology continues to overshadow other services the LDS church provides. Mormonism is built on the teachings of Smith as he is considered a prophet who restored the church and brought forth the Book of Mormon as an inspired record for humankind. It is enough to have a tangible book to emphasize how it is impossible for anyone to produce it. Joseph Smith devotion is kept alive today as he is the basis of the church's religious authority.

Shortly after Smith's death William W. Phelps published a song in the *Times and Seasons* titled "Joseph Smith" to be sung by the saints. The first stanza and chorus can be heard today:

> Praise to the man who commun'd with Jehovah,
> Jesus anointed "that Prophet and Seer,"
> Blessed to open the last dispensation;—
> Kings shall extol him, and nations revere.

> CHORUS—Hail to the Prophet, ascended to heaven,
> Traitors and tyrants now fight him in vain,
> Mingling with Gods, he can plan for his
> brethren,
> Death cannot conquer the hero again.

With advance technology, especially through the internet, the history, beliefs, and life experiences of Latter-day Saints are made available to those who search the web. Like searching for a book at a library an individual looks for reliable information. Most church sites only include what they want you to know rather than explain their faith experiences. History is usually exploited in order to further the continuing function of the organization.

Select Bibliography

Manuscripts and Publications

Joseph Smith Journals, LDS archives. See Dean C. Jessee, ed., *The Papers of Joseph Smith: Journal, 1832-1842*, Vol. 2 (Salt Lake City: Deseret Book, 1992); and Scott H. Faulring, ed., *An American Prophet's Record: The Diaries and Journals of Joseph Smith* (Salt Lake City: Signature Books in association with Smith Research Associates, 1987).

Kirtland Council Minute Book, October 10, 1832-November 27, 1837, LDS archives.

Kirtland Revelations Book, LDS archives. Manuscript book containing some of Joseph Smith's revelations, 1829-1834.

Nauvoo High Council Minutes, March 8, 1840-October 18, 1845, LDS archives, typescript.

Smith, Joseph. Manuscripts, LDS archives. Manuscripts include Joseph Smith Journals, correspondence including two letter books, addresses, legal and financial papers, Manuscript History, and the Revelation Collection are available on microfilm at LDS archives, Salt Lake City, Utah; RLDS archives, Independence, Missouri; and Special Collections, Harold B. Lee Library, Brigham Young University, Provo, Utah. Also on DVD in *Selected Collections from the Archives of The Church of Jesus Christ of Latter-day Saints*, 2 vols. Provo, Utah: Brigham Young University Press, 2002.

_____. *Book of Mormon*. Palmyra [New York]: E.B. Grandin, 1830. Current editions include Salt Lake City: Church of Jesus Christ of Latter-day Saints, 1981. Independence, Missouri: Reorganized Church of Jesus Christ of Latter Day Saints, 1908 [Authorized Edition] and 1966 [Revised Authorized Edition, 1992]; Church of Christ (Temple Lot), 1990. Original Manuscript, LDS archives and Printer's Manuscript in RLDS archives.

_____. *A Book of Commandments, for the Government of the Church of Christ*. Zion [Independence, Missouri]:

Phelps & Co., 1833. [in press 1833] Current edition includes *Book of Commandments*, published by the Church of Christ (Temple Lot), Independence, Missouri, 1960.

_____. Compiled by Joseph Smith, Junior, Oliver Cowdery, Sidney Rigdon, Frederick G. Williams. *Doctrine and Covenants of the Church of the Latter Day Saints: Carefully Selected from the Revelations of God.* Kirtland, Ohio: Frederick G. Williams & Co., 1835.

_____. *The Doctrine and Covenants of the Church of Jesus Christ of Latter Day Saints.* Nauvoo, Illinois: John Taylor, 1844.

Smith, Joseph, et al. *History of the Church of Jesus Christ of Latter-day Saints.* 6 vols. Introduction and Notes by B. H. Roberts. Salt Lake City: Deseret Book, 1959. Behind this revised history are preliminary manuscripts and the bound books of the compiled Manuscript History of Joseph Smith, also known as the Manuscript History of the Church, LDS archives. Most of the revelations in this manuscript from 1828 to 1834 were copied from the 1835 D&C. The history portion up to November 27, 1832 (except revelation texts) has been published in Dean C. Jessee, ed., *The Papers of Joseph Smith: Autobiographical and Historical Writings*, Vol. 1 (Salt Lake City: Deseret Book, 1989).

Smith, Joseph III and Heman C. Smith, eds. *The History of the Reorganized Church of Jesus Christ of Latter Day Saints.* 4 vols. Lamoni, Iowa: Herald House, 1897-1903. Reprinted 1967.

Smith, Lucy [Mack]. Preliminary Manuscript. Ms. 1844-45. LDS archives.

_____. "The History of Lucy Smith Mother of the Prophet." MS. LDS archives. Revised in 1845 from Preliminary Manuscript. A copy of this revision used for *Biographical Sketches of Joseph Smith the Prophet, and His Progenitors for Many Generations.* Liverpool, England: Published for Orson Pratt by S.W. Richards, 1853. Compared in Lavina Fielding Anderson, ed., *Lucy's Book: A Critical Edition of Lucy Mack Smith's Family Memoir.* Salt Lake City: Signature Books, 2001.

"The Book of John Whitmer Kept by Commandment," original manuscript in RLDS archives. Published in Bruce N. Westergren, ed. *From Historian to Dissident: The Book of John Whitmer.* Salt Lake City: Signature Books, 1995.

"The Conference Minutes and Record Book of Christ's Church of Latter Day Saints." Manuscript in the possession of the LDS church. Published in Donald Q. Cannon and Lyndon W. Cook, eds. *Far West Record: Minutes of The Church of Jesus Christ of Latter-day Saints, 1830-1844.* Salt Lake City: Deseret Book, 1983.

Books

Aland, Kurt and Barbara. *The Text of the New Testament, An Introduction to the Critical Edition and to the Theory and Practice of Modern Textual Criticism.* Grand Rapids, Michigan: Eerdmans/E.J. Brill, 1987.

Allen, James B. *No Toil Nor Labor Fear: The Story of William Clayton.* Provo, Utah: Brigham Young University Press, 2002.

Allen, James B. and Glen M. Leonard, *The Story of the Latter-day Saints.* Salt Lake City: Deseret Book, 1976; rev. ed., 1992.

Allen, James B., Ronald W. Walker, and David J. Whittaker, *Studies in Mormon History, 1830-1997: An Indexed Bibliography.* Urbana: University of Illinois Press, 2000.

Anderson, Karl Ricks. *Joseph Smith's Kirtland: Eyewitness Accounts.* Salt Lake City: Deseret Book, 1989.

Anderson, Richard L. *Joseph Smith's New England Heritage: Influences of Grandfathers Solomon Mack and Asael Smith.* Salt Lake City: Deseret Book; Provo, Utah: BYU Press, rev. ed., 2003.

Anderson, Rodger I. *Joseph Smith's New York Reputation Reexamined.* Salt Lake City: Signature Books, 1990.

Andrew, Laurel B. *The Early Temples of the Mormons: The Architecture of the Millennial Kingdom in the American West.* Albany: State University of New York Press, 1978.

Arrington, Leonard J. *Adventures of a Church Historian.* Urbana: University of Illinois Press, 1998.

Backman, Milton V., Jr. *American Religions and the Rise of Mormonism*. Salt Lake City: Deseret Book, 1965.

_____. *Joseph Smith's First Vision: The First Vision in its Historical Context*. Second ed., Salt Lake City: Bookcraft, 1980.

_____. *The Heavens Resound: A History of the Latter-day Saints in Ohio 1830-1838*. Salt Lake City: Deseret Book, 1983.

Barlow, Philip L. *Mormons and the Bible: The Place of the Latter-day Saints in American Religion*. New York: Oxford University Press, 1991.

Bates, Irene M. and E. Gary Smith. *Lost Legacy: The Mormon Office of Presiding Patriarch*. Urbana: University of Illinois Press, 1996.

Beecher, Maureen Ursenbach and Lavina Fielding Anderson, eds. *Sisters in Spirit: Mormon Women in Historical and Cultural Perspective*. Urbana: University of Illinois Press, 1987.

Bitton, Davis and Leonard J. Arrington. *Mormons and Their Historians*. Salt Lake City: University of Utah Press, 1988.

Black, Susan Easton. *Who's Who in the Doctrine & Covenants*. Salt Lake City: Bookcraft, 1997.

Bradley, Martha Sonntag and Mary Brown Firmage Woodward. *Four Zinas: A Story of Mothers and Daughters on the Mormon Frontier*. Salt Lake City: Signature Books, 2000.

Bringhurst, Newell G., ed. *Reconsidering No Man Knows My History: Fawn M. Brodie and Joseph Smith in Retrospect*. Logan, Utah: Utah State University Press, 1996.

Brodie, Fawn M. *No Man Knows My History: The Life of Joseph Smith, the Mormon Prophet*. Second ed., New York: Alfred A. Knopf, 1971.

Brooke, John L. *The Refiner's Fire: The Making of Mormon Cosmology, 1644-1844*. New York: Cambridge University Press, 1994.

Brown, S. Kent, Donald Q. Cannon, and Richard H. Jackson, eds. *Historical Atlas of Mormonism*. New York: Simon & Schuster, 1994.

Buerger, David John. *The Mysteries of Godliness: A History of Mormon Temple Worship*. San Francisco: Smith Research Associates, 1994.

Bushman, Richard L. *Joseph Smith and the Beginnings of Mormonism.* Urbana: University of Illinois Press, 1984.

Colvin, Don F. *Nauvoo Temple: A Story of Faith.* American Fork, Utah: Covenant Communications, Inc., 2002.

Compton, Todd. *In Sacred Loneliness: The Plural Wives of Joseph Smith.* Salt Lake City: Signature Books, 1997.

Cook, Lyndon W. *Joseph Smith and the Law of Consecration.* Provo, Utah: Grandin Book, 1985.

_____. *The Revelations of the Prophet Joseph Smith: A Historical and Biographical Commentary of the Doctrine and Covenants.* Provo, Utah: Seventy's Mission Bookstore, 1981.

Cooper, Rex Eugene. *Promises Made to the Fathers: Mormon Covenant Organization.* Salt Lake City: University of Utah Press, 1990.

Crawley, Peter. *A Descriptive Bibliography of the Mormon Church Volume 1: 1830-1847.* Provo, Utah: Religious Studies Center, Brigham Young University, 1997 [1998].

Cross, Whitney R. *The Burned-Over District: The Social and Intellectual History of Enthusiastic Religion in Western New York, 1800-1850.* New York, Harper & Row, 1965.

Ehat, Andrew F. and Lyndon W. Cook, eds. *The Words of Joseph Smith: The Contemporary Accounts of the Nauvoo Discourses of the Prophet Joseph.* Provo, Utah: Religious Studies Center, Brigham Young University, 1980.

Faulring, Scott H., Kent P. Jackson, and Robert J. Matthews, eds. *Joseph Smith's New Translation of the Bible: Original Manuscripts.* Provo, Utah: Religious Studies Center, Brigham Young University, 2004.

Flake, Chad J. and Larry W. Draper. *A Mormon Biography 1830-1930: Books, Pamphlets, Periodicals, and Broadsides Relating to the First Century of Mormonism.* Second ed., rev. and enlarged. 2 vols. Provo, Utah: Religious Studies Center, Brigham Young University, 2004.

Flanders, Robert Bruce. *Nauvoo Kingdom on the Mississippi.* Urbana: University of Illinois Press, 1965.

Godfrey, Kenneth W., Audrey M. Godfrey and Jill Mulvay Derr. *Women's Voices: An Untold History of the Latter-day Saints, 1830-1900.* Salt Lake City: Deseret Book, 1982.

Grunder, Rick. *Mormon Parallels: A Preliminary Bibliography of Material Offered for Sale 1981-1987.* Ithaca, New York: Rick Grunder Books, 1987.

Hallwas, John E. and Roger D. Launius, eds., *Cultures in Conflict: A Documentary History of the Mormon War in Illinois.* Logan: Utah State University Press, 1995.

Hansen, Klaus J. *Mormonism and the American Experience.* Chicago: University of Chicago Press, 1981.

Hartley, William G. *Stand by my Servant Joseph: The Story of the Joseph Knight Family and the Restoration.* Provo, Utah: Joseph Fielding Smith Institute for LDS History and Salt Lake City: Deseret Book, 2003.

Hatch, Nathan O. *The Democratization of American Christianity.* New Haven, CT: Yale University Press, 1989.

Hicks, Michael. *Mormonism and Music: A History.* Urbana: University of Illinois Press, 1989.

Hill, Donna. *Joseph Smith: The First Mormon.* Garden City, New York: Doubleday, 1977.

Hill, Marvin S. *Quest for Refuge: The Mormon Flight from American Pluralism.* Salt Lake City: Signature Books, 1989.

Holzapfel, Richard Neitzel and Jeni Broberg Holzapfel. *Women of Nauvoo.* Salt Lake City: Bookcraft, 1992.

Holzapfel, Richard Neitzel, Jeffery T. Cottle, and Ted D. Stoddard, eds. *Church History in Black and White: George Edward Anderson's Photographic Mission to Latter-day Saint Historical Sites 1907 Diary, 1907-8 Photographs.* Provo, Utah: Religious Studies Center, Brigham Young University, 1995.

Howard, Richard P. *Restoration Scriptures: A Study of Their Textual Development.* Independence, Missouri: Herald Publishing House, 1969; Second ed., 1995.

Hullinger, Robert N. *Joseph Smith's Response to Skepticism.* Salt Lake City: Signature Books, 1992.

Jackson, Kent P., comp. and ed. *Joseph Smith's Commentary on the Bible* Salt Lake City: Deseret Book, 1994.

Jessee, Dean C., comp. and ed. *Personal Writings of Joseph Smith.* Salt Lake City: Deseret Book and Provo, Utah: Brigham Young University Press, rev. ed., 2002.

Johnson, Clark V., ed. *Mormon Redress Petitions: Documents of the 1833-1838 Missouri Conflict*. Provo, Utah: Religious Studies Center, Brigham Young University, 1992.

Kenney, Scott G., ed., *Wilford Woodruff's Journals*. Typescript, 9 vols. Midvale, Utah: Signature Books, 1983-85.

Knecht, Stephen R. *The Story of Joseph Smith's Bible Translation: A Documented History*. Salt Lake City: Associated Research Consultants Publication, 1977.

Larson, Charles M. *By His Own Hand Upon Papyrus: A New Look at the Joseph Smith Papyri*. Grand Rapids, Michigan: Institute for Religious Research, revised ed., 1992.

Launius, Roger D. and Linda Thatcher, eds. *Differing Visions: Dissenters in Mormon History*. Urbana: University of Illinois Press, 1994.

Launius, Roger D. and John E. Hallwas, eds., *Kingdom on the Mississippi Revisited: Nauvoo in Mormon History*. Urbana: University of Illinois Press, 1996.

Leonard, Glen M. *Nauvoo: A Place of Peace, A People of Promise*. Salt Lake City: Deseret Book and Provo, Utah: Brigham Young University Press, 2002

LeSueur, Stephen C. *The 1838 Mormon War in Missouri*. Columbia: University of Missouri Press, 1987.

Madsen, Carol Cornwall. *In Their Own Words: Women and the Story of Nauvoo*. Salt Lake City: Deseret Book, 1994.

Marquardt, H. Michael and Wesley P. Walters. *Inventing Mormonism: Tradition and the Historical Record*. San Francisco: Smith Research Associates, 1994.

Marquardt, H. Michael, comp. *The Joseph Smith Egyptian Papers*. Cullman, Alabama, 1981.

_____. *The Joseph Smith Revelations: Text and Commentary*. Salt Lake City: Signature Books, 1999.

Matthews, Robert J. *"A Plainer Translation:" Joseph Smith's Translation of the Bible, A History and Commentary*. Provo, Utah: Brigham Young University Press, 1975.

McConkie, Mark L. *Remembering Joseph: Personal Recollections of Those Who Knew the Prophet Joseph Smith*. Salt Lake City: Deseret Book, 2003.

Metzger, Bruce M. *The Text of the New Testament, Its Transmission, Corruption, and Restoration*. Third ed. New

York: Oxford University Press, 1992.

Miller, David E. and Della S. Miller. *Nauvoo: The City of Joseph.* Santa Barbara: Peregrine Smith, 1974; reprinted Salt Lake City: Publishers Press, 1996.

Newell, Linda King, and Valeen Tippetts Avery. *Mormon Enigma: Emma Hale Smith.* Urbana: University of Illinois Press, Second ed., 1994.

Nibley, Hugh W. *Since Cumorah: The Book of Mormon in the Modern World.* Salt Lake City: Deseret Book, 1967.

Nyman, Monte S. and Robert L. Millet, eds. *The Joseph Translation: The Restoration of Plain and Precious Things.* Provo, Utah: Religious Studies Center, Brigham Young University, 1985.

O'Driscoll, Jeffrey S. *Hyrum Smith: A Life of Integrity.* Salt Lake City: Deseret Book, 2003.

Ostling, Richard N. and Joan K. *Mormon America: The Power and the Promise.* HarperSanFrancisco, 1999.

Palmer, Grant H. *An Insiders View of Mormon Origins.* Salt Lake City: Signature Books, 2002.

Persuitte, David. *Joseph Smith and the Origins of the Book of Mormon,* Second ed., Jefferson, North Carolina: McFarland & Company, Inc., 2000.

Petersen, LaMar, *The Creation of the Book of Mormon: A Historical Inquiry.* Salt Lake City: Freethinker Press, 1998.

Peterson, H. Donl. *The Story of the Book of Abraham: Mummies, Manuscripts, and Mormonism.* Salt Lake City: Deseret Book, 1995.

Porter, Larry C. and Susan Easton Black, eds., *The Prophet Joseph: Essays in the Life and Mission of Joseph Smith.* Salt Lake City: Deseret Book, 1988.

Pratt, Parley P. [Jr.], ed. *Autobiography of Parley P. Pratt.* Salt Lake City: Deseret Book, 1994.

Prince, Gregory A. *Power From On High: The Development of Mormon Priesthood.* Salt Lake City: Signature Books, 1995.

Quinn, D. Michael. *Early Mormonism and the Magic World View.* Salt Lake City: Signature Books, rev. and enlarged, 1998.

_____. *The Mormon Hierarchy: Origins of Power.* Salt Lake City: Signature Books in association with Smith Research

Associates, 1994.

———. *The Mormon Hierarchy: Extensions of Power*. Salt Lake City: Signature Books in association with Smith Research Associates, 1997.

Robison, Elwin C. *The First Mormon Temple: Design, Construction, and Historical Context of the Kirtland Temple*. Provo, Utah: Brigham Young University Press, 1997.

Rhodes, Michael D. *The Hor Book of Breathings: A Translation and Commentary*. Provo, Utah: Foundation for Ancient Research and Mormon Studies, Brigham Young University, 2002.

Romig, Ronald E. *Early Independence, Missouri "Mormon" History Tour Guide*. Independence: Missouri Mormon Frontier Foundation, 1994.

Shipps, Jan. *Mormonism: The Story of a New Religious Tradition*. Urbana: University of Illinois Press, 1985.

——— and John W. Welch, eds. *The Journals of William E. McLellin 1831-1836*. Provo, Utah: BYU Studies; Urbana: University of Illinois Press, 1994.

Skousen, Royal, ed., *The Original Manuscript of the Book of Mormon: Typographical Facsimile of the Extant Text*. Provo, Utah: Foundation for Ancient Research and Mormon Studies, Brigham Young University, 2001.

———, *The Printer's Manuscript of the Book of Mormon: Typographical Facsimile of the Entire Text in Two Parts*. Provo, Utah: Foundation for Ancient Research and Mormon Studies, Brigham Young University, 2001.

Smith, Andrew F. *The Saintly Scoundrel: The Life and Times of Dr. John Cook Bennett*. Urbana: University of Illinois Press, 1997.

Smith, George D. ed. *An Intimate Chronicle: The Journals of William Clayton*. Salt Lake City: Signature Books in association with Smith Research Associates, 1991.

Southerton, Simon G. *Losing a Lost Tribe: Native Americans, DNA and the Mormon Church*. Salt Lake City: Signature Books, 2004.

Todd, Jay M. *The Saga of the Book of Abraham*. Salt Lake City: Deseret Book, 1969.

Underwood, Grant. *The Millenarian World of Early Mormonism.* Urbana: University of Illinois [Press], 1993.

Van Wagoner, Richard S. *Mormon Polygamy: A History.* Second ed. Salt Lake City: Signature Books, 1989.

_____. *Sidney Rigdon: A Portrait of Religious Excess.* Salt Lake City: Signature Books, 1994.

Vogel, Dan. *Early Mormon Documents.* 5 vols. Salt Lake City: Signature Books, 1996-2003.

_____. *Indian Origins and the Book of Mormon: Religious Solutions from Columbus to Joseph Smith.* Salt Lake City: Signature Books, 1986.

_____. *Joseph Smith: The Making of a Prophet.* Salt Lake City: Signature Books, 2004.

Vogel, Dan and Brent Lee Metcalfe, eds. *American Apocrypha: Essays on the Book of Mormon.* Salt Lake City: Signature Books, 2002.

Walker, John Phillip, ed. *Dale Morgan on Early Mormonism: Correspondence and a New History.* Salt Lake City: Signature Books, 1986.

Waterman, Bryan, ed. *The Prophet Puzzle: Interpretive Essays on Joseph Smith.* Salt Lake City, Signature Books, 1999.

Welch, John W., ed. with Erick B. Carlson. *Opening the Heavens: Accounts of Divine Manifestations, 1820-1844.* Provo, Utah: Brigham Young University Press and Salt Lake City: Deseret Book, 2005.

H. Michael Marquardt Papers
Accession 900, Manuscripts Division, J. Willard Marriott Library, University of Utah, Salt Lake City, Utah (currently 288 archival boxes)

Web site
Mormon Central
http://tinyurl.com/45c4o
[http://www.xmission.com/~research/central/index.htm]

Index

Joseph Smith), 38, 41, 59-
61, 109, 138, 144, 148, 150,
152-53, 156n29, 159, 162,
164, 205, 214-15, 372, 379,
395, 413, 415, 417, 419,
422, 447; alphabet, 124,
405; appears before Nathan
Pierce, 156; articled for
land, 6, 114; assessment
records 1821-23, 7-   ;
baptism in Manchester,
New York, 216-17, 219;
cake and beer shop in
Palmyra, 4; census 1820, 7;
census 1830, 162;
complaint before Peter
Mitchell, 111-12; cooper,
108; favorite evening
hymn, 43; first vision of,
41-42;   handles plates in
frock, 118; highway tax
record, 2-3, 9; married
Lucy Mack, 38; moves to
Palmyra, 1; owes Russell
Stoddard for work on frame
home, 111-12; placed
advertisement in
newspaper, 11n28, 36;
plates not present for
translation, 98-99; received
Palmyra newspaper, 36;
revelation to, 212; seventh
vision of, 47; signs
agreement on selling Book
of Mormon, 153; signs
articles of agreement 1825,
64; signs 1818 note, 104;
sixth vision of, 42; taught
family in home, 43; taught

school, 40; testimony at
1826 examination, 71; told
story about plates, 77-78,
82-83; treasure seeker, 54,
56; 110; Universalist, 38-
39; visions and dreams, 42-
43; works for Lemuel
Durfee Sr., 116, 120; works
for Jeremiah Hurlbut, 103-
107; works for Josiah
Stowell, 62, 113
Smith, Joseph, III (son of
Emma and Joseph Smith),
411, 450-52, 525, 556, 622,
635
Smith, Joseph F. (son of
Mary and Hyrum Smith),
250, 618
Smith, Julia Murdock
(adopted daughter of Emma
and Joseph Smith), 556
Smith, Lovina, 117, 162 (see
also Lovina Smith Walker)
Smith, Lucy (sister of Joseph
Smith), 9, 162
Smith, Lucy Mack (mother of
Joseph Smith), 1, 7, 10-11,
39-40, 63-64, 86, 91,
96n44, 109-15, 117-19,
121, 124, 135-36, 146, 149,
152, 159n36, 162, 164, 214,
365, 404, 525, 629, 636;
arrives in Palmyra, 1;
baptism in Manchester,
New York, 217-19; baptism
in Randolph, Vermont, 40;
dream, 39; diversity of
churches, 51; family moves
to log house of Hyrum,

LaVergne, TN USA
24 March 2011
221426LV00001B/253/A